Dashiell Hammett

HAMMETT IN *REDBOOK* AD FOR *THE THIN MAN*, 1933

Selected Letters *of*

Dashiell Hammett

1921–1960

Edited by
Richard Layman

with
Julie M. Rivett

Introduction by
Josephine Hammett Marshall

COUNTERPOINT
WASHINGTON, D.C.

Book design and composition by Mark McGarry, Texas Type & Book Works
Set in Fairfield

Library of Congress Cataloging-in-Publication Data
Hammett, Dashiell, 1894–1961.
[Correspondence. Selections.]
Selected letters of Dashiell Hammett / Richard Layman, editor; Julie M. Rivett, associate editor; foreword by Josephine Hammett Marshall.
p. cm.
Includes index.
ISBN 1-58243-081-0 (alk.paper)
1. Hammett, Dashiell, 1894–1961—Correspondence. 2. Authors, American—20th Century—Correspondence. 3. Detective and mystery stories—Authorship. I. Layman, Richard, 1947– II. Rivett, Julie M. III. Title.
PS3515.A4347 Z48   2000 813'.52—dc21
[B]   00-055494

COUNTERPOINT
P.O. Box 65793, Washington, D.C. 20035-5793

Counterpoint is a member of the Perseus Books Group

FIRST PRINTING
10 9 8 7 6 5 4 3 2 1

CONTENTS

FOREWORD

"A Reasonable Amount of Trouble"

I COULD NEVER have gotten away with publishing Papa's letters while he was alive. He would have hated it. He was a private person, kept himself to himself, told you only what he wanted you to know. The idea of strangers peeping into his personal life would have appalled him, probably as much for the tender sentiments as for the grubbier bits. God knows there were enough of those, lots of stuff he wasn't proud of: the drinking, the sleazy women, the wasted years. But he wasn't ashamed either. It was what he did. Take it, or leave it and go to hell. "Go to hell" was a favorite expression, one he suggested Mama use on persistent landlords. Of course she couldn't.

Although my father appeared indifferent to what people thought about his personal life and put up an almost impenetrable front, sometimes I thought I could read him—the times he was sidestepping or deflecting the unwelcome question; the times when he thought words were useless, or only made things worse. He was very much aware of the limits and dangers of language.

I doubt the idea of publishing his letters would even have occurred to him. He seldom saved letters he received and would have been surprised that anyone saved his. This collection began with those written to me—that is, those that survived moving and child- or cat-damage—and those to my mother and my older sister, Mary, which were retrieved after Mary's death in 1992. The others were gathered with the help and generosity of many people.

But why publish them now? Well, first of all because I am still around to help make sense of them, to sort out his life from his fiction. I don't pretend that I, or the letters, can explain him. Papa was lots of people. Some of them show in his fiction. He's there when Spade tells Brigid

O'Shaughnessy that he "doesn't mind a reasonable amount of trouble." I can hear him in that cool understatement that must have left Brigid wondering, "Just how much is a reasonable amount, Mr. Spade? And how will I know when you've reached it?" And he's there in the implication behind the words—He'd do the job, take the risks, but he was no white knight; he wouldn't "play the sap" for her. That was pretty much how my father met his obligations in life—personal and otherwise. He did what he thought he had to; then he was history. But if you tried to read his life from his work you'd get it wrong. Yes, there's a piece of Sam Spade in him, the Op, Ned Beaumont, even Nick Charles, but there's much more: the man who loved hunting, fishing, and babies, who listened to Gershwin and Haydn, who read Moon Mullins, Doc Savage, and Dostoyevsky, who was a womanizer and a Victorian father. The man I knew and the one I only knew about.

People are always asking me how he sounded. Well, his letters, though they can't replicate the special quality of his voice, sound like him. They are full of sharp observation and the self-deprecating humor he liked. I was surprised how many people he corresponded with and how often he wrote some of them, but not that most of them were women. Papa liked women. He was most open, unguarded, and fun with them. He was a fluid, casual, but not careless letter writer. There are few typos or spelling errors (though he has a running battle with "occasional"). His words come out easily, in logical order, to the point, clear, and most of the time very funny.

That is what I like most about his letters. After all these years he can still make me laugh—the colored stamp BIBLES FOR RUSSIANS on the back of an envelope, the cutout signature of Erle Stanley Gardner at the bottom of a page. He was a funny, funny man. A lot of his humor was just seeing things for what they were, clichés stripped away.

And mostly he is truthful. He may not tell you everything but what he tells is for real. The worst thing he could call someone was "a phony." He is usually charitable about people's faults; when he's not it's because he's harried or really irked. I always think of my father as fitting the old definition of a Southern gentleman: He never insulted anyone by accident.

Still, he was born into a time and place in which views on race, gender, and sexual orientation were less tolerant than today. Over the years he came to realize that these stereotypical attitudes were often unjust.

But some remnants hung on and appear in his letters: what seems to be real prejudice and bias is sometimes just that. Other times he is like a little boy showing off how many bad words he knows. He would have considered it dishonest and cowardly to launder any of it out.

The letters, of course, don't show much of his drinking side. "Most of my friends drank too much," Scott Fitzgerald wrote. "The more they were in tune with the times, the more they drank." Well, Papa was mightily in tune with the times. Plus, he had come from a family rife with alcoholics. But I could never really understand his drinking, because it seemed to make him miserable. His humor took a nasty, sarcastic turn, and he was a pain to be with. I don't know if he realized how awful he was at those times. Once, in an out-of-character moment of valor, I told him I didn't like to be around drunks. "Yeah," he said, nodding his head in total agreement and making a sweep with one arm, "I always tell 'em to get the hell away from me." He was quite soused at the time. It's the kind of story he liked.

It was largely through his letters that Papa kept in touch with his family during the New York years. For Mary and me there were always postcards, birthday telegrams, letters with enclosures—clippings, drawings, matchbook covers from the tonier dives, Stork Club pins, Scotties off the Black & White bottles, Christmas boxes, and toys from FAO Schwarz for no reason at all. Mama got fancy boxes of chocolate and a regular check. Well, pretty regular. Sometimes it was late, but we always knew it would come.

My mother's role in his life, for me anyway, is partly defined by his letters to her that do not appear here. Those that were lost, or she chose not to save. The one written to her after he'd left the Public Health Service Hospital where they'd met, after he'd learned that she was pregnant. The letter making arrangements for her to join him in San Francisco and planning for their marriage. And he would have written her after the fall of '26 when, very nearly dead, he had sent the three of us to stay with her Montana relatives. "Dear Jose, have decided not to die. Come home," I imagine it reading. And there would be letters from the glitzy, gin-soaked New York of the thirties. These I can't imagine.

Though he gradually stopped writing to Mama, he continued to send her checks into the fifties, when he had little money to send. When they separated in '29 he had promised her, "You take care of the girls, and I'll take care of you." That's what she did, and that's what he did, for as long as he could.

His letters to Lillian, I think, give some balance to her share in his life. They put in proportion the myth of the Great Romance, which she dramatized and exploited after his death. He would have been irked and embarrassed by it. But he would have understood. He knew Lillian, her need to rewrite life so it played better, with herself in the dramatic lead.

What his letters to her do show is the delight and enjoyment they got from each other and his genuine pride in her success as a playwright. They had been lovers and remained best friends through the second half of his life. But before their meeting in 1930 he had had a whole lifetime of experience—his youth, the Pinkerton years, marriage and children. He had done the best of his writing before he met her. And even after they'd met he had friends, lovers, a political life apart from hers. Lillian was a constant in his life but not the everything she would have liked to be. No one was that; he wouldn't have it.

All that seems minor to me now when I remember how kind she was to him at the end. She didn't want him on her hands, would have gotten out of it if she could. But in the last days, she was there for him.

The letters also are witness to the surge and ebb of his political life. In those to my sister (five years my senior) he closely follows events in pre-war Europe and Japan. His opinions are acute, shrewd, and often wrong; but, as always, they are his own. He had joined the Communist Party in the early thirties and was involved in all sorts of left-wing causes and Party activities. At the time of the Spanish Civil War the Party considered his volunteering as an ambulance driver. Considering his disastrous experience in World War I when he turned over an ambulance, I'm sure it came as a relief to him when it was decided that he would be of more use at home.

Still, he never thought of himself as a Party member; he thought of himself as a Marxist. What he said was, if the Republican Party suddenly turned Marxist then he'd be a Republican. All other labels aside, he thought of himself as an American.

Enlisting in World War II, not a very sensible thing for a man of his age and health, was partly a show of bravado—thumbing his nose at age—but also a sincere display of what he felt. He was proud of his country, never wanted to live or even travel much in others, thought

Americans were damned good soldiers. His time in Alaska was one of the happiest of his life. He liked being with the guys; he loved the country. It was his last happy time.

His enthusiasm for the Party had dimmed over the years. The early fervor turned to a wry cynicism and then to silence. If he ever acknowledged to himself that he had made a mistake in his allegiance, I can't know. There were no explanations, no excuses; that wasn't his style.

When he was given the choice of naming contributors to a bail bond fund or going to prison, it was no choice at all. His letters from prison were stoic and uncomplaining, but when he came out his health was permanently shattered. He turned away from politics, and told himself there were other things in the world—he sketched, played around with photographing insects, made his own fishing lures, and, as always, read. He'd gradually given up on his own writing, disappointed with himself that he hadn't gone beyond the mystery to make it in the mainstream. But then it's not that simple. Nothing about him is. He knew what he had written was good.

What he didn't know was its lasting effect, how readers half a century later would still find his words as sharp and true as when they were written; how his work would continue to be studied, admired, and shamelessly copied; how deep his fiction had sunk into the American consciousness. And that people would want to know more about him as a man and an author. He knew he was good. He just didn't know how good.

And that, Papa, is why your book of letters got published. You see, it's your own damn fault.

JOSEPHINE HAMMETT MARSHALL
DECEMBER 2000

PREFACE

THE CORRESPONDENCE in this book is selected from nearly one thousand letters, most of them newly discovered, in four major collections.

The most important source was the Hammett family papers, which includes letters to Hammett's wife, Jose, and to his daughters, Josephine and Mary. Josephine saved most of the letters her father sent her, and 133 survive. At the insistence of Lillian Hellman, who was Hammett's literary executor until her death in 1984, Josephine carefully guarded access to these letters. Diane Johnson saw them when she wrote her 1983 biography of Hammett, as did Joan Mellen when she wrote her 1996 book *Hellman and Hammett*, published twelve years after Hellman's death. Josephine's elder sister, Mary, also saved her father's letters, though the 164 that survive were not found until well after her death in 1992, when Mary's husband and his family invited Josephine to go through her stored effects. Also among Mary's papers were many of Hammett's letters to Jose. None but a handful of Hammett's letters to his wife and his elder daughter are known to have been seen outside the family, except in connection with this book.

The second source of letters is a privately held archive of Lillian Hellman's papers that contains photocopies of some four hundred letters from Hammett to Hellman. The location of the originals is unknown, but Rita Wade, Hellman's extraordinarily well-organized secretary, kept copies for her files. They were made available for this book by the generous consent of the Literary Property Trustees appointed in Lillian Hellman's will, particularly Miss Wade's employer, Peter Feibleman. Certain of these letters, chosen by Hellman, were made available to Diane Johnson for her biography. Others were made available to Hellman trustee William Abrahams, named in Hellman's will as her biographer, and he, in turn, showed a batch of them to Joan Mellen.

The third source is a scattering of about eighty letters from Hammett to his friend and lover Prudence Whitfield. These letters were purchased in a lot from Ms. Whitfield by a consortium of book dealers. Through the kind assistance of Otto Penzler, James Pepper, Peter Stern, and Rushton Potts, copies of many of these letters were made available to us for inclusion here.

Finally, there are the Lillian Hellman–Dashiell Hammett papers at the Harry Ransom Humanities Research Center at the University of Texas, Austin. The HRC has long been the primary source of Hammett letters open to researchers. Although the provision of Hellman's will that bequeaths her papers to the University of Texas specifically excludes correspondence to and from Hammett, some forty letters from Hammett to Hellman, as well as a scattering of his correspondence with others, have found their way into the collection. The HRC also houses the archives of Hammett's publishers, Alfred A. Knopf, Inc. Twenty-eight letters from Hammett to Knopf editors, as well as some sixty letters from them to him, were made available to researchers when the archive was catalogued in the mid-1990s.

This, then, is as close as readers of this generation can get to Hammett. Though much of his correspondence is lost, what remains are letters to the people he cared about most. The personality that emerges from these letters is that of a self-sufficient man who assiduously guarded his privacy. He was witty, sarcastic, thoughtful, and eclectic in his interests; he was devoted to his beliefs and loyal to his friends. He had a sharply refined literary sense, and he suffered during his entire life from a creative urge that he had difficulty satisfying. He was a careful correspondent, who generally avoided written political discussions. It is interesting that, in his voluminous correspondence with Hellman, Hammett rarely mentioned his political dealings in Hollywood during the 1930s, though he was very active. There is no mention of the House Committee on Un-American Activities hearings in 1949, at which many of his Hollywood associates were called to testify, or even those in 1952, when Hellman was supoened, or of the McCarthy hearings. The frankest discussion of his political beliefs and activities is in his letters to his daughter Mary, who, as a strategy for engaging her father, asked him questions about his beliefs. Nor did Hammett talk about his own work, except to report with sad regularity after the mid-1930s that he was working on a new novel, which he never finished.

Hammett could be gregarious, especially when he was drinking, and he reported his social life with wry amusement to friends, Hellman in particular. In his letters from the 1930s it is not unusual for him to refer to a dozen or more people with whom he had some contact. When Diane Johnson asked Hellman to help her identify Hammett's references, Hellman replied that she had no idea who a third of them were. We have been able to identify or make informed guesses about most of the people he mentions, but some have eluded us.

This edition of Hammett's letters was begun in 1996 by Josephine Hammett, working with researcher Don Herron. Together they organized the family correspondence and began planning the form of publication. In 1998 Mr. Herron excused himself from the project. He made an important start. The present editorial collaboration was formed through introductions made by producer Josh Waletzky, whose documentary on Hammett for the PBS "American Masters" series focused our attention on this project in its current form.

Publication of Hammett's letters was made possible by a grant of rights from the Literary Property Trustees of the Estate of Dashiell Hammett: Peter Feibleman, Richard Poirer, and, before his death, William Abrahams. Nancy Wechsler, attorney to the trust, and Amy Ardell and Evan Marshall, representing the family, provided the agreement. Moreover, Mr. Feibleman and Mr. Poirer allowed Rita Wade to make copies of letters in Lillian Hellman's personal archive that would not otherwise have been available. After Mr. Abrahams's death in 1998, his literary executor, Professor Peter Stansky of Stanford University, generously allowed us to examine Mr. Abrahams's papers, which included copies of Hammett's letters. San Francisco book dealer Thomas Goldwasser shared his inventory of the archive with us, making the collection accessible. Through Professor Stansky's intercession and the cooperation of the staff at the Stanford University Libraries, especially Roberto Trujillo, William McPheron, and Polly Armstrong, we were able to use a valuable resource.

The editors are indebted to many others for assistance, including several Hammett relatives. Mary's husband, Kenny Miller, saved her effects after her death, and his brother and sister-in-law, Wally and Bonnie Miller, with his sister and brother-in-law, Miriam and Harry Newton, saw that what they thought were all her personal papers, including letters from Hammett to Jose, were turned over to Josephine. The earliest and the latest of Hammett's letters to Jose were discovered by the Millers and Newtons in a forgotten cache of materials in the spring of 2000, just in time to be included in this collection. A second important discovery was made shortly after this book was submitted to the publisher. Corinne Hammett, the wife of Dashiell Hammett's nephew, contacted Josephine Marshall to say that her daughter, Judi, had letters from Hammett to his brother, Richard, and his sister, Reba. Several of these letters are included here, and we are grateful to the East Coast Hammetts for their gracious and timely contribution to this project.

Thomas Staley and the staff at the Harry Ransom Humanities Research Center are always accommodating. They made our work at that fine library easy. We are also grateful to the staffs of the New York Public Library (especially the curators of the Schomberg Collection), the Wisconsin State Historical Society Archives, Madison, and the Margaret Harrick Library of the Academy of Motion Picture Arts and Sciences, Los Angeles. Roger L. Mayer, president of Turner Entertainment Company, provided us M-G-M file correspondence from Hammett.

The unfailing goodwill of people we have called on for assistance has been gratifying. Vince Emery is a friend who shares his expert research selflessly. Muriel Golden is unfailingly loyal to Hammett's memory. Virginia Chilewich is as charming today as she was must have been when she played Ping-Pong with Hammett in the 1950s. Cathy Kober shared her memories of the gentle man who let her run her feet through his hair when she was a child. Susan Finn, daughter of Peggy O'Toole, offered generous assistance. Larry White, Hammett's agent for his radio serials, has been an important source of information. Richard Dannay provided us letters from his private collection and good advice as well. William Arney, who lives in Hammett's apartment at 891 Post Street in San Francisco, is the most dedicated of Hammett's fans. English book dealer Mark Sutcliffe, who has added significantly to what we know of Hammett bibliography, is ever gracious about sharing what he has learned. Matthew J. Bruccoli saved me again from embarrassing errors and

Joseph M. Bruccoli provided scanned images for all the illustrations in this book.

Because their lives were so interesting, Hammett and Hellman have attracted an unusual share of biographers. We are indebted to them all. Hammett biographers Diane Johnson, Joe Gores, and William Nolan; Hellman biographers Carl Rollyson and William Wright; Joan Mellen, who has written the lives of both—all have all provided invaluable help through their books with the identification of people Hammett mentions in his letters.

Our editor Chris Carduff has provided reliable advice and sound judgment that has made our work better than it was.

Jane Gelfman deserves special thanks. Through her editorial savvy we found the right publisher. She is unfailingly supportive, providing knowing reassurance in necessary measures.

The impetus for this collection is, in large part, family devotion. We are particularly mindful of and grateful for the support provided by our own families.

RICHARD LAYMAN
JANUARY 2001

A NOTE ON THE TEXTS

Most of Hammett's letters are legibly typed and thus presented few problems for the editors. Most letters to Lillian Hellman, however, are available only in the form of file photocopies, some of which are faded and very difficult to read. Punctuation for these letters, and especially those of the war years, is often unclear; we have made our best attempt to transcribe them faithfully.

In an effort to provide an easily readable text for a general audience, the editors have corrected Hammett's occasional spelling errors, marking corrections with brackets. In a few cases inferred readings have been necessary, and these are also bracketed. We have silently made minor copyediting changes, primarily in capitalization of proper nouns and in standardizing the treatment of published works by inserting quotation marks or adding italics. Hammett's underlined words have been printed in italics.

In order to include as many letters as possible, we reluctantly cut passages of passing interest, such as observations about the weather and information repeated in other letters. These omissions are indicated by a row of centered asterisks. No cuts have been made that in any way serve to censor the letters, except in two cases when a name is supressed because Hammett's comments about the person or the person's family might be libelous. The form and location of each letter is noted after the closing, using a three-initial abbreviation to describe the form. The first initial, either A or T , indicates whether the letter is handwritten (autograph) or typed; the second initial, L or P indicates whether it is a letter or postcard; and the third initial, S or U indicates whether the letter is signed or unsigned. Telegrams are so indicated. Locations are as follows:

Finn is Susan Finn, whose collection is private.

HRC is the Harry Ransom Humanities Research Center, University of Texas;

LPT indicates Literary Property Trust, the legal entity formed under the terms of Lillian Hellman's will to administer Hammett's literary property that she owned. Copies of some letters privately held by the Literary Property Trust are included in the William Abrahams Collection at the Stanford University Library;

Marshall is Josephine Hammett Marshall;

Schomburg is the Schomburg Center for Research in Black Culture, New York Public Library.

The letters of Prudence Whitfield were purchased and offered for sale by a consortium of dealers, including Otto Penzler, Peter Stern, and James Pepper. Copies of those letters were obtained from the following sources:

> *Black & White* is Black and White Books, Hyannis, Massachu-setts; *Penzler* is Otto Penzler, The Mysterious Bookshop, New York City; *Pepper* is James Pepper Rare Books, Santa Barbara California; *Stern* is Peter L. Stern and Co., Boston.

Correspondence in this volume was selected from Hammett's letters available to us from the following recipients:

> Kermit Bloomgarden: 2; Nancy Bragdon: 52; Muriel Golden: 22 (none of which are included at Ms. Golden's request); Reba Ham-mett : 13; Richard Hammett: 4; Jose Hammett: 89; Josephine Hammett: 134; Mary Hammett: 172 (one of which is to both Josephine and Mary); Lillian Hellman: 308; Knopf: 28 (including letters to Alfred and Blanche Knopf and employees of the firm); Margaret Kober 21; Marjorie May 4; Peggy O'Toole: 2; Public Letters and Miscellaneous correspondence: 30 ; Jean Potter: 2; Herman Shumlin: 4; Hal Wallis: 2; Pru Whitfield: 61

R.L.

PART ONE

Writer
1921–1930

Hammett, near San Diego, California, 1921

"He knew then that men died at haphazard like that,
and lived only while blind chance spared them."

The Maltese Falcon, Chapter 7

SAMUEL DASHIELL HAMMETT was born on May 27, 1894, in rural Saint Mary's County, Maryland. His father, Richard Hammett, was an opportunist who tried his hand at several occupations, none very successfully. His mother, Annie Bond Dashiell, was trained as a nurse, but respiratory illness kept her at home most of the time—that and the demands of her three children, Dashiell, his older sister, Reba, and his younger brother, Richard, called Dick. At the time Dashiell was born, his family was living with his paternal grandfather on a plot of land the Hammetts called "Hopewell and Aim."

When Dashiell was six, his father failed in a bid for political office after an acrimonious campaign and felt compelled to leave the county. He took his family to Philadelphia, where the prospects did not meet his expectations, and, after a year, they turned to Mrs. Hammett's mother for support, moving in with her in the house she rented in Baltimore. Richard Hammett was struggling to support the family and Dashiell dropped out of high school after one semester to help. He never returned to the classroom. His early education came from the streets, from his avid reading, and from a series of odd jobs he held during his teens. When he turned twenty-one, he began what he considered a career as an operative for Pinkerton's National Detective Service. The job suited his intelligence, his sense of adventure, and his curiosity.

Hammett was still living with his parents in 1918 when he took leave from Pinkerton's to join the army during World War I. Though he did not travel more than about fifteen miles from his home during the war, the experience turned his life upside down. He was stationed at Camp Mead, Maryland, and assigned to a Motor Ambulance Company, transporting wounded soldiers returning from Europe. The worldwide Spanish influenza epidemic was especially evident in the United States at military installations, where soldiers returning from foreign service spread the disease that killed more people during the war years than warfare did. In 1919, Hammett was struck, and he spent the rest of his military service recuperating.

"I have always had good health until I contracted influenza, complicated by bronchial pneumonia treatment," Hammett told a doctor during his predischarge medical exam on 24 May 1919. The army pronounced his tuberculosis "arrested," and he was able to resume his prewar occupation as an operative for the Pinkerton's National Detective Service, working first in Baltimore, and then, after the beginning of 1920, in Spokane, Washington. Eighteen months after his discharge, however, his TB flared up again and he "broke down," in the words of a medical report. In November 1920 Hammett was among the first patients admitted to the newly opened Cushman Institute, a U.S. Public Health Service hospital in Tacoma, Washington.

Josephine Dolan, a pretty twenty-three-year-old from Anaconda, Montana, was among the staff of half a dozen nurses in the respiratory illnesses ward at Cushman. She and Hammett struck up a friendship that quickly became amorous. (She never believed that his tuberculosis was confirmed, despite the doctors' reports, and so discounted the possibility of becoming infected herself, a measure of how lovestruck she was.) Within a month they were dating; within two they were intimate. By the end of his third month, Hammett was among a group of tubercular patients transferred south to USPHS facilities in a warmer, drier climate. She stayed behind; he was admitted to the hospital at Camp Kearney near San Diego, and they continued their courtship by mail. These letters are the earliest surviving correspondence from Hammett. He was twenty-six years old when he began writing to Josephine Dolan in February 1921. They apparently did not know she was pregnant.

When Hammett was discharged from Camp Kearney in May 1921, he went first to see her in Spokane, stopping at Cushman to complain about his labored breathing. He then went to San Francisco, to search for an apartment where they could begin their married life. He and Josephine, whom he called Jose (pronounced "Joe's"), were married in the rectory at St. Mary's Cathedral in San Francisco on 7 July 1921. Their daughter Mary Jane was born on 15 October. Hammett returned to work as a private detective, but soon found he was not physically fit for the job. He stood six foot one and a half inches, weighed 135 pounds, and suffered from dizziness, shortness of breath, and chest pains on exertion. He told a Health Service nurse that he was employed as a detective "at intervals" in the fall of 1921, earning $21 per week when he worked, to supplement his disability income of $40 a month. By the end of December he was too sick to work at all. His disability rating was revised to 100 percent, but his pension, though increased to $80 a month, barely paid the rent, and he had a family to support.

Hammett began vocational rehabilitation at Munson's Business College in February 1922, training as a reporter. That fall, he began writing fiction on spec to supplement his income, and soon afterward reported to a visiting nurse that he was writing stories four hours a day. The pulp magazines were an easy market to crack, and though the pay was only a penny or two a word, an industrious writer could make $30 or $40 a month. Hammett had his experience as a private detective to mine for material, and he soon became a favorite of detective pulp readers for his tough stories that had the ring of truth. He churned them out at the rate of better than one a month, and the paychecks bought groceries.

That was how he lived until 1926. Jose was pregnant with his second daughter. Hammett needed more money. When he failed to get it from the editors at *Black Mask* magazine, his most reliable publisher, he decided to venture again into the workforce. This time, he determined to draw on his writing ability and the journalistic skills he had learned in his vocational training course. He answered a want ad for an advertising copywriter/ad manager at Albert S. Samuels Jewelers. The pay was $350 a month—about four times the income from his writing and pension combined. The job seemed perfect for him. Samuels was a congenial boss, and the social aspects of the job were very attractive to a man who had been a virtual shut-in for most of the past six years. Hammett enjoyed the freedom of the workplace; he enjoyed it too much. He began drinking heavily, spending too many evenings in speakeasies with cronies. Within six months the pace caught up with him. He collapsed at his office in a pool of blood, suffering from hepatitis and a recurrence of tuberculosis. Once again he was unable to hold a full-time job. That was his situation in winter 1926–7, when Joseph Shaw, the new editor at *Black Mask* magazine, wrote to Hammett with ambitious plans for revamping the magazine with a stable of star writers.

Shaw was a promoter with business savvy. He understood that the fortunes of his magazine were directly related to the success of his writers. He also recognized that readers respect novelists more than short story writers, so he encouraged his stable to undertake longer works and to aspire to book publication. Meanwhile, he began promoting them as an elite group pioneering a new type of mystery fiction. Shaw bragged that Herbert Hoover, J. P. Morgan, and A. S. W. Rosenbach read *Black Mask*, and that Hammett's contributions to the magazine were some of the best mystery fiction ever published. Soon Hammett had completed his first novel and submitted it unsolicited to Alfred A. Knopf, Publishers, who had just launched an imprint called Borzoi Mysteries. Within a year's time, Hammett had emerged as the most celebrated young mystery novelist in America, and respected reviewers were declaring him as good as if not better than Ernest Hemingway.

While Hammett's reputation soared, his personal life deteriorated. When his second daughter was born, Health Service nurses advised that Jose and the girls should not share quarters with the tubercular writer, who was sometimes too ill to walk unassisted to the bathroom. Jose and the girls went to Montana to visit her relatives in the fall of 1926, then they took a rented house fifteen miles north of San Francisco, where Hammett visited them on weekends. Such conditions made married life difficult; soon even the pretense of a marriage was abandoned. Hammett loved and supported his family, but he looked elsewhere for companionship and found it easily. His brief experience with family life had proven what he had clearly suspected: that it was not for him, especially when so many opportunities were available. He had a career to develop that required all his energies.

Within two years after his collapse at the jewelry store, Hammett had written three novels. *Red Harvest* and *The Dain Curse* were among the most prominently reviewed books of 1929, and *The Maltese Falcon* was recognized as possessing, in the words of one reviewer, "the absolute distinction of real art." Hammett was not satisfied, though. He saw greater opportunities in the writing game.

In 1927, Darryl F. Zanuck introduced sound to motion pictures with *The Jazz Singer*. By Valentine's Day 1930, when *The Maltese Falcon* was

published, studios had already abandoned silent films because they recognized the enormous audience for talkies. That, in turn, created an
unprecedented need for writers to provide scripts. The money was huge,
even during the Depression, and Hammett capitalized on the opportunity to turn his reputation as a writer into pure gold. He left San Francisco for New York in the fall of 1929 and kept steady company with
writer-musician Nell Martin, to whom he dedicated *The Glass Key* in
1930. They both had interests in Hollywood. *Roadhouse Nights,* a movie
adaptation of Hammett's *Red Harvest,* was released by Paramount in
February 1930, and her novel *Lord Byron of Broadway* was released as a
movie by M-G-M in March. That year Hammett claimed to be making
$800 a week—twice as much each month as the average American
worker made in a year. And he spent it all, on starlets and hotel suites
and limousines and chauffeurs and bootleg liquor and speakeasy nights.
When he had money left over, he gave handouts to his friends.

To Josephine Dolan

On 21 February 1921 Hammett was transferred from Cushman Hospital, in Tacoma, Washington, to the U.S. Public Health Service hospital at Camp Kearney, near San Diego. He and Josephine Dolan, one of his nurses at Cushman, had fallen in love just after he arrived, in November 1920, and she was pregnant, though neither seems to have been aware of her condition.

27 Sept [i.e., February] 1921, [Camp Kearney, California]

Dear Little Fellow—

We had just enough excitement on the trip down to keep away monotony, and landed here yesterday afternoon in pretty good shape.

This will be a pretty fair sort of a place, I reckon, after we get accustomed to it, but the going hasn't been any too smooth so far. Before we had our bags unpacked they flashed a set of rules on us (I mailed my copy to Larry Brazer—he'll get a kick out of 'em) but we have broken all but a couple and none of us have been shot yet, so I think we'll get along all right.

The food and the weather here are good so we should be able to put up with the rest of it.

But that's enough of the Kearn[e]y talk—now for a little Cushman.

Which lunger are you taking out now and dragging into town when he should be sleeping? Or are you storing up a little sleep before you start off again?

(If I put in two or three months of this life don't trust yourself out on the bridge with—not even a middle-aged, homely and legless woman would be safe with me.)

The lights have gone democratic, so I'll have to stop this.

When you answer this *tonight* give me all the latest Cushman gossip—just the same as if we were sitting in the Peerless Grill.

   Love
   Hammett

ALS MARSHALL

To Josephine Dolan

Friday [probably 4 March 1921], Camp Kearney, California

Dear Lady—

I didn't intend doing this—writing you a second letter before I got an answer to my first—but that's the hell of being in love with a vamp, you do all sorts of things. Before long, most likely, I'll have fallen into the habits of your other victims and will be writing you frequent and foolish letters, which you won't trouble yourself to answer. And then I'll be getting so I can't eat or sleep, and will lose my immortal soul lying to you about the 15 and 18 hour naps I'm taking and the pounds of meat I am eating—for I'd never admit that I allowed you to interfere with my comfort and health. You'd enjoy that too much!

I've been chasing the cure since I landed here, partly from choice but mostly from poverty. Most of the crew went into San Diego the other night, but I am holding just about enough money to keep me in Bull Durham and postage till my check comes (that should be in about two weeks) so I am sticking at home and spending my days reading or playing lady-like games such as Hearts and Five Hundred. She is a great world!

Richards and I have become quite chummy and ever so often he starts telling me what a wonderful person "little Miss Dolan" was. I usually change the subject as soon as possible, for he has the regular and usual opinion of you: that the Virgin Mary was a wild woman in comparison. Seriously, tho—he has a glorious opinion of the Little Handful, so you can add his name to your list—unless you already have.

The Cushman party has been split up—Goodhue and I are in the same ward. (I'll probably kill the God-damned fool one of these days!) The nurse here, a Miss Brown, is a friend of Mrs. Kelly's.

I like this joint very much and shall put in at least two months here. I've gained five pounds since I left Tacoma but I am pushing the thermometer up to 99° too often to please me.

The worst part of the day is when the clock shows 740 P.M., and I know that I should be down in front of the office, in the rain, waiting for Josephine Anna.[1] Six o'clock worries me, also—occasionally, when I figure it's time for your afternoon off and I should be standing on the People's Store corner, still in the rain, cursing you because you are fifteen minutes late and haven't shown up yet. I'll never awake at eleven, or I reckon I'd be thinking we ought to be out on the bridge—in the rain, of course—staging our customary friendly, but now and then a bit rough, dispute over the relative merits of "yes" and "no."

Are you still thinking of leaving Cushman? And do you think you could be persuaded to come to California? Has Miss Squally resigned yet?[2] Has Mr. Brown left for Texas? Is Miss Jacobs as sweet as ever?

If you answered my other letter at all promptly (and God help you if you didn't) I should hear from you tomorrow or Monday, at the latest. And if my memory is right, you were to inclose a picture in the first letter! The question is: will it be there? You're such a dear little liar, Sweet, that I'd hate to bet my right arm on it being in the letter. If I'm ever to get it I'll most likely have to come up and take it away from you. Maybe that's what I should have done about something else I wanted.

I've just time for a shower before lights-out

Love
Hammett

1. Josephine Dolan's middle name was Annis, not Anna.
2. Inge Qually was on the nursing staff at Cushman Institute.

ALS Marshall

To Josephine Dolan

9 March 1921 [Camp Kearney, California]

Dear Dear—
Your letter of the fourth got here this afternoon—so you see it does take nearly a week.

I was tickled pink to get your letter. I wasn't at all sure you'd write till some tiresome, draggy evening when you couldn't find anything else to do. But the letter came and so I feel as if I had the world by the tail—it was better than a shot of hooch.

I'm still a long way from finding anyone to take part of your place. (I don't expect to find any one who could completely fill it.) All the nurses here are impossible. A few with fair ankles but, My God! the faces—like cartoons! But, seriously, I am being remarkably faithful to you. Some day I may partially forget you, and be able to enjoy another woman, but there's nothing to show that it'll be soon. If anything, I'm a damnder fool over you now than I ever was.

Mr. Brown is one fine ass, isn't he? I wonder where he got all his information. Dream Book? Or Ouija board? But I reckon it was half guesswork and half based on information furnished by Jacobs. Now you can paste the following in your hat:

I may have done a lot of things that weren't according to scripture, but I love Josephine Anna Dolan—and have since about the sixth of January—more than anything in Christ's world. I know you don't expect or want me to deny Mr. Brown's news, so I won't bother you with it.

Meldner and Goodhue were kicked out a couple days ago for putting on a booze-party. I think they are at Alpine now—a san[i]torium about 30 miles out of San Diego.

You can't be missing me any more than I'm missing you, Sweet. It's pretty tough on these lonesome nights.

I'll have to cut this off now and fall in bed.

Yes'um, I deserve all the love you can spare me! And I want a lot more than I deserve.

> Love
> Sam

ALS MARSHALL

To Josephine Dolan

11 March 1921 [Camp Kearney, California]

Dear Little Handful—

Your letter deserved at least two answers, so here goes for the second. First for the news, of which there isn't very much.

Armstrong is in the venereal ward. For a while it looked as if Byrd,

Shell, Richards and a couple others would join him there, but they didn't.

I had a letter from Larry yesterday, giving me all the latest doings in the old home. He cheered me up by telling me he thought you were missing me. I don't know how he could tell, but I am anxious to believe him.

No one here has heard from Meldner or Goodhue since they left us.

My hands are usually quite warm nowadays so you needn't be afraid of 'em. But if you write me very much of that "in your nightie," "feeling chilly," "need someone to warm you" stuff I'll be climbing on a north-bound train and coming up to take the job.

I wouldn't want to give you any advice as to whether or not it's best for you to be going out with patients. Some day another "tall man" will come to Cushman and you'll have him losing his head over you and keeping you out on the bridge at all hours, and freezing you.

But the chances are I'll never hear of it and I'll go to my grave thinking you were true to me.

In spite of the fact that I know you are a liar I really think you love me a little—just because you said you did—for I've nothing else to base such a bel[ie]f upon. So if you don't, why then lie to me about it. I'll be happy that way till I find you out—and that may take months.

> Love in chunks
> Hammett

ALS MARSHALL

To Josephine Dolan

13 March 1921 [Camp Kearney, California]

Dear Nurse—

I should have started this "Dear Mama," for quite a bit of your last letter was most motherly—the advice about being a good boy and taking the cure and so forth. It only fell short of being a maternal letter in that you didn't give me any advice about my underwear. Don't forget that next time.

I have been following your orders tho—a few weeks more of this life and I'll be ready to grow a pair of downy wings and a pair of blue eyes. But my check should arrive (God only knows if it will) this week. Tijuana is open again so I reckon I'll make a trip down there as soon as I've something in my pockets besides my hands.

Altho it is none of my business, I'm glad you are sticking to your resolution about keeping away from the patients after hours. Even if it only lasts a little while. This is the first time I ever felt that way about a woman; perhaps it's the first time I have ever really loved a woman. That sounds funny but it may be the truth.

All the Cushman crew are quiet and well-behaved these days, except that Albert is becoming a chronic gambler. I'm afraid the boy is going to hell proper!

If I didn't know that you are an angel—even when the devil is looking out of your eyes—I'd begin to think you hard to get along with; after reading of all these scraps you are having, and the "I hate him," and "I don't care if he never comes back," and the rest of it.

What was the trouble with McDermott? Or shouldn't I ask?

If you and anyone fall out I am willing to gamble it's their fault. And when you can't get along with the rest of the world, look me up. I'll let you walk all over me—I'd get a good view of the pretty legs while you were doing it.

> Lots of love to the dearest small person in the world, and
lots of thanks for her dear letters
> S.D.H.

ALS Marshall

To Josephine Dolan

21 March 1921 [Camp Kearney, California]

Dear Josephine Anna—

After a long while of waiting—an even week it was—a letter from you came Saturday. I was beginning to think that another "tall man" had shown up and was dragging you into town every evening or so, and not leaving you time to write to me.

Meldner was up from Alpine a couple days ago. Said he liked it down there as they had no more rules than Cushman had.

That's all the news there is—nobody ever does anything here. And if they did I'd probably be asleep at the time and miss it. I'm the sleeping kid these days. It's about all I do—besides write letters to you when I am lucky enough to have one to answer.

I'm glad you're keeping your promise to "try not forget me for a couple weeks." You always were a mystery to me, Little Chap. I never could figure out whether you liked me a little (I mean "love"—I wouldn't give a God-damn to have you "like" me) or were just giving me your evenings because you hadn't anything else much to do with 'em, or merely vamping me to keep your hand in. Whichever it was tho, I had a mighty enjoyable time of it and right now I'd like to be anyplace at all with you.

If you'll live up to your dream and join me in a Los Angeles hotel (any time you say) I'll do my share and buy all the hot-water bags you want—if you think you'll need 'em.

You aren't the only one to dream these days. Even I, who have about three a year, dreamed of you during rest-hour yesterday. It was quite a remarkable dream—and I want a little information. Has the lady a mole on or near one hip? I want to know—if that part is true I can rely upon the rest coming true.

How about the picture, Sweet?

I'll be a "good boy" if I get enough letters from you to keep my mind occupied. If I don't I can't say what my behavior will be.

> Lots of the meanest sort of love—
> Daddy L. L.

ALS Marshall

To Josephine Dolan

Friday [March 1921, Camp Kearney, California]

Dear Boss—

Yes, Ma'am, I'll try to remember that I'm to say nothing when you load me with advice. Anyhow I don't have to take the advice. I can write that I'm obeying all your orders, and I can do as I please. I really like to have you tell me what to do and what not to do. It's like being married to you.

I reckon when 1921 is year before last Miss Qually will still be resigning every day or so. P.H.S. nurses are as bad as the patients that way—they are forever talking about quitting or being transferred.

Jacobs sent me a card telling me he had moved to Arrowhead. "I love it here," he wrote.

Albert isn't speaking to me nowadays (God only knows what I did to deserve such a cruel fate!) so you can't blame me for his going astray. I wanted to take him down across the line when my check comes and turn a wild Senorita loose on him, but unless he makes up with me, I reckon it's all off.

You shouldn't blame all men because Lilly didn't write his wife. I, for instance, always take particular pains to write frequently to all of my wives who happen to be pregnant.

Are you going back to Anaconda for your June vacation? Or haven't you decided yet where?

The picture with the motto—which I hope holds good—was very nice; but it reminded me of a much nicer promised picture. I am waiting for it with no patience whatever.

How are you feeling now, Sweetheart? Don't you think you should have taken Miss Weaver's advice? As Miss Qually used to say, "Little Miss Dolan is not very strong and she should be careful." Personally, I think a "southern trip" would be the best thing in the world for you.

I went into San Diego last Tuesday for ten hours, got fairly well lit up and had a very pleasant evening. Also I returned from town as much a virgin as when I went—so I am following at least part of your advice.

While there I met Meldner and Goodhue but had only a few minutes conversation with them. Since then I have heard, in an indirect way, that they have been thrown out of Alpine. It may or may not be true.

I'm hoping to get my check tomorrow so I can get down to Tijuana for Sunday's races—but I doubt that I'll make it.

Mrs. Hammett's boy is feeling top-notch these days—the pulse and temp. are behaving themselves. So I am looking for an early discharge. There's no fun in a hospital where there's no Josephine. I think there should be at least one in every U.S.P.H.S.H.

It's twenty minutes to eight. I wonder if you are waiting at the office for me—and if you are going to say "yes" tonight

All sorts of love
S.D.H.

ALS MARSHALL

To Josephine Dolan

24 April 1921 [Camp Kearney, California]

Dear Lady—

Here's a snap-shot of our hour-walk-gang, with Cushman represented by Max, Farrer, Taylor, Albert and I. Notice how plump young Albert is getting!

Yesterday I went down to Tijuana and misbehaved delightfully. Had a high, wide and deep time, and returned to the convent this morning as drunk as a lord and, of course, flat broke. But she was an enjoyable trip and I'm content to stick to my camp-fire for two or three weeks now. If I missed anything in the town it must have been hiding out while I was there.

I had a tearful letter from Miss Jacobs early in the week, inviting me to come up to Los Angeles for three or four days. He'll "keep" me while I am there, he writes. Ain't that sweet of him? But, somehow, I'm not hungering for his company, so I reckon I'll let the *wonderful* opportunity slide by.

What do you mean, I'd "never get well" with you around? You surely were not ruining my health to any great extent! If I remember right I didn't have to use crutches when I left Cushman. And I'd a lot rather be made an invalid by little Miss Dolan than cured by anyone else I can think of.

And, Sweetheart, I am not a "terrible man"—not by any manner or means. But I haven't any God except Josephine. That's all there is to it.

I'm having one hell of a time getting this letter down straight—the Mexican hooch hasn't all passed away yet.

What I would like to write would be a letter of the most passionate sort—one that would knock you off your chair—but I remember you saying that you were going to cut one bird off your list because his (it was your travelling man) letters were too loving; so I think I'll play safe.

I wish you were down here, Sweet, what a corking time we could have! Trips to Tijuana together; miles of country to roam around on evenings when we didn't want to go to town; San Diego, Coronado and Los A. now and then; warm evenings where you wouldn't be freezing and my hands would not be cold. But—oh hell!

I hope you are feeling better now.

> All the love north of hell
> Hammett

ALS Marshall

To Josephine Dolan

30 April 1921 [Camp Kearney, California]

Dear Josephine—

In your last letter you said you were not feeling well, and now I have not had a letter from you for a flock of days. So I've been picturing you sick a-bed, maybe dying: all the things a chap in love can think of when things don't go just right.

I hope I am all wrong: that you have been neglecting me through laziness, or anything except illness. I'd rather, even, that you had grown tired of writing—tho Christ knows that wouldn't be easy to take!

I haven't been out of camp this week. I've been sticking at home fighting a cold that is doing its damnedest to turn into bronchitis. But I think I have it licked now.

If tomorrow is warm and clear I shall most likely go up to Oceanside for an afternoon and part of an evening at the beach.

Richards is leaving for Seattle Monday night—discharged as an arrested case. Clements will go the same route in a few days.

That's all the news there is.

Love
Hammett

ALS Marshall

To Josephine Dolan

8 May [1921, Camp Kearney, California]

Dearest woman—

Your letter from Seattle came yesterday and I never in my life was gladder to get anything. She was a long, dry stretch: that letterless space.

I hope you are feeling lots better now, and stay that way. Now that you are thru with that damned night work perhaps you'll get back in shape. For the love of God, Sweet, take care of yourself!

That picture was taken about half a mile from the hospital and is a fair sample of the scenery here. Some of it is better and some worse, but that's about the average.

This isn't always "warm country"—the past few days have been mostly rainy and cool and altogether dismal. I've had a rotten cold but it is better now.

My going is still dependent upon my check, so continue addressing me here as usual until I tell you I am on my way. I may be here a couple weeks yet—tho I hope to get away this week.

I haven't heard from Brazer for a month or two, but I won't be at all surprised at anything he writes about your admirers. There's no reason in the world why all the patients in Cushman shouldn't be chasing you from morn till night. (Do you remember how I used to hang by your side from the time you came on duty in 35 until you went off?)

I didn't know whether you were a "wild woman" or not before I went out with you, Lady, but I did know that you were a wonderful little person from head to heels, from shoulder to shoulder, from back-bone to wishbone, inside and

[The rest of the letter is missing.]

ALS MARSHALL

To Josephine Dolan

10 May 1921 [Camp Kearney, California]

Dear Little Chap—

Your letter of the sixth came a few minutes ago.

You should have known better than to think I'd be angry because you hadn't sent me a letter for a few days. It was not comfortable, that row of days with no word from you, but I certainly couldn't get up on my ear until I knew how it happened.

The Lady has been much too nice to me for me to let a thing like that set me a-scolding.

Unless a hitch of some sort shows up, I will leave San Diego for Baltimore on Friday the 13th. I may possibly stay here until Saturday or even Monday but I think Friday night will see me on my way. That will put me in Baltimore Wednesday morning.

So you can address your next letter to:

1419 W. Lexington St.
Baltimore, Maryland[1]

There's no more news of any sort—except that I'm still loving you to beat hell, and that shouldn't be news to you.

> Love
> Hammett

1. The address of Hammett's parents.

ALS MARSHALL

To Josephine Dolan

Hammett was discharged from Camp Kearney on Sunday, 15 May 1921. Soon afterward Jose quit her job and went to Anaconda, Montana, to stay with her family while she and Hammett made plans for the future. He moved to San Francisco later in the month, and they were married there in the rectory of St. Mary's Cathedral on 7 July. Their daughter Mary Jane was born on 15 October. Hammett resumed work as a Pinkerton's detective, but by the end of the year, his health worsened and he was forced to quit detective work permanently.

Thursday [postmarked 2 June 1921], Davenport Hotel, Spokane, Washington

Dear Josephine

I didn't expect to land here, but here I am.

At the last minute the fat heads who run Camp Kearn[e]y decided that I'd have to take a ticket to Spokane or nothing. I was flirting with poverty so I took the ticket.

How long I'll be here depends upon my financial progress, but I am going to see you before I go east, regardless of how things turn out.

Now that I am here I haven't any sort of plans for the future but I reckon things will work out in some manner.

When do you start on your vacation? And what and where?

If I can't get to Tacoma before you go I may get to Butte later.

I'll write you a decent letter as soon as I am settled

      Love
        Hammett

ALS Marshall

To Allan Carter, U.S. Veterans Board

On 31 May 1923 Hammett was judged by the U.S. Veterans Bureau to be rehabilitated, and his disability compensation was discontinued.

11 June 1923, 620 Eddy St., San Francisco

Dear Mr. Carter:

I have your letter of June 8th notifying me that from May 31st my compensatory disability is rated at less than 10%.

Mr. Bourne, of your division, told me this afternoon that this rating was based upon my last physical examination: made by a Dr. Seid, I think, some time last month.

I do not feel that my condition at this time—which is certainly no better than it was before I entered training—justifies this rating and I wish to appeal from it.

If possible I should like another examination, preferably by a lung specialist, so that we may know definitely where we stand without putting me to the expense of getting the opinions of outside specialists.

Sincerely yours,

TLU Marshall

Letter to the Editor, *Black Mask*, 15 June 1923, pp. 126–7

After a vocational rehabilitation course at Munson's Business College, Hammett began writing for pulp magazines, primarily Black Mask, in October 1922. In this letter to the editor, he comments on his story "The Vicious Circle," published in the 15 June 1923 Black Mask under the pseudonym Peter Collinson.

[San Francisco]

I have been out of town for a couple of weeks—I have to go up in the hills to see some real snow at least once each winter—which is why I haven't answered your letter before this.

About the story: None of the characters is real in a literal sense, though I doubt that it would be possible to build a character without putting into it at least something of someone the writer has known. The plot, however, is closer to earth. In the years during which I tried my hand at "private detecting" I ran across several cases where the "friend" called in to dispose of a blackmailer either went into partnership with him or took over his business after getting him out of the way. And I know of at least one case where a blackmailer was disposed of just as "Inch" disposed of "Bush."

I like Rose's cover on the February 15th issue!

> Sincerely,
> S. D. Hammett

To Allan Carter, U.S. Veterans Bureau

19 September 1923, 620 Eddy St., San Francisco

Dear Sir,
    I had a letter from you, dated June 14th, 1923, advising me that my file had been forwarded to the District Board of Appeals for review, in connection with my protesting the rating of less than ten percent given me after my rehabilitation.
    Since that time I have received no information concerning this matter.
    Will you kindly advise me what action was taken by the District Board of Appeals, and what my status is now.

> Very truly yours,

TLU Marshall

Letter to the Editor, *Black Mask*, 15 October 1923, p. 127

"Slippery Fingers," a story about a blackmailer who has a set of fingerprints laminated onto his fingertips, was published in the 15 October 1923 Black Mask *under the pseudonym Peter Collinson.*

[San Francisco]

    Since writing "Slippery Fingers," I have read an article in the San Francisco *Chronicle,* wherein August Vollmer, chief of police of Berkeley, California, and president of the International Association of Chiefs of Police, is quoted as saying that although it is possible successfully to transfer actual finger-prints from one place to another it is not possible to forge them—"Close inspection of any forged finger-print will soon cause detection."
    It may be that what Farr does in my story would be considered by Mr.

Vollmer a transference rather than a forgery. But whichever it is, I think there is no longer reasonable room for doubt that fingerprints can be successfully forged. I have seen forged prints that to me seemed perfect, but, not being even an amateur in that line, my opinion isn't worth much. I think, however, that quite a number of those qualified to speak on the subject will agree with me that it can be, and has been, done.

In the second Arbuckle trial, if my memory is correct, the defense introduced an expert from Los Angeles who testified that he had deceived an assembly of his colleagues with forged prints.[1]

The method used in my story was not selected because it was the best, but because it was the simplest with which I was acquainted and the most easily described. Successful experiments were made with it by the experts at the Leavenworth federal prison.

> Sincerely,
> S. D. Hammett

1. Fatty Arbuckle, a movie actor-comedian, was tried for the rape and murder of an actress who attended a party in his San Francisco hotel suite on 5 September 1921. Hammett claimed to have worked as a detective for the defense. The time of the first trial, which ended in a hung jury on 4 December 1921, coincides with Hammett's employment at Pinkerton's. Hammett was retired at the time of Arbuckle's second trial, on a reduced charge, which ended in an acquittal on 3 February 1922.

Letter to the Editor, *Black Mask*, 1 January 1924, p. 127

In Hammett's story "The Tenth Clew," first published in the 1 January 1924 Black Mask, *Creda Dexter "was pronouncedly feline throughout. Her every movement was the slow, smooth, sure one of a cat; and the contours of her rather pretty face, the shape of her mouth, her small nose, the set of her eyes, the swelling of her brows, were all cat-like."*

San Francisco

Thanks for the check for "The Tenth Clew."

And I want to plead guilty to a bit of cowardice in connection with the story. The original of Creda Dexter didn't resemble a kitten at all. She looked exactly like a bull-pup! Believe it or not, she looked exactly like a young white-faced bull-pup—and she was pretty in the bargain!

Except for her eyes, I never succeeded in determining just what was responsible for the resemblance, but it was a very real one.

When, however, it came to actually putting her down on paper, my nerve failed me. "Nobody will believe you if you write a thing like that," I told myself. "They'll think you're trying to spoof them."

So, for the sake of plausibility, I lied about her!

Sincerely,
Dashiell Hammett

Letter to the Editor, *Black Mask*, 1 March 1924, p. 127

In "Zigzags of Treachery," published in the 1 March 1924 Black Mask, Hammett wrote: "There are four rules for shadowing: Keep behind your subject as much as possible; never try to hide from him; act in a natural manner no matter what happens; and never meet his eye."

San Francisco

I'll have another story riding your way in a day or two: one for the customers who don't like their sleuths to do too much brain-work.

The four rules for shadowing that I gave in "Zigzags" are the first and last words on the subject. There are no other tricks to learn. Follow them, and once you get the hang of it, shadowing is the easiest of detective work, except, perhaps, to an extremely nervous man. You simply saunter along somewhere within sight of your subject, and, barring bad breaks, the only thing that can make you lose him is over-anxiety on your own part.

Even a clever criminal may be shadowed for weeks without suspecting it. I know one operative who shadowed a forger—a wily old hand— for more than three months without arousing his suspicion. I myself trailed one for six weeks, riding trains and making half a dozen small towns with him; and I'm not exactly inconspicuous—standing an inch or so over six feet.

Another thing: a detective may shadow a man for days and in the end have but the haziest idea of the man's features. Tricks of carriage, ways of wearing clothes, general outline, individual mannerisms—all as seen from the rear—are much more important to the shadow than faces. They can be recognized at a greater distance, and do not necessitate his getting in front of his subject at any time.

Back—and it's only a couple years back—in the days before I decided that there was more fun in writing about manhunting than in that hunting, I wasn't especially fond of shadowing, though I had plenty of it to do. But I worked under one superintendent who needed only the flimsiest of excuses to desert his desk and get out on the street behind some suspect.

> Sincerely,
> Dashiell Hammett

Letter to the Editor, *Black Mask*, 1 March 1924, pp. 127–8

In the story described below, also published in the 1 March 1924 issue of Black Mask, *Owen Sack is a man afraid of guns until he is shot and finds that the wound doesn't hurt as much as he feared. It is set on the Kootenai River, which runs from Canada through the northwest corner of Montana.*

San Francisco

Thanks for the check for "Afraid of a Gun."

The *Owen Sack* I knew was a kid of fourteen, with a fast pair of legs and a great fear of fists. He might have grown up to be the man in my story; but he was overtaken one day by a lad with faster legs. *Owen* had to fight then. He lost the fight, and lost his fear, too. After that he collected skinned knuckles as men collect old pewter and first editions.

The most difficult part of writing the story was to keep out my—in this case—quite irrelevant enthusiasm for the country around the Kootenai River. For a man who likes his scenery big but not raw—wants trees and rivers and lakes in his mountains—northern Idaho and northwestern Montana were made to order. And if he likes to knock over an occasional deer, elk, or bear in season—I'd suggest that he buy his ticket to Libby, Montana, and set out from there. But if he goes in the winter, he ought to take his overcoat along.

In Australian roads, the ruts do sometimes stand "perversely up out of the ground like railway tracks." Where the soil is a loose sand, a strong wind will blow the road completely away except for the ruts, where the pressure of the wheels has packed the sand tight; and these ruts will be left sticking up in the air.

Dashiell Hammett

Letter to the Editor, *Black Mask*, August 1924, pp. 127–8

In a headnote to this letter, Phil Cody, who had become editor of Black Mask *six months earlier, reported on an editorial conference in which he rejected two of Hammett's stories. Hammett's letter in response was disingenuous. "Women, Politics, and Murder" was published in the September 1924* Black Mask; *and "The Question Is One Answer" was apparently retitled "Who Killed Bob Teal" for publication in the November 1924* True Detective Stories. *In the next nineteen months, Hammett published fifteen short stories, an article, two book reviews, and a poem.*

San Francisco

I don't like that "tragedy in one act" at all; it's too damned true-to-life. The theater, to amuse me, must be a bit artificial.

I don't think I shall send "Women, Politics, and Murder" back to you—not in time for the July issue anyway. The trouble is that this sleuth of mine has degenerated into a meal-ticket. I liked him at first and used to enjoy putting him through his tricks; but recently I've fallen into the habit of bringing him out and running him around whenever the landlord, or the butcher, or the grocer shows signs of nervousness.

There are men who can write like that, but I am not one of them. If I stick to the stuff that I want to write—the stuff I enjoy writing—I can make a go of it, but when I try to grind out a yarn because I think there is a market for it, I flop.

Whenever, from now on, I get hold of a story that fits my sleuth, I shall put him to work, but I'm through with trying to run him on a schedule.

Possibly I could patch up "The Question's One Answer" and "Women, Politics, and Murder" enough to get by with them, but my frank opinion of them is that neither is worth the trouble. I have a liking for honest work, and honest work as I see it is work that is done for the worker's enjoyment as much as for the profit it will bring him. And henceforth that's my work.

I want to thank both you and Mr. Cody for jolting me into wakefulness. There's no telling how much good this will do me. And you may be sure that whenever you get a story from me hereafter,—frequently, I hope,—it will be one that I enjoyed writing.

Dashiell Hammett

Letter to the Editor, *Black Mask*, November 1924, p. 128

[San Francisco]

I was born in Maryland, between the Potomac and Patuxent rivers, on May 27, 1894, and was raised in Baltimore.

After a fraction of a year in high school—Baltimore Polytechnic Institute—I became the unsatisfactory and unsatisfied employee of various railroads, stock brokers, machine manufacturers, canners, and the like. Usually I was fired.

An enigmatic want-ad took me into the employ of Pinkerton's National Detective Agency, and I stuck at that until early in 1922, when I chucked it to see what I could do with fiction writing.

In between, I spent an uneventful while in the army during the war, becoming a sergeant; and acquired a wife and daughter.

For the rest, I am long and lean and grayheaded, and very lazy. I have no ambition at all in the usual sense of the word; like to live as nearly as possible in the center of large cities, and have no recreations or hobbies.

Dashiell Hammett

To Editors of *The Forum*

6 March [1925], 620 Eddy St., San Francisco

Dear Sirs,

If you use the review of Sinclair's *Mammonart* I sent you on the 4th, will you please substitute "Ode on a Grecian Urn" and "Ode on Melancholy" for the atrocious free-hand titles I gave Keats' poems in the 14th and 15th lines of the first page of my manuscript.[1]

Sincerely,
Dashiell Hammett [unsigned]

1. Hammett's review of Upton Sinclair's *Mammonart: An Essay in Economic Interpretation* (1925) was not published. This letter is on the verso of a page from a draft of Hammett's unpublished story "The Secret Emperor."

   For publication data on this and other books that Hammett mentions reading, please consult the Appendix.

TLU HRC

To Philip C. Cody

Hammett had an uneasy relationship with Philip C. Cody, editor of Black Mask *from 1 April 1924 to October 1926. He did not write another long story for Cody after "The Gutting of Couffignal," published in the December 1925* Black Mask. *He responded to Cody's insistence on action-packed stories with "The Nails in Mr. Cayterer," featuring an effeminate detective, in the January 1926 issue of the magazine, and he published only two more stories before he quit in a dispute about money. He did not write for Cody again, but Joseph Shaw, who became editor in November 1926, lured him back.*

[November? 1925, San Francisco]

Dear Cody,

Thanks for the "Nails in Mr. Cayterer" check.

I've put THE novelette aside for a while, since I'm not due to knock at your door again with a long story until November, but, for better or worse, you can count on surely seeing it then.

Something I forgot to mention in my last couple of letters: through some sort of mixup with your rubber stamps, your check for "The Gutting of Couffignal" read all rights instead of first American and British serial rights. A paragraph in your next letter will straighten it out and save my literary executors trouble.

About the critical opinion: I'll be glad to let you have it, but remember I'm hard to get along with where fiction's concerned.

Here goes for the October issue: I liked Cummings' "The Mystery at Cragmoor," though I think it would have been a better yarn if the counterfeiting had been left out and Sir Henry had killed Griswold because of ill treatment of his wife, whom, as in the story, he still loved though his pride wouldn't let him admit it. However, I thought it a good story, well done—one of the best you've had. (Maybe it's just as well Cummings didn't use my motive—I can use it myself sometime.)

"Alias Buttercup"—if you like Race Williams, this is a good story; if you don't it isn't.

The three short stories in this issue I didn't like at all. Not that they were offensive, but simply that they didn't mean anything. People moved around doing things, but neither the people nor the things they did were interesting enough to work up a sweat over.

I always like Somerville's articles.[1]

Yours,

1. Hammett's remarks about the October 1925 *Black Mask* refer to Ray Cummings, who was the creator of series detective T. McGuirk and who published fifteen stories in *Black Mask* between December 1922 and September 1926. "The Mystery at Cragmoor" was Cummings's only *Black Mask* story in which McGuirk was not the detective. Race Williams was a hard-boiled series detective created by Carroll John Daly, who published sixty-one stories in *Black Mask* between October 1922 and December 1938. Hammett liked Daly and felt that he had contributed to the eclipse of Daly's career because Daly was unfavorably compared to Hammett as a practitioner of the hard-boiled style. Charles Somerville's "A Weird Detective" was one of the forty-seven ostensibly true crime stories in the Manhunter series.

TLU HRC

To Veterans Bureau Claims Division

In March 1926, two months before his second daughter, Josephine, was born, Hammett began working full time as advertising manager at Albert Samuels Jewelers in San Francisco. He collapsed in his office in July 1926 hemorrhaging blood from his lungs and suffering from hepatitis.

27 September 1926, 20 Monroe St., San Francisco

Gentlemen:

My compensation was discontinued on June 30, 1924.

Hemorrhages, weakness and the rest of the things that go with tuber-culosis forced me to give up my work a couple of months ago.

I enclose an affidavit to that effect from my former employer.

I should like to have my case reopened so that I may be awarded compensation again.

Will you kindly advise me when I should report for examination.

> Yours truly,
> Samuel D. Hammett [unsigned]

TLU Marshall

To Josephine Dolan Hammett

After a brief convalescence, Hammett began working part time for Samuels again in October, the month his family took up separate residence, at the recommenda-tion Health Service nurses, to protect the children from infection. Mrs. Hammett and the girls, five-year-old Mary and the infant Josephine, spent the fall with rela-tives in Montana, then moved to Fairfax, California, about fifteen miles north of San Francisco.

4 October 1926, 20 Monroe St., San Francisco, California

Dearest,

I did like the pictures very much: you look quite intellectual, or maybe it's artistic, with the bob.

I missed Samuels Friday. Harry was still away on his vacation.[1] I'll probably try again this week. I'd like to know whether anything is going to come of the advertising racket or not. What he's afraid of is that I'll die on his hands. I'm not altogether sure I want the blooming thing. Of course it will be easy insofar as actual work is concerned, but I'll have all the responsibility, and the arguing with him and Harry, that I had before, and I don't know whether that will sit well on my lungs or not.

I haven't heard from the Veterans Bureau since I filed my papers, but

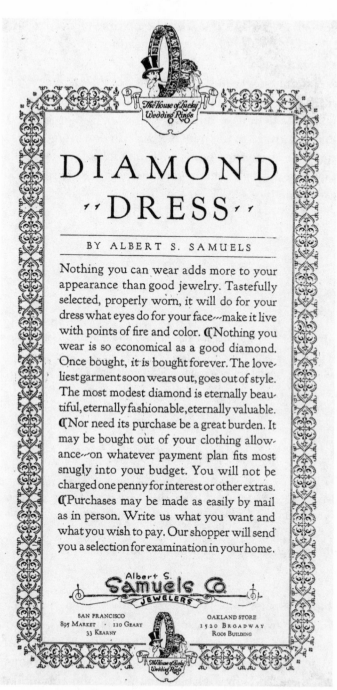

DIAMOND
''DRESS''

BY ALBERT S. SAMUELS

Nothing you can wear adds more to your appearance than good jewelry. Tastefully selected, properly worn, it will do for your dress what eyes do for your face---make it live with points of fire and color. ⸿Nothing you wear is so economical as a good diamond. Once bought, it is bought forever. The loveliest garment soon wears out, goes out of style. The most modest diamond is eternally beautiful, eternally fashionable, eternally valuable. ⸿Nor need its purchase be a great burden. It may be bought out of your clothing allowance---on whatever payment plan fits most snugly into your budget. You will not be charged one penny for interest or other extras. ⸿Purchases may be made as easily by mail as in person. Write us what you want and what you wish to pay. Our shopper will send you a selection for examination in your home.

Albert S.
Samuels Co
JEWELERS

SAN FRANCISCO
895 MARKET · 110 GEARY
33 KEARNY

OAKLAND STORE
1520 BROADWAY
ROOS BUILDING

Proof for Samuels Ad Hammett sent to Jose.

that's less than a week ago, and a week's no time at all for a government body. Of course I'm sure of the compensation—there's no question of yes or no, just of when.

Here's the customary portrait for the nitwit. Ask her what kind of dumbbell she is, and tell her to kiss Josephine Rebecca for me. I imagine the youngster is a darling by now.

I'm looking forward to the new pictures, so don't forget them.

And don't be worrying about my financial affairs. God knows we always staggered through somehow in the past, and I still can. I haven't missed any meals.

Yesterday I wrote four poems, and I think maybe one of them is some good.

> Love,
> D.

Walter's $50 just came[2]

1. Harry Sloss was Albert Samuels's cousin and a member of his management team. He was known for his inflated ego.
2. Walter is presumably Jose's younger brother, Walter Dolan.

TLS MARSHALL

To Peggy O'Toole

Peggy O'Toole was a secretary at Albert Samuels Jewelers. Albert Samuels said Hammett confided that he was thinking of her when he wrote about Brigid O'Shaughnessy in The Maltese Falcon. *Chipman was a member of Samuels's management team.*

10 November 1926, 1509 Hyde St., San Francisco

Sweet,

My God! this is terrible! I've just remembered that we had a bet and I lost it and ergo owe you a box of chocolates. It's your fault; you should have hinted at 'em. It'll serve you right if I can't finance the purchase for months. The only solace I have in my humiliation is the thought of you waiting all this time, divided between greed and the feeling that it wouldn't be "nice" to remind me. Aren't you a lil?

After several careful subsequent inspections, I've decided that you were—peculiarly—wrong in assuming that I think you lovelier now because I don't see you as often as I did. You are lovelier. If it were a glandular delusion, it would work the other way round: I'm not a Chipman. I love you more when I'm with you than when I'm away; and more when I'm touching you than when I'm merely looking at you; and most of all when I'm tasting you—but that's not happened often enough to be talked about very much. So you must be actually improving; perhaps the doubtless considerable spiritual benefits of being loved by me are showing themselves physically. I've always known I had a good [e]ffect on you.

The plans for my return to advertising are coming along nicely. I'm going to have a lot of fun next year, if boredom doesn't set in too soon.

> I love you, dear animal.
> Hammett

TLS Susan Finn

To Peggy O'Toole

[San Francisco]

Here, sweetheart, are the gems.[1] No doubt you'll be somewhat disappointed in them—having expected God only knows what monstrosities! If you find them too tame I'll gladly do some richer ones for you—ones that I held up, hoping to get into print with these before turning myself loose. I, in a manner of speaking, love you, or words to that effect.

1. The "two gems" Hammett refers to are the story "Seven Pages" and a poem, enclosures that survive in fragments. Peggy O'Toole's daughter recalls that her mother had about twenty letters from Hammett, most of which were destroyed. Miss O'Toole and Mr. Niederholzer, also a Samuels employee, were married in 1928.

ALS Susan Finn

To Josephine Dolan Hammett

When Joseph Thompson Shaw became editor of Black Mask *magazine in November 1926, he promptly began recruiting a stable of writers, including Hammett, who insisted that he be paid $300—money he felt Cody owed him—as a condition of his return.*

[November? 1926, San Francisco]

Dear Jose,

A telegram from Shaw woke me up this morning. It was all about how glad he was to have me back in the flock and so on. The only important thing in it was that he's sending me $300. That's what the fight was about in the first place, and so I won after all.

I wrote Dick a little while ago, sending him one of the pictures of the little hippo.[1]

Tomorrow morning I'm going to start in on the *Black Mask* junk, putting my mornings in on that and my evenings on the novel. So you won't

```
Upon these lips in touch sublime
And gives me ease until you come                    again ?

O happy sun, that though it sets,
Shall rise to gaze again on thee.
Had I his place no shade of night
Should on the face of heav'n be seen
While yet thy vision fell on earth
And hills resung thy gracious mirth's               refrain.

O, that my eyes might form its rays
And seek thee wantonly all day,
My lips the shafts of sunny haze,
To kiss thy cheeks, thy brow, and hair
In rapturous confusion lost
While joy unto my heart were host                   in vain.

How did I die? By my own hand
They say. 'Tis wholly false indeed,
For I was dead ere yet I planned
The act which vort response decreed,
    When naked to the night and you
    My soul I bared, but met rebuke.                "Abstain !"

Not then it came; but soon, when calm
Reflection cooled thy heated heart,
While sober thought lent passion balm
And haven from erotic dart.
Then, then I died by your command
That we should rend this human bond                 in twain.
```

One of the "two gems" Hammett sent to Peggy O'Toole

Dashiell Hammett
20 Monroe Street
San Francisco
California

800 words

Seven Pages

By Dashiell Hammett

One

She was one of the rare red-haired women whose skins are without blemish: she was marble, to the eye. I used to quote truthfully to her, "Thou art all fair, my love; there is no spot in thee." She was utterly unpractical. One otherwise dreary afternoon she lay with her bright head on my knees while I read Don Marquis' Sonnets to a Red-Haired Lady to her. When I had finished she made a little purring noise and stared dreamily distant-eyed past me. "Tell me about this Don Marquis," she said. "Do you know him?"

Two

I sat in the lobby of the Plaza, in San Francisco. It was the day before the opening of the second absurd attempt to convict Roscoe Arbuckle of something. He came into the lobby. He looked at me and I at him. His eyes were the eyes of a man who expected to be regarded as a monster but was not yet inured to it. I made my gaze as contemptuous as I could. He glared at me, went on to the elevator still glaring. It was amusing. I was working for his attorneys at the time, gathering information for his defense.

One of the "two gems" Hammett sent to Peggy O'Toole

Three

We would leave the buildings in early darkness, walk a little way across the desert, and go down into a small canyon where four trees grouped around a level spot. The night-dampness settling on earth that had cooked since morning would loose the fragrance of ground and plant around us. We would lie there until late in the night, our nostrils full of world-smell, the trees making irregular map-boundary division among the stars. Our love seemed dependent on not being phrased. It seemed if one of us had said, "I love you," the next instant it would have been a lie. So we loved and cursed one another merrily, ribaldly, she usually stopping her ears in the end because I knew more words.

Four

He came into the room in brown stocking-feet, blue policeman's pants and gray woolen undershirt. "Who the hell moved that pi-ano?" he demanded, and grunted and cursed while wheeling it back into the inconvenient corner from which we had dragged it. "It's my pi-ano, and it stays where I put it, see," he assured us before he went out again. His daughters were quite embarrassed, since Jack and I had bought the whiskey that was in him, so they didn't object when, just before we left, we took all the pictures down from the walls and stacked them behind the pi-ano. That was in the part of Baltimore called Pig Town, a few blocks from another house where we had found one night two in the company who would not drink alcohol. We gave them root beer into which had been put liberal doses of aromatic casca.

Five

her four time

have to be economical any more. We'll pay off the debts gradually and everything will be great until I decide to quit again.

But I really think this time I'll do enough of the murder-and-so-on to make a book. It's time we were trying prosperity for a while. Pray God I can keep my thoughts on it!

See you Sunday. Kiss the little ladies for me.

Love,

D.

1. Hammett called his brother Richard "Dick." "Little Hippo" was Hammett's pet name for his daughter Josephine.

TLS Marshall

To Josephine Dolan Hammett

Monday evening [1927? San Francisco, California], between sips of gin

Dear Jose,

This day's mail brought seven bucks from the *Saturday Review*, and a letter from Dick with the enclosed snapshot of his cub.[1] He says it looks like me, and he thinks our little Jo looks like him.

Nothing exciting has happened in Mr. Samuels' well-known jewelry store since I last wrote you, except that a couple of out of town folks have sent in the picture of the ring perched on the cactus points with orders for it. That impressed the well-known Mr. Samuels quite a bit, since he has always protested quite strenuously against having his hard-earned money "wasted" in the *Chronicle's* rotogravure section. Lucky for him I don't pay any attention to him!

I'll see you Thursday—put a plate on the table for me, but if anything should happen to make me late don't wait—just save my share.

Now for some paragraphs of Blackmasking.

Kiss the reptiles for me.

Love,
D.

1. Hammett reviewed mystery novels for *The Saturday Review of Literature* from 15 January 1927 to 26 October 1929.

TLS Marshall

To Josephine Dolan Hammett

Mrs. Hammett, Josephine, and Mary lived in Fairfax, where Hammett visited them on weekends. To get to their home, he rode a ferry across the San Francisco Bay and took a train to Fairfax.

24 May 1927, 891 Post St., San Francisco

Dear Jose,

I got back home safe and practically sober, which made me very nearly the only sober passenger. What a gang of riff-raff travels over that line on Sundays!

* * *

The weather has warmed up here, so I suppose you are baking prettily over there.

In the good old government fashion, my dentist was off on his vacation when I reported for punishment yesterday, so I'll have to wait until late next month to get a crack at him again. Lucky my teeth have stopped bothering me!

Kiss the animals for me.

> Love,
> D.

TLS MARSHALL

To Josephine Dolan Hammett

31 May [1927], 891 Post St., San Francisco, California

Dear Jose,

Home safely again, as usual. There wasn't such a mob last night.

I left fountain pen and pencil with you. Don't let the children play with them, unless, of course, they cry for them.

What do you guess I did last night? Went to a movie—John Barrymore in *Don Juan*. I got home feeling bored and not like reading or sleeping, so I thought of that as something to do. And now I'm cured of movies for another couple of years. It was lousy—bad taste, bad acting and stupid ignorance can't go any further than last night's show carried them.

Nothing exciting in the morning's mail, except another tempting invitation to buy an *Encyclopaedia Britannica.*

Kiss the insects for me,

Love,
D

TLS MARSHALL

To Josephine Dolan Hammett

[postmarked 1 June 1927, San Francisco]

Dear Jose,

Got home tonight to find a stack of letters from the *Black Mask:* one from Shaw telling me how good I am, one from Cody telling me the same thing with further trimmings, and one from Gardner telling me the last dingus he read of mine was not only the best ever printed in the *Black Mask,* but the best he had ever read anywhere, and so on and so on and so on.[1]

Overwhelmed by this applesauce I'm wiring them to shoot me some dough and I'll do them some more of the shots-in-the-dark.

On the strength of that I'm putting in an order for an *Encyclopaedia Britannica* and some gin.

Merry Christmas!
D

1. Erle Stanley Gardner was an editorial consultant at *Black Mask.* "The last dingus" refers to Hammett's Continental Op story "The Main Death," published in the June 1927 issue of *Black Mask,* which would have been on the newsstands in May. The Continental Op is the nameless operative for the Continental Detective Agency who narrates many of Hammett's short stories and his first two novels.

TPS MARSHALL

To Josephine Dolan Hammett

Sunday [June 7, 1927? San Francisco]

Dear Jose,

Got back all in one piece and reached the store a little before five to find that somehow in spite of my lateness the place seemed to be running all right.

I had a letter from Shaw of the *Black Mask* yesterday—nothing very exciting, just acknowledging my letter of thanks for the check and cautioning me against trying to follow too faithfully the advice he, Gardner and Cody had sent in their letters.

The story goeth along slowly but nicely. I got a good hunk of it done this day of our Lord.[1]

Yesterday I went down early enough to have luncheon with the Messrs Samuels (senior and junior), Sloss, and Chipman.[2] Before we went Miss O'Toole told me she had had another morning of being put through the third degree about the advertising. So at the luncheon table Chipman and I put on a swell argument. It lasted from quarter to one till half past two. I was in good shape for battling. I had a hell of a lot of fun: I hit him with statistics and flourished percentages and the like in his face and quoted all the authorities from Moses to Babson and smothered him with incidents from the experience of the National Biscuit Company and General Motors and sent up assorted facts like fireworks. Some of all this had something to do with the case and some didn't, but it was all amusing. Finally I got him indignant, peevish, and then to save his face he had [to] admit that he wasn't as sure of his side as he had seemed.

I was surprised and quite elated to have talked him down and won my case. Al was quite tickled. He and Harry are afraid of Chipman, and so they were pleased to have somebody in the firm who could make him back up. The only bad feature is that Chipman can't afford to let it rest at that. He's a high-class expert, and nobody pays men a thousand dollars a month to be stumped by youngsters who have only been in the business world a few months. So I'll have to keep my eye on him or he'll slit my throat one of these mornings. But, having licked him once, I think I can keep it up. It's a lot of fun anyway!

I'll put Reusche's check in the mail so he'll get it the fifteenth.[3]
I've only had one drink since I left Fairfax. Temperate, eh, what?

1. Presumably the writing Hammett refers to is one of the sections of "Poisonville," which was serialized in four parts in *Black Mask* beginning in November 1927 and published as *Red Harvest* by Knopf in 1929.
2. Chipman was Samuels' advertising manager.
3. Reusche was Jose Hammett's landlord.

TLU MARSHALL

To Josephine Dolan Hammett

Hammett appeared twice in Stratford Magazine, *a little magazine that published verse: "Yes" in the March 1927 issue, and "Goodbye to a Lady" in June 1927.*

Tuesday in the Morning [June? 1927, San Francisco]

Dear Jose,

There isn't any excitement to report today.

I didn't see Chipman yesterday, but Miss O'Toole told me he had been busy all morning prying into the advertising—so I reckon the fight is still on.

Had a letter from *Stratford* saying that copies of the issue containing my verse were being sent me. Thank God, he didn't embarrass me by asking about the book I was to have reviewed.

I'm mailing Reusche's check today.

The publisher of the Oakland *Post-Enquirer* sent word to me that he thought the stuff I have been running is the best advertising his paper has ever carried. (Probably applesauce, since he knows I'm thinking about cutting down the space used in the Oakland papers.)

That's all I know. See you Thursday. Spank the children for me.

Love,
D.

TLS MARSHALL

To Josephine Dolan Hammett

Sunday afternoon [late June 1927? San Francisco]

Dear Jose,

I've been Blackmasking all day and expect to put in a couple of hours more at it before I knock off.

I've even been too busy to go to mass—the first Sunday I've missed church since the last part of June, 1927![1]

Here's something for the yellow-head.[2]

Tomorrow afternoon I start playing with the dentist again. A couple of more weeks should clean me up.

I left a library book behind me. Hold it for me.

Not being able to fight with Chipman the last two or three days, I've been carrying on a war with Sloss—over the credit department, which he thinks, or pretends he thinks, a good department, though it's really the bunk. I think I'll prove that it's lost us more business than we've ever had.

How did you like today's tricky advertising?

Kiss the germs for me. I hope all your colds are gone.

Love,

D.

1. Hammett was joking about going to church. Josephine Hammett Marshall comments: "That papa was not a churchgoer is perhaps an understatement. He was zealously scornful of the Church for its history of siding with the establishment and ignoring the social problems of the people. He could be very sarcastic on the subject but never forced his opinions on the family. In our San Francisco days he often stayed with Mary and me so Mother could go to Mass—usually Old St. Mary's in Chinatown."
2. Hammett called his daughter Mary "Yellow-head."

TLS Marshall

To Josephine Dolan Hammett

Tuesday evening [June 1927? San Francisco, California]

Dear Jose,

This is just a line: I spent most of the afternoon with the dentist and my mouth hurts too much for me to feel like writing—even if I had anything to say.

Tell Mary Jane that's the reason I couldn't send her a picture this trip.

I haven't got my copy yet, but I hear that *Western Advertising*[1] reprinted another of my ads this month. Getting to be a habit.

I got another gallon of gin today, so I'll bring a bottle over with me Thursday.

Here's something today's mail brought.

Kiss the dingbats for me.

> Love,
> D

To Josephine Dolan Hammett

The opening of the letter is missing.

[June 1927? San Francisco]

Today's filling was the last, thank God—a couple of treatments for pyor[r]hea and I'll be through with the gent.

Don't wait dinner, or get anything for me, Thursday. The chances are I won't be able to catch so early a boat, and even if I do I'll eat on the way over.

The landlady came in yesterday morning and begged me to let her send in the janitor to scrub the kitchen and bathroom. We measured the dirt and it wasn't quite knee-deep so I told her she'd have to wait a little longer.

That just about winds up the news. I'll write again the day after tomorrow, so you'll get it Wednesday.

Convey my profoundest respects to your dear, beautiful, well-behaved, quiet, intelligent, cubs.

Love,
D.

1. Hammett wrote five articles for *Western Advertising*, the first published in December 1926, the last in March 1928.

TLS MARSHALL

To Josephine Dolan Hammett

Sunday evening [3 July? 1927]

Dear Jose,

I did around 2000 words on Blackmasking yesterday, which isn't so bad, though I had hoped to knock out 5000. However I've got tomorrow to spend on it, but I know I won't be able to finish it.

I went to the dentist yesterday morning, and had a swell time. He let a drill go through and hit a nerve. That's a lot of fun! I go back to him Tuesday afternoon.

It has been quite cool since I got back.

The *Blue Book* story came sailing home yesterday.

Here's the usual dingus for Mary Jane Ignatz.

I hope you'll all have a glorious Fourth and so on and so on.

My love to the splinters,
D

TLS MARSHALL

To Editorial Department, Alfred A. Knopf

11 February [1928], 891 Post St., San Francisco

Gentlemen,

Herewith an action-detective novel for your consideration. If you don't care to publish it, will you kindly return it by express, collect.

By way of introducing myself: I was a Pinkerton's National Detective Agency operative for a number of years; and, more recently, have published fiction, book reviews, verse, sketches, and so on; in twenty or twenty-five magazines, including the old *Smart Set* (when your Messrs. Mencken and Nathan ran it), *Forum, Bookman, Saturday Review, Life, Judge, Sunset, Argosy-Allstory, True Detective Mysteries, Black Mask* (where "Poisonville" ran as a serial), *Mystery Stories, Stratford,* and *Western Advertising.*[1]

> Sincerely yours,
> Dashiell Hammett

1. Knopf published the *American Mercury* magazine, which H. L. Mencken and George Jean Nathan founded and edited. No Hammett contribution to *Life* or *Mystery Stories* has been identified.

TLS HRC

To Blanche Knopf

Blanche Knopf was editor of Borzoi Mysteries, the line of mystery novels published by her husband's firm beginning in 1929. She accepted Hammett's "Poisonville," which was published on 1 February 1929 as Red Harvest.

20 March 1928, 891 Post St., San Francisco

Dear Mrs. Knopf,

Many thanks for your kind letter and its suggestions for "Poisonville"'s improvement.

The middle of the book, as it now stands, undoubtedly is more than somewhat cluttered up with violence, and I am thoroughly willing to make whatever changes you consider necessary. But, if possible, I'd like to keep Lew Yard in the story, as most of the second half of the book hinges on Reno's break with him.

In the enclosed revised pages I have cut out the dynamiting of police headquarters (page 134); have cut out the attack on Reno's house (page 176), which shouldn't have been put in in the first place; and have changed the dynamiting of Yard's house (page 149) to simple shooting off-stage. These changes will, I think, relieve the congestion quite a bit. If you think additional revision advis[a]ble, please let me know.

In connection with these cuts, the following chapter titles should be changed:

Chapter XVI, page 128, to "Exit Jerry"
Chapter XVIII, page 149, to "Painter Street"
Chapter XXI, page 169, to "The Seventeenth Murder"

You will notice that I have left the bombing of Pete the Finn's estab-lishment (page 209) as it was. Since both of the other dynamiting episodes have been removed, I think this one might be retained, espe-cially as it is further along in the story, not in the congested area. But it can be easily enough deleted if you so desire.

Somehow I had got the idea that "Poisonville" was a pretty good title, and I was surprised at your considering it hopeless—sufficiently sur-prised to ask a couple of retail book sellers what they thought of it. They agreed with you, so I'm beginning to suspect which one of us is wrong. Here are the only new titles I've been able to think up so far:

THE POISONVILLE MURDERS,	THE CITY OF DEATH,
THE SEVENTEENTH MURDER,	THE CLEANSING OF POISONVILLE,
MURDER PLUS,	THE BLACK CITY,
THE WILLSSON MATTER,	RED HARVEST [✔]

Maybe I'll be able to do better later, or maybe you can help me. The only prejudice I have in this connection is against the word "case" used where my sleuth would use "job" and, more officially, "matter" or "operation."

I've another book-length detective story—tentatively entitled *The Dain Curse*—under way, using the same detective I used in this book, but not using him so violently. I hope to finish that next month. The first serial rights have been sold to *The Black Mask*.

Then I want to try adapting this stream-of-consciousness method, conveniently modified, to a detective story, carrying the reader along with the detective, showing him everything as it is found, giving him the detective's conclusions as they are reached, letting the solution break on both of them together. I don't know whether I've made that very clear, but it's something altogether different from the method employed in "Poisonville," for instance, where, though the reader goes along with the detective, he seldom sees deeper into the detective's mind than dialogue and action let him. If I can manage it, I want to do this one without any regard for magazines' thou-shalts and thou-shalt-nots. I hope to get it finished by late summer, in time to do another—a plot I've been waiting to get at for two years—before 1928 is dead.

I'm one of the few—if there are any more—people moderately literate who take the detective story seriously. I don't mean that I necessarily take my own or anybody else's seriously—but the detective story as a form. Some day somebody's going to make "literature" of it (Ford's *Good Soldier* wouldn't have need much altering to have been a detective story), and I'm selfish enough to have my hopes, however slight the evident justification may be. I have a long speech I usually make on the subject, all about the ground not having been scratched yet, and so on, but I won't bore you with it now.

I want to thank you again for your interest in "Poisonville." I hope you'll find the changes I have made sufficient, but if they aren't I'll appreciate any further suggestions you may make.

> Sincerely yours,
> Dashiell Hammett

TLS HRC

To Blanche Knopf

6 April 1928, San Francisco

HAVE YOU REACHED VERDICT ON POISONVILLE YET STOP AM NOT TRYING TO HURRY YOU BUT HAVE REQUEST FROM WILLIAM FOX STUDIO FOR MATERIAL AND YOUR DECISION WILL DOUBTLESS AFFECT PRICES I CAN GET STOP[1] ALSO PLEASE ADVISE IF I SHOULD INCLUDE POISONVILLE IN NEGOTIATIONS OR LEAVE THAT TO YOU=

> DASHIELL HAMM[E]TT

1. William Fox was head of Fox Film Corporation, one of the big five Hollywood studios at the time. Hammett did not make a sale to them.

TELEGRAM HRC

To Blanche Knopf

9 April 1928, 891 Post St., San Francisco

Dear Mrs. Knopf,

I am returning the *Red Harvest* contract, signed and witnessed.

This new title is, I think, a satisfactory one; though my first choice probably disqualifies me as a competent judge.

Many thanks for the acceptance, and also for your wire concerning the motion picture dickering.

I included *Red Harvest* in the half a dozen stories submitted to the Fox Studio, and have hopes that something will come of it.

In accordance with the terms of the contract, I shall, of course, pass on to you any offer Fox may make for *Red Harvest*.

If, as seems quite likely just now, I make a more than transient connection with Fox, I'll probably let the stream-of-consciousness experiment wait awhile, sticking to the more objective and filmable forms.

Meanwhile, I'll have at you with another book next month.

Will you kindly put this dedication in *Red Harvest*:

"To Joseph Thompson Shaw"

> Sincerely yours,
> Dashiell Hammett

TLS HRC

To Blanche Knopf

25 June [1928], 891 Post St., San Francisco

Dear Mrs. Knopf,

Here's the second detective novel. I hope you'll like it.[1]

My Hollywood trip didn't carry the Fox negotiations much ahead. So far I haven't managed to trade them any of my published stuff for money, and a tentative agreement concerning some original photoplays is still very tentative.

Sincerely yours,
Dashiell Hammett

1. Knopf published *The Dain Curse* on 19 July 1929.

TLS HRC

To Harry Block

Harry Block was the editor at Knopf who did the line editing of Hammett's novels.

16 June [1929], 891 Post St., San Francisco

Dear Mr. Block,

I started *The Maltese Falcon* on its way to you by express last Friday, the fourteenth. I'm fairly confident that it is by far the best thing I've done so far, and I hope you'll think so too.

Though I hadn't anything of the sort in mind while doing it, I think now that it could very easily be turned into a play. Will you let me know if you agree with me? I wouldn't take a chance on trying to adapt it myself, but will try to get the help of somebody who knows the theater.

Another thing: if you use *The Falcon* will you go a little easy on the editing? While I wouldn't go to the stake in defense of my system of punctuation, I do rather like it and I think it goes with my sort of sentence-structure. The first forty pages of *The Dain Curse* were edited to beat hell (hurriedly for the dummy?) and the rest hardly at all. The result was that, having amiably accepted most of your changes in the first part, I had my hands full carrying them out in the remainder, trying to make it look like all the work of the same writer.

Like most of the world most of the time I am just now rather desperately in need of all the money I can scrape up. If there is any truth in these rumors that one hears about advances against royalties, will you do the best you can for me? If my appreciation equals my need I can promise to quite overwhelm you with gratitude.

How soon will you want, or can you use, another book? I've quite a flock of them outlined or begun, and I've a couple of groups of connected stories that can be joined in a whole just as I did with *Red Harvest* and *The Dain Curse*. The best of them were written just before *Red Harvest*, a group that would make a book as exciting as *Red Harvest*, though less complicated, with *The Big Knock-Over* as title.

Also I've about two hundred and fifty thousand words of short stories in which the Continental Op appears. I know you're not likely to be wildly enthusiastic about the short-story idea; but don't you think that something profitable for both of us could be done with them by making a quite bulky collection of them—selling it by the pound, as it were? I don't know anything about the manufacturing costs—how far bulkiness could be carried at a fairly low price without eating up the profits. I'd want to rewrite the stories we included, of course, and there are possibly fifty or sixty thousand words of the quarter-million that I'd throw out as not worth bothering about. In the remainder there are some good stories, and altogether I think they'd give a more complete and true picture of a detective at work than has been given anywhere else. And I think *The Continental Op* would be a good title.

Also I've a horror-story I'd like to get to work on—a variant of the Frankenstein idea—tentatively entitled *AEAEA*; a pure plot detective story, *Two Two's Are Twenty-two*; a political murder mystery, *The Secret Emperor*; one something on the order of *The Maltese Falcon, That Night in Singapore*; and an underworld mystery, *Dead Man's Friday*. (All these titles are tentative, of course.)[1]

I had intended doing the story of a gunman next, but, according to Asbury, *Little Caesar* was *that*.[2] So, until I've read it I'm holding off. I'm a little afraid anyhow that gunmen and racketeers, as such, are going to be rather sour literary material by this time next year.

> Sincerely,
> Dashiell Hammett

1. Drafts for "AEAEA" and "Two Two's Are Twenty-Two" are at the Harry Ransom Center, University of Texas. The archive includes a character list, outline, and a fragment for "The Secret Emperor." "That Night in Singapore" and "Dead Man's Friday" are not located.
2. Herbert Asbury was a journalist, book reviewer, and aspiring screenwriter. He enthusiastically reviewed W. R. Burnett's *Little Caesar* (1929). The classic movie made from this gangster novel was released in January 1931 by Warner Bros.

TLS HRC

To Harry Block

14 July 1929, 891 Post St., San Francisco

Dear Mr. Block,

I'm glad you like *The Maltese Falcon*. I'm sorry you think the to-bed and the homosexual parts of it should be changed. I should like to leave them as they are, especially since you say they "would be all right perhaps in an ordinary novel." It seems to me that the only thing that can be said against their use in a detective novel is that nobody has tried it yet. I'd like to try it.

Since writing you I've reread some of the short stories and novelettes I mentioned. I don't think I want to do anything with them. Most of them could be rewritten into fair shape, I think, but only fair shape, and I'd rather forget them. I've a title I like—*The Glass Key*—and at least part of a plot to go with it. I'll probably get going on it next week.

I like the *Dain Curse* jacket.

About the advance: I've no objections at all, of course, to drawing up a new contract for three more books, but I need more than a thousand dollars. As a matter of fact I'd like to have twenty-five hundred. This doesn't seem an at all unreasonable figure to me, since, after all, it would be actually, from my standpoint, an advance against six books.[1]

> Sincerely,
> Dashiell Hammett

1. Apparently Hammett's first contract with Knopf was for three books and did not stipulate an advance against royalties. In July, before royalties had yet been paid on *Red Harvest*, which was published in January 1929, Block offered Hammett a $1,000 advance payable under a new contract for three more books.

TLS HRC

To Harry Block

31 August 1929 [San Francisco]

Dear Mr. Block,

OK—go ahead and change them. I don't imagine a few words' difference will matter greatly, and, anyway, I'll soon be on hand to do in person whatever crying is necessary.

I won't try to express my gratitude for the *Times* page. It was, well ...

I've just finished reading *Monks Are Monks*, and liked its insolence a lot.[1]

The Glass Key is going slowly, but I expect to have at least a third of it done before I go East, and I think perhaps it'll amount to something.

> Sincerely yours,
> Dashiell Hammett

  1. George Jean Nathan wrote *Monks Are Monks*. See appendix.

TLS HRC

To Alfred A. Knopf

12 September 1929, 891 Post St., San Francisco

Dear Mr. Knopf,

Many thanks for the movie check, which arrived at a time when I was considering hocking my typewriter.[1] Thanks also for the *Times* page: I hope we'll make slews of money for each other in the not too distant future.

The Glass Key is coming along slowly but not badly.

I shan't leave for New York next week as I had expected, but shall be there in any event by the first of October.

> Sincerely yours,
> Dashiell Hammett

  1. In February 1930 Paramount Famous Lasky Corporation released *Roadhouse Nights,* a movie very loosely based on *Red Harvest*. Hobart Henley was the director; Helen Morgan, Charles Ruggles, and Jimmy Durante were among the cast.

TLS HRC

To Mr. Burton, Alfred A. Knopf, Inc.

Nell Martin, to whom The Glass Key *is dedicated, lived at the same address as Hammett in New York.*

18 October 1929, 155 E. 30th St., New York City

Dear Mr. Burton,

I've found a place in town, at the above address, and am banging away at *The Glass Key,* hoping to have it out of the mill by the middle of December at the latest.

Will you be good enough to pass my address on to the Manufacturing Department so they can send my proofs, etc. direct?

>Sincerely yours,
>Hammett

ALS HRC

To Herbert Asbury

Hammett was responding to a fan letter from Asbury.

6 February 1930, 155 E 30th St., New York City

Dear Mr. Asbury,

I can't tell you how pleased I am with your verdict on *The Maltese Falcon*. It's the first thing I've done that was—regardless of what faults it had—the best work I was capable of at the time I was doing it, and, well......

The Glass Key, held back thus far by laziness, drunkenness, and illness, promises to get itself finished somehow by the latter part of next week. As soon as it's out of the mill I think we ought to get together and celebrate whatever there happens to be to celebrate.

My best to Helen.

>Sincerely,
>Dashiell Hammett

TLS HRC

To Manley Aaron

The movie The Glass Key, *starring George Raft, was released by Paramount in 1935.*

19 July 1930, Hollywood, California

MISS MANLEY AARON, CARE A A KNOPF INC=
730 FIFTH AVENUE NEW YORK NY=

JUST HOW ARE WE TIED UP WITH WARNER BROTHERS ON THE GLASS KEY
STOP THINK I CAN PUT OVER BETTER SALE WITH PARAMOUNT HERE STOP
RUMOR THAT WA[R]NER WILL NOT MAKE FALCON[1] STOP SEND ME PROOFS
OF KEY=

DASHIELL HAMMETT

1. Warner Brothers released *The Maltese Falcon*, starring Bebe Daniels and
   Ricardo Cortez in May 1931.

TELEGRAM HRC

To Alfred Knopf

The Glass Key *was first published in London on 20 January 1931.*

14 August 1930, Roosevelt Hotel, Hollywood, California

Dear Alfred,

Thanks for the note about the *Mercury*. I've delayed answering it until
I could get myself a more or less permanent address.

For the next couple of months my address will be 1714 Ivar Avenue
(the Hollywood Knickerbocker). Will you kindly see that Miss Aaron and
whoever else is supposed to be interested gets it.

So far the Hollywood expedition has been a lot of fun, except that I
haven't found time to do much work on the new book. I'm tied up with
Paramount for a few weeks doing a Bancroft.[1]

Anything new on the matter of publishing or not publishing *The Glass
Key* next month? I hope to have the movie rights profitably placed before
I turn to the East again.

My best to you and Blanche.

Sincerely,
Dashiell Hammett

1. The Bancroft reference may be to the actor George Bancroft, who was under contract to Paramount at the time.

TLS HRC

To Alfred A. Knopf, Inc.

20 December 1930, Hollywood, California

Gentlemen,

I am returning your invoice for excess corrections on *The Glass Key.*

These corrections were made necessary by someone in your editorial department who, with unlimited amounts of time, energy, and red ink at his disposal, simply edited the Jesus out of my MS.

Mrs. Knopf may remember that I spoke to her about this at the time. In any case, if you'll take a look at the MS, which I think is still in your hands, you'll see you're very lucky I haven't billed you for the trouble I was put to unediting it.

Sincerely yours,
Dashiell Hammett

TLS HRC

PART TWO

Celebrity
1931–1942

Hammett on Tavern Island, Connecticut, 1938

He looked down at his plate and muttered:
"I hope you like it when you get it."

Ned Beaumont to Janet Henry, *The Glass Key*, Chapter 8

On 22 November 1930, the Saturday before Thanksgiving, Hammett attended a Hollywood party hosted by Darryl F. Zanuck, then supervisor of production at Warner Bros. In addition to *The Jazz Singer,* Zanuck had produced *Little Caesar* (1930) and *Public Enemy* (released April 1931), movies that initiated the gangster-film genre, and he had bought movie rights to *The Maltese Falcon.* Also at the party was Lillian Hellman, the wife of Hammett's colleague at Paramount, screenwriter Arthur Kober.

Hammett and Hellman left the party together that night, and they were companions for the rest of his life. The effect they had on each other was altogether remarkable. Though they were lovers, neither was ever faithful. Yet when together they were a formidable team, he providing the image of authority, and she its voice. Within a year of meeting Hellman, Hammett all but quit writing fiction for publication, though he entertained vague ideas for a sixth novel and continued, as he had for at least five years, to mull over various ideas for plays. He concentrated instead on screenwriting and mentoring others, often young women. When Hellman and amorous writing partner Louis Kronenberger were unable to complete a satiric drama they were attempting and threatened to go away together to work on it, Hammett responded by giving her his idea for dramatizing a true crime story by William Roughead called "Closed Doors; or the Grand Drumsheugh Case" about a girls' school in Edinburgh forced to close in 1810 because its owners were rumored to be lesbians. Hammett and Hellman worked on successive drafts together, and when it was produced under her authorship in 1934 as *The Children's Hour,* she was an overnight sensation. The play ran on Broadway for 691 performances, and by the year's close, Hellman was a name that could be uttered in literary circles in the same breath as Hammett.

The letters from this period paint the fullest available portrait of Hammett as a working writer. He was serious about his writing, but he was also an opportunist—a man born poor who had lived through illness and who now wanted to wring all the benefits he could from success. Hammett was a literary man, but he was too much of a pragmatist to devote himself to literature. Like his characters the Continental Op and Sam Spade, he was contemptuous of images and the people who traded in them. When reviewers began to make too much of his work, he lost interest in their opinions; when editors or moviemakers or other writers began to take themselves too seriously, Hammett ridiculed them. Gradually the company he kept became too ludicrous in his eyes to abide sober. He opted for the solace of drunkenness.

His initial collapse came in stages, beginning in Hollywood. In spring 1931 he had a recurrence of venereal disease, which he had first contracted as a teenager. In winter 1931 he was charged with sexual assault against one of his girlfriends, Elise DeViane, and found guilty of civil charges the next summer. By mid-1934, his drunkenness was so alarming that his friends confided their concern about him to one another. In the winter of 1935, he sank into suicidal despair. Another attack of venereal disease and alcoholic depression landed Hammett in Lenox Hill Hospital in New York. He was physically and psychologically broken, yet his celebrity remained untarnished. He recuperated at a rented house in Princeton by attempting to drink himself well, and finally the parties became so raucous that he was evicted.

Hammett went back to Hollywood in spring 1937, a place as uncertain about its responsibilities as he was. On the one hand, Hollywood was still the nation's capital for crassness, shallowness, greed, arrogance, hypocrisy, licentiousness, and intemperance. On the other, the Hollywood image makers, attempting to avoid government regulation, had since July 1934 accepted the strictures of their own Production Code Administration, known as the Hays Office, designed to rid movies of unwholesome content. The movie industry stood for values that Hammett despised, and some that he couldn't resist. He was contemptuous of Hollywood, and he reserved some of the contempt for himself because he gave in so easily to its temptations. Hammett found it easy to rationalize his work there when he was drunk. But during this, his last extended stay, he was mostly sober. He found a purpose in politics, and that work required a clear mind.

Hollywood developed a social consciousness of sorts in the last half of the 1930s. The Hollywood section of the Communist Party USA was newly formed, and Hammett was an active member. It was the time of the Popular Front, when, upon orders from the Comintern, the international policy-making body of the Communist Party, national parties worked to promote social change within established political structures. In 1937 Communist Party membership required a commitment to civil rights and to social equality, and opposition to exploitation of workers and to Fascism. It explicitly did not advocate subversion of the government or anti-Americanism. It was easy for a conscientious citizen with a liberal bent to be a Communist sympathizer in the 1930s. But to be a card-carrying member required unqualified submission to Party discipline, which was strict and often severe. Hammett managed somehow to reconcile the demands of the Party with his anti-authoritarian convictions.

Communism provided a more or less formal expression of values that Hammett believed in well before he joined the Party in the mid-1930s. At the simplest level, Communists championed the equality of all people. They opposed class systems that subordinated one person to another and supported their beliefs with a web of complex arguments that, in their public expression, focused more intently on social and economic theory than on practical solutions to the problems they identified. While Hammett held to a rigorous personal code of values, it seemed out of character for him to advocate a political party actively, however idealistic. Yet he was an unapologetic Marxist who found Communism the best political option available to him. Communism isn't perfect, he said, but it will do until something better comes along. He worked, when he worked at all, for the rights of the workingman, and he enthusiastically studied the political situation around the world.

The Spanish Civil War was a major Communist cause in 1937. There, in the prequel to World War II, the Italians and the Germans supported a coalition of Fascist forces, ultimately led by Francisco Franco, that were attempting to overthrow the Republican government. European Communists, particularly Soviets, sent weapons and soldiers, in what were called International Brigades, to oppose the Fascist threat. Hammett believed in the cause fervently enough to attempt to join, at the age of forty-one, the Abraham Lincoln Battalion, the American volunteer group. Communist leaders told him he could do more good at home, and he followed their advice.

Hammett was an organizer. He attended meetings, took leadership roles in Communist organizations, and donated money to Party-sponsored causes. He also became involved in Hollywood union activities, fighting the corrupt International Alliance of Theatrical Stage Employees and Playwrights Guild, whose leadership had sold out to studio bosses. When the Screen Writers Guild reorganized in 1937 after a false start earlier in the decade, Hammett and Hellman were members of the board of directors. He worked diligently and effectively to gain formal recognition for the organization as an authorized agent for screenwriters, and he used the influence he garnered in his SWG work to support other leftist causes.

On the whole, however, the late 1930s were depressing times for social libertarians. Hammett despaired as the Republican cause in Spain went from doubtful to hopeless. To him the Fascist victory in the face of American neutrality signaled a threat to personal liberty in the United States, especially in those prewar years when many Americans found much to admire in the strict order of Fascist states. Anti-Semitism and racial segregation, generally accepted as middle-class values during the Depression, were moral issues that Hammett reacted to sharply because of his basic belief in civil rights. His awareness of worldwide persecution of Jews was amplified by his relationship with Hellman and her circle of Jewish friends. There was little cause for optimism about workers' rights in the eighth and ninth years of the Great Depression, as long-term unemployment drained whatever sentiment people had for union-organized work disturbances.

Hammett's personal world was equally glum. The more independent Lillian Hellman became, the more flagrant she was with her sexual dalliances (and he with his), the more steadfast his love for her seemed to become. When she got pregnant in the fall of 1937 and pressed him to marry her, he took steps to oblige her by obtaining a mail-order Mexican divorce from Jose that was probably not valid in the United States. Hellman averted the crisis by getting an abortion, after which neither saw the point in legalizing their relationship. Having spent the spring and summer in Hollywood with Hammett, she left in the fall and began a romance with another lover.

That fall of 1937, Hellman was gone, and he missed her. While he never lacked for girlfriends, he had discovered the gulf between sex and love. He was lonely and isolated. His paychecks came from MGM, where he labored over the third of the *Thin Man* movies based on the characters of Nick and Nora Charles introduced in his 1934 novel. The work went slowly and without enthusiasm. He wrote three drafts of the screenplay for *Another Thin Man*, and while his work impressed his bosses at the studio, his work habits did not. For his own part, Hammett considered the results embarrassing. In 1933, when he wrote *The Thin Man*, he had been like his charming drunken hero, Nick Charles, but not now. Hammett wrote Hellman in January 1938 that he had not had a drink in ten months. His political work gave him a reason to get up in the morning, but without her for support, he became overwhelmed by frustration and a sense of futility. He had to be drunk to face the world, especially the world of Hollywood in those days; and when he began drinking again, he showed no restraint. The breakdown came in summer 1938. Although over six feet tall, Hammett had shrunk to 125 pounds, and he was helpless, both physically and emotionally. He felt he had nowhere to turn; he was in a state of collapse. Hellman took him in and nursed him out of the darkness of depression.

In New York, Hammett's health improved with his spirits as he worked out a new accommodation with Hellman. They could love each other without being possessive. He had a permanent room at Hardscrabble Farm, in Pleasantville, New York, which she purchased in her name in the summer of 1939 but which was a joint investment between them, and they entertained friends—and often lovers—independently there. They recommitted themselves to each other in a relationship as strong as marriage but with a different set of vows. Their lives took separate paths, which intersected at intervals. What they shared was a home base.

Hammett liked most of Hellman's lovers and treated them as friends. Arthur Kober, her former husband, was the first. Now, as Hellman's affairs more frequently blossomed into serious relationships, Hammett remained tolerant. In 1939, he worked closely with Ralph Ingersoll, though he rarely missed a chance to sneer at his idealistic naïveté.

Broadway producer Herman Shumlin, *PM* Washington bureau chief Kenneth Crawford, and *New Yorker* editor St. Clair McKelway were others among Hellman's many lovers whose company Hammett tolerated if not enjoyed. Likewise, he had romantic entanglements with Laura Perelman, Jean Potter, and a bevy of actresses and hangers-on whom Hellman, in turn, endured. They could not make themselves invulnerable to jealousy, but they did resolve, more or less successfully, not to allow its destructive effects.

A sure sign that he was on the mend, Hammett announced late in 1939 that he was ready to begin work on his sixth novel. He resumed an active role in politics, backing up with action the principles he endorsed. He helped start a magazine, *Soviet Russia Today*, and he joined with Ralph Ingersoll in planning and organizing the Communist-supported newspaper *PM*. He was working with purpose again.

To Lillian Hellman

4 March 1931, Hollywood

Darling:

It's 10 o'clock and you haven't come back, so maybe you didn't miss the train after all.

I've finished *The Illustrious Corpse*—amusing, but unfortunately transparent—and have started *China Seas*, which thus far isn't so bad.[1] My headache is gone, my respiration seems normal, and if I had a thermometer I'd give you a report on my temperature. I think I've been to the toilet twice since you left: I'll try to keep more complete records hereafter.[2]

The Asburys were in for an hour to bring me a smug celluloid dog, to drink Bourbon, to borrow books, to tell me you had inadvertently said "An equitable young man," to tell me they were going to give Fox only one week from today to reach a decision, to argue about how early they should go to the Adirondacks, to inform me again that their car was good for another five years (Helen told Jones this afternoon they were going to trade it on a Lincoln), to discuss the economics of home keeping, and, finally, to depart.[3]

I've been to the toilet again. There were no unusual idiocies in the Parsons column for tomorrow. Skippy was adequately amusing, the weather remains warm and clear, Mono Port Cement pfd closed at 4 3/4.[4] The motmot is some sort of bird. I don't know whether to have something sent in or sup on beef tea. The roses are holding up pretty well against their blowness and the heat of the room. The Powell story will probably have things done to it tomorrow—yeah, always tomorrow![5]

If that doesn't exhaust the available news it at least exhausts my memory.

Don't forget to write to me your impressions of the aquarium, the Chrysler building, traffic, the Great White Way, Wall Street, the subway, greed for gold, Central Park and Anna Held.[6] Maybe you'd better wire me—prepaid—about her.

The emptiness I thought was hunger for chow mein turned out to be for you, so maybe a cup of beef tea....

65

love in quantities that permits you to pass some on to Laura,[7]
Dash

1. *The Illustrious Corpse* by Tiffany Thayer and *China Seas* by Crosby Garston.
2. Hammett was recovering from venereal disease, probably gonorrhea.
3. The Asburys are Herbert and his wife, Helen. Jones was Hammett's chauffeur and Man Friday.
4. Louella Parsons was a gossip columnist, and "Skippy" a comic strip by Percy Crosby. Both were widely syndicated.
5. Hammett was working on an original Sam Spade story for Warner Bros. to star William Powell.
6. Anna Held was a Polish entertainer who starred in the Ziegfeld Follies.
7. Laura Perelman, sister of writer Nathanael West, married S. J. Perelman in 1929.

TLS HRC

To Lillian Hellman

Hollywood in California on the fifth day of March in 1931 A.D.

Sweet,

The day has been full of people getting me out of bed to wander to the telephone to tell them how I felt, as if I knew, and which was probably none of their business anyhow.

Jones rescued the pajamas from the cleaner's this evening. I'll dispatch them to you presently.

Arthur was in for a couple of hours, left just a few minutes ago for an early bed so he could rise early.[1] If I can make it we'll probably do the fights tomorrow night.

Your telegram came a few minutes ahead of Arthur. What is the boy fish doing that far inland?

I've been to the toilet approximately eight times today, with hopes of running it up to a round ten before bedtime, and I've shut the door each time, and locked it once.

To get around to the news an anxious world is waiting for: I'm feeling a lot better today, but a couple of hours of being up convinced me I'd better stay home, so I spent the day on my spine reading, had dinner sent in from the Brown Derby, and let my whiskers hang down on whichever side of my chest they chose.

I daresay my absence from the Brown Derby, coinciding with your departure, has started a crop of fresh and juicy rumors. I'll see they don't die from want of feeding.

A gem from the day's reading:— "Stegall took Harp's own butcher knife...and taking Harp by the hair of the head, drew the knife slowly across the back of his neck, cutting to the bone; Harp staring him full in the face, with a grim and fiendish countenance, and exclaiming, 'You are a God Damned rough butcher, but cut on and be damned!' Stegall then passed the knife around his neck, cutting to the bone; and then wrung off his head, in the same manner a butcher would of a hog.... Passing an outlying cabin, they were delighted to find that the farmer had plenty of roasting-ears of corn, and was willing to spare some.... Harp[]'s head, bloody and contorted, had been loaded in the only sack they carried, but that only bothered them a moment: with a shrug, they dumped the corn in with it. 'He won't eat it!' they said. And so, that night, they feasted...."[2]

Jones did two errands without a mistake today: I'm suspicious: the chances are an imposter has slipped in.

Beginning a thousand-stanza narrative verse:

> *In San Francisco, Elfinstone*
> *Fell in with a red-haired slut*
> *Whose eyes were bright as the devil's own*
> *With green-eyed greed, whose jaw was cut*
> *Wolfishly. Her body was lean and tough as a whip,*
> *With little of breast and little of hip,*
> *And her voice was thin and hard as her lip,*
> *And her lip was hard as bone.*

The weather remains warm. My sheets were changed today. Old-time ballads by the boys in "Wesley's Barber Shop" will be broadcast by KFVD at half-past nine tomorrow night. Grigsby-Grunow closed at 5 1/2. The mangour is an obsolete Turkish copper coin. Gary Cooper is in the Hollywood Hospital, reputedly being treated for alcoholism. It ain't the 'eavy 'auling that 'urts the 'orses 'oofs, it's the 'ammer, 'ammer, 'ammer on the 'ard 'ighway.

Lecherously,
Dash

1. Arthur Kober and Lillian Hellman were married in 1925 and divorced early in 1932.
2. The reference is to a true crime story. The Harp Brothers, called Big and Little, have been called the first serial murderers in America. At the end of the eighteenth century they terrorized the country on the Western Kentucky–Tennessee border. Big was killed after murdering the Stegall baby. A posse caught him and Mr. Stegall cut off his head and mounted it on a stick by the road, now called Harp's Head Road, near Dixon, Kentucky.

TLS HRC

To Lillian Hellman

Friday [10 April 1931, Hollywood]

Dahlink,

Up at noon and to the doctor's. He couldn't find anything to put under his microscope, so we'll try again Monday, and if—pray God—we have the same luck then we'll call it quits, and I'll doubtless throw a "purity party" Monday night.

From the doctor's—to continue my probably fascinating log—I went to Paramount to see Herzbrun—about the release on my Bancroft story, and was stalled off till tomorrow, all the time hoping they'd decide to pay me the five thousand b[o]nus and keep the piece of cheese.[1]

Thence bookshopping, coming out with *The White Paternoster, The Pinkertons, Sanctuary, The Everlasting Struggle,* and *Apache,* and home to find part of the American Play Company waiting for me.[2]

I've a date with Thalberg next week to talk terms on a Wallace Beery story after I return from New York.[3] What's that? Uh-huh, you guessed it, I'm going to sell him that hobo story we were fooling with for Bancroft.

RKO seems to be seriously considering *The Dain Curse.* I ought to have an answer out of them next week.

Leland Hayward wired me again today, still trying to hurry me up on the serial for *Cosmopolitan.* Tsk! Tsk! Tsk! How business keeps up!

I had dinner with the Hammetts this evening, coming home tired and early, but now, having rested with Jeans's *The Mysterious Universe*, I feel able to essay the Brown Derby.

Oh yes! Florence Lawrence, the *Examiner*'s drama editor, has been quoted as saying that La Parsons has quite a yen for me. Hm-m-m!

It's a little cooler tonight. SJL&P pr pfd 7% closed at 117. I love you. Torii are Japanese gateways or archways. It is now eleven-twenty-nine P.M., Pacific Standard Time.

> Be seeing you,
> Dash

1. Bernard Herzbrun was an art director for Paramount during the early 1930s. Hammett did not receive credit on a movie starring George Bancroft in 1931 or 1932.
2. *The White Paternoster* by C. F. Powys; *The Pinkertons* by Richard Wilmer Rowan; *Sanctuary* by William Faulkner; *The Everlasting Struggle* by Rowan Bojer; and *Apache* by Will Levington Comfort. Leland Hayward, then director of the American Play Company, was Hammett's agent. Without proper authorization, American Play Company sold rights to an early version of *The Thin Man* written in May 1931. The sale had to be canceled. Hammett abandoned the draft and started from scratch with the novel published by Knopf in 1934.
3. Irving Thalberg was production manager at MGM, and Wallace Beery was a star under contract to the same studio.

TLS HRC

To Lillian Hellman

A Tuesday [14 April 1931, Hollywood]

Dearling,

What bad two days did my letters have to carry you through? You mean the street-cleaner's band wasn't at the station to greet you? And nobody gave you the keys to any cities?

I haven't seen Arthur for a couple of days. I dare say he's too busy whoring around. Last night I ran into Sid in the Brown Derby, brought him home with me, gave him some Bourbon, and wound up doing a little pimping for him.[1] God knows I'm doing my best to keep celibacy from rearing its ugly head in Hollywood! But something's got to be done to keep the gals moderately content while I'm out of order.

Tonight I had dinner with Sydney Fox, Frances Dee, Joe Sternberg, Dudley Murphy, and I forget who else. I also saw Joe March with the blonde Peggy Prior, and Jeff Sherlock.[2]

I still haven't done a great deal on the Powell story, but may work through the night on it. This is income tax week, I owe all Southern California money—I've got to do something approaching the desperate.

This morning I finished *Sanctuary*, and, without actually disliking it, am of the opinion that Mr. Faulkner is rather overrated by such people as have heard of him at all. He has a nice taste in the morbid and gruesome, but doesn't seem to do much with it. I also read Will Levington Comfort's *Apache*, and enjoyed it. I finished *The White Paternoster*—most of the stories are more than a little silly.

I haven't heard yet whether Bertie got his Fox contract: I imagine I would have heard if he'd had any luck.

Today's been warm again. Web Sh Cse pfd closed at 16 _. Dagan was the Babylonian god of the earth. Senator Borah will be heard on KHJ tomorrow.[3] The Farmers Saving Bank of Alden, Iowa, was robbed of $4,000 yesterday. I—but that doesn't matter.

> Ovelay.
> Dash

1. S. J. Perelman was known as Sid.
2. Sydney Fox and Frances Dee were movie actors. Josef von Sternberg was a director, producer, and writer whose films included *An American Tragedy* (1931), which starred Dee. Dudley Murphy was a writer and director for various studios, Joseph Moncure March was a writer in the Paramount stable; and Peggy Prior was a writer for Pathé. Jeff Sherlock is unidentified, as is Bertie (below).
3. Senator from Idaho for 33 years, William E. Borah, though a Republican isolationist, advocated diplomatic recognition of the Soviet Union and helped establish the Good Neighbor policy toward Latin America. During the Depression, he supported many of the New Deal measures intended to relieve domestic economic conditions.

TLS HRC

To Blanche Knopf

17 April 1931, Hollywood, California

THOUSANDS OF APOLOGIES FOR NOT HAVING ANSWERED YOUR LETTER
BEFORE THIS AM JUST BACK FROM A FEW WEEKS IN SAN FRANCISCO EXPECT
TO STAY HERE SEVERAL MONTHS BUT HOPE TO HAVE NEXT BOOK THE THIN
MAN FINISHED IN A COUPLE OF MONTHS BEST REGARDS TO YOU AND
ALFRED=

        DASHIELL

TELEGRAM HRC

To Alfred Knopf

27 April 1931, 1714 Ivar Avenue, Hollywood

Dear Alfred,

Your hopes for *The Glass Key* aren't any more ardent than mine. If its sales aren't what they should be—and what *The Maltese Falcon's* should have been—I think *The Thin Man* will be my last detective novel: we'll try our luck with another genre.

The Thin Man, by the way, is the nearest to a straight detective story I've done.[1] I'll send you a slice of it presently. *Collier's, Good Housekeeping,* and the *Cosmopolitan*, all of whom have seen about a third of it, seem to like what they've seen—I had a wire about it from the Hearst pair today—so I'll probably catch a good magazine market for it and have hopes of raising its movie price above *The Glass Key's* twenty-five thousand.

I hadn't heard about the closing of your London office.[2] Cassell & Co. is of course perfectly satisfactory to me, but I don't think I want my stuff edited for the British reader henceforth. The Anglicization of *The Glass Key* didn't please me much. Changes that might reasonably have been made weren't, unnecessary ones were, and there were such absurdities as translating the verb "stall" into "bluff."

The Hollywood venture has been fairly successfu[l] thus far—though I know I ought to chuck it and keep my nose to the novel grindstone—

even if I haven't saved any of my take. Just now it looks as if I'll have to go around and around in a court-room with the Warner Brothers to straighten out my financial difficulties: they seem to have outslickered me—or are trying to—in connection with a Powell story.[3]

I haven't seen Eddie for some time, but may do a short stretch of story-carpentering in the same factory that employs him.[4]

With all good wishes,

Yours,
Dashiell

1. The "Thin Man" Hammett refers to is not the published novel, but an abandoned draft.
2. On 17 April 1931 Alfred Knopf wrote to Hammett that he had closed Knopf's London office and had arranged for Cassell & Co. to publish his list in London.
3. Darryl F. Zanuck at Warner Bros. hired Hammett in January 1931 to write an original Sam Spade story as a vehicle for William Powell. The terms were $15,000 payable in three installments. Hammett took two $5,000 payments for his story "On the Make" before Zanuck rejected it and refused further payment. Hammett eventually sold the story to Universal, who used it as the original for *Mr. Dynamite* (1935).
4. Alfred Knopf's half brother Edwin H. Knopf was a screenwriter at Universal in 1931.

TLS HRC

To Lillian Hellman

City Streets, for which Hammett wrote the original story and received his first screen credit, was released in April 1931 by Paramount. It starred Sylvia Sidney and Gary Cooper.

[About 27 April 1931, no address]

Angel,

Thanks a lot for the clippings. In spite of good reviews, the picture did only a fair $50,000 or $60,000 in New York and seems to be going at about the same proportionate gait here, though pretty good in the tank towns. I haven't seen it yet.

Alcohol has had me pretty much out of touch with whatever local situation there's been the last couple of weeks, but now that I'm on the wagon again—this is my third day—I'll no doubt presently be more or less au courant again, which'll be a lot more than I ever was.

I've just finished a book called *Thunder Above the Sea* and think—though I don't trust my jedgment, having read it while under the inflernce—it a swell bit of work.[1] In spite of trickiness—I'm always saying that—I think the author, a gent named Hauser, succeeded in doing the futile-ships-that-pass-in-the-night-business better than most, and in most I include one who shall be designated E. H. (To hell with A.H.)[2]

Otherwise my reading has consisted chiefly of Jeans's *The Mysterious Universe*, nice; Moley's *Our Criminal Courts*, nice; *Plagued by the Nightingale*, a good enough job if you can stay awake through it; *Gay Agony*, monstrously overwritten; *Darkness at Noon*, not too bad; and *But It Still Goes On*, which has a couple of worthwhile things in it.[3]

Given energy enough, I'm to edit an anthology of ghost stories for John Day, to be published in the fall.[4]

I suppose it's not news to you that Knopf has shut up his London office. My English editions pass into the hands of Cassell.

Between Warners and me there seems to be some sort of misunderstanding—vague, but potent enough to hold up my final check—Thalberg left for Europe before I was sober enough to talk to him—the Colman-story dicker with United Artists has come to nothing thus far—I'll probably either have to eat Jones or starve to death.

I, as the saying goes, miss you terribly.

> Love,
> Dash

1. *Thunder Above the Sea* by Heinrich Hauser.
2. E.H. probably refers to Ernest Hemingway. A.H. possibly refers to Albert Hackett, screenwriter who later, with his wife Frances Goodrich, wrote the script for *The Thin Man.*
3. *Plagued by the Nightingale* by Kay Boyle; *Gay Agony* by H. A. Manhood; *Darkness at Noon* by Harry Carlisle; and *But It Still Goes On* by Robert Graves.
4. On 8 October 1931 John Day published *Creeps by Night,* a collection of stories selected and with an introduction by Hammett.

TLS HRC

To Alfred A. Knopf

Josephine Hammett recalls that this telegram was written about the time the Packard that Hammett had bought for Jose Hammett was repossessed, much to Mrs. Hammett's relief, because driving made her nervous.

29 April 1931, Hollywood, California

IN DESPERATE NEED OF ALL THE MONEY I CAN FIND STOP CAN YOU DEPOSIT THOUSAND DOLLARS IN MY ACCOUNT IRVING TRUST COMPANY FIFTY NINTH STREET BRANCH AND DEDUCT FROM MONTHLY PAYMENTS STOP IF CONVENIENT PLEASE WIRE ME AS SOON AS POSSIBLE STOP WROTE YOU YESTERDAY STOP BEST REGARDS=

        DASHIELL HAMMETT

TELEGRAM HRC

To Lillian Hellman

A place called Hollywood on what's known as the thirtieth of April [1931]

Darling,

Further thanks for press shipment number two. Can I ask that it be kept up, since it's my only source of reviews?

I ran into Arthur, Sid, and Laura at the Brern Doiby night before last and we're all going to dinner together tomorrow evening. I tried to pump Laura about your conduct in New York, but she was so circumspect, gave you such a respectable tint, that I'd have suspected you of the loosest sort of conduct even if I hadn't previously received reports about you. Ts! Ts! Ts! Just a she-Hammett!

Last night I went to see *City Streets,* and found it pretty lousy, though Sylvia Sidney makes the whole thing seem fairly good in spots. She's good, that ugly little baby, and currently my favorite screen actress.

Alfred wired me this morning that *The Glass Key* has got off to a swell start and would probably go over big. I daresay he means it'll sell fifteen thousand copies. Anyhow, I made him come across with a thousand dollars, so I won't have to eat Jones until perhaps the latter part of next week.

My ambition now is to collect enough money to be able to take a couple months to finish *The Thin Man,* which, God willing, will be my last detective novel. (So I'm being intimidated by Mrs. Parker, eh?)[1]

This is my seventh day on the wagon.

When are you coming home?

>Love,
>Dash

1. Writer Dorothy Parker was a friend of Lillian Hellman's. As a reviewer for *The New Yorker*, she gave rave notices to Hammett's novels.

TLS HRC

To Lillian Hellman

Hollywood at four by the clock on a May morning in 1931 A.D.

Angel,

It was nice of you to phone me, even if you did have to get plastered to do it.

The inseparable Arthur-Laura-Syd combination ran into me at the Brown Derby last night, on their way, as usual, from looking at a picture show they didn't like. They see more pictures and like fewer of them than any trio I know, though if you ask me how many trios I know I'll have to fall back on Jesus, Mary, and Joseph.

I've been reading Gorky's *Magnet* and, as with most of his stuff, like it well enough without being anywise excited about it.

Your rival, Marlene, is back in town with her offspring and reputedly living in sin with that great, if somewhat stunted, genius of the flickers and lisps, Joe Steinboig.[1]

If, as doesn't seem likely, I get my finances straightened out this week I'll probably run up to San Francisco for another go at the dizzy whirl.

People like Harpo Marx and Dudley Digg[e]s have been telling me about a swell review Hansen gave me in the *World-Tel.*[2] Did you by any chance see it? Maybe I ought to subscribe to a clipping bureau again. Will you do it for me? Whichever one you think best. If I remember when I get through I'll enclose a check. Otherwise just hock something.

So you're not coming home, eh? I suppose it doesn't make any difference if I have to go on practically masturbating!

> Love and things,
> Dash

1. Marlene Dietrich became a star with her role in the German movie *Der blaue
   Engel,* directed by Josef von Sternberg. In 1930, Sternberg, Dietrich's lover,
   brought her and her daughter Maria to the United States. Sternberg directed
   Dietrich in six movies, including *Morocco* (1930) and *Dishonored* (1931), both
   released by Paramount.
2. Dudley Digges played Caspar Gutman in the 1931 Warner Bros. movie version of
   The Maltese Falcon. Harry Hansen was the book reviewer for the *New York
   World-Telegram.*

TLS HRC

To Alfred A. Knopf

6 June 1931, 1714 Ivar Avenue, Hollywood, California

Dear Alfred,

Thanks, sincerely if belatedly, for the thousand: it saved my life.

I suppose you've heard that *Cosmopolitan* bought an option on the
serial rights to *The Thin Man* at $26,500, a fair enough price, I think.

Is *Variety's* report that the price of *The Glass Key* has been boosted
50¢ correct?[1] I'd like very much to know what it does to the sales.

Naturally I've done a lot of worrying about titles, but I'm damned if I
can see anything wrong with either *The Maltese Falcon* or *The Glass Key,*
and most of the outside opinion—including that of a few booksellers—
has been favorable. I don't mean it would be impossible to pick better
titles, but I do think they are at least better than average.

Would it be convenient to let me see the jacket of the next book
before publication? I think the current one was an awfully unfortunate
choice, tying the book up with a gal who couldn't possibly have anything
to do with it and who furthermore is already beginning to turn the customers away from box-offices all over the country. Clara's been slipping

badly ever since talkies came in, and now, of course, with the help of a scandal or two, is altogether through.[2]

Since this seems to have become an argumentative letter, I may as well go ahead and whine that there are things wrong with the front-flap blurb too, several things, beginning with the incomprehensible thinness and fatness attributed to Madvig and O'Rory respectively.

What's really wrong with me, of course, is that it's past five in the morning, I haven't had a drink for a week, and I'm supposed to be doping out a picture story for Gloria Swanson.

Best wishes to you and Blanche,

> Sincerely,
> Dashiell

1. *The Glass Key* was published at $2.50. An ad in the 23 May 1931 issue of *Publishers Weekly* announced a decrease in the price to $2.00, with a return to $2.50 on 1 June 1931.

2. The dust jacket featured a photo of Clara Bow, a Paramount star known as the "It" girl after the success of her 1927 silent movie *It*. Bow had a thick Brooklyn accent that made her transition to the talkies difficult. She was the iconic flapper, whose movie persona was fun-loving and sexy. She sued her secretary in 1930 for compiling a list of her lovers for publication by the New York City tabloid *GraphiC*. Though she won the suit, the publicity and resulting damage to her career led to her nervous breakdown and retirement from the movies in 1933 at the age of twenty-eight.

TLS HRC

To Alfred A. Knopf

6 August 1931, Los Angeles

WANT TO RETURN TO NEWYORK NEXT WEEK BUT AM IN TERRIFIC FINANCIAL DIFFICULTY STOP CAN YOU DEPOSIT TWENTY FIVE HUNDRED DOLLARS TO MY ACCOUNT IRVING TRUST COMPANY FIFTY NINTH STREET OFFICE THURSDAY BEST REGARDS=

> DASHIELL HAMMETT

TELEGRAM HRC

To Alfred A. Knopf

Knopf published an English translation of Alfred Neumann's The Hero *in 1931.*

1 Sept 1931, Los Angeles

FOR BEAUTIFUL SHEER BRUTALITY I KNOW NOTHING IN LITERATURE TO
TOUCH THE LAST CHAPTER OF THE HERO STOP IT MAKES ME FEEL LIKE A
PANSY STOP BEST REGARDS TO YOU AND BLANCHE=
        DASHIELL

TELEGRAM HRC

To Alfred Knopf

30 October 1931, Hotel Elysée, New York City

Dear Alfred,

    Thanks for forwarding Delany's letter. I like Bill, but I'm afraid nei-
ther he nor his firm has enough of an in with the studios to be very valuable as an agent. There's little doubt that the American Play
Company–Myron Selznick combination (formed this summer) is by far
the best bet on picture rights.

        Yours,
        Dashiell

TLS HRC

Presumably to Lillian Hellman

23 March 1932, Hotel Elysée, New York City

        Statement
        Too many have lived
        As we live
        For our lives to be

Proof of our living
Too many have died
As we die
For their deaths to be
Proof of our dying.

—*D.H. 3–23–32*

HOLOGRAPH POEM HRC

To Lillian Hellman

When Hammett wrote this letter Hellman was on her way from Manhattan to her hometown of New Orleans by train, a route that took her though Salisbury, Maryland, in the southeastern part of the state, along the train route from Manhattan to New Orleans.

5 May 1932, The Biltmore Hotel, New York City

The second day of the hegira

Darling,
    Your wire from Salisbury was here when I got back from breakfast and a look at Grand Central, which had changed but little over night.

When I finish this I'll do a telegram designed to catch you at Atlanta, and then to work on the masterpiece.[1]

"Mr. Hammett, when interviewed, said:

'A bed without Lily ain't no bed.'"

I finished the Russian primrose's memoirs last night. What a guy![2]

The missing of you is terrific!

There are more people on the streets today than are shown in this stationery's illustration, but on the other hand the flags aren't flying. The X marking my window doesn't show on account of my room being around the corner. The other building is Grand Central. I go there sometimes.

Huey Long called up this morning to ask when you'd reach New Orleans. I stalled him. Was that all right?[3]

If I pay any attention to what you said this will be the last letter I can send south.[4] Why don't you keep your silly mouf shut?

> With love of the lewdest sort,
> Signature illegible

1. The second draft of *The Thin Man*.
2. The "Russian primrose" is probably Feodor Chaliapin, whose *Man and Mask: Forty Years in the Life of a Singer* (1932) is the holiday reading of Nora Charles in *The Thin Man*.
3. Huey Long, former governor of Louisiana, had just become U.S. senator. Hammett was joking.
4. Hellman's divorce from Arthur Kober, whom her family liked, was in the final stages. She apparently warned Hammett not to write her to avoid the impression that she was leaving Kober for him.

TLS HRC

To Lillian Hellman

5 May 1932, The Biltmore Hotel, New York City

Later on that same 5th of May

Dear Madam,

And in this week's *Judge* that dirty bum Pare Lorentz says the divine

Greta shows delirious love in *Grand Hotel* by dancing around the room in such a manner that "at every gallumping whirl she seems in danger of breaking a leg or all of MGM's modern furniture." What a cad the fellow is![1]

So far the work hasn't gone so rapidly today—only a page or two—though the evening's not very far gone yet.

If I weren't broke I'd go up to Moriarity's and probably find you there playing bagatelle with Buck Crouse, because I for one don't take much stock in this rumor that you've left town.[2] For a small fee any Pullman porter would have sent that wire from Salisbury. I, for instance, had no trouble at all bribing a bellboy at the Biltmore to handle mail for me while I'm living here on Lenox Avenue with a woman named Magda Klemfuss.

And, while I'm at it, I don't believe there's any General Pershing Street in New Orleans or anywhere else.[3] What would be the sense of it? It'd lead to things like Former Secretary of the Navy Josephus Daniels Boulevard, or First-Class Private Smith Alley.

> Much love from I and Magda.
> Mr. Hammett

I give you an "E."

To continue:
Your telegram from Atlanta arrived while I was spitting on the flap of this envelope.

You probably missed my wire to Atlanta. Lackaday!

Watchout for strangers on those late trains. Them fellers are likely to take you for a Yankee and not respect you. Maybe you'd better use your accent—and be taken for Anna May Wong.[4]

All New York mourns your absence.
> Bud

1. Greta Garbo starred in *Grand Hotel*, released by MGM in April 1932. Pare Lorentz's review of the movie appeared in the 7 May 1932 (p. 20) issue of *Judge*, a popular humor magazine.
2. Moriarity's was a Manhattan speakeasy. Russell Crouse was a boyfriend of Lillian Hellman's. With Howard Lindsay, he wrote and produced a string of hit Broadway comedies, including *Anything Goes* (1934; music and lyrics by Cole Porter) and *Life with Father* (1939).

3. Lillian Hellman's paternal aunts, Jenny and Hannah Hellman, lived on General Pershing Avenue in New Orleans.

4. The most famous Chinese American movie actress of the day.

TLS HRC

To Josephine Dolan Hammett

Jose and the girls had moved from Fairfax, first to Burbank, then to Santa Monica, California.

22 January 1934, The Lombardy Hotel, New York City

Dear Jose,

At last—and I hope forever—our financial troubles seem to be over. Barring acts of God, this week should see us out of debt and well on the road to some decent sort of security.

First, the book is going swell. It got very fine reviews—as you can see from the enclosed clippings—and last week sold better than any other book in New York, Philadelphia, and San Francisco, besides being near the top of the list in most other cities.

Second, MGM is buying the movie rights for $21,000, which is four thousand less than Paramount paid for *The Glass Key,* but a pretty good price this year at that. I ought to have the check in a day or two and will send you a thousand at once and then some each week regularly thereafter.

Third, I'm writing a story for a cartoon strip for Hearst's syndicate, which will bring me a regular and, I hope, growing income perhaps forever. If it goes over well it can make me a lot of money.[1]

So it looks as if we were out of the woods, and this time I mean to stay out. No more nonsense. If I can get away I may go down to Florida for a while to try to finish my next book.

I didn't thank you all for the swell Christmas gifts. Thanks a million. Tell Mary I'm blowing my nose on one of her handkerchiefs now, and tell Josephine I shaved with her shaving soap this morning. Also, if the three of you will write me right away and tell me what kind of gift you'd each *most* like to have, I'll send them.

I know how you feel about having the Kellys on your hands, and I don't envy you.[2] Can't you tell them you haven't room?

Sis is still with me and, of course, all excited over the book.[3] I'm feeling pretty well and hard at work. I've got to run now.

> Love to all,
> D.

I'm on the radio—NBC—at two Friday afternoon, Los Angeles time.

1. On 30 January 1934, King Features, owned by William Randolph Hearst, launched "Secret Agent X–9," a daily comic strip with a story line by Hammett and drawings by Alex Raymond. To promote the strip, King Features serialized *The Thin Man* in daily installments running from 18 March 1934 to 16 April 1934. The novel was published by Knopf on 8 January 1934.
2. After Jose's father died when she was seven, the Kellys—her maternal aunt and her husband—raised her in their home in Anaconda, Montana.
3. Hammett had a sister, Reba, who visited him in New York. Her full name was Aronia Rebecca; Hammett appropriated her name for the charlatan Aaronia Haldorn in *The Dain Curse*.

TLS Marshall

To Josephine Dolan Hammett

[February 1934] Post Office Box 1195, Homestead, Florida

Dear Jose,

I came down here this afternoon after a four-day stay in Miami and hope to stay here at least a week or two, getting plenty of rest and plenty of work done.

The place is a fishing camp on Key Largo, an island about forty miles southeast of Miami and there is absolutely nothing to do here but fish and swim and eat. The lights go out at half-past ten, so maybe I'll get back to regular and early hours.

I'm glad the youngsters are getting along so well in school. Tell them that just before I left New York I bought a watch for Mary and an Alice-in-wonderland bracelet for Josephine, but I haven't had a chance to send them yet. I will either tomorrow or the next day. Tell Mary I was afraid to send a puppy all that way by train as the men on the trains don't always take very good care of them, and I thought Jo would like the bracelet better than a game.

I hope you all like your new house and are comfortable in it.

Thank the youngsters for their letters to me and tell them to write me how they like their presents.

The book is still selling pretty well, though of course not as well as the first two or three weeks, and the strip in the papers seems to be doing well too, though I haven't seen a statement yet. Have you seen it in any of the Los Angeles papers?

Kiss the little mugs for me.

> Love,
> D

TLS Marshall

To Mary and Josephine Hammett

23 February 1934, Post Office Box 1195, Homestead, Florida

Dear Mary and Josephine,

I finally sent your presents off to you, so you should get them at about the same time you get this letter. I hope you will like them, and I think you will. You must take good care of the watch, Mary, because it cost an enormous amount of money. It may not run very well at first, because new watches often don't, and if you have any trouble with it have Mama take it to a good jeweler. I think your Alice-in-wonderland bracelet is very cute, Josephine, especially the Cheshire Cat and the March Hare.

I suppose you are both such big girls now that I would hardly know you. I want to come out to see you some time this year, but it won't be for a few months yet, as I will probably stay here for a month or so, and then I have to go back to New York for a while to see about some business.

The place I am now is an island off the coast of Florida, with coconut trees and all sorts of things. Yesterday I went fishing out in the Atlantic, trying to catch a sailfish, which is about seven feet long and looks like the picture on the top of this match-book I'm enclosing. I didn't have any luck, though: all I caught was a grouper (a fat ugly fish that looks something like a catfish) and a couple of barracuda, which are fish with great big teeth like dogs, and they are supposed to be more dangerous than sharks. This afternoon I'm going out and try again. Maybe I'll catch a dolphin: they are great big fish, all green and gold and very beautiful.

Tell Mama I go to bed every night at ten o'clock and get up at six in the morning and am as sunburned as a Zulu, and am feeling better than I have felt for years. Tell her also that I couldn't find a present I was sure she would like, so she is to use the check I am enclosing to buy herself something.

I hope you are both well and strong and still doing well in school, and, *most important,* I hope you are being good girls and doing everything you can to help Mama.

Here's a kiss for each of you:
X...for Mary
X...for Josephine
Kiss Mama for me.

> Love,
> Papa

TLS MARSHALL

To Josephine Dolan Hammett

22 March 1934, Post Office Box 1195, Homestead, Florida

Dear Jose,

I'm glad the youngsters liked their presents. Jo's letter was very cute. What happened to Mary's?

I'll probably be here another week or two, and a stop over in Havana for a few days on my way north. You'd hardly know me. I've been on the wagon for ten days, look as if I'm gaining weight—whether I am or not—and am burned brown as a native. Tell the youngsters I'm not freckled, just tanned. Here are a couple of snapshots, not very clear, but they at least show me in my new sunburn.

If the present deal goes through I'm going to write a picture story for either Powell or Claudette Colbert. Everything seems all set, but you know what can happen to those Hollywood deals. I won't come West to do it—probably start it here and wind it up in New York. I'll send you some money the first of the month.

Yes, *The Thin Man* did very well and is still dragging along with fair sales. *The Maltese Falcon* comes out in a Modern Library edition in a week or two, and should bring me in some more dough. The newspaper strip seems to be going over very well, though I haven't collected any money on it yet.

I like this place a lot and am planning to come back here next winter, by which time I'll no doubt be an expert deep sea fisherman and general out-door man, to the amazement of everybody including myself.

It's past ten o'clock now, my bed-time, so I'll say good-night and crawl in. Kiss Mary and Jo for me.

> Love,
> Dash

TLS Marshall

To Josephine Dolan Hammett

[Summer 1934] Post Office Box 271, Huntington, New York

Dear Jose,

I'm up here on Long Island for the summer, comfortably settled and hard at work on a moving picture and a play, both of which I hope to have finished by the middle of September so I can get going on the next book.

I think your going to Montana is a good idea, especially since Los Angeles seems to be having an infantile paralysis epidemic. I hope you and the youngsters have a swell time.

There isn't a great deal of news. I saw the film version of *The Thin Man* the other day. They made a pretty funny picture of it and it seems to be doing good business wherever it is being shown. Select Pictures— a new independent company—is making *Woman in the Dark*—which I sold to *Liberty* a couple of years ago—and it'll probably be pretty bad.[1]

I doubt now that I'll be able to get West before early fall.

Here's a check for five hundred.

Kiss Mary and Josephine for me and tell them to write to the old man.

> Love,
> Dash

1. Select Pictures and RKO Radio released the movie adaptation of *Woman in the Dark,* with a screenplay by Sada Cowan, in 1934. Hammett's story was published in three parts in *Liberty* (8 April–22 April 1933).

TLS MARSHALL

To Lillian Hellman

The movie of The Thin Man, *starring William Powell and Myrna Loy, was released by MGM in June 1934. In the wake of its success, the studio asked Hammett to come to Hollywood to work on the sequel. Hammett sent the following telegrams while on a train trip from New York to Los Angeles.*

27 October 1934, Kansas City, Missouri

MRS. LILLIAN KOBER=

HOTEL ELYSEE=

SO FAR SO GOOD ONLY AM AMISSING OF YOU PLENTY LOVE=
>   NICKY

TELEGRAM LPT

To Lillian Hellman

27 October 1934, Albuquerque, New Mexico

MRS. LILLIAN KOBER

HOTEL ELYSEE=

HAVE NOT GOT USED TO BEING WITHOUT YOU YET WHAT SHALL I DO LOVE=
>   DASH

TELEGRAM LPT

To Lillian Hellman

Tuesday [29 October 1934], Beverly Wilshire Hotel, Beverly Hills, California

Darling—

And so passed the first day of laboring in the picture-galleries. I think it's going to be all right. I like the people thus far and have a comfortable office.

We're going to make the picture with all the surviving members of the first cast—which won't be silly if I can devise a murder that grows with some logic out of the set-up we left everybody in at the end of the *T.M.* and I think I can. We may title it *After the Thin Man*.

I saw Sam Spewack—who sends his regards—and also those dear friends of yours, Bart Cormack and David Burton.[1] As I told you last night, I am going to the Asburys' for dinner this evening and will no doubt run into dozens more of your friends and worshippers.

I miss you awfully, honey—it would be so thoroughly nice being back here if you were only along.

I hope the rehearsals are going smoothly and I hope you are being a good girl.[2]

> I love you v.m.
> Dash

1. Sam Spewak was a writer at MGM in 1934; Bartlett Cormack was a screenwriter at Columbia; David Burton was a director at Columbia Pictures.
2. Lillian Hellman's first play, *The Children's Hour,* written with Hammett's assistance, opened in New York on 20 November 1934 and ran for 691 performances.

ALS HRC

To Alfred A. Knopf

Knopf, whose contract with Hammett called for a sixth novel, was eager to take advantage of the success of The Thin Man *and its movie adaptation.*

31 October 1934, Beverly Wilshire Hotel, Beverly Hills, California

Dear Alfred—

So I'm a bum—so what's done of the book looks terrible—so I'm out here drowning my shame in MGM money for 10 weeks.

> Abjectly,
> Dash

ALS HRC

To Lillian Hellman

31 October 1934, Beverly Wilshire Hotel, Beverly Hills, California

Sweetheart—

And so—besides loving you very much—I went to the Asburys' for dinner last night and there were N. Johnson and the J. Sayres and the L. Hubbards and the B. LeVinos and the J. Dunns and so on and the food was surprisingly good, but people went around muttering that the cocktails were too weak, which was funny, because Herb had told me early in the evening that he made "the best dry martinis in the world"—honest![1]

Herb's got a job again—doing a prison story for Fox. He's fatter than ever.

After the party broke up Mrs. Joel Sayre and I did a little town-roaming until nearly five this A.M., but I was up at ten and so to work on my *Thin Man* sequel, but still without the exact murder hookup I want, but still loving and missing you very much all the time. And I do and I do and I do! Want to make something of it?

> Several kisses,
> Dash

1. Nunnally Johnson was a short-story writer and journalist working as a screenwriter at 20th Century-Fox. Joel Sayre was a screenwriter at various studios in 1934 and 1935. Lucien Hubbard was a producer, director, and writer at MGM. Margaret P. LeVino was a screenwriter; B. Levino is unidentified. James Dunn was an actor. Herb is presumably Herbert Asbury.

ALS HRC

To Lillian Hellman

1 November 1934, Beverly Wilshire, Beverly Hills, California

Angel—

And so I took Thyra to dinner last night and so I got very—not to say disgracefully—drunk and so I saw Ben and Ad—who are back together again—and Reuben and Marlene and the Tuttles and the Dick Wallaces[1] and nine tenths of Hollywood and lost a lot of money betting Ben was right in a crap-game where he was always wrong—and so home at what hour I don't know and too hangovery to go to the studio today[2] and god help me you'd better come on out and take care of me.

 BUT ALL THE TIME I'M LOVING YOU VERY MUCH PLEASE!
   Dash

And so this afternoon I'm going to the Eddie Robinsons for cocktails and to Nunnal[l]y's to see 'em off for N.Y. and then to my folks' for dinner and I.L.Y.V.M.
   D.

1. Thyra Samter Winslow was a writer in Hollywood. Her volume of short stories, *Picture Frames,* was published by Knopf in 1923. Ben and Ad are B. P. and his wife Adeline Schulberg. He had been head of production at Paramount until 1932, when he began producing movies independently. Other apparent references are to Marlene Dietrich; Frank Tuttle, a movie director at Fox who specialized in crime movies; and Lurene Tuttle, an actress who was later the voice of Effie Perrine in the radio production of *The Adventures of Sam Spade,* 1946–1951. Richard Wallace was a director. Reuben is possibly Rouben Mamoulian, who directed Hammett's first screen story, *City Streets,* and Marlene Dietrich in *Queen Christiana* (1933).
2. On 29 October 1934 Hammett began a contract with MGM, working on a sequel to *The Thin Man.*

ALS LPT

To Lillian Hellman

5 November 1934, Beverly Wilshire, Beverly Hills, California.

Darling—

 I haven't written to you for a few days because I've been too ashamed of myself. I've been faithful enough to you, but I went back on the booze pretty heavily until Saturday night—neglecting studio, dignity, and so on. And was I sick Sunday and today! This morning I showed up at M.G.M. for the first time since last Tuesday and squared myself, but didn't get much work done, since the publicity department took up most of my time, what with photographs, interviews and the like.

I'm still surprised at the fuss the *Thin Man* made out here. People bring the Joan Crawfords and Gables over to meet me instead of the usual vice versa! Hot-cha!

Arthur and I had lunch and got pretty tight together Saturday afternoon. He looks well and seems more cheerful. He has another job at Fox.

I saw Ad and the Jaffes the other night and lost some dough betting—but I think I wrote all this the other day.[1]

Miss Winslow is a bit of a problem: she seems to think I should take her out two or three times a week. We dropped in at the Eddie Robinsons' and saw the new baby the other day. Eddie's going to play in Warner's new version of *The Maltese Falcon*.

Tonight I'm home and hope to be in bed by ten. I've been making too many dates. Tomorrow I'm going to dinner at the Spewacks who want to rent me their house—and afterwards to the Perelman's, whom I haven't seen yet.

Miss Deviane caught up with me and so my pay-check is sewed up, but I hope to get it fixed up tomorrow so that only a little is taken out each week—if $300 a week for 9 weeks can be called a little. But I'm stuck for it so I suppose there's no use bellyaching.[2]

Your sweet letter with the clippings came today. The Weiss evening sounded like a Weiss evening, but the Eric evening didn't sound like an Eric one. I'm tickled to death that your cast still looks good![3]

The lads with the car arrived O.K. I've got 'em out learning something about the town before I start riding in wrong directions with them.[4]

I love you something awful and days are years till I see you again! And I'm not five feet nine and I'm not going to be an actor and don't pay any attention to the publicity the studio is sending out on me: I gave 'em a free hand and they've gone pretty nutty.

I suppose you'll see the Johnsons on their Eastern jaunt—the[y] said they were going to look you up.

I love you and miss you and love you and miss you and not much else.

Dash

1. The Jaffes were Adeline Schulberg's family. Her brother, Sam Jaffe, was studio manager at Paramount.
2. In June 1932 Elise De Viane, a girlfriend of Hammett's, sued him in Los Angeles Superior Court for sexual assault and battery. She asked for $35,000 and was awarded $2,500. When Hammett failed to pay, she garnisheed his wages.
3. Weiss and Eric are unidentified. There was difficulty casting *The Children's Hour* because actresses offered the job of the spinster schoolmasters were anxious about the lesbianism implicit in the play and the effect such roles would have on their reputations.
4. Hammett often rented limousines and drivers. He was sued repeatedly in Los Angeles Municipal Court for failing to pay for them.

ALS HRC

To Lillian Hellman

26 November 1934, 18904 Malibu Rd., Pacific Palisades, California

Darling,

Here is the thingamagigger and I love you very much please.

I haven't a single bit of news beyond what I told you over the phone except that I still love you very much please and would ask that you might find it possible to return my affections if it so happens you could do it without too much trouble.

I've been reading the new Millay book and a French novel called *The Wolves* and Waldo Frank's new novel and find them all pleasant enough going without being exactly hairraising and I love you very much.[1]

Carricature by an unkown artist Hammett sent to Jose and his daughters in the early 1930s

Alfred's been bothering me with pleas that we bring "The Big Knock-Over" out between covers with a foreword saying it was written long ago and we don't think much of it, but there it is.[2] He claims he's being hounded by my public—the rats!—and I love you very much, but I don't think I'll let him do it.

Now—still loving you very much—I'm off for another crack at the thinmansequel, on which I'm pretty cold at the time, but will probably be highpressured by Hunt Stromberg into the wildest enthusiasm before long[3]

I love you very much.
Dash

1. Edna St. Vincent Millay's new book was *Wine from These Grapes*; Guy Mazaline wrote *The Wolves*; Waldo Frank's novel was *The Death and Birth of David Markand*.

2. Hammett published "The Big Knockover" in *Black Mask* in February 1927. Knopf proposed that it and a related story, "$106,000 Blood Money" (*Black Mask*, May 1927), together would make a book, which might have satisfied Hammett's contractual obligations to the house.

3. Hunt Stromberg was producer of the Thin Man movies.

TLS LPT

To Alfred A. Knopf

4 June 1935, Metro-Goldwyn-Mayer Studios, Culver City, California

Dear Alfred,

Yellow fellow that I am, I turned tail before the difficulties the new book was presenting and scurried back here to comparative ease and safety. I think I'm a cinch to be here through the summer, but will try to get in some licks on the book meanwhile.

I haven't found a house yet, so this is the nearest thing to a permanent address I have.

If you've anything coming out that looks like picture stuff you might shoot it to me, as we are hunting for some material. (I'm working with Stromberg, the chap who produced *The Thin Man*, and he listens to reason.)

My best to you and Blanche.

> Yours,
> Dash

TLS HRC

To Lillian Hellman

[About 17 September 1935, no place]

Darling,

So after I phoned you I took a shot of scotch, the first I've had since when was it? and it didn't seem to do me any good, but I suppose it hardly ever does anybody any good except those who sell it to get enough money to buy detective stories or tickets to Elliot (41st week) (D–929-$3.30)[1] and that damned barking bird is at work outside and if I don't look out I'll become a stream of consciousness writer and be discovered by Whit Burnett. (If you committed a crime and left an incriminating letter behind I Whit Burnett.) Want to see me do one with Martha Foley?[2] In the screen version of *The Children's Hour* Karen says, "Martha, Foley we could make Mary tell the truth we..." Oberon could do that nicely: it's the way English actors talk normally. (I hear the editors of *Story* are no longer Whit Burnett Cerf.)[3] I hope you can stop laughing long enough to read the rest of this letter: It gets better as it goes on.

> That's what I'd like to think,
> and like to have you
> think, but I know
> as well as you
> do that just
> about now
> what lit-
> tle im-
> agin-

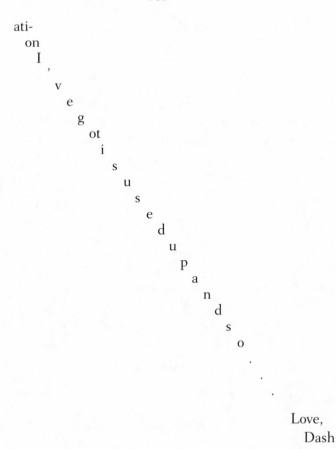

ati-
on
I
,
v
e
g
ot
i
s
u
s
e
d
u
p
a
n
d
s
o
.
.
.

Love,
Dash

1. Hellman's play *The Children's Hour* opened at Maxine Elliott's Theatre in New York on Tuesday, 20 November 1934.
2. Whit Burnett and Martha Foley were the founding editors of *Story* magazine.
3. In Hellman's play *The Children's Hour,* Karen is one of the unmarried women who run a girls' boarding school, and Mary is a student who tells a vindictive lie about them. Merle Oberon played Karen in *These Three,* the movie version of *The Children's Hour,* released in March 1936 with a screenplay by Hellman. Bennett Cerf co-founded Random House in 1927.

TLS HRC

To Alfred A. Knopf

24 September 1935, Los Angeles, California

WILL YOU DEPOSIT MY CCOUNT GUARNTY TRUST SIXTIETH AND MADISON
ONE THOUSAND DOLLARS AND WIRE ME THREE TWO FIVE BELAIR ROAD
WESTLOSANGELES STOP THANKS AND BEST REGARDS AND DON'T BE SUR-
PRISED IF YOU GET A BOOK BEFORE SNOW FLIES=
DASHIELL HAMMETT

TELEGRAM HRC

To Alfred Knopf

28 October 1935, Los Angeles, California

CAN YOU DEPOSIT THAT SECOND FIVE HUNDRED TODAY AND LET ME KNOW=
DASHIELL HAMMETT

TELEGRAM HRC

To Josephine Hammett

13 January 1936, Wichita, Kansas

AND AS FOR YOU MY FINE FEATHERED FRIEND I AM STILL ON THE WAY AND I
LOVE YOU AND YOUR RELATIVE=
GUESS WHO

TELEGRAM MARSHALL

To Mary Hammett

*Hammett entered Lenox Hill Hospital on 17 January 1936 to be treated for venereal
disease and general ill health. He took a heat treatment current at the time. During
one session a protective blanket fell from his legs and he was burned severely, leaving permanent scars.*

[postmarked 16? January 1936] The Plaza, New York City

Dear Mary—

Your note came yesterday.

I had a swell trip east: we got in a half hour or so ahead of time. It's mighty nice being back in New York, though I haven't been feeling well enough to get around very much.

Tomorrow I'm going to the Lenox Hill Hospital, 76th St. and Park Avenue for a week or two to see what's the matter with me. Don't any of you worry too much about it. My doctor seems to think it's only that I'm run down and need a good rest.

Here are some match covers for Jo. Kiss her and Jose for me.

Love,
Dash

ALS Marshall

To Josephine Hammett

[postmarked 20 January 1936] Lenox Hill Hospital, New York City

Dear Jo—

I haven't been able to get you any more match covers because they've still got me cooped up in this place, but I expect to get out at the end of this week—and then I'll try to make up for lost time.

Tell Jose I'm feeling a lot better (they've been keeping me in bed—the nurse even scrubs my face for me) and there is nothing to worry about.

Yesterday it snowed all day and from my window now I can see hundreds of roofs covered with white.

I liked the note you sent along with Jose's letter.

When I leave here I am not going back to the Plaza—the service is too lousy—so I'll have to send you my next address. Until then, write me here.

Love to you and Jose and Mary.
Dash

ALS Marshall

To Josephine Dolan Hammett, Mary Hammett, and Josephine Hammett

23 January 1936, Lenox Hill Hospital, New York

Dear Jose —

Dear Mary —

Dear Jo —

It was two or more degrees below zero earlier in the day, so God only knows how cold it is outdoors by now — nearly midnight — but here in my bed it is warm and snug enough for anybody.

I'm still busy taking tests and examinations (I had my head X-rayed this afternoon and was told I had a thick skull) and will probably be here at least another week. There doesn't seem to be so awfully much wrong with me, though, outside of being pretty badly run down. So nobody should do any worrying.

Now I'm going to bite into some cold duck a kind friend sent me and try to get some sleep.

> Love to all of you
> Dash
>
> Mary — you spell it p-n-e-u-m-o-n-i-a.

ALS MARSHALL

To Mary Hammett

As a young girl, Mary Hammett attempted to attract her father's attention by writing him questions about matters she thought interested him. She was fourteen when she received this letter.

21 February 1936, The Madison Hotel, New York City

Dear Mary,
What happened to that report on the Youth Movement (and a lousy movement it is!) in Germany you were going to send me?

You asked me a couple of weeks ago to tell you about the present German government. It would take a couple of books to do that, so you'd better just ask me about the particular part you're interested in. Roughly, the way things seem to stack up now, it seems only a matter of time before von Blomberg (who controls the Reichswehr, or national army) and Goering (who is Hitler's minister of war) will split with Hitler and Goebbels (who is the head of the propaganda department and a real madman); and then there's no telling what will happen. Hitler isn't as strong a man as any of the others I've mentioned, and has only stayed in power this long because he has played along with them and Schacht (who is probably not a Nazi at heart, but is a swell financier.)[1] Meanwhile our Communist Party there has some forty thousand members and, with the help of Russian money, may be getting itself in shape to do something when the blow-up comes—but nobody is counting much on that. It looks too much as if some sort of Nazi rule will continue in Germany for a few more years, especially since the new king of England is supposed to be a Nazi sympathizer and is in a position to give them a lot of help.[2]

* * *

You'd better not count on the Florida trip: it's pretty certain that my doctors are going keep me here in New York the rest of the winter, though I may try to find a house in the country near here after the first of the month.

Tell Jo I'm mailing her some more of those match folders, and kiss her silly little nose for me, the fine-feathered fiend.

Last week I went to see the Chaplin picture,[3] but didn't like it very much. Parts of it are funny, but not enough parts. I've also seen Ziegfeld's Follies, which is all right when Fanny Brice is on the stage and terrible when she isn't, and a show called *End of Summer*, which was dull.[4]

I've got to dress now to go to some affair up in Harlem where we're trying to raise money to help those poor negroes they've got in jail down in Scottsboro.[5]

Be a good girl and don't keep on endangering your life by studying so hard.

Love,
Dash

1. Gen. Werner Von Blomberg was Hitler's minister of war (1933–8) and Gen. Herman Goering a leader in the Nazi Party who held several important positions, including head of the Luftwaffe. In 1937 he succeeded Hjalmer Schacht as minister of finance in the National Socialist government. Joseph Goebbels, a skillful journalist and orator, had the job of marshaling popular support for the Nazi Party.

2. King Edward VIII of England assumed the throne on 20 January 1936 upon the death of his father, George V. On 10 December 1936 Edward voluntarily abdicated to marry Wallis Simpson, a divorcée whom influential officials felt was unsuited to be queen. In October 1937 the former king, now Duke of Windsor, visited Germany and was honored by the Nazi Party. Hitler later devised a fanciful plan to recoronate the duke King of England.

3. *Modern Times*, directed by Charles Chaplin, was released in February 1936.

4. S.N. Behrman's *End of Summer* opened at the Guild Theatre on 17 February 1936. It ran for 152 performances.

5. The Scottsboro Boys were nine black males charged with the rape of two white women in Scottsboro, Alabama, in March 1925. Doctors who examined the women found little evidence of rape, but an all-white jury condemned eight of the defendants to death and the youngest (who was thirteen at the time) to life imprisonment. A series of trials and appeals lasted through 1937. The cause of the Scottsboro Boys was championed by many Northern liberal and radical groups, especially the U.S. Communist Party. The state of Alabama eventually freed or paroled all but one of the defendants, and he escaped from prison in 1948.

TLS MARSHALL

To Josephine Dolan Hammett

21 February 1936, The Madison Hotel, New York City

Dear Jose,

I wired you a hundred dollars yesterday and hope you can get by with that until next week, when I'll try to get some more to you.

I'm still seeing doctors every two days, but I seem to be coming along all right, so there is nothing particular to worry about. (I'm still pretty likely to outlive all the rest of you.)

There isn't much news. I haven't been able to get much work done, but hope to have better luck next week. I turned down an offer this morning to come back to Hollywood—still want to get the book finished before I do anything else.

Take care of yourself.

> Love,
> Dash

TLS Marshall

To Josephine Hammett

14 March 1936, The Madison Hotel, New York City

And as for you, my fine feathered friend—

I've some more match-books for you and will mail them as soon as I find something to wrap them in.

Have you ever heard the little verse that goes something like this?

> *Yesterday, upon the stair*
> *I saw a man who wasn't there.*
> *He wasn't there again today.*
> *Oh, how I wish he'd go away!*[1]

In a picture called *These Three* that will soon be showing there is a little girl named Marcia Mae Jones who looks—especially around her mouth and eyes—quite a bit like you and sometimes talks exactly like you, and everybody thinks she's swell. Be sure to see her.

Take care of yourself, pardner.

> Love,
> D

1. Hammett is quoting from memory Hugh Mearns's poem "The Psychoed," also known as "Antigonish."

TLS Marshall

To Josephine Dolan Hammett

14 March 1936, The Madison Hotel, New York City

Dear Jose,

Don't let the weather reports worry you: millions of people have lived through eastern winters and always will, including me. I've had a touch of grippe, but think it's a lot better today.

I haven't been able to find myself another place to live yet, and, with the strike on, hotels here aren't the most comfortable places in the world to live nowadays; especially if—like me—you don't like scabs. Maybe I'll be able to get out in the country the first of the month.

There's not much chance of my coming back to California in the immediate future. If I do some picture work in the next few months— and I probably will—it will be done in the east.

Kiss the youngsters for me.

> Love,
> D

TLS Marshall

To Josephine Dolan Hammett

[postmarked 29 April 1936] The Madison Hotel, New York City

Dear Jose—

Here's the check I wired you I was sending. I'll send you some more in a few days as I think I have my affairs partly straightened out at last. There's no sense in your moving to save money—only if you find a place you like better.

I haven't read Kelly's letter yet—and probably won't.

After having been sick as hell for some time I'm up and around again—and hope to stay that way. I'll write you more fully in a day or two.

Kiss the youngsters for me.

> Love,
> Dash

ALS Marshall

To Lillian Hellman

6 June 1936, The Madison Hotel, New York City

Darling,

I hope whatever was wrong about the beginning of your trip is all gone now and you're having the swellest time you ever had in all your silly little life, so help me!

My trouble seems to be better. It was chiefly in the prostate and, what with hot sitz baths and rectal irrigations, I'm feeling almost human again and the toilet seat's getting a chance to rest up.

I haven't seen anybody but Kenyon since you left, so I'm not exactly top-heavy with news.[1] Lois is coming in this evening to talk about the play.[2] That's going to be nice, though she'll probably do most of the talking. I think I've a vague idea of how the thing might be fixed up, but...

The first of the King Features stories started this afternoon: "Flypaper," now called "Girl Hunt," and it reads pretty awful.[3]

La Paterson, in tomorrow's "Books," has a go at Edm[u]nd Wilson in her very best manner.[4] I'd send it to you if it weren't that anger is probably not good for you in the tropics, and I don't want anything to happen to you.

The Thin Man goes on the air Wednesday for an hour, I think, with Loy and Powell. I guess I'll have to sneak up on a radio and regret it.[5]

I'm missing you terribly. Last night I almost phoned Rhinelander 4–4108 just to hear it ring, but that seemed a little too silly.

A note in one of the papers says Thyra is in Hollywood working for RKO. (I've a feeling that's not news, maybe you told me she was going.)

I've decided not to go to the Louis–Schmelling fight[6] and wouldn't be surprised if a lot of other people come to the same decision. The more you read about it, the duller it sounds.

Rusty White phoned to invite me to spend a month with him in Darien.[7] His family is away. If it had been anybody else I'd've been tempted, but he's a hard boy to be around alone.

With that last snappy paragraph I seem to have wr[u]ng myself dry of news-bits — unless you want some stock market quotations — so I'll go see if I can find out where to send this.

> I love you.
> Dash

1. Kenyon was Hammett's physician.
2. Lois Jacoby was a friend of Hellman's who had amorous designs on Hammett. "The play" is Hellman's *Days to Come,* which opened on Broadway on 15 December 1936 and closed after seven performances.
3. After 1934, King Features syndicated a series of Hammett's short stories and the complete text of *The Thin Man.* "Flypaper" was first published in *Black Mask,* August 1929.
4. Isobel Paterson was the book review editor for the New York *Herald Tribune.*
5. *The Thin Man* radio play was broadcast on the Lux Radio Theater on 8 June 1936.
6. The Joe Louis–Max Schmeling heavyweight championship boxing match on 19 June 1936 was expected to be an easy win for Louis, but Schmeling knocked him out in the twelfth round.
7. Rusty White is unidentified.

TLS LPT

To Lillian Hellman

11 June 1936, The Madison Hotel, New York City

Dear Leelee,

I'm sorry about that first letter, but, not being a very up-to-date fellow, I stupidly forg[o]t all about air mail and sent it off to be conveyed to you by a wind-jammer, no doubt. You ought to have it by now.

I'm awfully glad you like Havana and are having a good time. Things have been kind of dull around here since Laura Riding threw herself....[1]

This noon, after visiting Kenyon, I went to see *Fury,* but he had given me an injection, so after seeing not quite half of the picture I had to run for home and my every ten minutes' toileting.[2] It seems to be easing up a bit now.

While out, I bought myself a pipe and a can of tobacco and all afternoon, between trips to the toilet, I've been practicing looking like Corey Ford, so you've got that to come home to.[3]

Variety reports that your show did $4,500 last week;[4] Lois told me Arthur may go back to Hollywood to work on the Eddie Cantor picture; I haven't had a drink since Lois was here last Saturday; I haven't heard from Mrs. W.; Fox and some other company are nibbling at the King Feature story (probably under the impression that it is a "new novel," as advertised);[5] The *Thin Man* broadcast was last Monday, but I didn't start hunting for it until Wednesday, which I discovered didn't work out very well; and I love you and miss you.

King Features invited me to contribute, free, one of those columns they use in Winchell's place while he's vacationing. They said he'd appreciate it!

It's raining.

A couple of days ago I had a letter, about a house in Huntington the gent wants to rent, from a member of the firm of Milbank, Tweed, Hope & Webb.

Variety says the N. Johnsons are leaving for a holiday in Europe the first of July. (Well, where else am I going to get news if I don't go out?)

I guess that's the crop.

> I love you, as you may remember.
>   Dash

1. Riding was an American poet who lived in London from 1926 to 1929 in an unorthodox relationship with Robert Graves and his wife, Nancy Nicholson. When Irish poet Geoffrey Phibbs urged Riding to leave the household with him in 1929, she jumped from a second-story window, fracturing her spine.
2. *Fury* is a movie by Fritz Lang, starring Spencer Tracy and Sylvia Sidney.
3. Corey Ford was editor of the humor magazine *Judge*. A Yale graduate, he cultivated an Ivy League persona.
4. The "show" is apparently *These Three*, released in March 1936.
5. Presumably a reference to the syndication of Hammett's long story "The Big Knockover."

TLS HRC

To Josephine Dolan Hammett

c/o Herman Shumlin [Summer 1936?], Tavern Island, South Norwalk, Conn.

Dear Jose,

I'm in New York for a couple of days to see a doctor or two and to have myself fitted with new glasses, but expect to get back to the above address by the first of the week and will probably stay there for at least a fortnight. It's a swell place for summering, a four-acre island three-quarters of a mile from shore, with a marvelous beach and all sorts of other pleasant things. Thank God one of my friends found it, since there was no chance of my getting a place this summer.

The hospital stay was short, but plenty tough while it went on. I took one of those new fever treatments. They put me under a stove, ran my temperature up to a hundred and seven and kept it there for fourteen hours straight. You can imagine how much fun that was, but it seems to have done me a lot of good. The first eight days out of the hospital I gained seven pounds and seem to be still putting on weight.

I'm wiring you a hundred dollars, which you will or should get before this letter reaches you and I hope you have a nice time in Catalina. How do you feel since you had your teeth pulled?

You all might just as well give up the idea of seeing me in September. There's no chance of my getting West until I've finished the book, and I'll be very lucky to get that off my hands before November.

Tell Mary I've enjoyed her letters very much and will write her as soon as I get back on the island. Kiss her and Josephine for me.

Love,
Dash

TLS MARSHALL

1936

To Josephine Dolan Hammett

11 September 1936, The Dorset Hotel, New York City

Dear Jose,

I've been laid up for a week with a cold in my back or something of the sort, which is why I haven't written before this. It's much better now; it was more painful than serious at its worst.

I gained thirteen pounds this summer, which makes me heavier than I have been in years.

I'll wire you some money this week, trying to get it to you before Mary's birthday.

The chances are I won't stay in New York this fall, but will go down to Princeton until I finish the book at least, but I'll let you know about that when it happens.

Kiss the youngsters for me.

Love,
Dash

TLS MARSHALL

To Mary Hammett

11 September 1936, The Dorset Hotel, New York City

Dear Mary,

I'm glad you like being in school again and, since you say you're doing swell in all your subjects, I hope you'll put in a few odd minutes now and then on your spelling. It's not exactly swell.

No, there's no truth in the statement that the Communists are supporting Roosevelt; that's just the old Hearst howl. They've been against Roosevelt from the beginning and, though they'd rather have him elected than Landon, it's only because they think he'll do less harm. Meanwhile they're busy trying to get all the votes they can for their own presidential candidate, Earl Browder. They don't expect to win, of course, but the idea is that if the Communists and Socialists and Farmer-Labor interests make a pretty good showing this time, the Democrats will try to win their support by doing something for the workers between now and the next election. If the Republicans get in, all the workers can expect is a kick in the seat of the pants no matter what happens.

And no again, the Spanish government isn't Communist. The Communists aren't much stronger in Spain than they are here. At the beginning of the revolution there weren't any Communists at all in the government and now there are only two Communists in the cabinet, which has twelve members; but as time goes on the Communist strength will very probably increase.

Here, roughly, is what happened in Spain:

Spain has for years been a land of terrible poverty. Most of the money and land were owned by a very few people—many of whom didn't even live in Spain anymore—and our old friend the Catholic Church, which, according to some accounts owned very nearly one third of all the land. The workers were paid little or nothing, the people were much poorer than the poorest in the United States. So they decided to change things by chasing out their King and setting up a Republic, which they did a few years ago.

Unfortunately, it's not enough to get rid of a bad government; you must make sure you're getting a good one in its place. After various troubles, the Spaniards found that their government was in the hands of the same old gang, except for the King, who had only been a figurehead anyway. The things that the people wanted, the things they had thrown the King out for, the things the government had promised them hadn't come. They were as bad off as ever. So last February the people went to the polls and voted; they defeated the politicians in power and elected their own men— men they knew they could trust to carry out the laws they had passed.

Things began to look better for the small business man, the storekeeper, the working man, the peasant. It was *their* government and it was going to help *them*—even if it had to hurt the very rich people like Count Romanones, big land and mine owner, Juan March, tobacco, and Francisco Cambo, financier and electric-power magnate. Those three didn't like the setup, so they got together to see what they could do about it.

They couldn't do anything legally, because the people had voted for what they wanted and would vote the same way again. So they decided to buy a revolution. They had money enough to pay for one. Many of the army officers were hang-overs from the King's day and had never got used to the new government, so they were willing enough to talk business. As for the privates in the army, they were used to doing what their officers told them, and would probably keep on doing so. Across the water in Spain's African colony there were black soldiers who didn't care who they fought as long as they got their money and loot, and a Foreign Legion composed of white men of all nations who felt the same way about it. Through Spain, outside the army, there were 3 or 4 million people (out of a total of about 24 million) who wanted the King back, or wanted another king called Carlo, or who for one reason of another didn't like the present government. But the chief idea was that the army could grab everything quick, set up a ruler the moneyed folk liked, and everything would be hotsy-totsy. So the Romanones-March-Cambo group put up the money and the shindig was on.

Franco began to bring his blacks and his hired soldiers from Morocco, General Mola called out the army in Spain. In the big cities of Madrid, Barcelona, and Valencia, the common soldiers either refused to rebel with their officers or were quickly overwhelmed by the people, but in the rest of Spain perhaps as many as 80,000 soldiers joined the rebels. In the Navy, the crews of one or two boats joined the rebels, but the rest arrested their officers and remained faithful to the government, making it impossible for the rebels to bring over their African troops rapidly enough to grab everything in a flash. And so the revolution settled down into the hard bitter struggle it now is.

At present it looks very much as if the rebels will take Madrid. In that case, Italy and Germany, perhaps followed by other countries, will immediately recognize the rebels as the real government and a great attempt will be made to convince everybody that the revolution is over. But don't let them fool you: this is a fight that's going to last a long, long time.

It's not possible in smaller space than a book to give you the principles of the Republican, Democratic, Communist parties and the Fascists. I'll give you a political rule though: be in favor of what's good for the workers and against what isn't. Follow that, and you may not be the most brilliant person in the world, but you'll at least be able to hold your head up when you look at yourself in the mirror.

> Love,
> Dash

TLS Marshall

To Josephine Dolan Hammett

14 September 1936, c/o Herman Shumlin, Tavern Island, South Norwalk, Conn.[1]

Dear Jose,

Here's a hundred and fifty dollars. I'm sorry I couldn't get it to you earlier. Tell the youngsters everybody admired their photos a lot—or said they did. I suppose they're busily engaged in getting back into the school grind.

I'm feeling a lot better than I have felt for a year or so, so the hospital venture seems to have been worth all the hell I went through.

There's no news. I'm hard at work on the book and will probably return to the city in a week or ten days. I don't know where I'll live. Kiss the young for me.

> Love,
> Dash

1. Herman Shumlin was a theatrical producer who staged Hellman's early plays. She had an affair with him, making little effort to hide it from Hammett.

TLS Marshall

To Mary Hammett

17 September 1936, Tavern Island, Connecticut

Dear Mary,

And how does it feel to be a schoolgirl again?

I'll probably go back to New York next week and hunt for a place to dig in while I finish the book, which, God knows, is going along slowly enough. I think I'm going to call it, "Death Is for Suckers." This one isn't a detective story.[1]

My health has been improving steadily since I left the hospital — helped along no doubt by my not having had a drink for three months — and I think I'm putting on some weight. I wear silver-rimmed glasses all the time now. I guess your old man is getting to be an old man.

I hope you are taking some interest in the war in Spain. It is tremendously important, since if the rebels win it will be a great set-back for the cause of working people everywhere. Don't believe too much of what the papers say: they are largely on the side of the rebels, and so are such Fascist countries as Germany, Italy and Portugal. The truth is that the present Spanish government is far from perfect, but it at least tries to be on the side of the poor people, while its enemies (including the Catholic church, which never in its whole history has believed that poor people should do anything but go to church, put money in the collection, and do as they are told) are the sort of people that most of our ancestors came to this country to escape. It looks just now as if the government will win, though it will be a long and bitter war unless, as I hope, the French radicals force the French government to help them.

What do the people in Santa Monica think about the presidential election? And what do you think about it?

Good night, darling. I want to write Jo a short letter and then get to work.

> Love,
> Dash

1. Aside from his mention in his letters, there is no known manuscript for this or most of the other novels-in-progress Hammett refers to.

TLS MARSHALL

To Josephine Dolan Hammett

13 November 1936, 90 Cleveland Ave., Princeton, New Jersey

Dear Jose,

I'm sorry I can't send more than this, but I'll try to get some more to you as soon as possible. What money I've got coming to me has been tied up in a law-suit all summer, and, since most of the people I know are broke right now, borrowing isn't so easy.[1]

The book has been giving me plenty of trouble, as usual, but of course it will straighten itself out sooner or later. I doubt if it will be finished before the first of the year however. And while I'm pretty sure of a movie sale on it, I'm not too hopeful of being able to sell it to a magazine. But we'll see…

My health is so-so; not bad enough to do a great deal of worrying about, and, by staying down here, away from New York, I hope to get myself back into pretty good shape again.

Tell Josephine I've got another little black dog like Flic and I'll send her a picture of it as soon as I get a chance to take one. Its name is Blakeen Babs and it's a hundred percent devil. Thank her and Mary for their letters. I'll write both of them in a day or two. Meanwhile, kiss them for me, and tell them to stop whatever it is they are doing that is wrong.

> Love to all,
> Dash

1. Between 1933 and 1936 five lawsuits were filed against Hammett in Los Angeles Municipal Court for non-payment of debts. All were settled by default judgment.

TLS Marshall

To Lillian Hellman

SCENE—The library of a rented house in a college town in New Jersey, U.S.A.

TIME—Late at night late in December late in 1936 A.D.

Dear Lilushka,

What kind of nonsense was that about your scow leaving at two o'clock? It was still there when I passed Princetonward an hour later. I'd've stopped if I'd thought there would have been any chance of finding you. But you're so little and the boat's so big.

As usual, it was nice getting back here. I was in bed by ten last night and camped there until five this evening, mostly reading, for the first time, *Gil Blas,* and finding it unexpectedly charming, which I suppose is late news to most literates. It's been hot as hell all day: I've been sitting around tonight with the doors open.

The drawing things, for which thanks, arrived, but I haven't had at them yet.

I imagine, and hope, that what is tough weather for this time of the year ashore is all to the good for you sea-going folk, and I also hope you're having a swell time romping across whatever ocean lies between here and wherever you're bound.

Most of the lists of the best pictures of the year, with which the papers are lousy nowadays, seem to include *These Three. After the Thin Man* got for the most part at least as good reviews as it deserved. Robert Garland, who hadn't seen the first one, had an orgasm, but then I always say an orgasm by Robert Garland is an orgasm by Robert Garland.[1]

Baby was very glad to get back, is in fine fettle so far as friskiness, noisiness and weight-gaining go, and sends you her love, or if it isn't that what the hell has she been yelping and growling about all day?[2]

Sleepiness is crawling up on me and I can't fake any more news. I haven't seen or heard from anybody (oh, yes, I had a Christmas card from those charming Dignans and a phone call from Prue) and they probably wouldn't have told me anything if I had.[3] Tomorrow I'm settling down to work.

I love and miss you. Give my love to Rita and tell her it's very silly of her to waste more time in a country that definitely won't let members of its ruling house marry American women. For God's sake, she doesn't want to content herself with an earl of a marquis, does she?

> Love,
> Dash

1. Garland was movie and drama reviewer for the New York *World-Telegram.*

2. Baby was a brown standard poodle given Hellman's childhood nickname.

3. Pru Whitfield, Hammett's lover in the late 1930s and 1940s, was the former wife of *Black Mask* writer and novelist Raoul Whitfield; they divorced in 1932. The Dignans are unidentified, as is Rita (below).

TLS HRC

To Lillian Hellman

29 December 1936, Princeton, New Jersey

Operative D. H. reports: —

Rather than get a haircut I went to work after I had finished writing you yesterday and rather than do what my more rabid fans would call creative work I spent most of my time rewriting most of what I had already written. I bet if I worked hard enough on those few pages I could whittle them down to a phrase.

This afternoon I applied myself to my other art, doing two pictures of Baby, neither of which was a howling (ah, talkies!) success, neither of which was as bad as I expected after seven years of non-drawing. I'll try again tomorrow, and the next day, and the next, if she'll stand for it. Between being photographed and drawn these last couple of days she's getting the suspicion that her full name is Baby Rose Marie.[1] When she hears another dog bark now she gets up and takes a bow, or is it a bow-wow? (Jesus, I'm a scream!)

Last night the temperature dropped some 23 degrees to around 35, which is a lot nicer for this time of the year. I woke up with a terrific cold in my head, but three aspirins seem to have killed it. I haven't even the sniffles now. Everybody in New York has the flu. (Is there any connection between the last sentences?)

I hope you are praying for the Pope's rapid recovery. You take care of that and I'll do my best to forward the Mary Pickford–Buddy Rogers wedding and maybe we can find somebody else to do something for my sister.[2]

Now to settle down to an evening's toil among those God-damned Yules, the silly jerks.

I love you, if that's any business of yours.
Dash

1. Baby Rose Marie, born in 1925, was a child actress who starred in six movies before 1934.
2. Actress Mary Pickford ("America's Sweetheart") married Charles "Buddy" Rogers ("America's Boyfriend") on 26 June 1937. He was eleven years her junior. Hammett's sister Reba was unmarried. When Hammett's daughter Jo asked him why Reba had never married, he said, "Well, she was never exactly a hot number."

TLS LPT

To Lillian Hellman

30 December 1936, Princeton, New Jersey

Dear Lilushka,

It's raining today, but nothing can spoil my day now: Woolcott Gibbs sent me a dollar check for that Raised Eyebrow Department Colony Club contribution, so I'm going into the New Year well-heeled financially as well as with the knowledge that I can still sell stuff.[1]

Eddie Robinson, on his return from Europe, is quoted as follows: "I think the movies are one of the finest gifts the world has received since the beginning of history. Of course there are others." See if you can come back with something that good. You might work out something along the line of: "I think history is one of the finest gifts the movies have received since *Clive of India*. Of course there is George Arliss."[2]

Powell, I hear, is fighting with MGM over a new contract, holding out for $200,000 a picture. MGM's recent statement that there will be no more sequels to *The Thin Man,* no matter how well this one does, is, I suppose, just a piece of iron pipe to slug him with.

Cooped-up indoors by the rain, Baby and I are so full of animal spirits and physical energy that we'd be unbearable if there were anybody around who had to put up with us. I've even been thinking that I ought to provide myself with means for getting regular exercise. (See what four days without a drink does for the lug! He'll—two to one—have a hemorrhage tomorrow.)

I've been looking through a copy of *Le Faucon De Malte* and have decided that what I had last night was either a *mouillé songe* or a *humide rêve.*[3] When I can take time from reading my own opera I'm rereading *Don Quixote,* and liking it a lot better than the times I tried it before. Do you suppose I'm going to discover Spanish literature? I bet I'll get around to everything if I live long enough. I missed a lot of things in that San Francisco Public Library.

> *Tu es un ange.*
> Dash

1. Gibbs was a *New Yorker* writer-editor.
2. *Clive of India* was a 1935 hit movie starring Ronald Colman and Loretta Young. George Arliss (born 1868) was an Englishman who specialized in playing such historical figures as Benjamin Disraeli and Cardinal Richelieu in Hollywood movies.
3. The French edition of *The Maltese Falcon, Le Faucon de malte* (translated by Henri Robillot), was published by Gallimard in 1936. Hammett's imperfect French translates as "wet dream." His closing is "you are an angel."

TLS HRC

To Lillian Hellman

[February 1937, Princeton, New Jersey]

Thoughts of a middle-aged and slightly tight guy sitting around alone at home on a rainy Sunday night:

I love you and miss you.

Herman was very charming last night, very, but very, much in love with Arthur's play, and very cute and boring with the intimate details, all very mellow-voiced, of his dog's carnal knowledge of yours.[1]

Our Doctor Sobel, who liked the play (as who didn't) got — on my dead mother's grave I swear it — tight on sidecars in 21 with us.[2] His last and feeblest excuse was that he was trying to show me a horrible example for my own good.

La Dowling, who obviously is fascinated by you, spent a fair part of the evening telling me how much she'd like to go to Hollywood, with the idea, I gathered, that maybe I'd mention it to you and you would send for her.[3]

From La Dowling: she says your Maria and Domingo are half-nuts from fear that you're not going to send for them.[4]

From La Dowling (2): Irwin's mother has insisted that he should not use your sheets and towels, apparently because she's afraid he might spoil one and you might sue him, though he is quoted as begging her to let him at least use the towels, since he's never had such nice ones.[5] Ma, it seems, has also insisted that when Maria and Domingo leave the new servant must not be trusted with a key to the apartment. "Irwin can get up and let her in in the mornings." (I suspect Irwin's Ma of being a character.)

Rose—in case you couldn't guess it—entertained me with the usual kind but firm constructive criticism of the way *Having Wonderful Time*'s leading lady (who really did a marvelous job) handled her role.

I had a couple of drinks with Ralph after the show, which, so far as I can figure out, he liked.[6] I've decided I can't understand what he's talking about most of the time. A sweet guy, I think, but dull.

Ed Sullivan, in case you missed it, reported from Miami that the man with the "most interesting face" in Florida was our own dear Dave Curtis.[7]

I saw Maggie Sull[a]van last night, and does she look scrawny and bedraggled. She wanted to tell me a story about herself, but Leland wouldn't let her. Leland—who also liked the show—said he thought maybe our deal with Warner's for *The Maltese Falcon* would go through.[8]

Speaking of my saying everybody liked the show, I wouldn't be surprised if it got mixed reviews—though they must be largely favorable— but I don't think even bad reviews would hurt its business a lot: it's a really charming evening in the theatre, though I do think Arthur should have been a bit sterner with Marc.[9] The things that are wrong with it are obviously 90 per cent Mr. C.'s slicking-up of it. And the direction is by no means too hot.

> I love and miss you.
> Dash

1. Hellman's ex-husband Arthur Kober's *Having a Wonderful Time* opened on 20 February 1937 at the Lyceum Theatre in New York.

2. Louis Sobol, a columnist for the New York *Evening Journal,* called himself "The Voice of New York."
3. "La Dowling" is presumably former Ziegfeld Follies star Rachel "Ray" Dooley, wife of producer and actor Eddie Dowling.
4. Maria and Domingo were Hellman's servants. Hellman was in Hollywood working on a screenplay for Sidney Kingsley's *Dead End.*
5. Irwin and Rose (below) are unidentified.
6. Ralph Ingersoll, then general manager at Time, Inc., was a Hellman paramour. He later founded the liberal newspaper *PM,* with Hammett's editorial assistance.
7. Ed Sullivan was a gossip columnist for the *New York Daily News.*
8. Margaret Sullavan was a wealthy, impetuous actress. In 1936, the year of her hit performance in the Broadway play *Stage Door,* she married Leland Hayward, her third husband. Hayward was Hammett's agent.
9. Marc Connelly directed the stage version of *Having a Wonderful Time.*

TLS LPT

To Lillian Hellman

13 March 1937, Princeton, New Jersey

Darlink,

This is not an answer to your letter. This is just because I want to write you.

This is my last week-end in Princeton and I feel kind of gloomy about it, though the truth is the house has never been the same to me since Baby died. That sounds a little maudlin for a grown man, but facts are facts.

Lois is coming down this afternoon to stay till Monday morning. She was rather nice the last time she was down, didn't do the drunken act until everybody had gone, and everybody liked her very much. There was a bit of comedy attached to it, which I'll tell you about when I see you, but nobody noticed it.

I gave André Malraux your address and phone number last night.[1] I think you'll like him—very intense, dogmatic, actorish, with a very interesting face, looking somewhat like a soft hawk. He lectured here yesterday afternoon. I didn't hear it, but met him last night. I don't think we understood one another very well. He insists that I'm the "technical link" between Dreiser and Hemingway and I don't exactly know what he means by that. On the other hand, when I suggested that he might be the French O'Flaherty he didn't seem to know what I meant by that.[2] But we got along all right and I really liked him. Which is more than I can say for your friend MacLeish (or however you spell it) who is a stuffed shirt if I ever saw one.[3]

I had a letter from Beatrice Kaufman thanking me for a modest contribution to the medical fund for Spain and asking me to come in and talk about doing an original for Goldwyn, which as you know I've no intention of doing.[4] I suspect the Jacoby hand. By this time everybody ought to know that if I want to work in pictures I'll work for Hunt Stromberg, but even Leland Hayward agrees with me—against his pocketbook—that I've got no business working in pictures at all.

> Jesus, do I love you.
> Dash

1. The novelist André Malraux, who wrote about war and revolution in such novels as *Man's Fate,* commanded a squadron of foreign soldiers during the Spanish Civil War. He left Spain at the beginning of March 1937 to speak in pro-Communist forums at several American universities, including Princeton. His tour took him to Hollywood, where he arrived with a copy of *The Maltese Falcon* in hand.

2. Like Malraux and Hammett, Liam O'Flaherty dealt with political questions in harshly realistic novels such as *The Informer* (1925).

3. The poet Archibald MacLeish joined with Hammett, Hellman, and others early in 1937 to form Contemporary Historians, a group to support a Communist-backed documentary to be written by Ernest Hemingway and John Dos Passos and directed by Dutch Communist Joris Ivens.

4. Beatrice Kaufman was the wife of George S. Kaufman. She dabbled in many projects and held several editorial positions from the mid-1920s to the mid-1930s, including head of the editorial department at Boni & Liveright and editor at Coward-McCann and Viking. For fourteen months, ending in November 1936, she was fiction editor at *Harper's Bazaar,* a position she left to become East Coast story editor for movie producer Samuel Goldwyn.

TLS HRC

To Lillian Hellman

In the fall of 1937 Hellman was pregnant in New York and had been pressing Hammett to marry her. At the time of the telegram, she was in Europe, where she had an abortion.

7 September 1937, Los Angeles, California

HAVE DIVORCE AND FLU STOP REMAINING HERE UNTIL TWENTIETH STOP
MUCH LOVE=
> DASH

TELEGRAM LPT

To Lillian Hellman

9 September 1937, Beverly Wilshire Hotel, Beverly Hills, California

Dear Lilishka,

There's a lot of missing of you going on around here, personally speaking, and maybe it's not only me: I seldom see Charley Brackett that he doesn't put in his vice-presidential two-cent's-worth.[1] Maybe you've got something there.

The Gershwin concert last night seems to have been a smash. I didn't go, afraid to take a chance on the great out-doors with tail-end of my flu (practically gone now, thank you) but it sounded swell on the radio.[2]

I saw Lou Holtz night before last.[3] He's taking a screen test for David Selznick, thinking about marrying a girl with two children, and has had a successful eight weeks in a Chicago night club. Don't say I don't give you the news.

Willie Wyler is giving a cocktail party for John Huston tomorrow, and the Arthur Sheekmans' one for themselves Saturday.[4] No, I'm not going.

The Hacketts cabled me from Stockholm that Hunt had wired them from Biarritz to cable me asking about the story. Hunt will be back on the 19th.

Eddie Knopf phoned me yesterday with his tongue hanging out trying to get hold of you. He had just run across the *Hollywood Reporter*'s little item saying you had left Goldwyn in a huff over the *Follies*, and seemed disappointed when I told him it wasn't exactly so.[5]

Dead End, I suppose you know, is doing terrific business and a lot of nice things are being said about what you did to the play.

Life this week has pictures of you week-ending at the Kauffmans': one bad of you playing tennis, one good of you knitting, so I guess you're more the domestic type.

I haven't seen the Goldwyn's since you left; I ran into Haight one night at the Clover—where he was gambling and I wasn't—and saw Freddy and Maxine at the Trocadero.[6] Freddy, very drunk, was trying to find out if it was wrong of him to think that Lois got on his nerves sometimes.

Speaking of Lois, believe it or etc., she borrowed thirty dollars while she was here and sent it back as soon as she got home. I think she's a little peeved because I didn't take her out, but maybe that is just my male vanity.

Arthur's play, according to always reliable *Variety*, has picked up again and is good for a few more months.

Moss Hart's mother died a day or two ago;[7] the 21-Trocadero deal has fallen for the twentieth and supposedly last time; our Labor Board hearing is slated for the 27th of this month; I was divorced in Nogales, Sonora, Mexico, on the 26th of last month; Al Lichtman still says the chemin-de-fer's no good since you left town;[8] my gambling has not been doing me any good financially; the Guild has been signing up an average of about twelve members a week, including a few from the Playwrights;[9] and the weather remains pleasant enough, though I've been out only twice briefly in the past two weeks.

I hope and imagine you had a swell time in Russia.

> Love,
> Dash

1. Charles Brackett, one-time theater critic for *The New Yorker*, left Manhattan for Hollywood in 1929 to be a screenwriter. In 1937 he worked for MGM, earning co-credit on *Live, Love, and Learn*. He was vice president of the Screen Writers Guild in 1937–8 and president in 1938–9.
2. On 7 September 1937, a memorial concert at the Hollywood Bowl was broadcast to the largest radio audience to that time for a concert of Gershwin's music.
3. Holtz was a Yiddish-dialect vaudeville comedian and comic actor whose last credits were for Columbia Pictures in 1934.

4. William Wyler directed Hellman's adaptation of *The Children's Hour, These Three,* and *Dead End* (1937), with a screenplay by Lillian Hellman based on Sidney Kingsley's play. The latter movie, produced by Samuel Goldwyn, starred Sylvia Sidney and Humphrey Bogart. In 1937 John Huston was a screenwriter; in 1941 he would direct his first movie, *The Maltese Falcon,* starring Humphrey Bogart. Arthur Sheekman was a screenwriter and bit-part actor.

5. Hellman was working as a screenwriter for Samuel Goldwyn in 1937 when *The Goldwyn Follies of 1938* was being produced. She did not receive a screen credit for that movie, and at the time complained about script difficulties.

6. George Haight was associate producer of *The Goldwyn Follies.* The Clover Club was a gambling establishment that was periodically closed down by the police. The Trocadero was a supper club on Sunset Boulevard in Hollywood. Freddy and Maxine are unidentified.

7. Moss Hart was a playwright who, like Hellman, worked as a screenwriter in Hollywood.

8. Al Lichtman was a producer working at MGM in 1937.

9. Both Hammett and Hellman served in 1937 on the board of directors for the Screen Writers Guild, which sought to be recognized as the bargaining agent for writers with studios. MGM led the fight to keep the studio-backed Screen Playwrights Guild as the bargaining agent. The case was argued before the National Labor Relations Board, which supervised an election in August 1938 won overwhelmingly by the Screen Writers Guild.

TLS HRC

To Lillian Hellman

24 September 1937, Beverly Wilshire, Beverly Hills, California

Dear Lily,

I haven't seen Stromberg yet, but I hope to have the story cleaned up by the first of the week, and then…

We go to bat before the NLRB Monday.[1] Rumor hath it that the Playwrights may fold this week, probably in an attempt to swing their membership over to the IATSE,[2] which seems to be the producers' weapon against the CIO and other 'radical' organizations now.[3] Last week the IATSE came out with a claim of jurisdiction over all studio employees, and they are evidently going before the NLRB with an attempt to have the election held among studio employees en masse and not by crafts. That complicates things, since the idea of industrial unionism is sound, but, unfortunately, the IATSE isn't sound. The producers have evidently come to terms with them, or at least have decided that they know Browne and Bioff can be persuaded to play ball when it comes to a pinch. I think our side is inclined to under-rate the danger: the IATSE big argument is that they have got a ten per cent raise for most of their people immediately, and you know how big that can look to anybody.

We, the Directors, and the Actors came out with a joint statement saying we'd do our own dickering and wanted nothing to do with IATSE, to which they replied, fairly effectively I think, that they weren't interested in us big-salaried folk who could all deal directly with the producers and to whom a 10 per cent raise was no item, but in the little fellows who couldn't expect much help from us.

So that's the way the merry-go-round spins now. Our inter-guild affairs go as usual: the move for constitutional changes has reached the point where we are inviting La Silcox to come out here and talk to us.[4] I think we'll get what we want without as much trouble as most of the boys seem to expect. As far as I can see, it's more a matter of tying Silcox down definite points than h[a]ving to fight for those points. But maybe I don't know her.

The Clover Club has been closed for several weeks, but, figure this out, Lew Wertheimer is now executive assistant to Joe Schenck.[5]

You know now, I dare say, that *Stella Dallas* has turned out to be only a pretty good box-office flicker while *Dead End* is something else; and you'll be glad to know that Willy doesn't bat an eye when people call on him to take the lion's share of the bows.[6] I haven't seen Goldwyn, but I hear he still leans pretty heavily on his broken arm in arguments.

I enclose some literature and I miss you something terrible.

> Loads of love,
> Dash

1. The National Labor Relations Board was a federal agency established in 1935 by the Wagner Act to oversee union elections.
2. The International Alliance of Theatrical Stage Employees (IATSE), the oldest show business union, was mob-dominated in the 1930s. In 1936 Joseph M. Schenck, chairman of 20th Century-Fox and one of the "five moguls" in Holly-

wood, agreed, as spokesman for the studio heads, to pay off IATSE Hollywood representative Willie Bioff to avoid a strike. Schenck paid with a personal check, which provided evidence of the extortion and led to a charge of tax evasion. In 1942 Bioff and George E. Browne, president of IATSE, were convicted of extortion for having accepted money from the heads of major studios. They were controlled by Chicago mobster Frank Nitti, Al Capone's successor.

3. The Committee for Industrial Organizations (CIO) was formed within the American Federation of Labor in 1935 to organize factory workers by industry. The left-leaning group was expelled from the AFL in 1938 in a dispute over whether workers should be organized by craft or by industry and was renamed the Congress of Industrial Organizations.

4. Louise Silcox was executive secretary of the Authors' League of America, which became affiliated with the Screen Writers Guild in 1933, though the two remained separate entities.

5. Lew Wertheimer was the manager of the Clover Club.

6. *Stella Dallas,* starring Barbara Stanwyck, and *Dead End* were both produced by Samuel Goldwyn. Willy is William Wyler.

TLS LPT

To Lillian Hellman

27 November 1937, Beverly Wilshire, Beverly Hills, California

Dear Lilishka,

Since you've never been to Hollywood, I suppose I should try to show you what kind of a place it is. Perhaps you can get some idea from this: when Ethel Butterworth and her newest collaborator had a row the n.c. suggested that perhaps Ethel's lack of literary experience made her judgment of story values not too good, whereupon Ethel is quoted as having said, "That's silly! Why, I've criticized George Kauffman!"[1]

Or maybe this will supply a better clue: Tommy Manville, Jr., is trying to get a picture job through Earl Carroll, with some idea that he might be connected with Paramount's *Bluebeard's Eighth Wife*, as technical advisor, I hope.[2]

Or there is the strange marriage of Noel Langley, whose bride is supposed to have said that the only reason Noel married her was that he was jealous of Charles Bennett (what! what!) who had a yen for her.[3] She told Frances Goodrich that as soon as Noel gets a thousand dollars he wants her to have her breasts lifted (I think he means a boyish bob) and her nose fixed. Noel, by the way, was given *The Foundry* to do some months ago and told the Hacketts he was very enthusiastic about it because he "had always wanted to take a crack at those labor unions."[4]

But I don't suppose that's enough yet: well, the last time I saw Ogden Nash he was on his way to see an eye-doctor who guaranteed that after one half-hour treatment, that's all, anybody could throw his glasses away and never need them again.[5] I haven't seen Ogden since: he's probably too busy walking into walls.

Then there was the radio announcer at the Stanford-California game who said into my ear personally: "We'll now go down to the field microphone and see if we can pick up some of the cheers and innuendo from the stands."

So you can see that, in spite of the Buddy Rogerses' preferring a cottage to Pickfair, life is not and cannot be simple out here.[6] There is Morrie Ryskind writing a guest column for the *Citizen-News* in which he says that if Black's past is to be forgiven there is no reason why Al Capone can't some day be a member of the Supreme Court;[7] there is Jane Withers to be given "a skating audition by Sol Wertzel," according to the same paper; there is...but you'll think I'm exaggerating.[8]

The Hacketts had a party last night, but I didn't get away from my groupie meeting in time to go. Bruce Lockwood, who has been borrowing money from me, sent me a dozen of his wife's horrible watercolors, from which I'm supposed to select a couple to be gifted with. Sidney Skolsky has had a fight with the *Examiner* and is shifting his column back to the *Citizen-News*.[8] There's a poker game at Billy Wilkerson's tonight, but I'm still playing hookey from them.[9] It is rumored that the American Tel. & Tel. is thinking about backing a chain of ten-cent movie theatres. Want any more news today?

> I love you and Maria.
> Dash

1. Ethel Butterworth is not identified, but perhaps she was the wife of Paramount actor Charles Butterworth, who in 1937 appeared in *Every Day's a Holiday*, directed by Hammett's friend Eddie Sutherland.

2. Tommy Manville, Jr., was an often-married playboy. Earl Carroll was a stage and movie producer best known for the annual *Earl Carroll's Vanities*, a musical stage revue. *Bluebeard's Eighth Wife* (1938), for which Hammett's friend Charles

Brackett wrote the screenplay, was about a rich man who is married for the eighth time.

3. Noel Langley was a young South African screenwriter at MGM; Charles Bennett was a British screenwriter who worked with Alfred Hitchcock.

4. *The Foundry* is a proletarian novel by Albert Halper. MGM bought the rights at Hammett's suggestion and assigned him to write the screenplay. The project was aborted.

5. Humorous poet Ogden Nash worked as a screenwriter at MGM in 1937.

6. Rogers married Mary Pickford on 26 June 1937. Pickfair was the mansion Pickford and her previous husband, Douglas Fairbanks, had built in Beverly Hills.

7. Morrie Ryskind was a screenwriter who specialized in screwball comedy. In 1937 he worked on the screen adaptation of Arthur Kober's play *Having a Wonderful Time.* Hugo Black was a senator from Alabama who was nominated as associate justice of the Supreme Court by Roosevelt on 12 August 1937. Black was opposed by conservatives for his liberal views and by liberals for his past, which included membership in the Ku Klux Klan and opposition to anti-lynching legislation. He was confirmed the week after his nomination.

8. Jane Withers was an eleven-year-old actress for 20th Century-Fox in 1937, and Sol Wurtzel was a producer of crime movies.

9. Sidney Skolsky was a journalist and occasional screenwriter sometimes credited as naming the Oscar. He played himself in *Sunset Boulevard* (1950). *The Examiner* was a Hearst paper;

10. Billy Wilkerson was publisher of the *Hollywood Reporter*. Hammett enjoyed playing poker. "Poker game" was also a euphemism in Communist circles for a political group meeting.

TLS LPT

To Lillian Hellman

29 November 1937, Beverly Wilshire, Beverly Hills, California

Dear Lilishka,

> **Austria Bans 'Dead End'**
> Vienna. — Austrian censors have banned Samuel Goldwyn's "Dead End" because its social message is "too strongly presented."

I passed our telephone conversation on to C. Brackett, who was in complete agreement (can we be wrong?) with both of us on all the details of the ALA dickering.[1]

For political purposes I think the rumor that you, Dotty and Alan are due back here any moment should be kept alive so that the Tony Ve[i]llers can't go around saying, "Oh, I'd vote for them myself, but they won't be here."[2]

The Clover Club, I hear, is wide open again, but I haven't been around to pay my dues.

> But I love you.
> Dash

1. The Authors League of America (ALA) had formed an amalgamation with the Screen Writers Guild to force writers to join the SWG rather than the more conservative Screen Playwrights, which the SWG called a company union. The SP filed a $250,000 libel suit against the SWG board, which included Hammett, Hellman, Charles Brackett, and others. The case was thrown out of court.

2. Dorothy Parker and Alan Campbell were married. They worked off and on as screenwriters in Hollywood during the thirties and were active in the Screen Writers Guild as well as other leftist political organizations. In 1937 each received a writing credit for *A Star Is Born*. Anthony Veiller was a screenwriter on the negotiating committee of the Screen Writers Guild. He later resigned to take a studio job at Paramount.

TLS LPT

To Lillian Hellman

26 December 1937, Beverly Wilshire, Beverly Hills, California

Dear Lilishka,
Christmas was for me what it should be on this frontier, a nicely dull day spent at home brooding over nothing. The youngsters came in for lunch to bring me their presents: otherwise I saw nobody. My contacts with the world consisted

The Beverly Wilshire
APARTMENT-HOTEL
WILSHIRE BLVD. BETWEEN EL CAMINO AND RODEO DRIVES
Beverly Hills, California

of those telegrams agents, producers, and people who either owe or hope to owe you money send wishing you unbelievably happy futures.

I'm in the middle of the usual so-the-script-is-done battles with my own dear producer, who insists that it's all right, but it's not exactly like the two previous scripts. The Hacketts sit on the sidelines and tremble while Hunt and I pace his floor and yell at one another. My latest line of attack is to point out that since he doesn't seem to know what was good and what bad in the two previous pictures they were so far as he is concerned just lucky flukes. It's good clean fun and can't lead to anything more serious than blows.

The morning Hearst paper had a pro-rebel news item dated, "Hendaye, Franco-Russian Border."[1] I imagine it was more dream-writing than propaganda.

The local Christmas decorations are up to par, what with the illuminated Santa Clauses sitting on Beverly Hills walls, cactus trees hung with colored lights, and the like.

I had a nice Christmas Eve dinner at the Hacketts', with most of the evening spent over their new pool-table. Henry Myers and friends, in costume, came in for a while to sing carols, making up in earnestness for what they lacked in the musical line.[2] I don't think that sort of thing will ever replace the machine.

The rainy season has set in, but I hope to get out to Santa Anita this week if it so happens I have anything to go out there with. The local newspapers are in the middle of what seems to be a campaign to bore everybody stiff with racing news: does a mediocre horse of Bing Crosby's win the cheapest race of the day against an assortment of plugs that haven't enough legs among them to furnish one horse, it's front-page headline news.

I should stop this and go to work on some changes in my charming fable of how Nick loved Nora and Nora loved Nick and everything was just one great big laugh in the midst of other people's trials and tribulations. Maybe there are better writers in the world, but nobody ever invented a more insufferably smug pair of characters. They can't take that away from me, even for $40,000.[3]

The studio having failed to talk Miss Shearer out of it, *Marie Antoinette* goes into production this week with very little hope on anybody's part of getting out of it what it will cost.[4]

X marks my windows—wish you were here.[5]

> Love,
> Dash

1. Hendaye is a town in southwest France, just across the International Bridge on the Spanish border
2. Henry Myers, a screenwriter at Paramount, was an active member of SWG and author of the humorous "Screen Writers Marching Song."
3. On 11 February 1937 Hammett granted MGM perpetual rights to the *Thin Man* characters—Nick, Nora, and their pet terrier Asta—for $40,000.
4. *Marie Antoinette,* starring Norma Shearer, was released by MGM in August 1938.
5. Hammett lived in a six bedroom penthouse at the Beverly Wilshire.

TLS HRC

To Lillian Hellman

15 January 1938, Beverly Wilshire, Beverly Hills, California

Dear Lilishka,

Lucky you! Right at this moment you're doubtless either trying to pull fish out of the Gulf Stream or making mots for folks in a Presbyterian church, and who can say which is most fun?

I see by *Variety* that your beauty, Tim Durant, has finally found his sucker: he is polishing the Goddard script for Chaplin.[1]

It's a good thing I really didn't expect that promised copy of your Madrid radio talk: it hasn't arrived. I may as well face the facts: my Lilishka may be generous in most things, but she's a postage-stamp miser.

For the records, this is my tenth month without a drink. A curious thing is happening: guys like Dudley Nichols and Sam Hoffenst[ei]n are becoming proud of the ease with which their former drinking companions like me and Fitzgerald and O'Flaherty stay on the wagon, and they encourage us to continue: we've become their assurance that they are not slaves of alcohol, that they too can stop drinking without much trouble when the time comes.[2]

Did I forget to tell you that the John Brights' Christmas card was a picture of a Spanish loyalist bayonet charge, with the greeting, "Viva!"?[3]

I must go now.

> Love,
> Dash

1. Paulette Goddard appeared in *The Great Dictator*, written by, directed by, and starring Charles Chaplin, her husband at the time. Hammett considered her one of the most beautiful women he had ever seen. Tim Durant did not receive a credit for this or any other movie.
2. Dudley Nichols was a screenwriter for Goldwyn and others who served as president of the Screen Writers Guild in 1937–8. Samuel Hoffenstein, a popular humorous poet, was a screenwriter at MGM.
3. John Bright was a flamboyant radical who had come to Hollywood from Chicago in 1930 to adapt his novel *Beer and Blood* into the movie *The Public Enemy*. He was a successful screenwriter.

TLS LPT

To Lillian Hellman

12 May 1938, The Beverly Wilshire, Beverly Hills, California

Dear Lilishka,

I hope you like your eastern circumstances a little better by now, but, if you don't, you know California will be mighty glad to welcome you back—the part I know about will be, anyhow.

MGM and I are still at odds over the price on the new story, so I told my agent fellow to say bye-bye to Hunt for me and begin talking to Dave Selznick and maybe Sam the Good.[1] Some little technicality about $5,000 I owe the studio on the *Foundry* deal of a couple of years ago is holding up my get-away check, but I dare say that will be straightened out in a day or two.

Phil Dunne phoned me today, but couldn't get away from the studio to turn in his report on doings in Washington.[2] I'll probably see him tomorrow.

The political committee seems to be coming along in most promising shape: it'll make a stir in local circles, no matter what else we accomplish.[3] There is a great deal of undercover muttering about it already. Most unprejudiced folk think it a swell idea. We should have a pretty good idea of how it is going by this time next week. I don't see how it can go badly.

Today I went book-purchasing to the extent of *Hope of Heaven, Reader's Digest of Books, Long Haul, The History of Motion Pictures, I Should Have Stayed Home, The Folklore of Capitalism, Dashiell Hammett Omnibus,* and *The People's Front.*[4] Rangey, eh?

> Love,
> Dash

1. David O. Selznick had left MGM in 1936 to form Selznick International. Sam the Good was one of Samuel Goldwyn's nicknames.
2. Philip Dunne, son of humorist Finley Peter Dunne, was vice president of the Screen Writers Guild in 1938. His public letter to P. G. Wodehouse charging Screen Playwrights with being a company union prompted the union's lawsuit against the SWG for libel in 1938.
3. In May 1938 Hammett was working diligently as an organizer for the Communist Party. He was the newly elected president of the Motion Picture Democratic Committee.
4. John O'Hara, *Hope of Heaven*; A. I. Bezzerides, *Long Haul*; Maurice Bardeche, *The History of Motion Pictures*; Horace McCoy, *I Should Have Stayed Home*; Thurman Wesley Arnold, *The Folklore of Capitalism*; Earl Browder, *The People's Front.*

TLS LPT

To Mary Hammett

In mid-May 1938 Hammett had a physical breakdown. Philip Dunne and the Hacketts called Hellman on the East Coast, who, on doctor's advice, arranged for him to fly to New York, where he was admitted to Lenox Hill Hospital.

20 June 1938, Tavern Island, South Norwalk, Connecticut

Dear Mary,

Here's the story of my life since I left Beverly Hills:

The plane trip east was very rough. Lillian and my doctor met me at the airport and took me straight to the hospital, where I weighed in at—believe it or not—125 pounds. After spending two weeks in bed, and another week up and around part of the day, I left the hospital weighing 135 pounds and with the assurance that my lungs and heart were all right and that there was nothing organically wrong with me—simply run down. The day after I left the hospital—a week ago today—I came up here (you may remember that I came up here from the same hospital two years ago) and after a week of loafing like a sundial and eating like a wolf and his brother now weigh 143 pounds. So I reckon you all might as well stop worrying about the old man's health. I'll probably come back to California looking like a football team in a huddle.

My plans—subject to change with or without a minute's notice of course—are to stay here until the end of the summer, by which time I hope to have my book finished, then to put in a couple of weeks with a New York dentist, and to be back in California in time for the wind-up of the political campaigning—around the first of October. If, however, I should finish the book ahead of schedule, or get too restless for all my California committees, I'll be home sooner.

You can believe practically anything that you read or hear about Mayor Hague of Jersey City as long as it is bad: he is a bastard with hemstitching; but I am afraid there are political reasons that I don't like to put down on paper—remind me to tell you about them when I see you—why too much can't be done about him just at this time.[1] Maybe a little later....

I'm sorry I can't help you with any hints on halibut fishing. The halibut is a gent I never tried to catch.

Tell your mother not to worry about all those tax bills: it's just money we owe that we can't pay yet. Speaking of money, she told me she got the second $100 I sent her, but she didn't say anything about the $100 I wired her a couple of days after I arrived in New York. Did she get it? I'll send some more late this week or the first of next.

I told Jule to have my *New Masses* sent to you each week. Are you getting it?

Is school over yet? And what good or bad news have you and the daffy princess to communicate to me about it?

I've got a date with the sun now on some rocks out over the water.

Kiss your mother and Joseph Northeast for me.

> Love in hug quantities,
> Dash

1. Frank Hague was a political boss who served as mayor of Jersey City from 1917 to 1947. In return for Hague's political support in his presidential campaigns, Franklin D. Roosevelt funneled New Deal money through New Jersey, solidifying Hague's power.

TLS Marshall

To Nat Deverich

Nat Deverich was a junior partner in Leland Hayward's agency on the West Coast. He was handling Hammett's contract negotiations with MGM. Hammett was paid a total of $35,000 to write Another Thin Man —$5,000 *for the synopsis,* $10,000 *for the story idea, and* $20,000 *for the complete screen story. On 23 March 1938, Hunt Stromberg wrote a memo complaining that the Hacketts, who were writing the screenplay, were at a standstill "owing to lack of knowlege of that last situation with its needed motivation for the whole treatment." About seven weeks later, Hammett suffered his breakdown without having finished his work. On 15 July 1938, Hammett granted MGM a one-year option on all his writings for* $5,000, *and on 25 December 1938, his contract was suspended. Hammett wrote three drafts of the original story for* Another Thin Man, *which was released on 17 November 1939.*

25 June 1938, Tavern Island, South Norwalk, Connecticut

Dear Nat:

I'm sending this MGM stuff back to you unsigned, which I don't suppose will surprise you. Under these 10-days-for-Metro-to-meet-anybody-else's-terms arrangements I'd be behind the eight-ball for a year, since it is pretty obvious that no other studio would be interested in dickering for either services or material along those lines. So it would be pretty much a case of working for Metro at their price or not working—and I think that's too much to give for $5,000.

I've gained twenty pounds since leaving Beverly Hills and am beginning to feel like something human again. I've dug out the partly finished book, *My Brother Felix,* and hope to get it done here this summer. I think it's going to be pretty good both for magazines and movies—which is another reason for not snapping at that tiny piece of bait on Hunt's hook.

I hope your health is ok again.

Yours,
Dash (Dashiell Hammett) [unsigned]

c.c. Messrs: Selznick, Kaufman, Marcus, Winkler, Gurney, Townsend, Wolff, Young, Hayward (2) (original to file)

Discussed above letter with Mr. Mannix,[1] 7–6–38. He requested that I ask Deverich what disposition Hammett intends to make of the $5000.00. He also advised that it was in order to pay Hammett the balance of $2500.00 due him after deducting the $5000.00 in question.

FLH[2]
7-6-38
K

1. Eddie Mannix was general manager of MGM.
2. FLH is unidentified.

TLU MGM

To Josephine Dolan Hammett

27 June 1938, Tavern Island, South Norwalk, Connecticut

Dear Jose,

Here's a check for $100.

I'm still putting on weight, though naturally not as rapidly as at first. This morning's figure was 146, which is pretty good for me even when I'm feeling O.K. I'm still not any too spry on my feet, but I suppose that will come.

There isn't anything I can tell you in the way of news: I eat, sleep, work a little on my book, and loaf.

Kiss Mary and the dippy princess for me.

Love,
Dash

TLS Marshall

To Josephine Hammett

1 August 1938, Tavern Island, Connecticut

Dear Princess,

I liked your letter, especially the suggestion that you might be willing to renounce your title and your claim to the throne and join the Communists. All the Communists I know would be very glad to have you: they feel that as a rule they don't get enough royalty.

Did you get the bales of match-covers and clippings I sent you by carrier pigeon and dog-sled a week or so ago? Here are a couple of more of each. The dogs and pigeons are eating now, so I'll have to send this by Indian runner, which takes longer. (My Indian is a movie fan and stops every time he sees a double bill advertised.) (When he's not doing that he's fixing his moccasins, which keep coming untied. Sloppy fellow!)

I've got to go out now and wind up the sun dial. Give my love to any sisters or mothers you may have.

> Love and kisses,
> Big-belly Hammett

TLS Marshall

To Nat Deverich

26 August 1938, Tavern Island, South Norwalk, Connecticut

Dear Nat,

Here's the MGM agreement, properly signed and so forth. It's an OK deal as far as I can see. I should have sent it along weeks ago, but between working on the book and trying to get in my usual number of hours of daily loafing I haven't had much time for anything else.

About Metro's deductions from the $2500: the deduction for California Income Tax bolli[x]es things up a little, since I am, and have been for 16 years, a California resident, but I can straighten that out with the State Tax Department without much trouble so there's no harm done.

I'm in first rate physical shape again—got myself up above the 160 pound mark—and the book seems to be going along nicely, so I've got nothing to bellyache about. I hope your ills have cleared up as easily.

Give my best to Hunt and Myron.[1]

> Yours,
> DASH (DASHIELL HAMMETT) [unsigned]

c.c.Messrs: Selznick, Marcus, Winkler, Hayward (2), Gurney, Townsend, Wolff, Ham, Brickley, NY Office. (original letter to file)

1. Myron Selznick was a Hollywood talent agent and brother of David O. Selznick, whose wife, Irene Selznick, was the daughter of MGM head Louis B. Mayer.

TLU MGM

To Mary Hammett

26 August 1938, Tavern Island, South Norwalk, Connecticut

Dear Mary,

Will you give the enclosed check to your Ma?

I don't know what has happened to the *New Masses* subscription—they're always getting things bolli[x]ed up—but I'll try to find out and have it headed your way.

The book, which is coming along not too badly, is for the time being entitled *Toward Z* but I may change it to something else any minute now. Don't ask me what it's about—about people, maybe.

I'm still picking up a little weight there and there, wherever anybody's left any lying around. The present total is a hundred and sixty-one pounds, which is heavier than I've ever been before.

Your letter makes you sound like a very bored young squirt. Maybe you need a new boy or a spanking or some school work to do—or all three.

How about that picture you were going to send me? You might tell Joseph Northeast, the crackpot princess, to send me one of he[r] too.

I hear the lunch-bell, so to hell with this. Give my love to various members of your family.

> Much love,
> Dash

TLS Marshall

To Mary Hammett

27 September 1938, The Plaza, New York City

Dear Mary—

Please give this check to your Mother and tell her I am—as usual—sorry to have kept her waiting for it. Maybe those people are right who say money doesn't grow on trees—the dopes!

I came into town this afternoon and shall stay here till Thursday; then I go back to the Island until the fifth or sixth of October. I don't yet know what my address will be after that. I'll let you know as soon as I find out.

Tonight I went to see *Room Service* and thought it pretty dull for a Marx Brothers picture.

I'll try to tell you about the Czech situation when I get back to my typewriter. The present trouble is largely the fault of that group of British capitalists which backs Chamberlain. They have been building Hitler's Germany up to weaken France—which immediately after the World War became to[o] powerful for England's liking—and it's a little difficult to know what they're up to now—except you can go on not trusting Chamberlain. But more of that later.

Give my love to your mother and the demented princess, and kiss yourself for me.

D.

ALS Marshall

To Mary Hammett

13 October 1938, The Plaza, New York City

Dear Mary,

Now for a stab at trying to answer your questions about Europe:

"Isn't England worried that she might be building Germany up for her own destruction?"

Many Englishmen are worried, including the capitalist groups that are represented by Lloyd George, Anthony Eden, Duff Cooper, Winston Churchill, and their like, which is why those gentlemen opposed Chamberlain, even though their opposition was pretty mild.[1] But to Chamberlain and his backers—of which the most prominent are the Astors and others of the Cliveden set—it seems that the next World War will be between the Fascist countries and Russia, and Britain should do what it can to help the Fascists and to keep that war from spreading to Western Europe.[2] It seems to them that the war will be a very long and fierce one that may result in the Fascists and Communists destroying one another, but will certainly result in considerable damage to both sides—leaving England sitting pretty, holding once more the balance of power.

"Is France communist at the present?"

France is not, and never has been, communist. There are, I think, about half a million French communists. They have been very active in the labor confederation—which has nearly five million members, but have never controlled it, just as the American communists are very active in the C. I. O. and the A. F. L., but have never been able to control either organization. The French communists also had working agreements with the Socialist and Radical-Socialist parties—the United Front—on which the Daladier government was supposed to be based, but could not persuade those two parties to go along with them in blocking the Czech sell-out. Daladier—supposedly a Radical-Socialist—is now far over to the right. The French Fascists are growing strong again. From here it's impossible to guess what the final outcome will be. The communists have not yet withdrawn from their bloc with the other radical parties, hoping that they may be able to take the wavering Socialists with them if they wait till Daladier shows his hand a little more.[3]

"Why does England feel Russia is her worst enemy?"

Capital in the stage it has reached in England today needs three things in ever-increasing quantities: 1. markets for the products of its industries; 2. raw materials to supply its industries; and 3. new places to invest capital at a profit. Even in a country like the United States capital cannot supply these needs at home; how much less then can English capital stay home. Well, Russia is an immense country, occupying a sixth of the world, a country that used to sell its raw materials and buy manufactured products. Now Russian industry grows steadily while the industries of capitalist countries move jerkily, growing in boom years, shrinking in hard times. Russia, once an agricultural country—that is, a country that could buy from British manufacturers—is now an industrial country—that is, a country that sells to the world in competition with British manufacturers. (Russian oil, for instance, not having to make a fancy profit for stockholders, is sold abroad at lower prices than Shell can sell it. Sir Henry Deterding of Shell doesn't like that—and some people say Deterding is probably the most influential capitalist in England.)[4] Instead of selling her raw material to other countries—and buying it back later as finished products—Russia now uses it for her own factories. That takes care of two points; for the third, how in hell can you invest capital in Russia for a profit? So England doesn't like it. There are other things about it she doesn't like—for instance, if Russia stays in existence there's always a chance that the British workman might begin to think those reds aren't so dumb—but the real core of the trouble lies in the three points above. (By the way, the shrewder American capitalists are beginning to believe that the coming antagonism in the capitalist world will be between the United States and Britain.)

"Does Germany really hold all Czechoslovakia or just Sudetenland?"

She holds, officially, a good deal more of it than anybody could call Sudetenland, with still more divided among Hungary and Poland. Whether Czechoslovakia is within the next few months officially wiped off the map or not isn't important; she can only exist in either case as—officially or unofficially—a part of Germany.

So much for today's lesson in history! If there is anything in what I've written that isn't clear to you, or if you'd like additional information on any point I've passed over too rapidly, or if there's anything new that's bothering you, speak up! I like doing this: it's easier than standing on a soap-box and the audience is prettier.

Tonight I went to see George Kauffman's revue, *Sing Out the News*,[5] and enjoyed it very much, which was lucky, because I ran into him at 21 afterwards and had to say something about it.

The week's reading has consisted of Farrell's *No Star Is Lost*, which I think is the best of his books, Tolstoy's *War and Peace*, which has some swell stuff in it but is a bore, and Romain[s'] *Death of a World*, the seventh volume of his *Men of Good Will*—a little work that will probably run into twenty or more volumes and is likely to be the best book of our time. I should have been reading material for a paper I've promised to do comparing the modern utopian socialists like Upton Sinclair, Townsend, etc. with the earlier ones like Owen, Fourier and Saint-Simon,[6] but I'm putting it off as usual until the last minute. I've also got to find something to talk about at a dinner to raise money for the Lincoln Battalion members who are now being shipped home.

In return for this very long letter I expect many letters of a very superior sort from you.

Kiss the Princesse de Madhouse and your mother for me.

> Love,
> D

1. David Lloyd George, Anthony Eden, Alfred Duff Cooper, and Winston Churchill were all members of Parliament in 1938. Neville Chamberlain, British Prime Minister from 1937 to 1940, rejected Franklin Roosevelt's proposal for a world conference to reduce armaments and avert a world war. Chamberlain favored appeasement of Germany.

2. Cliveden is a 17th-century estate, about twenty-five miles west of London, with a grand three-story mansion built in the mid-19th century. Cliveden was owned by a succession of illustrious figures in British history, including the great-great-grandson of American investor John Jacob Astor, Waldorf Astor, who used it as his summer home. In 1906 Waldorf Astor married Nancy Witcher Langhorne, and they became among the most celebrated hosts in England at Cliveden, entertaining power brokers and celebrities, including Winston Churchill, Neville Chamberlain, George Bernard Shaw, and Charles Chaplain. Waldorf Astor, who controlled the London newspaper *The Observer*, was a member of parliament and later viscount, as was his father before him; Lady Astor became the first female member of the House of Commons in 1919, succeeding her husband. Waldorf Astor's brother, John Jacob Astor, also a member of parliament beginning in 1922, owned controlling interest in the *Times* of London. British journalist Claud Cockburn coined the term "The Cliveden Set" to refer to the British power elite, and it was widely adopted by other journalists.

3. The Popular Front ended in France when the government of Radical Socialist Prime Minister Edouard Daladier failed to support the Communists in opposing the Munich Agreement, advocated by Chamberlain, which allowed Germany to annex parts of Czechoslovakia. Critics felt that the independence of Czechoslovakia had been sacrificed to Fascist interests.

4. Sir Henry Deterding was director general of the Royal Dutch/Shell Petroleum group, which had worldwide interests.

5. *Sing Out the News* opened on 24 September at the Music Box Theatre in Manhattan. It ran for 105 performances.

6. Robert Owen (1771–1858), Charles Fourier (1772–1837), and Claude Henri Rouvroy, Comte de Saint-Simon (1772–1837), were social scientists mentioned by Marx in part 3, section 3 of *The Communist Manifesto*.

TLS MARSHALL

To Mary Hammett

25 November 1938, The Plaza, New York City

Dear Mary,

Many thanks for the lovely photographs. I guess I'll have to make up my mind I'm stuck with a couple of good-looking daughters. Tell the demented princess her long hair is very becoming.

I've been laid up for a week or two, but am getting back on my feet again and expect to survive as usual. I would probably have been all right before this if I hadn't sneaked out of bed to attend some meetings I had promised to show up at. There doesn't seem to be anything seriously the matter with me—just my old friend the-run-down-condition. I lost sixteen pounds of the fat I picked up during the summer, but I think I'm getting it back again now. (As soon as I get hold of one I'll send you a picture taken of me speaking at Madison Square Garden this week, and you'll see I'm still a lot beefier than I used to be.)[1]

Tell your mother I hope to get my finances straightened out within a week and—if she can hold on that long—will send her a check then.

Now for a whack at the questions in your last two letters, with apologies for not having answered them before this:

Olson was certainly "the man" for governor, and he's just about as "red" as Roosevelt, which is my book is hardly red at all.[2]

Blum is the leader of the Socialist Party in France.[3] He supported the French government in the World War, he supported Daladier in the Munich agreement, and he has not opposed him very actively in any of the Daladier policies since then. None of these actions fits in at all with the Communist program. The French Communists had a working agreement with the Socialists, but it's pretty shaky right now, as Blum has a habit of giving in to the reactionaries whenever the going gets tough. The Communists still hope that they can win a good number of Socialists away from Blum's leadership. They have never trusted Blum—though they supported his government because it was a case of choosing between that and a pro-fascist government—and it's unlikely they will ever learn to, thank God.

Yugoslavia has had to do what most little nations in Europe have had to do, that is play along with whatever neighbor or group of neighbors seemed strongest at the time. Thus Yugoslavia stooged for Italy in Mussolini's boom days, then shifted to an alliance with Ro[]mania and Czechoslovakia when they seemed to have French support, and now is doomed to fall under the thumb of Germany. There is not much to be learned by watching what little countries do or say: their destinies are decided in London, Berlin, Paris, Washington, Rome and Moscow.

On the "king-democracy" question, the whole point lies in how much authority the king has. You say that in a democracy all men are supposed to *be* equal. That isn't necessarily so. In a democracy all men are supposed to *have an equal say* in their government, but their equality need not go beyond that.

The problem of what to do with the Jewish refugees is still high in the air and not very near practical solution. I don't think the African colony idea will be tried, though Germany's objections to it aren't important because there are still no indications that Germany will do anything that Chamberlain doesn't at least condone; so if he says Africa it'll be Africa. But, in the first place, the most likely African spots to be allotted are bad for the Jews both from a standpoint of health and of economics; and, secondly, once you set up dumping-grounds where any nation can send citizens it wants to get rid of (after, as in the case of Germany, having robbed them) to become wards of the civilized world, you've really helped the oppression of millions. Poland, for instance, would probably throw out a million Jews immediately, confiscating their property of course. (I'm sorry this is a bit muddled, but I'm in a hurry—ten minutes late to meet a mug from Washington with some Labor Board information—and I'll try to go over it more clearly in a later letter.)

(Because I'm still in that same hurry I'll have to give a quick brush-off to those two arguments against Communism—and I'll promise to do better later.) (1) "Neither communism nor socialism take into account human nature. So long as people have a pride in possession neither can work." We reds usually roll on the floor when we hear those two sentences. The most optimistic thing communists and socialists do is taking "into account human nature." Jesus, they dote on it! Their argument against capitalism is that it doesn't "take into account human nature." You don't have to read much history to know that capitalism has not yet existed two hundred years. How long has man existed? So for this little splinter of time man has been turned into a machine for making money for somebody else, and all the communists and socialists say is that it can't last, that capitalists don't take into account human nature. For a brief instant they can impose on man the delusion that making money (for whom?) is the aim of life, but that it isn't human nature for man to go on thinking that. As for "so long as people have a pride in possession"—what possession? Do ninety percent of the people in the world have any possessions to be proud of—even an ashtray?

"A leveling of incomes fails to provide an incentive for the exercise of ability etc." First, under socialism there is not necessarily—as there is not in Russia today—any leveling of incomes. (There is not under communism either, but that is arranged in a different way.) Second, in a country such as ours where there are say ten million people who can't find work, I should say that any kind of an income was an incentive. Third, in a country such as ours where so many of those who can find work are not paid enough money to keep them healthy, I should say that a living wage would be an incentive. Fourth, I should think that the worst incentive would be that which exists today: the knowledge that, if you work in a box-factory for instance, the more boxes you turn out, the sooner will the market be flooded with boxes, and therefor[e] the sooner will you be laid off.

Now I've got to run.

Kiss the different sized Jo's for me.

Lillian sends her love and say[s], after looking at your pictures, you're a very beautiful girl. Unless my memory is bad she's right.

> Love and pats,
> D

1. Hammett was a speaker at a mass meeting at Madison Square Garden on 21 November 1938 organized by the American Sponsoring Committee Against Nazi Outrages.
2. Cuthbert Olson was elected governor of California in 1939. He called a parole hearing for Tom Mooney, a radical union leader convicted of murder, that resulted in Mooney's release from prison.

3. Léon Blum was the premier of the French Popular Front government in 1936–7 and in 1938, when he was replaced by Daladier, who broke with the Communists.

TLS MARSHALL

To Mary Hammett

19 December 1938, The Plaza, New York City

Dear Mary,

I'm awfully sorry all of you, even to the dog, are on the sick-list, and I hope that by the time this reaches you you'll all be on the upgrade again.

Here's your Christmas present. Will you pass your mother's and Josephine's on to them? I'm doing it this lazy way because I haven't the slightest idea of what any of you really want.

It would have been nice if you could have come on to visit me for the holidays, because I miss you a lot, but it couldn't be managed this year. Maybe if I take a place in the country this summer you and Jo can come east to spend your vacations with me. But I'll see you before that: my present plan is to come out to Hollywood in February or March for three months.

Never mind about school's being tough: get to work and get it over with. There are a lot of things to be done in the world as soon as you've got yourself some kind of an education, so hurry up.

I didn't see the newsreel shots of the meeting, so I don't know whether I was in them or not. Yes, it was a good meeting. The Garden was packed—around 22,000 people—and there were five or six thousand more outside listening to the loud-speakers. Your old man is becoming a talking fool: he spoke four times last week, at an afternoon affair at the Commodore for Spain, at a dinner for the League for Peace and Democracy, at a Mecca Temple anti-Nazi mass meeting, and over the radio for Jewish refugees. I'm going easy this week and next if I can, then I'm scheduled to go down to Washington for three speeches in two days. By the time I get through there won't be a healthy ear left in the East!

I'm feeling better these days, but I have not been able to do anything about my weight. I suppose I was born to be skinny and to hell with it!

My conduct is excellent, probably because I'm too antique to do much cutting up. How is your behavior?—and no lies about it!

Your letter was very sweet, and I liked the message in French. Tell me more.

> Love, kisses, and things,
> D

TLS MARSHALL

To Mary Hammett

21 January 1939, The Plaza, New York City

Dear Mary—

I'm glad you finally got the glasses and I hope you'll wear them most of the time. How about a picture so the old man can see how you look in them?

How did the dog make out? Your mother said he had distemper.

New York days for the past week have been very snowy, very cold, or very both—but pleasant.

I'm back in a streak of speech-making again, which isn't my idea of fun, but there is, as usual, so much to be done and so few people to do it that none of us can pick the things he likes to do. And that's the best reason I know for your plugging away at school—no matter how discouraging it may be at times—until you've got at least the basis of an education. I promise you that when you're ready—and if you still feel as you do now and as I hope you always will—I'll introduce you to the most interesting, exciting, and important work in the world. "We" and I both need you, darling, so don't disappoint us. (I don't mean to sound as if I am afraid you will, because I've a great deal of faith and pride in you.)

Your hero Freddie March opens in a play (*The American Way*) tonight.[1] My spies tell me it's a stinkeroo. Lillian's play (*The Little Foxes*) is in rehearsal now. It opens in Baltimore on February 2nd and here on the 15th.

I had my palm read at a cocktail party a day or two ago and was told that the most successful years of my life would be from 1941 to 1948, that most of my real troubles were behind me, that I was going to make a lot of money out of two entirely different lines of work, plus a side-line, and that I'll have most luck with women born in December. So I'd be sitting pretty if I could make myself believe in palmistry, and if I knew any women born in December!

Kiss the two Josephines for me.

Love,
D

1. *The American Way* by George S. Kaufman and Moss Hart opened at the Center Theatre in Manhattan on 21 January 1939 and ran for 244 performances that year. In 1938 Rep. Martin Dies, chairman of the House Special Committee on Un-American Activities, had accused the film and stage actor Fredric March and his wife, the actress Florence Eldridge, of being Communist sympathizers. When they angrily challenged him, Dies retracted the charges.

ALS MARSHALL

To Mary Hammett

7 February 1939, The Plaza, New York City

Darling,

Once again I have to apologize for not having written you sooner, but I got stuck down in Baltimore for a week with my long nose to the grindstone night and day, with hardly a chance to go to the toilet, let alone write a letter. I'll try to do better from now on, but you must do better too, and write me oftener even if I don't always answer on the dot. I look forward to your letters as much as you say you do to mine and you've got less excuse for being so god-damned lazy.

Your school record sounds pretty good, but the main thing is to keep it up so we can get you going in the world as soon as possible. Don't forget I'm waiting.

I saw my old man in Baltimore—for the first time since 1931—and I'm damned if he looks any older than your old man. He's seventy-six, has got a twenty-seven-year-old girl who seems really in love with him, and I took him to a wild theatrical party at Tallulah Bankhead's—where the parties are really wild—and at two o'clock in the morning he was still fresh as a daisy. Maybe I shouldn't worry about growing old—if that's the way old Hammetts are.

There's no use pretending the Loyalists aren't in a tough spot right now, but it's still a matter of munitions and food.[1] If the embargo is lifted they can still not only hold out but go ahead and win—which means it's pretty much up to the people of the United States and France.

Tell your mother I wired her what I could scrape up at the moment and will get some more to her in a day or two. Kiss her and the dizzy duchess for me.

I'm off to bed now, not having been in one since some time yesterday morning.

> All kinds of love,
> D

1. The United States, which had adopted an official position of neutrality in the Spanish Civil War, maintained an embargo on arms and support to either side in Spain. The Civil War ended with the surrender of Madrid on 28 March 1939 and the defeat of the Communist-backed Loyalists.

TLS Marshall

To Mary Hammett

10 March 1939, The Plaza, New York City

Darling,

I was awfully glad to get your letter—after all this time. And thanks for the snapshots. I like them, especially the one with the hand on the hip.

I've been working like hell, but am feeling all right and having a good time in my quiet old man's way, though I still seem to be losing weight. That's nothing to worry about, however.

I'm sorry you're not going to hear me on the radio tonight. I simply couldn't make it. I hope you like what they do to *The Glass Key*.[1] Write me what you think of it. I'm not sure I'll be able to hear it myself.

Nobody seems to know exactly what is happening in Spain at the present moment, except that it's pretty bad. Generals, it seems, are seldom worth a god-damn except to sell out to the other side as soon as the going gets tough. I suppose the Los Angeles papers are carrying the same sort of news as most of the New York ones—that the Communists are making all the trouble, that everything could be wound up peacefully if it weren't for them. The truth is that the Negrin government—the Popular Front government that has been carrying on the war—wanted to continue to carry on the war, but the military clique headed by Miaja & Co. saw a chance to make a deal for themselves with Franco by handing the Loyalists over to him; and the present row is the result of that—a fight between those who are willing to fight until they are offered a decent peace and those who want to buy peace with their comrades' lives.[2] The result is that Spain is doomed for the time being, with England and France (who are backing the traitor clique) squabbling with Italy over who's to get what. The terrible thing about it from an American standpoint is that if we had lifted the embargo last year none of this would have happened.

Don't overlook Dorothy Parker's story in this week's *New Masses*. It's a swell job.

Kiss your mother and sister (have you got any brothers?) for me.

> I love you, toots.
> D

1. A radio play adapted from *The Glass Key* was performed on Orson Welles's *Campbell Playhouse*.
2. Juan Negrin, the Socialist prime minister of Spain, assumed office on 17 May 1937. He formed a leftist government and took the position that he could not continue the social revolution until the war was won. Negrin was replaced in a military coup by General José Miaja, who adopted the policy of "peace with honor."

TLS MARSHALL

To Lillian Hellman

10 March 1939 [no address]

Dear Lily—

Since you left I haven't seen anybody but busboys and waiters, haven't had letters or telegrams from anybody but folk who either wanted me to contribute time or money to something or didn't want to contribute time or money to something I wanted them to, and haven't spoken on the phone to anybody who had anything to say (except Irwin, who told me that Lois wouldn't be worked on until today), so if I'm to give you any news I'll have to fall back on the newspapers—and I don't read good in my old glasses.

You'll be glad to know that, though Judith Anderson got good reviews herself, the show got very tepid notices.[1] That ought to learn her! You'll also be glad to know that Dorothy Killgallon described me in her column yesterday as "a fiction-writer's version of a hard-boiled Dream Prince."[2] That ought to learn all three of us!

I wish I could cheer you up by telling you the weather here has been terrible, but since I haven't been out I've no idea what it's been like.

Alan Campbell phoned me yesterday, but I've forgotten what he said, if anything.

I decided not to speak on the Orson Welles program tonight. (I hope I remember to listen to it: I always like to hear myself not speaking.) Arthur's really responsible. He didn't think $200 was enough money. (Christ knows where I'll wind up taking his financial advice!)

Now I'm going to get up and type a long letter to Herbert Biberman on the State of the Nation and how to keep from Viewing the Future through rose-colored testacles.[3]

I love you and miss you.

* * *

Thine,
PIUS XIII[4]

I've just read Dottie's piece in the *Masses*. A really fine job! Ralph phoned—will pick me up at 10:00 AM tomorrow to go to the country.[5]

1. Judith Anderson was in the musical *One for the Money*, which opened at the Booth Theatre in Manhattan on 4 February 1939. It ran for 139 performances. Anderson had turned down the role of Regina in Hellman's *The Little Foxes*. Tallulah Bankhead premiered the part of Regina on Broadway.
2. Dorothy Kilgallen was a gossip columnist for the New York *Journal-American*.
3. Herbert Biberman was a Hollywood director and founder of the Hollywood chapter of the Anti-Nazi League. He was later one of the Hollywood Ten who refused to testify about Communist activities before the House Un-American Activities Committee.

4. Pope Pius XII was elected on 2 March 1939. Hammett enjoyed making fun of the Catholic Church.

5. Dottie is Dorothy Parker. "Not Enough!" appeared in *New Masses*, 30, 12 (14 March 1939): 1–4. Ralph is Ralph Ingersoll.

ALS HRC

To Mary Hammett

PM, *a liberal New York daily without ads, published its first issue on June 18, 1940. Founder Ralph Ingersoll resigned as publisher of* Time *in April 1939 to plan the paper. He sold investors shares for $100,000 each, and was capitalized at over $1.5 million, with major support from Marshall Field, the Chicago department store owner. Hammett wrote for pre-publication dummy issues of the paper. Though the paper continued until 1948, by the end of 1940 it was considered a commercial failure that stayed alive only through the support of its rich backers.*

19 March 1939, The Plaza, New York City

Dear Mary,

To get the worst news over with first, it looks very much as if I'm not going to be able to make a trip to the Coast this spring, though there is still a faint possibility that I may manage a short trip, say a week.

I've got myself involved in helping start a new afternoon newspaper, which could be terrifically important in national affairs and which is quite likely to make me a hell of a lot of money in the course of the next few years, so there is not much chance of my taking time off to write a movie. We're working day and night on the paper, hoping to get it out on the streets this summer. It will be an altogether new sort of newspaper and it's all very exciting at this stage and will get more exciting as it goes along.

The weather has gone a bit cold again, but bright and sunny, though I've been too busy to get out in it much except when I go to see friends who are in hospitals.

Lillian's play, *The Little Foxes,* is the big hit of the straight dramatic shows in town and looks as if it will run well over a year.[1] She has just returned from a couple of weeks in Cuba.

My old man's girl is in town and I got stuck with her for dinner tomorrow night. I wish he would keep his women home.

I haven't done any work on the book in days. I hope what I've done hasn't been shrinking while my back's turned. I still haven't found a title for the damned thing.

That about exhausts my supply of news.

Kiss your mother and the crazy princess for me and for anybody else who wants them kissed.

Love and kisses,
D

1. It ran 410 performances.

TLS MARSHALL

To Lillian Hellman

20 March 1939, The Plaza Hotel, New York City

MEMO
FROM: D. H.
TO: L. H.

The English contract came through today. 1 Terms: £250 advance against royalties of 15 % on first 4,000 copies, 20 % thereafter. Cheque (ah, there Albion!) should come through in two or three weeks.[1]

Took the old man's girl to dinner at 21 and to Billy Rose's thereafter.[2] Summary of evening: dull. Best break of evening: she had to catch a ten o'clock train for Baltimore.

Plans for tomorrow: interviewing sundry applicants for jobs on proposed gazette; phoning Oscar Levant and Quent Reynolds anent same.[3] Tentative plan for same day: get hair cut. Plan for evening: class.[4]

Weather: clear and cold.

Mood: missing you.

Feelings: love.

Time: 11:30

1. Probably a reference to the contract for the British edition of *The Little Foxes*, published by Hamish Hamilton in 1939.
2. Billy Rose's club was The Diamond Horsewhoe.
3. Oscar Levant was an eccentric concert pianist known for his acerbic wit.

Quentin Reynolds was a news reporter and associate editor at *Collier's* magazine; he later distinguished himself as a war reporter.

4. Hammett taught classes in writing at the Marxist Jefferson School for Social Sciences in lower Manhattan.

TLS LPT

To Bennett Cerf

1 June 1939, The Plaza, New York City

Dear Bennett,

For a specimen dummy of the new paper I've done a review of *Finnegans Wake,* and to go with it I'd like some dope on Joyce if you've got it handy; to wit

Has he any plans for another book? Is he working on anything now?[1]

Does he live in an apartment or a house, and what's the address?

How many copies of *Finnegans Wake* do you expect to sell?

How many copies of *Ulysses* did you sell? How many would you guess were sold in other editions, including the pirated ones?

Are there any photos of him that haven't been used by anybody, especially an unusual sort of picture, and where is it to be had?

Don't go to any trouble on this—it's simply for a dummy that will never be seen by more than a couple of dozen people—but if you happen to have the answers at your fingertips I'd appreciate it.

> Yours,
> Dash

I think *Finnegans* better than *Ulysses,* though God knows it's hard work.

1. Bennett Cerf, president of Random House, published the first U.S. edition of *Ulysses* in 1934. Cerf enjoyed a warm personal relationship with Joyce thereafter. *Finnegans Wake* was published by Viking, with whom Cerf maintained cordial relations.

TLS LPT

To Mary Hammett

14 June 1939, The Plaza, New York City

Dear Mary,

I owe you so many letters—though you haven't written me as often as you should—that it's kind of hard to know where to start.

I got rid of that cold some time ago and feel as well as an old guy like me has any right to feel, though I'm a little tired from what I call being overworked. In another few weeks I'll be able to let up a little and try to get some meat back on my bones.

The paper—which is to be a regular afternoon newspaper, though a better-looking one than anybody has ever seen so far—is coming along nicely, but still won't be out for several months. We haven't even raised our second million dollars yet, and we need at least three. Besides that there is still a hell of a lot of work to be done lining up writers for it, deciding how the different departments are to be arranged, getting artists and photographers who can do good news pictures, and so on and so on.

I haven't heard any likely rumors of sabotage in connection with the sinking of the two submarines, but nobody can tell what's going on in the world these days.[1]

I never liked that Ernst Toller very much, never trusted him completely, but there was a lot more good in him than bad.[2] He wasn't a Communist—I don't think he was ever able to decide just what he was—though he was one of the leaders who tried to establish soviets in German Bavaria at the end of the World War. He was usually on the right side of things, but his mixed up political notions made him hard to work with. I never knew him very well.

It's been hot as hell for a few days, but a thunderstorm has cooled things off tonight.

Kiss those people for me.

> Much love,
> Hammett

1. The U.S. submarine *Squalus* sank off the coast of Portsmouth, New Hampshire, on 23 May 1939 due to a malfunction of induction valves. Many of the crew were recovered by a diving bell. The British submarine *Thetis* was lost on 1 June 1939.

2. Ernst Toller was a German expressionist playwright who committed suicide in New York City on 22 May 1939. He had written screen treatments for MGM in the mid-1930s and raised funds to aid children affected by the Spanish Civil War.

TLS MARSHALL

To Mary Hammett

17 June 1939, The Plaza, New York City

Dear Mary,

You and that sister of yours look very lovely in the snapshots your female parent sent me, only I wish when you are being photographed you would rub off at least some of the lipstick. You can put [it] back on again afterwards, but in a black and white picture it makes your mouth come out too damned dark, so that the rest of your mug seems to fade off. All blonds have that trouble if they're not careful. If you have a copy of a picture you sent me some time ago (taken indoors: you're standing with one hand on your hip) you can see what I mean. In that one, because your mouth isn't too dark, your eyes—helped by the use of a little eyebrow pencil—come out the way they should.

Now that the French submarine has been lost, I suppose the rumors of dirty work at the crossroads will increase, but there's still nothing to show that there is any connection between the American, British and American sinkings, beyond the fact that they all happened within a few weeks. Japan, by the way, lost a submarine with 81 aboard earlier in the year.

The British government is still stalling Russia, hoping somehow the treaty can be made to fall through without the British public knowing it is their government's fault, hoping somehow Hitler can be made to pick a fight with Russia.[1] But since Russia and Germany both know what Chamberlain is up to, it isn't very likely that his plan will work out. Hitler wants easy pickings, not a war; Russia wants neither pickings nor war.

It's hot as hell here today.

How did you make out in school?

Kiss Josephine 1 and Josephine 2 for me.

> Love and kisses,
> D

1. The treaty is the nonaggression pact Great Britain was negotiating with the Soviets. As Germany continued its aggression eastward, annexing Czechoslovakia and threatening Poland in the summer of 1939, the United States and Great Britain anxiously awaited the Soviet response and, as Hammett suggests, secretly hoped they would help stop the German advance westward. The Soviet-German nonaggression pact was signed on 23 August 1939, and in September first Germany from the west then the Soviets from the east invaded Poland and divided the country.

TLS MARSHALL

To Theodore Dreiser

Theodore Dreiser was a leftist activist throughout the 1930s. His literary prominence, based on the success of Sister Carrie *(1900),* An American Tragedy *(1925), and other works, coupled with his carefully promoted social consciousness, marked him as an important advocate for Communist-sponsored causes. Dreiser joined the Communist Party in 1945.*

13 November 1939, Hardscrabble Farm, Pleasantville, New York

Dear Mr. Dreiser:

Will you join me and a few others in constituting a committee to sponsor the enclosed statement. My plan is to circulate this declaration over the name of the initiating committee, and solicit the signatures of other leading and representative Americans. Once signed by a number of these individuals, the statement will be released to the press. This I hope can be done before news of the actual events in Mr. Browder's trial will be likely to crowd it out of the papers.

Do you approve of the statement? What changes would you suggest? If you are willing to participate will you please let me know at once by collect telegram?

Before circulating the declaration over your signature, I shall, of course, submit to you the final draft, together with the names of the others who have expressed willingness to be on the initiating committee. And if you wish to look at evidence supporting any assertions made in this statement, I shall be glad to supply it to you.

> Yours sincerely,
> Dashiell Hammett

TLS SCHOMBERG

14 WEST 9TH STREET
NEW YORK CITY

GRAMERCY 5-3409

January 1940

Sir:

On December 14, 1939, the day before the 148th anniversary of the Bill of Rights, the enclosed statement—signed by 65 prominent citizens—was sent to the American press.

So far as I know, no newspaper except the Communist "Daily Worker" printed a fair version of it, though most of the New York papers commented editorially—for instance, the "New York Times":

> *. . . we have had a timely warning this week from a group of some sixty educators, scientists, and writers who have urged us to be on guard against the incitement of "witch hunts" and the persecution of minorities. Particularly in times like these, when freedom and tolerance and good-will are in danger of extinction in so many quarters of the world, we ought to conserve with scrupulous care the fundamental liberties of the American system and its Bill of Rights.*

I feel, however, that editorial comments—no matter how favorable—are not so important at this time as the statement itself and, therefore, am sending you this copy of it.

Sincerely yours,

Dashiell Hammett

Form solicitation letter and statement, signed by Dreiser, as Hammett requested in his 13 November 1939 letter.

In Defense of the Bill of Rights

We, the undersigned, believe that civil liberties are the distinguishing mark of American democracy. We believe, furthermore, that the Bill of Rights must apply to the rights of all Americans —or that it will prove a cheat for all. We do not accept the dangerous proposition, now being broadcast from certain quarters, that civil rights can be withheld from this dissident minority or that, at the pleasure of those who may have the power to do so.

Therefore, we feel compelled to speak out sharply and boldly at this moment. When forces exist, as we believe they do now exist, whose objective effect—if not their secret purpose—is the destruction of civil liberties, blindness to facts becomes dangerous, pious protestation of liberalism becomes mockery, and failure to speak out courageously becomes criminal. The objective effect, furthermore, is to create war hysteria and to incite witch hunts at a time when unity for peace in the face of international events is a condition for our further progress as a nation of free men.

We recognize the following blunt facts: 1. that the Dies Committee is talking openly of the suppression of dissident groups and that in this it has secured the support of influential newspapers throughout the country; 2. that open incitement to vigilante activity against labor, against minority radical groups, against national and religious groups is increasing in this country, 3. that various discriminatory and repressive measures against the foreign-born have been passed by the House of Representatives and have become law in many states.

We recognize particularly that serious efforts are being made to silence and suppress the Communist Party. We regard as significant the fact that precisely now Earl Browder, its General Secretary, has been indicted on data which the government has evidently had for years. We observe that a charge four years old has just now been revived against another official of the Communist Party, Sam Adams Darcy. Similarly, a minor technicality was invoked in order to rule all Communist candidates off the New York City ballot. Without legal right Representative Dies and his aides have conducted raids on Communist Party headquarters in several cities. Detroit police failed to give adequate protection to a legally held meeting addressed by William Z. Foster, National Chairman of the Communist Party, and an organized gang was allowed to assault people as they left the hall. Harvard University cancelled a speaking engagement previously arranged for Mr. Browder.

We record as well that a speech which Mr. Browder recently delivered in Boston was inaccurately reported in many newspapers throughout the country and the false impression was thereby created that he had in effect called for armed insurrection against the government of the United States.

We point out sharply that this concerted campaign to lay the basis for outright suppression of the Communist Party is reminiscent of the post-war hysteria which culminated in the now universally condemned Palmer raids. We are not Communists, and we are not concerned at this moment with the merits or demerits of the doctrines advocated by the Communists. We are interested only in the indisputable merits of our American tradition of free speech and in the consequences to the non-Communist majority of the suppression of the Communist minority. We have before us the example of many European countries where suppression of the Communist Party was but a beginning, followed by a campaign against trade unions, cultural groups, Jews, Catholics, Masons, and ending with the destruction of all freedom. It is in our own interest, therefore, and in the interest of those rights for which America has struggled these many years that we raise our voices in solemn warning against denying to the Communists, or to any other minority group, the full freedom guaranteed by the Bill of Rights.

Signed by:

Scientists and Educators

Professor THOMAS ADDIS *of Stanford University*

Professor HAROLD CHAPMAN BROWN *of Stanford University*

Professor GORDON W. ALLPORT *of Harvard University*

Professor JOSEPH WARREN BEACH *of the University of Minnesota*

Professor FRANZ BOAS *of Columbia University*

Professor HADLEY CANTRIL *of Princeton University*

DR. P. McKEEN CATTELL, *editor of "Science"*

DR. BELLA VISANO DODD, *teacher and leading trade unionist*

Professor IRVING FISHER *of Yale University*

Professor RICHARD FOSTER FLINT *of Yale University*

DR. H. RAWLE GEYELIN, *New York physician*

Professor FRANK H. HANKINS *of Smith College*

Professor BENJAMIN HARROW *of the College of the City of New York*

Professor MELVILLE J. HERSKOVITS *of Northwestern University*

Professor ELLSWORTH HUNTINGTON *of Yale University*

Professor PAUL H. LAVIETER *of the Yale School of Medicine*

Professor ROBERT S. LYND *of Columbia University*

Professor KIRTLEY F. MATHER *of Harvard University*

DR. KARL MENNINGER, *Director of the Menninger Clinic of Topeka, Kansas*

Professor CLYDE R. MILLER *of Columbia University*

Professor WESLEY C. MITCHELL, *President of the American Association for the Advancement of Science*

Professor O. H. MOWRER *of Yale University*

Professor GARDNER MURPHY *of Columbia University*

Professor JOHN P. PETERS *of Yale University*

Professor WALTER RAUTENSTRAUCH *of Columbia University*

DR. RANDOLPH B. SMITH, *Executive Secretary of the Cooperative School for Teachers*

Professor HANS OTTO STORM *of Stanford University*

Professor C. FAYETTE TAYLOR *of the Massachusetts Institute of Technology*

Professor HAROLD C. UREY *of Columbia University*

Professor J. RAYMOND WALSH *of Hobart College*

Professor LOUIS WEISNER *of Hunter College*

Writers

JOHN D. BARRY, *San Francisco columnist*

VAN WYCK BROOKS, *author and critic*

MALCOLM COWLEY, *editor of* The New Republic

COUNTEE CULLEN, *Negro poet*

MARTHA DODD, *journalist*

WILLIAM E. DODD, JR., *journalist*

THEODORE DREISER, *novelist*

SARA BARD FIELD, *poet*

DASHIELL HAMMETT, *novelist*

LILLIAN HELLMAN, *playwright*

MATTHEW JOSEPHSON, *author and critic*

ARTHUR KOBER, *playwright*

OLIVER LAFARGE, *author*

JOHN MURRAY, *playwright*

CLIFFORD ODETS, *playwright*

ARTHUR POLLACK, *theatrical critic*

RALPH ROEDER, *author*

GEORGE SELDES, *journalist*

GEORGE SOULE, *editor of* The New Republic

IRVING STONE, *biographer*

CHARLES ERSKINE SCOTT WOOD, *author and poet*

Artists and others

FRIEDA ALTMAN, *actress*

CHARLES BELOUS, *lawyer and former member of the New York City Council*

AARON COPLAND, *composer*

WILLIAM E. DODD, *former Ambassador to Germany*

THE REVEREND WILLIAM LLOYD IMES, *leading Negro clergyman*

ROCKWELL KENT, *painter*

PHILIP LOEB, *actor*

FANYA MINDELL, *Theatrical Designer*

THE REVEREND HERMAN F. REISSIG *of New York City*

HERMAN SHUMLIN, *theatrical producer*

SANFORD SOLENDER *of New York City*

HELEN TAMIRIS, *dancer*

DR. MAX YERGAN, *Secretary of the International Committee on African Affairs*

To Theodore Dreiser

15 January 1940, 14 West 9th St., New York City

Dear Mr. Dreiser,

The response to our statement, In Defense of the Bill of Rights, has been so good and its potential effectiveness seems to me so great that I think it would be a shame not to push it along as far as we can. Every day I hear from people who would have signed it if they had been given the opportunity, and there must be hundreds of others in various professions throughout the country who feel the same way about it. My present thought is that these hundreds might be reached best through "key" people in the different professions and localities, but I have not yet worked out any details. As a matter of fact, I am not even sure that this would be the best plan. Have you any suggestions, any advice on this?

> Sincerely,
> Dashiell Hammett
>
> DH:LJ

TLS Schomberg

To Mary Hammett

15 February 1940 [New York City]

Dear Mary—

I'm writing this sitting at the speakers' table at a meeting—pretending I'm making notes of what's going on. Some ass is talking about Finland as if he thought it was a breakfast food. Maybe he does.

The dog-show was nice, though there weren't many bloodhounds this year. I like them. The best-looking dogs were—as usual—Great Danes. There were a couple of honeys!

We had eight inches of snow yesterday—it's a foot and a half deep in my little yard—with plenty of wind; so I stayed in all day, cooking myself some hamburger for dinner.

Ass #1 has finished his lecture on Finland and a lug who looks like one of his relations is speaking his piece. He seems to think Finland is a patent medicine, but—fortunately—he ran out of words soon and sat down. Some old duffer is up on his tottering legs now mumbling so that there's no way in God's world of knowing what he is talking about, though I just heard him say "civil liberties." Some crackpot just passed me a note asking if I thought we ought to say something about F.D.R. and the Youth Congress. I'm going to suggest that we say something about Aztec pottery.

Great-grandpa has sat down now and a woman with woolen eyelashes is asking a question from the audience; something about the Starnes Bill.[1] The chairman answers her without making much more sense than her question made.

In a couple of minutes it'll be my turn to get up and add my 2¢ worth to the general ignorance and confusion. Then I'm going to duck out, catch a bite of food, and go off to a meeting of German refugee writers. At least I'll come as close to understanding them as I do these mugs.

I hope big and little Jo are all well again. Give them my love and kiss yourself hard for me.

> Love,
> D

1. The Starnes Bill, sent to President Roosevelt for signature on 28 March 1940, required the mandatory deportation of aliens convicted of or admitting to spying, sabotage, or violation of state narcotic laws. President Roosevelt vetoed the bill on 8 April.

ALS Marshall

To Mary Hammett

27 February 1940, 14 W. 9th St, New York City

Dear Mary,

Let's see, what have I done since I last wrote you?

I liked *Pinocchio*. It's a much better picture than *Snow White*, which had too many tiresome and silly stretches to suit me.

The Lou Ambers–Al Davis fight at the Garden was only so-so. Davis is a young man with a terrific left hand, but after three or four rounds old man Ambers began to make a monkey of him. Davis didn't like the going when it got tough, and spent most of the fight trying to hang on.

I went to the country Saturday morning and stayed until Monday. It was bright and cheerful, but I spent most of the time indoors trying to get rid of a cold.

Tell your Mother I got the papers she sent me and will get them fixed up as soon as I can.

What ever happened to that picture of you wearing glasses that you were going to have taken for me?

What magazine subscriptions have you? Or have they all run out? Let me know. I've got to renew some of my own and I might as well take care of yours at the same time.

Kiss those people for me.

Love,
D

TLS MARSHALL

To Mary Hammett

29 March 1940, 14 W. 9th St., New York City

Dear M. J. H.,

You'll have to forgive me again for being such a lousy correspondent, but I've been up in the country banging away on the book, and that's given me about all the writing I've felt like doing. I'm going back up there tomorrow and, as I'm in New York only for a day or two every week or ten days, you'd better send your letters there until I tell you different. The address, in case you've forgotten, is Hardscrabble Farm, Pleasantville, N.Y.

My daily schedule up there goes something like this: breakfast in bed at 10 a m, newspapers and other reading until a little after noon, then up for lunch and out at 2 P M with the dogs for a walk through the woods until 4 or 5, back to the house to loaf, read or nap until dinner at 7:30, then a couple hours for digesting, and to work until I run out of words, which may happen at midnight or may not happen until 4 or 5 in the morning. It's a marvelous life, particularly since there is seldom anybody else up there.

I remember *Fortitude* as the only book Walpole ever wrote that was worth a damn.

Speaking of books, I've bundled up a few to send you, but don't be too sure I'll remember to get them off before I leave tomorrow.

Joe Louis is fighting a tramp named Paychek or something of the sort tonight, but I decided to stay home and try to get some letters written instead of going to see what will probably be a grade B sporting event.[1]

I'm sending you a letter I just got from a chap who has gone down into *Grapes of Wrath* country for the first time.[2]

Marc Blitzstein has written an opera called *No For an Answer* that we're all very hopped up about now, which gives us something else to try to raise money for.[3] It will take about thirty-five thousand to produce it, and a good investment, I think. It's a damned good job.

That's about all I know except that I love you and miss you. Kiss J–1 and J–2 for me.

Love and things,
D

1. Joe Louis knocked Johnny Paycheck out in the second round of their heavyweight championship fight on 29 March 1940.
2. Enclosed was a letter from a communist organizer reporting on conditions among itinerant farmers.
3. Composer Marc Blitzstein's *No for an Answer* opened on 5 January 1941 at the

Mecca Temple in New York City. It closed after three performances. He later wrote an opera, *Regina* (1949), based on Hellman's *The Little Foxes*.

TLS Marshall

To Theodore Dreiser

19 September 1940, New York City

COMMITTEE ON ELECTION RIGHTS 1940 SO EAGER FOR YOUR PARTICIPATION IN MASS MEETING ON ELECTION RIGHTS AT ASTOR HOTEL OCTOBER 9 THAT IF TELEPHONE MESSAGE FROM YOURSELF COULD POSSIBLE BE ARRANGED IT WOULD PROVE OF INVALUABLE HELP PLEASE WIRE COLLECT VIA POSTAL-TELEGRAPH YOUR DECISION=
DASHIELL HAMMETT 10 FIFTH AVE NYC

Telegram Schomberg

To Mary Hammett

26 November 1940, Fifth Avenue Hotel, New York City

Dear Mary,

I'm just in from a couple of weeks up in the country working on the book and haven't even looked at my mail yet. I hope there is a letter from you in it. I suppose you would write me more often if I wrote you more often, so it's probably all my fault.

How's school coming? And what are you doing with yourself generally?

In another envelope I'm sending you some clippings and a copy of a folder that will answer some of the questions in your last letter. I've got a lot more stuff on the same points and will send some of it to you if I can remember to dig it out of the files in my office.

About your other questions: If the United States and Great Britain continue to fiddle around with Japan in their present fashion it is quite likely that Japan and Russia will have to come to some sort of agreement between themselves, possibly even involving a division of influ-

"In the maintenance of free elections rests the complete and enduring safety of our form of government"

AN OPEN LETTER TO THE PRESIDENT OF THE UNITED STATES

A MEETING
on
YOUR RIGHT TO VOTE AS YOU PLEASE

Victims of suppression at the polls will come from West Virginia, Pennsylvania, Arizona, New Jersey, Maryland and all corners of the nation to tell of the battle for election rights.

You will hear from:
* THEODORE DREISER
* OSMOND K. FRAENKEL
* WALTER RAUTENSTRAUCH
* DASHIELL HAMMETT and others

TONIGHT · 8 P. M.
HOTEL ASTOR—B'WAY & 44 ST.

Auspices
COMMITTEE ON ELECTION RIGHTS—1940

Dear Mr. President:

"In the maintenance of free elections rests the complete and enduring safety of our form of government."

You spoke these great words on September 20 at the University of Pennsylvania.

We interpret the words to mean that every citizen must have the right to vote as he pleases and for whom he pleases; that every citizen is entitled to call upon the forces of government to guarantee his right to exercise his franchise without hindrance by force or intimidation.

We subscribe wholeheartedly to your statement, but we are disturbed by the facts. We are disturbed because certain Americans, with whom we may seriously disagree, are being denied the right of free election.

In many States the right of suffrage is being unlawfully withheld from Socialist, Communist, Socialist-Labor, Prohibition and various independent, minority groups.

In some States attorneys-general and secretaries of state have ruled minority parties from the ballot by arbitrary fiat without recourse to law.

Officers sworn to uphold the Constitution and the laws of the United States, have in some places encouraged vigilantism and themselves have resorted to this un-American device in the denial of suffrage rights. They have made arrests for the acknowledged purpose of preventing the fulfillment of statutory requirements to place candidates on the ballot.

A candidate for Governor has been sentenced to 15 years in prison on the charge that he misrepresented his petition, despite the fact that the face of the printed petition was in the form prescribed by law.

Petition signers have been intimidated by a Congressional committee which has made a common practice of sending them communications of seeming official character, with inevitable coercive effect.

Officials in many places have invited petition signers to repudiate their signatures under pain of losing their employment in industry. Under such intimidation signers have been induced to "withdraw" their signatures or consent to cancellation of their signatures.

Some newspapers have published the names of petition signers with the open suggestion that employers discharge the signers.

An official of Ohio ruled signatures illegal on the sole ground that he had received a number of telephone calls purporting to repudiate the signatures.

In California legislative action was taken to rule candidates of a party from the ballot.

In view of what is happening, we do not believe a free election can be held on November 5, unless you take immediate steps.

We take this means of appealing to you, Mr. President, because as Chief Executive of this nation you bear a large part of the responsibility for the preservation of the Constitution of the United States.

We believe that the sanctity of the ballot and the right of every American to vote as he pleases is at stake in this matter, whether he be a Democrat, a Republican, a Socialist, a Communist, a Farmer-Laborite, a Socialist-Laborite, an American-Laborite, a Prohibitionist, a Progressive, or something else. If one or more of these parties proposes a program contrary to the interest of the nation, the remedy lies in the people's right to vote against such a party, and not in the denial of that right.

We believe that the safety of our form of government is secure so long as we preserve the rights of minorities to participate in the elections and be defeated by a free electorate. You can do much now by speaking out against these political outrages, and by taking such official actions as are within your power.

We ask that you do this in the name of American freedom.

Respectfully yours,

COMMITTEE ON ELECTION RIGHTS—1940
DASHIELL HAMMETT, *Chairman*

COMMITTEE ON ELECTION RIGHTS—1940, 100 Fifth Avenue, New York City
is a sub-committee of the
NATIONAL FEDERATION for CONSTITUTIONAL LIBERTIES, 1410 H Street, N. W., Washington, D. C.
Rev. OWEN A. KNOX, *Chairman*

For Free Elections: This is a reproduction of the full page advertisement which was inserted in the New York Times yesterday by the Committee on Election Rights—1940, headed by Dashiell Hammet, prominent author, a sub-committee of the National Federation for Constitutional Liberties.

ences in China. The same sort of foolishness (actually it's worse than foolishness) drove Russia[] and Germany into the same sort of agreement last year.

I don't think Roosevelt wants to be a dictator. What is really happening is that American big business is trying to take the British Empire away from British big business—trying to do the same as an ally that Germany is trying to do as an enemy. (In the early days of the war France was in pretty much the same position in relation to Britain that Britain now is in relation to us, and decided in the end that she could make a better bargain with the Nazis than with the British. It is not inconceivable that Britain will eventually follow in France's footsteps.)

About Browder not being allowed to leave the state to make campaign speeches. He's out on bail awaiting an appeal on his conviction for making a false statement in procuring a passport. When you're out on bail you can't leave the jurisdiction of the judge who set the bail without his permission. So holding B. here was legal enough—though the motives were political, and it seems pretty definitely established that the orders to do this came from Washington.

Most good lawyers consider the draft bill unconstitutional, but it's very unlikely that the present Supreme Court would so rule. Men like Frankfurter—ordinarily trustworthy on problems involving the violations of civil liberties—are too pro-British, or at least anti-Nazi, at the moment to care much about anything else.

The Communist Party, so far as I know, does not now and never has advocated the overthrow of the United States government by force or violence. Their stand on overthrowing governments is pretty much the same as Lincoln's—that you only use force and violence when *most* of the people want a change and the *few* in power won't give it to them peaceably.

The Poll Tax is a device used, chiefly in Southern states, to make it harder for the poor to vote. I think it runs from $1 in some states to $5 in others—though I'm not sure of these figures—and if you can't pay it you can't vote.

The opposition to the anti-lynch bill comes from those Southerners (aided by their friends in the North) who believe that lynching and the threat of lynching are important to keep the negro principally, but also the radical and labor union organizer, in their "places."

This has taken me longer than I thought. I've got to run to a meeting. More later.

> Much love,
> D

TLS Marshall

To Josephine Dolan Hammett

6 February 1941, 14 West 9th Street, New York City

Dear Jose,

I'm finally getting my government compensation straightened out, so in a little while you should be getting a check for fourteen or fifteen hundred dollars from the Veterans Administration, and twenty dollars a month thereafter. Make it last as long as you can—will you?—because I'm going to have a hell of a time scraping up any other money in the near future. Kiss the youngsters for me.

> Love,
> D

TLS Marshall

To Mary Hammett

12 February 1941, Fifth Avenue Hotel, New York City

Dear Mary,

It seems at least fifteen years since I last plopped my behind down to a typewriter with the intention of writing to you. I don't suppose it is actually that long, but God knows it's long enough. I've got the usual excuse that I've been busy as hell and that I've been out of town a good deal. And I'm making the usual promises that I'll try to do better from now on—and will try to.

The pipe—which is in my mouth as I write—is swell. Thanks and thanks and thanks.

How are you? And what are you doing with yourself in general? And how are your near kinfolk? And what are they doing with themselves? I'm sorry your mother had the flu and hope she is well for keeps by this time.

About the literature you asked for: I'll try to make up a selection to send you. *Capital* is tough reading for a beginner—for anybody else as far as that goes—and far from the best book to start with.[1]

Of myself there isn't a great amount of news. I keep plugging away at the book—which I hope to have finished next month—between committee meetings, conferences, speech-makings and so on. Lillian has finished a new play—untitled as yet—which will go into rehearsal as soon as it is cast, and which will probably open late in March.[2] *The Thin Man* may go on the air, starting in June. My book will most likely not be published until fall.[3] My health is pretty good for me and I think I'm putting on a little weight again.

That's about all except that I send great quantities of love. Kiss the folks for me and write me a long letter about you and them.

>   Love,
>   D.H.

1. The English translation of Karl Marx's masterwork *Das Kapital* completed by Freidrich Engels after his death.
2. Hellman's anti-fascist play *Watch on the Rhine* opened at the Martin Beck Theatre in New York City on 1 April 1941.
3. The radio serial *The Adventures of the Thin Man* debuted on NBC on 2 July 1941. No book by Hammett was published in 1941.

TLS Marshall

To Mary Hammett

[24 April 1941] Hardscrabble Farm, Briarcliff Manor, New York

Dear Mary—
    I'm doing this in a boat in the middle of the lake with forsythia to the right of me, dogwood to the left, a couple of pintail ducks swimming at a

safe distance ahead of me and bass refusing to bite all around me. The weather has been like August the last few days, but there's a sharp wind blowing through the sunshine this afternoon.

The snapshots of you and Jo were lovely. I guess I'm stuck with a couple of attractive daughters, all right, all right. How about sending me some more? (More snapshots—no more daughters!)

The book—thank Christ—will soon be finished except for some changes I want to make. My health is OK again and, though I still can't manage to fatten myself up, I'm feeling good. So I have a tough time finding anything to bellyache about.

As you know, I still haven't sent you those books I promised—I haven't been in to New York for several weeks—but I'll get around to it some day. Be patient with the old man!

Since I've been playing hookey from the city I've been letting my beard grow on my chin. It's mostly white and makes me look a little like a decrepit Italian general—one of those who are always being defeated by the Greeks or captured by the British.

I suppose by the time you get this the fighting in Greece will be all over. It was a foolish thing for the British to have got into. That crackpot Churchill has always been a political soldier and apparently he's never going to learn anything from his or anybody else's mistakes.

The big war question just now is Turkey—whether Russia's pact with Japan, and whatever the U.S.S.R. is doing in the Balkans, will keep Germany's hands off Turkey.[1] Hitler's Spanish stab probably won't be made until he's pretty sure of Suez. My guess is he'll try to bottle-up the British Mediterranean fleet, though he may have to close the Gibraltar door earlier to keep reinforcements and supplies away from Wavell's troops.[2] (But who in hell said I was a military expert?)

Lillian Hellman's new play—*Watch on the Rhine*—seems to be a big hit. Paul Lukas is in it and gives a swell performance.

The Thin Man may—if everything goes along without a hitch—start on the radio in June. I don't yet know who the actors will be.

I haven't sent in for my mail for ten days or so. I hope there's a letter from you in it when it comes.

Kiss the two Josephines for me.

> Love,
> D

1. On 6 April 1941 German troops invaded Turkey. On April 23 the Greeks signed an armistice and King George II was exiled to Crete. Within a week, German troops had taken Athens and the British Expeditionary Force had been evacuated. Turkey's official position was to refuse military engagement and to remain friendly with Great Britain and the Soviets.

2. Gen. Sir Archibald Wavell commanded the British Imperial divisions in North Africa.

ALS MARSHALL

To Josephine Dolan Hammett

27 June 1941, Fifth Avenue Hotel, New York City

Dear Jose,

I'm sorry I couldn't get around to this until now. Here's a check. I've been working like hell, but feel better than I've felt in years, even though I'm way under weight.

I'm not likely to be able to get out to California for even a short trip this summer, so how about letting the children come east to visit me for at least a couple of weeks in August? Ask them how they feel about it, and if they like the idea I'll send them money for the tip and set a date for it.

I'm still spending most of my time up in the county, so if you write me there I'll get your letters sooner.

Kiss those gals for me.

> Love,
> D

TLS MARSHALL

Public letter

24 July 1941, 381 Fourth Avenue, New York City

Dear Friend:

The funds you have contributed to the Exiled Writers Committee of the League of American Writers for the rescue of anti-Nazi refugee writers are at last bearing fruit.

But—

A few weeks ago, Anna Seghers and her family landed in Vera Cruz without money enough to complete their flight, although the Exiled Writers Committee emptied its pockets to cover the last mile.[1]

Last week eight other anti-Nazi writers reached Ellis Island, only to be held there by a ruling which prevents aliens of Axis nationality from entering or leaving or passing through the country. If they are not to be detained there indefinitely, or even sent back to overseas camps, we must meet the legal expenses of presenting their cases in Washington.

If all the long work in which you have helped us is not to prove futile, the Exiled Writers Committee must complete the cases it has undertaken. Others are on the way; others yet are still in concentration camps. For these we must

—continue to send food.

—be ready to buy passage whenever a way out opens, and the situation changes daily.

—be able at all times to meet emergencies as they arise.

The Committee must raise $5,000 within the next few weeks. Will you mail me TODAY your contribution toward the final solution of these problems—legal fees, food, clothing, medicine, transportation, — Life? Will you add the last miles to the thousands that these anti-fascist writers have already travelled?

Please make your check payable to Dashiell Hammett, and mail in the enclosed envelope.

> Very sincerely yours,
> Dashiell Hammett

1. Anna Seghers was a respected anti-fascist German writer, exiled first to France, where she became friendly with André Malraux, and then to Mexico, where she joined a community of German communists. Her *Das siebte Kreuz,* first published in Mexico in 1942, translated as *The Seventh Cross,* was internationally acclaimed.

To Mary Hammett

1 October 1941, Hardscrabble Farm, Pleasantville, New York

Dear Mary,

Thanks for the pictures, but I look mighty old and frail in them.

We've had a taste of almost winter weather, with the thermometer down to 34 night before last.

I don't think the Russian news is as bad as you seem to consider it. I don't mean it's completely cheerful, but the war on the eastern front isn't one that can be judged by looking at maps.[1] It's primarily a killing war rather than a geographical one, as both sides have announced several times, and victory will only come to the side that succeeds in destroying the other side's armies, regardless of where that wiping-out takes place. Unfortunately there are no figures on casual[]ties that can be trusted enough even for guessing purposes. It looks at the moment as if a British Army—at least a "token" army—may be on its way through Iran to help out Budenny's Soviet forces in the south.[2] Our aid to Russia is still being slowed up by pressure of the Catholic Church, but Roosevelt's quotation from the Soviet Constitution yesterday to show that they have the same sort of religious freedom as we may do some good there. It at least shows that he hasn't yet knuckled under to the church as he did during the Spanish Revolution.

I'll probably check out of the hotel next week and move up here for the winter and spring, that is if Lillian can find an apartment by then. Her itch has stopped; Shumlin is out of the hospital; I'm all right—that's all the health news.

I still miss you and Jo and it's a waste of time.

Give this check to your mother and give my love to her and to that sister of yours whose name I can't remember at the moment.

Love,
D

1. The German invasion of Russia began on 22 June 1941. On 1 October the United States and Great Britain agreed to supply materials to Russia for nine months to aid them in resisting the Germans. The British had invaded Iran on 25 August 1941. At a press conference on 30 September 1941 President Roosevelt responded to religious groups who opposed foreign aid to Russia on the grounds

that the Soviets were intolerant of religion by citing Article 124 of the Soviet Constitution, which states, "Freedom of religious worship and freedom of anti-religious propaganda is recognized for all citizens."

2. Marshall S. M. Budenny was Soviet commander of the South-Western Front.

TLS MARSHALL

To Josephine Dolan Hammett

20 October 1941, Hardscrabble Farm, Pleasantville, New York

Dear Jose,

Thanks for the snapshot of Jo: it was cute or something.

Today is a bright snappy one and the shooting season opens, so I shall probably spend it out in the woods and fields trying to slaughter squirrels, rabbits, miscellaneous birds and whatever else comes along.

Tell Jo I saw that thing she thought was a snake—in the same spot she saw it—and it was a dark mink.

Have you seen *The Maltese Falcon* yet?[1] They made a pretty good picture of it this time, for a change.

Here's a check.

Love to everybody.
D

1. *The Maltese Falcon,* directed by John Huston and starring Humphrey Bogart, Mary Astor, Peter Lorre, and Sydney Greenstreet, was released in 1941 and is now considered one of the classics of Hollywood film.

TLS MARSHALL

To Josephine Dolan Hammett

11 December 1941, Hardscrabble Farm, Pleasantville, New York

Dear Jose,

I hope you are not just trying to keep me from worrying about the children; I hope they are really all right—or close to it—by now. If they aren't, please tell me the truth about it.

There is no particular reason for believing that any of the Pacific Coast cities are in actual serious danger at the moment, but in a war like this you never can tell; so if you folks feel at all nervous, I'd suggest that you pack up and move. It probably wouldn't be sensible to take Jo to a cold part of the country so soon after her illness, but there are places like Tucson (you've been in that part of the land) that might be very nice to winter in.[1] Think it over, and if you make up your mind to go I can manage the money part of it.

I haven't been in the city since the war started, so I have yet to go through my first air alarm. In New York they seem to have been rather confused, but then things are in the early days of any war, no matter how well prepared everybody thinks they are.

I'm feeling pretty good, gaining a little weight again, and looking around to see if there is any part of the government branches that doesn't mind being handicapped by a doddering old man.

Kiss the youngsters for me.

> Love,
> D

Here's a check.

1. Jo was recovering from pneumonia.

TLS MARSHALL

To Josephine Dolan Hammett

16 January 1942, Hardscrabble Farm, Pleasantville, New York

Dear Jose,

Here's a check.

The weather is fine and bright and just cold enough to keep the snow from melting, which makes my morning snowshoeing through the woods very pleasant these days.

I'm glad both youngsters are recovering so well from their respective diseases. Why don't you get some healthy children?

I've put the book aside for a while. Tonight I have to make up my mind whether to do the movie adaptation of *Watch on the Rhine* or a play that I have been talking over with Shumlin.[1]

That exhausts the news on this end.

Kiss the gals for me.

> Love,
> D

1. Herman Shumlin, who had directed the stage play, directed a movie adaptation of *Watch on the Rhine* with a screenplay by Hammett and starring Bette Davis and Paul Lukas. The movie, "with additional scenes and dialogue" by Hellman, was released in August 1943 by Warner Bros.

TLS Marshall

To Mary Hammett

9 February 1942, Hardscrabble Farm, Pleasantville, New York

Dear Mary,

Nothing much has been happening in this part of the world except that last week I was laid up with a fairly mildish case of laryngitis; and the week before that I spent in Baltimore, where my father had gangrene in one foot and had to have his leg amputated, but seems to have stood the shock pretty well in spite of his being seventy-nine; and this week I'm hard at work on the motion picture version of *Watch on the Rhine*— a dull life.

What's the news on your exam?

Please give this check to your mother, and kiss her and Jo for me.

> Love,
> D

TLS Marshall

To Theodore Dreiser

New York, March 1942

YOU ARE CORDIALLY AND EARNESTLY INVITED TO WIRE COLLECT IMMEDI-
ATELY ENDORSEMENT OF NATIONAL FREE EARL BROWDER CONGRESS ALSO
CONFIRMING THAT YOU WILL MAIL MESSAGE TO BE READ TO THE CONGRESS
MARCH 28 IN NEWYORK FULL DETAILS ON CASE AND CONGRESS AIR MAILED
YOU TODAY. AWAIT YOUR REPLY INFORMING AMERICAN PUBLIC OF YOUR
STAND ON THIS EXCEEDINGLY IMPORTANT ISSUE. NUMEROUS WRITERS
TOGETHER WITH LEADERS IN ALL FIELDS PARTICIPATING=

LEAGUE OF AMERICAN WRITERS DASHIELL HAMMETT PRES. 381 FOURTH AVE
NEWYORKCITY.

TELEGRAM SCHOMBERG

To Hal Wallis

*Producer Hal Wallis was concerned about Hammett's reputation for missing dead-
lines. Wallis agreed to pay Hammett $30,000 to write the script for* Watch on the
Rhine *only after Hellman and Herman Shumlin took responsibility for timely
delivery.*

13 April 1942, Pleasantville, New York

IF I DON'T BREAK A LEG WILL FINISH SCRIPT THIS WEEK=
                    DASHIELL HAMMETT

'1004AM

TELEGRAM HRC

To Hal Wallis

23 April 1942, Pleasantville, New York

DONE=

HAMMETT.

450PM

TELEGRAM HRC

To Josephine Dolan Hammett

11 May 1942, Hardscrabble Farm, Pleasantville, New York

Dear Jose,

Here's the monthly thingamajigger. Sorry to be late with it, but I've been kept hopping since the first of the month.

I finished up the screen version of *Watch on the Rhine*, and have to make up my mind this week whether I'm going to do another picture— probably a sequel to *The Maltese Falcon*—next, or something else. Maybe I'll do some short stories.

Week before last I was down to see the Old Man, whose leg has now healed nicely. He seems in pretty good shape again. I'll probably ship him over into the West Virginia mountains for the summer.

I've got to start going to the dentist's pretty soon and will most likely l[o]se a few teeth, but outside of that I feel top-hole.

Kiss the youngsters for me.

> Love,
> D

TLS MARSHALL

PART THREE

Soldier
1942–1945

Army portrait

I looked at the boy. His face was proud and flushed and every few seconds he looked at the girl in the window while he listened to the jabbering of the worshipful group around him. I knew he wasn't any Apollo-Socrates-Alexander but he managed to look the part. He had found a spot in the world he liked.

The Continental Op in "This King Business"

WHEN THE UNITED STATES entered the World War II, Hammett's convictions, which were based on unflagging patriotism, left him one course of action only. Though he was initially turned down by recruiters, he persisted and was inducted into the U.S. Army, despite being forty-eight years old and still on a disability pension from World War I. It was the start of the happiest time of his life.

With the exception of the few months in 1926 when he worked full time for Albert S. Samuels, Hammett's military service was the only time since he was a teenager that he had a daily schedule imposed by someone else. In the army he had assigned tasks each day, and he performed them, however mundane, with no more than a common amount of grumbling. He got up at a prescribed time in the morning and went to bed at an assigned time most nights. Because of his age and his celebrity, he enjoyed enough privileges to satisfy his need for freedom, but, for the most part, he lived by army rules. He drank in moderation, except for an occasional binge, and he ate regular meals. He maintained close contact with the people he loved—his daughters and Jose, Hellman, his lady friends Prudence Whitfield and Maggie Kober (Arthur's second wife), and he seemed content with the terms of his separation from them. He read with pleasure and with boundless curiosity.

The isolation on Adak Island in the Aleutians, where Hammett spent most of the war, suited him. The weather was cold and the conditions were often brutal, but Hammett was robust. He gained weight and enjoyed good health and peace of mind. He had a job that mattered. He had progressed from his first assignment, rewriting training manuals, to the kind of creative project he enjoyed—launching a camp newspaper. *The Adakian*, his four-page daily, consumed him as he was planning it, gathering his news resources, organizing his staff, and acting as chief writer and editor. He enjoyed both the journalism and the teaching his job entailed. He liked being an authority, interpreting the news on his weekly radio show, and counseling soldiers less than half his age. He liked being respected and being in control of his project.

The Adakian was Hammett's creation, and it reveals as much about him as his letters of the period. It was a serious newspaper of fact, and it informed those soldiers on the island who cared about world events. As his letters reveal, Hammett was not content to rely on the traditional news sources available to him—the Associated Press (AP), Army News Service (ANS), Camp Newspaper Service, the Armed Services Radio Network, and the camp's short-wave radio. He insisted on supplementing his sources with a steady supply of publications otherwise unavailable to Alaskan soldiers, including such left-wing papers and periodicals as *PM*, the *Daily Worker*, and *New Masses*. He read British Communist Claud Cockburn's opinionated *The Week* regularly. He received reports of foreign short-wave radio broadcasts that provided information about war progress from perspectives different from the standard United States sources. Hammett digested this material into a paper, which he edited and partly wrote. *The Adakian* concentrated on international stories about the war and domestic news in the States. Camp news, sports, and entertainment appeared on page 4. Frequently a story relating the history of a military company or campaign was included. Soldiers were informed about post facilities, including the four post theaters and the library, which had over 8,500 books in addition to free Armed Services Editions. There were typically two opinion cartoons per issue, often with captions by Hammett.

The purpose of *The Adakian* was to inform and to instruct—not to proselytize. Hammett provided gentle history and geography lessons along with his war news so soldiers could understand the war they were a part of. He took care to make the paper personally relevant to the soldiers on Adak. A remarkable fact, given the peacetime work record of its editor, is that *The Adakian* appeared with the regularity one expects of newspapers. In the Aleutians, Hammett did not miss deadlines.

He did get bored when the challenges faded, though. By late 1944, Hammett's newspaper was well organized, and his staff was trained. He was no longer needed, and he got restless. He eagerly accepted those assignments that took him off Adak to the Alaskan mainland, back where he had access to something like civilian life. The old temptations still held their power over him, but the effects were softened somewhat by his age. Hammett was over fifty in an army that considered soldiers past thirty-eight over the hill. The trips exhausted him; the bars sometimes bored him; the women were more appealing when they had something interesting to say.

As the war wound down, Hammett had visions of remaining in Alaska. He even bought a bar in Anchorage, but when the war ended he gave it to the black woman who ran it for him. Attractive as life in Alaska may have seemed, it was not a real option. He had to go back to the States because the work he had committed himself to before the war remained to be done. The Allies had been victorious in the battle against Fascism, but the fight was not over. He planned a life as a politician, and speculated what offices he might seek so that he could continue to fight for the principles he believed in. His exile on Adak had allowed him to exorcise some personal demons, and now he had a winner's confidence. He looked to the future with eager anticipation of the important work that lay ahead. And, as always when he was feeling healthy, he resumed work on a novel.

To Lillian Hellman

Hammett joined the army at the Whitehall Street recruitment center in New York City on 17 September 1942. After a week at the Camp Upton Reception Center, he was assigned to the Signal Training Unit at Fort Monmouth, New Jersey, where he stayed until 29 June 1943. Beginning 1 July, he spent ten days at Camp Shenango in Transfer, Pennsylvania, rumored to be a holding camp for politically suspect soldiers before Eleanor Roosevelt learned of it and challenged that use. On 12 July Hammett went to Fort Lewis, Washington, to await deployment to Fort Randall, Alaska, which came on 31 July, and then to Adak. Hammett returned to home on 28 August 1945 and was honorably discharged at the Fort Dix Separation Center on 6 September.

27 September 1942, Fort Monmouth, New Jersey

Dear Lily—

Army manners seem to have changed a lot for the better since my last experience with them. For instance: our food is put on the table in platters, from which we dish it into our mess-kits. The man who takes the last full portion from a platter carries it back to the counter to be refilled. If someone asks for, say, a piece of bread, nobody is supposed to take a piece from the bread-plate while it is being passed down the table to him. To do so is called "short-stopping" and is considered very low practice indeed, almost as bad as sitting on another man's bed.

There are a great many young men in the Army who look, talk, act and snigger like Bennett Cerf; also there are far too many carbon copies of Jimmy Cannon—but most of these are your people.[1] In addition to all this I encounter a surprising number of finger-nail biters. (Try to keep your tact from relaying this item to Dotty even if you think it would cheer her up to know that Mr. Campbell is among his ilk.)[2]

Love—
Pvt. S.D.H.

1. Bennett Cerf, president of Random House, was affable and urbane. Jimmy Cannon was a sports writer, who in 1942 was a correspondent for *PM* and for *Stars and Stripes*.
2. Dotty: Dorothy Parker, married to Alan Campbell.

TLS LPT

To Josephine Dolan Hammett

[Postmarked 28 September 1942] Fort Monmouth, New Jersey

Dear Jose,

Well, here I am, back where I started twenty-four years ago—a private in the United States Army.

I enlisted ten days ago, was sent to Camp Upton—out on Long Island—for a week, and then came down here for training.

This time I'm in the Signal Corps and am training for combat duty, with, I think, a fair chance of making it, though Army regulations say men over forty-five must be non-combatants.

So far my middle-aged bones are holding up pretty fair under the strain of romping around on the drill field with a lot of kiddies, and I feel fine—have even put on some weight—but, oh, boy!—am I tired when I hit my bed at night.

There'll be the usual amount of money for you and the children for some time to come, but I don't know how the more distant future will work out, so I'd suggest that you try to save as much as you can.

I took out $10,000 insurance—$5,000 in the name of each of the children—and the Army allotment—I don't remember the exact amount—will come to Josephine each month. I couldn't claim Mary as a dependent, since she is more than eighteen. All in all, if you're reasonably thrifty—I don't mean downright stingy with yourselves—I think we'll make out all right financially.

I've got to rush off to company headquarters now. Kiss Mary and Josephine for me and tell them to write.

Love,
D

Address me:

Pvt. Samuel D. Hammett
Company G
1st Signal Training Bn.
Camp Monmouth, N.J.

TLS MARSHALL

To Lillian Hellman

28 September 1942, Fort Monmouth, New Jersey

Dear Lilishka,

So you get up at five-thirty (or 0530, as we say in the Signal Corps) and dress and make as much of your bed as possible before five-forty, when you turn out for morning assembly and roll call. Then you pick up cigarette butts and matches around the barracks, finish making your bed, and so on until six, when you go to breakfast: oat meal, hot cakes, bacon, apples, bread and coffee.

After breakfast you stand in line awhile to wash your mess-kit and then have nothing to do except get your laundry together—making out the slip in triplicate—and finish straightening things up until seven.

At seven you go over to an auditorium and look at movies of first aid work until eight; then have an hour of extended order drill—which consists of learning to flop down on your face while running, how to crawl along the (this morning) very muddy ground without raising face, chest or stomach from mother earth, then jump up, run in zigzags for a space, then fall and go through the whole thing again; at nine you have an hour of first aid lecture with demonstrations; at ten you have an hour of regular, or close order, drill; from eleven to twelve you learn to splice electric wires; and then until one (or 1300 as we say in the S. C.) you have nothing to do but eat dinner. From one to three you listen to a talk on the Articles of War (the Army criminal code) by a lieutenant who keeps saying "excape"; then back to the drill field for another hour of "columns left," "columns right," and so on; followed by an hour of playing soft ball or football (compulsory) and then some more drilling until six; then to supper and to mail-call where you receive a note and some welcome money from a very nice girl's secretary; followed, at six-thirty, by a visit to the infirmary for a shot in the arm. After that your time is your own, except that you have to shave for the next day and finally can take a shit, for which you literally haven't had time up till then—oh, yes, and your shoes have to be polished because it has been raining, but no longer is, so there's no excuse for leaving little orts of mud on your hoofs.

All of this brings you up to about nine o'clock and you're a pretty tired old fellow who feels at least fifty-eight as you sit down to dash off a few lines to some sweet young thing on Eighty-Second street whose life is some bed of roses, eh, kid? But you eat like a wolf and sleep like a log, so you know you're not tiring yourself out too much and you still think you'll—what with one thing and another, including chiefly the increasing bitterness of the war—be able to get past the rule that no men over forty-five can be fit for combat duty.

Love and thanks for the money.

> You're a cutie.
> Dash

TLS LPT

To Lillian Hellman

1 October 1942, Fort Monmouth, New Jersey

Dear Lili—

Your letter—the one written ten days ago—came and was very well liked, but no more have come: what about that constant stream you were going to emit? Busy, I guess. It's funny to think of civilians being busy. (Ah, that military smugness!)

* * *

Since I last wrote you I've gone through classes and drill periods too lengthy and varied for me to list at the moment, and I've looked at God knows how many movies showing what to do and not do under different circumstances. The active day ordinarily runs from five-thirty in the morning until six-something in the evening, and more than half of the time there's something to do till later. Things like washing, shaving, shining shoes, keeping your clothes in shape and so on—and all studying—have to be done in our "spare" time between six or later in the evening and five-thirty in the morning. She's a long and wearing day!

I'm still feeling fine, though tired and a little grippy, and think I've put on some weight.

A couple of days ago I blossomed out as the camp celebrity—somebody got past that Samuel to the D.—so I have a great many dull conversations with people, and quite a few autograph requests, including one from my company commander. I had one rather nice talk with a lieutenant here, who, after bumbling uncomfortably for a long time, said what he really wanted to do was thank me for, through my books, having given him back his self-respect at a time when he had got himself in a very bad hole. I can't figure it out, but it was—as I told him—probably the nicest thing anybody could say to a writer.

Tomorrow we try out our gas-masks—we've been drilling with them for a couple of days—in the gas chamber; after that we spend four hours pitching and unpitching tents, making up and unmaking packs, which is a lot of work.

That, I think, is the crop.

> I love a girl like you,
> Dash

TLS LPT

To Lillian Hellman

4 October 1942, Fort Monmouth, New Jersey

Dear Missie:

I'm kind of like Alphonse: I'm writing this in a recreation room while listening to the radio report of the Cardinal–Yankee ball game.[1]

* * *

The only new item is that I've been tapped for training as an instructor, and may take it. It would mean that I'd stay here in Edison for six months or more, but it would—or with breaks it would—pave the way for combat duty eventually, while, if I don't take it, I'll probably be classified as a "specialist" this week, which—ten to one—would mean my winding up in a public relations post and having a hell of a time ever getting out of it. Another thing, I'd like to teach for a while: it would give me the feeling that I was actually having a hand in making an Army instead of just drilling along preparing myself to be part of it. (It wouldn't interfere with my training: that goes on when the instructor is not instructing.

True, he has even less spare time then, but nothing minus any number you think of is still only nothing.) (I bet you the Army don't like philosophical soldiers!)

One of my scouts has just returned with the intelligence that the latrine is practically devoid of bathers and shavers, so I think I'll deploy down there and make myself one of each.

>Love,
>Dash

1. Alphonse was apparently a house servant dismissed by Hellman.

TLS LPT

To Mary Hammett

30 October 1942, [no address]

Dear Mary—

Please give one of these checks to your mother. The other is to buy something for your twenty-first birthday. I am sorry to be so late with it, but the Army has kept—and is keeping—your old man so busy that he usually waits till Sunday to go to the toilet. Anyway, it's almost that bad.

I think the idea of your finding something to do in one or another sort of war work is a good one. We are in for a long tough fight and anybody who can help ought to.

Roughly, the Signal Corps takes care of all means of communication in the army, from radio, messengers, pigeons and field telephones to the moving pictures that are used in training soldiers. Since most of our work is done in the field, we are given combat training as well as the technical stuff, which is sometimes tough on my old bones, but so far I have held up all right.

Give my love to your mother and Josephine and tell them I'll write soon.

>Love
>D

New address –
Pvt. Samuel D. Hammett

Co. G, 2nd Sig. Tng. Regt.
Fort Monmouth, N.J.

ALS MARSHALL

To Mary Hammett

4 December 1942, HQ, Co, 2nd Sig. Tng. Reg't., Fort Monmouth, N.J.

Dear Mary—

I'm very pleased with your going to work at Douglas and I hope your back lets you stick it out.[1] Regardless of the optimistic view everyone is taking towards happenings in Northern Africa and Russia, this still looks like a long and tough war—and it's no time for able-bodied people to be fooling around with things that don't count.

Another reason why it might be just as well for you to have a job is that my radio program goes off the air this month and—while we hope to find another spot for it in a little while—there's no telling what will happen to my income.[2] There's no immediate danger of my not being able to take care of you all, but, on the other hand, there's no reason for thinking I'm going to be making much money till the war is over.

I'm a couple of miles from my check-book just now. Tell your Mother I'll put the check in the mail either tonight or tomorrow morning.

We had our first snow of the year day before yesterday. It didn't amount to much, but we have had a couple of days of cold wind that's kept our tents rocking like ships in a storm.

My cold seems to have cleared up and I'm feeling top-hole.

Herman Shumlin goes into the Army next week and the chances are we'll get him in the Signal Corps, since we get most of them who have had anything to do with movies.

Kiss Jose and Jo for me.

> Love
> D

1. Mary Hammett worked briefly at the Douglas Aircraft plant in Santa Monica, California.

2. NBC dropped *The Adventures of the Thin Man* at the end of 1942. The show resumed on CBS in 1946 and continued until 1948, when it switched to NBC, where it ran until canceled in 1950.

ALS Marshall

To Lillian Hellman

In December 1942 Hellman left New York for Hollywood to work on the script for The North Star: A Motion Picture About Some Russian People.

14 December 1942, HQ, Co, 2nd Sig. Tng. Reg't, Fort Monmouth, N.J.

Dear Lily—

Now you are speeding—if that's what trains do nowadays—towards your new home in the west and I am left behind to face the war practically single-handed.

This afternoon my war effort takes the form of trying to revise, correct, rewrite, co-ordinate, deshit and otherwise make sense of three divergent courses in what they humorously but solemnly call Army Organization. For instance, and I quote: "A regiment is composed of units smaller than itself," as who isn't? Or are we all regiments?

Tonight, after I've had my pecker peeked at by a physician, I'm going into Red Bank for my first meal off the reservation since Wednesday, or maybe Thursday. But do not fret yourself into a quivvie: I shall bundle up in a great coat and muffler, I shall wear my finest woolen socks and gloves, and I shall return early to the protective arms, or at least the semi-protective tent, of your country and mine.

I know you're gone, but I suppose I'll first really miss you when I can't phone you in the morning. Maybe I'll phone anyhow just to keep my hand in.

      Love
       D

ALS HRC

To Josephine Dolan Hammett

6 January 1943, Company B, 2d Signal Training Reg't, Fort Monmouth, New Jersey

Dear Jose—

As you can see by the new address above, I have moved again—into another company in the same regiment. The chief difference it seems to make is that I'm now back in barracks—and it's a lot colder in the morning than my tent was—and I'll probably get fewer passes.

The Christmas gifts were fine and handsome and warm and I am wearing several of them right now. Thank you all very much.

I, as usual, am way behind-hand with my Christmas gift to you. Anyhow, here it is. (It's the extra over $400 on the check—to be divided among you in three mathematically exact parts—and I hope you all buy something you like with it.)

I'm sorry not to have written in so long, but I've been pretty busy, what with one thing and another. I'll try to do better in the future.

The weather has been lousy here most of the winter. If it isn't freezing—which I like—it's all rain and mud—which I don't like. My health—in case you're worrying about that—stays good.

Kiss Mary and Jo for me.

> Love,
> D

ALS Marshall

To Lillian Hellman

7 January 1943, Co. B, 2nd Sig Tng Rgt, Fort Monmouth, N. J.

Dear cutie and good writer—

Last night I read the script and I kind of guess it's kind of all right.[1] I like. Maybe you're going to have to cut the early parts a little—as who doesn't?—but you've done what you set out to do, and what's wrong with that? The desired documentary effect comes over nicely. It's nice and warm and human and moving.

And so are you

> Love
> Rookie

1. Hellman was working on the movie script for *The North Star*.

ALS LPT

To Mary Hammett

11 January 1943, Co. B, 2d Signal Tng. Reg't, Fort Monmouth, N. J.

Dear Mary—

I don't know whether I've written you since I moved into Co. B., but anyhow there's my new address up top. I'm back in barracks and they aren't as warm or otherwise as comfortable as tents. I've also risen in the military world. I'm a corporal now. Think of that!

There isn't much news. The Army may lend me to the Office of War Information for a few weeks to make a propaganda film, and then again they may not. I'm thinking of asking for a transfer to the Engineers, and then again I may not.

Except for a lame arm, a cold in my chest, and—today—a pretty bad hangover, I feel swell. I'm going to be in bed by six-thirty tonight unless Germans invade New Jersey.

Kiss those other Hammetts for me

> Love
> Cpl. Hammett

ALS Marshall

To Lillian Hellman

12 January 1943, Co. B, 2d Sig Tng Reg't, Fort Monmouth, New Jersey

Dear Lily,

Spewack phoned yesterday afternoon to ask if it would be ok by me if the OWI tried to borrow me from the army.[1] I said it would be very OK if it was only for one job, but not for any sort of permanent-arrangement. (I ain't going to give up my army career and my new corporal's stripes for nobody!)

I wasn't in bed at 6:30 last night as I had planned. A dental examination at 8:30 interfered, but I was tucked in by 9:00 and slept like the innocent child I am until 5:30 this A. M.

I've just finished reading the lurid end of your script.[2] She's very much all right, honey, so you'll have to find something else to worry about or, God forbid, go worryless.

Insult to injury department: I have a letter from Kermit saying I owe the Great Big Doorstep Co. an additional $23.10.[3]

The weather has been surprisingly pleasant the past three days, which means in Camp Wood in New Jersey that it hasn't been windy or rainy.

Today I'm working hard, so Army Organization will be cleared up if the OWI deal goes through; which I don't actually care about, on second thought, except on a kind of anything-for-the-sake-of-variety basis.

Tonight I'll probably go into Red Bank for dinner, unless something like a cadre meeting or a company duty rears its pretty little head.

You know, I haven't been up to Hardscrabble since you left. I guess I can manage to live there when you are away, but don't like to visit it when you aren't there. It's awfully nice waking up in your apartment Sunday morning. In some ways it's more comfortable than the barracks.

> Love
> That middle-aged man

1. Sam Spewak had produced a movie for the Office of War Information (OWI).
2. Hellman wrote additional dialogue and added some scenes to the movie adaptation of her play *Watch on the Rhine,* with a screenplay by Hammett, released in August 1943. She also wrote the script for *The North Star,* which was released in November 1943. Hammett probably refers here to an early draft of *The Searching Wind*, her play-in-progress.
3. *The Great Big Doorstep,* produced by Kermit Bloomgarden, adapted by Albert Hackett and Frances Goodrich from the novel by E. P. O'Donnell, and directed by Herman Shumlin, opened at the Morosco Theatre in New York on 26 November 1942. It ran for twenty-eight performances. Hammett invested in the play.

ALS LPT

To Lillian Hellman

14 January 1943, Co. B, 2d Sig Tng Rgt, Fort Monmouth, New Jersey

Dear Lily—

Once again it's a well-rested, late-sleeping soldier boy who's writing. Yesterday and today for the first time since I've been in the army I haven't been prepared, or, rather, anxious—to lie, sit, or lean and go off to sleep on a minute's notice. And I find it's nice to be caught up on sleep; it makes one's skin fit more comfortably.

* * *

The asterisks represent a nine-thirty breakfast of tomato juice, ham and eggs, cherry pie and coffee. I feel better.

Irwin Shaw sent word that I should hurry up to Astoria, where everything goes beautifully at the moment.[1] I don't understand him: he's working on a picture about General Somerville (remember him?) who is now in command of the Service of Supply, and thus our big boss, George Cukor, bivouacking at the St. Regis, also thinks Astoria is pretty good.[2]

The latest bright idea in our department is that we might get permission from Washington to make a Signal Corps propaganda film here. If anything comes of it—a great deal doesn't come of many of our ideas— it will be dumped in my lap. (I) That may be good. (II) That may not be good. (III) That may be bad; (IV) That may be very bad; (V) That may keep me from being sent to the OWI.

* * *

And those asterisks represent noon chow plus half an hour of drilling, which we did pretty sloppily today.

I'm thinking about maybe going into New York tonight since I'm caged in camp this weekend—but it's nice not being sleepy tomorrow, so maybe, again, I won't. It's a little problem to occupy my afternoon. I haven't any other problems to consider. I have problems, but not the kind anybody would consider; not even Lin.[3]

Duty calls now.

Love,
SDH

1. Irwin Shaw was at the beginning of his career as a fiction writer. He had worked on screenplays and received sole credit for *Commandos Strike at Dawn* (Columbia, 1943). The Kaufman Astoria Studio in Queens was converted for the production of training and propaganda movies during World War II. Gen. Somerville had been New York City Administrator and was considered unfriendly to the New York Arts Project before the war.
2. George Cukor was a highly respected MGM director. His many credits include *Dinner at Eight* (1933) and *The Philadelphia Story* (1940). The St. Regis is a posh midtown Manhattan hotel.
3. Lin S. Root was a theater friend of Hellman's and Hammett's. Her play *One Good Year* ran on Broadway for 223 performances beginning on 27 November 1935.

ALS LPT

To Lillian Hellman

16 January 1943, Co. B, 2d Sig Tng Reg't, Fort Monmouth, New Jersey

Dear Lily—

Up for reveille this morning, it being Saturday inspection. Morning, and to breakfast on prunes, cereal, scrambled eggs and coffee. But no butter! What do they think we are? Civilians?

* * *

So far I've seen or been sent a dozen or more clippings of that item about my promotion.[1] I guess newspapers have as little to do as the army. Maybe if the army finds out it can get its name in the papers by promoting me I'll turn out to be a general or something step by step, if they don't find out they can get their name in the paper by demoting me.

Maggie reports that the L. Kronenbergers have a son and Emmy had a tough time of it, culminating in a caesar[e]an.[2] (It's difficult not to just shrug and say, "I knew that little snot wouldn't be able to do anything right.") She also reports that Shummy returned from his OWI chore pretty displeased by one of those Washington run-arounds. I guess a lot of people don't like dealing with our government. What do you say we all get together and have a great big revolution and overthrow it? Huh? You want to play?

Financial report: statement and no check yesterday from Watch on the Rhine Co.; statement and no check yesterday from The Great Big

Doorstep Co.; statement and $109.21 check yesterday from The Corn is Green Co.[3]

If you're leaving Beverly Hills on the 26th or thereabouts, this will be the last letter I'll send you there. Army camp mail service being what it is, it's doubtful if this one will reach you in California. But that's where I'm a-sending it.

> Love
> Signal Corps Laddie

Now I won[']t have to spend that 6¢ a letter for a stamp—but can send them free like the other soldiers.

1. Hammett had been promoted to Tec 5 on 7 January 1943.
2. Louis Kronenberger was a longtime friend and former lover of Hellman's. He was an editor at Knopf and, a decade earlier, had attempted to collaborate with her on her first play, which was aborted.
3. Emlyn Williams's play *The Corn Is Green,* starring Ethel Barrymore, opened at the National Theatre on 26 November 1940 and ran for 477 performances; it was revived at the Martin Beck Theatre on 3 May 1943 and ran for 56 performances. Herman Shumlin was the director of both, as well as *Watch on the Rhine*, which ran for 378 performances. Hammett invested in all of these plays.

ALS LPT

To Josephine Dolan Hammett

21 January 1943, Company B, 2d Sig. Tng. Reg't, Fort Monmouth, N. J.

Dear Jose—

I like the snapshot of Jo, even if she does still sulk in front of cameras.

We've just got through—temporarily, of course—another long rainy spell and it's all clear and cold, though it's beginning to look like snow.

If you believe in dreams, one of the officers in my company says he dreamed the other night that I came into the supply room all dressed up in ski clothes and with a white hood over my head.

John Huston, who is now a captain in the Signal Corps, has just come back from a three-month job in the Aleutians and is getting ready to go off on another one somewhere overseas. He sent me word that if I wanted to go along he thought he could get me transferred. I wired him "Yes" this morning, so we'll see what comes of it, if anything.

Company duties of one sort or another have kept me out of New York for ten days or more, so I think I'll catch the 5:58 train, which will put me there at 7:10 and then catch the 12:15 back, which will put me in bed a little before 3 A.M. I sleep till 7:30 these mornings, so I won't be going around all day tomorrow with my eyes shut.

Kiss the children for me

Love
D

ALS Marshall

To Lillian Hellman

23 January 1943, Fort Monmouth, New Jersey

Dear Lily—

No news from Sam Spewack of the OWI. No news from John Huston of the ASC.[1] What kind of a war is this? Don't they want to win it? Then why don't they get Hammett, the demon corporal of Co. B?

Had a nice box of nice cookies from the Benéts yesterday.[2] In my barracks the life expectancy of a package of food is something less than eight minutes from the time the string is cut. Your aunt would say it's a pleasure to watch the boys eat. Most of them are learning to be field switchboard operators or radio operators, with a few student truck drivers. A good deal of their training consists of setting up and operating equipment out of doors under simulated field conditions, and when they come in out of the cold to find themselves face to face with food, they know what to do about it.

New York tonight and dinner with Pat Baltwood and his wife;[2] then to the Kobers'; and, with very pleasant finality, to the quarters of a girl named Hellman, who had better be heading in that same direction herself. It is nice waking up there Sunday mornings, as you could find out for yourself if you only gave it a trial. Maybe I can show you how to do it.

Love,
Whitey

1. ASC is Army Signal Corps.
2. The poet William Rose Benét was an editor at the *Saturday Review of Literature*. Hammett met Dorothy Parker at Benéts' home in the early 1930s.
2. Pat Baltwood is unidentified.

RETYPED LETTER LPT

To Josephine Dolan Hammett

30 January 1943, Co. B, 2d Sig. Tng. Reg't, Fort Monmouth, N. J.

Dear Jose—

I'm glad you feel all right about the operation and I'm glad it's not a serious one. But don't be foolish about putting it off or trying to save money. Be sure you do and get whatever is necessary, so you can get it over with as quickly, safely and with as little discomfort as possible. No nonsense now!

I haven't heard anything new on my overseas journey. If it happens I'll probably leave in about a month, or perhaps three weeks.

It has been snowing here for a couple of days, and it looks as if it'll keep it up for a couple more. I'm staying in camp this weekend on Alert Duty, though I'll probably run over to nearby Red Bank or Long Branch for dinner.

Next week I shall probably—if I don't put it off again—start having my teeth fixed up. I'm afraid there is a lot of work to be done on them and I'd like to have it done before I ship out.

Kiss Mary and Jo for me—and the best of luck to you.

Love,
D.

Be sure to let me know just what's going on from day to day.
D.

ALS MARSHALL

To Lillian Hellman

1 February 1943, Co. B, 2nd Sig Tng Rgt, Fort Monmouth, New Jersey

Dear Lily—

So Sunday in camp is like this:

You hear reveille at seven and go back to sleep. At nine-thirty you wake up. Somebody is complaining, "This god damned fire is going out." Somebody else yells, "Hey, Odell, get up and fix this fucking fire." Odell says, "Anybody wants the fucking fire fixed fixes it theirself"; Odell is barracks orderly today. He is a gangling blond pimply boy of perhaps 21—you've seen him in Pleasantville—with a pleasant, silly face. He was out late last night. You saw him around nine-thirty on his way to the skating rink—the boys' favorite hunting-ground. Somebody fixes the fire while Odell is getting up.

You get up, put on your clothes, gather up your toilet things, towels and a clean pair of sox, and go across the company street to the latrine. The sun is shining and last week's snow, it is becoming slush except in the shadow of the latrine, where it is hard and slippery. In the latrine three men are washing clothes and half a dozen others are shaving. You urinate and take a drink of water. Then you find you've forgotten clean underwear. It doesn't bother you. You're in no hurry. You could shave and then go over to your barracks for the underwear, but you decide against that and go back to your barracks to sit by the stove and smoke a cigarette.

The men in the barracks—there are about six—most of the others are away on week-end passes—are proing and conning over a rumor that there is to be a practice evacuation. The rumor has been going around for a couple of days. You say you don't think there's anything to it, but soldiers want to believe rumors, so some of them begin to roll their field packs. This entails taking down their shelter-halves, which are hung beside their beds to make triangular screens. Odell is working on the stoves: there are three of them. "How are those for fires?" he asks proudly. "OK," you say. "How'd you make out at the rink?" "Jesus, I was pissed," he says. "I was pissed when you saw me, and then going around on skates. I got two new addresses. I always get a couple of new ones and I never go around to the same one twice. How's that?" "That's all right," you say, "as long as there are enough new ones to see you through the war."

You dig out a suit of clean underwear, a woolen one, which isn't too logical, since you've been wearing cotton shorts for a month, and today is warmer than most of the month—but you don't feel logical. In the latrine you shave, shower, put on clean clothes, and return to your barracks moderately hungry. It's somewhere around ten-thirty. You can walk down to the Phillips House and have a leisurely breakfast of ham and eggs, but you're in no hurry about anything today and the barracks seems kind of homey, so you decide to wait for noon chow at the mess-hall. Meanwhile, taking your time, you do your housework. There's no use making your bed on Sunday, but you smooth out the blankets and comforter and arrange the pillow for your comfort when you lie down to read later. Then you attack your footlocker and are surprised at the number of clean handkerchiefs and sox you find hidden in the bottom. The amount of dirty clothes doesn't surprise you even though some of it has been there for months. You knew about that. You repack your locker so you can find everything and then begin to get your laundry together. You haven't sent out any for a couple of weeks. It must be longer than that: you list, in triplicate according to regulations, 24 pairs of sox, 49 handkerchiefs and so on. You dump these things into one of your barracks bags and stick it under your bed, ready for delivery to the supply room in the morning. Then you unwrap the shirt you got from the cleaners last night and put it on one of the hangers suspended from the rod over the head of your bed. You look at your shoes, the pair you are wearing and the two pairs—one GI, the other civilian—under your bed. None of them needs polishing, but you will polish them after chow.

A short swarthy switchboard operator trainee with the face of a dwarf is looking at a booklet on Army signs and symbols which you had found in your locker. He seems interested in it and it's no good to you, so you say, "You can have that if you want it." He says something like, "Aw, gee, thanks," and goes away with it. In a couple of minutes he comes back, the book in one hand, a fountain pen in the other. "Will you do me a favor, Cpl. Hammett?" he asks. "Sure," you say. "Will you write your name on the cover of the book?" You write "Dashiell Hammett" on the booklet cover while a voice comes over the public address system speaker: "All out for chow."

You go up to the mess hall. There is fried chicken, lima beans, carrots, and pease, sliced tomatoes and lettuce, bread, butter, coffee, and chocolate ice-cream. It all tastes good and you all stuff yourselves. Then you go back to the barracks and smoke a cigar by the fire. Men come in with extra boxes of ice-cream they've brought back from the mess hall, but everybody is too full to be interested. One man has brought back two chicken legs. He locks them in his foot locker for later. You finish your cigar. So far you haven't thought about anything since waking, and it seems unlikely that you'll think of anything before you go back to sleep at night. There is something in your head about the newspapers, but it isn't really a thought; it's not even strong enough to make you try to get a news broadcast on the radio. You shine your shoes, all three pairs. They don't really need it, so you don't use much paste, but you rub them down long and thoroughly, liking the shine you get on them. You've been wearing one pair of your GI shoes for weeks, leaving the other one properly laced and under the edge of your bed. Now you put on that pair and set the pair you have been wearing, properly laced, under the edge of your bed.

Your shoes finished, you put on a field jacket and go out. It is sunny and spring-like, and you feel fine, without any excess energy to bother you. You walk up to the Recreation Hall. Forty or fifty soldiers are in the building, a few talking to visitors, a few reading, writing, playing pool, most simply waiting for the free movies at two o'clock. You go into a phone booth and call Rhinelander 4–4328. There is no answer, so you drink a bottle of Coca-Cola and go across the Bataan Avenue to the Post Exchange. You don't really need anything, but you buy a key-ring for 25 cents. Then you remember you liked shining your shoes, so you buy a new dauber and a bottle of liquid polish. You can put the liquid polish on first, rub your shoes to shininess, then put on paste, and rub them to still greater shininess. This increase in shininess is probably only theoretical, but in any case it isn't important. The thing is you can now make the business of shining your shoes a more complicated and a lengthier one.

You go back slowly to your barracks, carefully put the new dauber and shoe polish in to your—for the moment—very orderly locker, put your old dauber in the stove and lie down on your bed to read. Little, Brown & Co. has sent you a copy of a book called *Experiment Perilous* by a woman named Carpenter. It starts very slowly and you dislike the principal character, but a little more than half-way through the book suspense is built up very prettily, so for a while you are quite excited. The near-ending and ending go flat and foolish. You are sorry. You look at your watch. It is five o'clock. You doze for three-quarters of an hour, then get up, put on your overcoat and go over to the orderly room. You pick up your pass and, since this is your week on Alert Duty, tell the C.O. that you are going into Red Bank for dinner and can be reached by phone at the Strand if there should be an air-raid warning. There are only half a dozen others in the Red Bank bus. When you get out, in front of the movie in Broad Street, you run into a couple of men who were in your group at Sea Girt. You talk to them for five minutes and go down the street to get a newspaper. The only New York Sunday papers left are *PM* and the *Journal-American*. You buy a copy of the Hearst paper and go around the corner to the Strand. It is fairly crowded as usual and you are lucky to get one of the small tables out in the middle. You order a double pinch-bottle with plain water and your waiter tells you he will have a booth for you in a minute or two. But when the booth is empty, a young lieutenant and a girl are waiting for a place, so you tell the waiter to let them have the booth. You think the young lieutenant is rather matter-of-course in his thanks (after all it's the girl you gave the booth to) but presently he calls to you and points to a booth being vacated, so you know he's been looking out for you. You move to the new place and eat a shrimp cocktail, clam chowder, pork chop and sliced tomatoes, drink beer, coffee and one more pinch bottle, and read the *Journal-American*, a clipping from which is enclosed.

When you leave the Strand you mean to buy a shaving mirror, but a Camp Wood bus is waiting in front of the drug-store and you get in. You can always get the mirror. Cpl.PL Tschirky, a grandson of Oscar of the Waldorf, is on the bus and he tells you about the nice weekend he spent with his wife, who had come down to the Molly Pitcher Hotel.[1]

Back in camp, you remember you had promised to take bed-check for a non-com who didn't want to come back that early. So you go over to the orderly room and are told some lieutenant is going to take bed-check, so you needn't stay up until eleven. So you sit around talking about training camp incidents and personnel with a sergeant whose name you don't know and an E Co. lieutenant whose name you don't know until about ten-thirty, and then you cross the company street to your barracks and go to bed and go to sleep.

     Love
     Dash

1. Oscar Tschirky, known as "Oscar of the Waldorf," was the maître d'hôtel and
   official greeter of dignitaries at the Waldorf-Astoria in New York City. Reputedly
   the first employee of the hotel after it opened in 1893, he is credited with creating Thousand Island salad dressing, Waldorf Salad, and Veal Oscar.

ALS LPT

To Mary Hammett

3 February 1943, Co. B, 2d Sig Tng Reg't, Fort Monmouth, N.J.

Dear Mary—

Today is warm and sunny, though there is still plenty of snow and ice
left on the ground. It's a sort of dull day for me. I was supposed to go over
to Sea Girt—about eighteen miles from here and part of the Fort Monmouth post—to start making some changes in Basic Training Guides—
things designed to show instructors how to teach new soldiers—but the
lieutenant I'm working with went on the sick list today, so I've been sitting
around twiddling my thumbs, and it's dull. I'll probably go up to New York
tonight to liven myself up. Lillian is having Dorothy Parker, the Gerald
Murphys, and George Bacher—he owns the *N.Y. Evening Post*—for dinner.[1] I can leave camp at five, catch the five-twenty-five out of Red Bank,
get to Jersey City by six-thirty and arrive in uptown New York—via ferry-
boat and subway—by seven or seven-fifteen. And the twelve-fifteen train
out of New York will—with the help of a taxi from Red Bank—put me in
bed by two in the morning. Of course, it may be dull at Lillian's dinner—
but you have to take your chances on things like that.

Warner Bros. asked me to do the screenplay of Prokos[c]h's *The Conspirators*—they would get me 10 weeks leave of absence from the army—
but it wouldn't make a very good movie, so I turned it down—though
God knows the money would come in handy, and even a little rest from
the army might have been pleasant.

I guess I'll go out and get some coffee.

Kiss the two Jos for me.

Love,
Old Soldier

1. Gerald and Sara Murphy were important figures among the Paris expatriates of the 1920s, hosting F. Scott Fitzgerald, Ernest Hemingway, John Dos Passos, Pablo Picasso, Fernand Léger, Cole Porter, Dorothy Parker, and Alan Campbell, among others, at their home on the French Riviera. In 1943 Gerald Murphy owned and managed Mark Cross leather goods in Manhattan.
2. The screenplay for Frederick Prokosch's novel *The Conspirators* was written by Vladimir Pozner. The movie was released by Warner Bros. in 1944.

ALS MARSHALL

To Josephine Dolan Hammett

11 March 1943, I. T. Co—1st Sig. Tng Reg't, Fort Monmouth, New Jersey

Dear Jose—

Now that you are out of the hospital I have gone in for a few days, but my trouble is nothing worse than bronchitis and the need of a little rest.

I'm glad you are coming through your trouble all right (if you're not lying to me to keep me from worrying).

As you can see from the address above I moved again before coming to the hospital. The new set-up gets me out of doors more. (The "I. T. Co." stands for "Instructor's Training Co.") And so far—I moved ten days ago—I like it much better than my previous spots.

* * *

Kiss the girls for me and tell Mary I know I owe her a lot of letters but I've been busy as hell.

Love,
D

ALS MARSHALL

To Lillian Hellman

9 May 1943, I. Co., 1st Sig Tng Reg't, Fort Monmouth, N. J.

Dearest Lily,

The toothless one has to report that he is now completely out of teeth, having given up his last nine yesterday morning, along with some pieces of his jawbone. In return he has some stitches in his mouth and a swollen jaw, none of which are much good for chewing with. He'll probably be going around like this for three or four weeks, gumming eggs and soft bread and looking like an English character actor. You should hear him trying to say, "Message Center School," on the telephone: there are no sibilants, but a lot of spray.

I still like my new set-up down here—school and company—and am looking forward to a pleasant summer. The weather has finally turned good and this isn't a bad camp when such is the case.

Remember my speaking of the lawyer named White whom I liked? This afternoon I found out he is Irving White's brother.[1] Irving is now a corporal at Wright Field.

You should like this. There are two sergeants down here—one in the infirmary and the other in the school, and they don't know each other—who call me "Dashie." Shall I tell them to stop it?

It seems—and as a matter of fact is—a long time since I have seen you. What do you look like? Do you appreciate good music and flowers? What are your hobbies? Would you like to correspond with one of our soldier boys in a New Jersey camp? He is a dandy fellow. His hobby is Jewish playwrights.

There undoubtedly is more news than this and I will write it to you later, but now I must go up and get some ice cream, of which I eat incredible amounts these days.

> Meanwhile hold tightly on to my love,
> Dash

1. Irving White was an actor and playwright. His best-known play, *Fly Away Home*, ran for 202 performances on Broadway in 1935.

TLS LPT

To Josephine Dolan Hammett

15 June 1943, Co I—2d Sig. Tng. Reg't, Fort Monmouth, New Jersey

Dear Jose—

I had just mailed a letter to Mary, enclosing a check for you, when your letter came. Here's another check, but go easy, sister, because this is going to be a long and complicated war and nobody can tell how it is going to work out for any of us. I don't mean you are not to have as pleasant a vacation as possible—you need and deserve one—but the future, especially if I go overseas for any considerable length of time, ain't at all what anybody could call a certain one.

I still don't know where I am going or when, but it still seems sure that I am going somewhere soon.

The weather has been practically perfect the last week or so—and that makes a lot of difference in camp life. I've just finished a dullish job writing a training film and had hoped to be sent back to my trainees at Sea Girt to await my shipping orders, but they are holding me here and I'm bored.

My new teeth ought to be coming out of the factory tomorrow or the next day and I'm looking forward to learning to eat solid food again. I've found plenty of things to eat but I am tired of *having* to eat certain things.

I'll let you know as soon as I have any news.

> Love to you and the girls
> D

ALS MARSHALL

To Mary Hammett

[2 July 1943] Co. A, 12th Tng Bn., T–1823, Shenango PRD, Greenville, Pennsylvania.

Dear Mary—

That, all of it, is my present address. I don't know how long I will be here, all I know is I got my new teeth, passed my physical examination for overseas duty, and now am presumably on my way.

I arranged with the County Trust Company, Pleasantville, N.Y., to send your mother a monthly check amounting to $100.00 a week as long as there is that much money available—which I hope will be a long, long time.

If anything should go wrong with this arrangement, or if any other emergency should arise, get in touch with Lillian Hellman. I've left most of my affairs in her hands and she knows more about them than anybody else. Her address is—

> HARDSCRABBLE FARM
> PLEASANTVILLE, N.Y.
>
> or
>
> 5 EAST 82D STREET
> NEW YORK CITY

I'm still fighting with my teeth, which give me hell when I eat, but outside of that I'm in good shape, as I had to be to get overseas at 49.

Give my love to the two J's when you write them.

> Love and kisses
> D

ALS MARSHALL

To Lillian Hellman

14 July 1943, APO 7082, Seattle, Washington

Dear Lily—

That's the new address and I can't tell you where I think I'll be when your mail catches up to me, but I hope there will be mail and it does catch up with me.

To answer a question in Nancy's report: the arrangement with the bank was for them to send the ex-wife and youngsters $100 a week, but to mail a check for the amount due once a month. There will be fractions involved, but I dare say they won't bother the bank as much as they do you and Nancy. Banks are used to unround sums.

Army regulations being what they are, there isn't much news I can give you just now, except that I am in the pink and mighty glad to be stirring my brittling bones at long last. Peculiarly, those ten months in train-ing camps now seem—for the first time—more like years.

I've got to go eat now.

> Love,
> Dash

ALS LPT

To Mary Hammett

15 July 1943, APO #7082, Seattle, Washington

Dear Mary—

I don't remember whether I've told you or not, but your name and address are on my dog tags and you are the one the government will notify if it has any news to give out about me, like "ARRIVED SAFELY IN GRAUSTARK," or "DESERTED," or "MISSING IN ACTION," or "WE CAN'T GET RID OF HIM."[1] If any such news comes along, wire Lillian, will you. I sent you her address a week or so ago.

Tonight I'll probably go into Seattle for dinner. I haven't been there since 1921, and that's a long time ago.

Take care of yourself,

> Love,
> D

1. *Graustark* (1901) was a courtly romance by George Barr McCutcheon set in an eponymous fictional land.

ALS MARSHALL

To Lillian Hellman

17 July 1943, Seattle, Washington

I AM A PATIENT ELDERLY MAN WHO SAYS TO ARMIES QUOTE ALL RIGHT I

WILL LIE ON THIS BUNK UNTIL YOU TELL ME WHAT TO DO UNQUOTE AND
WHO LOVES YOU=
                DASH.

TELEGRAM LPT

To Mary Hammett

18 July 1943, Seattle, Washington

Dear Mary—

There are clouds over the sun today. I'm up against another Army doctor who thinks I'm too old to be sent anywhere. He hauled me in for a re-
examination yesterday and told me he intended to find something wrong
with me physically to back up his turning me down because of age. So I
was blood-pressured and eye-charted and thised and thated, and when
we got through he still had only my forty-nine years to mark up against
me. He's to give me his answer Tuesday. He told another medical officer
that he wouldn't take the responsibility for OK'ing me, so I don't know
how I'm going to make out. Pretty much the same thing happened the
first time I took my overseas physical at Fort Monmouth, but somebody
higher up said age by itself wasn't sufficient reason for rejecting me—so
they gave me another exam and passed me. I hope history repeats itself.

                Love,
                    Papa

ALS MARSHALL

To Lillian Hellman

19 July 1943, Seattle, Washington

Dear Lily—

I'm just back from questioning the medical examiners about my status. (I couldn't wait until Tuesday—ah, hot-headed, impetuous youth!)

The answer: no verdict yet. At this point that's more good than bad, since the man was reported as being pretty emphatically thumbs down Saturday. I shall go back and nag them again tomorrow morning, and the next day and the next if necessary.

A German-born self-styled premature anti-fascist bent my ear for an hour this morning. He hopes to be sent (A) to Europe, or (B) to work in a German concentration camp, as a translator. I think he's a dreamer.

The $50 to Nancy was OK of course.[1] As a matter of fact, I think you ought to put her on my payroll. She's always done a good deal of work for me and now will most likely have to do more rather than less.

This afternoon finds me too lazy to go into Seattle—though I will no doubt have found enough energy by tonight—so I shall let the shopping expedition wait till later in the week. I haven't done any work for so many weeks that I'm practically out of any condition I was ever in. In self defence I'm going to have to start going along with those who follow some sort of training program here. I don't know what it consists of, but anything is better than this lying around gathering lethargy.

Maybe I won't loaf this afternoon. Maybe I'll find things to do. I'll take a suit of OD's to the cleaners;[2] I'll get a haircut; I'll go up to the post office for some air mail stamps; I'll shine my shoes; I'll take a shower; I'll mark the rest of my equipment; I'll—boy, ain't I mapping out a mess of activity? It's practically the afternoon of a chorus boy.

> Love,
> Dash

1. Nancy Bragdon was Hellman's secretary.
2. ODs are olive drabs, a uniform.

ALS LPT

To Mary Hammett

20 July 1943, Seattle, Washington

Dear Mary—
Today's big news for me is that I finally got an OK from the Medical

Department for overseas duty. Of course some other bright boy can always gum things up before I get off, but I'm keeping my fingers crossed while I go around grinning.

I'm glad you liked the photos. I haven't seen them.

I can't tell you where I'm going, baby, and I couldn't have told Jose when I was going to pass through Montana. This is a war: don't you remember?

> Love,
> D

ALS Marshall

To Lillian Hellman

22 July 1943, Seattle, Washington

Dear Lily—

I've eaten too much already and I've still got at least one more meal to go today. (I sound like you.) My appetite has finally come back—in spades—and I seem to spend most of the day running down food and devouring it. I suppose sooner or later I'll get used to this always-stuffed-to-the-gills feeling.

And, come to think of it for the first time, I haven't had a drink of hard liquor since the day before I left Shenango—one day short of two weeks—and not because I decided not to either. I just haven't got around to it. So I'm an alcoholic, eh? Do you want to apologize for anything?

Tonight I think I shall go see a baseball game. Seattle is playing Hollywood—and a lot you care about it. Well, just the same, it's pretty close to *my* heart.

Maybe I'll go get a dish of ice cream now, and then walk up and down some hills to joggle it down into place.

> Love,
> Dash

ALS LPT

1943

To Lillian Hellman

28 July 1943, Seattle, Washington

Dear Lily—

Notes of an elderly enlisted man:

(1) Just as every woman thinks any woman five years older is a hag, so every man thinks any man five years older must be growing feeble.

(2) Quotation from one of your people: "With that last name of mine"—it's Glick—"thank God my people had sense enough to give me a good American first name, Irwin."

(3) This is the first time I've ever loafed in the Army without drinking: it can be done.

(4) Rumors—though my informant spelled it "rhumor"—reach me that Camp Edison and Camp Wood are to be taken over by the Air Force next month.

(5) There's more gambling here than I've found in any other camp. Most of the men figure they're not going to be able to spend much where they are going.

(6) It's not the endless horseplay of the young that annoys the elderly; it's the endless capacity for horsing.

(7) Trees, mountains and ocean water make a nice combination.

(8) Cities in the Northwest are dull, without flavor or chic; it's the country that's swell.

(9) The coast newspapers seem to have the Italian king and Mussolini's heir confused with Garibaldi and Thomas Jefferson.

(10) A WAC sitting beside me at the PX cafeteria this morning had for breakfast a piece of lemon meringue pie and a cup of tea.

(11) Most of the men I came west with have been shipped, and here I linger.

> (12) I love you
> Dash

ALS LPT

To Josephine Hammett

29 July 1943, Seattle, Washington

Dear Princess—

Men come and men go, but I linger on. It's only been a day or two over two weeks, but when you are young and impatient that can seem like months.

I'm awfully glad you had such a good time in Montana. Lovely country, that northwestern part of the state. When I came out here three weeks ago I got glimpses from the car window of places I visited back in 1919–20, Libby, Glacier National Park, etc., and I was sorry I had stayed away so long.

* * *

My tailor-made choppers have at last adjusted themselves to me—or I to them—so that I'm usually not conscious of them and can once again eat anything. At the moment I am eating everything that will lie still on a plate long enough for me to get a fork into it, making up for lost time. From the feel of my clothes I imagine I'm getting back some of the weight I lost during the eating-is-hell period.

Kiss your mother and Mary for me.

> Love
> D

ALS Marshall

To Lillian Hellman

29 July 1943, Seattle, Washington

Dear Lily—

So men were going some places but I wasn't going anyplace, so I went to my immediate boss and said, "How come? Are the docs double-crossing me, sir?" So he phoned the proper place and then told me, "No, you are marked available." So I said, "Good, but I want to go quick." So we talked back and forth for a little while and then he phoned another proper place and asked them if they would put my name on the next shipping list, and, when he hung up, he told me, "You're OK, you'll go soon." So I came home to write you.

>Love,
>>That man

ALS LPT

To Lillian Hellman

8 August, 1943, 14th Sig. Serv. Det., APO 944, c/o Postmaster, Seattle, Washington

Dear Lily—

So this is still the Army— A guy just rushed over to the radio, dialed in George Jessel—they make platters of the big radio shows for our local station to play—and then went back to his shaving, loudly whistling tunes from *Coney Island*, which he had seen this afternoon.[1]

Me, I didn't see *Coney Island* this afternoon, though I may see it tomorrow night. Last night I saw a picture called *False Faces*.[2] Night before last I saw a B picture called something about being alone, about a career woman in the advertising game. I don't know whether I like these pictures. I lack film background. I have nothing to compare them with. (Films now have spoken dialogue: tell Louis).[3]

Here at this post men talk too, a great deal. Of course enlisted men in the Army everywhere talk a great deal. They don't like being alone—no soldier ever does anything or goes anywhere unless he can get somebody to put in with him—and they don't like being quiet. Usually they don't talk about anything, they just talk. But here most of the men have been out of the States for from ten to twenty-some months and there is a touch of the missed-too-many-boats about their chatter. Maybe I'll be like that some day, meanwhile I'm more the sour silent type.

It seems to be supposed that I will settle here for a while, but I don't know. The new address at the top of this letter is the fourteenth I have had in less than eleven months in the Army and I don't see any reason for thinking I'll keep it much longer than I did any of the others.

The trip here was one of the nicest I've ever had anywhere, any time, and my health is of the best. I haven't weighed myself since I left Seattle, but I suspect I'm still picking up an ounce or two here and there.

I like what I've seen of it here, which isn't so awfully much, but I think I'm going to get along all right with rest of it too. It's very airy and just enough on the primitive side to be nice. There are nice things to look at in the distance on days when you can see that far, and nobody has to be afraid of sunstroke here.

A very vocal repair gang—I think they were all acrobats in civilian life—has come back from its labors and is rocking my new home, so maybe I'd better wind this up and save whatever else I've got to say for other, quieter times.

If I stay here I'll probably want you to send me a large number of things of all sorts, so stand by for requisitions.

I'm hoping mail from you via the old address catches up with me soon. I want to hear of and from you.

Love,
Dash

1. George Jessel was an entertainer who often served as master of ceremonies. *Coney Island* was a popular musical comedy starring Betty Grable released by 20th Century-Fox in June 1943.
2. *False Faces* was a movie mystery released by Republic Pictures.
3. Louis B. Mayer was head of MGM.

ALS LPT

To Lillian Hellman

11 August 1943, Alaska (which is a fine large address)

Dear Lily—

The biggest thing that's happened here since I last wrote you is that for the first time beer came to this post—8 bottles of 3.2 per enlisted man. In that quantity and with that alcoholic content you can understand what came of it all was a lot less than an orgy.

Here's a clipping to hold onto until I start thinking of things I want. We can have cameras here, so maybe I'll be begging you to borrow the Ikon I gave you. It's not that I'm an Indian giver, but it would probably be handier here than either my Contax or Graflex, besides being light enough to come by mail. But wait till I make up my mind. I may be able to pick up something here.

I'll probably do some broadcasting over the post radio. I'm to talk to them about it tomorrow. Also I'm to be photographed for *Yank*.[1] (Jesus, how us writers cram ourselves down the public's throat! Or do you want to make out you're different?)

I'd planned to visit a nearby settlement this Sunday, but it seems to be quarantined with mumps, so maybe I'll look into the fishing situation instead. Salmon are running now and the trout here are said to be worth having a go at. If I can get hold of some tackle I'll find out.

My sleeping and eating these days would satisfy you at your maternal crankiest. I ordinarily sleep from ten to six, with brief naps after breakfast and noon chow; and I eat three solid meals with chocolate bars and similar truck in between.

Love,
Dash

1. *Yank* magazine, "The Army Weekly."

ALS LPT

To Josephine Hammett

12 August 1943, Somewhere in Alaska

Dear Princess—

I'm trying you again at the old homestead, taking it for granted that you and your Ma will be back from Montana and San Francisco by the time this letter gets to the States. Or are you going to spend all your lives roaming around like a couple of Irish gypsies? And did you have a good time?

So far I've had a quiet but pleasant time up here and I'm pretty sure I'm going to keep on liking it. After all, your old man is past the age when he needs cities and bright lights and such stuff to keep him happy, and this corner of the world has things I like. (Now don't ask me about polar bears: the only animals I've seen are dogs and gophers.)

Somewhere in transit from Fort Monmouth I lost the pictures of you and Mary, so you're both to repair that loss immediately if not sooner. That's an order!

I do a great deal of very sound sleeping up here, which may not be an immediate contribution to the war effort, but it certainly should put me at decided advantage if I happen to meet a Jap who's got insomnia—unless, of course, his troubles have made him bad-tempered. I also eat a lot, which should help me if that Jap is underfed. (Boy, am I whittling this Jap down to suit myself!)

What's ahead of you this school term? And then what? And have you made up your mind what you want to do when—say in 1955—you've finished school? I'll try to have the war over by then—if I can get any decent cooperation out of MacArthur and Eisenhower and those other sluggards.

Meanwhile kiss your mother and Mary for me and write me. Letters are like pearls up here.

> Love,
> Papa

ALS Marshall

To Lillian Hellman

13 August 1943, APO 944

Dear Lily—

Keep plenty of room open under the H's in your address book. I'm still bobbing around and will probably move over to an infantry outfit for a while the first of the week. Don't use that as an excuse to put off writing me: my mail will follow me, and some of it that follows me had better be from a certain well-known Jewish woman playwright.

The infantry thing promises to be a tough go, as we say, but I've had so little exercise in the past two or three months that a general shaking up ought to be good for my old bones and joints, if they don't shake apart. Anyhow, for all my laziness, I'm usually happier moving around, and I guess the infantry will have me hopping around abundantly.

I did my mugging for *Yank's* photographer this afternoon, a couple of kind of dull and probably silly-looking poses.

Sunday the fifteenth.

Day of rest. Brilliant thought while walking back from breakfast (we usually ride a truck to and from meals, but this morning nobody else in my hut chose to get up in time to make seven-thirty chow): Alaska is one of the few places that looks just like Alaska.

I miss newspapers, though I often enough didn't even glance at them when they were available. I haven't seen even a month-old one since I left Seattle. The radio keeps us up to date on war and sports news, but the rest is a vacuum. When I get around to it I want to send you a list of publications to renew my subscriptions to. The number of them on sale at the PX here is limited, and chiefly limited to ones I don't want.

You can disregard that stuff about the new address. I'm going to be with the infantry only a couple of weeks and, since they are crowded for quarters, I'll go on living here.

Give my best to Herm, Max, Peggy, Jerry, Lin, Irene, Elizabeth, George, Louis, Ken, Jed, Leane, Carl and my sister and the Pope, if you see them.

      Love,
       Dash

ALS LPT

To Lillian Hellman

22 August 1943, Alaska

Dear Lily—

* * *

The *Variety* man liked *Watch on the Rhine* all right, all right, and I hope he's right.

Your report on the play sounds exactly like a girl named Lillian Hellman I used to know, when she was writing a new play.[1]

All we know about the Harlem affair are vague references like yours in our mail. What happened?[2]

I had a nice long letter from Herman, a sort of love letter to one of the puppies, who's obviously too young to read. So I'll keep the letter for it till it's older. The pups look like honeys in the picture.

Frances Pindyck wrote that you "have been more than helpful and things have cleared immediately," meaning, I suppose, that I'm the one who held things up. My thanks to you for speeding me to wealth![3] I wrote Max a couple of days ago.[4] Is Windsor Hotel the right address? Right or wrong, that's where his letter went.

Florence Monash wrote me that Paul is very busy and happy writing radio stuff for the Far or Middle East section of OWI.[5] Is everybody in New York working for OWI? If not, what are those three people doing?

Everybody writes me how hot it is, so I guess it must be hot down there. It ain't hot up here, though it ain't so damned cold either.

I still like *The Searching Wind* for your play, so don't let's have any more dilly-dallying about it.

Now that the Japanese are gone from Kiska, there are all sorts of rumors, guesses and hopes about what will be done by or to the Alaska Defense Command, but of course none of us really knows anything.[6] It seems logical that something should happen to some of us, but— —

Today is Sunday: I'm making it a day of rest in a big way, recovering from a week of slogging over the landscape most of the days and cleaning rifles at least part of the nights. The coming week promises to be no less active, and maybe more so. I'm getting good and tired so I'll be entitled to years of complete rest after the war is over. Jesus, the things I can think of not to do! Starting with not helping you rearrange the living room furniture! And not painting anything! And never, never picking vegetables or flowers!!! It's almost going to make peace worth while.

> Love,
> Dash

1. Hellman was working on *The Searching Wind,* which opened on Broadway on 12 April and ran for 326 performances.
2. On 2 August 1943 a black soldier was murdered in Harlem by whites. A riot followed that left five people dead and caused an estimated $5 million damage.
3. Frances Pindyck was one of three people in the New York office of Leland Hayward's agency, which was run by Lawrence White.
4. Max Hellman was Lillian's father.
5. Paul Monash was a writer who later became a screenwriter and producer and produced, among other movies, *Butch Cassidy and the Sundance Kid* (1969).
6. The Japanese landed on the Aleutian Island of Kiska in June 1943. The U.S. Marines landed on the island on 15 August to find that the Japanese had abandoned it.

ALS HRC

To Lillian Hellman

29 August 1943, Alaska

Dear Lily,

Last week was like this: machine guns and hikes over tundra, bayonet practice and hikes up mountains, hand grenades and hikes through swamps, and, after each day's doings, rifles to clean and machine guns to clean and a tiredness that made letter writing something only heroes could have done. And that's why, honey, this is my first letter since last Sunday. I never hope to be any tireder than I was practically every night. My ancient bones really took a lot of punishment, but that routine is over now—at least for the time being—and I dare say I'll be all rested up and as good as new in a couple of months. But don't ever let anybody tell you that infantrymen don't earn their pay in this neck of the woods.

Food note: wild strawberries are plentiful here, and large and tasty. We scouted the tundra with one eye alert for a theoretical enemy, the other skinned for berries. (After all one can flatten oneself just as expertly in a berry patch as elsewhere; and eating doesn't interfere with one[']s alertness—nobody expects to taste the enemy.)

One night there were stars. You don't know that's news.

About the book of short stories, I'm still of the opinion that problem should be put off until the day when you, as literary executor, can face it by yourself.[1] Don't let's be in any hurry about it, huh?

A nice letter from you, dated the 19th, arrived on one of my tiredest (if there were actually any degrees of tiredness) nights and was a sort of spiritual liniment, if you know what I mean. Air mail reaches us fairly regularly, no other kind has come since I've been here, though we constantly expect it.

Pru Whitfield wrote me that Raoul is dying of T.B. in a San Fernando hospital and that Lois, his third wife, "fell" (the quotes are Pru's) out of a window in San Francisco recently and is pretty badly banged up.[2]

I enclose a snapshot of the old corporal returning from chow. At first glance I thought he looked like a sort of benevolent hired man, but, looking again, he's more like a girl's school French teacher on a fishing trip. Nowhere can I find any signs of the hardy martial appearance the old corporal would like to think he presents.

Will you have some magazine subscriptions renewed for me? (It isn't necessary to make a separate deal with each publication: most magazine shops take subscriptions and you—I guess I mean Nancy—can clear it up in one fell swoop.) The ones I want are:

> *Field and Stream*
> *New Yorker*
> *New Masses*
> *Time*
> *Popular Mechanics*
> *Alaskan Sportsman*
> *Variety*

I'll do better on letters this week.

> Love
> Dash

1. On 15 June 1943 Lawrence Spivak published $106,000 *Blood Money,* the first of nine paperbound volumes published over the next eight years reprinting stories by Hammett.

2. Hammett had a long-term romantic relationship with Prudence Whitfield. Raoul, Prudence's ex-husband, was a drinking friend of Hammett's in the late 1920s and a *Black Mask* writer. His novels, notably *Death in a Bowl* and *Green Ice,* were published by Knopf. He and Prudence divorced in 1933. Raoul's second marriage was to Emily Davies Vanderbilt Thayer, a wealthy socialite, who was found shot to death at the Whitfields' ranch in Las Vegas in 1935 shortly after their separation. The death was ruled a suicide. Having run through his wife's money and suffering from ill health, Whitfield married a third time. Destitute, he died of tuberculosis in 1945 at the age of forty-six.

ALS LPT

To Prudence Whitfield

30 August 1943, 14th Sig. Serv. Det., APO 944, Alaska

Dear Pru—

You don't get your wish, but I got mine: I finally talked my way up here. And so far it's been a rugged go, but I kind of like it. The chances are this will be the last war they'll let me into and I'd like to make the most of it—especially since I'm more in favor of this one than I ever was of the last.

I'm sorry about Raoul. That's really no fun. There's nothing I can tell you about beating t.b. It's nearly altogether a matter of temperament, which is why medical aid isn't a hell of a lot of use to you. Even determination is by itself as much a handicap as a help. Many of those who most firmly chased the cure were among the earliest to die in our groups in the 20's. It's probably true that reasonable amounts of rest and nourishment and freedom from excessive worry are the chief things, but I think it's also necessary to be having a relatively good time. That means as a rule having something you're interested in. I don't mean something to get well for. I mean something that interests you sick or well—something you don't have to get well for. Writing did that for me when I had t.b., though I doubt that it would serve now. And temperament comes in there: it isn't possible for some sick people to be sufficiently interested in anything except getting well. I wish I could write something more helpful than this, but I honestly don't know anything.

Will you give my best to Raoul when you write—and tell him I'm writing him?

> Love,
> Dash

ALS PEPPER

To Lillian Hellman

30 August 1943, APO 944

Dear Lily,

Pictures, pictures, pictures! All he does is grow fat on the Army and send people pictures of the face. That's a bad sign on a man. Anyhow here they are. These were taken for *Yank* and they make me look like a Long Island clam digger who isn't doing so well against more vigorous competition. The garments, in case you can't place them, are fatigue clothes and arctic field jacket. They are our work clothes, but what am I doing?

I am one who does not always figure things out with quickness. For instance, I have had a mild puzzle. Some time ago I—slowly, of course—learned that I could no longer go without sleep. If I cut much under eight hours, the next day I paid and paid for it. Well, I said, that's age. So I came to Alaska and for a couple of weeks I found myself working harder than I had ever worked—I mean physically—and, try as I would, unable to catch more than six hours sleep a night—sometimes not much more than three. But I didn't miss the lost sleep. So far as sleep was concerned I felt fine. Why? I asked myself, why? Now comes an inkling. Before the tenth of July I drank a lot, since July tenth I have had just one drink. Can it be that going to bed with at least a mild snootful every night—and not age—was what called for at least eight hours of rest? I wonder. Meanwhile I work on the problem, thinking slowly, slowly.

I sent Raoul Whitfield a check for $500.00 today, so don't think it's a forgery when the bank sends it through.

Men in my hut—we live in quonset huts, those semi-cylindrical gal-vanized iron affairs you've seen in pictures of the army in Iceland—are talking, loudly, but not about anything, with much laughter, but without much humor. Maybe I'll go out for a walk. I am not fond of the men in my hut this week.

A batch of mail came in while I was walking—it's nice out tonight, with no wind for a change—but there was only one letter from you, an earlier letter forwarded from my old APO address.

So the Kobers are really coming home? I'll owe Maggie $20.[1] I haven't heard from her since I left Seattle.

The press-trade-what-you-call it on *Watch* came from the Shumlin office and reads good. Maybe we've got something.

Stop moping, honey, you're a great and elegant woman and I love and miss you.

> Love,
> Dash

1. Maggie was Arthur Kober's second wife.

ALS LPT

To Lillian Hellman

8 September 1943, Alaska

Dear Lily—

I've just come back from my weekly chore at the Post radio station. This week's sermon—no more brilliant than previous ones—was on Mari Santoz's *Old Jules,* which isn't a bad book, however dull I may have made it seem.

There's a USO show in camp tonight—some burlesque old-timers who, I am told, are pretty good—but I go to the theatre no more readily than I did in civilian life, so it's not likely I'll see them. So I can keep on thinking they're pretty good.

Sept. 9
Business picked up this morning. There's something stirring that I'm

in favor of and I ought to have news for you in my next letter, though of course you'll probably still be left pretty much in the dark.

There should be mail in today—and it better include something from you. The last batch didn't and once is enough of that.

Well, that's all right: there were two mighty fine letters from you, and the review clippings. Miriam Howell also sent me a set of reviews, so I now have one for each eye.[1] Along in the same mail came a letter from Maggie and a long and newsy one from Max.

It's nice I'm rich and likely to grow richer, and you can borrow all you want. (How could I stop you?) Do what you think best about the savings bank accounts and such, but don't make me any investments in anything except U.S. Bonds and Shumlin Productions, and leave me a thousand or so in the checking accounts in case I want to write a check now and then. I also leave the matter of new radio contracts in your and Larry White's hands.[2] Just be sure you do things that bring me great gobs of money. (By the way, what happened to Larry's merchant marine plans? And give my best to him.)

I'm glad the *Watch on the Rhine* reception was so good. The reviews don't seem so hot to me—but I've never believed in the influence of NY movie critics on box-office.

I don't think you should be too hasty in deciding not to marry Sulzberger; and, if you do marry him, I hope you don't neglect taking Alphonso back.[3] Think what he could do with a hammock in the living room!

Here's a clipping from a Southern newspaper that may interest you for various reasons. Reba sent it to me. She says the old man is getting an artificial leg.[4] (Jesus, those Hammetts! You can't say they give up without a struggle.) Max sent me a clipping of the Theodore Strauss story on you.[5] You're, it seems, and I've never doubted it, a noble woman, which is one of God's fairest creations, and it was very smart of me to have been so fond of you all these years. Now I think I'll keep it up.

> Love,
> Dash

1. Miriam Howell is unidentified.
2. Larry White ran Leland Hayward's New York office. He negotiated radio contracts for Hammett.

3. Arthur Hays Sulzberger was publisher of the *New York Times* from 1935 to 1961.
4. Hammett's sister.
5. Hellman's movie script for *The North Star* attempted a realistic depiction of life in a Russian village. Director Lewis Milestone Americanized the set and cast. Associate director William Cameron Menzies commented on Hellman's dissatisfaction with Milestone's tampering to Theodore Strauss in a 29 August 1943 article in the *New York Times*.

ALS LPT

To Mary Hammett

21 September 1943, Alaska

Dear Mary,

Here's a check to buy yourself something for that new birthday (How they roll around! You must be an old lady by now!) and I hope it's a gay and happy one, and I hope you have a lot of gay and happy ones ahead of you.

I've moved again, but the only difference in my address is that the APO number is now 980 instead of 944. The rest remains the same. I like the new spot more than the old one—there is more doing here and I'll probably be doing work I know more about and like better.

You can break the news to your mother that I haven't seen an Eskimo nor chewed a piece of blubber since I've been here, and don't expect to if I stay five years.

I read *Days of Our Years* when it first came out and found so many contradictions in it that I decided Van Paa[s]sen was either a crackpot or a liar, or, most likely, both; and the gent's career since then hasn't done much to change my mind.[1]

Kiss your mother and Jo for me and tell Jo I'll write her either tonight or tomorrow.

Be a good girl and write soon.

Love,
Papa

1. Pierre Van Paassen was a political travel writer. *Days of Our Years* is a political memoir that concludes: "Only radicalism which grows out of a principled oppo-

sition to capitalism and which acts according to its own scale of values can lead to victory over Fascism and imperialism, over poverty and war and ignorance."

ALS MARSHALL

To Lillian Hellman

23 September 1943, Alaska

Dear Lily—

You are a very rich woman and this next play will only make you still richer. You say you love me, but you haven't yet given me the birthday present due last May, which is pretty disgraceful. I'll let bygones be bygones, but I want a ring. I would prefer that the mounting be platinum, but I'll leave the details to you. All I ask is that the ring be sturdy, beautiful and valuable: I don't want any Japanese hacking off my finger to get at some trifling bauble. Also there should be something engraved inside the band. Enclosed you will find my size and an order for the Post Office. I have spoken. (Sometimes in the Army you're like a pregnant woman waking up at three in the morning asking for strawberries and cream right away.)

These are nice days and—even without a ring—I am at peace with the non-fascist part of the world. I'm pleasantly occupied and full of plans for the future, both in the Army and afterwards. Want to guess how many of them I'll even remember when the time comes, let alone carry out?

Mail from APO #944 still hasn't caught up to me; I suppose they forwarded it by wheelbarrow. Oh, well, if I can't read letters from you tonight I'll wash some sox. I ought to wash a suit of woolen underwear too, but it'll take a few more letterless evenings to push me that far. I push kind of slow.

Such other news as I have is of an inferior quality and not worthy of being sent to a New York girl who is in constant touch with the latest hot news flashes from all the big time wire and radio services, besides probably going to a tea-leaf reader.

Love,
Dash

ALS LPT

To Lillian Hellman

28–30 September 1943, Alaska

Dearest Lily—

* * *

Another batch of forwarded mail arrived yesterday, and this time I was luckier: there were several letters from you and one from Nancy enclosing a couple of very lovely pictures of your face. Thanks, honey. Presently your face will be over the head of my bunk and I can go to sleep at night safe in the knowledge that you're guarding those two bottles of Pepsi-Cola and the one of orange pop on the floor beside my rucksack.

A check from Knopf arrived via Monmouth, Shenango, Seattle and APO 944. I'm sending it to you for proper disposition.

All right, so I "look like an aging tulip tree." What am I supposed to look like? A budding lily-of the-valley? Josephine wrote, "You look just like the frontispiece in that intrepid explorer's (Lord Whosis R.R.G.) book 'Down the Nile With Pack and Gun.'" Maybe I'll stop jumping in front of cameras. That color picture you sent ought to discourage me. In it—if I can put in my two cents' worth along with everybody else—I look like a brown diagonal about to bisect a void.

I'm glad you had sense enough to go to a doctor—instead of a hairdresser—at last, and if it does turn out to be tobacco poisoning I hope you'll be sensible about it. That stuff can be nasty and—regardless of what you think—the prevention is so easy that it's sheer idiocy to go on knocking yourself out. Get well and stay well—and that's an order!

The Ben Hecht poem was really something.[1] Does he think we ought to tell Hitler we'll call the war off if he won't kill any more Jews? There are quite a few too many anti-Semites here. I tried the poem out on them and it went over big: they never doubted that it was anti-Semitic— to them it said plainly that Jews ought to shut up about their little troubles while there were big things afoot—and they posted it on a bulletin board for our few Jews to see. (I'm a little ashamed of myself, but, by God, fun is fun, and if his own people encourage Hecht I can't always be expected to suppress the Nero in me.)

Paul Streger sent me a set of *Watch* reviews—so I've had three.[2]

Thanks for the new batch you sent. I'm glad all's going well. If you had any memory—or I'd saved such letters as you may have written me while you had previous work in progress—you'd know that your present dithers over the play are only the normal bellyaching of La Hellman at work.[3] You still think you dashed those other plays off without a fear, a groan, or a sigh; but you didn't, sister. I haven't had a dry shoulder since your career began, and I was an amphibian long before the Army and Navy ever heard of combined operations.

And, speaking of combined operations, some day, when it can be done, I'm going to do a book or a saga or something on this Alaskan-Aleutian operation.[4] It's really a honey, and there's never been anything like it. Most of the people up here are too close to it to have any perspective, and wish they were in Italy or the South Pacific or someplace where newspaper stories are born; while those who aren't here don't know enough about it and, likewise, are more interested in the gaudier happenings in Eastern and Southern Europe and the tropics. (Most soldiers, like all civilians, are too impatient about their wars.) What we've got up here isn't gaudy, but it's history—and may well be *the* thing of the war when everything's sifted. I don't mean only our having taken an army where no army was supposed to be able to go and function. (Though look at all the fuss made over Hannibal's dopey elephants in the Alps, and that was not as new, not as daring, not as difficult, and, more important, not as lasting as this.) Nor our going out on the rim of the world and inventing procedures and technics to fit it. They're fine big things to have done, but they're only means to an end. What I think we've done is built a wall and a path that changes the shape of the world.

It's eleven o'clock. I guess I'll take my elation up to the mess-hut and feed it.

On my way back from chow I picked up another letter from you, written before the others, before you went to Martha's Vineyard. Also there was one from Lin, quite lyrical about her Hardscrabble week-end.[5] "A merry crew and thirsty," she writes, an old-fashioned girl to the last.

Don't be too pessimistic about the South American project: something could well come of it. All is not yet either black or white.

I like the picture of your indignation in re the spelling of names, but I guess you know how I would have voted.

Anyhow you are cute and I love you and if it weren't for you there wouldn't be anything I really miss up here.

> Love,
>> Dash

1. Ben Hecht was a prominent literary figure who frequently wrote topical political poems for newspapers and magazines.
2. Paul Streger produced and directed plays.
3. Hellman was working on *The Searching Wind*.
4. Hammett collaborated with Robert Colodny on *The Battle of the Aleutians*, a short history of the successful U.S. defense of the Aleutian chain against Japanese invasion from June 1942 to May 1943. The pamphlet was published in 1944 and "produced by the intelligence section, field force headquarters, Adak, Alaska, October 1943." Hammett wrote the text; Colodny, the captions.
5. Lin S. Root wrote *One Good Year*, which ran for 223 performances on Broadway in 1935.

ALS LPT

To Mary Hammett

28 September 1943, 14th Sig Serv Det, APO 980 (i.e., The Aleutians), Alaska

Dear Mary—

Let's not get fussed up about the mail deliveries. I don't live on a city street these days, and the mail service is surprisingly good taking one thing and another into consideration. Air mail is still the fastest way of reaching me here—so stay with it.

I wrote you in the spring of 1942 that I was doing the *Watch on the Rhine* script. I suppose you had forgotten. I've seen some of the New York reviews and they were pretty good. Warner Bros. thinks it has a big hit—but they always think that.

That isn't thinness showing up so much in my recent pictures as old age. And don't tell me I'm not really old. That's not the point. The point is that the last couple of months I've begun to look oldish, with lines and things in my face and neck; and now and then my voice seems to crack a little. So when I come back from the wars you can be ready to welcome something resembling a Civil War veteran. Well, youth was good when I had it—though I could more easily resign myself to its loss if there wasn't so damned much of it around me. Sometimes I think I'm living in a blooming kindergarten!

I like this spot better than any I've hit so far in the Army, and I have liked most of them; I feel well and I'm having by no means a bad time. If it keeps on like this I'll start feeling sorry for civilians.

That, honeybunch, just about winds up today's crop of news.

Kiss your mother and Jo for me.

> Love,
> Papa.

ALS MARSHALL

To Josephine Hammett

2 October 1943, 14th Sig Serv Det, APO 980 (i.e., The Aleutians), Alaska

Dear Princess—

We live here in Quonset huts—those semi-cylindrical metal things you have seen in pictures—strung out down along both steep walls of a little

valley, close to the walls, half dug in sometimes and spaced well apart so that if some dope wants to bomb us he can't bag too many with one shot. The huts have no openings in the sides, but a door and two square windows in either end. My hut is so well concealed under sod, tundra, and stuff, spread over chicken-wire, that little light comes in even on those days when we can leave our doors and windows open. If our generator is functioning we have electric light, and can get our armed forces station (short

Enclosure in 2 October 1943 letter to Josephine

wave) or Radio Tokyo (where all our navy is sunk every day) on our radio. And most of us have rigged up some sort of reading light over our beds.

Our beds are the regular metal Army cot. We have plenty of blankets and comforters, but of course no pillows and sheets. A Diesel-oil stove keeps the hut warm and—what's more important—dry, and our beaver-board wall lining makes a good background for pin-ups—mostly Vargas girls that look too much like Vargas girls.[1] Long cracks between the floor and the walls let in enough fresh air to keep our canteens of water—and bottles of Coke when we have them—cool, but not enough of the out-doors to really bother us. (We're pretty comfortable when we're not wet *and* in the wind.)

The prevailing wind—and it can do a mighty fancy piece of prevailing when it sets its mind to it—turns our valley into a funnel, and you think it's rugged going until you climb up the steep green sides to the terrain above. Then, lady, you've really bought yourself a hunk of air in motion. The only reason we don't sound like liars when we tell people how hard it blows is that we don't know. Our machine only registers up to 109 miles per hour. So we can just say it's blown harder than that.

A brook winds down our little valley, and winds is the word. Between my hut and the mess-hut—only a few hundred yards away—we cross the brook eight times, mostly on impromptu footbridges that are as eas-ily missed in the darkness as washed away when the brook cuts up. The brook is a lively one, busy and bustling and clear and cold, with rocky pools that sometimes have fish in them. (There's a report that a couple of pound Dolly Varden trout was seen this morning in a pool some twenty feet from my hut. I may hike that way after I finish this letter and see if I can do anything about it. I think I know where I can borrow some patchwork fishing tackle.)

I worked all night, until seven this morning, and should be sleeping now. Maybe I'll do that instead of going fishing. Or maybe I'll wash some sox and things. That's what I really ought to do, so maybe I won't. Maybe I'll take a nap after all.

Kiss your mother and Mary for me—and don't bite 'em.

> Much love,
> Papa

1. Alberto Vargas drew sexy young women in provocative poses for *Esquire* magazine.

ALS MARSHALL

To Lillian Hellman

2–3 October 1943, Alaska

Dearest Lily—

I'm glad you're sending some books. I can feel a reading streak coming on, but there's nothing here except a small selection of popular magazines and pocket mysteries. Thank you, ma'am. Another boat should be in from my last home in a day or two, and maybe it will bring things from you. And if you're as well-behaved a correspondent as I hope, mail should start coming direct from you in three or four days—if nothing happens to disrupt our air-mail service.

I served my country all last night, till around seven this morning, and should be in bed now, but another night-country-server beat me home and is snoring like a B-38 on the other side of the hut, so I think I'll wait until he wears some more of the lining out of his nose and throat—or wears his teeth down grinding them. He is one of three very bearable teeth-grinders in our hut. When they all get going together it sounds like we're infested with beavers.

* * *

3 October 43

See, I told you—this is a Sunday. And it looks as if it's going to be a nice one. (It's still early; I've got a lot of work to do and want to get this off first.) A nice day here is where the wind doesn't blow the rain through the seams of your clothes. And when there's no rain *and* no wind the oldtimers go around complaining that it's going to give newcomers a false idea of things. The oldtimers worry a good deal about that sort of thing. You can get them pretty mad by saying, "Oh, yeah, this is a lousy day, all right, but I remember once in Sea Girt, N.J., we had etc., etc., etc." You don't have to lie very much. They don't like to think of other places having *any* bad weather.

I'm still having more or less of a love affair with this country. Once on a boat with islands looming up half-real in fog and rain I suddenly thought how nice it would have been to have been born on one of them and to be coming home to it—and I'm a white-haired son-of-a-gun if I wasn't actually sorry for myself for a moment, like Cliff Odets not having had any skates.[1] APO 944 had grander distant scenery than this place, but this—in spite of having even fewer modern conveniences—is much homier for Army-style living.

It will be nearly the middle of October when you get this letter. There will be leaves on the ground at Hardscrabble Farm and fat and edible gray squirrels scampering through them. (I haven't seen a tree since July.) Indoors you will be burning some of the apple trees that were cut last year and I hope you'll have sense enough to broil some food—apple wood's especially good for fowl—over it. (There are things wrong with that sentence: I write what Maggie calls fallen English.) The thermostat on the oil heater will be cutting up a little and you will be having a monstrous time getting your bedroom and study heated and/or ventilated to suit you. There is also the problem of where the puppies should sleep now that the cold weather is coming on. (I take for granted that you have already decided there's nothing to be done to the main driveway until Spring.) You are already thinking about giving skating parties. If there were no war I'd now be in the living room listening to a football game—no, it would be a World Series game—on the radio and (if I wished to talk to you, which I do) I could simply yell through the dining room into the study, where you'd be pretending to work to avoid listening to the radio—and that would be a lot intimater than this.

> Love,
> Dash

1. Clifford Odets was a proletarian playwright.

ALS LPT

To Lillian Hellman

5 October 1943, Alaska

Dearest Lily—

This morning I slept late, babying myself because I'd worked from around 7 A.M. until after 11 P.M. yesterday. Your behind gets pretty tired sitting in one place—and it hard metal—practically all that time. Mine does, anyhow, not being very well upholstered, if you remember.

Such news of the war as reaches us here is all pretty good, so I reckon we'll be out of this in another year or two—those of us who don't [get] tapped for armies of occupation. And if we stay on good terms with all our allies. Last month I passed my one-year-mark in the Army. If I had thought of it I could have set myself down and tried to sum up, but one year in the Army is probably pretty much like another, so maybe I'll do it next September. I wouldn't want to let it go any longer than that—my memory may begin to fail me.

Finance department: I leave entirely in your hands the matter of whether and what I should invest in the forthcoming A. Kober show when and if there is a forthcoming A. Kober show.

Still the same department: you know, cutie, it would be a lot simpler all around if you would simply enter that $5000 you are "borrowing" from me as, "Payment of Loan." I'm still carrying on what I ostentatiously call my "books," a lot of "loans" from you.

Notes for Post-War Lies: Remind me to tell you some time about the five days I once spent in a hundred-foot or so boat on the Bering Sea with, among others, a Medical Corps captain who was always sea-sick, a corporal who had been in command of an island for four months, a cowboy who was all broken up over having been transferred from the infantry to a Graves Registration Co. (they do the Army's burying), and an ex-Shanghai policeman who thought I looked like Neville Chamberlain.

It's about time to get into boots and an outer garment and go wandering up in our little valley in search of chow. I'd like to be eating one of your gumbos tonight, but I don't guess you can get it cooked and delivered up here in time. Oh, well, no hard feelings. I know you just didn't happen to think of it in time—probably working too hard on the play.

> Love,
> Dash

ALS LPT

To Lillian Hellman

7 October 1943, Alaska

Dearest Lilishka:

I've got a little headache tonight, maybe from the shot in the arm I had—some of the others were complaining earlier.

I managed to get a fifty-dollar bet down on the Cardinals just before they lost their second game of the series, but I had to hurry.

Something else you can send me please: a chain on which to wear my dog-tags; light, strong, and naturally, expensive.

(I broke off there to help scrub—with lye and soap and brooms and mops—the floor of our hut. We track in gobs of mud and thus every couple of days our Diesel-oil burning stove explodes, showering one end of the place with soot.)

I have a couple of other topics I want to take up with you tonight, but sometime soon I intend to go into the peculiar military role played by the Army's Special Services branch. Special Services supplies us with shows and other morale builders, not always in a manner that does us much good. This isn't altogether Special Services' fault: its chief job is to keep civilians always aware that the boys in the Army are having a lot of things done for them. Sometimes the boys—well, like once at Camp Upton we didn't stand retreat there, but we had a formation after evening chow. So this time after the regular business of the formation was over, first sergeant said, "There's a show at the open-air theater tonight. Anybody don't want to see it, fall out." Well, a lot of us had been in the Army too short a time to miss shows yet, and were pretty tired, so most of us fell out. So he blew his whistle and yelled, "Everybody fall in." And we did and they marched us up to see the show.

Notes of an Elderly Enlisted Man, Cont.

A. Notes for Post-War Lies.

(1) Remind me to tell you about the time I was in love with a volcano named Pavlov. That was in another part of Alaska many miles from here. Early on a clear morning—after it didn't rain until later in the day—I could go to the door of the hut I was living in and see Pavlov

smoking against the sky. Its main crater was crusted over. The smoke came out in slow-paced smallish dark puffs from a vent near one edge of the top and usually hung for a while just atop the mountain before the wind blew it away.

I could walk from the door of my hut fifty yards to the crest of the hill and—on a very clear morning—see another volcano. It was larger than Pavlov and had a prettier name, Shishaldin. A lot of people say Shishaldin is second only to Fujiyana—or however you spell the Japanese showpiece—in perfection of form. It was a beauty all right, but— maybe because I could see Pavlov oftener, maybe because I liked the little dark smoke-puffs—Pavlov seemed cozier to me and I stayed pretty faithful to it.

At first it was dark, but, as the summer got along, snow appeared and each morning the snow would reach further down towards Pavlov's foot. Later I passed that way in a boat. It was a sunny morning and Pavlov was solid white against a luminous mirror-grey sky. Its base was hidden by mist that was glowing white in the sun and two long thin cloud streaks cut shiny white cross-sections out of the volcano. The puffs of smoke were very dark against all this bright gray and white. It was lovely—two-dimensional and unreal as fairyland, as that part of Alaska often is—only I wouldn't be surprised if Pavlov that morning was lovelier than anything else ever was. See what I mean? I liked it.

B. Notes on the Art of War.

There's more to modern warfare than just going out to try to kill a man who's coming out to try to kill you. For instance:

(1) Military Urination.

To make civilian urination is a relatively simple matter. He simply walks into a readily recognized room, faces familiar white fixtures, unbuttons his fly, and gravity and either Crane or Kohler of Kohler take care of the rest of it. But there's more to it than that in the Army.

Here we ordinarily urinate out of doors, into oil drums that have been split lengthwise and mounted on two-foot lengths of pipe. The pipe is driven down into the ground, whence it is supposed to carry such urine as gets into it. On an average it may be estimated that sixty or more percent of urine output does get into and run down through these pipes, though the percentage will vary widely with the weather, as wee shall see.

These urinals—they look like large unornamented bird baths—stand completely open to the elements—no walls, no shed, no nothing—and here there is usually a wind. Now it's pretty obvious that if you try to urinate facing the wind you're going to get wet. So what? Do you merely turn your back to the wind? That's not so good. A strong wind—and that'[s] a mild way to describe the kind we have most of the time—then creates a vacuum in front of you, the process that propels sail boats forward. But this time it won't so much propel you forward as whip the urine back in a fine high spray. Face to the wind's no good, back to the wind's no good, so you try side to the wind. Now you're getting somewhere—but you've still got some delicate problems. If you turn your—say—left side directly to the wind, it's naturally going to spray your right side. You've got to shelter your front a little, inching your back diagonally into the wind, and as soon as you inch it the least bit too far you start creating that dangerous vacuum again. Then, too, the wind doesn't always blow steadily, but in gusts that upset the carefully calculated physics of the operation. You try regulating the flow of urine—on and off with the gusts—and you learn to shift your stance to compensate for constant shifts in the wind, and you learn to work it out pretty well at times, but the results are seldom altogether happy.

Many men say it is better not to go out to urinate at all, but simply to wet your pants. Then you are at least sure of being dry above the waist. But I don't know anybody who practices this.

> Love,
> Dash

<small>Retyped at Lillian Hellman's direction; LPT</small>

To Lillian Hellman

12 October 1943, Alaska

Dear Lily—

Another letter—written at the Plaza—came from you today, still via 944. You are a good girl and a better correspondent than I often make out.

* * *

That's awful about Maggie.[1] Or—I hope—isn't it as serious as it sounds at this distance? She's never mentioned it in her letters.

I read the Warner short stories this evening and had a good time.[2] Thank you again, ma'am.

I'm glad you're going to look at the Ellery Queen introduction, and hope you'll be strict about it: the Ellery Queen taste can be pretty bad at times.[3]

I got to go back to work, lady; I can't lie here on my bunk writing letters all night even to you.

> Quantities of love,
> Dash

1. Maggie Kober was diagnosed with multiple sclerosis.
2. Presumably Sylvia Townsend Warner's *A Garland of Straw* (1943).
3. *The Adventures of Sam Spade*, with an introduction by Ellery Queen, was published 14 April 1944 by Lawrence Spivak as Bestseller Mystery #50.

ALS LPT

To Lillian Hellman

13–14 October 1943, Alaska

Dearest Lilishka—

At last we've got direct contact. Your letter postmarked the 7th arrived this morning. It seems to take my letters longer to get to you than yours to me, which is a break for the old corporal and no particular hardship on you, since I—except for unavoidable lapses—write oftener than you.

Paul Monash writes me that *The Thin Man* is *back* on the air. What goes on? I hope the cutie-pie hasn't been hiding things from the old corporal. Don't let's have any nonsense of that sort—or I will take my trade to some other financial manager. (You're scaring me anyhow with those threats about taking a firm stand on money matters. Lady, I didn't join the Army to get rich: it had something to do with fighting fascism.)

I will—footsteps are squinching through mud out there in the dark. It's nearly 2300, so I guess it's the man coming to relieve me, and not the ghost of Col. Oldfitz, who was foully murdered by his daughter's Hessian lover way back in the Eighteenth Century. It is. So more tomorrow.

14 Oct. 43

What I wanted to say was, I'm glad you asked for requests because I am in a requesting mood these days. You shall have requests till they run out of your ears. As a starter—though by now you have some of my previous letters and know it's been going on a while—how about a minor matter like about a dozen pairs of light-weight wool-mixture socks, either gray or white, size 11 1/2? The wool and cotton mixture holds up better than the pure wool, which I would otherwise prefer as more expensive. But, alas, the mixture disintegrates less in washing. Thank you.

I got a sore left thumb, unheroically sprained when I fell carrying cases of Coca-Cola down the steep slippery slopes of the little valley in which we live. I'm a clumsy oaf.

Today we signed the payroll, so I'll draw two months' pay the last of the month. I'm a rich old man; and you won't be able to get your pretty but niggardly little hands on my 2 x $78.20 – 2 x $11.40.

It's probably good for you not to know exactly where I am and precisely what I am doing: it'll teach you patience, maybe, and, perhaps, something about that world in which women wait at home while their menfolks range afield or in ships or something. It all has a doubtless nice other-worldish aroma.

It's as late now as it was last night when I stopped writing and I'm sleepy. Ordinarily I sleep pretty late by Army standards—till 6:30—but that's not so awfully, awfully far away from the 11:30 or so it will be by the time I've got myself tucked in.

> Mountains of love and such,
> Dash

TLS LPT

To Mary Hammett

16 October 1943, Seattle, Washington

TWENTY TWO YEARS AGO I WAS WORKING A HORSE SHOW WHILE YOU WERE BEING BORN AND A STRANGE REDDISH ORANGE CREATURE YOU WERE

COMMA[1] MOSTLY EYE =LASHES AND MOUTH BUT YOU SOON IMPROVED STOP
HAPPY BIRTHDAY WITH LOVE PAPA=

S D HAMMETT.

1. Mary was born severely jaundiced.

TELEGRAM MARSHALL

To Lillian Hellman

17 October 1943, Alaska

My dear Miss Hellman—
Your undated favor postmarked the 9th inst. is at hand and contents duly noted, to wit; paragraph by paragraph:

¶ 1. I'm glad you're glad I asked for the ring and I'm glad you're glad to send it. But keep Army psychiatrists out of it: my two contacts with them have been pleasantly off-hand and I don't want to change my luck. The first one, at Fort Jay, when I took my physical for enlistment, said, "After reading your books I'm not going to ask you if you've ever had a nervous breakdown or things like that. You probably know more about all this than I do." And then we talked about detective stories. The second one—at Fort Monmouth when I was taking my overseas physical— asked as an afterthought when we'd finished talking about various Hollywood progressives of the 30's, and he had picked up his pen to OK my papers—"You're not nervous, are you?" He was already scribbling his signature when I said, "Oh no," mildly and uneagerly.

¶1, SEC.2. It's nice that your old man should like and have a high opinion of me. If his unemployment should ever become a problem I am sure we can get him a job as an Army psychiatrist.

¶2. I'm sorry to hear the bad news about what they've done to *The North Star,* but—well, *now* you know about Hollywood. And if I were you I'd take Kenneth's word for the importance of what the picture— however bitched up—says.[1]

¶3. We don't shine our shoes in Alaska, but I'm not aiming to spend the rest of the war here—as much as I like it—and the rest of the Abercrombie package sounds immediately useful and you are a sweetheart and I am grateful. And I will thank you again when the stuff gets here and I can see what I am thanking you for.

¶4. As you know by now you're not going to be allowed to complain about a lack of requests from me. I have a sleeping bag, probably not as good as the A & F one, but I've got to keep it and haven't room or back-muscles for another—no matter how lightweight. We're fairly bowed down under arctic equipment.

¶5. Give my best to Major M[c]Kelway when you write him.[2] Is he still in India? Things ought to be opening up down there now—or soon.

¶6. Joya's mother wrote me an ecstatic letter about the puppy the morning it arrived, and practically invited me to come there to live when I returned to the States.[3] That's all to the good as far as my matrimonial plans are concerned. But I don't know. It seems Joya thinks I ought to write a book in which she is the heroine and in which she can star on the screen. Do you suppose she's just trying to use me to further her career? I wouldn't want to be caught in that kind of trap.

¶6. SEC.2. Flora's a cute name for a poodle pup. And she sounds cute and I'm too pigheaded to admit this soon the possibility of her turning out unbeautiful.

That disposes of your letter for the time being, so let[']s put it aside for later rereading and go on to other matters.

I heard—over our radio this afternoon—a nice recording of Oscar soloing with the Philharmonic in Gershwin's Concerto in F.[4] Today I loafed, but tonight—all night and god knows how far into tomorrow— I've got to do some extracurricular work—some four thousand words of—of all things—writing! I could scream, chum. But as long as I can keep on writing this I won't have to start writing that, though I guess that's what you call pampering myself.

Addenda to previous notes on military urination, from Army Field Manual 211–11, page 55: "Prevent freezing of the penis when urinating by protecting it from the wind and afterwards by carefully buttoning the clothes."

The lights went off in my hut, so I've had to hunt up another place— the Message Center—in which to do my work. Having found a place in which to do my work I guess the logic of the situation suggests that I stop this and do it—and where logic leads there I stumble along; I'm that big a sucker for logic.

Take care of yourself, honey, for me and don't worry too much—some is natural and perfectly permissible—about the play.

>   Much love,
>   Hammett of the North,
>   big brother of Nanook

1. Ken Crawford was chief of the Washington bureau for *PM,* and one of Hellman's lovers.
2. St. Clair McKelway was managing editor of *The New Yorker* in charge of nonfiction from 1936 to 1939, when he gave up his editor's duties to concentrate on writing. He was a respected Profiles writer with whom Hellman had an affair.
3. Joya Johnson was the young daughter of a friend of Hammett's for whom he bought a poodle puppy.
4. Oscar is Oscar Levant.

ALS LPT

To Lillian Hellman

19 October 1943, Alaska

Dearest Lily—

Baby boy is restless today and unsettled and far from cheerful, probably because he has not finished a job he should have done some time ago, and what might be called his conscience is not at rest. (Or maybe he thinks somebody might give him hell about it.)

Anyway a box of Martin's food and beau-ti-ful pipe from the Plaza did a lot to pull him together again. Thank you, and thank you, and thank you, toots! You are a kind woman, and even I am not altogether worthy of you, I sometimes think.

And, lo! even as I write, what is that shining in the east? A new star of Bethlehem? Far better, it is a tobacco pouch and another pipe—this one a chubby briar easily carried in pockets—sent from Dunhill's by my Lily. (Reread the second paragraph from midway the third line.) Three packages from you in the last two mail deliveries is pretty swell stuff. Of course there was no letter, but——

There was a letter from my father who has "ordered a leg but can't tell when" he will get it. Further, he writes, "Reba sent me a clipping with Dick's picture taken with Annabella the Movie Star."[1] Now you know about my family. Aren't you glad we never married?

This is a bad time of the day, just after evening chow. Men come into the hut not knowing how they are going to kill the hours between now and bedtime. They fidget and make conversation and turn the radio up too loud and constitute an annoyance to elderly grouches. It's possible that they should be beheaded. They sometimes do not make me love them. They sometimes get themselves onto the nerves, if I make myself clear. It is that I am in possession of whims tonight. It is also that irritation comes upon me with an easiness. In addition, it is that they should cease the tapping of the foot in faulty concord with the dubious music on the radio of an inferior tone and go fuck themselves. What I mean is tonight I would not buy Victory Bonds.

(Come, come, Hammett, leave us stop this foolishness! Leave us resolve now to have at our chores tonight and clean them up if it takes to the morrow's noon. That's what's gnawing at your vitals, ain't it? And now that you've faced it, don't you feel better? I thought so!) Actually I feel better because I went up on the hill for a while and looked at boats at anchor in the dusk, with dim hills behind them, and a few planes coming in from their errands and tiny truck-headlights running along roads way down below me. But I guess I'll work tonight anyway. And something called Phil Spitally's Girl Orchestra—or something of the sort—on the radio is making me feel no longer better. It is an orchestra your enemies should not miss.

I hurry off to my duties before returning ill-humor turns me—god forbid—into a neglectful soldier.

I kiss your hand.

> Love—and thanks
> Hammett

1. Annabella was a French actress in several Hollywood movies from 1938 to 1947.

TLS LPT

To Lillian Hellman

27 October 1943, Alaska

Dearest Lily,

This typewriter is, I realize, out of place in my barabara: Pishtush, the Aleut squaw I am living with at the time, shivers a little as she looks at it with her beady black eyes and pulls the collar of her sealskin Mother Hubbard closer around her brown neck and her fingers are a bit unsteady as she engraves tomorrow's menu on a tusk by the light of a whale-oil lamp; and my pet blue fox Sasha (named after Heifitz, of course) whimpers a little and stirs restlessly on his bearskin rug.[1] But I'm a creature of civilization and must use modern implements wherever I find them. I think this typewriter was left here by a naturalist who came to these parts in the early '30s for *National Geographic*. Anyhow it was pretty rusty, but I worked on it with pieces of fat seal-meat—till the carriage would slide back and forth and, while God knows I'm not one to sneer at notch-cutting in sticks, still and all I do think that this is a more flexible means of communication, if you know what I mean. I mean, you can get more nuances into what you're saying this way, don't you think?

I do not think this is funny. I do not think anything about it. I simply report it as I remember it and as I am told about it. So...Raoul has been, for fourteen months, in a lung-hospital in San Fernando. His second wife, you too will remember, committed suicide in Las Vegas. His third wife recently jumped out of a hotel window in San Francisco, and has just died. This news comes to me from his first wife, who is in a hospital in Pittsburgh, having fallen down cellar steps one night while selling War Bonds. Do you want to write a book called *Journey into the Night*? Or do you think *Sanctuary* is a better title?

Not writing you for a few days hasn't been altogether my fault: I've been kind of on the jump, what with one little military duty and another. War isn't what it was in the good old days when, unless we have been lied to, a warrior could sulk in his tent and catch up on his correspondence, not having a typewriter to be heard tapping inside.

Sometime in the next couple of days I'm supposed to be photographed—Army publicity—and if the result is any good and I can get hold of a print I will send it to you so that you can continue to build up the largest collection of pictures of any one soldier since Napoleon, who was also a corporal, though at an earlier age than I.

One of the things wrong with this Army is that everybody thinks he had a better time in civilian life than he actually did have.

Tell me about women. Are they still the same? (Don't just say, yes. Are they still the same as what?) I have seen four women since July, but not to speak to. The last one I spoke to was a girl in the PX at Fort Lawton, in Seattle. My conversation went like this, "Coffee and doughnuts, please." I probably didn't even say, "Please, darling," because I was in a hurry to catch the boat. Tell me about trees too. I haven't even *seen* one of them since July.

Tonight I go on duty a little before midnight and wear the night through till breakfast time. Sleep well, honeybunch; no harm will come out of the northwest tonight; Hammett keeps watch there; even God can catch a nap.

> Love in great quantities,
> Dash

1. Hammett refers to the violinist Jascha Heifetz.

TLS LPT

To Lillian Hellman

29 October 1943, Alaska

Dearest Lily,

* * *

All right, so you told me so. I admit it, so don't let's have any more gabbing about it. Anyway, what with reading being as scarce as it is here, I worked on *The Circular Staircase* for quite a while—it took that long because I put it down on the slightest excuse and sometimes on none—and finally finished it, finding it as shabby as I remembered; and then today, wearing gloves, I picked up *Wuthering Heights*, which—remember me?[1] I never could get into—and guess what? That's right: I haven't finished it yet—am less than half through—but I'm having a good time reading it. Does that mean I should try some of those other pompous hacks you've tried to foist on me? Of course not. You were right this time and I was wrong, but that proves nothing—purely an isolated instance. (Crawl back into your kennel, Proust, and take Melville with you.) However, I guess I ought to thank you or something.

Is it true what I hear, that the Perelman–Nash musical is a big hit?[2] You New Yorkers had better reconsider while there's still time. That's going to make an awful lot of people awful mad, and all those people who are mad aren't going to be residents of Buck County either.

I hear mighty nice things about *The Watch on the Rhine* from my agents in various states, though the agent who reported from Georgia is the type of agent who writes to Alaska complaining about how cold and wet it is in Georgia, and the agent who reported from Pennsylvania is Pru Whitfield; but some of the other agents are not that type of agent at all.

No[w] I am going to get some rest. The Notre Dame–Navy football game will be shortwaved here starting at eight-fifteen in the morning which means that my hut will be no good for sleeping purposes until nearly noon.

> Love in quite noticeable quantities,
> Dash

1. A popular mystery novel by Mary Roberts Rinehart published in 1908; Emily Brontë wrote *Wuthering Heights*.
2. *One Touch of Venus*, a musical with music by Kurt Weill, book by S. J. Perelman, and lyrics by Ogden Nash, opened on 8 October 1943 at the Imperial Theatre in Manhattan and ran 567 performances.

RETYPED AT LILLIAN HELLMAN'S DIRECTION LPT

To Lillian Hellman

31 October 1943, Alaska

Dear Lily—

All letters from you are nice; but now and then comes one that's so extra-special double portion triple-ply nice, like yesterday's, that I don't exactly know what to do about it. I can't say, "Gee, I'd like to see her!"

and phone you for a date. And I can't go send you some flowers that would get to you right away. And there's not much use of my promising I'll never again complain about your twisting your hair, is there? You'd know I meant a lot by that, but you wouldn't believe I'd stick to it. There must be something I can do, if I can only hit on it. Meanwhile—it *was* a nice letter and I thank you.

The approaching chill of winter led me to get out my sleeping-bag and spend last night in it. So today I've gone around emitting a corpse-like aroma: the bag had been packed in my rucksack along with some clothes chemically treated for use in gas attacks and the stuff they were treated with smells like embalming fluid, and, for all I know, in some two-birds-with-one-stone twist of the Army's, may actually be that.

I finished *Wuthering Heights* and had a good time throughout, though I'm not sure the book isn't a rather shameful waste of some good characters.

* * *

Things to think about sometime, no. 204: the Texan who sleeps across from me was telling me about one of his brothers. "They call him Catfish," he said. "You know, he's kind of dark."

It is latish now and I must be breakfasted and on duty by seven or so in the morning; so—

> Love and love and love,
> Dash

I'm told it's now permissible to tell you I'm in the Aleutians—and after all these lies I've written you about floating down the Nile!

ALS LPT

To Lillian Hellman

6 November 1943, Alaska

Dearest Lily,

You'd be surprised how little I've seen, heard, and done since I last reported to you. Even if it had happened to the Benets' relations they couldn't make a story out of it, though God knows that's a daring statement to make.[1]

So, if I've got nothing to tell you, it's obvious that I'm writing this because I want to talk to you, which makes it a kind of love letter, only I'm too old to write love letters. I've been looking at that picture in *Yank* again. I think I sent you a copy of it: it's the one sprawled on a bench with a pipe in hand and radio tubes on shelves behind me. I look like God's older brother, the one that always stuck up for Him but never thought the Kid had enough gumption to make His mark in the world. Or maybe I look more like Asey Mayo.[2] Anyway I don't look like the type that ought to be writing love letters, so even if I love you and miss you and you have got beautiful wrists I'll have to just let it go at that. Those things happen; they are facts: I accept them; I do not have to go into an unseemly song and dance about them. (No temper now! Leave us be adult. And leave us have no caustic remarks about the goyim.) I will go so far, however, as to say you are a sweetheart, I mean even in addition to the wrists. Maybe I'll even write you a love poem, to wit:

LOVE POEM

I am silly
About Lily.
Without Lily,
I am silly
Willy-nilly.

Kind of a nice old-English air about it, eh? All right, all right, I like it, moderately, though I'm not really sure I'd want it included in the definitive edition of my works.

It approaches four o'clock in the morning of 7 Nov and I still have about three hours of on-duty ahead of me, to be followed by breakfast and perhaps a couple of hours of listening to the Army–Notre Dame football game, which starts on our radio, via shortwave, at seven-forty-five. Thereafter I will sleep the day away, fitfully, of course, as Louis and the old do.

> Mountains of love,
> Dash

1. William Rose and his younger brother Stephen Vincent Benét were prominent literary figures, both poets, and both associated with the *Saturday Review of Literature*, for which William Rose Benet served as editor.
2. Asey Mayo was the detective in novels set in Cape Cod by Phoebe Atwood Taylor. In *Punch with Care* (1946), Mayo's housekeeper-cousin Jennie describes him as "Tall, lean, salty Asey Mayo, the Codfish Sherlock, the Hayseed Sleuth."

TLS LPT

To Lillian Hellman

17–18 November 1943

CPL. S.D. HAMMETT, 3118358
14TH SIG. SERV. DET.
APO #980, C/O PM
SEATTLE, WASH.

Dearest Lily—

I suppose no great harm will come from letting you go on juggling the parts of my address around hither and yon on the envelope, and it probably does get pretty dull always writing them in the same order. So the GI form above is not to be considered in any way as a criticism of your [arrangement]: it's simply there for you to refer to someday when you get the whole thing hopelessly tangled. After all, you *do* want your letters to reach me, *don't* you?

Speaking of things from one person reaching another, did [you ever get the] radiogram I sent you on 14 Oct.?

You are please to pick me out a lawyer, a young one who will have reached his prime when I come home from the wars. What we are going to due is sue a Philadelphia newspaper. I don't know which one, but I am in possession of a clipping that reads—listen!—:

"RICH SHIRKERS

"Dashiell Hammett, novelist and reformer said in an interview:

"'If it wasn't for the poor the world would become depopulated. The rich don't seem to seem to have [any] children.'

"Then he added with a smile:

"'The rich have their twin sixes, the poor have their six twins.'"

Old Henry Ward Hammett himself—with dialogue by Kay Kaiser's gag-men![1]

You may think we're pretty much out of things 'way up here—oh, yes, you do! but you're wrong. Special Services keep up to the dot. For instance, last Monday we had a re-broadcast of Jack Benny's Mother's Day program, with timely gags about the Kentucky Derby and everything. It was pretty difficult to imagine we weren't sitting in the waiting room at 21, with Jimmie at the dial, and you late for dinner—held up by a Dramatists Guild meeting no doubt. (Stop flirting with Arthur Richman!)[2]

It's nearly one in the A.M. and I've just come in from my soldierly duties—stopping at the messhut for fried eggs and coffee on my way home—and now I have smoked my old man's post-meal pipe and am ready for sleep. So what's stopping me?

> Love,
> Dash

1. Henry Ward Beecher, brother of Harriet Beecher Stowe, was a celebrated nineteenth-century minister and moral crusader. Kay Kaiser was a band leader whose radio variety program was called *Kay Kaiser's Kollege of Musical Knowledge*.
2. James Coslove, known as Jimmie the Doorman, was a fixture at "21" from its days as a speakeasy until his retirement in 1955. Arthur Richman was a playwright who flourished in the 1920s.

ALS LPT

To Lillian Hellman

19 November 1943, Alaska

Dearest Lily,

Three letters from you yesterday made it kind of like Bastil[l]e Day for the French or May Day for the Rooshians. That sort of thing has my approval: the whole trouble at Valley Forge was doubtless with the mail deliveries, maybe coupled with the fact that most of the members of *that* army seem to have been chumming around with illiterates, there being a pronounced shortage of female playwrights at the time.

Poor baby! you are having a tough time of it with the dentist, aren't you? That tittying around is no fun! I took the easy way, having them all out and the bone whittled down in practically one fell swoop. God knows I wouldn't advise you to do that; but it *is* easier than "having them taken care of." I hope you're past the bad part by the time this gets to you, and don't go having any more misunderstandings that lead people— named Tushnett or not—to take you apart. I like it up here, but you will spoil it for me if I have to sit around and worry about what you are up to. You're supposed to worry about me, not me you!

Lin wrote me she had a job: "I just run around and read up things for a lady radio announcer. She's really top man in the fashion world; but she likes to talk about penicillin and basic English." Lin seems to like it as much as she'll like any until Albertus Magnus gives her one. She sent me some toiletries for Christmas, no Kotex, and—you could knock me over with an iceberg—the right tobacco mixture from Dunhill's. I know they have my recipe on file there, but who ever supposed Lin wouldn't have thought up something different? It was sweet of her, and, what's more important, I now burn mighty nice-tasting tobacco in my pipes.

* * *

Much love,
D

TLS LPT

To Lillian Hellman

Thanksgiving Day, 1943 [25 November], Alaska

Dearest Lily—
So we had Turkey Day, 1943, and the rest of that holiday meal the Army likes to publicize so much, and most of us overate, hoping we would not have to skimp too much the next week or so to make up for the day's feasting, which no doubt goes to show we are an ungrateful lot. The day wasn't a holiday, but I managed to trim a couple of hours off my labors, and I figure an hour saved is an hour earned.

I've been reading at Howard Spring's *My Son, My Son* and as fresh as ever is my amazement that anybody could write so long a book without ever once letting his imagination get a word in edgewise. Even Montgomery Ward loses out to the muse once in a while, but Howard Spring never. No wild-eyed poet he.

Some time ago I wrote you that I had some extra-curricular work in the shape of writing to do, well for a miracle, I did it and a major and a sergeant are now winging their way to San Francisco with a 4000 word M.S. that's to be hatched into a booklet called *The Battle for the Aleutians* or something of the sort. The local army folk think it's hot stuff. If it turns out fairly all right I'll see that you get a copy. (I could have wrangled a trip back to the states for myself, but only at the risk of finding myself trapped there for other writing jobs.)

Yes, ma'am, it's thirteen years just about this day. And that's nice, that is, and I thank you, I do. They have been fine grand years and you are a fine grand woman and for all I know I must have been a fine grand man to have deserved them and you. And, with such a start, think of, not only the next thirteen, but the next after that! A lot of very great poetry has been written about much less, and I mean that.

Raoul Whitfield, writing me about the death by suicide of his second wife in succession, says: "I felt pretty much lost—I don't seem to get over these things easily." You can have that for your scrapbook.

I haven't asked you to send me anything for more than a week. That won't do, you'll begin to think I don't love you. So will you send me some foodstuffs? Non-sweets are best. We eat too much candy and sugars here. A cheese would be nice, but I leave it in your hands. Things that come in cans or containers in which they'll keep, and preferably, that can be eaten cold. The dingus for the Postmaster is attached hereto.

[end of letter missing]

ALU LPT

To Lillian Hellman

29 November 1943, Alaska

Dear Lily,

The grouchiness has abated enough, maybe, for you to get a civil word or two out of me today, unless, of course, you are going to start an argument or something with me before I get this letter finished. But if you'll just shut up and keep quiet until I get it done we'll get along all right. And don't sit there sulking about it either.

A fruitcake and some sardines from Herman arrived today, as did a package of Martin's goodies from Nancy, which—am I on the right track?—is one of your pen-names, I imagine. Thank you, Ma'am, very much indeed. You help keep me a very well fed soldier. It's probably too late in this war, but in the next one I'm going to see if I can have you made Quartermaster General. You seem to be able to give more attention to the individual needs of the man in uniform than he does.

Tomorrow's payday, thank God, so I won't have to be going around with only $837.76 in my pockets. (I just counted it, having nothing else to do.) Money is a problem here: what to do with it. Such gambling as I do usually leaves me a little ahead, and you'd get bowlegged carrying back from the PX more than a couple of dollars' worth of goods. Maybe I ought to start buying liquor. I feel like a Dupont making money out of a war.

* * *

Today you're in the hospital. I hope you're OK and not frightened or any of that foolishness, but I imagine you won't be with Stettin running the show.

I may shift over to another job, something to do with orientation; you know, trying to tell the troops what the hell they are fighting for and the like. It's up in the air just now, but if it looks as if it might be reasonably reasonable I think I'll give it a try.

It's time I was stumbling over to the mess hut for some eggs and coffee before I go to bed, so....

Get through that hospital stuff and that stuff with your teeth and then stay all in one piece. You're not supposed to start falling apart as soon as my back is turned. I'd figured that with reasonable care you could be made to last a number of years longer, and I haven't made any plans for replacing you. So cut it out.

> Much love,
> SDH

TLS HRC

To Josephine Dolan Hammett

30 November 1943, Aleutians

Dear Jose,

Here's a check to split three ways for Christmas, unless you and the girls would rather match for it, winner take all.

And I hope you all have a very, very Merry Christmas and a happy Happy New Year.

And I also hope that none of you will be dopey enough to go round kidding herself that the old man is having a sad holiday season in the north country. I can promise you he'll be doing at least all right and, the chances are, a lot better than that, and he hopes you all do as well.

* * *

Kiss the youngsters for me.

> Love,
> SDH

TLS Marshall

To Lillian Hellman

20 December 1943, Aleutians

Dear Lilibell—

I read *The North Star* last night and am very fond of you today. The *N. S.* is a simple, compact, neat and moving piece of work and you are all right, you are, and in many ways you have my approval, you have.

* * *

Just because I am away you are not to construct any batty notions about the course of this war. The Italian campaign can be viewed in whichever of the following forms you like, but in no event is to be considered important in itself, a., as a simple sop to newspaper readers until we do whatever it is we are going to do next; b., as a get-Rome-for-prestige affair with or without additional trimmings; or, c., as a matter of getting protected air and sea bases for other invasion operations, perhaps across the Adriatic, as some recent doings seem to hint. That's all! Anything else is nonsense, even if it happens, and you are not to believe in it.

Now about peace offers and such. Here I must be stern. Under no circumstances are you to visualize a world without at least 18 months of European war, and an additional 18 of Asiatic, ahead of it. Of course things could happen to cut that time down, but that still doesn't keep it from being silly to think it's going to happen. (The later success of parachutes didn't keep early crackpots who smashed themselves up jumping off roofs with big umbrellas from still being crackpots.)

I read your letter while eating noon chow and, going back to work, I had to go through a sort of very short tunnel through the snow, and as I went into the sort of tunnel I unbuttoned my parka, and some of the snow ceiling of the sort of tunnel broke off and went down the back of my neck and I wished to god I was in that cozy Lenox Hill Hospital with you.

Now I haven't got any snow down my back, so I just wish I were with you.

> Love,
> SDH

ALS LPT

To Mary Hammett

Christmas Day 1943, The Aleutians

Dear Mary,

This is far from being the worst Christmas I have ever spent—figure it out for yourself: out of forty-nine of them some *must* have been sour—

and, as a matter of fact, it stacks up pretty well against the best of them. It was a holiday—the first we've had up here, and that includes Sundays—for those of us who didn't have duties that had to be done no matter what the day, so we slept until around eleven. Early noon chow was at eleven-fifteen. That was our big meal of the day—our Christmas dinner. For those of us who slept late it was, of course, breakfast, and shrimp cocktails, turkey, and the rest of the trimmings, including mince pie, pumpkin pie and fruit cake, make a substantial breakfast; so naturally there was nothing to do afterwards but go back to our huts and lie down while the stuff digested. We hadn't been up long enough to be sleepy, no matter how much we had eaten, so what's easier than to get to talking back and forth? And talk in the army, after it's exhausted furloughs and rotation, gets around to women and liquor, and, in Alaska at least, finally settles on liquor. Liquor, of course, is illegal on Army posts, so what finally appears—just out of this talk, mind you, though it seems to come from under bunks and loose floor boards and such—cannot be liquor, though it looks like, tastes like it, and has pretty much the same effect. So we spend the afternoon talking—a great many things are remembered out of our pasts, but few of them are told straight: most of them are dressed up beyond recognition—and taking what seem to be authentic swigs of this liquor that is against army regulations and therefore must be imaginary, since it is inconceivable that any of us would break the rules. So along about five o'clock we're all feeling pretty good, and there is an issue of beer to be had at the mess-hut—not much, it's true, but we haven't had *any* beer for a couple of months. In a box under my bed there are some cans of pâté de foie gras and caviar and lobster and smoked salmon in olive oil and one thing and another that ought to go pretty well with beer, so we throw it into a sack and go up to the mess-hut; and mighty pretty going it is too, with our little valley all white under a clean fresh coating of snow. And in the mess-hut we eat and sip beer for a couple of hours until we're stuffed to the ears. And then I know where there is a vacant typewriter—so I come over to write this. (You can't call what I've described an exciting day, but try to find anything unpleasant in it, any worries, any sources of irritation, any of the things that ordinarily spoil people's days!)

I read *Under Cover* in the condensed *Omnibook* version and didn't think much of it.[1] Anybody who was in on as much as the author claims would know a lot more than he tells. As a matter of fact, he tells nothing that hasn't been widely printed before, and a great deal that he leaves out—particularly about the people higher up—has been told by others. He reads to me like a rat who failed to make much money out of one side and is now trying to play the other, without hurting anybody who might stand in his way [i]f he wants to jump back again.

I've got to go back to my hut now and see what's cooking.

> Mountains of love,
> Papa

1. *Under Cover* by John Roy Carlson.

TLS MARSHALL

To Lillian Hellman

28 December 1943, Aleutians

Dearest Lily,

Again it's been some time since I have set myself down to do this, and again the excuse is about the same: I haven't yet tamed all the details of the new job. And, added to that at the moment, the weather has gone whimsical and doesn't give us very many really dull moments. If one thing isn't becoming impass[a]ble another is caving in. I think the island is having a lot of fun with us. It's a little rough on us sometimes, but I dare say it serves the purpose of keeping us from mildewing in the absence of much activity on anything you could call a fighting front.

I've been looking at my calendar: six months ago tonight—and it's night now—I said goodby to you and went back to Wood, to take off for Shenango and eventually these parts. That's kind of a long time to be without seeing you and I don't know that—except for a war—I would for a moment consider it practicable. Sometimes I think I must really hate fascism and such to do the things I do and put up with the things I put up with. The only other explanation would be that I'm a strong character, and somehow that doesn't seem reasonable to me.

Christmas was a nice day. I ate a lot of turkey and things at noon, had a few drinks in the afternoon, and did myself very grand in the evening with a cold supper of beer—we had a couple of bottles apiece, the first since some time in October—and pâté de foie, caviar, anchovies and the like from your boxes. I've had more exciting Christmases, but I don't remember many that were freer from any sort of irritation or small bothers. It was a nice serene day, and I hope you did as well for yourself.

Now do you want to tell me what I gave you for Christmas?

It's getting on toward eleven o'clock, so I reckon I'll insert myself into sheepskin and parkas and things and go down to the mess hut for something to eat on my way home. Thank god the weather will be beating on my back all the way: this is no night to be facing the elements, or the ghosts of dead Aleuts, or whatever it is that's abroad.

My new guess on things military is that when we open our western European front the Germans will try to persuade the Japs to strike north at Russia, to lighten the pressure on the German eastern front. (That's the kind of wishful thinking we go in for in my neighborhood. Jesus, do we pant for something to happen on our side of the tracks!)

> I love you, madam, and trust you are trying to deserve it.
> S.D.H.

TLS LPT

To Lillian Hellman

30 December 1943, Aleutians

Dearest Lily,

Well, by one means or another, we've finally got this year on its last legs or thereabouts. I don't see how it can last more than another day at the most. It hasn't been such a bad year, taking it all in all, but I expect better things of 1944, though it would be a waste of time to try to pin me down to any detailed account of what I expect and why. I just expect.

A letter and a pair of socks came from you today and both were received with thanks and things.

You sound as if you're having a good time with the butchering and harvesting and other bits of husbandry, and I shall certainly send you an order for the ham. But this week I must use my order for tobacco. Will you have Dunhill send me another pound of my prescription (it's #A 10432) and, while they're at it, I'd like some cigars, fairly heavy Havanas; preferably in the panatela size, but that part isn't too important. And, come to think of it, I don't know why I should wait a week for the ham. I can write Nancy—can't I—and she won't think I'm blackmailing her.

In re Nancy: I'm meddling with soldiers' training again and from time to time there will be a good deal of material I want that'll take too long to get through military channels. So (a) can you spare her for some chores, and (b) will you arrange to reward her for the additional toil, and (c) will you stick your pretty little nose into the matter now and then so that I will have—at no cost to myself—the advantage of your sagacity anent world affairs. What I'll be primarily interested in is what's cooking in the national mind, and what people say and print about the origins of the war, the conduct of the war, and what's going to happen at home and abroad after the war. (While I think of it, I'd like to have the "News of the Week in Review" section of the Sunday *Times* airmailed me as soon as it comes out each week.)

The North Star is scheduled for our Post theater on 9 and 10 January. I need not tell you I'm agog. (Did I write you that I'm trying to get 16mm prints of it and *The Watch* to use in the training program?)

The next time you think of it will you stick some County Trust Company blank checks in a letter or two for me. I used up the last blanks I had sending various Hammetts Christmas presents. (What *did* I give you this year?)

Joya's mother, I figure, can help our romance most by aging rapidly. She is a Kentucky girl, suh, and "cain't figuah out why people always know right away she's a southe'nah, suh." I'm sorry about the puppy, but I hope you paid no attention to the encores.

Duty calls.

> Much love,
> SDH

TLS LPT

To Nancy Bragdon

Hammett was founding editor of a camp newspaper, The Adakian, *which published its first trial issue on 19 January 1944. The paper was published daily in print runs between 3,000 and 6,000 copies and was distributed on Adak only.*

1 January 1944, Aleutians

Dear Nancy,

* * *

A couple of days ago I wrote Lily asking her if she could spare some of your time to do some chores for me, if you'd be willing to do some chores for me, and if the two of you would make some sort of what are sometimes called "arrangements" covering the chores for me. Actually, of course, I did not really *ask* her: I assumed—in the slightly high-handed manner you learn by the time you send your first uniform to the cleaners—that *everybody* is just simply tickled to death to do *anything* for our soldiers. Still so assuming—What else can I do? Wait a month or six weeks for an answer?—here's what's what:

I'm fooling around with training programs again (the Hammett-trained soldier will win the war) and at the moment my principal interests are:

1. The causes of the war.
2. The progress of the war.
3. What the people in all countries including the U.S. are bothering their pretty little heads about.
4. How the same folk are affected by the war.
5. What comes after the war (a) international, and (b) domestic.

I can get practically anything I want through military channels, of course, but it often takes too long, and the time-lag is one of our major problems. So do you want to be a speeder upper of dope and data to the troops?

Good! Here's what I'd like to have as a starter:

The *Sunday Times* has a *Review of the Week* section. I'd like to have that sent me by airmail as soon as you can get hold of it. (If it, or anything else of the sort, is too heavy for overseas airmail, rip it into suitable fragments and send them on.)

The *Times* usually prints in full all more or less important statements of more or less important people, and it's seldom that *Time* or *Newsweek* give more than a condensation. So there's something else for airmail.

I'd like a daily, if possible, airmail batch of clippings from the New York press—cartoons, editorials, news, letters to the editor, anything that comes under heading #3 above, or under any other heading.

I'd also like a heavy dose of columnists and those dreamers who write for the *Nation*, *New Republic*, etc. (I get the *New Masses* here.) And don't let's save postage stamps; send me things when you find them, if it's a dozen times a day. And when in doubt, send it.

On books, as a rule, the simplest and quickest way is probably for me to order them direct from the publisher and have him bill me in care of Lily. I've already done that with Random House, and will probably do it with others from time to time. But I would like a charge account opened for me with Paul Elder's Book Co. (I think that's how he does business), San Francisco, Calif. Maybe the easiest way would be to keep a credit there. In any event, will you fix it up so he'll send the books here as I order them and bill me there?

I've got to see about some mail arrangements so I can get stuff that exceeds the authorized dimensions—I want a lot of maps and stuff—and I'll let you know about that when I know about that.

You are to involve Lily heavily in all this and she will explain anything that this letter doesn't make clear (or has she been lying to me all these years about being psychic?) but you aren't to let her pay for anything. She is not to get off that easy: she is to nose out items for me, and she is not to suppress those she thinks might have a bad influence on me.

This will do for the nonce, but you can expect to be flooded with increasing requests for this and that, and, if sometimes there's a certain vagueness about what I ask for, just send me something, so long as it comes by airmail.

Gratefully,
SDH

TLS HRC

To Lillian Hellman

2 January 1944, Aleutians

Dearest Lily,

* * *

Last night—taking for granted that you had spoken to Nancy about the chores for the Army and that everything was hotsy-totsy—I wrote her what I want to start with. (In the event that she can't do it, will you find somebody who can? And, in any case, it would be nice if you could get some of your more knowing friends to send me what they can when they can.)

I'm not sure I gave you a clear idea of what I'm up to in my other letter, so I'll try again. The radio news we get here is up-to-date but necessarily very sketchy; *Time, Newsweek, Life,* daily newspapers, etc., as well as the Army publications, are usually weeks and weeks old. This time-lag makes it difficult to tie in background stuff with current news. Any reduction in this lag, no matter how slight, is all to the good. Also, *Time, Life* and *Newsweek*—so far our main sources—actually don't have a hell of a lot to do with—or even knowledge of—what's going on in people's heads: they represent a sort of college graduate dream world. And the letters most soldiers get from home aren't much help.

Now the program I'm working on is designed to tell him as clearly as possible what's cooking—why we got into this war and what we stand to get out of it, good or bad; how the war is progressing, and what people at home and any place abroad think of it; what's going on in the U.S. and elsewhere, what people think and do; what plans are being concocted at home and abroad for post-war life, and what people think of them; in short, we want to produce a soldier who, up here, knows more, not less, than he ever knew about his world in civilian life down there.

To do this we have—or will have in a few days—a daily newspaper, a local radio station, moving pictures, lecturers, bulletin boards, and weekly classes; and, which is not to be sneezed at, we have our public penned up on an island where they can't get away from us without swimming in some of the coldest water known to whales.

So there's my problem; and the answer is largely you, Nancy and airmail. You want to win the war, don't you? Well, then?

> Love,
> SDH

TLS HRC

To Lillian Hellman

5 January 1944, Aleutians

Dear Lilishka,

It's after one in the morning and I am tired, though I didn't start to work until after noon today, and it is cold in my office hut in spite of the Diesel burner's being on full blast, and I guess I've got all of a mile to walk home, the way the path winds, if you can find the path, and if you can't you're likely to plop down through a soft snow crust into the brook, and how would *you* like that? So I reckon I'll write the cutie a letter to keep her from sulking and then light out for home and bed.

Have you read Ralph's story of his doings in Africa, "The Battle Is the Pay-Off"?[1] I've only had time to glance at it, but believe me or not, it looks pretty good, and the *Infantry Journal* calls it "one of the finest if not the finest battle report to be written on this war." It may be that our boy has found himself. In that case, since I certainly helped him with his early editorials—something about which I have heretofore seen no reason for boasting—I shall claim that he is my protégé. (You need not tell Leane about this just yet.)[2]

I'm in process of flooding Nancy with requests for this and that. Do not let her weaken. Encourage her, tell her an airmail stamp is not something to wince at the sight of, point out how airmail deliveries at Valley Forge might have changed the outcome of the battle of Germantown. (If she does not know what the outcome of the battle of Germantown was, tell her; if you do not know, look it up.)[3]

I cannot explain about Frank Sinatra to you. I think it is that he looks hungry, sings slow, and does not bellow. At least two of these things should not be discouraged in singers. But I cannot even now explain the considerably greater to-do that was made over Rudy Vallee back when you and I and love were young, and it is not my intention to take up any new subjects while the old ones remain unmastered. I am slow but thorough.

* * *

Folk who know I know you ask me what you are doing now. I am tired of just telling them you are writing a play. I think I will start quoting Louis about your collaboration with Edna Ferber.[4] (When I first came to this island the Texan who sleeps across from me used to tell people who asked him what I was like, "He's just like anybody else except he's got more sense," until he got tired of that and for a week or two went around replying, "He's the meanest, most disagreeable old son of a bitch you ever saw," until he got tired of that. Now I think (a) nobody asks him, and (b) he wouldn't pay any attention to them if they did.)

I ran across a nice quotation from Frederick the Great today: "It is not sufficient to kill Russians. One has to knock them over."

That, deviously, reminds me. I could use some quick stuff, with pictures and human interest and all, on the destroyer explosion.[5] (Am I going to be a nuisance!)

My God, it's after two o'clock, and now I am really tired.

> Much love, darling,
> SDH

1. A story by Ralph Ingersoll in *PM*.
2. Leane Zugsmith wrote special features for *PM*.
3. On 2 October 1777 Americans were defeated when one of four attacking columns got lost in the fog.
4. In his letter to Hellman of 31 December 1943, Hammett referred to a letter from Louis Kronenberger: "He wrote, and I quote, 'The other day there was a large lunch in honor of Miss H., who sat hearing herself praised from 1 to 4 and then (I'm told) burst into tears because they wouldn't continue with the eulogies until 6. She and Edna Ferber have started collaborating on an Old Testament play laid mostly on Mr. Sinai and tentatively called Jahveh." Ferber was a Jewish novelist (*Showboat, Giant*) and playwright who in the 1920s and 1930s collaborated with George S. Kaufman on three Broadway hits (*Dinner at Eight, The Royal Family, Stage Door*) that were later made into hit movies.
5. On 3 January 1944 the U.S.S. *Turner* blew up in the Atlantic off Ambrose Channel near New York Harbor.

TLS HRC

To Lillian Hellman

8 January 1944, Aleutians

Dearest Lily,

A package of food came from you yesterday, a package of nice thick socks today. Thank you, darling, you are an elegant woman and I was no fool when I took up with you some years ago. Buying you those drinks in Tony's was one of the best investments I ever made. I haven't sampled the cheese yet, but it has the proper look; the rest of the groceries are fine and the socks are just what I wanted. Thank you, Ma'am.

Each mail brings me letters of thanks from the folk whose Christmas presents you picked out, and you seem to have behaved nobly about it and I thank you for that too. Leane, Maggie, Herman and Nancy have been heard from and seem enthusiastic about their gifts, though it's true Herm had at the time he wrote only your promise that you were getting a robe for him. My instinct was always right in trying to make you do my yule shopping for me, so that is established precedent from now on out; be I at home or abroad!

Your financial explanations muddle me a little, but I like those large round figures and even the thought that you may not know what you are doing does not disturb me. It is only money and what is there is yours and I only ask you to continue your reports to me because I like to hear about having or having had money. You and Nancy are very cute about the whole thing and as soon as I can I am going to send each of you an ivory abacus.

The coat sounds good. All I ask is that you buy an extravagant one so that when you tell people I gave it to you for Christmas they will say, "Ah, that Hammett! He certainly treats his women well!" (I'm thinking primarily of debs and shopgirls; you may tell actresses that you won the coat in a crap game.)

It is nearly eleven o'clock and I am going down to the mess hut to eat and will go on with this when I return. I have eaten and I have returned. Hamburger, sweet potatoes, coffee and a few-minute chat with a Venezuelan dancer or some such who is USO-showing here.

The pamphlet I mentioned some time ago is now coming off the presses in far San Francisco, should arrive anon, may be mailed home;

so you may expect a copy.[1] I saw an advance copy a day or two ago and it isn't bad for its purpose, but do not expect anything approaching *War and Peace*, which is by a Russian (pre-Soviet) author.

I don't know why you shouldn't be able to send me a copy of the play. I'll look into the matter and, if some sort of super-permission is necessary, will see what can be done about getting it. I don't have to tell you I am anxious to see it. Tomorrow I go down to see *The North Star*, which I hear is a worthy effort though probably propaganda.

I had—maybe I wrote you this before—a Christmas card from Irene and am about to write her a letter.

Leane wrote me that you had probably told me all about Carl's book, which you had not and which you need not.[2] A good many of your friends seem to think you and I devote a large part of our correspondence to them.

I did not exactly understand what you wrote about entertaining soldiers for me at Christmas so it is but only natural that I should not exactly understand your entertaining limey sailors unless, in your twisted oriental way, you look on Christmas as an extra day of atonement for your people.

I came up here tonight to work and now I have got an idea of something to work on, so your loss will no doubt be the Army's gain as I quit this and become once more a small, brittle, false-toothed cog in the United Nation's War Machine.

> Love,
> SDH

1. "The Battle of the Aleutians," a 24-page pamphlet by Hammett and Robert Colodny, was published early in 1944.
2. Carl Randau was a playwright married to Leane Zugsmith.

TLS LPT

To Lillian Hellman

11 January 1944, Aleutians

Dear Lilishka:

Climatic conditions have been such that the hoods you sent me could be tested in God's own laboratory, and I have to report that they held up nobly. The chamois face-piece was no go, but I ripped it out and carried on with the rest of the rig and very fine carrying on it was. The fact that I have any face at all now—wait till I put my hand up and see if I have—is all due to you and I shall try to repay you some day in case an otherwise busy posterity overlooks it, the lice. The socks too stand between my feet and the unkinder elements—though I *am* compelled to wear boots also—so I may say truthfully that you've clothed me from head to toe.

Today I had a letter from Santa Monica, California, postmarked January 31, 1944, which makes me think that maybe a man is safer up here than in your mad civilian world—unless a month has slipped by us unnoticed—a thing that could happen.

Such news as we have is such news as we can't write home. It would as likely as not bore you anyhow. It may be that in a little while we'll be a little less hush-hush and can babble a bit about this and that. Meanwhile I hope you think I'm the repository of a great many military secrets— which I am not—and know just what's going on—which I suspect nobody does, not even Raymond Gram Swing, or is that going too far?[1]

After a great deal of early foolishness the Japanese propaganda machine—we get Radio Tokyo and Domei—seems to be doing a pretty skillful job on New Asia. I've got a suspicion that Hitler took a leaf from his partner's book in his New Year's Day speech, which, considering the spot he is in, seemed to me to be a very unclumsy affair. You might call it kind of nimble, as a matter of fact—remembering Smuts's recent statement on the future of the British Empire in Europe.[2]

The night calls me—and boy, oh, boy has it got a loud voice—so this, my own dear, is all of this for the time being.

You are to take care of yourself. You are not to overeat. You are to keep your feet dry. You are to wrap up when you go out. You are not to sit in drafty places. You are not to sit up late in smoky rooms. You are to avoid committee meetings and other such rat-races where flu germs are rife, nothing healthy being able to stand the atmosphere. If you do those things I will continue to love you—

> Like now for instance,
> SDH

1. Swing was a respected political commentator during the war.
2. Jan Christiaan Smuts was prime minister of South Africa from 1939 to 1948.

TLS LPT

To Lillian Hellman

0130 Sun, 16 January 1944, Aleutians

Dearest Lily,

Maybe it's because it's soothing or something that I do this before I drag myself off to bed, though today I only worked thirteen hours, which is kind of like a holiday. Boy, am I glad I got in plenty of loafing on Army time before this: it'll still take them a little while to break even with me—and there is always a good chance that I shall presently get things well enough organized to take life reasonably easy again; and if you can't take life easy in the Army where can you?

Tomorrow morning, if everything goes well, or if it doesn't, at this time I'll be almost ready to go to press with the first issue of a daily news-paper—just one of my works-in-progress: I've got more irons in the fire than the wind's got compass-points to blow from. And, believe it or be stubborn about it, starting a paper in the Army is just as dizzy a business as starting a New York daily in Brooklyn, though I will say I've got more confidence in my hastily gathered staff here than I had in that net-full of zanies we got together under *PM*'s roof three or four years ago. (The paper won't be mailable—we'd have to pass up too much stuff of inter-est to the men here—so you'll probably never see a copy of it and can't disprove any lies I tell you about its high quality.)

Most of my tentative staff are youngsters who haven't been up here very long, who are fascinated by a chance to work with the old master on something like this, and who, when they need hopping up, respond immediately to any pointless tale of your and my and Ralph's early days with *PM*. Many of the faultily educated look on that sheet as a milestone or something, and the better educated have a good deal of respect for you.

A letter came from you this afternoon and that didn't hurt the day at all. I never saw the day it hurt.

Your instinct is right: you can't have a character say, "Everything can't be put in words." That's as bad as, "It's just like in a book," "These thing's just happen—you can't explain them," or, as everybody has written at one time or another, "I don't know—it's all so crazy." So mend your ways and do not wear your pretty little finger nails out against the bottom boards of the barrel.

I see, according to Leonard Lyons—whose column reached me because it had the usual inaccurate account of my Aleutian booklet— that you've torn up two acts of your play and started all over, which means, I suppose, either that you've never started a play or that you have finished one.[1] I get an oc[c]asional clipping, but few from our clipping bureau, meaning, I dare say, that I seldom make the movie page of the Round Rock, Texas, *Bugle-Bulletin*.

* * *

This is the bottom of the page; this is 2:20 in the morning; this is time I went home to bed; this is the end.

> Much love,
> SDH

1. Leonard Lyons was a syndicated gossip columnist.

TLS LPT

To Lillian Hellman

24 January 1944, Aleutians, early A.M.

Dearest Lily,

Very fine large batches of clippings have been coming in daily, with a lot of mighty useful stuff among them. You and Nancy may consider yourselves practically indispens[a]ble parts of the Alaskan Department Army Training Program. My thanks to you both.

I had a letter from Max this morning. He still complains of his health and loss of weight—also of the quality of horseracing in New Orleans. He does seem to have lost a lot of poundage, not necessarily a good thing at his age even if he is overweight.

My own old man, dissatisfied with the first artificial leg he got in Baltimore—it probably wasn't youthful enough in contour for him—has sent it back and is getting another. Maybe it didn't fit his dancing pumps.

Repaying clipping with clipping in a manner of speaking I enclose some from my newspaper—at present in crude-young or mimeograph shape. We may make the whole sheet mailable, in which case your name will of course be high on the mailing list. And if you make your reports on the nation as good as the first sample I'm quite capable of running them over your name, giving us a very hightone New York correspondent indeed.

Thanks for the Critics' Circle and *NY Times* clips on the *Watch*. I suppose it is no news to you that *Red Book* also gave it some kind of nod. Folk up here are very impressed and I may have to—the Ralph Ingersoll touch—put something in my daily hoot about it. I've avoided that so far, but my superiors are becoming a little insistent, and who am I to go contrary to the wishes of anyone more powerful than, say, a sick midget.

There is a sort of scheme afoot in what might be called relatively high places which may, if it comes to anything, take me to other scenes of action (The lights went out and I had to stop and rig up a flashlight arrangement by which I now carry on—*nothing* can stop the American soldier.) in the more of less near future. It might be nice, but I have no control over, and no part in, the bringing about of it, and it is as vague as I make it sound here.

I'm treating myself to an eight-hour day for a change and expect to be back in my bunk and asleep by three o'clock. And that—the way I've been going lately—will be a real touch of luxury.

So, if I'm going to do that, it's high time I got the clippings ready for you and took off down Pneumonia Gulch.

> Much love,
> SDH

TLS LPT

1944

To Lillian Hellman

24 January 1944, Aleutians

Dear Lilishka,

If one and one make two, then this is my second letter to you today. Remember me? I'm the boy who wrote you before he went home to bed this morning. (In case one and one don't make two—and I am not too sure—just forget the whole thing.) And when I finish this I am going home to bed again, even though it's still a couple of hours short of morning. You seem to be a kind of bedtime story for me, and a lot better than that three bears stuff that tots have to put up with.

The local newspaper situation has been snagged up by supply and equipment failures; the lilting voices of newsvenders will not be heard on our streetcorners tonight and tomorrow; I've been swooping around in wide circles repairing my logistic deficiencies and now I have an evening of non-printing while I wait for my day's efforts to bear fruit—which it ought to along about tomorrow or the next day. Meanwhile I champ at the bit in the best manner of a road-company Roy Howard whose presses have stopped—and I rest tonight.[1] Also I have a date with a general in the morning and it may be if I am well rested and look young and pretty when I show up he will make me a colonel, or at least not make me a KP. You've got to figure angles in this man's army.

I know there's some mail down in my hut, but I don't know whether any of it's from you, but I do know what I hope.

Will you ask Nancy to throw in some gossip column stuff now and then. The Elsa Maxwell clipping was a gem, but my people would only be confused by it. And they'd like a bit of the none-genuine-without-this-label WW and Sullivan and such canaries now and then.[2] (All right, so I'm pampering depraved tastes. So what? It's a newspaper, ain't it?)

Sleepiness is putting its muddling fingers on my whitened skull. So ...

> Much love, darling,
> SDH

1. Roy Howard was editorial director of Scripps-Howard newspapers and president of UPI.

2. Elsa Maxwell, Walter Winchell (WW), and Ed Sullivan were widely syndicated gossip columnists.

TLS LPT

To Lillian Hellman

1 February 1944, Aleutians

Dear Lily,

A letter from you today made it a better day than a lot of days are, and almost any day I can think of would be improved by the same means, a message which, I hope, you will take to heart.

I know how you feel at this stage of working on the play and it is nice of you to even think of writing after your day's stint is done, so don't let my piggish complaining bother you. Write me when you can and to hell with me!

I by all means still want the weekly summary of what you've heard and what you think about it. When I run through clippings and similar reports of what's going on back home I'm usually a little bewildered and start thinking maybe it's me, maybe even seven months away from the familiar paths has addled my memory and I'm glad to have your assurances that things are as dopey as they seem.

When are the short story books coming out? Or has the first one already emerged? Send me copies when they pop, will you? Fran Pindyck sent me a copy of the paper *Red Harvest,* which I mean to re-read some day when I get around to it.[1] Just now I'm so busy reading news and Army stuff that I can't even keep up with what I'm supposed to consume of the latter.

This English I'm writing the last few days is a far more horrible thing than I ever knew, proving, possibly, that Alaskan journalism don't help nobody's style. A good man[y] of my contributions to our paper, I'm ashamed to admit, are beginning to read thisaway too.

I had a letter from Lois today. She's wondering why she didn't nag Dick into marrying her—and she actually means why she didn't try. She's got the best trained—for comfort rather than accuracy—memory I've ever heard of.

But this is the Lois you'll like, and I quote: "The usual mid-winter doldrums are upon us and out of sheer boredom, I'm thinking of writing a play. Since I have been around here and seen the jerks who do it, I think I must be a sucker not even to try." That handy memory again. It's not going to stop her from dashing off a little something that'll make her a few hundred thousands.

That, for the evening—or morning—is all you're going to get.

> Love in great quantities,
> SDH

1. *The Adventures of Sam Spade and Other Stories*, a collection of Hammett's stories, was published by Lawrence Spivak on 14 April 1944. *Red Harvest* was published in paperback form by Pocket Books in October 1943.

TLS LPT

To Nancy Bragdon

2 February 1944, Aleutians

Dear Nancy,

The *Christian Science Monitor* seems to be double-crossing me by not running any more of those swell maps that were my chief reason for wanting it, so maybe we might as well cut them off the list.

On the other hand, the *Herald-Tribune* stuff you've sent has been mighty nice, so let's have batches of stuff clipped from it daily.

Cable stuff such as Ernie Pyle's (*World-Tel*) are fine when I get it—them (to try to match up that "are" earlier in the sentence) fairly early. My people are interested in knowing what men on other fronts do and think about and eat and so on. So any of the homey details about them are what's wanted.

Small items that give examples of the whackiness inseparable from civilian living are also good—and the little worries that will seem funny to a man who's had to crawl out of a snow-smashed hut at three in the morning.

Thank you, ma'am.

Yours,
SDH

TLS LPT

To Lillian Hellman

3 February 1944, The Aleutians

Dearest Lily,

Madam G. Tabouise—all right, so I don't know how to spell her name—writes, as you're ignorant if you don't know—for a French publication in New York, the name of which is not in the memory at the moment, but I dare say it has something to do with victory.[1] But what I am getting at is that her recent predictions on things European-political have been what I always like to call uncanny, and I would be oh, so happy if I could get hold of her material a little quicker. So it occurs to me that, since you are of the a[c]quaintance of Madame and she is one cannot doubt a patriotic daughter of la belle France, it might be put to her that advance sheets—proofs, possibly—dispatched hither by airmail for use in my racket through radio and newspaper channels might be of benefit to her country in some roundabout way, the details of which escape me at the moment, and would certainly help my patients toward a clearer understanding of what goes on in the world—since they would help guide our radio and newspaper utterances. If, as it may be, things cannot be arranged thus, then will you have Nancy get hold of Madame's product when available, airstamp, mail?

Another message for Nancy, and then I will turn my attention to you. I've written her that the *Christian Science Monitor,* [h]aving failed me in the matter of maps, should henceforth be unmailed. Will you ask her—I know you are not going to like this entirely—to mail me fair-sized chunks of *PM* fairly regularly. Its childish simplicity might make it useful, and it does have good maps.

Now we'll move over into the next column and deal with you, as soon as I've said I can have G.T. translated here, so don't worry about its being in French.[2]

It's close to five in the morning and today's issue of my little daily is being ground through the mimeograph machines, so there's nothing left for me to do but worry about distribution, which always breaks down on at least one part of the island, and to shave in preparation for a 9 o'clock date with the general, presumably to discuss Aleutian journalism and a good deal of fancy equipment that's being bought by radiogram. It may be that I shall come out of the whole thing a Private First Class, a one-striped ex-Hearstette, or a sort of former Ochs of the williwaws.[3]

This was the column in which we were going to talk about you. Well, we're getting warmer: we're as close to you as me—even if that isn't as close as I'd like to be just now.

Oh, yes, about you: I hope the play is coming along better than if I was on hand to get into quarrels with you about it, and that therefor[e] you are devoting to sheer writing those periods you used to take out for sulking because I was hampering your art or objecting to a glittering generality, which, it's possible, is the same thing. And I hope you are not paying too much attention to what people—I still distrust everybody's advice but my own—tell you about what you are writing.

I have a play to read, but it's already not as good as yours is going to be. It was put in my hands by a character who is radio officer on a ship plying between here and Seattle, and is about the Murmansk run. I haven't read enough of it to know how it shapes up. If it's any good I'll no doubt pester Herman with it.

> That's all for now, toots, except much love,
> SDH

1. Geneviève Tabouis was a prominent French anti-fascist journalist. She fled occupied France in 1940 for New York and established the weekly magazine *Pour la Victoire* in the United States.
2. This letter is typed in two columns. The first column ends here.
3. William Randolph Hearst owned a string of newspapers, magazines, and newspaper syndicates. Adolph Ochs was owner and publisher of the *New York Times*.

TLS LPT

To Lillian Hellman

6 February 1944, Aleutians

Dearest Lily,

Bennett Cerf sent me a copy of his ms for the February *Esquire*, "not because it is important in itself, but because it is small evidence of the fact that what you are doing is not being overlooked by your friends." So help me, that's what he wrote in his letter![1]

* * *

Me, I sit around and think up ideas for gag cartoons. One of the eagles on a colonel's shoulders lays an egg there. A non-com lies sleeping in bed with his stripes sewed on a comforter over his arm. A rat coming down a rope from a ship says to one behind him, "Go back, this is the Aleutians." A bedraggled raven swoops down saying to another, "Look, I'm a dive bomber." A bottle of milk and a morning paper stand at the door of a Quonset hut. A soldier sits on his bunk dressing, saying, "I dreamed about Evelyn again. Gee, travel improves her." And on and—ho hum—on and on. Sometimes I think I've missed too many boats.

I'm going to stop this and pull myself together. Pretty soon my rumor sheet will be off the mimeos and it will be time to face breakfast—fried eggs this morning, I believe—and that's no time to be caught off-balance.

You are a cutie who—have I said this before?—uses her play-writing as an excuse for not writing where it would in the long run—after all, what are money and fame and the admiration of thousands?—do most good. You wouldn't want to be cut off with a phrase in my memoirs, would you?

Mountains of love,
SDH

1. Cerf had just taken over the monthly column "Esquire's Five-Minute Shelf," an overview of the book trade. In his February 1944 column he wrote, referring to mystery writers: "The greatest of them all, Dashiell Hammett, has chucked everything and at the age of forty-nine, enlisted as a private in the Signal Corps. He was last reported in Alaska promoted to corporal, asking no favors and doing his job. If he ever gets round to doing another murder story, a hundred thousand readers will be waiting to buy it. (why doesn't M.G.M. revive the original *Thin Man*?)"

TLS LPT

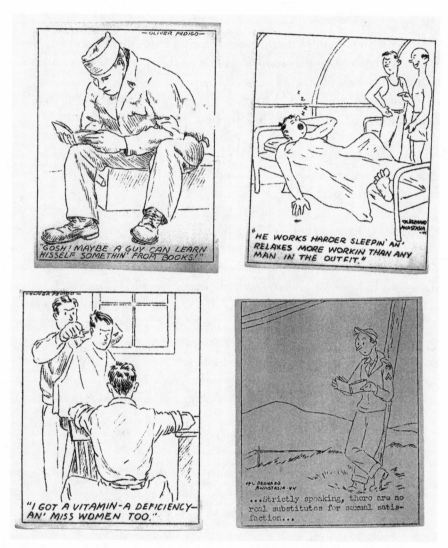

Sample cartoons that Hammett sent to Mary and Josephine.

To Mary Hammett

6 February 1944, Aleutians

Dear Mary,

It's early on a wintry morning and all that kind of stuff and I'm waiting to go down the gulch for a breakfast of, I hope, fried eggs and then on to my hut and blanketed bunk.

By this time you should have given up any hope of getting much news from me—there simply isn't any up here, unless you want me to make reports on my daily routine.

I wrote a booklet for the army to describe our situation up here—a short booklet of maybe 10 pages—but I can tell you the whole story in a very few sentences.

Back in June 1942 the Japs bombed Dutch Harbor and landed troops on Attu and Kiska. That wouldn't do, so we came down the Aleutians, almost island by island, setting up a chain of well-defended air and naval bases and, in 1943, chased the last of them back to Japan. Now we develop and improve and strengthen our chain of bases and wait to see what the Japs will do next, what Washington decides we will do next. Meanwhile, just to keep our hands in, we bomb the Jap instal[l]ations at Paramushiru lightly from time to time, and trust to our air and naval patrols to keep the Japs from playing the same game with us.

That's the set-up—except that most of us hope and believe that there will be something doing in this corner of the world sometime reasonably soon.

And now it's just about time to go down and lift a couple of those eggs off the stove.

I get tired of writing that my health is still good, but it is, and I hope you all are doing as well.

Kiss Jo and your Mother for me.

> Lots of love,
> Papa

TLS Marshall

1944

To Nancy Bragdon

12 February 1944, Aleutians

Dear Nancy,

Should I do anything about my income tax? My very vague notion was that soldiers overseas can postpone everything until some four months after they get back home. That, and the twenty percent pay raise, were practically the only things I left the states for. Will you find out if I'm nuts.

No, *The Week* hasn't started coming yet, nor *Newsweek*, but I manage to limp along. Your clippings have been a great help and the island is practically lousy with information about the state of the world. Guys who at home thought it was all right are finding out plenty different and it may be that some of the home news will send them off in rowboats to join the Japs at Paramushiru.

I hear that winter has really hit you all, and I'm looking forward to letters telling me all about the horrors of it and as good as saying I'm pretty fortunate to be snugly tucked in up here. (The truth is I have fallen into a fairly comfortable—for here—routine, and since the snow collapsed the hut I used to live in I've moved into another that can be reached without crawling through the night along an ice shelf.)

> Yours,
> SDH

TLS LPT

To Mary Hammett

13 February 1944, Aleutians

Dear Mary,

Come, come, now, my blonde darling, I may have not written for a little longer than usual, but it couldn't have been that "over a month" you mention. And you mustn't worry about not hearing from me now and then. A lot of things can happen in a wartime Army to make writing difficult, and they don't all have to be bad. If anything should happen to me, the good old USA would notify you: your name and address are on my dog tag. (The new dog tags, not yet issued to us, have no name and address of next-of-kin on them.)

I think anybody who looks for the fall of Germany within a month, or within a few months, is dreaming. It could happen, of course, because we have to more or less guess at what's going on inside Europe, but, in spite of the retreats in Russia and Poland, there is not the slightest indication that the Nazi army is cracking, and none that they are running short of either men or—except possibly some types of planes—equipment. It might even be in the cards that Japan will go under first.

Jack Woodford was never a very good writer—too much of the hack in him—but his books and articles on writing (he wrote a great many of them) were usually pretty good reading.[1] I used to like them, though I don't remember learning very much from them.

I imagine house-hunting is going to be a problem, if you have to do it. Tell your Mother not to worry about the higher rent—the amount I'm sending monthly can be increased easily enough if you need it. I probably have saved a good deal of money since I've been in the Army, though I don't know how much. It's been going automatically into War Bonds.

Now I'm going to run along through whatever kind of weather happens to be filling the night and get myself a bite of breakfast—should be hot cakes this morning—before I go down to my hut and insert my antique frame into my blankets and comforter.

Kiss Jose and Jo for me.

> Lots of love,
> Papa

1. Jack Woodford was a crime writer who also wrote books about authorship, including *Why Write a Novel* (1943) and *How to Write for Money* (1944).

TLS MARSHALL

To Lillian Hellman

14 February 1944, Aleutians

Dearest Lily,

A nice, nice letter from you today: hence it's been a nice, nice day, showing woman's control of nature.

What happed to you, clumsy ox, that you fell and hurt your back? And how badly? And are you all right now? You think of the damndest things to do as soon as my back is turned.

A letter from your McCarthy—he of *Yank*—came today, offering to do what he can for my publication, which I suspect isn't much, since my problems are mostly just the teeny-weeny ones that can't be fixed up very much unless we stop the war.

I also had a letter from Nels Jorgensen, in India, where he ran into McKelway mailing a letter to you.[1] Mac—not liking Nels, I dare say, as many people don't—told him he didn't know me.

I finished reading the maritime gent's play and think maybe it's got something in it in a very naïve way if anybody wants to go to the trouble of working it out.[2] Anyhow, I'm writing Herm about it, and if he wants to take the trouble to look into it, it's his own fault and not mine. It's about a convoy run to Murmansk, written as only a socially conscious merchant mariner could write it, full of priggish utterances and black and white characters, but with, I think, a kind of simple charm. And, boy, oh, boy, do things happen to that boat!

* * *

And that is my little budget of chit-chat for this morning.

> Mountains of love,
> SDH

1. Jorgensen is unidentified. Hammett elsewhere spells the name "Jorgessen."
2. Lt. Sam Hakam, with the U.S. Maritime Service, gave Hammett a play to read. Hammett sent it to Herman Shumlin. The play was apparently never produced.

TLS LPT

To Lillian Hellman

17 February 1944, Aleutians

Dearest Lily,

Another night gone, another two dollars and sixty-four cents earned—and, oh, boy! I get my food and bed free, and my clothing too.

So I spend an hour tonight—you know I mean last night, so don't make out you can't understand me—thinking up cartoon gags like a man is lying on the snow under a beach umbrella and is wearing a bathing suit and sun glasses and one other man is saying to another other man, "He was transferred from Nome." Or a soldier is showing the sights to a visiting Senator and points to the left and says, "And that is snow." Or like two men are being blown through the roof of their hut and one says to the other, "I guess that wasn't Diesel oil." Or like, but I guess you get the idea along about now. When I want a change of pace I think up ideas for topical cartoons like an American eagle looking toward Asia from an island marked Green Islands, or like Hitler sitting in a blasted tree like a buzzard against a ruined background and labeled, "The bird who croaks, 'At any cost!' " Or like, but I guess you get *that* idea. It's not always birds—Mountbatten's forces, for instance, are going to be a leopard stretching a paw out toward Burma or something—but you can see now why I sometimes say, "Let's run a map in that spot tonight."[1] I tell you this thing of being a north country insular Ingersoll is not always better than a poke in the eye with a sharp stick.

* * *

Much love,
SDH

1. Louis Mountbatten was supreme allied commander of the Southeast Asia Theatre. He directed the recapture of Burma.

TLS LPT

To Lillian Hellman

18 February 1944, Aleutians

Dearest Lily,

Some places in the world people are looking at calendars and saying, Ah, February eighteen...another month and Spring will be a-coming! But not on our little island. We look at the calendar and remember that last year the toughest weather of the Winter cut loose around the sixth of April. But things ought to be tapering off along about June. And I saw a patch of earth—and mighty dirty looking it was too—a couple of days ago, the first I've seen in weeks and weeks. It's going to be strange to see a landscape that isn't white: we have no trees to break the monotone. And then in, say, August there will be flowers—flocks of them—but before that, and during that, and after that there will be mud and mud and mud in incredible quantities. That part of it I don't even pretend to like. It's the one thing up here I really hate, though I wouldn't go so far as to say that I'm always queer for the wind either. But there are times when I find it in my heart to forgive God for the wind; but for the mud, never ...

I gave myself a very royal day[']s sleep of about twelve—give a half, take a half—hours and am much the better man for it. Also—what hurts the disposition not at all—I had to spend no time devising cartoon gags. Instead I put in that time whipping up a polar projectory map of the Pacific Ocean fighting area from Truk to Henderson Field to Wewak, with 10 Jap and 7 Allied bases all neatly indicated—and a neat, if slightly off-scale job it was, if I do say so. It may be that even you could have found places and directions with its help, though now I guess I'm bragging.

Our mail has been laggard the last couple of days, so I don't know whether you've been doing the right thing by me. Some ought to come tomorrow, and then I'll know.

I haven't heard from Maggie in weeks so your bit of Frohnknechtana was new to me—or would have been new if I hadn't known her.[1]

How about the Kober play? I see a note about casting now and then in *Variety*, but what I always say a note about anything in *Variety* only means that they put a note in about it.[2]

I wrote Herm about the seafarer's play, and the rest of it's on his own head, unless he's got sense enough to duck.

And how about your play? How does she go? Does it go forward with running or acrawl? I gathered from your last letter that you'd decided to put it on this year, which—I remember you—is what I thought you'd decide.

That just about drains dry my little stock of news, chatter, leading questions, small talk and the like.

> A great deal of love,
> SDH

1. Maggie Kober's maiden name was Frohnknecht.
2. No play inolving Arthur Kober was produced in the 1940s.

TLS LPT

To Richard Hammett

Richard Hammett was Dashiell's younger brother, a businessman with conservative political views. They had a strained relationship.

18 February 1944, Aleutians

Dear Dick,

An Air Force lieutenant whose name I thought I'd remember, but didn't, came in a couple of weeks ago and told me he used to sell, or try to sell, you billboard space in Charlotte—so I came 5,000 miles to hear about you, proving that we're a close-knit family.

I've been up here about seven months. The only thing I really dislike about the place is the mud, and that's been buried under layers of snow for some time now, so I am, for the Army, moderately happy.

* * *

I've got no younger with the years, but have managed to weather most of the stuff that the Army chucks around. In places I may creak, but I've kept myself clear of the shadow of limited service and the like. Basic training had me bleeding from the pores and then, at my first station in Alaska, I put in a few weeks romping over the tundra with an infantry outfit, dragging machine guns through mud, toting rucksacks and rifles on nice little forced marches up mountains—and it wasn't too jolly. Sometimes I was pretty surprised to find myself turning out in the morning for another go at it. At present I am having a fairly good go of it, with nothing much on the strenuous side except the daily battle with the elements—a thing that uses up most of our energy here.

Drop me a line when you get a chance.

> Yours,
> Dashiell

TLS Judi Hammett

To Lillian Hellman

22 February 1944, Aleutians

Dear Lilishka,

I woke up this afternoon to find a nice letter from you beside my bed, and that stacked the cards in favor of the day's being a nice one.

So I came up to the hut out of which I excrete my daily paper and found myself with temperaments that needed to be dealt with. I am not such a one as likes to have to deal with temperaments except in a chilly four-letter-word manner. So what ensued was polite but cold-blooded and I have for the present no more temperaments that need to be dealt with.

That, and reading your letter again, made it once more a nice day—only I am tired. It may be that I am too old for fifteen-hour days, even if they do involve no great amount of physical exercise.

A letter from Maggie came along with yours, and she sounds as if she had been, and still is, pretty sick. But it was written in penmanship—Arthur seems to have moved his typewriter to the Gladstone—so I do not pretend to understand everything she wrote. Maggie is often willing to settle for the small child's conviction that any mark you make on a piece of paper conveys whatever you happened to be thinking at the time.

Also came a letter from Raoul Whitfield, who hopes to be discharged from his hospital next month. He is broke and I am sending him $500.

You are not to sulk about that and you are not to mislead the bank with hints that my check may be a forgery. I know this is asking a lot of you, but you must be brave and kind and—mind your own business.

I let one of your admirers read your letter and it quite overwhelmed him. Do you wish to marry a young man of perhaps 24, certainly not handsome, but very interested in films and the stage? Your name would be Mrs. Glackin, which in itself should be no mean inducement.[1]

I think, however, it would be better all around if you did not marry anybody, but stuck to me.

I have a warm, if small, heart and it may be assumed that I've sown my wild oats.

Love,
SDH

1. William Glackin was the associate editor of *The Adakian*.

TLS LPT

To Nancy Bragdon

25 February 1944, Aleutians

Dear Nancy,

Thanks for the *Hollywood Reporter* page. I'm glad to know the country's in safe hands once more.

About the PEN bill: nobody, so far as I know, has ever given them a cent of dues and I don't feel the necessity of breaking any precedents.[1]

The girl at *Fortune* kept her promise and sent me the usual dreary list of the usual dreary forthcoming *Fortune* guess-as at what nobody who can't pay ten bucks a year for a magazine could possibly be interested.

If Mrs. Her[r]man[n] is knitting a helmet I guess I'll have to send an order for one, but, until I grow another head, and so far there's no sign of that, I'm pretty thoroughly helmeted up, and seldom [wear] them anyhow except in the wickedest weather.[2]

On the bond purchases—news of which sometimes cheers me with the feeling that I'm betting on my side, and sometimes depresses me with the notion that I'm having to buy my own food and ammunition—

will you let me know how many of this year's Serie[s] E's you've bought. I may want to buy some up here—I'm carrying around too much cash—and would like to know whether my $5000 limit has been reached. (Also it may be that I've a suspicion that you and Lillian, being big traders with eyes only for large round figures, may be ignoring such small stuff even though its yield is higher than most other classes of War Bond.)

I thought I was getting pneumonia or something yesterday, but it was probably just lack of sleep, because I went to bed at five this morning and knocked off a good straight eleven hours, rising heavy of leg, but otherwise fairly pert and chipper, at four this afternoon.

The clip selection you send is excellent, though I could use a few more cartoons, both gag and political-war.

It's getting cold in here and it's getting along towards five in the morning again, so I reckon I'll leave the wind-up of the night's issue to the help and go home and try yesterday's p[re]scription again.

Yours,
SDH

1. PEN is an international writers' organization. The name is an acronym for "poets, playwrights, editors, novelists."
2. Peggy Herrmann was the wife of a farmer at Hardscrabble Farm.

TLS LPT

To Lillian Hellman

29 February 1944, Aleutians

Dearest Lily,

* * *

I'm sorry I can't help you on the Herman thing, honey, but I've never understood your relations with him. The professor's store of knowledge is—now the truth comes out—not limitless and that whole set-up has always been a closed book to me, which, somehow, I've always thought you understood. I'm not—I hope I don't have to tell you—talking about things being kept from me or anything of the sort. I simply mean that I've never been able to understand what you and he—as a pair—were all about; you never made any recognizable pattern for me. I couldn't say that the two of you together didn't make sense—as I could, for instance, in the case of you and Arthur—but I never could see *what* sense you made or *whether* you made any.

Cockburn's *The Week* has at last begun to arrive and very glad I am to have it.[1] He's even sprier, and not much less intelligible than of old, and it's good to have the old gossip about folks in high places again. Now, when I start getting Tabouis, I can give afternoon teas and it'll be just like back in Bloomsbury with Ivy.[2]

If I play my cards right, and choose to try, it's likely that I can wangle either (A) a sort of roving job up and down the Aleutians and through and roundabout Alaska, or (B) a few months back in the States.

A tempts me, though I'm not nuts about being on the loose in the Army. Being part and parcel of a definite outfit at a definite station is pleasanter for me, gives me more of a feeling of belonging, and that's one of the nicer Army feelings. B wouldn't tempt me at all except that— without anything at all being wrong, and without it itself being within a hundred miles of seriousness—I'm a bit run down at the moment, off my feed, and without too much physical vigor. I blame that on dietary deficiencies and have already written Nancy for vitamins and the like, but the notion is not to be escaped that maybe a semester with the flesh-pots of the USA might do me more good.

What I'll no doubt do, of course, being me if you remember, is noth-ing one way or the other and just let things turn out as they turn out. So far as anything being a matter of principle is involved, that's been my Army practice.

Look, I write like this after reading only two issues of *The Week*. Are you going to have fun trying to read me after I've been Cockburnt for a few months!

> Much love,
> SDH

1. Claud Cockburn (pronounced Coburn), born in China and educated at Oxford, was a British journalist and Communist. *The Week* was a news and commentary journal that was unabashedly partisan and freely reported rumors as diligently as facts. Cockburn was also a correspondent for the *Daily Worker* under the pseudonym Frank Pitcairn. *The Week* was used by Cockburn to disseminate Comintern-directed propaganda, manipulated by Hellman's close friend Otto

Katz, who was the model for Kurt Müller, the anti-Fascist hero in *Watch on the Rhine*.

2. Bloomsbury is a district in west central London around the British Museum where a group of artists and intellectuals, including Virginia and Leonard Woolf, John Maynard Keynes, and Lytton Strachey, formed a circle that came to be known as the Bloomsbury Set beginning about 1905 and flourishing into the 1930s. The group was characterized by radical politics and a Bohemian lifestyle.

TLS LPT

To Nancy Bragdon

1 March 1944, Aleutians

Dear Nancy,

A soldier just asked me: "Do you read much? I mean other authors' books." So help me, that's what he said.

The stuff is coming in fine—*The Week* now arrives in about two weeks' time, which is swell from London—but we're a little top-heavy on the *Herald-Tribune*.

My objection to that is not that the *H-T* isn't a good newspaper, because it's good enough, but that it's not a very good indicator of public opinion and such in the States, since, outside certain fundamental Union Club beliefs of a simple nature, it's never known exactly what anybody thinks, including the Ogden Reids.[1]

So will you mix up the press a little more, not forgetting Hearst and the *Daily News?* (I can't reprint much of anything—War Dept restrictions—but I'm primarily interested in what goes on in the home head as reflected by the home papers.)

If the calendar and the experiences of those who have spent more time here didn't say different, these last few weeks would have me thinking that maybe spring is just around the corner. Even our harbinger mud is raising its unpretty head here and there.

> Yours,
> SDH

1. Ogden Reid was publisher of the *New York Herald Tribune*. His wife, Helen, was the paper's advertising manager and vice president.

TLS HRC

To Lillian Hellman

1 March 1944, Aleutians

Dearest Lily,

I like the snapshot of you—you're very hellmangay in it—and the Salud one also: he's got that nobody-ever-does-anything-very-much-for-me look and pose.[1] He may be coming to resemble me as I was in my earlier years, but I doubt that he's growing to look like me now.

A package of edibles came from you, but I haven't had a chance to sample them yet. A close inspection of the labels, however, justifies my thanking you very much, and so that is what I do here and now.

The new Randau–Zugsmith novel came from Random House, but I haven't yet had a chance to dip—or whatever one does—into it.[2] Also came a letter from the authoress, with a dullish story about a German going to hell and not much news in it. The authoress is too chained "to our desks" to get around very much, and so only knows what Barney Gallant tells her when he phones to ask them to dinner Monday evenings when business is not good in restaurants.[3]

Today was payday, which mostly means to me that all the folk who owe me money come around and pay me back and I may not have to lend the lucky ones money again for as much as ten days. Meanwhile I feel like an unusurious money-changer who was not driven from the temple.

I wrote Bennet[t] Cerf a note a few weeks ago, chiefly so I could make a point of not saying what I thought about his sending me the ms, but you snub Bennet[t] only for the record: it doesn't do anything to him. I had a letter from him today, saying he was sending me some books.

I don't have to tell you how I'm looking forward to the arrival of the play script.[4] Until it gets here and I've reported on it you've nothing to worry about, so you're to stop your fidgeting. It will give Zilboorg a bad name.[5]

This is my eighteenth month in the Army, my eighth out of the States. Neither period seems that long, but then I'm not very good even at figuring out how long a week ought to seem. And my memory of civilian and continental US ways is certainly none too good most of the time, though things like the snapshots bring it back sharply enough now and then. It may be that most of the time I don't want to think about the outer world: an Army station is, if not a fine safe place in actuality, at least as good a substitute as you're likely to find anywhere.

Now it is that I am a little drowsy, but also hungry, and the time of this is ten minutes before five in the morning. With my usual mental agility I've solved the whole thing by deciding to catch an hour and a half nap atop a table before going down to breakfast and thence to my bunk.

Love in large quantities,
SDH

1. Salud was Hellman and Hammett's standard poodle.
2. Leane Zugsmith and Carl Randau's novel *The Visitor* was published by Random House in 1944 and adapted as a play, which opened at the Henry Miller Theatre in Manhattan in October 1944.
3. Barney Gallant was a legendary Greenwich Village restaurateur, who often befriended literary leftists. He was reputedly the first man to go to jail (for twenty days) for violation of Prohibition laws.
4. *The Searching Wind.*
5. Gregory Zilboorg was Hellman's psychoanalyst.

TLS LPT

To Lillian Hellman

2 March 1944, Aleutians

Dear Lilishka,

Here it is not the next morning yet and I'm writing you already. It must be that I've cleaned up most of my work early or something.

I see by the *Herald-Tribune* that Shumlin has engaged Cornelia Otis Skinner, Dennis King and Dudley Digges for your opera and that you go into rehearsal on the sixth.[1] True? False?

By the *Mirror* I see that Thyra for probably no very many pieces of silver does quite a drooling act over the Lonergans, managing to be far more disgusting than they ever did manage to be.[2]

From many papers I fail to see that anybody mentions what—in the simplicity of my long-range view from here—seems screamingly obvious about the presidential veto of the new tax bill; to wit, that he deliberately taunted Congress into overriding his veto—thus, not for the first time, making his own campaign issues and, thanks to Willkie's having declared himself ahead of time, leaving the opposition even more muddled than they could have been if left to their own crackpot devices.[3]

* * *

I must stop this now and come up with an idea for a stirring cartoon on the war or one of its fronts or something. I'm tired of thinking up new ways to dramatize our taking of another Pacific Island. You'd think somebody would take a peninsula or a cape once in a while, just for the novelty of thing. But, no, just one damned island after another. It's becoming as tiresome as those Red Army pincer movements. They had our cartoonists drawing sickles in their sleep.

I love you more than I do islands.
SDH

1. Skinner, King, and Digges played in the Broadway production of *The Searching Wind*.
2. The Lonergans—Lester, Lenore, Lester Jr., and Lester 3rd—were a theatrical family active on Broadway and in the movies. Thyra Samter Winslow wrote a piece about them in the New York *Mirror*.
3. President Roosevelt submitted a bill requesting more money to support the war effort. The Republican-controlled Congress refused the request and passed a bill instead that generated less revenue than Roosevelt requested and introduced payroll tax withholding, which was very unpopular, while granting tax concessions to business interests. Roosevelt vetoed the bill, and the veto was overridden in Congress. Wendell Willkie had run for president against Roosevelt in the 1940 election and was a major contender in 1944 but lost the Republican nomination to Thomas E. Dewey.

TLS LPT

To Prudence Whitfield

5 March 1944, Aleutians

Dear Pru,

Your letter was nice and full of nostalgia, making me think of things that hadn't wriggled around in my memory since God knows when. Fifteen years is a long time even for me. And my recollection of a great many of those years has to pass through an alcoholic cloud. But I remember that you were very exciting—and annoying, though all of that wasn't your fault.

Anastasia is a good-looking dark sullen boy of twenty-something, who sulks a little because the Army won't call the war off and let him go back to Cleveland to his wife.[1] He used to be a clarinet player with dance bands, but became a commercial artist so he wouldn't have to roam around the country. About a month ago I started—and still edit, though it's beginning to bore me and I'm going to move on as soon as I can—a newspaper for the troops here. Anastasia is one of my staff.

I had a letter from Raoul late last month, sounding fairly cheerful. He said he was taking his test the next day and hoped to be saying goodby to the hospital in March. Of you he wrote: "Pru is also busy, but she writes quite often and has really been a big help—though I'll probably never admit it again."

About the rifle: no, I don't tote it up here to the newspaper hut. There was a time when rifles and steel helmets had to be worn here by anybody going one hundred yards or more from his quarters, but we're comparatively civilized now and there's even an order against wearing hunting knives on our hips.

I would like to see more of the poetry. And why should you be shy about it with me? Don't you remember that I was always in favor of it?

It's almost breakfast time and I've got to stop on my way to the mess hut and wake a man up. So...

Love,
Dash

1. Albert Anastasia was a cartoonist on the staff of *The Adakian*.

TLS Penzler

To Lillian Hellman

5 March 1944, Aleutians

Dearest Lily,

Anything can happen. Like I got a letter from Dick—you remember the kid—today. He's still Standard Oiling in North Carolina and he and

Judith are wrangling—he does not see why she needs a lawyer—over money matters incidental to their separation or divorce or whatever it is.

He thinks I'm probably a little bats to have enlisted in the Army, though he would have understood my sliding into some kind of Public Relations berth. Of the *Watch* he says, "It was by much the best picture I saw last year and the only war picture or play I have seen with a shred of integrity." All right, all right, but he gets pretty indignant about FDR and seems foolishly certain that we're going to have a new president next year. Also he thinks the sales tax is about the only way to pay for things. In other words, his mental processes are those of the true Hammett, uncorrupted by any glimpse of the world as it really is.

Here's a statement from Knopf, to add to those records of mine that I am idiotic enough to suppose you and Nancy are keeping.

With that, I guess I've just about shot my bolt as far as news is concerned. I've had letters from Fran Pindyck and Pru Whitfield, but if there's anything in them to interest you I've forgotten what it could be. Josephine's going to the U.C.L.A. in the fall, so I suppose I should get around to what I've been putting off for some time and raise the western Hammett family allowance. I might just as well face the fact that they're three adults now and can no longer be fed on Nestlé's food. Should I double it?

The mechanics of getting out the Post newspaper are beginning to bore me and I'm trying to keep myself from taking something I don't really want just because it is something else. Maybe I'll go back to my outfit and become a radio operator—except they all walk around in a kind of haze most of the time, though, come to think of it, so does nearly everybody else who has been in the Aleutians any length of time.

I dreamed about Lee Gershwin the other night and was very glad to see her, only the dream stopped—as they usually do in my brief and dull freudian-life—before she got close enough to speak to.[1]

The weather is still such as to make us think spring is coming, though that hardly seems reasonable. Still, it was a very early winter for these parts.

Me, I know go eat.

> Much love,
> SDH

1. Ira Gershwin's wife.

TLS LPT

To Maggie Kober

5 March 1944, Aleutians

Dear Maggie darling,

* * *

Of news I have none except what people write me from the States, like the Randaus are working on their fortieth or sixtieth book—they sent me a copy of *The Visitor*, but I haven't had time to read it yet—and my brother—in the first letter I've had from him in well over fifteen years—doesn't like Roosevelt and Leland Hayward is back in town and very chipper—you don't know how I'd worried about *him*—and a lot of oh, so exciting thinks like that.

I suppose the die is more or less cast with Lily's play, having seen a note about the cast—do you want me to make a mot about its dying— and rehearsal dates in the *Herald-Tribune*. Lily's last direct report to me had the whole thing still more of less hanging in the air.

What stirs with Art's play?

My feet are cold in this joint, so this is going to stop right along about here. It will be warmer in the mess hut and breakfast should be on the stove by now.

But that does not mean that I do not love you. But I can love you just as well if my feet are warm and I am eating. Anyhow that is what I mean to try.

> Much love,
> SDH

TLS HRC

To Lillian Hellman

At the top of this letter, Hellman has written in script, "Isn't this a special, nice letter? L."

10 March 1944, Aleutians

Dearest Lily,

You're practically breaking my heart with your letters about the play. I think we're going to have to make a rule that you're not to tackle any work when I'm not around to spur, quiet, goad, pacify and tease you, according to what's needed at the moment. It is obvious that you're not capable of handling yourself.

I am sorry, though, baby, and hope that now—since the die seems finally cast—you'll at least go fatalistic on the whole thing. And I will write you in great detail—if I can trick myself into thinking in terms of the theater from way up here—as soon as I've read the script. And I hope it comes soon. Meanwhile, what the hell—you did your best and you'll have to let it go at that no matter what you'd like to do.

Now let's talk about me. I think it would be nice to have one of those Martin's boxes again and, counting on your kindness, enclose the official document necessary thereto. Thank you.

You may as well put away that Pinchot photograph and your memories now so you will be in shape for my return on some distant day. You will not—unless you've developed a newer and higher order of idiocy—find me very beautiful—not even if I let my hair grow long and wavy. What the Army will be giving you back is definitely a scrawny who shows plenty of signs of wear and tear and on whose face Father Time has left a footprint or two. The best I can say for myself is that I probably still look intelligent, though maybe a better fitting lower plate might help a little. But even at that I feel that I'm going to have to do business with little shop girls on the strength of my beautiful nature and my wealth and fame and low animal cunning. I no longer can count on dazzling the eye.

I have an idea that will annoy some people. I must beg you to excuse me now while I try to work it out before breakfast time.

> With much love and protestations of this and that,
> SDH

TLS LPT

To Richard Hammett

10 March 1944, Aleutians

Dear Dick—

Getting into the Army was no trick at all—just a matter of passing their physical tests—so why should they bother about history? Getting overseas was a little more trouble—they had me tied up as an instructor at Monmouth for some months, and there's a tendency to keep enlisted men over 35 in the States—but nagging took care of that in the end. At the moment I'm tied up with training programs again, here, but I hope to get back to my own outfit—or some other Signal Corps organization— soon. I like communications work, and, while it's not my line, I *have* strung wire.

Unfortunately, I'm a pretty good instructor, so I'm always being borrowed for somebody's training program. Public relations is another—and much worse—pitfall that keeps gaping in front of me, but so far I've managed to sidestep it with a couple of brief exceptions. It, in the Army, is the crap of the crap.

* * *

I hope the eyes are being licked into shape. That kind of thing can't be much fun.

> Yours,
> Dashiell

ALS Judi Hammett

To Lillian Hellman

12 March 1944, Aleutians

Dearest Lily,

This early Sunday morning the world is not as I would have it, taking one thing with another. There are people and things in it that I don't like over-much. Events run in a pattern that is not always to my taste and my patience with the ways of my Maker is by no means inexhaustible, as He is going to find out if He keeps on like this.

For instance, I do not like your friend André Gide's comment on *Red Harvest* as quoted by *Time* and I wish the old fairy would keep his lecherous tongue to himself and his ilk.[1]

For instance, I have reason to suspect that I am going to be transferred from the 14th Signal to Headquarters here and they can take Headquarters and stick it for my part. I do not like any Headquarters. They are vacuums and I, with nature, do that well-known thing to vacuums.

For instance, I have had no letter from you in several days and the script—for which I wait impatiently—has not come.

* * *

For instance, my favorite pair of pants—my only pair of kersey-lined ones—have reached a stage of filthiness beyond even me and so, until they are cleaned, I must wear OD's.

For instance, but that ought to give you a rough idea of how he who writes you is greeting the Sabbath. In a pet, that's what I am.

I read Carl and Leane's *The Visitor* and—hold on to your chair—it really isn't bad at all except for their dull insight into character and a tinny and foolish ending. I wrote 'em I had a good time reading it—which I did—and think it would make a play and movie—which it would. Never did I think I would have to encourage them to go on writing by telling them I'd liked something they did!

The enclosed check from Knopf you may do what you like with—be sensible and buy yourself a birthday present with it, or devote it to some slightly less worthy cause, or be unimaginative and deposit it in my account. I point out possibilities, I don't tell people what to do, though I do judge them by their actions.

Much love,
SDH

1. In "An Imaginary Interview" (*New Republic*, 7 February 1944), Gide called *Red Harvest* "A remarkable achievement...Hammett's dialogues, in which every character is trying to deceive all the others and in which the truth slowly becomes visible through a fog of deception, can be compared only with the best of Hemingway." During the middle 1930s, Gide was considered an important fellow traveler in international Communist circles. The Party looked to him particularly

for support of the Popular Front. After a visit to Russia in 1936 to deliver a funeral oration for Maxim Gorky, Gide published *Retour de l'URSS*, an attack on the Soviet system. Thereafter he was considered a traitor to the Party, all the more loathsome because so much effort had been invested in soliciting his support.

TLS LPT

To Lillian Hellman

The play discussed here is Hellman's The Searching Wind.

13–15 March 1944, Aleutians

* * *

Last night the play came, so I pushed the War up a couple of hours so I could read it before breakfast. Now, having breakfasted, I report as follows:

You must understand first that I am not a man who knows very much about polite comedy and what makes it tick. You have, in this one, a defter touch than in any of your other plays, and it may well be that that is what makes light comedy tick and will make this one click. I don't know. It doesn't seem to me that you make your points, but it may [be] the nature of light comedy that its points aren't so much made as revealed in passing.

My feeling is that you should have told your story in chronological order, running the triangle straight through with history from the dawn of Mussolini up to today. The best of the play is in the historical scenes and, in the present form, they seem to me to be in effect subordinated to the triangle—and to make the closing of the play anti-climactical. Now, one section of the play is seen in the light of the other; it is said, and is of course inherent in the whole thing, that each had a bearing on the other—but for me that part is not sufficiently shown.

Another thing: catching these characters now here, now there, doesn't—it may be different seeing them on the stage—give me a chance to know, to *feel* them and what they do to one another. Cas, as a matter of fact, seems to me a not altogether necessary character in the play. What I'm trying to say is that there are too many things—too much rounding out of personality and even event—I have to supply for myself, and I'm not sure that audiences can be trusted to do that accurately.

The essential frivolity that fucked things up—and I take it that's the real point—isn't *shown*. No answer is provided to the question, "But what else could these people have done?" And there isn't—except of course by inference—any statement that the kind of people who couldn't do anything else should never have been there.

(You understand, of course, that I read the script for the first time only a few hours ago, know very little beforehand of what you were trying to do, and am coming to the whole thing not only cold but with practically no time to have let it sink in or to have thought it over. This kind of snap jud[g]ment is not likely to be of the best. I'm just putting down what I feel on practically the spur of the moment, and I hope you don't give it any more value than that. There's no excuse for either of us considering this anything like considered judgment.)

Characters of the sort you've chosen here are—you've learned before now—sons of bitches to handle on the stage unless, of course, you load them down with idiosyncrasies or something, because they are essentially characterless characters. I don't know how you're having the two gals directed, but they don't come through to me from the typed sheet with any bite to them.

None of this is doing you much good, of course, and I'll try to do better after I've had a little while to think, but I dare say we'd be better off if I just kept my big mouth shut. After all, if you're opening on the 26th and this, at the fastest, can't get to you before the 22d—how can it do anything but perhaps disturb you?

I will try, though, to get something maybe useful to you as soon as I can.

And it is in ways the most interesting play you've done, and it's got swell stuff in it, and, as I said before, it's defter than any of the others, and you are a cutie.

> Much love,
> SDH

(who does not always know as much about everything as he acts like he does and who hopes the play gets its points over in a manner that'll make this letter sound like the work of a smart-alek)

TLS LPT

To Lillian Hellman

21 March 1944, Seattle, Washington, APO 980 (i.e., The Aleutians)

Dearest Lily,

This—the calendar and nothing else tells me—is the first day of spring, so by now I've had a look at at least of piece of all four seasons up here, since I came to the chain—though not to this island—in the summer. Come to think of it, I *have* seen a bit of all four seasons here. I arrived just a couple of days ahead of autumn last September. (I'm glad I got that point settled without taking all morning, tho god only knows just what difference it makes.)

I understood about your not writing, honey, so don't bother your pretty little head over it. And that goes for the rest of those weeks of rehearsal and while the show's on the road. I'll just be happy and grateful to get what I get when I get it—but you are supposed to make up for it later, when you otherwise have not a thing to do but figure out how to spend your royalties and what to say to interviewers.

I'm still a cluck on the play. Maybe I can't advise you what to do because there isn't so much you should do. In that case I am showing a certain amount of taste, even if in a stupid way. Do you think that could be it? (I'm not trying to dismiss it, darling, and I'm still trying to jockey things around so that I can devote at least one solid day to it. So far I haven't been able to manage more than a solid hour or two, and nothing much good to either of us can come out of that.)

You'll notice I got a new address. The change is a small one as far as you're concerned—simply substitute Post HQ for 14th Sig. Serv. Co. The rest stays the same. The transfer—so I understand—went through a couple of days ago, but nobody has yet given me any official notification. Also I seem to have taken a downward step in rank—from corporal to Technician 5th Grade. (They pay the same and a T/5 carries the courtesy title of corporal, but they are by no means the same, though it's likely that only an enlisted man really feels the difference.) However, I haven't been officially told about this either and thus haven't been able to squawk. It's probably one of those roundabout moves designed to get me a promotion in the end, but even at that I don't like it and I'm by nature distrustful of these delicate organizational maneuvers. Half the time you wind up being screwed by them. And, anyway, I wasn't too dissatisfied with my dinky but honestly earned two stripes and I'd like to have them back without any lousy T underneath them. I don't know why I'm giving you hell about this, since it's obvious that your part in it couldn't have been a very large one.

I give you free hand in the matter of my Broadway investments and anything you did on the play is very fine and pleasing to me.

If you and John Huston had to talk about me, we are more or less even. Olivia De Havil[l]and is up here and I have to talk to her about John.[1] She, by the way, hadn't known he was back from Italy until I told her about your letter. I think she wanted a look at the part of the letter mentioning him, but you had fixed that with your Hellmanisms about his maybe being queer for me, so—not knowing how long it might take me to prepare her properly for what she was going to read—I kept it in my pocket. She seems very nice. As a matter of strict fact, she seemed a little more than that to me, but I'm not unmindful of the fact that she's the first woman I've really talked to in nearly 9 months. The softness is what really gets you. Suddenly you realize that everything you've touched for months and months has been harsh in texture. A handkerchief—and ours are far from silken—is the closest you've come to tactile smoothness. The snow here is granular, with a good deal of ice in it; the tundra is coarse; even the mud is gritty. Visually there is no softness here. I'm, if possible, more convinced than ever that this is the most beautiful part of the world, but it's an almost metallic two-dimensional beauty with no warmth or gentleness to trick or woo you into liking it. Its great bleak loveliness is just there hard and sharp forever and ever and to hell with you and your red-headed sister. So after a while you forget about softness, gradually, not even knowing that you've forgotten anything. And then you are reminded. If you are a Hammett—which is to say, if you are very smart and lucky—you presently discover what it is you have been reminded of and then it's all right. If you don't discover what it is then you are in for a rather bad time of it.

A chap name Wallace, who once took some publicity pictures for *The Watch on the Rhine*, took a pip of me the other night. As soon as I can get the prints he promised me—or if I get them—I'll send you one. I look kind of like an old character actor and kind of like Groucho Marx in a white fright-wig and kind of like me showing off, but I think it's one of the best I've ever had taken—lately anyhow—and in any case, as they say, it's very interesting and well-composed.

This morning I wrote Peggy Herrmann to thank her for the knitted thing, into which I thus far have been afraid to insert my noodle, not knowing whether I can get out again. But it was nice of her, I guess, and I will try to give it to somebody who needs it.

I'll try to obey all your orders on the vitamins and such when they get here. But it is only fair and just to remind you that it was always you, and not I, who never read the instructions on things. I am, as I wrote you before, back in good shape again, but the little odds and ends to eke out dietary deficiencies can't do me any harm and, who knows, may plump me out, a thing I had counted on dentistry for, but, alas, in vain.

Once again I've fallen way behind on sleep. It's past noon now and I've been up since around four yesterday afternoon, with only about three hours sleep yesterday. So I reckon I'll go lie down when I finish this, though I'm more tired than sleepy. I think I'm falling into your old way of being afraid I'll miss something if I stay in bed.

I'm glad you liked Hakam's bracelet. I was afraid you had a horror of some sort coming to you. And thanks for fixing up the Tabouis matter. There is a character up here who was wounded in Spain and who practically lives on political salon intrigue and who is drooling himself into a permanent mildew at the prospect of reading Mme's proofs.[2] I haven't yet decided how much I'm going to charge him for the right to translate them for me—only I'll have to be pretty firm to keep him from reading them to me. Cockburn's news-letter has him on the verge of pregnancy once a week. Cockburn, by the way, is usually at his very good—if quaintly phrased—best these days, particularly when he is dealing with the antics of the Conservative Party.

By the time you read all this tinified V-mail form you'll probably have no eyes whatever and I do not want you to stop having eyes.[3] They are very nice eyes, as I remember. So it may be that I had best save them by stopping this.

> Mountains of love,
> SDH

1. Both John Huston and movie star Olivia De Havilland made Office of War Information documentaries and traveled to the Aleutians.

2. Robert Colodny, one of Hammett's *Adakian* staff, as a member of the Abraham Lincoln Battalion had been wounded in the Spanish Civil War. He was eager to read *Tabouis*.

3. V-mail was a wartime innovation to reduce the volume and increase the efficiency of overseas postal deliveries. Letters were written on special, already stamped sheets available at the post office and sent to an APO address, where they were microfilmed. The film was flown overseas, or back to the states, where letters were printed on special paper and delivered to the addressee. The page size of V-mail correspondence is reduced about 75 percent from the original.

TLS LPT

To Lillian Hellman

25 March 1944, Aleutians

Dearest Lily,

Yesterday brought a very nice small flood of packages from your generous and pretty little hands: tobacco and much very fine food, some of which has already been guzzled and some of which awaits that rainy day. Thank you very much, darling.

There was also a package of food from Herman, so I guess I'm not going to have to take any lip from the mess hut if worst comes to worst.

Today there was a letter from you, sounding very tired and making me wish I could do something for you, but I guess that ain't so easy at this distance, so I'll have to just take it out in feeling for you, which doesn't help either of us so awfully much.

* * *

You can use Swope in your novel, of course, but that gives you no exclusive right to him. He is public domain stuff if I ever saw any.[1]

I know one has to put up with a lot from folk in your profession, where the theater takes up so much of your time, but, just the same, it seems to me you're going a little too far—being just a little too narrow, shall we say?—when you send me "loge" instead of love. Let's have no more of this talking shop.

I still think I'm pretty nearly right on FDR vs Congress and, no matter how the anti-administration papers interpret things, the members seem to me to be stepping very carefully around at the moment. As for Barkley, don't forget it was he who said, after his first visit to the White House subsequent to the blowup, "You would never have known anything has happened—if it did."[2] Southern Democracy may squawk and cut up and sulk and roar, but they need the man from up on the Hudson and they know it. The coming campaign may be a nasty one, but I don't see how it can be a very close race—not with Willkie busy as he was four years ago undermining all the campaign issues that would give the GOP a chance.

The Italian thing isn't pleasant of course, but it's downright delightful compared to what could be cooking over there on the Indian border. Mac may yet be cabling you for some of Max Factor's heavy sunburn grease paint.[3]

I suppose you read what your friend and bracelet giver Sam Hakam had to say about me in *PM*. He seemed to find it remarkable that I could still breathe at my age, the louse, and I've hardly been out of my wheel-chair since I read his piece. One bit especially I liked. I repeat it to myself often—when my staff isn't reciting it to me: "He had recaptured the zest, the very essence of life." Old Lazarus Hammett himself, ignoring the grave-clods still clinging to his shroud! No amount of practice in s[c]hmaltz-spreading will ever make your people a really tactful race.

Now I've got to go see a man about an artist, and then wander on home for a nap. (Yesterday I got a lot of sleep; today I go short.)

> Great quantities of love,
> SDH

1. Herbert Bayard Swope was former executive editor of the New York *World* newspaper.
2. Alben Barkley from Kentucky was majority leader in the U.S. Senate. He was a centrist. When President Roosevelt was preparing to run for his fourth term, he invited both Barkley and James F. Byrnes to the White House and led each to believe he would be the choice for vice presidential running mate, then FDR chose Harry S Truman without informing them. Barkley was elected Truman's vice president in the 1948 election.
3. On 15 March 1944 Allied forces began a bloody assault on the German Gustav line in central Italy. General Douglas MacArthur led an assault on Burma to establish an air route to China at about the same time. St. Clair McKelway was in Burma.

TLS LPT

To Mary Hammett

27 March 1944, Aleutians

Dearest Mary,

Here's a clipping from *PM* which just goes to show what people can put on paper when they set their minds to it. It makes me sound—and for a day or two had me feeling—as if I'd been dug up from the grave and am now racing around to keep the sexton from finding me and putting me back in. The clothes in the illustration seem to have been stolen from a dead Russian.

Thin Man's Father

By Lt. (j.g.) Sam Hakam, USMS

It was quite by chance, while making a survey for the United Seaman's Services, that I met the famous author of *The Thin Man*. I stumbled across him in one of the Aleutian Islands . . . Where he runs the camp newspaper.

When I met Corp. Dashiell Hammett he received me heartily, this tall spare man who had chucked an income of a hundred thousand dollars a year to go into the army as a buck private. He took me over to the radio station to meet the bunch there. We trudged over the snow.

Hammett was in the lead, his long legs making firm, vigorous strides, while I, a much younger man, panted along behind. He discoursed with sparkle and vitality as we walked and I could scarcely believe my host was a man past 50 and one whose health was at one time shattered almost beyond repair.

At the radio station Hammett was warmly greeted by the staff. I was amazed at the vitality of this writer turned soldier.

After a short stay we returned to the office to get out the morning's paper.

Hammett perched himself on a desk, feet in laced boots draped over a chair, a GI hat cocked over the right eye, partly covering his shock of iron gray hair. His voice, as he barked out instructions, had an almost belligerent tone. He had everything under firm control.

Writers brought him their copy. He scanned it rapidly and pointed out necessary corrections, additions or deletions. Invariably the criticism would end with a word of praise . . . Steadily and surely, an excellent camp newspaper took shape.

The guy was enjoying himself hugely. He was living! One could almost say he was young again. He had recaptured the zest, the very essence of life.

This was a vigorous, patriotic, fighting man doing his bit for his country—a corporal in the Army of the United States. This was Dash Hammett, Soldier!

* * *

Your dope on furloughs from Alaska and the Aleutians is wrong, honey. The present period of service—or tour as the Army calls it—in this part of the world is two years. Then you can—if the transportation and the replacement are available—either take a 30-day furlough or go off somewhere else on "rotation." And your old man has only been up here eight months. So, in the normal course of events, he hasn't anything to bother about for a long time yet.

I don't know whether I wrote you, but a couple of months ago I started, and am still running, a daily newspaper—still on mimeograph while we wait for other equipment to be shipped from the Coast—for the troops on the island. It's been kind of fun, but it's running fairly smoothly now and beginning to—if not exactly bore me—make me look around for something else to try my hand at.

The paper, by the way, is the reason for my having been transferred from the Signal outfit to Headquarters—a change I'm not too heartily in favor of. Oh, well, the war will probably last long enough for me to get around to a lot of other things.

My antique health remains excellent and I hope you all are as well as I.

A great deal of love and many kisses,
Papa

TLS MARSHALL

To Lillian Hellman

Hellman's play, The Searching Wind, *was in tryouts before the Broadway opening on 12 April.*

27 March 1944, APO 980 (i.e., The Aleutians), Seattle, Washington

Dear Lilishka—

It's a cinch you'll be off to Delaware parts, doing what playwrights call work, when this gets to you. I do hope it's all going well, darling, and that your fears are by now past history and your play a coming honor to the American stage. Anything I say from this distance now will sound lame—though it needn't be as flat as the beginning of this paragraph— but I don't have to tell you how unlame and unflat my wishes and hopes are. And I hope I don't have to tell you that I'm not just wishing for the play to be a "success"—though that ain't bad, either—but for it to come out right for you, which, after you've spent the zillion or so it might make you, is the only thing you're left permanently with. I do hope it does, baby! Along about dusk I went up on the hill that overlooks our bay and practically talked to god about you and it.

There's very little—that's putting it mildly—news of or from me at the moment. I eat better than usual. I sleep spottily but—in the long run—amply. I do work that doesn't bore me too much, my prospects of the future are limited but not unpleasant. I live among inconveniences that are no longer discomforts. I know where I stand with god and the world. I am a dull but not unkindly vegetable.

Everybody in the Army...Oh, all right, then! Nearly everybody in the Army thinks a good deal about what they'd like to do after the war. Being, as you know, very slow on some things, I've just recently got around to that. It's still kind of an idle game in which I've not yet involved myself very deeply, but I think maybe politics. I mean politics of an office-holding—or at least office-running-for-with-a-chance-of-getting-in—kind. What does Madam think? Would Madam speak to me when I was, say, a City Council member in Detroit, for instance, or a legislator in California? It would, of course, be best—or, in any event, would make me feel I was being a shrewder jobbie—if I picked whatever geographical spot seemed to offer the best pickings for an earnest left winger who was willing to spend a year or two digging in. There is always the chance that I may have forgotten all about this by the time you reply, but, on the other hand, things like this sometimes sneak up on me and stick, and this may be one of them. So it might be just as well for you to think it over some night when you're having trouble getting to sleep and don't want to wonder why Irene is sulking.[1]

(But, remember, first thing, after the war, I am going to loaf—and I mean really loaf—not just idle around the way I used to—for quite a stretch, maybe with cameras in my hand, maybe not.)

Speaking of cameras reminds me that I haven't yet had the censor OK a print of my new portrait so I can send it to you. I'll try to get that done tomorrow. You should not be deprived of this gem any longer than necessary. It will make you count the silver.

* * *

With mountains of love,
    SDH

    1. Irene is presumably Hellman's housekeeper.

TLS LPT

To Mary Hammett

31 March 1944, Aleutians

Dear Mary—

    I had a nice letter from you today—except that the part about having to have a wisdom tooth yanked mayn't be nice from where you sit, but I reckon it's over with by now.

Let's see what I've got in the way of news. Lillian and Shumlin are down in Wilmington, Del., where her new play, *The Searching Wind*, was to have opened its out-of-town tryout last night. I read the script and can't make up my mind whether I like it—though parts of it are very, very fine. Neither can I decide whether it will be a hit. My guess is that it'll not make a great deal of money. (I have a moderate investment in it.)[1]

Olivia De Havilland spent last week up here on our island, chiefly visiting the men in the hospital, and Yehudi Men[uh]in stopped overnight to fiddle a little, so we're practically as cluttered up with people like that as the Brown Derby; and then *The Adventures of Mark Twain*—not yet released in the States—was shown somewhere on the island last night. By golly, it's getting to be like living in Glendale!

I put that photograph in the mail today, so you'll soon see what the old man is looking like these days—or, anyway, what he looked like last week.

I'm trying out a new schedule, by which I get some sleep during the night so I can get up around noon, and if I'm going to stick to it tonight it behooves me to put this away and get going down the gulch to my hut.

> Love and kisses,
> Papa

1. *The Searching Wind* ran for 326 performances at the Fulton Theatre in Manhattan.

TLS MARSHALL

To Lillian Hellman

In April 1944 Hellman was denied a passport to go to London to work with movie producer Alexander Korda on a script for Tolstoy's War and Peace. *The reason given was "the present military situation," though a year earlier she had been denied a passport because she was "reported to be an active communist."*

31 March 1944, Aleutians

Dearest Lily—

Yes'm, you've been swell with your letters this week. They've been coming in nicely and I am very grateful and ungrouchy about the whole thing. This is the way wars ought to be fought and you may quote me. But you're not very psychic over salt water. I've been as spry as that elderly goat your nautical friend wrote about all week and feeling very well indeed.

I liked the FBI clipping very much: it approaches the whole post-war question from the true FBI angle and was addressed to the perfect FBI audience. At the moment I'm trying to figure out what I can do about it. Maybe your sergeant on *Yank* might take hold of it if you prodded him. The *New Statesman* you mentioned hasn't come yet, but I always await with great interest any inkling as to what our cousins across the sea are thinking if that's what it is.[1]

Yesterday I had a letter from Lois, who seems to like the political parts of the play, but thinks the other scenes are let-downs. She always writes me kind of loftily about the dull people we know, although she never sounds as if she thought them dull until she sums up at the end of the letter.

You never can tell—the Korda thing might come through. *War and Peace* would be something nice to get your teeth into, except that the English sometimes do funny things to pictures, or so I—who haven't seen even an English movie since along about 1914—am told. So you have to figure it this way: if the deal goes through, it's swell; if it doesn't, you haven't missed anything maybe.

I finally got around to preparing that photo for shipment to you and it should go off today.

A long letter from Nell Martin came today, giving me a great deal of very detailed information on the latest happenings to a great many people whom I no longer remember at all. Reading it was practically like having a[p]hasia.

All my hopes are that, as I write, everything is very hotsy-totsy in Wilmington, Del., and that, as you receive it, everything will be the same, only more so, in Baltimore, Md., all of which is simply building to the real hoopla in New York, N. Y.

Now I go off to bed, wishing I were going to dream of you, but knowing it's ten to one I don't dream of a damned thing.

Much love,
SDH

1. Founded in 1913 by the Fabian Socialists Sidney and Beatrice Webb, the *New Statesman* is a literary and political weekly magazine published in London.

TLS LPT

To Lillian Hellman

3 April 1944, APO 980 (i.e., The Aleutians), Seattle, Washington

Dearest Liliaska—

The first of the Tabouisouis articles came today, for which thanks.

This morning we were awakened by rumors that the invasion of Europe was under way, but—as of three-thirty P.M.—no confirmation or even supporting rumors have come through. My guess is that it's happened, but most of the local Army is pretty thoroughly disgusted by now, apparently because they've seen no troops marching down to board ships.

Last night I finished the Si[m]one book and had a good time reading it.[1] I think he's a satisfactory writer, not because he shows you a hell of a lot that's so right, but because he does not give you anything that's wrong. And that is more than a negative virtue in a novelist.

This is the 4th of April (pay no attention to the dates at the top of my letters: I sometimes just stick a sheet in the typewriter and head it up so it'll be ready when I want to write you) and in another couple of days I ought—if I'm lucky—be getting your report from the road. It passes not quickly, that bit of time. And my conscience acts as if I were shirking by being up here instead of down in Wilmington with you. (Oh, well, I'll make up for it, you'll have dozens of out-of-town openings for me to go along to between this and the next war.)

I mailed you—the same day I sent the photo—an advance copy of the "Battle of the Aleutians" booklet. The text is mine, the stuff under the illustrations Colodny's. It is no *War and Peace* you understand, and it was [meant] primarily for the troops up here, so you are not to quarrel with its rather severe tone of understatement. That was my own idea and I like it. As a matter of fact the Army gave us a remarkably free hand. They just said, "Write a booklet about the Aleutian campaign," and when we'd written it they said, "That's fine," and printed it.

The April issue of *Field & Stream*—read on a rainy Sunday afternoon—gave me the god-damndest dose of homesickness I've had since I've been in the Army. For a day and a half I went around seeing very little besides the pond, the green boat with six inches or so of rainwater in it, and the flyrod with the adhesive-tape bandage around the loose place in the wrapping.

But that too passed and today I'm once more that perhaps dull but not too discontented middle-aged member of the armed forces who, recognizing the fact that his age makes it more than doubtful that he'll ever see actual combat duty on an active front, accepts this as perhaps the next best thing, and who, in any event, does not need to bruise his white head against things as they are.

This afternoon's mail brought me a long and dull letter from Nels Jorgessen—still in India. I don't know what's given him the notion that I'm vitally interested in all the details of his inner and outer life. He must think absence has done it, I never let him have any illusions like that when he was around me.

I'm interested in the details of your inner and outer life, though, and your sidewise life if you have one.

Mountains of love,
SDH

1. The name is unclear in this v-letter, but it seems to be Simone, a reference to André Simone, the pseudonym of Otto Katz, the model for the anti-fascist hero of *Watch on the Rhine*.

TLS LPT

To Lillian Hellman

9 April 1944, APO 980 (i.e., The Aleutians), Seattle, Washington

Easter Verse
(for L.H)

That Christ has risen
And this be true:
You've been good for me
And I for you.

D.H.

TLS LPT

To Lillian Hellman

17 April 1944, APO 980 (i.e., The Aleutians), Seattle, Washington

Dearest Lilishka,

Tomorrow I embark on my twentieth month in the Army. Does that kind of historical trivia interest you? Well, then, in those twenty months I've been a member of, or on special duty with, no less than seventeen different companies, proving that nobody seems to have wanted to hold on to me, I guess. With such a past, however, I need, I hope, never fear that I will be finally bogged down anywhere, or at least that's what I keep telling myself on those occasions when life seems not as highly spiced as it might be and today too slightly distinguishable from yesterday.

Not that that has any bearing on my current days, most of which flow past evenly and swiftly enough. If I'm not exactly getting all the excitement that a war has to offer, I'm probably getting as much as a man my age can expect and what I say is, let's be humble and not demand what is beyond our deserts.

Having run out of Milton I now go to bed of mornings with Donne, of whom I've got hold of the Everyman's volume. And, if I've got to insist that nobody can actually substitute for M, yet D is pretty good in his own right and I could be doing a lot worse than reading him. You may quote me on that too.

It's latish morning—that is, latish in a pre-breakfast sense—so it may be that any minute now I will chop this off and run for my hot cakes or eggs or whatever it is that the best-fed soldiers in the world are being fed this spring morning. (We had some very creditable corn fritters last night.)

Believe it or not, I just stopped for a moment to give my staff an opinion on which, if one's wife were having a baby and it was a matter of saving the life of one or the other, one should save. Have you any ethical-moral problems you want an easy answer to?

I thought not. All right, then I'm wasting my time on you and had better go spend it eating.

> Which I'm going to do—though not without much love,
> SDH

TLS LPT

To Lillian Hellman

17 April 1944, APO 980 (i.e., The Aleutians), Seattle, Washington

Dearest Lily—

There's no sense in my telling you that you can't imagine how happy your telegram about the play's success made me because unless you are a dope—which I sometimes doubt—you ought to be able to imagine it pretty accurately. I just go around muttering, "Fine, darling, fine, fine, fine!" and grin into my mustache.

And let this be a lesson to you, my fine buxom cutie. You are a big girl now and you write your own plays the way you want them and you do not necessarily give a damn for the opinions of Tom, Dick and Dashie unless they happen to coincide with your own. No matter how close to you T, D, or D may be, and no matter how hard they try to think in terms of your play, you must always bear in mind that what they're actually fooling around with is some slightly different idea of their own, which may be all right, but with which you have no business involving yourself. So maybe sometimes you *are* too close to what you are trying to do and it *doesn't* quite come off. So what? So you've certainly inched yourself closer to being able to do what you want to do than if you had let yourself be talked into doing something you didn't want to do just because it would come off. And when—as now—you've done what you wanted to do and it has come off, why you've made a sap of the author of that stuff about not eating your cake and having it too and you are of the elite...with hemstitching.

I've just finished thumbtacking to the wallboard over my desk the portrait from the Sunday *Herald-Tribune*. You may sneer at it, but I who have not seen you since June 28 find it warm and lovely and it makes me think that maybe it would be a mistake to stay up here after the war is over. After all, I've probably only got fifteen or twenty years of youth left and it seems needlessly spendthrift to waste them away from you. So you may definitely expect me back!

Day after tomorrow is the one on which I expect that veritable river of letters from you to me to start flowing—maybe the next day, because you may have been too tired on opening night, but certainly no later than that . . . else I'm going to be very, very irritable and that's not good for either of us.

I shall now take my happiness for a walk up on the hill before I settle down to the night's work of breaking in a couple of new staff members, which will of course resolve itself into my more or less secluding myself in my cubbyhole inner sanctum while the more experienced staff members work over the less. All I really have to do is be a little bland about mistakes, and I've had practice.

> Mountains and mountains of love,
> SDH

TLS LPT

To Lillian Hellman

28 April 1944 [no address]

Dearest Lily—

At last that letter came, permitting me once more to write you direct without too much loss of pride and one thing or another; but I reckon I'd better make this a long letter, because you said you were going to write again the next day, and when you say that our post office department takes a week off, knowing there won't be much doing for at least that long.

* * *

Go easy on those plans, darling, you're scaring me. Remember this is the Army and the Aleutians and there's a war and August is a long time off, allowing for many untoward intervening happenings. And even if everything goes along like a dream, I won't know things like where and when till the last minute; and it's quite likely to be a bit later than you think. The last of July is the minimum-date, but, since only five per cent of us can be gone at any one time, there undoubtedly will be a back-log of those ahead of me to wait out—if you can make any sense out of the way I tell it.

Subject to all of those things—and to your ability to get transportation when you want it—the nicest plan—when and if I get going—

would be for you to meet me in Seattle; then we could go down to Los Angeles for a couple of days and then East—or wherever we felt like going. But there's no use—though I know this won't stop you: you've already started changing furniture and things around—doing much in the planning line just yet.

I don't know about Pleasantville as a political arena. Westchester County is largely populated by people I don't understand and, in any event, is probably best by-passed until the forces of darkness have had more harrying by local guerrilla forces. My own inclination at the moment is toward the fat lands that lie between—say—Michigan and Nebraska inclusive, in many parts of which there also is admirable shooting and fishing, which hurts nobody. But—and don't think I'm giving up the idea—sticking the pin in the map comes fairly late on the agenda, so there is no immediate hurry about that. The larger plan, the grand strategy, should be worked out—see, there's planning to be done: so stop sulking—before we come down to working out tactical details. I'm trusting you to put your mind to it.

Sure, yes, of course, naturally, you know I will, why do you have to ask? and uh-huh are some of the answers on the play-reading, mulling and advising question. I may not be able to do you much good in a hurry, but if I can take my time, maybe…though, as I wrote you a couple of times before this, I'm inclined to think you're about ripe to go on ahead and play your string out in your own way and to hell with the no-matter-how-well-meaning-or-even-shrewd counsel of no-matter-whom.

I'm glad you liked the picture: I liked it, though I wouldn't want to go on record as saying it didn't maybe give me just a little bit the best of it.

Again, last week, I walked into a mess hut in time to see the last few minutes of something called *Higher and Higher,* with Jack Haley, who seemed to be playing straight (isn't he even as much of a comedian as he used to be?) and Frank Sinatra, who in the end was left standing on a cloud, deserted by director, cast and even lighting. And *that,* my darling, catches me up with the movies for at least fifteen years ahead, I hope. There is now little doubt that the true three-dimensional film will have arrived before I get around to them of my own will and accord again.

Now I must sever myself from this and turn to what may be called my duties.

Much love and many kisses,
SDH

TLS LPT

To Lillian Hellman

On 25 April 1944, the New York Drama Critics Circle failed to select the best play of the year, though Hellman's The Searching Wind *received seven of the fourteen votes and four judges abstained. The group's constitution had been lost, and the secretary had failed to record in the minutes a resolution about voting procedures, which revised the system that allowed judges to cast an unlimited number of ballots. The Circle determined that as of 1944 a majority vote was required for a winner, and Hellman's play fell one vote short.*

3 May 1944, APO 980 (i.e., The Aleutians), Seattle, Washington

Dearest Lily—

* * *

Lin on Hellman at the opening of the *Wind*: "She was beautiful in a fine red suit and golden tan. The Kohinoor swung from her throat on a golden rope best of all she was serene...you could tell by her voice, which always gives her away.[1] I've never seen her so calm." So.

Lin seems very pleased about a radio program, *Listen: The Women*. As a matter of fact, if Lin ever finds anything to settle down to—and to even suggested that she might takes a lot more brashness than mine—it's more likely to be radio than anything else.

I also had a letter from Maggie—the first in quite a while. She says she is sure the *Wind* will win the Pulitzer, but has not "irritated" you by mentioning it to you, and she's trying to wheedle me into making a $100 bet on it, but as much as I would like to give Maggie the money—knowing how she needs it—I don't think I'll do it that way.

The NY critics' comedy, as reported in the press, sounds very much like something staged by the NY critics. I think once they get their charter as the Manhattan chapter of the College of Cardinals they'll behave a little less foolishly: they won't be under so much strain.

I'm sorry about you and Louis only because you're probably sorry.[2] It has been a long time since there was any reason for anybody supposing he was heading in any direction at all in any field whatever and, even if you're moving at a snail's pace, it takes a loud voice and very sharp ears to carry on any kind of intercourse with one who's lying down.

* * *

Mountains of love and many kisses,
SDH

1. The Kohinoor is a 186 carat diamond that dates back to the 14th century. In 1850 the East India Company presented it to Queen Victoria, who had it recut to 108.93 carats. It is presently housed in the Tower of London.
2. In a review of *The Searching Wind* in *PM* on 13 April 1944 Louis Kronenberger criticized the play as unbalanced and failing to integrate the political plot with the personal lives of the characters.

TLS LPT

To Albert Hackett and Frances Goodrich

6 May 1944, APO 980 (i.e., The Aleutians), Seattle, Washington

Dear darlings—

It was swell hearing from you after all these thirty or forty years, and that is what you can send me instead of cookies and gay colored neckties—letters. Lying around on the beach all the time here with your head in a native girl's lap—or whatever it is Charles Laughton's always doing—you get out of touch with things back home and the first thing you know you're going around not caring whether your sheep-skin-lined sarong is cleaned and pressed properly or not.[1] It was different in my first war—they kept us pretty busy twisting spare bow-strings and rubbing dents out of our shields—but nowadays everything—except, of course, transportation and things you can use—is so highly mechanized that time—which is generally shaped like a five-gallon can of Diesel oil for the stove in your hut—hangs pretty heavy on our hands.

If I didn't guess you were pretty tired of *The Virginian,* I'd say it wasn't a bad assignment.[2] It's—unless my memory is no good at all—by far the best of the all-time Westerns.

That booklet on the Aleutians that I worked on was only a ten or twelve page affair and there wasn't anything in it to make Korda change his mind about producing *War and Peace*. (That Hellman–Korda deal has been cooking or hanging fire for months, and Lily never seems to have thought it would come to much.)

For the past three or four months, I have been editing a daily—mimeographed till our equipment comes—newspaper for the troops on this particular island. It's a soft go, I reckon, but being an Aleutian Ingersoll was never my chief aim in life. So I'm kind of looking around...just shopping. Sometimes I think I'd rather be back in the Signal Corps stringing wire—but that's sheer insanity.

This is my tenth month in this corner of the world and it doesn't seem anywhere near that long—nor does it seem possible that I'll have been in the Army two years by the end of this summer. The weeks really click by. It worries me sometimes. The first thing I know the war will be over and there I'll be out of a job again. Oh, well, there's no use being pessimistic about it.

Much love, and if you hurry through those cross-word puzzles just a little faster you'll have time to write me some afternoons.
Dash

1. The British actor Charles Laughton played Chester Tuttle the 1942 Hollywood film *The Tuttles of Tahiti*. Tuttle was a feckless hedonist who frittered away his family's fortune on the tropical island.
2. There had been movie versions of Owen Wister's novel *The Virginian* in 1914, 1923, and 1929. The Hacketts received writing credits for the Paramount remake released in 1946.

TLS LPT

To Lillian Hellman

6 May 1944, APO 980 (i.e., The Aleutians), Seattle, Washington

Dearest Lily—

I had a letter from Frances and Albert this afternoon and will be glad to pass on to you all the Hollywood news you can't get from Lois and Celia Ager.[1] Want to play like that? They're finishing a re-do of *The Virginian*, having finished something called *Hitler's Gang* for Paramount after having done an Army orientation picture called *Know Your Enemy—Japan* for Colonel Capra.[2] If you want to know more, just say so? God knows I've got no secrets from you!

They also said Herman was due out there soon to make his next picture for Warners. I dare say now that Wallis is gone he—H.S.—faces this next chore with a shake or two.

* * *

How could I have pretended to forget it? Came in the mail today a sort of diploma thing from the Academy of Motion Picture Arts and Sciences with a shiny seal and everything and all signed by—you'll never guess—Walter Wanger in person.[3] I'm afraid to read what it says on this document. It's sure to be a let-down, and as long as I don't read myself face to face with harsh reality I can go around thinking maybe I've been appointed ambassador or something to some place or am entitled to buy something at wholesale prices. Whatever it is, it was nice of them to think of me. In the same mail, by some kind of coincidence, came an invitation to join the Academy, which costs two dollars—and it wasn't *that* nice of them.

I'm having a pretty good time with Romains's *Work and Play*, so maybe I'm not condemned to poetry after all. So that takes *that* load off my mind. (My literary style this morning seems to consist of underscoring the word *that* wherever it appears: well, there are worse ones.)

The Japs in their English-language press dispatches now call their Chinese enemies "Chungkingers," and I like it and wish I could use it without seeming to reflect on one of our Allies.

I hope I also like the breakfast of creamed chipped beef on toast for which I am now heading...but not without much love,

SDH

1. Celia Ager is unidentified.
2. Movie director Frank Capra joined the Office of War Information.
3. Walter Wanger was a producer and at the time president of the Academy of Motion Picture Arts and Sciences.

TLS LPT

To Lillian Hellman

The opening references are to Lillian Hellman's father, Max, and probably to Aline Bernstein, set designer for The Little Foxes *and costume designer for* The Searching Wind.

10 May 1944, APO 980 (i.e., The Aleutians), Seattle, Washington

Dearest Lily—

The Maxisms and the La Bernsteinism were both very typical and I liked them. I like to feel that those things—and what else are we fighting to preserve, may I ask?—continue, come rain, war, high water or the devil, because they are what I understand by freedom of speech. If they ain't that, what are they?

As always, however, I like most in your letters the parts—when any— which speak favorably of me, for that too is somehow an integral part of my conception of freedom of speech. (By god, I'm going to get some good out of the otherwise slightly fantastic notion of the import of freedom of speech if it's the last thing I do!) But what you had to say this time pleased me very much, and you are a cutie-pie, and, if I had any sense, I would stay away forever so that you could build up a kind of dream picture of me without ever coming up against old bubble-prickler reality, but I haven't got sense enough, so do not throw away the clothes and things I left around the house.

For instance, if you do not think I am worn down you are nuts—very lovely and sweet and all that stuff, no doubt, but nuts! I am worn down to a fine frazzle and I would not kid you about it. I don't mind kidding the Army about it because it is all right to kid armies except on the enemy's behalf, and I can still go through most of the necessary service motions, but the truth is I am only a hollow shell, inside which is nothing but bones, blood, flesh, anatomical sundries and chemical doings. There are no diamonds in me, no pearls, and damned few divine souls. I am a husk, that's what I am, and five or six years more of this are going to begin to tell on me. Only yesterday I thought I saw a soft flicker in the hard gem-like flame with which I used to burn and there's no longer any use denying that I've more than a sprinkling of grey on my temples, though perhaps if I wear my hair longer that won't show so much—and I could keep my parka hood up.

This week has been W. H. Auden week (*The Double Man*). He is neat, but I am not sure that's all a poet needs to set up shop. You do not have to treat that as a question. Nowadays I limit literary discussions sharply to: "Do you like Whosis's novels?" "Yes." (or, "No.") End of discussion. To say, "Yes, but" (or "No, but") is to turn the whole thing into a lecture and I do not care for lectures.

But I care for you and thus do not mind sending you great quantities of love,
SDH

TLS LPT

To Maggie Kober

11 May 1944, APO 980 (i.e., The Aleutians), Seattle, Washington

Dear Maggie darling—

This is W. H. Auden week in the Aleutians, but I'm not sure his week isn't going to be whittled down a little, because it did not start until yesterday morning, which was a Wednesday, and, after I have eaten and picked up my laundry this morning, which I don't have to tell you is a Thursday, it's more than likely that I'll go to bed with *Bar 20 Rides Again* or a copy of this week's *Yank*. I do not want to run down any friend of Gypsy Rose Lee's, you understand, and W. H. A. is a tidy enough man with his phrases, but sometimes when the torrents of spring are all asurge in me I do not feel that "the better the manicure, the better the poet" is necessarily true.[1] Well, there's no use being nasty about it, I suppose, so let him go his way, at least this morning, and I'll go yours.

I'm still having trouble with my prose reading: I seem to enjoy *Work and Play* while I'm reading it, but I intermit a great deal. (That brings my reading pretty much up to date. In my next letter I'll report on my writing and arithmetic.)

I saved you a pretty penny by not betting on the Pulitzer, though I guess it would have been too late by the time my taking-up of your offer got back to you.[2] What else do you want to bet on? And did Nancy ever pay you that twenty bucks? She didn't say anything about it in any of her letters to me, and she and Lily are inclined to be thrifty with my money, so don't let them beat you out of it with that "how can you take it from a poor soldier boy overseas?" stuff.

I'm feeling sort of twice be-widowed this week. The two most satisfactory guys-to-be-around that I've run into thus far in the Army were transferred out of my hut into another outfit and I miss them when I remember to.

And if I don't stop this I'll miss breakfast.

           Mountains of love,
           SDH

1. In 1941 W. H. Auden managed a house in Brooklyn Heights for writers, which was owned by George Davis, an editor at *Harper's Bazaar*. Boarders included Carson McCullers and the burlesque stripteaser Gypsy Rose Lee, who wrote *The G-String Murders* (1941) while she lived there.
2. No Pulitzer Prize in drama was given in 1944, though a special prize for musical presentation was awarded to *Oklahoma!*

TLS LPT

To Mary Hammett

13 May 1944, APO 980 (i.e., The Aleutians), Seattle, Washington

Dearest Mary—

Our days are getting long: it's not yet five-thirty in the morning, but it's almost full daylight outside. Except for the mountains and here and there in the valley, our snow is practically gone and we—I mean those of us who are young and spry enough for such doings—are trying to lay out baseball grounds on the tundra.

Two weeks from today I'll be fifty. It seems a little incredible. I suppose it's always almost impossible to remember how long you've actually lived. I've been thinking too much about my age the last couple of years. Maybe, once I'm past the half-century mark, I'll stop it. It's a foolish sort of occupation and can in the end lead only to thinking you're pretty good just because you're pretty old. And, boy, oh, boy! can you go wrong on that!

I haven't been doing much of anything worth writing about. A little, not too much, work. A little reading, chiefly Milton and Donne because prose doesn't seem to hold my attention very well nowadays, though I have been slowly threading my way through Jules Romains's *Work and Play*, and seem to like it—except, if I like it as much as I seem, then why do I dawdle through it? (What are we playing? Riddles?) Every once in a while I bring out the notion of writing some fiction while I'm here, but so far all that's come of it is that I've dusted off the notion and put it back where it came from. Maybe someday...

Earlier this week I lost—by transfer to another outfit—a couple of hut-mates I kind of liked. One of them, a Texan named Colvin, had been with me since I hit this island last September. You see 'em come and you see 'em go.

If this letter isn't exactly the gayest one you ever saw it's probably because I'm hungry and sleepy and my vitality is low, all of which I will fix up *very* shortly by means of tomato juice, scrambled eggs, coffee and bed.

> Much love darling, and many kisses,
> Papa

TLS LPT

To Lillian Hellman

15 May 1944, APO 980 (i.e., The Aleutians), Seattle, Washington

Dearest Lily—

Life on islands between the Bering and the Pacific is very dull around four o'clock some Monday mornings to which this one isn't much of an exception. I don't know just how anybody except maybe the Japs—god forbid—could go about livening it up, and I'm not one to hanker after *too* much excitement, but just the same anybody's heart that's beating this morning is doing it on its own hook... The *Variety* with the New York review of the *Wind* came today and read reasonable enough. I haven't yet seen the *New Yorker*'s or the *New Masses*'s—magazines are in one of their slow-arriving streaks nowadays, except for *Newsweek* and *Time*, which come in the first class mail...If I ever get around to having my hair cut I'm going to have a portrait painted for you so that I won't be altogether at a loss for words should I find myself in a taxi with D. Parker on my return to what we call the old country...will you ask Nancy if she ever paid Maggie that twenty buck bet for me. She, N., hasn't mentioned it and her, M's, reference to it was too ambiguous for me to figure out whether any cash had changed hands...Frances Pindyck wrote me about some other deals she was fixing up for the Spade book, and which she would take up with you when the contracts were ready—and I don't know why in hell I'm bothering to mention it, since I don't know anything about it and she'll certainly tell you. I guess it just comes from wanting to stick my nose in my own business, where, god knows, it doesn't belong...There are undoubtedly a great many fanciful things going on in international and domestic politics at the moment, but, to one who would have to have very long fingers indeed to be in touch with the world-pulse at the moment, it seems that you're letting them over-worry you a little. (This isn't true of you only, of course, but is fairly general among the serious.) There's no question that a great deal of trouble is looming, but—what the hell!—history railroaded us into an approximately ideal set-up (if you look chiefly at its possibilities and don't pay too much attention to some details) and you have to pay for that sort of thing sooner or later. You can't beat the spiral and there are few short-cuts to the third step in the dialectical process. But so long as there *is* a spiral and there *is* the process, then the rest of it's more or less a matter of paying a high price or a little lower one, of having to wait till tomorrow or till the day after. (See? I'm going into my fiftieth year with the deep conviction that man is young and rich.)...I had a letter from Paul Monash, who pretends not to be proud of his analyst's having sent one of his dreams to the *Psychoanalytic Quarterly*, or whatever it is...The Wallis deal sounds okey-dokey: about as close as you can come to a stomachable Hollywood deal is probably a not-too-tight tie-up with somebody you respect[1]...

A great deal of non-Hollywood love,
SDH

1. Hal Wallis was the producer of the movie adaptation of *The Searching Wind*, released by Paramount in 1946.

TLS LPT

To Lillian Hellman

16 May 1944, APO 980 (i.e., The Aleutians), Seattle, Washington

Dear Lilishka—

I don't know exactly why I'm up this early afternoon, except for *this*. I got to sleep around five this morning, woke up at ten, rose for early noon chow that was hardly worth it, and am now probably staying out of bed through inertia. I wish inertia would take me down to the PX for a haircut, but I guess that's asking too much of it: I doubt that anything else will get me there, though what wind there is is blowing in that general direction. But that won't be enough: no leaf in the breeze Hammett...I read the Gibbs review last night and a nasty little puppyish affair it is.[1] Jesus, the impudence of the little when they happen not to like something! It fills them with all the power of a beauty contest judge...My other reading consisted of finishing Romains's *Work and Play* (I guess it's safe enough to say that *Men of Good Will* is going to be a very large minor novel) and Bob Carse's *There Go the Ships,* which makes it safe to say that foolish men will always write foolish books on no matter what subject of no matter what degree of closeness to their hearts. And that just about runs me plumb out of literary pronouncements for the nonce...Except that Max Yergen, a piece on Africa by whom I've just read in the *NM,* is possibly as dull a writer as he is a talker, and I wouldn't want to go any further than that[2]...I forgot to tell you that this isn't afternoon anymore, but the morning of the 17th. A little man who does movie reviews for our paper came into the hut and, though he tries not to bother me, he is a depressant with no sedative effect and I am a coward who took to the hills for a little walk and then to bed for a little nap and did not get going on this letter again till my night's chores had been done and were being immortalized on mimeograph paper...Another non-sedative the day brought my way was a stray copy of *The Country Gentleman,* which started me thinking about farms in New York that I haven't seen since a year ago next month and *that,* by mighty easy stages, led me, in what you might call the twinkling of an eye, to thinking about sex.[3] Needless to say, I arrived at no new conclusions about it, which possibly proves that my memory is not as bad as it could be. And the only old conclusion I came to was that I could give in to a temptation if it played its cards right. In my present situation this is a completely impractical decision, since there is no way to implement it: I'm up a blind alley if you ever saw one and will probably go down in history as the Lord Dunsany of the Aleutians[4]... On the other hand, I may go down in history as the Rip Van Winkle of the Aleutians because I am going down to my hut and even if I can't find any little old men with casks and bowling equipment to bed ...

> Mountains of love,
> SDH

1. Woolcott Gibbs, "The Theatre: Miss Hellman Nods," *The New Yorker* (22 April 1944): 42–44.
2. NM is New Masses.
3. *Country Gentleman* was a monthly magazine from Curtis Publishing Company.
4. The prolific Irish dramatist and story writer Edward John Dunsany (1878–1957) was acclaimed for his fantasy and science fiction.

TLS LPT

To Lillian Hellman

21 May 1944, APO 980 (i.e., The Aleutians), Seattle, Washington

Dearest Lily—

Life sent me a tear-sheet on General Montgomery that makes him out just a little too cute for even a British officer and—not consciously, of course, because the Luce publications seldom get anything right that way—more or less one with the picture your Englishman gave[1]... My only comment on "A" is that if he'd spend less time at Moss Hart's and more time at brushing up on tactical operations we might be getting further with the loss of less. I'm not one to sneer more than the ground forces have to at those propeller fellows, but it does seem to me that when we're flying something smaller than the *Queen Mary* at less than 20,000 feet of altitude over a target that twitches we somehow fail to squeeze the last drop of utility out of the Wright brothers' invention...

This week's news from the States that you didn't send me is the birth, on April 30, of Jill Clayburgh.[2] Don't you think I care about these things? Do you think I intend to spend my declining years among those who have grown old too? Have I, in your opinion, no foresight?... Hammett the scholar has just received a bundle of books from Paul Elder's and should now be visualized as yawning his way through Count Sforza's *Contemporary Italy*, some woman's *Yankee from Olympus*, and E. E. Cumming[s]'s *1 x 1*.[3] Hammett the writer received a letter from one David Morton, poet, who said H's books were just about all that saved his sanity while undergoing a three-way spinal operation in a Boston hospital. Next week I'm going to save a hat designer's masculinity... My week-old—or older—grouch seems to be peeling off a little, chiefly, I suppose, because I haven't been able to find anything to blame it on, but I'm still looking around and may still come up with something before it's all gone. It's been a beast and I'd hate to lose it... Hammett the reader just took time out to look at the title poem—the last one in the book—of *1 x 1* and begs to report that he was favorably impressed. In fact, I'm ready to quote, though from elsewhere in the book, first an epigram,

> "*A politician is an arse upon*
> *which everyone has sat except a man*"

and, second, cross-page, four lines on Louis Untermeyer:

> "*mr u will not be missed*
> *who as an anthologist*
> *sold the many on the few*
> *not excluding mr u*"

You think *you* have trouble getting news? You should have to depend on AP and ANS as it comes to us; that is, whittled down to interfere as little as possible with military communications traffic, which is of course necessary, but which also of course allows for plenty of slanting in the whittling. And then, for your sins, you should try to put it in the morning's paper in such form as will not completely misinform everybody.

330

And this trick you must do wearing handcuffs labeled Army Regulations and War Department Orders...Sometimes I think it'll turn my hair gray...but I guess that's an exaggeration...

> Much love, cutie, and that's no exaggeration...
> SDH

1. Field Marshal Bernard Law Montgomery was commander in chief of British-Canadian forces in France in 1944.
2. The actress Jill Clayburgh's mother, Julia Door, worked for a time as a theatrical production secretary for Herman Shumlin, Lillian Hellman's producer. Hellman and Door were friends.
3. Paul Elder's was a San Francisco bookshop Hammett frequented. *Yankee from Olympus* was Catherine Drinker Bowen's biography of Oliver Wendell Holmes.

TLS LPT

To Lillian Hellman

23 May 1944, APO 980 (i.e., The Aleutians), Seattle, Washington

Dearest Lily—

The old professor is tired this morning, so the class in natural history will please come to order without too much fuss and feathers. In fish circles—at least among the bass and sunfish I was raised with—the male fish guards what may be called—since mama fish has gone off to write a play or attend a meeting of the League of Women Shoppers or something—*his* eggs. I do not know why anyone should care about the sex of a fish, but if you're of the opinion that this information will upset Herm's affair in any way you are at liberty to withhold it from him until such time as the fish is free to look out for himself...All right. Now we turn to the class in psychology. A long time ago I pointed out to you certain points of resemblance between Lois and Maggie. You did not like the idea and chose to push it aside. You may continue to do as you like about it, my fine feathered friend, but you'll never understand Maggie *that-away*...All right. That brings us up to the class in personal relations. For many years you've thought it cowardice not to take pretty definite sides on people and things without bothering very much about the question of whether any pretty definite sides existed to be taken. You couldn't be indifferent to baseball, for instance: you had to hate it. You couldn't think a canoe was a nice light vessel for water: you had to love it. And so with people: they had to be lovable or hateful and they, of course had to feel the same way about you. It's doubtful that anybody ever loves or hates anybody anyhow; though of course they may love or hate the *idea* of them. For the rest, we get along on loving, liking, hating, disliking or being indifferent to this or that part of them...School's out...Burke was her name, though now I think she is—or will soon be—named Morrow. She was—the last time I had a report—about to marry the ex-husband of a girl who has since married Ralph Trealor, a chap I used to hang around the neighborhood of Fort Monmouth with...For the first time in many, many months there is now a case of Coca-Cola under the Hammett bunk; yesterday I sent out both laundry and dry cleaning; there no longer can be any doubt that civilization has come to APO 980...Did I tell you I'm tired this morning? Well, I am and I've got to shave before I go to bed, and maybe wash a couple of pairs of sox, and as long as I'm doing all that I might as well take a shower—though I'll bet you when it comes right down to it I don't go *that* far—so perhaps you would be so kindly as to excuse me...

> Much love,
> SDH

TLS LPT

To Josephine Hammett

24 May 1944, APO 980 (i.e., The Aleutians), Seattle, Washington

Dearest Princess—

So now you're eighteen and I'm all out of child daughters. My family is cluttered up with grown women. There's nobody who has to say, "Sir," to me anymore and there are no more noses to wipe. I feel old and caught-up-with. But there's no use sulking about it, I guess, and I might as well try to make the best of it and welcome you into the ranks of the adult. I'm sure you'll like our little club.

Josephine Dolan, Hammett, and an unidentified nurse at Cushman Institute, 1921

Hammett in his apartment at 620 Eddy Street, San Francisco, circa 1924

Hammett on the roof at Eddy Street, 10 August 1925

Jose, Mary (age 6), and Josephine (age 13 months) in Fairfax, California,
June 1927

Albert S. Samuels, Sr.
(by permission of Peter Samuels)

Peggy O'Toole, who, Hammett said, was
the model for Brigid O'Shaughnessy in
The Maltese Falcon

Postcard from Hammett to Mary, postmarked 10 May 1928. On back: "I'll be home
for luncheon Saturday. Papa."

Josephine, age 6, 1932

Josephine and Mary with the Raggedy Andy doll their father sent them, circa 1930

Hammett, circa 1932

Mary and Hammett in Malibu, California, circa 1934

Josephine, age 13, on the day of her confirmation into the Catholic Church

Mary in Santa Monica, circa 1937

Tavern Island, 1938. On back in Hammett's hand: "The clouds are your old man. I don't know who that apparently naked native in the lower left corner is."

Mary in Santa Monica, 3 February 1942

Jo, about age 15

Portrait of Lillian Hellman from
Jose Hammett's photo album

Ralph Ingersoll in front of a display of PM
front pages (Bettman / CORBIS)

Herman Shumlin and Hellman

Hammett in Adak, Alaska, circa 1944

*Hammett to Hellman, 29 August 1943:
"I enclose a snapshot of the old corporal returning from chow."*

Hammett circa 1945

On back in Hammett's hand: Back row: Alva Morris, Hammett, Bernie Anastasia, Dick Jack. Front Row: Oliver Pedigo, Hal Sykes, Bill Glackin, Don Miller. On floor: Al Loeffler, 1944"

On back in Hammett's hand: "Corrine's, Anchorage—June 1945. Goldman, Kierce, Joe Louis, K, Ruby Goldstien, Hammett, Capt. (?)"

Hammett and Josephine in the backyard of the house he bought Jose and the girls on Purdue Street in West Los Angeles

Jean Potter, Anchorage, 1946

Hammett and Mary at a restaurant in Greenwich Village, circa 1948

Hammett, late 1940s

Virginia and Kermit Bloomgarden with Lillian Hellman
(courtesy of Virginia Chilewich)

Hammett with Josephine on
her wedding day, 6 July 1948

Hammett with his granddaughter Ann, age 3 months

Jose and granddaughter Ann, age 9 months, at her home on Purdue Street in Los Angeles

Hammett, Ann Marshall, Hellman, Loyd, Julie, and Evan Marshall on the porch of Hellman's house on Martha's Vineyard, Spring 1960

As you've probably found out by now, this world of grown-ups into which you have been admitted is a very, very superior world indeed, inhabited only by people of sound, mature and mellow mentality—all of which they can of course prove simply by showing the dates on their birth certificates.

But what you may not yet have noticed is that all these people stand on their own feet as independently as all get-out, being beholden to their fellows only for food, shelter, clothing, safety, happiness, love, life and picture post cards.

Another thing you'll discover is that one of the chief differences—some cynics say it's the only difference—between a child and an adult is a child is under some sort of obligation to grow, while an adult doesn't have to if he doesn't want to. Isn't he already grown up? What do you want 'im to do? Try to make himself into God or something?

You'll *love* our little club.

Actually, it's nice thinking of you as grown up, darling. You were a nice child and you'll make a fine woman and it may not be necessary to disown you for many, many years to come.

> Until then, much love and kisses,
> Papa

TLS MARSHALL

To Lillian Hellman

3 June 1944, APO 980 (i.e., The Aleutians), Seattle, Washington

Dearest Lily—

Your birthday cable came belatedly, but none the less welcomely and you are a cutie and now let's talk about your birthday which my calendar says isn't very far off. You are to start thinking of something you want and I will send you a check between now and the great day because I can no longer trust you to buy things on your own...There's no reason for your explaining to me why you don't like John. It's easy enough not to and I've never been what you could call wild-eyed about him myself...The citation

would be swell, honeybunch, and I do hope it comes through. God knows you deserve it…The Wallis deal on the *Wind* sounds pretty good…Speaking of deals, I didn't cable you on the Warners deal because (a) cabling presents certain difficulties at the moment and (b) I trust you to do right by me without any interference on my part…It's as stinking a June morning as anybody's likely to see, or maybe that's just me, though when I peeped out of the door just now what I saw out there wasn't me and was stinking…I finished the Sforza book on Contemporary Italy. Career diplomats are strange empty people…I'm now reading a book on astronomy and Willard Price's book on Micronesia, which seems to have [been] written with an old set of crayons that were found among Ralph's childhood effects…Did I tell you that nowadays it's not quite dark when we go down the draw for late chow at eleven at night and it begins to get light around four in the morning? I didn't? Well, it's a fact and possibly the only fact that has nothing to do with you in this letter…This is another of those days that find me kind of aimlessly up. I went to bed around three this morning, slept until nearly six, couldn't get back to sleep, got up at six-forty-five for breakfast and decided to stay up until I got sleepy, which ain't yet…I sent you a copy of the "extra" my staff got out on the occasion of my natal day. I think it amusing enough, but I hope I don't have to point out that I'm a far finer character than they make out…I have two or three photographs of the island to send you as soon as I get something to wrap them in…I suppose you've seen—or at least been told of—the item in La Parson[s'] column saying I'm up here "entertaining the boys." Good old USO (or Three-shows-a-day) Hammett doin' his bloomin' bit!…Memorial Day I was a one-minute part of a local radio program and if you've got a hat handy to drop I dare say I could find a draft of my speech handy to quote in full, so it's up to you and Johnfred…I'd better write the turtle-catching instructions to Nancy. If I haven't got you mixed up with somebody else you have nice wrists but do not get much out of written instructions, having a tendency to go into action long before you've read as far as the first comma…Now I think I'll read the full text of Churchill's last speech to see if it's as appalling as excerpts make it seem, but didn't I always tell you not to write off the British people?…I keep telling myself that now…What I've got to tell you has to do with love and kisses and such…
SDH

TLS LPT

To Lillian Hellman

12 June 1944, APO 980 (i.e., The Aleutians), Seattle, Washington

Dearest Lily—

* * *

I'm awfully sorry you've been out of sorts and I hope that's all just so much case history by now…Have I really sounded upset? I don't think I've been, though my memory for that kind of thing is not always so good. (Did I ever tell you that the strong of heart never remember how badly off they've been at one time or another, which is what leads you, for instance, to the eventual belief that each of the past plays wrote itself.) Anyway, it's easy to read too much into a series of letters from a place like this. Ordinarily one goes around all day neither up nor down in spirits, but when one sits down to sum it up in a letter (you always have an idea that your addressee wants to know how you feel) one falls into habits of cheerfulness for awhile perhaps, and then of lesser degrees of cheerfulness, and so on down the scale to gloominess. And then there's another thing you should discount. I nearly always write you at the end of my night's work, when the hour and fatigue both work towards a letdown, or later in the morning of days when, for one reason or another, I've not been able to sleep…So far as I know I'm running along normally these days. My appetite isn't all I would like it to be, but it's not too bad. I'm now feeding myself Hexebox, though with no clear knowledge of how many I should take in the course of twenty-four hours, and maybe that'll pick me up. But there's nothing for anybody to worry her pretty little noggin over. Don't you remember me, the fellow to whom *but nothing* happens?…One of Mike Quill's transport workers came in last night and brought me a book of poetry by a Navy flier named William Meredith who had put in some time up in the Aleutians.[1] As verse most of it's not bad, though a bit obscure and diffuse, but what I wanted to say is that in the title poem, "Love Letter From an Impossible Land," he mentions Shishaldin and Pavlof, the volcanoes I once wrote you I was in love with in another part of this north countree. Only he called Pavlof "the black volcano!" I guess he was never lucky enough to see it in the sunlight in September, all silver white. I may write him an indignant letter!…Night before last a Major Obermeyer, a relation of Alfred Knopf's, phoned me and we chatted for a while about how much he disliked Blanche. I think people bring that up too quickly, defensively...You can see by the two foregoing paragraphs that my little newspaper hut is practically a Bloomsbury salon, only better heated no doubt...I had a letter from Leane which—you'll never believe me and there's no reason why you should—had nothing in it about the Randau literary labors, though there were nice things about your play...I go now ...

> Mountains of love ...
> SDH

1. Quill was president of the Transport Worker's Union, CIO.

TLS LPT

To Josephine Dolan Hammett

18 June 1944, Post HQ Co DEML APO 980 c/o PM Seattle, Wash.

Dear Jose—

There's not much news, as usual. The furlough deal does not look any too bright at the moment, though I may get away for a week or so on the mainland of Alaska.

The weather's been pretty good—for here—and my health runs along in its customary nothing-hurts-a-Hammett form. Once in a while boredom sets in, but that happens to practically everybody everywhere, and it only means that you've got to stir yourself to find something else to do or think about.

I had a letter from Dad a couple of days ago. It was cheerful enough, but short—his hand goes to sleep when he writes. He didn't say how he's making out with the new artificial leg.

The bank check should come at the rate of $200 a week. Let me know if there's any hitch in it, though I don't imagine there will be.

The summer's wild flower crop has actually begun to show itself, sparsely, it's true, but this is pretty early for it to be showing at all. By next month, however, we should be fairly giddy with colors.

We now have ice cream at least once a week, there are rumors that we're soon to have real milk, and the new latrine is to have flush toilets. Civilization is moving right in among us. Maybe before I leave here we'll even have a paved road, though that seems kind of far-fetched.

Breakfast ought to be about ready, so I reckon I'll go down and see about it before I go to bed.

Love,
SDH

TLS Marshall

To Lillian Hellman

26 June 1944, The Aleutians

Dearest Lily—

Among things going on today are my purchase of $20,000 worth of Series F bonds, which takes $14,800 out of that sacred account; good weather; a general feeling of well-being, induced I suppose by a good day's sleep and some rather nice ham for chow this evening; and a vague feeling that the world in general is going along as well as anybody has any right to expect and there's no reason for examining the seams too closely.

About the turtles (snapping): it's safe enough to pick them up by their tails if your grip is firm enough. Towing them across the lake by the hook is kind of risky, unless you're sure the hook is set solidly in good strong tissue; otherwise the big ones can tear themselves loose sometimes, even if they lose half of their guts in the process. The simplest way of bringing them back in the boat is to put them in a burlap sack.

The play hasn't arrived yet, so I'm still walking the floor.[1]

One of my mates just got himself transferred to the small boats section of the Army Transportation Service and, the weather being what it is and these islands what they are, I could be tempted to try to make the same kind of deal for myself.

The fellows fishing in one of the enclosed cartoons would be standing about ten feet from my office-hut door. There used to be fish in that brook, but too much Diesel oil gets into it nowadays, though once in a while a foolish Dolly Varden trout gets itself in there, until the oil seals up its gills and smothers it.

That just about concludes my report from the Aleutians for this day of our Lord.

Much love and many kisses,
SDH

1. Hellman's screenplay for *The Searching Wind*.

TLS LPT

To Prudence Whitfield

27 June 1944, The Aleutians

Dear Pru—

It's almost summery enough these days to make us believe in summer again and I'm feeling almost spry enough to start rebelieving in youth. When I was in my teens and my maternal grandfather, then in his 70's, got himself a new bride and began turning out a new crop of uncles for me I thought him a little touched in the head, but I now find myself less critical of him: maybe he wasn't as batty as he seemed to me then, though I still claim he was the most longwinded grace-sayer that god ever put between a hungry child and his food, and I've disliked few people as much as I disliked him. One of my pet fears used to be that— since I looked a little like him, had been named after him, and had even been born in the same room he was born in—I might grow up to *be* like him. In his old age he became very religious, wouldn't raise tobacco— the only really profitable crop in his part of Maryland—because it was sinful, and squandered what means he had putting up churches for some obscure Holy-rollerish cult. Rather than have that kind of future I'd stay in the Army.

Love,
SDH

TLS Penzler

To Lillian Hellman

2 July 1944, APO 980 (i.e., The Aleutians), Seattle, Washington

Dearest Lily—

I don't know about your handsome Russian colonel except that I'm sure I don't approve. And what the hell's he doing in Canada? Are we fighting them? And are you sure there wasn't something significant about the color of his uniform? Maybe he's been in Toronto, in that same uniform, since 1918 or thereabouts. And, anyhow you ought to be careful about foreigners. They have strange customs and on the whole don't, for all their fancy la-de-da's, really respect women the way wellbred Americans do. Now understand, this is just for your own good...I had a letter from the "kid" in which he expressed surprise at learning I'm now 50.[1] He thought I was 49, so, since he knows he's 2 years younger than I, I suppose he's been going around lying about his age until he fooled himself. The last sentence in his letter—in a paragraph complaining about the limitations of Public Relations work he does for Standard Oil—was, "Incidentally, I got myself divorced yesterday morning." I don't always understand the Hammetts, but you can't fool me about the priggishness (pronounced with a very hard g as in Klondike) of that "incidentally." My Joya in New Castle sent me a picture of herself and poodle and it looks large and fine with its tongue hanging out like any one of the generations of poodles we've had grow up around us...Last night, or rather this morning, I finished reading Sigerist's *Civilization and Disease*, and had a very good time with it in spite of its limitations. Hurriedly, before you are roiled, I say these limitations are those imposed by the nature of the book: it's based on six lectures at Cornell—the "Messenger Lectures on the Evolution of Civilization"—and therefore barely skims the surfaces that he will plow in the history of health that he's got to do *sometime*. The book has a great deal of his own charming simplicity...Of the Wertenbaker stories I've only seen one—on the Normans—and thought that very fine, so I'll be on the watch for the others.[2] There seems to me to be something criminal, using the word precisely, about *Time* nowadays...I'm not surprised by Ed's having seen that paragraph. He also is a subscriber—maybe he's the *other* subscriber—to the *Alaska Sportsman*. I think that's where I first saw the magazine...Frances Pindyck wrote me that she had got married to a Morton Thompson or something in the Army, so will you—or your delegate—send her a wedding gift for me? Something around $100, say...Here I am, rambling on about other people and using up all the paper I could be writing about myself on. But there's no use starting now. I couldn't do myself any kind of justice in this mingy little bit of space that's left. So the hell with it. I'll go eat ...

> Much love, Madame, and many kisses ...
> SDH

1. The kid is Hammett's brother, Richard.
2. Charles Wertenbaker was a foreign correspondent for *Time* who was among Hellman's amorous interests. He wrote the text for *Invasion* (1944) about the Allied landings in France June 1944, with photographs by Robert Capa, as well as novels.

TLS LPT

To Lillian Hellman

5 July 1944, The Aleutians

Dearest Lily—

I enclosed a clipping Sis sent me, in case you missed it and want to know how you seem to a bit of Southern womanhood, sir, writing for Southern womanhood. I remember that girl now. We once got tight together and she wrote a very silly interview, and later did a foolish one on Dotty, which I think I sent you from here. There doesn't seem to be any malice in her—just foolishness—and her story on you taught me quite a few things that I was glad to learn, such as, for instance, that Dick Maney is now your adviser as well as friend, and how can you go wrong listening to him?[1] I'm also glad to know that you are neither cynical nor naïve, but engagingly feminine and devoted to practical jokes. I can see you now hanging that bucket of cold water over the door so it'll upset on Fred Her[r]mann's head when he comes in with the egg money and a flower catalog. I bet I'm missing a barrel of fun up there in the country! The headline—Lillian Hellman's Happy When Writing Her Plays—left me speechless. Even service in two wartime armies doesn't make a man's vocabulary able to cope with things like that.

Yesterday was a pleasant quiet sunny day and today is a pleasant quiet only slightly less sunny day and a small batch of books—Dalí's *Hidden Faces*, Franklin's *Rise of the American Nation* and Selsam's *Socialism and Ethics*—arrived from Paul Elder's and that would be all the news you could get out of me if you ran me through an orange squeezer.

If you could find it in your heart of such well-known generosity to send me a box of sweets, you would also find me very grateful, to which end I append a ducat for the postmaster.

> Thank you, dear, and with mountains of love,
> SDH

1. Maney was Herman Shumlin's press agent.

TLS LPT

To Lillian Hellman, as "Corporal Hammett"

Hammett bought $20,000 worth of savings bonds, and found that the account he drew from, which was managed by Hellman, had insufficient funds. In response to her letter informing him of the mixup, Hammett sent this reply.

6 July 1944 [no address]

Dear Corporal Hammett,

This is the way it went:

Hardscrabble Farm has for many years needed a washing machine. But it was not until after the war started, when they were no longer available, that I decided to buy one. A year passes and the curtain comes down.

On Wednesday, June 28th, Miss Hellman and Miss Bragdon, two unmarried and dislocated women, saw an ad in the newspaper saying that Gimbel's, at a War Bond Rally, would auction off many things, including an electric washing machine. The two ladies figured out what Miss Hellman had in the bank and what Corporal Hammett had in the bank, and Miss Bragdon took herself to the auction. Missing the washing machine by a thousand dollars, annoyed at missing it, she then bid $30,000 for an inner spring mattress which had not previously appeared in the conversation. She pays for the mattress with a $22,200 check on

Cpl. Hammett's account and on her way out buys a $1000 bond for some nylon stockings. Happy in this victory she goes home. The curtain goes down on Act 2.

The curtain comes up one week later with Miss Bragdon and colored maid on stage, with Miss Bragdon inquiring from Gimbel's whether this is a single or a double mattress. Shortly after this a letter arrives from Cpl. Hammett saying that he has withdrawn $14,500. I am not in a temper nor is the weather good enough to describe the scrambling around to put back in Hammett's account money which was removed for the purchase of the mattress. The curtain comes down on what many foolish folk would call a happy ending: Gimbel's has the mattress, the account is well covered for your check, and the $22,200 bond will be destroyed. Miss Hellman has taken an oath that she will not again use your bank account for evil purposes, and both ladies request that you send sufficient notice when you intend to draw large sums of money.

Miss Hellman is interested in enclosing a letter from the Veterans Administration, and wishes to assure you that she will stand by you in any ugly emergency.

> Most sincerely

TLU LPT

To Lillian Hellman

9 July 1944, APO 980 (i.e., The Aleutians), Seattle, Washington

Dearest Lily—

Some people say it's raining out, but I say there's just enough moisture in the air to keep the skin from cracking.

Some people were in from *Yank* to tell me what a fine paper I run and to give me Joe McCarthy's regards and I sent him my regards and told them what a fine weekly he and they were running, and so the loving cup passed around for an hour or so and no great harm done one way or the other, I dare say.[1]

The AP last night carried a rumor which I choose to believe about Russian troops massing on the Siberian borders of Jap-controlled China.

I hate to believe anything that comes out of Chungking—including the communiqués—but this looks like the move that's got to be made if China's to be kept in the war and Henry Wallace shouldn't have been sent to Asia just to carry the season's greetings.[2] Me, I've always wanted to go to Kamchatka.

I'm still full of unseemly spryness and cockiness, trotting around coatless and with my head bared to the elements except when there are cloudbursts and acting in general as if I weren't a day over forty-nine. You wait and see: I'm going to be one of those silly old men who pretend they are sound as a dollar, deny their lumbago is bothering them and are always challenging younger men—who have nothing to gain and wish the old buzzard would go off and die—to foot-races and wrestling matches.

Well, that just about drains the last drop of my store of wit, chitchat and pleasantries this morning.

Take mighty good care of yourself and I'll do the same with me.

> Much love,
> SDH

1. Joseph McCarthy was editor of *Yank: The Army Weekly*.
2. Henry A. Wallace, a friend of both Hammett's and Hellman's, was vice president of the United States from 1941 to 1945.

TLS LPT

To Lillian Hellman

As Hammett was serving in the Army during World War II, the Veterans Administration discovered that he was still classified as disabled as a result of his service in World War I. His disability pension was discontinued as was the pension paid to his daughter Mary as a dependent of a disabled veteran.

14 July 1944, APO 980

Dearest Lily—

I'm sorrier than I can say about the bond mixup, but Nancy wrote me that there was around $23,000 in the account and it was all right to go ahead and use any part of it, or so I understood her, and I took *that* for an indication that you knew—or at least were prepared for—what I was going to do—or that I was going to do something. I'll move slower after this, and you're not to take any oaths—or keep them if taken—about tampering with my account...I'm writing the Veterans' Administration about the disability pay. I never thought they'd've gone along this far with the payments, but the idea of drawing disability pay for one war while serving in another, twenty-five years later, was too funny for me to do anything to stop it. I'll have to give 'em back some $1100, I dare say, but let me handle it from up here because it may be that I can still get some fun out of it and, in any event, need something to occupy my mind and this will do that without overburdening my mind. So will you send along any more correspondence that comes along in re this, as we used to say in Wolf's office?[1]...I had a letter from Lin, who described a cocktail party she had given and said of you: "Lily looked but too too...in a soft black satin, with a hat the color of her hair and tanned skin ...bound in black. She has lost weight again...very becoming...she looked so tidy and all together and very very pretty." Are you sure there was never anything between you two? Or do you suppose she was just having that orgasm on my account? She also wrote: "Joel Sayre came late and tight. Whenever anyone made a bad joke or even a not bad one, he focussed heavily and said, 'Do you know men are dying out there?'"...I don't know why that didn't make me homesick...The book I mentioned is, published by the Oxford Press. You'll like it and it's got a lot of sensible stuff in it on the importance of long-range planning for woods, ponds, pasture and tilled land, though you'll have to go further of course for technical details...I'm now about to inject myself into Selsam's *Socialism and Ethics* and Runes's *Twentieth Century Philosophy*...The group photographs as well as a smaller shot of island scenery, are packaged and stamped and will go out in the same mail as this, but probably won't arrive as soon. There's nothing in them though to make you walk any floors until they get to you...I've also filled out my application for a ballot so that I may cast one vote for FDR when the time comes...There is a nasty rumor around that some work has accumulated for me. I may not have to do anything about the work, but I'm going to have to stop this and extinguish the rumor ...

Mountains of love and many kisses ...
SDH

344

1. Eleanor Wolff was Hammett's secretary in the late 1930s.

TLS LPT

To Lillian Hellman

15 July 1944, APO 980 (i.e., The Aleutians), Seattle, Washington

Dearest Lily—

Last night we caught some crabs in one of our lagoons and cooked them for midnight chow, and very good going it was. They're much like the ones we're used to except that the claws are smaller and the legs or flippers have little hairy spines on them. They don't seem to have so much taste, either, but after you've eaten three or four of them it's easy to tell yourself that the seeming lack of taste is only a greater delicacy of flavor. I'll try to verify this when we catch and cook another batch tonight, when there'll be a beer ration to go along with them...Now do you see why it was necessary to defend these islands against the Japs?...Yesterday was not altogether a good day. Along with your letter giving me hell about the bond mix-up, and the one you enclosed from the Veteran's Administration telling me they were disinheriting me, came one from the Post Chaplain taking me to task for taking God's name in vain in our columns. (My feeling in the matter is that God's doing pretty well to be mentioned at all, space limitations being what they are, and He and His representatives had better leave well enough alone.)...After thinking over that Veteran's Administration deal I find myself growing indignant. That seems to me very small potatoes for a big country like ours and if they're going to put their wars on a retail basis then I shan't enlist in any more of them and they can get along the best they can with whatever paratroopers, Eisenhowers, tank-drivers and tail gunners they can scrape up at their cut rates...I've just been out to look at the dawn and it is a very nice gaudy little thing with red bands behind snow-capped mountains and the like, and possibly forecasts a pleasant day, though only a stock broker would do that for more than five minutes at a time here, so I shall stay up for breakfast and see what comes of it, though I'll have to either make my bed or get into it before inspection time...I've just got hold of my first copy of *Guinea Gold*, the letterpress daily MacArthur's crew got out in New Guinea. It's only a small affair of four undersized pages, but the amount of news they get into it makes me envious. Maybe I ought to try to swap my multilith equipment—now supposedly en route—for a newspaper press...A lad just phoned to ask if I wanted to play some ping-pong before breakfast. I don't know what he's doing up at this hour. Strange things go on on our island. But maybe I'll go up and see if I do want to play. I haven't touched a paddle since I came up here and it'll at least be a way of seeing how much age has stiffened my [illegible]. If I don't mention this incident in later letters you'll know that the whole thing didn't turn out too well...So now off I go to be a god-damned (that for the Chaplain!) pre-breakfast athlete, but not without sending you

> a great deal of love and those things that go with it ...
> SDH

TLS LPT

To Prudence Whitfield

Hammett sought Lillian Hellman's assistance in arranging publication for a collection of cartoons that had appeared in The Adakian. *Ultimately Hammett paid for the private publication, titled* Wind Blown and Dripping (1945), *for which he wrote an introduction.*

17 July 1944, The Aleutians

Dear Pru:

It's a damp and coolish day, but not too bad, by which I suppose I mean my ancient joints aren't actually creaking, or at least not loudly enough to be heard up here where my ears are.

Here are some more of the little pictures purporting to show what we're like up here. Viking Press is toying with the idea of bringing out a selection of them in book—or booklet—form so the world—or that part of it that's foolish enough to waste on printed matter the money with which it could buy liquor, women, men, raiment, crêpe[s] suzettes, phonograph records and dogs—can get a glimpse of our own mild horrors of war.

Once upon a time, way back in my foolish youth, I got myself involved in philosophy to the extent that thereafter I've tried to keep in some kind of touch with what's going on in that field. Not in too close touch, you understand—just one eye open to see that nobody did anything behind my back. But it's been a long time since I got any fun out of it and it really bores the bejesus out of me now. Like a great many early habits, however—breathing, for instance—it's hard to shake off, which is why I'm now laboring through a thick and dull compendium of 20th century philosophy which has me pretty well convinced that nothing's been going on while my back was turned except flea-cracking, which sounds better in German, but not in *my* German.

I guess that about covers the fields of weather, art and philosophy from the local angle for the time being. Economics, bee-keeping, homeopathy and parlor card tricks will be discussed later.

> I kiss your hand, Madame.
> Love,

TLS PEPPER

To Mary Hammett

20 July 1944, The Aleutians

Dearest Mary—

No, I don't know a thing about my furlough chances, but I'm going to see if I can find out anything today. The truth is I haven't been bothering about it much, but now I shall try to hump myself and see what's what. Don't count on it too much.

The DEML is Detached Enlisted Men's List and entitles me to wear that green cord on my cap instead of the orange and white of the Signal Corps. Most Post Headquarters outfits are DEML and it is just a little like being born out of wedlock.

I've got a new habit of playing Ping-Pong for an hour or so before breakfast each morning. I do not know exactly how that's going to help win the war—unless perhaps by puzzling the Japs if they ever hear about it—but anyhow that's what I do.

I read a somewhat condensed version of *The Lost Weekend* in *Omni-book* and thought parts of it interesting because they were authentic, but there were other parts that didn't seem to ring true and as a whole—except to make me shudder at parts I'd gone through myself—I found it just so-so.[1] (Don't pay too much attention to my verdict on novels: I'm not the best customer in the world for anybody's fiction anymore.)

Now I'm going to stop and sew on some shoulder patches, a job I've been putting off for weeks.

> Much love, darling, and many kisses,
> Papa

1. *The Lost Weekend* was a 1944 novel about alcoholism by Charles Jackson, filmed the following year by Billy Wilder, starring Ray Milland. *Omnibook Best-seller Magazine* was a monthly that published condensed versions of popular books.

TLS MARSHALL

To Prudence Whitfield

20 July 1944, The Aleutians

Dear Pru—

Thanks very much for the clippings and very, very much for the lettuce seed, for which I am now trying to find a bed where they won't be trampled under foot.

I saw the Parsons's item about my entertaining the boys, but it didn't arouse any indignation in me. It is quite natural that she should think that the most worth while endeavor I could be up to. The boys thought it the funniest thing they'd read since Leonard Lyons's story about my having refused a commission. My favorite one, though, is still the one about my having given up an income of $100,000 a year to come into the Army. (The truth is (a) it's many a day since I worked hard enough to make that much money, and (b) as nearly as I can figure it out, coming into the

Army hasn't cost me a nickel: my income has stayed just about where it would be if I were a civilian.)

I told you before what I thought of the photo—that you are very lovely and desirable in it and my only objection to it is that it makes me write you too many letters...like now, when I'm already late for a date up in the dayroom to play Ping-Pong, at which I'm now in the habit of romping for an hour before breakfast.

So I'm off to romp.

> Much love,
> SDH

TLS BLACK AND WHITE BOOKS

To Lillian Hellman

26 July 1944, The Aleutians

Dearest Lily—

Here are enclosures, about one of which you will know what to do. Though I am the last one in the world to cause anybody any trouble, I would kind of like it sometime, if it can be done without upsetting things too much, if one of the people who use "Two Sharp Knives" in an anthology would do so under its original—and so far unused—title of "To a Sharp Knife," which, while certainly no world beater, has at least the merit of pertinence, which god knows nobody could say the other title—which was thought up by *Collier's*—has.[1]

I slept beautifully from two to nine o'clock (P.M.) yesterday and am thinking about making them the standard hours. But, always cagey, I'll try them out again today before really deciding.

Sex—and by that, up here, we seem to mean chiefly the absence of women—has been bothering me a good deal lately, and, while I'm not one who thinks he's too old to be bothered that way, still I feel that my age should have let me off more lightly. However, always the scientist, I have roughly traced it to the small streak of sunshine we had some time ago and shall certainly include the relation of sunshine to sex in my ecological studies. Some work has been done in that field, of course, but I don't think the surface has been scratched, except perhaps in the narrower field of biology, which by no means covers the whole subject.

Now I've got to go see a man about a news story on the advisability of having published which those who are higher and I do not see completely eye to eye. Editing an Army newspaper in such a theater as this is often like walking an invisible tight-rope between two moving towers while juggling hot stove-lids and trying to eat a sandwich.

I'm off.

Much love and many kisses.

> Salud!
> SDH

1. "Two Sharp Knives" was published in *Collier's* on 13 January 1934. It was republished as "To a Sharp Knife" in *The Avon Annual* (1945).

TLS LPT

To Prudence Whitfield

27 July 1944, The Aleutians

Dearest Pru—

Tonight I need a soothing hand and I wish yours were around. It's been a day of petty—what the Army calls chicken-shit—annoyances and he who writes this letter is an irritable and somewhat disgruntled old man who wishes they would get their God damned war over with and let him go home, even if that *would* mean the loss of the only steady employment he has had since the Army let him go home in 1919. The way I feel tonight, I may not enlist in any more of their lousy wars; but I guess that's going too far.

* * *

The war news continues good. I imagine we've landed enough stuff by now to mount a fairly large-scale offensive and that things will soon be humming in Western Europe.

I liked the Cummings verse you sent: I had forgotten it, and there wasn't any censor for it to puzzle. Incoming mail isn't examined.

And you'd better not complain about this being a short letter, darling, if you know when you're well off. A long one would be full of whining complaints, self-pity, pleas for your tears and miscellaneous belly-aching, because I've really got the vapors.

> Much love, dear …

SDH

TLS Black and White Books

To Lillian Hellman

27 July 1944, The Aleutians

Dearest Lily—

Pessimism is the opium of the middle-class intellectual and you are to stop it. Of course there are some dark clouds in the sky, but you are no doubt too young to remember how tired everybody once got of those Maxfield Parrish blue heavens. And the whole picture is good, good even though we lost the election this fall, though I don't think that's going to happen. I still think it was wise to have sacrificed Wallace rather than have him become the focal point of the Democratic anti-FDR forces.[1] I love him as much as you do, but you simply can't make a politician out of him and a politician is what you've got to have in that second-place spot. Far more useful places can and no doubt will be found for Henry. I think the Democrats are going to be scared into turning out the vote—something they too often neglect—and there will be a lot of work done on the she-vote between now and November, especially by the CIO's PAC.[2]

Being stingy, I'd like not to give more than two to one on my election betting, but I don't think there's going to be a great deal of that kind of money, so I'll take what I can get—meaning twelve to five is acceptable if that's the current price. You could bet up to say twenty-five hundred dollars for me if you would be so kindly.

I'm tickled to death that your travel plans are shaping up so well and am keeping all my fingers, my legs and my eyes crossed for you, and if you think my dropping in at one of the Lord's outhouses for a spot of prayer would do any good I might even do that, though I get housemaid's knee pretty easily.[3]

Yesterday's was a fine sunny afternoon and I soaked up a great deal of it and when the morning mistiness thins out enough I hope to get some more today.

Early this morning I had a very satisfactory dream about you and it is my impression that you are a very sweet woman.

> Much love and many kisses,
> SDH

1. In 1944, President Roosevelt chose Harry Truman to be his running mate for his fourth term, passing over his current vice president, Henry Wallace.
2. The Political Action Committee of the Congress of Industrial Organizations claimed to have influenced the elections of seventeen senators and 120 representatives in the 1944 election.
3. Hellman was planning a trip to Russia for fall 1944.

TLS LPT

To Prudence Whitfield

30 July 1944, The Aleutians

Dearest Pru—

I had a letter today from an artilleryman I knew in another part of the Aleutians, a big red-haired fellow with a pleasant foolish face. He was going back to the States to get out of the Army on that 38-years-old deal and I gave him a note to a girl I knew who lived in a town not far from where he did his farming.[1] That was last fall. Now he writes that they're married and very happy and her sister is living with them. It is fine that people should be happy and it is much better for me to write you that she never had a sister than for me to write him, because you do not care either and sometimes red-haired ex-artillerymen are impulsive and if he is happy what difference does it make who is related to whom?

Because—and probably only because—the circumstances are such that I can't very well make a short story out of it, I've been thinking all afternoon how much I'd like to. I haven't willingly done a short story in

God knows how many years and must conclude therefore that this desire now is just perverse. Maybe my having passed it on to you will take it off my mind. (If that works you may be surprised—not to say smothered—by the number of odds and ends I pass on to you.)

It's been a quiet Sunday—not that the Lord's day differs much from any other with us except that we're likely to have chicken and ice-cream for dinner—and I hope those armies engaged in the active part of war have not been overdoing things, so there will be just enough news to fill our paper neatly and I can be in bed with a book at three or so in the morning. I do not feel like having to whittle down monstrous Soviet successes to fit available space tonight. Let 'em save their victories for the nights I'm restless enough to want something to do. Tonight is a night for moderation. And I might start it off on the right note by taking a moderate nap before it's time to see what AP and ANS are selling.

He who is about to spread himself out on a table beside the mimeograph machine sends much love...

SDH

1. The "38-years-old deal" refers to age deferment policies enacted in December 1942 that provided for "termination of voluntary enlistment of individuals 38 years of age."

TLS Penzler

To Lillian Hellman

30 July 1944, The Aleutians

Dearest Lily—

You'll be interested to know that the talking animals are back in my dreams again. This one was a yellow cat that belonged to you. Besides being witty, she was very pretty, and sexy too, I might add; though nothing much came of that. I hope you will not get rid of her before I come home.

I've discovered a magazine that runs neck-and-neck with *Natural History* for ph[o]tographic reproductions, and am sending in a subscription for you. It's called, of all things, *Arizona Highways*.

We're going through a pleasant period with a new and better mess sergeant. The steak and French fried potatoes last night were very fine and the chicken with stuffing equally good today, in spite of the sage. We eat heartily and hope that it will take him a little longer than is normal to slide downhill. We've even got a cook who breaks eggs for frying into a bowl first instead of just crushing 'em over the stove. Don't tell me about the Colony!

I had a letter from Maggie yesterday, who has new servants to write about and who is expecting a visit from her father to give her new inconveniences to write about. She's already looking forward to Arthur's having to go visit the Gershwins. I guess the smaller your world the gladder you are to have *anything* happen in it. I don't know why I'm complaining. I always said without levity that she was really—technically—crazy. As a matter of fact I've always said that American middle-class women are the loveliest in the world; but they are all crazy—though not *all* technically. (You, of course, may not be middle-class. You may be an intellectual. I do not wish to become involved in any Marxian discussions on this point. I cannot think of *any* point at the moment on which I wish to become involved in any Marxian discussions. Do I make myself clear?)

It is time to eat again and grow fat on the people. It is Sunday evening. There will be cold-cuts—spam, canned corned beef, bologna, cheese—and perhaps corn fritters.

> Much love, my little cabbage, and many kisses...
> SDH

TLS LPT

To Prudence Whitfield

31 July 1944, The Aleutians

Dearest Pru—
The last of another month, ending my first year in this north countree...payday, another well-earned $79.80 less insurance and laundry to invest at 3 and 1/3 per cent so I may spend my declining years reclining in the lap of luxury or something.

The only other news is that I'm breaking in a new pipe, which used to mean nothing to women and now means very little to anybody, since most manufacturers at least partially break 'em in. There was a day when a new pipe could be counted on to give you a very bad smoke for about a week and a great deal of foolish care was devoted to guiding the new hod through this critical period. It was swell. There were different schools of thought on the proper technique and you went about the whole thing like a conductor breaking in a new orchestra. But progress spoiled all that: today if you get a good pipe you like it right from the beginning and so, of course, it never comes to represent so many man-hours of nursing and a lost throat-lining to you. It is much better this way and I only complain because one more knack that I learned at my father's knee is now useless. The same thing happened to pencil-sharpening. I don't think the old man taught me very much that had a future in it and I don't see how he missed giving me lessons in making wax candles.

The Dalí book returned home today—a little battered, but still with all its pages—so I shall take it on presently.

I've been half-seriously monkeying with the notion of doing—or trying—a longish poem that would be called "The Aleutians Don't Give a Damn" if that s sound followed by d weren't so awkward. (This notion too, naturally, will likely as not be put away in the drawer marked *Projects thought up in the absence of women,* which already is pretty full.)

I should shave now, before the rumor gets around that the American Army is full of greybeards. That sort of thing might encourage the enemy. Or discourage our Allies.

He who will presently be clean-scraped of face as the merest lad kisses your hand.

> Love ...
> SDH

TLS Stern

To Lillian Hellman

2 August 1944, The Aleutians

Dearest Lily—

For a couple of days we've had no mail at all and, because it's the first time that's happened in quite a while, you'd think, to listen to us, that we'd been betrayed by the whole world.

Day before yesterday I picked myself up a small chest-cold, but, between aspirin and one thing and another, it's showing no signs of developing into anything that'll give me a day or two of idleness. Anyhow I'd just as lief wait until the new hospital is finished. It's more conveniently located than the old one and should be more comfortable. Come to think of it, I'm way overdue. I have not been on sick call since the spring of 1943, which isn't right at my age: it looks as if I'm trying to show off.

I'm about half-way through Dalí's *Hidden Faces,* which seems sort of watered Van Vechten to me, with a great deal of perversion and very little sex. But I guess most perversion is kind of like that. If you've got more in your mind than you've got in your glands I dare say you have to think up tricks.

I'm also reading the Random House anthology of horror and supernatural tales.[1] It's got some nice stuff in it, but you'll go a long way before you'll find any worse taste than's displayed in the little intro[d]uctory notes over each item. (I mention this knowing that you're a connoisseur of Random House tastelessnesses.)

Now I leave you and go spread myself on my cot for a couple of hours until the night's labors begin.

I'm still waiting impatiently—which I know makes at least two of us—for news of your international project.

> Much love, sweetheart,
> SDH

1. Edited by Herbert Wise and Phyllis Fraser.

TLS LPT

To Lillian Hellman

4 August 1944, The Aleutians

Dearest Lily—

I don't want to do you an injustice, and it may be I'm just an impatient type, but it seems to me I haven't had a letter from you in at least a week. What kind of shenanigans are those? Is it going to be necessary for me to speak sharply to you again?

Tomorrow is Saturday, inspection day, and I've just come from scrubbing my corner of the home hut, straightening out shoes and shelves and clothes racks, and burning rubbish. It all takes about twenty minutes and gives you a feeling of soldierly virtue—especially those of us who will be sound asleep in our beds when the inspecting's going on. I may stay up tomorrow morning, though: I haven't had any pre-breakfast Ping-Pong in days.

I finished the Dalí novel, which was by no means as bad as it could have been, but makes you wonder why anybody should have bothered to write it. It must be—hard as it is to believe—that there are people in this world who just naturally *like* to write.

Me, I'd like to keep on writing to you, but I've got to go out into the early evening weather and find out how the news is shaping up for tomorrow morning's product.

> Much love, darling, and many kisses...
> SDH

TLS LPT

To Lillian Hellman

7 August 1944, The Aleutians

Dear Lily—

Two letters came from you today and all I've got to say is it's about time. The news about your trip was very fine and I'm holding my breath for you, though I've an idea that it would take some kind of disagreeable major event to block things after they've gone this far. And I do hope everybody will be nice about your transportation so you can be sped on your way with dispatch and comfort and those honors worthy of you, if any such there be. From now on I'll be writing to you in a kind of semi-vacuum, not knowing whether you are yet off to the other side of the world. How long—you've never said anything about that part of it—do you expect to be gone?

Life up here on the northern highway—it's more like the northern treadmill most of the time—to victory continues quietly, with little things looming large in our lives. For instance today I got a new and lovely knife designed by Santelli, the fencing bloke, and it pleases me greatly—remember me and knives?—though I certainly have no immediate intention of engaging any Japs with any knives, no matter how beautifully lethal they may be.

Besides the cartoons I enclose a couple of snapshots that'll show you what summer looks like in my immediate working vicinity. The hut whose end looms round and dark beside the brook is the one in which we get out the local daily. The brook, by the way, is now cutting up, washing away bridges and hunks of its banks. Both of these snapshots were taken from about the same point.

Thanks for sending the stuff to Viking. You can imagine how much strength of character my lads have to show to keep from asking me every day if there is any news, because if it should so happen that Viking does the book it'll be *the* event in their three lives, shrinking the war to the size of a baby's sock.

I'm ordering *A Walk in the Sun* from Elder's.[1] I've been reading Hervey Allen's *Bedford Village,* and though I'm a sucker for frontier fiction I have a hard time standing this gent's wooden characters and general naïveté, though not so hard a time as standing Orson Welles's hamming on the radio in *Suspense,* which I've just dialed out.[2]

Now I've got to go up on the hill and see how the traffic in news from the great outer world is doing tonight, or am I going to have to make tomorrow's paper up out of my head?

Bon voyage and things, of course, and I'm starting as of almost immediately to look for Russian stamps on letters.

Much love, darling, and may you have a very fine time on a very fine trip,

SDH

1. *A Walk in the Sun* by Harry Brown.
2. *Suspense* was a CBS radio dramatic anthology series that ran from 1942 to 1962.

TLS LPT

To Josephine Hammett

8 August 1944, The Aleutians

Dearest Princess—

The first part of *Dracula* is fine and scary—though the garlic always brought in a touch of comedy for me—but I could never get much out of the last half. It's pretty difficult to make horror last throughout a whole book, which is why most good shock stuff has been either short story or novelette length.

I liked the pictures Jose sent me—taken at the lake—and it's a shame they were a bit light-struck. Both of you look very lovely indeed.

I've got a new toy—a very lovely knife designed by Santelli, the fencing master, on the model, I imagine, of an Italian or Spanish dueling dagger. It is beautifully balanced and lethal and also, in the complete absence of anybody into whom it can be stuck without too much ado, very good for opening mail.

Lillian Hellman got herself an invitation to go to Moscow as the guest of a theatre and movie workers' union and, if things have progressed as smoothly as they should, is probably sitting right now in a plane somewhere along the Cairo-Teheran-Moscow air route. If she isn't, she's probably in bed crying.

Herewith another batch of life-on-the-Aleutians-as-it-may-very-well-be-for-all-I-know.

Something—I guess it must be the watch on my wrist—tells me it's just about time to go downhill through the elements and get something to eat and I don't feel much like arguing with jewelry, so

With much love and many kisses, cutie...
Papa

TLS MARSHALL

To Prudence Whitfield

11 August 1944, The Aleutians

Dearest Pru:

Today's big news is that late this afternoon the sun showed itself for about an hour; very modestly, however, so nobody could possibly be tempted to dash naked out into it, but it was definitely that same sun we haven't seen for days and days and it's nice to know it's still around. The rest was and is rain.

I finally got around to Dalí's *Hidden Faces,* and I don't think I liked it very much. On the other hand, I *did* finish it and I don't often do that unless I'm getting some sort of enjoyment. Off-hand I'd say there was too much perversion and not enough sex in it, but I guess that's what's wrong with most perversion, so it would be unfair to blame Dalí, and I don't want to be unfair to him. With all his foolishness—and often he's downright childish—I think he's a very fine painter.

And that reminds me that you asked about a very unfine painter recently. I haven't touched even so much as a drawing pencil in several years, which, believe me, is no great loss to the world of art—though I did have fun. I don't know whether I told you that the toy with which I was spending my declining years—just before the Army rejuvenated me—was the photography—several times life size and in color—of insects. It was wonderful. To get any sort of decent results you have to take incredible pains—no matter what you do to a dead bug the result looks like the picture of a dead bug, so you work with live stock—and the whole thing drives you nuts. It also drives your cook nuts, since you keep little boxes of bugs in the icebox.

Today somebody told me about riding along with a man who really hates the Army and everything connected with it. And it began to rain pretty hard and the Army-hater left his feet out where they were getting soaked and, when my informant looked questioningly at him, the Army-hater said in a tone of complete satisfaction, "Ah, look at it dripping on their shoes!"

I reckon that's about all the news I have to report from this front today and it's getting along towards that hour when I have to hunt up news from other fronts to report to this one, so it behooves me to stir my old stumps.

> Much love, darling ...
> SDH

TLS PENZLER

To Lillian Hellman

11 August 1944, The Aleutians

Dearest Lily:

* * *

Today I heard that a letter of commendation on the Aleutian booklet was on its way from a couple of generals, which is very nice, but you cannot hang letters on your chest for warmth, as you can medals. By the way, I got my Good Conduct medal the other day, a bronze thing with an eagle on it, not unlike the stickers boxed candy manufacturers paste on the ends to hold the cel[l]ophane outer wrapper in place, with Efficiency, Honor and Fidelity on it, which sums the whole thing up very neatly, and all hanging from a red ribbon with six white stripes. I don't for the life of me see why people say republics are ungrateful.

I don't remember whether I wrote you yesterday that some time in the near future—near future to us means the same year—I shall probably get up to Mt. McKinley for a little holiday. Pedigo and I plan going together, thus leaving our publication for a while with neither art nor articulation.[1] (I don't know why I thought that was going to be a joke. Oh, well...)

There is a very pleasant little bird up here in quantity. I think it's a longspur. (You may look it up for me.) It's something like a sparrow, brownish, and the male has black markings on its throat and a bright chestnut patch on its noodle. It's cheerful as most sparrows and has a tinkling gay voice which it uses a lot flying around. Here, perhaps in the absence of trees, they stay on the ground a lot and no doubt nest in flower clumps.

On this nature note I will bow myself out, not however without sending much love and many kisses, toots ...

SDH

1. Oliver Pedigo was a cartoonist on the *Adakian* staff.

TLS LPT

To Lillian Hellman

13 August 1944, The Aleutians

Dearest Lily—

It's a quiet rainy Sunday vastly improved by two letters from you as what day wouldn't be?

I'm still holding my breath for you on the passport and transportation, and I don't think a week's delay means anything at all these war days, but of course it may be that I want the trip for you too strongly to see anything as a sign of anything untoward.

* * *

Strict orders, to be carried out to the letter and with absolutely no use of what you perhaps call your own best judgment: *You are to have Luis Quintinilla paint you for me.*[1] I have spoken.

Yes, ma'am, I'd like you to put some money in the Randau–Zugsmith show for me.[2]

If you don't think it necessary for me to give anybody else a power of attorney while you're gone it's OK with me. I could always send one down to Nancy in case anything came up. And I haven't anything but confidence in her ability to cope with things.

I may get up to Mt. McKinley for a week next month, or I may even be changing my address before that, so I won't send any orders for all the things I can think I want until I know what's what, or at least as nearly what's what as you ever know in the Army.

Of course there's a great deal of good in Dotty, darling, which is one of the reasons I don't like her, maybe the chief one; but there's no reason why you shouldn't be fond of her if it doesn't lead you into thinking that she's ever actually going to do anything worthy of her—and not just through sentimentality or for the applause of the part of society she wants to be patted by at the moment.

> Much love, honey…
> SDH

1. Luis Quintinilla was a leftist Spanish painter.
2. Leane Zugsmith and Carl Randau's dramatic adaptation of their novel *The Visitor,* produced by Herman Shumlin, opened on 17 October 1944 at the Henry Miller Theatre and ran for 23 performances.

TLS LPT

To Lillian Hellman

16 August 1944, The Aleutians

Dearest Lily:

I'm halfway through a novel called *Little Coquette,* by a Frenchwoman who married one of the batty McCormicks and it's kind of cute in a way I think you'd like, though you will miss nothing of earth-shaking importance by ignoring my advice.

My chances of moving on to another part of Alaska—except for the McKinley furlough, which I still expect to manage early next month— seem to have been knocked on the noggin at least for the nonce and I hope you are doing better with your trip. (I'm having to build up my disappointment, since actually I hadn't been sure I wanted to go until after I found out I couldn't.)

To return to literature, I read Muriel's *Beast in View,* with my usual feeling that she still hasn't managed to pin anything down so you can say, "This is it," which is what I ask of my poets.[1]

In my stupid little way I'm at a loss to figure out what the landing in the south of France was for unless there are to be some more in other places, but military men often do things that are not crystal-clear to me.

I could go further, in fact, and say that the whole Italian campaign has been somewhat less than mud-clear to me thus far. (And in passing I should like to remind you that my usual optimism does not extend to any business in which Jumbo Wilson is the least bit involved.)[2]

Of me, except as reported above, there is little to say. I'm still coughing a little, but musically, I trust, and a recent still of my chest—I have it photographed every now and then as people do growing children—showed no cavities, depressions, knobs or frayed spots. It is the local medical consensus that I am hale...and I find myself seeing eye to eye with science.

Science is about the only thing I do see eye to eye with this morning, however, since I'm in a kind of pettish mood and inclined to be on the outs with most of the world.

But not of course with you, my fine blonde playwriting cutie, with whom I wish to be on nothing but the warmest and closest ins.

> Much love, darling, and many kisses,
> SDH

1. Reference is to Muriel Rukeyser.
2. British Gen. Henry Maitland "Jumbo" Wilson was Supreme Allied Commander in the Mediterranean in 1944.

TLS LPT

To Lillian Hellman

18 August 1944, The Aleutians

Dearest Lily:

It's fourish of a Friday morning as they say in circles where I wouldn't be found dead, though it's not clear in exactly what circles I would care to be found in that condition, and it's pretty safe to say of any letter that the more rambling the opening the less likely is there to be anything in it worth reading, and I'm not one to try to undermine my own generalities.

What passes for news of interest with us is that the new offset printing equipment is on the high seas and a new hut is being erected to house it and us, so for a while I'll think I'm very busy with my new toy, learning how it works and what can be done with it, if—as often happens in the Army—some of the more important parts have not been shipped somewhere else.

That there cough that was bothering me a bit has gone, leaving me with less than ever to do, and it may be that's the gap I'm trying to fill by staying up for pre-breakfast Ping-Pong again this morning.

Of my cultural side I've only to report that I've just started a novel by Victor White called *Peter Domanig*, which so far has all the signs of being not too disagreeably another of those studies of adolescence in European cities—Vienna this time, and it seems pre-war Vienna was like a beautiful woman or something, as you may have heard if you listen to gossip. Also, in this same department, I have to report that there are some very fetching pieces of drawing in Steig's *All Embarrassed*, especially the couple bestrung together on page 89, though I don't know why I'm singling that one out.

We now, thanks to the Red Cross, have a man in a car stop by at two in the morning to bring us coffee and doughnuts, the best innovation we've had since they built a laundry on the island.

Yesterday I had a letter from Lois who has written "fifty-eight pages of something that might turn out to be a book," and which—guess what?—she'll send me "if it turns out to be anything at all," because she has "just been writing it to let of[f] steam" from her "unconscious" and can't "really evaluate it properly." The man situation, she says—and when doesn't she?—is terrible. She also reports that [***] is having an affair with his daughter-in-law, which makes me suspect that maybe your set is fast. I hope you are not acquiring any racy habits such as ogling grenadiers or taking a dash of lime in your coca-cola. On my return I should like to find you the same simple county maid who was content to sip brandy strained through marajuana or however the hell you spell it.

> Much love, darling and many kisses...
> SDH

TLS LPT

To Lillian Hellman

21 August 1944, The Aleutians

Dearest Lily—

You're a nice, kind and sweet woman, but the small edition of the cartoons probably wouldn't be good for the boys and so I thank you, but think you should not do it. As a matter of fact, now that the new equipment is supposedly practically here, it might be well to lay off the whole idea until they've turned out some stuff in the more usual—and certainly freer techniques—than mimeograph.

I'm going to be away from the paper for at least a few weeks, and will be able to write you about it later, though I can't right now. It'll be—or so I hope—a pleasant change for a while, though in the Army "pleasant change" is tautological.

I'm glad you finally succeeded in getting money down on the election for us. We'll never make a fortune at those odds, but winning—I don't know why it seems especially true—will be very satisfactory.

In re Pindyck and White, I can only fall back on the notion that agents—all of them—are a completely inexplicable people.[1]

I hope you're out of bed with your cold long before this, and you're to stop that kind of thing. *My* cold is gone and you are to leave colds and such to me.

Between *Searching Wind* negotiations and transportation dickerings, you must be leading a full life these days. I hope both in the end go the way you wish—and quickly. And I'm not worried about your making a fuss. What I say is, Lily is a cutie and if she wants to make a fuss, why then let her make a fuss to her heart's content.

You may laugh at it as much as you like, but I *am* flattered by the Dashiell, Inc., and I don't like it's being referred to as a dubious honor.[2]

In my next letter, for which you may as well wait before replying to this one, I hope to have more—though not necessarily world-shaking in its importance—news.

Now I must be off, my fine blonde darling; so, with much love and many kisses ...

SDH

1. Frances Pindyck worked in Larry White's office, the New York branch of Leland Hayward's literary agency.
2. Dashiell, Inc., was a stock corporation set up by Hellman to handle investments in movies and stage productions. Movie rights to *The Searching Wind* were the first property sold through the corporation.

TLS LPT

To Josephine Hammett

Hammett's new assignment was Fort Richardson, near Anchorage, headquarters from which he traveled the entire Aleutian chain on orientation missions that took advantage of his celebrity.

23 August 1944, Alaska

Dearest Princess:

This is going to be a short and stingy note from your tall and stingy old man, with hardly any more news in it than that I've said goodbye to my island for a few weeks and am now on the mainland just like people in St. Louis.

My new address is Als Dept S S Office, APO #942, c/o PM, Seattle, Wash.

I'm now near a town, a very small one, but to me, after a year and more out on the tip of the world, it is a completely satisfactory metropolis. Saloons, stores, restaurants, taxis, cement sidewalks—boy, oh, boy! This is high life!

I've got to take it on the lam now, darling, and I'll try to get off a more satisfactory letter when I settle down in a day or two.

> Meanwhile much love and many kisses...
> Papa

TLS MARSHALL

To Mary Hammett

3 September 1944, Alaska

Dearest Mary:

Your old man has been a lousy correspondent the past couple of weeks, but God and the Army have been working together against him. I came up here on a three-week loan and have been kept humping on a hurry-up job. But most of the pressure should be off now and I'll try to do better.

I've been into town only three or four times since I've been here. It's not a bad town at all, rather like the oil-boom towns of Montana and Wyoming in 1919–1920, and I have a good enough time when I go in, but the novelty of having women around and stores and restaurants and being able to get a drink whenever you want it has worn off pretty quickly. I don't think any of us down on the islands miss those things as much as we think we do—though it's often hard to make us believe that it's all in our minds.

Or maybe it's just that I've finally become old enough to not care so much for the fleshpots—though somehow I don't think that's quite true yet. After all, that hasn't happened yet to my father, and he's well into the 80s.

I'm supposed to go back to the Aleutians in another week or so, but write me here until I tell you, because what you're supposed to do in the Army and what you actually do aren't always the same thing. On the whole, I like it down on the island more than I do here, but this has—or could have—its good points too and I'm not particularly fussy about what the Army does with me.

Last night I won a couple of hundred dollars in a latrine crap game—the first time I've had dice in my hands in nearly a year. But I still find gambling kind of dull and wonder why I used to spend so much time at it. I imagine I'd still have fun at the race-track, but the rest of it seems to me a pretty heavy way of killing time.

I had some photos taken a day or two ago—I'm still going through the "visiting celebrity" phase of my stay here, but it should wear itself out in a little while—and if they turn out well and I can get hold of extra prints I'll send 'em along.

I hear I'm a sergeant now, or am to be one when I return to my home station, but there's been no official notice, so for God's sake don't start addressing me thataway until I let you know. I was promised a staff sergeancy some months ago and nothing came of *that*. It's a good thing I'm not trying to make a career out of the Army. In two years of service this time I haven't reached the grade at which I was discharged 25 years ago. At this rate in the next war I'll have to put in five years to make Pfc.

I know where there's some pickled pigsfeet that needs eating, so, my fine blonde cutie,

> with much love and many kisses...
> Papa

TLS Marshall

To Mary Hammett

5 September 1944, Alaska

Dearest Mary—

I guess I'm a hell of a father, but I've been trying all afternoon to remember whether you were born in September or October—and I still don't know.

But, whenever it happened, it was one of the nicest things that ever happened to the world and to me and I hope you'll buy yourself a pretty with the enclosed check. It ought to be for at least $1,000,000 of course, but you know how stingy I am.

Have a nice birthday, darling.

> Much love and many kisses—
> Papa

ALS Marshall

To Lillian Hellman

5 September 1944, APO 948, Seattle, Washington

Dearest Lily:

There was a letter from you in the batch of mail that was forwarded from the island today, but it was dated the 25th, so I still don't know what's new in your mission to Moscow. I take it out in hoping, though. Also it's about time I was hearing from you direct. Sometimes I don't understand what God's up to if anything.

About the house, why should I be angry?[1] I certainly don't know enough about New York City real estate trends at the moment to say whether it was a good investment. My own guess would be that the high rent area wouldn't be a good buy near the end of a war, but, after all, you're as much interested in solving your apartment problems as you are in making money out of real estate, so if you want to buy yourself a house, my blessings light upon you. And, since you *have* bought it, let's have the news about it. How much work has to be done on it? And when do you expect to be able to move in?

I think you were wise to get rid of Irene. There's no use of battling your nerves with people that get on them—unless there were some sort of question of justice involved, which certainly couldn't have been true in this case. It's likely a good idea to change domestics once in a while anyhow, just as you do wallpaper.

You didn't have to be very smart to guess about my visitor, so you needn't show off about it. All you had to do was to be able to read a booklet and a newspaper, certainly no great feat for America's foremost playwright—or do I overestimate playwrights?

I hope you are all over your grippe by now, darling, and I agree that you don't know how to take care of yourself and only know how to be snippy giving other people advice on how to take care of his or herself, and you are a silly little woman to whom nobody ought to pay any attention, as I wouldn't if I didn't love you.

Nothing's new in any of my affairs. I haven't been into to town since I wrote you, though I'll probably go in to do some shopping in a day or two.

This afternoon I wrote Nancy that I'd probably draw $2500 or so out of the account to open one up here, where it will be handier if I'm to spend much time on the mainland.

At the moment there's a deal afoot that will send me roaming the mainland and islands for a few months before I get back to my own station—to stay, that is: I'll probably include it in my tour. I don't know whether it'll work out: we Army folk change our plans with a speed that is as miraculous as it is often aimless. But I should know in a day or two.

After a couple days of rain—a softish, windless affair in this place—we've had one of very fine sunshine. The two kinds of weather seem to run in two- or three-day groups here this time of the year. It's still quite warm and I'm beginning to find the climate a little vapid after a year in *my* part of the north countree.

The war news is really terrific nowadays, showing you can't go wrong by taking things out of the hands of a British general, no matter how tactful you have to be about it.[2]

A story you may like: The last time I was in town I was standing in a bar when a soldier came in with a native girl. Both were tight, but she could hardly walk. He half-carried her over to a booth and they had three quick drinks. When they got up to go she couldn't make it at all and toppled over backwards, sprawling out face upward on the floor. He turned around and with an air of utter surprise asked, "What the hell's the matter with you?"

Another, which I don't think I've told you. A man I know down on the island was riding in a jeep with a friend who really deeply hates being in the Army and everything connected with it. It began to rain and the man I know noticed that the Army hater hadn't pulled his feet in where they wouldn't get wet—it was pouring by now. Then the Army hater saw my friend was looking curiously at him and he smiled delightedly at my friend and, looking at his feet again, said in a tone of complete satisfaction, "Look at it raining on their shoes!"

Thus ends today's ration of anecdotes from APO 942 and thus also practically ends this letter. I'm trying once more to put on some weight while I'm in a place where such foods as ice-cream and pastry are available and I'm overdue to insert some in me.

> Much love, darling...
> SDH

1. Hellman had bought a house at 63 East 82nd Street in Manhattan.

2. In August 1944 Gen. Bernard Law Montgomery, known as "Monty," commander
    in chief of British forces on the Western Front, was promoted to Field Marshal
    in command of British and Canadian troops. Under General Dwight Eisen-
    hower, with whom he had numerous disagreements, Montgomery had con-
    ducted the pivotal Normandy invasion on D-Day, June 6, 1944.

TLS LPT

To Prudence Whitfield

6 September 1944, Alaska

Dearest Pru:

Today there is sun in large quantities, nicely filtered thru the Alaskan
haze and life is pleasant.

The trip was approved, so in ten days or so I'll be off bounding from
post to post in this part of the world for eight or more weeks. I'll hit my
home station among others, but continue to address me here—and with
frequency, I hope—and the stuff will be forwarded.

The war news continues swell and I don't think there's any doubt of it
now that the whole show will be over long before anybody makes me a
general, but I guess I mustn't be selfish about it and expect men to go on
fighting just so I can rise in the world, especially since, at my present
rate, I couldn't promise them that it would only be a matter of a few
weeks or months.

I'm getting plenty of sleep nowadays, so you can stop your worrying
over that. Going without sleep never bothered me much anyway, except
to make me irritable, which was worse on those around me than on me.

Finally I landed some Dewey money in New York—though I had to
give larger odds than I'd hoped—and have some $2500 riding on FDR.[1]
I'd like to get down just about that much more, but am holding off for a
little in hopes that the price will improve. Can you ask your man in Pittsburgh what the price is there? And whether there's likely to be any development that'll encourage the Dewey folk—a lot of whose bitterness is
based on a suspicion that they're backing a gone goose—to put up?
None of this is too important, of course, so don't go to any trouble; this
is all just for fun and if I were back in the States the chances are I
wouldn't bother about betting at all.

I suppose I ought to do a little work for the Army before it's time to knock off for the day, and that time isn't very far off, so, darling, with a great deal of love...

SDH

1. Thomas E. Dewey, governor of New York, was the Republican candidate who ran against, and lost to, Roosevelt in the 1944 presidential election.

TLS PENZLER

To Lillian Hellman

13 September 1944, Fort Richardson, Alaska

Dearest Lily:

What passes for big news with us today is that for this part of the mainland unit censorship of enlisted men's mail has been called off, and what's nice about that is not the possibility of passing on to you all the Alaskan Department's secrets, thus proving I'm in the know, but the fact that I can remember you in bed without feeling that I'm telling whichever officer in my unit happens to be unit censor about you in bed. Understand me, officers are very superior people, I am told, but there are some of them to whom I would positively not want to confide that in cold weather you sleep with your buttocks sticking out from under the covers.

Then there's another feature. Under the unit censor plan your mail is ordinarily being censored by either the officer under whom you work or one of your company officers, so it is seldom the smartest thing in the world to write, "Today we did that thing to that dog all day," or, "It's been months since I've done an honest day's work," or, "This morning we put a still in down behind the generator in the lower end of the draw," or even, "The CO thought up a new one this payday, show your dogtags or you don't get paid. The six pairs of dogtags that were available passed from hand to hand to pay of[f] a hundred and ten men. If the CO *can* read he didn't try it on the dogtags."

I slept late this morning and then was told there was a telegram for [m]e at HQ. I immediately thought, of course, that it would be from you saying you had at last taken off for Muscovy, but it wasn't. It was from Maggie, asking what I want for Christmas and where it should be sent. I

373

suppose it would be best to have stuff sent here, but, you know me, and when did I ever know what I wanted for Christmas.

About my own Christmas giving: if it looks as if I'll get to Nome in time, I'll do my shopping there. Otherwise it will be up to you or, in your absence, Nancy.

Tonight I'm going into Anchorage again, actually, to call on some people in a private house, which will be the first [I'v]e been in since yours. Tell me, darling, does one get a check for his hat and coat in residences too? And are there separate toilets for ladies and gents?

I've got to run now, baby. Much love and many kisses and that you are a cutiepie is the firm conviction of
SDH

TLS LPT

To Margaret Kober

30 September 1944, The Aleutians

Dear Maggie darling:

* * *

Life is very nice these days. This is the third island I've hit since I left Anchorage and—thanks partly to unusually good weather—it's been nice going most of the way. This is the first time I've been on this island—though I was very nearly sent over here instead of to 980 last year—and a very cozy affair it is. I wouldn't at all mind putting the rest of the war in right here, but I won't. I'll probably pull out along about Thursday for my next stop, making it part-way by boat, part by plane. My schedule calls for a jump every five or six days, but I'm already a week behind and if bad weather should set in I'll be lucky to get through—I'm supposed to wind up in Nome in December—a month or more behind. It doesn't make much difference to me: this is as nice a way of fighting a war as any, and I'm a fellow who has seen some mighty nice ways.

If you notice any slight stiffness in the tone of this letter it's doubtless due to the fact that I've recently been elevated to the dizzy heights of a sergeancy and, while God knows I don't want to be pompous, still and all

I do feel that with that third stripe should go at least a dab of added dignity or something. The whole thing has made me feel very encouraged about my military career. Here, in only two years, I've already worked myself up to the rank I held twenty-six years ago. Not bad going, eh? Now if this war will only last long enough...

I spent most of the afternoon crawling over rocks and such along the shoreline with a scientific gent, helping him bag mollusks and barnacles and other waterline specimens, including one very fine dead baby starfish and my antique legs are on the tired side and just about ready to be inserted into my sleeping bag, which is where I am going to insert them without much more ado.

With a great deal of love, darling, I beg to remain your obedient servant and things,

SDH

TLS HRC

To Prudence Whitfield

30 September 1944, Fort Richardson, Alaska

Pru darling:

* * *

It's nice being down on the islands again, especially since the weather has been practically perfect. This is the third spot I have hit since leaving the Mainland and they seem to get better as I go along. I'd settle for this one till the end of the war, but I'll probably pull out Thursday.

* * *

The promotion slipped my mind. In a very mild way I'm disgruntled. I'd been promised more sooner and when this thing came through it somehow failed to seem the most exciting thing that had ever happened to me. So far I've managed to have the new stripes sewed on only one shirt and go around some days with the corporal's still on and some days with none at all, which confuses people a little. Tomorrow's Sunday and I've nothing to do—unless I get in a bit of sight-seeing—so maybe I'll dig out the sewing kit and bring my arms up to date. There's nothing certain about it, though: in the last war I never did get around to putting my sergeant's chevrons on…which didn't keep us from winning the war.

I don't remember the yellow and green tie at all, but it's nice to think of something belonging to me wrapped around you when you step out to panic the natives.

Don't worry too much about your conversation with Raoul. T.B. convalescents run a fast gamut between optimism and the blackest of depressions. There is a definite toxic effect on the brain that keeps it over-stimulated either for good or bad most of the time and makes lungers mighty touchy folks to deal with, as I have good reason to know.

Some guys from an infantry outfit I trained with last fall on the peninsula have just come in for a visit, so I'm going to stop this now with a promise that I'll use some of tomorrow's time to do a more adequate job.

Much love, darling, and take care of yourself for me.

SDH

TLS Pepper

To Prudence Whitfield

1 October 1944, The Aleutians

Dearest Pru:

* * *

It's three in the afternoon here, so it's nine at night in New York and you've finished dinner somewhere and have had a couple of lique[u]rs and have forgotten about the hangover that bothered you earlier in the day and are having a very pleasant time cutting up old touches with somebody you knew in Paris or some place. And if I could get back here tomorrow or the next day I should very much like to be with you—only we wouldn't stay in town much longer tonight, but would go on up to the country, where I don't imagine the dogs would hate to see me and it would be still and lovely on the lake, and I could very easily give myself some synthetic twinges of nostalgia going on this way. What I really mean, baby, is of course that I'd like to see you. But I guess father time and the course of history can be trusted to take care of that.

Somebody's got Tokyo on the radio, a Japanese Christian program that seems to prove that Christianity doesn't pick up much in glamour by going abroad.

This typewriter, which I picked up on another part of the chain on a complicated dicker with a camouflage engineer, hasn't been used very much, but it's been on and off too many boats and little pieces have been knocked off it here and there, which doesn't make it any easier to handle. I must try to remember to have it patched up as soon as I hit a place where Ordnance has a repair shop. But I wonder where in hell the engineer is going to get a fix-up job on the combination egg-beater and motion picture projector or whatever it was that *I* swapped *him*.

I got company again, so this will be this for the time being, sweetheart. With much love,

SDH

TLS LAYMAN

To Lillian Hellman

5 October 1944, The Aleutians

Dearest Lily:

* * *

Now that I'm out here, there's not much use going into the ifs connected with meeting you in Fairbanks. I'd've tried it, but the chances of our making connections there would have been a bit more of a gamble than you and your map make it. Something more than getting "a day off" would be involved; in the first place, since it would take me at least three to make the round trip if everything went like clock work. Trains, for instance, run only every other day on that railroad and then— But I'm way over a thousand miles from that part of the country and still headed west, so there's no use etc., as I said up above. It was a nice idea though, baby, and I would've made a stab at it. Maybe God will make it possible on your return trip.

* * *

I saw the announcement of your intellectuals' committee in an early August issue of the *New Masses* that just caught up with me and thought it a good mixture of names;[1] but I don't pretend any longer that I really understand much of what's going on back in the States, so I just go along telling myself, "Well, there are a lot of competent folks back there who will do what's necessary without my bothering my white head about the ins and outs of it," which is no doubt a form of shirking…or may be becoming modesty for all I know.

What you're doing to the new house sounds nice and I'm looking forward to seeing it.

Also it's nice that you're feeling so well about the analysis—a feeling that you've earned by staying with it like a little major, and I guess maybe the eminent Doctor Z deserves some credit for his part in it.[2]

It's unfair to blame me bec[au]se I look like the kind of diplomats you associate with.[3] You understand I don't expect this to make any difference to you, but I just wanted to get it down for the record.

The fifteen day furloughs—for one of which you may remember I was trying—have been called off and in their place is a new deal by which you can get—if you're lucky—sixty days in the States, thirty of them to be spent at home and thirty in a rehabilitation center before you return to your Post. I may try for one of 'em when this rat race is over in the winter, though I've no idea how long a line is waiting back in my own outfit. But, for that matter, I don't even know whether I'll ever get back to my outfit again. And, if I should decide to try for rotation to another theater next summer, when my two year term in Alaska ends—which I won't do unless I'm pretty sure I'll be sent to another theater and not just back to the States—then there's a time element involved that will probably keep me from getting the sixty day deal. But all that's pretty far ahead, since I can't wind up this jaunt till sometime this winter and don't see much sense to trying to get back home before you do anyway. That— if you can make heads or tails of it—is my status as things now stand.

Our boat got in this afternoon, so we should shove off on the first leg of our trip to the next island tomorrow morning, going to an intermediate spot to pick up a plane for the second leg. Since mail service is speedier from that intermediate stop than from here, I'll probably carry this letter along with me and send it from there.

Now I've got a little packing to do, and some shaving and bathing, and then I'm going to bed fairly early because I was up early this morning listening to the second Card-Brown game—on which I won back what I lost yesterday—and am of a sleepiness.

Good night, honey—with much love and many kisses...

SDH

1. "The Arts Go to War," *New Masses*, 1 August 1944, page 19.
2. Gregory Zilboorg, Hellman's psychoanalyst.
3. Hellman had begun a relationship with an American diplomat named John Melby.

TLS LPT

To Mary Hammett

7 October 1944, The Aleutians

Dearest Mary:

* * *

Tonight's turning into the kind that's best spent snug in one's own hut. There's a pretty good non-coms' club here, with beer and pretty good steaks, and I was going up there for my evening meal, but, the weather being what it is, I think I'll do my eating in the nearby mess hall and then tuck myself in with whatever I can find in the way of reading matter. I think I saw a copy of Lamb's *Genghis Khan* around and I've never read it. The night before last—back on the other island—I read *A Tree Grows in Brooklyn*[1] for the first time and thought it a fairly empty affair, though readable enough in spots. It's been quite a while since I've got any reading done and I'm not too fussy about what I try. On the other hand, I've got some sewing that I ought to do, so maybe—just maybe—I'll do that instead.

It's getting along toward eating time and I'd look prettier if I washed and shaved a little, so I guess I'd better stop doing this and start doing that. I've been putting it off all day just out of laziness.

So a very good evening to you, my fine blonde cutie, with much love and a thick sprinkling of kisses...

Papa

1. *A Tree Grows in Brooklyn* by Betty Smith.

TLS MARSHALL

To Prudence Whitfield

16–17 October 1944, The Aleutians

Pru darling:

* * *

17 Oct 44

This letter didn't get much further than I imagined it would last night. Since I stayed till the party broke up a little before two o'clock this morning, I suppose I must have had a pretty good time.

After waking at five, hungry, and eating half a box of pretzels—the only food I could reach without getting out of bed—I slept through breakfast and got up barely in time to show up for my morning's work. It went fairly well today. This afternoon I spent cutting up old touches with soldiers I knew elsewhere and reading Laura Hobson's *The Trespassers,* which seems based chiefly on her love affair with *PM's* Ralph Ingersoll back in 1940 and thereabouts. I was more or less on the inside of both ends of that and it's kind of interesting in a gruesome way to see how the lady rehashes things in fiction form. She's got a problem: he's got to be a louse, of course, for throwing her over, but, also, he's got to have some fine things in him to justify her having fallen in love with him. And other people's love affairs usually seem to have a great deal that's silly in them, especially when they think they're important enough to write a book about. In short, I would prefer that you did not write a book about you and me: just paint a picture of it or something.

If the weather's not too mean tomorrow after we finish our morning session I'll probably go for a sight-seeing trip round about the island. Thus far I've seen very little of it and may not get another chance.

Last night I ran into a couple of officers from a post in which I spent two or three months last year and heard some untrue but very pleasant anecdotes about myself. The legends are occasionally better than the facts, though they're usually overdressed.

Now I'm going back to my bed and Laura and Ralphie and find out all about love in the great outer world. Meanwhile I send you all mine from the small insular one I live in...

SDH

TLS Penzler

1944

To Prudence Whitfield

21 October 1944, The Aleutians

Pru darling—

Today's another of those days—of which we have many—spent waiting for transportation. They're not bad days except for a sort of emptiness that gives the younger of us the fidgets. We lie around and talk a little and sleep a little and read a little and play a little Ping-Pong and write a little mail and maybe our transportation materializes presently or maybe it doesn't, and there is probably no great amount of harm done either way. There always is, I'm beginning to believe, tomorrow. Meanwhile, of course, we can't go visiting, or anywhere else, much because we're likely to be called any moment, but that's bearable—you're not here and who the hell else do I want to visit just now? Which brings me around to thinking that it's Saturday afternoon and, unless you're gone out of town for the weekend, you're most likely at loose ends, as everybody in New York is Saturday afternoons unless my memory is cockeyed. Maybe you'd be settling down in your new home. You'd have a date for tonight, of course, but after a couple of drinks—and if I played my cards very carefully—maybe you could be talked out of it. Anyhow, when I get back to New York—certainly not this afternoon, but possibly some time in 1945—I mean to try. (I'm that fellow I mentioned before who's beginning to believe there's always tomorrow!)

Now I think I'll go out for a short walk and try to figure out from whatever I can see of the sky what our chances are of making a getaway this evening—and you'd be surprised how small an effect what I decide will have on what actually happens. Sometimes I think this Army doesn't want to let me run it.

     Much love, dear,
     SDH

ALS Black and White Books

To Nancy Bragdon

27 October 1944, The Aleutians

Dear Nancy:

From the 1010 Fifth Avenue heading on your letter I—with the help of a cup of tea leaves and a crystal ball and male intuition—inferior as *that* is—come up with the supposition that Lillian has moved over to the Kobers' apartment, so I'm now writing her there. God knows what I'd do if I waited for you all to tell me things!

After being banged around all day by the Bering Sea we came ashore here last night, and, no matter what you choose to think, this also is a cozy island. We got two-story barracks here with built-in latrines and showers and stuff; and furthermore there's a "town" of almost two hundred—well, almost a hundred and fifty—people, with a couple of bars where soldiers can liquor up quickly from six to eight in the evening and a restaurant and practically everything that spells high life to us hut dwellers, and so we'll probably stay here in the fat lap of luxury for a week—and maybe even a day or two more.

It's just as well that you didn't congratulate me too soon on the sergeancy, since I'm still pretending I'm pretty disgruntled about the whole thing. Actually it didn't make much difference to me one way or the other, but, since I'd been promised something better—which I wasn't too sure I wanted—I took advantage of this dingus to try to wangle something else that I thought I might want and...If you can make much sense of that paragraph you're pretty good. I've been sampling the "town" tonight and am not what you could call blind sober. I'll try to remember to tackle the ins and outs of what I thought I was trying to say there some other time.

I intended—and still intend—if I can get up around Nome in time to buy Christmas presents to get everybody native atrocities from the far north; but I'm by no means sure I'll make it now; so it's quite likely I'll have to call on you for my Christmas shopping, in which I will send you a list, the amounts to be spent for each—that's the kind of gift-buyer I am—and a check—and the results, good or bad, will be on your pretty little head.

Some of my colleagues have come in with a problem having to do with this rat race we're on, so I've got to stop this for the nonce, but that is not to be taken to mean I won't go on with it later—say about tomorrow.

Love,
SDH

TLS LPT

To Lillian Hellman

29 October 1944, The Aleutians

Dearest Lily:

This has been a nice Sundayish Sunday, with nothing much done but eating, dozing and reading, and that's the sort of hardship I'm not likely to complain about.

The eating consisted mostly of fried oysters and sliced tomatoes for breakfast, cold cuts for a sort of snack, and a steak the size of a library door for late dinner.

The reading consisted of *Climate and the Energy of Nations*—a man named Markham's attempt to stack the cards to prove a thesis which I only read through because it comes roughly into the field of ecology I still claim I'm interested in—and a novel called *The History of Rome Hanks,* which has some good stuff in it but is a lot too highfalutin for my simple tastes.[1]

The dozing consisted of just dozing, and I'm likely to go back to that any minute now.

Yesterday I had better luck with my reading, thanks to you. A copy of *A Walk in the Sun*, ordered from San Francisco some time ago on your recommendation, caught up to me, and a very fine job it is! I also had just as good luck with my eating and dozing, but not with a four-five-six game—you do it with dice—later. Maybe I'm lucky in love!

* * *

I hope you and Moscow are doing all right by one another ...
SDH

1. *The History of Rome Hanks and Kindred Matters,* by Joseph Stanley Pennell

TLS LPT

To Prudence Whitfield

30 October 1944, The Aleutians

Pru darling:

A letter from you today made it an especially nice day because you'd at last got those letters from me and I don't any more have to go on sheepishly apologizing for that gap. Not that your complaining about it was as bad as you make it sound, but anyhow it's nicer this way. So, to celebrate, I went into "town" tonight and bought you a necklace of what's known as ivory in these parts, which comes from walruses or something and I guess is nice enough if you haven't seen better from elephants—as of course you have too—but what I always say hopefully is that it's not the gift but the thought behind it that counts and maybe I ought to scratch the thought behind this one on its beads with a pin or something, and if I don't sound a little tight tonight it isn't because I'm not. Do I make myself clear?

We did what we call work here today and it went very pleasantly, with no hard feelings one way or the other, which is the most you can ask of what you call work in the Army, and tomorrow morning I do what we call work again, and then I'm through till we hit the next spot, which may be late this week or may be next week, depending on how transportation makes itself available.

Tomorrow's Hollow-e'en plus payday and the bars will stay open four hours instead of the customary two, which will, so I'm of the opinion, make it one high old ripsnorting evening, goldurnit! It doesn't take much to make practically everybody happy as all git-out up here.

My man-in-London-who's-supposed-to-be-in-the-know reports that Von Papen and Ribbentrop have been in Portugal conferring with "Mr. Kirkpatrick," Britain's candidate for civilian government in Germany after the war—who, incidentally, was the first man to talk to Hess after his flight to England—and my-man-in-London-who's-supposed-to-be-in-the-know doesn't think that that's necessarily good news.[1] More cheerfully, however, he reports that the Spanish Republicans, encouraged by what's happened in France, have made enough of a show of strength that Franco is having to muster his Moorish troops again.

Me, I just report that I love you and am about to hit the sack, with maybe a box of pretzels to nibble on till the life of Rome Hanks puts me to sleep, which, unless he's livened up since I last read into him, won't be so awfully long.

> Much love, sweetheart, and many kisses…
> SDH

1. Hammett's "man-in-London" is probably Claud Cockburn reporting in *The Week*. Franz von Papen was a Nazi diplomat (acquitted of war crimes). Joachim von Ribbentrop was Nazi minister of foreign affairs (hanged in 1946 as a war criminal). Kirkpatrick is unidentified. Rudolf Hess was Hitler's deputy who in 1941 undertook a strange private mission to negotiate peace between Germany and Great Britain.

TLS PENZLER

To Prudence Whitfield

3 November 1944, The Aleutians

Pru darling:

Well, my dear, after I'd written you Wednesday afternoon and had gone up to see the major—which, as I suspected, wasn't about anything—somebody turned up with a bottle of rum and, drinking it, it occurred to us that since we would probably stop off here—where booze is hard to get—for a day, it might be pleasant to have another bottle or two of rum to bring along with us. So we sent out for a couple of bottles and then went into the village to drink till the bars closed at eight, and from there to one of the local restaurants for dinner—I seem to have got hold of the idea that you can't legally eat anything but steak in the evening—and then on to the non-com's club, where I drank a little beer and lost not quite five hundred bucks in a four-five-six game and went on back to the barracks to forget we meant to take the rum with us and by the time we had finished it it was around six in the morning—and we were supposed to be leaving before eight. That didn't leave much time for sleep, but, by skipping breakfast and getting somebody else to pack for me, I managed to get in an hour of it, which can't be said to have done me much good, but anyway it didn't matter much because our boat trip was a smooth one and so was the bunk that I stuck in most of the way till it was time to transfer to a barge and come on over here this Friday morning. Now we lounge and wait, with nothing to do till the next plane takes off for any one of three places...maybe this evening, maybe tomorrow. I'm afraid I'm losing my liking for boats: I've taken too many beatings running up and down this chain, or I'm getting too old for the cramped quarters into which the Army customarily puts its enlisted men, or something. When I get back into civilian life I'm going to travel in nothing but kiddie kars or ambulances.

Now it's time for me to scrape a couple of days' accumulation of beard off my face before turning out for chow. I've eaten in this mess hall before and the food is nothing to make the mouth of a decadent Roman emperor water, but I can't help it if I'm hungry.

> Much love, sweetheart...
> SDH

TLS Stern

To Lillian Hellman

5 November 1944, Fort Richardson, Alaska

Dearest Lily:

He who wishes he were with you in Moscow this Sunday night—where you are no doubt flirting with handsome colonels in chic white uniforms, and why aren't they at the front?—has to report that—his Aleutian task finished for the nonce—he flew back to this mainland oasis early yesterday morning. I won't know till tomorrow how long I'll stick around this time. I've still got Kodiak, Fairbanks, Nome and a couple of other spots to hit—unless, as can always happen behind your back in the Army, my itinerary has been changed.

Over in the office I've got half a closetful of very fine-looking Christmas packages and, since the chances are I'll be back here for the holidays, I've thus far resisted the temptation to open any of them. If, however, anything comes up between now and then to make it look as if

I *won't* be here Christmas, why then I shall tear into them in a fine frenzy, regardless of the date.

Remember the volcano I told you I used to be in love with — Mt. Pavlov? We flew past it the other night, on our way from down the chain, and it put on as fine a display of fireworks as anybody's ever likely to see. It's still my baby in spite of Shishaldin — which I missed this time — and Great Sitkin — which was as lovely a fawn-colored thing in the sunset as you'd want the afternoon we sailed out past it — and Mt. Cleveland — which I'd never seen before and which made headlines a few months ago by blowing up and killing one of the air force men stationed near it — and the one on Umnak with a crater six miles in diameter in which I poked around one day a couple of weeks ago until it got too hot on the soles for comfort. I'm by no means a one-volcano man, but I do favor Pavlov!

Anchorage seemed quite a city when I hit it last night — the only settlement I'd run into on my travels was the one of perhaps a hundred and fifty folk near Dutch Harbor on Unalaska — and the moderate amount of drinking and such that I did seemed to constitute quite a festive celebration. I still love the islands, but I'd be a liar if I denied that it's kind of nice to have a spot of highlife now and then.

What happens to me after I wind up this Orientation romp is still a moot point so far as I know, but at the moment the chances seem to be in favor of my being held here on temporary duty for a while even if I decide I wish to go back to my home station. Actually, it doesn't make a hell of a lot of difference to me, but I'm still holding out till I can see what kind of deal I can make. If, however, my commanding general should be transferred — a distinct possibility — then the ground will be cut from under my feet. It's only his refusal to OK my transfer unless I want it that gives me any bargaining power. And it's quite likely that his successor would feel capable of running the island with no help from me.

I've got to get up early tomorrow morning, so I dare say it behooves me to get to bed at a decent hour tonight and it's pushing midnight now.

Even though I know it's unavoidable, I can't help missing the letters from you which don't come these days, and probably won't be coming for many a day. I don't know how long you'll be gone, but maybe it'll lure you home earlier if I tell you that telephone communication is now to be had between here and the States. Also, if you can give me a hint at your possible return date it'll help me decide when I want to try to get my long over-due 30-day furlough. After all this time there doesn't seem to be much sense in my trying to get it while you are off in foreign parts—especially since I'll likely turn down rotation, which, as far as I can see, would only get me back to the States and not into another overseas theater, and serve out the rest of the war up in these parts. (All of this is predicated on the belief that one can plan ahead in the Army, and that's as false a premise as I've ever seen.)

Now I'm off to that bed, sweetheart, but not without sending you much love and many, many kisses...

SDH

TLS LPT

To Lillian Hellman

24 November 1944, Ladd Field, Alaska

Dearest Lily:

I've still had no word from you since your wire while you were waiting to take off—all my mail is still in other parts and probably won't catch up to me, or I to it, for another week at least—but Miriam Dickey tells me she's heard from Nancy that you arrived OK, for which I'm thanking the appropriate gods.[1]

I got up here Monday, couldn't get into Fairbanks that night, but made it the next, saw Miriam for a moment; went to dinner with her and Jean Potter the next and then went with her to the Wons' (is that it: the engineer and Stella) for Thanksgiving dinner last night—to have what was probably the finest conventional Thanksgiving dinner I've ever put in my mouth. You've eaten there, so I doubt if it's necessary for me to tell you that Stella's quite a cook. If I'm still here Saturday night I'm going there again, but it's not likely I will. As a matter of fact I'm waiting for a plane to take off for Nome tonight, which is why I am not in town right now.

I like Miriam, especially since she seems very fond of you, though she says you embarrassed her by giving her too many gifts. Cap isn't in town now—except that wherever Miriam is he'll always be present at least verbally—but I hear you made quite a hit with him. You seem to have impressed most of Fairbanks very nicely—in spite of their being puzzled by your political views—which isn't surprising to at least one skinny white-haired soldier.

Winter is beginning to set in at last, so I've had myself equipped with Mukluks and other dinguses to face whatever weather I happen to meet up with over at Nome. I'm not likely to stay there more than a few days, since I'm due at Mt. McKinley early next month and should pay a quick visit to Fort Richardson en route.

Miriam says she thinks you wrote me while you were in Fairbanks, so I'm a-hoping it'll be among those which should be waiting for me when I get back down below.

I've got almost no news that I can write except that I'm my usual completely well and practically completely happy self.

> Much love, darling, and many kisses...
> SDH

1. Miriam Dickey was a friend of Hellman's in Fairbanks who was secretary to Austin "Cap" Lathrop, a wealthy industrialist.

TLS LPT

To Lillian Hellman

At the time of this letter Nome was quarantined due to an outbreak of diphtheria.

26 November 1944, Nome

Dearest Lily:

We came over here yesterday morning, and very nice we have found it under a sun of days and a moon of nights. I know you won't admit cold country can be too nice, but this is as close as close.

I still haven't seen the town—which is quarantined—but I've two possible angles on that: (1) I'm trying with some hopes to find a loophole tomorrow, and (2) there's a report that the quarantine will be lifted Wednesday. In the latter case we'll probably hang around till about Friday so as to get a gander at the place. Then we'll go scurrying back to Anchorage so we can get back up to Mt. McKinley for a conference or clam bake we're supposed to attend early next week. And that'll leave us with only a couple of more spots to hit before the end of the tour—though I won't be surprised if it's called off after McKinley.

I don't remember whether I've written you that something else is cooking for me when this rat race is over—another more or less elaborate plan in which I'm supposed to be a necessary part. I'm neutral on this one too. It may work out fairly well for me, and it may not, but in the end the chances are I won't have much say over whether I'm to be involved in it. I still like the thoughts of my home island, but I'd be a liar if I didn't admit that being around the fleshpots of Alaska has softened me a little and somewhat reconciled me to the notion that I may never get back there. But we shall see what we shall see!

It's kind of nice seeing the Russians take the Russian planes through here, and the folks here consider them very hot stuff indeed. This part of Alaska—Fairbanks and here—is all completely new stuff to me, since I live and work in another theater completely and there is no connection between the two except they're both in a place called Alaska.

It's early to bed for me tonight, since it's to be early to rise for me in the morning, so...

> Much love, my fine blonde cutie, and many kisses ...
> SDH

TLS LPT

To Josephine Dolan Hammett

14 December 1944, Fort Richardson, Alaska

Dear Jose:

Will you split this check three ways to buy pretties for yourself and the girls for Christmas—and I'm sorry I haven't been able to do any shopping on my own account for you all up here. Maybe later ...

This morning I came down by train from Curry—where I'd stayed over-night on my way back from Mt. McKinley—and a very nice morning it was. There was a sunrise along about nine o'clock that was like nothing anybody's ever seen since the last ice cap receded. It was really a picture of what most of the world must've been in prehistoric times and made you understand people cowering and shuddering and trying to warm themselves with superstitions. There were a lot of moose to be seen running away from the train, and a couple of bears, as well as some ptarmigan and varying hares and the like. It was—since I'd a good night's sleep behind me and a hearty breakfast—a nice morning.

Tomorrow morning I shove off for Whittier—not very far from here—and then come back next week to stay till after Christmas, after which I'm supposed to report back to my home in the Aleutians. How long I'll stay there and what I'll do next are unknown to me at the moment. There are too many contradictory plans afoot and *all* of them can't work out. Meanwhile, back there, I've got a new printing plant—an offset process, if that means anything to you—to play with, so I can have my own quiet fun fooling around with it till I see what comes of what and why.

I haven't opened my Christmas presents yet—see what a strong character I am!—but I loved the pictures. And, if you don't mind my saying so, you really are a handsome old lady, toots!

It's not your fault about that Veterans Bureau deal. I should have told you that it was bound to come. My being in the Army and still drawing compensation didn't make sense and they were bound to see it sooner or later, but it was too funny a gag to give up. As soon as I get settled down and do a little bookkeeping I'll send you a check for what you had to give them back. I'm not sure I made a note of the amount, so maybe you'd better tell me what it was in your next letter. And if you're in a hurry for it—I mean if having to send it back pinched you—say so and I'll send it right away.

* * *

I'm still sorry about not sending you all stuff from Nome, but the diphtheria epidemic was pretty bad and—though, as I wrote, I managed to beat the rules and go into town for a couple of days—I didn't think it would be too smart to send things from there.

Kiss the youngsters for me and tell them I'll write them, if not tonight, then as soon as I can; and I hope you all have the merriest of Merry Christmases and the happies[t] of Happy New Years.

    Love,
    SDH

TLS MARSHALL

To Prudence Whitfield

16 December 1944, Whittier, Alaska

Pru darling:

* * *

There's still no way of telling—and there isn't likely to be any way till I get back to the island—what my chances are of getting down to the US for a month early in the year. I suspect my chances aren't too hot, but I haven't anything to lose by trying. And, with all the circumstances surrounding my immediate future as mixed up and contradictory as they are, I ought to be able to fish out something for myself.

Movie studios seldom read anything that comes in the mail, but it's not too hard to have them look at your stuff. Most of them have so-called story editors or material scouts of one kind or another in New York and it's usually not too difficult to make a date with them. And for some peculiar reason—I'll never really understood what goes on in moviemakers' heads—their reluctance goes away after they've seen you. It's as if they thought the post office serves nobody but ogres—which may be why they transact nearly all their own business by telegram or telephone. (Did I ever tell you about the time Leland Hayward phoned me from New York to Hollywood to tell me he had just written me a letter?)

Now I've got to go over and see what the local non-com's club is like, and to meet some of the fellows I came up from the States with in July 1943.

> Much love, sweetheart, and many kisses...
> SDH

TLS Stern

To Mary Hammett

16 December 1944, Whittier, Alaska

Dearest Mary:
Yesterday I came down here from Anchorage and—so shortly after

Mt. McKinley's 50 below zero—it seems muggy and almost tropical. It actually is kind of sloppy, though, with rain turning snow to slush underfoot. The chances are I will be here till Wednesday—which is the 20th—and then go back to lay around Anchorage through Christmas, trying to get back to my island before the first of the year. After that, who knows?

I've got some odds and ends of several letters of yours—at least one of them written as far back as October—which I'll try to answer even though you may have forgotten your questions before this.

About Henry Hoke I can't remember a thing, can't even remember having heard the name before, though of course I may have.[1] The Purple Heart was founded by old man Washington as a decoration for soldiers who had been wounded. Sometime later it was dropped, and was not revived until after the World War—some time in the 20s I think—when it was brought back to life to honor those who had been wounded in that row. It's still in effect, of course. If you're wounded as a result of "direct enemy action," and your wound is serious enough to need treatment by a commissioned medical officer, then you automatically get one of them. Which franking privileges do you mean? The one Congressmen have or the one us heroes can use?

The Chinese-Sti[l]well affair takes quite a bit of explaining, but there has probably been enough printed about it by now to make it fairly clear—if you keep away from *Time* and *Life,* which have done all they can to confuse the whole thing.[2] Why don't you go to the trouble to get hold of the *New Masses* every week? It's pretty good on things like that.

Los Angeles Times ** TUES., NOV. 28, 1944—Part II 9

PRIVATE LIVES — BY PAUL FORD

DASHING OFF THRILLERS IS OLD STUFF TO DASHIELL HAMMETT—

—BUT FEW HAVE CHALLENGED HIS RECORD FOR TURNING OUT A MYSTERY NOVEL IN 24 HOURS!

SINCLAIR LEWIS LIKES BEST TO WORK IN A HOTEL ROOM FURNISHED ONLY WITH TABLES—ON WHICH HE SCATTERS HIS MANUSCRIPTS.

Venison's pretty good eating if it's handled right, though for some reason there don't seem to be a great many people who know how to cook it. Caribou is dull: I agree with you on that. Sure, it's against the law to shoot anything on the islands, but things don't always happen by the book.

It's easy for me to tell you about writing that book in twenty-four hours. I didn't. Ben Hecht used to claim that he wrote *The Florentine Dagger* in that length of time—and that's what the muddled cartoonist probably thought he was thinking about. Don't start believing *anything* you read in the L.A. *Times*. It's always been one of the country's least reliable newspapers.

* * *

     My love, darling, and many kisses …
     Papa

1. Henry Hoke was a pioneer in direct-mail advertising. Among his books is *Black Mail* (1944).
2. Gen. Joseph "Vinegar Joe" Stilwell commanded U.S. forces in China. He strongly opposed support for Chiang Kai-shek, president of the Chinese Nationalist government, and was recalled to Washington on 28 October 1944.

TLS MARSHALL

To Prudence Whitfield

18 December 1944, Whittier, Alaska

Pru darling:

* * *

There's a faint possibility that when I get back to Anchorage I may be able to angle myself into an immediate 30-day furlough in the States before going back to my island. It's only a faint possibility, but it's worth a trial and, if I'm lucky, I might even hit California before the first of the year. I'm not counting too much on it, however: it'll take a fine and fancy piece of talking to manage it.

Otherwise—according to today's official version of my plans, which are always subject to change without notice—I'll go back to the Aleutians to start organizing a new *Information and Education* program—and that'll no doubt keep me humping for some time. (Tomorrow's official version of my plans may well be something altogether different. I only know what they tell me and I haven't much control over what comes to me—which is just as well, I reckon, since, within reasonable limits, I don't care a hell of a lot one way or the other.)

Now I'm off to try to find a book with which to read myself to sleep, not being at all sure I've worked hard enough today to earn my night's slumber honestly.

It's been days since I've heard a word of news from the great outer world and I've no more idea of how our war's going than if I were in Graustark,[1] but, anyway, I hope all's going well in your part of the world.

Take care of yourself, sweetheart.

> With much love and many kisses...
> SDH

1. A fictional country in George Barr McCutcheon's courtly romance *Graustark*.

TLS STERN

To Mary Hammett

26 December 1944, Fort Richardson, Alaska

Dearest Mary:

A very fine, fat and fruitful Christmas was had by all the Hammetts in these parts, thanks chiefly to all the friends and relations of Hammett in other parts. My warmest thanks to you and Jose and Jo for a swell selection of gifts, all of which hit the spot. You're a nice family.

I got back from Whittier on the 20th, but have been resting too hard to get going with any mail until today. It's a question whether I'll get back to the island in January or in February. Meanwhile my orders are to get a good rest here, and they're the kind of orders I can carry out whole-heartedly. True, I suspect I'm drinking a little too hard, but I can taper off on that, and the rest of my program is all to the good. I seldom get out of bed before early afternoon and then I usually manage to get quite a bit of rest—doing little else—before crawling in again around midnight. I suppose the tour had tired me out more than I'd supposed: I didn't know how good this rest was going to seem until I tried it out, but, now that I know, I'm planning to stay right with it until I get all I need—that is, of course, if my orders aren't changed again over-night.

Most places have no laws against cousins marrying and there's little reason for supposing it's harmful to the offspring unless—perhaps—it happens too often in succeeding generations. The Catholic Church has a sort of rule against it, but they've often made exceptions.

My memory of your birth is that it was on the 16th, but there's no use quarreling with your birth certificate. You can easily check up. You were born on Sunday and it isn't hard to find out what date that fell on.

"Blood Money" was written for *Black Mask* back in 1927, I think, just before I wrote *Red Harvest*. I'd never let Knopf publish it or the short stories, but I eased up [on] the cheap edition people. By the way there's an article about detective stories (and me) in the December *Atlantic Monthly* that you might like.[1] It's by Raymond Chandler and—though this may sound immodest of me—he does a pretty good job.

I hope you all had the Merriest of Christmases and are all set for the Happiest of New Years.

> Much love and many kisses ...
> Papa

1. "The Simple Art of Murder," by Raymond Chandler, *Atlantic Monthly*, December 1944.

TLS MARSHALL

To Isadore Gottlieb

Corporal Isadore Gottlieb was an army friend of Hammett's.

28 December 1944, APO 942, Seattle, Washington

Dear Gottlieb:

Don't let this paper fool you. It doesn't mean that I've switched deals again. It only means that I'm using *Yank*'s office tonight, and I'm going to stop it and take my trade elsewhere if they don't put darker ribbons in their typewriters.

You seem to have picked yourself a very fancy go this time. Boy, you certainly have had a tough time of it in this man's war, proving, I dare say, that you can't keep a good man down simply by not giving him a commission.

Me, I'm dumb and have to work for a living. Last week I wound up a four-month—some ten thousand miles in all—romp over an area roughly bounded by Attu, Kodiak, Fairbanks, and Nome. Anything you want to know about Alaska and the Aleutians, just ask me. Yes, the Eskimo girls at Nome are often very pretty, usually very good-natured and practically always very diseased. No, there's no sense in trying to rig up a sea otter poaching racket on Amchitka, because while you could angle it OK there, you couldn't peddle the skins anywhere except, perhaps, in the London black market. Yes, Kodiak is a little gem, whether you want to shoot, fish, drink or futz around with the dames. No, etc., etc. Go on, ask me.

What happens next I don't know. The chances seem to be that I'll hang around here—here is Fort Richardson, on the edge of Anchorage—doing nothing until along about the first of February and then go back to my Aleutian island. I'm trying to swing a 30-day furlough in the States first, but am not counting too heavily on it. At the moment I'm pretty tired—I don't suppose I have to tell you that an EM's trave[l]ing up here isn't always accompanied by any great amount of luxury—and haven't anything against the kind of rest I'm getting. (I'm averaging about 13 hours a day in the sack, seldom crawling out before one in the afternoon and sometimes—like yesterday—not managing it before six-thirty.)

The address on this envelope will get me no matter which way I jump next. And right now I'm going to jump over to the airport restaurant and get something to eat before I go back to bed—and with a bottle, brother, always with a bottle here!

> Luck to you, keed …
> Hammett

TLS Richard Davie, August 1996 catalogue

To Josephine Hammett

28 December 1944, APO 942, Seattle, Washington

Dearest Princess:

No, I didn't have to worry about a White Christmas this year—any more than last—as a heavy snowfall on Christmas Eve fixed everything up fine. In these parts I hum, "I'm dreaming of a white birthday," which I had last year and am as likely as not to have again this.

* * *

I liked the portrait of you and the new porcelain filling, though I hadn't known your Chinese ancestry was going to show up so early.

Yes'm, for a good part of summer mosquitoes and no-see-ums make life practically unbearable on a large part of the Alaskan mainland. Man and beast have to keep themselves netted to avoid being blinded. This isn't true of the Aleutians, where—probably because of the winds—there are less insects of any kind than you're likely to find anywhere else in the world. Did I ever tell you that just before I came into the Army a great deal of my time was being taken up by photographing insects in color? It was a lot of fun and I'm looking forward to going on with it after this fuss with foreigners is over. I took them larger than life, though not through a microscopic lens, and the whole thing took a great deal of patience, but, as I say, was a lot of fun. The thing is, that if you take a picture of a dead insect it looks—no matter how you fake it—like a dead insect. On the other hand, if you try to take a live insect in its natural state you've got to use too much speed to get any sort of accuracy as far as color is concerned. So what you do is catch the critter and put it in the ice-box till it's frozen stiff. Then you take it out, put it against the background you want, and turn on your lights. To get true colors you have to use a pretty strong light, which, very soon, warms your model back to life and activity. And there's your chance! You've got a matter of seconds, maybe even a full minute, in which the insect is alive enough to look alive, but not yet frisky enough to start moving around too much. You either get your picture in that little time or you don't. If you don't, he probably takes off and you chase him round the room till you catch him, and put him back in the ice-box till he's stiff enough to try the whole thing over again. It's a fine, fine way to spend your time. And then, as in the case of all color photography nowadays, if you've caught approximately true color values once out of twenty tries you're doing swell. But one bell-ringer more than makes up for any number of flops. After all, how many really good color photographs of insects has anybody seen so far?

I've still got God knows how many thank-you letters to pound out for Christmas gifts—maybe people are trying to keep me up here by a sort of bribery—so I guess I'd better quit this and have another hack at them.

Much love, darling, and a kiss for the china tooth...
Papa

TLS MARSHALL

To Mary Hammett

5 January 1945, Fort Richardson

Dearest Mary:

I read most—or at least a large part—of *Tales of Terror and the Supernatural* down on the island last summer and thought it a pretty good anthology.[1] Of course there's a lot of dead wood in it, but there has to be in any bulky collection. I remember "Silent Snow, Secret Snow" from 'way back in the early 30s, I think, when it was published in a magazine.[2] It is a swell job.

Once again—after loafing since I got back here in December—I'm hard at work, and it's no means bad, at least for a change; and I don't think this present spurt is going to last much more than a week. After that I will probably go into another rest period.

There's nothing new on the furlough. I still may be able to get it, may not be able to. There's no way of telling at the moment.

The sun's been shining at least some part of the last three days, which is always nice and not too usual up here. The temperature's been hanging around 8 to 20 above zero, which means nobody has to bother about bundling up when they go out of doors, and that's nice too. Having discovered that I was drinking too much and not eating enough, I went on the wagon three or four days ago and now I'm eating piggishly and feeling swell—and that also is nice. So you can see that everything is nice and all is practically fine and dandy in this probably best of possible worlds.

Much love, honey, and many kisses...
Papa

1. *Great Tales of Terror and the Supernatural,* edited by Herbert Wise and Phyllis Fraser.
2. Conrad Aiken's story was first published in *Virginia Quarterly,* December 1932.

TLS MARSHALL

To Lillian Hellman

10 January 1945, Fort Richardson, Alaska

Dearest Lilishka:

Today's the day Nancy says you're due in England on your way home, so I guess it's about time that I started seeing you have something worth coming home to—if that's what this is.

It's strange writing to you again after all this time—though it's going to be both strange and wonderful hearing from you again—so if I should sound a little distant or something at first it's because I don't want you to think me—by now comparatively a stranger—too fresh.

First, the Christmas gifts were swell, a marvelous assortment. (I'm taking for granted that the Abercrombie miscellany was from you: there were no cards in them.) Thank you very much, darling.

The holidays here were quiet but kind of nice. I got back up here from Whittier—winding up my tour—on the 20th and had nothing to do but lie around and celebrate till after New Year's Day, when I went to work again, and am now plugging away rather manfully at the dull task of organizing a new Information & Education program, which seems to hinge at the moment on a rather lifeless weekly publication, the first issue of which I'm about to see through the press. Maybe I'll be able to liven it up in later issues. Otherwise I'm likely to go over to the Japs.

Last month I very nearly snapped up that long overdue thirty-day furlough in the States, but your absence made me gamble on my chance of getting it after your return—with, of course, the possibility that I'll lose out entirely, or till late summer. The way things stand now—or, which isn't always the same thing, the way I've been told things stand now—I am being transferred from my old DEML HQ Company down on the island to Alaskan Department HQ; and when and if the transfer goes through—next week, next month, or next year—I can immediately put in for the furlough. Till then there's nothing I can do except sweat it out. The transfer, by the way, won't necessarily mean that I'll stay here instead of going back to the islands, though the chances are that's what'll happen. I'd rather work this job from the islands and still have hopes of managing it so that I can spend at least most of my time down there. This is a pleasanter part of the world climatically, but I don't know whether I've ever told you I hate working around HQ—any HQ.

The tour went along very nicely, starting in mid-September and winding up in late December. I got in, I suppose, some ten thousand miles in short jumps inside a territory roughly bounded by Attu, Kodiak, Fairbanks and Nome. So if you want to know anything about Alaska just open your mouth and ask me. This month there's a dog-sled expedition going up from Fairbanks to Point Barrow, but, try as I will, I haven't been able to dig up a water-holding reason for my going along.

* * *

Having done a lot too much drinking throughout the tour and having topped that a little while loafing through the holidays here, I've now gone on a small wagon that somebody left under my bunk and have not had a drink since the second or third of the month. It's nice to wake up hungry every morning and to feel good all day, so it's quite likely that I'll stay non-alcoholic for a long time. I don't know why I'm always surprised to find I can have a good time staying sober. I guess my memory only applies to what happens to others, and not to myself.

* * *

Now, my home-coming blonde cutie, I've got to go see about putting some lunch into me.

> Welcome home with much love and many kisses, baby...
> SDH

TLS LPT

To Nancy Bragdon

10 January 1945, Fort Richardson

Dear Nancy:

* * *

Life at the moment is quiet enough, but dull, dull, dull. I'm cooped up in an office most of the time readying a weekly publication that's supposed to be the backbone or something of a new information and education program. Sometimes I think it'd be better if the Army stayed dumb. Once upon a time I was in the Signal Corps and we "got the message through," and if the message was a silly one, or shouldn't have been sent at all, or was based on misinformation, that was none of our business: we just got it through and let the rest of the Army do as it pleased. That seems to me like the good old days now. I'm tired of fooling around this damned Headquarters with a lot of jokers who don't know what in the name of God they're doing, only they vaguely hope it'll somehow please the General.

Tonight I'm a testy old man.

> Love,
> SDH

TLS HRC

To Prudence Whitfield

11 January 1945, Fort Richardson

Pru darling—

Anything can happen in this kind of Army. So today arrives from Washington a Major Parker, who turns out to be none other than Johnny Parker, whom you may remember from the Village—a short, stocky fellow who looked a bit like Grover Wh[a]l[e]n, black mustache and all.[1] He was ship news man for one of the N.Y. papers and not doing so well with his pulp stories. The last time I saw him he was what the boys used to call "slatting on his uppers" and C. D. Russell (who draws a strip, "Petey the Tramp") and I took him out and got him drunk, whereupon he became tearful-truculent and accused us of patronizing him because we were successful and he wasn't. Finally he tried to take a poke at a bartender and we had to tote him off and put him to bed.

He told me that Jimmy Collins—another newspaper character of the time whom we often had to stake to gin—is now a full colonel. They're both in Public Relations, which seems to be a soft touch.

* * *

I'm glad you found an apartment you like and I don't think the lease is anything to be afraid of. After all, it's only words on paper. And I don't think the war's going to be over soon enough to ruin your sublease prospects should you have to give it up.

You don't have to tell me Lindy's is not everything anybody'd want in a restaurant. It was never one of my favorite spots and I don't think I've been in it half a dozen times.

No'm, I still haven't taken off for my home island, and as I wrote you yesterday or the day before, my chances of getting there in the immediate future seem none too hot. I don't know about that "excitement" you mention. It usually seems serene enough to us residents.

It's getting along towards late afternoon. Maybe I should see about doing a modicum of work before I knock off for the day. The fact that there isn't much to do is, I suppose, all the more reason for doing what there is. (God damn all offices and all office work!)

> Much love,
> SDH

1. Grover Whalen was a New York City public official who from 1919 to 1953 oversaw the city's tickertape parades. As police commissioner from 1928 to 1930 he hounded Communist organizations. He later became chairman of the board of Schenley Distillers. He called himself "Mr. New York" and was known as the official greeter of the city.

ALS Pepper

To Lillian Hellman

14 January 1945, Fort Richardson, Alaska

Dearest Lily:

Last night was a big night in town, so I didn't crawl out of the blankets till nearly two this Sunday afternoon. Then I breakfasted so heartily on roast turkey at the cafeteria that I had to go back—pausing en route to watch part of a not very exciting hockey game—and take to my bunk with a book while the turkey got itself digested.

The book—*Snow Above Town,* a simple narrative of life in a Wyoming settlement, by a man named Hough—turned out to be pretty good reading, so I had a nice afternoon till along about six-thirty, when, naturally, it was time to rise and eat again, which is what I've just come from doing.

It's been snowing merrily all day, the first snowfall to amount to anything that we've had in what seems a long time. I'm stuffy and unimaginative enough to like winter to be winter, so this pleases me, even though the temperature remains pretty mild.

The artist on whom I've been waiting for a week has managed to get himself into another stew with some higher-ups—he collects delinquency reports as other people collect stamps—and is faced with shipment out to the Aleutians—the local equivalent of the gallows—unless I can think up some way to stop it. So I'll probably spend the first part of the week running around in small irregular circles, trying out feeble schemes to save this drawing-fellow, and, at the same time, keeping my eyes peeled for another one in the likely case that this one's doom is inescapable. I guess that's one way of fighting a war.

Having gone without glasses for a week or two—till I got around to having the frames repaired—I now find I don't need them nearly as much as I used to. Reading, for instance, goes much better without them. Do you suppose I'm growing younger? I must check up on my gums and see if new teeth are growing out, and on my hair to see if it's turning dark. It would be nice to start all over and make the same mistakes again in slightly different form

Much love, darling, and many kisses…and keep on coming home …
SDH

TLS LPT

To Josephine Dolan Hammett

15 January 1945, Fort Richardson

Dear Jose:

I wish you'd stop thinking I'm having a tough time of it and being very rugged or something. I suppose parts of it have been, and are, what you could call tough, but, taking it all in all I have been having the best time

I've had in years. I feel top-hole most of the time; occa[s]ionally I'm bored, but it seldom lasts long; and I'm not young enough to kid myself into thinking I'd be having such a hell of a swell go someplace else. This is actually kind of made to order for me. There are things about the Army that nobody could be too fond of, but I'm close enough to being an Old Soldier to know how to cut corners here and there and find myself cushions against a good many of the sharp edges.

You're right, I still haven't gained much weight, but I guess I might just as well make up my mind that that's never going to happen—and it's probably just as well at my age. I doubt if I could get used to being tubby, and the extra weight would no doubt bog me down.

I'm sorry you're having to go to the trouble of house-hunting. If what I hear of housing conditions in your part of the world is true, you've got a sweet job ahead of you.

This morning I came to the office to find that the high command had decided over the weekend to completely reorganize my department, so now I'm engaged in (a) trying to figure out what in the hell they think they want, and (b) patching up something that they will think is it. Fortunately, there doesn't seem to be much of a hurry about it, so I shall coast along placidly waiting for them to change their minds again. Meanwhile I may go into Anchorage around noon and stay till tomorrow night or maybe Wednesday morning. It's not likely I'll do any work anyhow till the middle of the week, except maybe get a haircut. That's the way we fight our war up here.

Kiss the youngsters for me.

> Love …
> SDH

TLS MARSHALL

To Nancy Bragdon

24 January 1945, Fort Richardson

Dear Nancy:

* * *

The day before yesterday a letter from Lillian came by airmail from Russia. It was dated October 31 and was written from Kazan. She was still on her way to Moscow and had been grounded for the seventh time by bad weather. All this was nearly two weeks after she'd left Fairbanks, so I guess Alaska doesn't have all the bad flying weather.

Tonight I'm staying on the post, which is supposed to be punishment for coming in too late on too many passes and makes me feel quite small-boyish, only it comes at a bad time. I've been putting in non-Army work helping Jean Potter put the finishing touches on what promises to be a fine and exciting history of civilian aviation in Alaska, and this kind of foolishness is likely to set us back.

* * *

It's time I was sliding over to the cafeteria for a steak or something in lieu of the fleshpots of Anchorage.

Love,
SDH

TLS HRC

To Josephine Dolan Hammett

Hammett bought a house for Jose and their daughters because of the wartime housing shortage. He provided a substantial down payment and money to pay the mortgage.

23 February 1945, Aleutians

Dear Jose—

I think the FHA idea is a good one and here's a $2,500 check for the preliminaries. I hope you get the priorities OK and can get going without too much delay and at last have the place of your own that you've wanted. How long should the whole thing take?

I still haven't settled down in my groove here. As a matter of fact I'm not even sure I'm going to stay, though the chances are I will.

My health remains good as usual and I'm eating and sleeping plenty and well on the way to recovery from the fast life of the mainland. At least it seemed fast in comparison with life on the islands.

We're finally getting something like winter weather, which pleases me because I like winter to be like winter.

Kiss the children for me.

Love to all…
SDH

TLS Marshall

To Mary Hammett

24 February 1945, The Aleutians

Dearest Mary,

That date at the top isn't exactly right. It's actually about four in the morning of Sunday the 25th, and most of my chores on the paper are done and I've just filled myself up on chili con carne and stuff—we now have a one-burner gasoline stove in the office and some $20 worth of new-bought groceries—and I haven't a great deal to do but write a couple of letters, maybe read a while, and then stall around till breakfast is ready in the mess hall at 7:30. It's one way of fighting a war.

There isn't much news. I still haven't seen anybody to ask what, if anything, I'm going to do next or about my furlough. I've been putting it off until I make up my mind what I'd like to do—that is, within the range of things that are reasonably possible.

While up at Anchorage I put in practically all my spare time the last few weeks helping edit a book on early Alaskan pilots by an old friend of mine, Jean Potter. It will probably by called "Flyingest People" and should come out in the fall, or maybe late summer. It looks like a swell job and I would have liked to be able to see it into its final shape. Maybe I'll get another crack at it when—or if—I come back to the States on my furlough. She—Jean—should be back there by then.[1]

I'm reading a silly and empty book on the Polish underground movement—*The Story of a Secret State*—designed I suppose to convince people that the Polish Government in Exile—that collection of lice—had something to do with the resistance effort in Poland.[2] I don't know why I'm going back to the book: it's neither interesting nor informative. Maybe it's because there's not much else to read in the office. Anyway that's where I'm going.

Much love, darling, and many kisses…
Papa

1. Jean Potter's *The Flying North* was published by Macmillan in 1947. It is dedicated to Hammett.
2. *The Story of a Secret State* by Jan Karski.

TLS MARSHALL

To Lillian Hellman

25 February 1945, The Aleutians

Dear Lilishka,

My spies report that Fort Richardson has asked, or is about to ask, for my transfer there permanently. If it's the roaming job I had my eye on just before I left, then it's all to the good and I'm for it—though it may not make much difference what I think.

* * *

Let's see, what have I been up to? I read Selsam's *Socialism and Ethics* and Francis Franklin's *The Rise of the United States* and liked them both though both are a bit rigid and school-teacherish. I also read somebody's *Story of a Secret State,* a foolish and empty attempt to make believe the Polish Government in Exile had something to do with a legitimate underground movement in Poland. An amazing book in that nobody even faintly resembling a worker has anything to do—except perhaps by accident—with the resistance movement. I tell you, sister, the gentry can be trusted to save our world. Now, for a change of pace and something to enjoy, I'm reading *Donovan's Brain,* a pulp horror tale.[1]

It's seven-thirty, so if I'm going to catch that nap before I go to work it behooves me to cut this out and get myself sprawled on yon table top.

Much love, darling, and I hope you're at this moment speeding over the Atlantic in a generally westward direction…
SDH

1. *Donovan's Brain* by Curt Siodmak.

TLS LPT

To Prudence Whitfield

25 February 1945, The Aleutians

Pru darling,

* * *

I haven't seen Joe Shaw for god only knows how many years. Is he still in the agency business? Sure I was grey-haired back in those days: I've been grey since my middle twenties.

Up at Richardson I had another photograph taken—next to Olivia D[e] Havilland and Mt. McKinley I seem to have stood in front of more Alaskan cameras than anybody or anything else—which turned out dark and brooding and I'll send you one of them as soon as I can find anything big enough to wrap it in.

The war news is fine these days. The coordinated eastern and western offensives in Europe could turn out to be *it,* though I'm not one of those who expect sudden miracles. I'm one of those who think the Nazis will let Berlin go—or rather, use its defense as a delaying action—and go into their final stand in the south—trying to hold the Russians off along the Leipzig–Vienna line. The Asiatic end could go on for quite a while, especially if Japan succeeds in making us fight it out in China.

Now I'm putting my c[r]ystal ball away and heading for that nap before work.

> Much love …
> SDH

TLS PENZLER

To Lillian Hellman

27 February 1945, The Aleutians

Dearest Lily,

I got home from work this morning to find a wire from Nancy saying "HELLMAN COMING HOME TUESDAY ARE YOU ALL RIGHT SPEAK," so, since it's now Tuesday evening, I suppose you're home and I'm mighty glad of it even if I'm not there to welcome you. (I am not too credulous, however, and it wouldn't be an unexpected shock to get word that you'd changed your plans and hadn't made New York yet.)

* * *

For no reason at all except that it was available, I felt like reading and was too lazy to go to the library, I'm now reading a thing called *The Red Cock Crows*, about which there's no reason for anybody ever to have heard.[1]

Tonight for breakfast I had some fine steak and onions. Our chow here is pretty good. Did I tell you that during one stretch of time—from December 19, when I left Whittier, till February 17, when I stopped overnight at Port Heiden—I managed to get along without as much as a mouthful of Army food? Ah, those good old days when I was deep in the fleshpots of the Alaska mainland!

I like the Alaska mainland and am as likely as not to come back to it some day. There's a Major up here who thinks I should ranch on one of the islands after the war—he promises to get me all the backing I need from Maury Maverick—but, as much as I like the islands, I don't think that would make too much sense.[2] Of course Kodiak, possibly my favorite spot in all Alaska, is an island, but that's different.

A messenger just came in with the first batch of the day's news and I may as well accept that as a call to duty and start sifting the stuff to see what we can use and what we can't.

Much love, darling, and it's swell to think of you as once more safely e[n]sconced in residence...

SDH

1. *The Red Cock Crows* by Frances Gaither.
2. Maury Maverick was a liberal Texas congressman in the 1930s and mayor of San Antonio in 1939. In 1944 he was appointed vice chairman of the War Production Board in charge of the Smaller War Plants Corporation, with responsibility for providing small businesses a fair share of war-related contracts.

TLS LPT

To Lillian Hellman

27 February 1945, The Aleutians

Dearest Lily,

It's two-thirty of a Tuesday morning and the newspaper that runs itself has run itself into another day's issue, so I sip coffee and nibble doughnuts and do this while I wait four hours for breakfast.

* * *

The kid, who was divorced not long ago, seems to have got himself married a couple of weeks ago. The old man is still puttering round with his artificial leg, his crutches and his girls. Reba's working at something or other in Charlotte and smoking black market cigarettes. I'm here.

The Red Cross truck came along a few minutes ago with coffee and doughnuts (see above) and we lazily settled for that handout in lieu of the more elegant meals we usually whip up at this time o' day. Maybe we'll weaken in an hour or so and start cooking, but then that will mean little appetite for breakfast at six-forty-five. I tell you, sister, life is complicated as all hell.

Did I tell you (I know damned well I didn't have to tell you) I mildly disapproved of your exchange with La Bankhead?[1] Oh, all right; I just thought I'd mention it. A great many folks seem to think you did very well.

Gladys Percey, old friend of mine in Paramount's research department, from time to time sends me small color reproductions of paintings. The latest—Zuloago's *The Actress Consuelo,* which I didn't know at all—now looks down from the wall over my desk, and looks down very lovely indeed. But she's got tough competition beside her: a small color print of Rembrandt's *Young Girl at an Open Half-Door.*

* * *

Much love, darling, and many kisses ...
SDH

1. Tallulah Bankhead and Hellman regularly displayed their animosity toward each other in public. Bankhead played Regina in *The Little Foxes* in 1939. After Russia invaded Finland on November 30 of that year, Bankhead wanted to join in a dark

night on Broadway to show support for Finland. Hellman and Shumlin refused, and both women issued public statements attacking each other.

TLS LPT

To Prudence Whitfield

27 February 1945, The Aleutians

Pru darling,

A man who's spent all day in bed—as I've done—making up for not having spent any of the previous day there is not at all likely to have much news and I'm no exception. It may be that a lot of fascinating things were happening all over the island all day, but, if so, I missed them.

It's now around three in the morning and my chores are about over. My little factory practically runs itself as far as I'm concerned and I don't know what in the name of God I'm hanging around for.

* * *

I'm reading—Christ knows why—a Ben Ames Williams novel called *Leave Her to Heaven.* I don't know why I mention it either. There isn't anything in it to mention, except maybe it proves that with practice and enough paper anybody can write a novel the *Saturday Evening Post* could buy if it wanted to and if so many other people weren't doing the same thing. (This attitude on my part is, if I recognize the symptoms, an indication that if I stay here I'll get around in a little while, out of a sort of boredom, to at least starting to write a book. That would be a shock to me. I haven't written a book since 1933.)

Take care of yourself.

> Much love…
> SDH

TLS Stern

To Lillian Hellman

1 March 1945, The Aleutians

Lily dear,

No-news Hammett, they call me, the man who's sure to miss whatever's going on; and that fits me fine early this nasty morning.

* * *

I finished Fast's *Freedom Road* and found it pretty much like his other works with the exception of *The Last Frontier*—on the right side, but over-simplified to death. I'm finding out that that sort of stuff does have a place, though: I know at least a couple of readers whose, you might say, eyes were opened by the book and who at least think they'd like to know more about what actually went on down there in the old South, suh.

I hope Nancy warned you that I was going to expect some kind of explanation why you didn't write me all the time you were in England. It seems to me if Cockburn could keep in touch with me ...

My face has been full of those red blotches for quite a while— remember? that vitamin-A deficiency stuff—and I've been meaning to go over to the hospital and see if they can fix it up with capsules or a sun- lamp or something; but that too, along with a lot of other things, I keep putting off, thinking each day that maybe some information on what I'm going to do next will turn up and then I can start planning with some idea of what's ahead of me. But this kind of shilly-shallying doesn't seem to be getting me anywhere, so maybe I'd better take a firm stand or stir my stumps or something.

I'll probably stay up in the morning to hear FDR's report on the Yalta Conference, which seems to have been just what was needed to show everybody that the Big Three haven't any intention of letting anything or anybody split them at this moment.

I promised to do the office cooking tonight, so I reckon I'd better quit this and light the gasoline burner and start pushing soup and stuff around.

> Love and kisses and things...
> SDH

TLS LPT

To Lillian Hellman

4 March 1945, The Aleutians

Dearest Lily,

* * *

I'm still reading haphazardly—*The Big Rock Candy Mountain*, Simenon's *On the Danger Line*, and such like—without going to much trouble to find anything better than what's close at hand.[1] Laziness, I reckon. I seem to use this sort of reading chiefly as a sort of lead-in for thinking about other things. It turns out that I've got a lot of things to think about these days in an unhurried and unha[r]assed way.

I'm even thinking about maybe perhaps it might be possibly writing a novel, for which I've got a kind of feel if not exactly any very clear idea. We'll see. It's hard to convince me that I haven't all the time in the world ahead of me for practically anything I wish to do. It's a nice feeling even if it may when analyzed turn out to be just sheer shiftlessness. Maybe Alaska's got something to do with it.

* * *

Much love, darling, and many kisses…
SDH

1. *The Big Rock Candy Mountain* by Wallace Stegner.

TLS HRC

To Lillian Hellman

10 March 1945, The Aleutians

Lily dear,

This morning's news budget is moderately gruesome. On the basis of a conversation yesterday with my company commander I am in a position to report that I seem to have lost on my furlough gamble. If things go along as they now do I have a fair chance of getting my furlough early in the fall, but not before. Of course this is our Army and things can happen to improve or worsen my chances, so I'm not committing suicide just yet.

I spent Thursday on the rifle range and, not having finished up, was due to go out again yesterday, but the weather blocked us. I had as usual a good time, but it can safely be said, even with incomplete returns in, that I'm unlikely to set any world records. I could blame a swollen right hand—I must have knocked it against something or wrenched it somehow, but I don't remember anything of either sort—except that my trigger finger works as well as ever and that's the only part of your right hand that's got anything to do with rifle firing. The rifle we're firing is the most accurate of all the general issue models, but it's not particularly suited to me and I've been experimenting with changes in what I call my style, and that's fun. Then, late in the day when we were firing on the 300-yard range, snow began to blow up from the ground to blot out the bull's-eyes—and a 10-inch bull's-eye on the 300-yard range blots out very easily, being at best no larger, as we say in the Army, than a gnat's ass—so we shot where we "estimated" the black spot was, and that was very interesting. As you may or may not remember, I was never nuts about shooting at inanimate and inedible targets, so these novelties that can be worked in pleased me.

Mail deliveries have been pretty bad lately and so—though it's ten days since you've been home and I'm still without a letter—I haven't been blaming you. I only blame you for not having written from England, and probably wouldn't even do that if Cockburn's paper hadn't kept coming through on time to remind me of what you weren't doing.

I'm not sure we won't get out to the range later this morning, so I reckon I'd better play safe and try to catch a nap before breakfast.

Much love, darling, and I hope you came home to nice things...

SDH

TLS LPT

To Lillian Hellman

13 March 1945, The Aleutians

Dear Lilishka,

I remember you. You're the tart-tongued problematic woman in *Time* this week and I bet you're having fun.[1]

* * *

A small dark distant political cloud has appeared on my military horizon. It may fade or may loom large and is very interesting indeed. I wish I could write you about it. Or perhaps you're a constant reader of the *Chicago Tribune*.[2]

Much love, darling...
SDH

1. Hellman was featured in the "People" section of the 12 March 1945 issue of *Time* magazine. Having just returned from a four-month trip to Russia, she claimed to have discussed world politics with "high-ranking Red Army men" and to have been told that Stalin was "too busy with the Poles" to meet with her.

2. On 1 March 1945 the *Chicago Tribune* obtained from a house military affairs subcommittee investigation the names of ten commissioned officers in the U.S. Army who allegedly were Communists. The Communist Political Association (the organization formed from the Communist Party USA after it was dissolved in May 1944) claimed that 10,000 Communists were serving in the armed forces, of whom at least 500 were commissioned officers.

TLS LPT

To Prudence Whitfield

13 March 1945, Fort Richardson

Pru dear,

It was nice getting two proper letters from you this afternoon and knowing your touch of whimsy was a thing of the past. For all your charm you're a cantankerous bastard when you set your mind to it...sometimes.

* * *

Rumors still float around that I'll be transferred to the I & E section, but so far they're only rumors. The chances are—or did I tell you this before?—the transfer would help my chances for an earlier-than-fall furlough, though there's nothing sure about that either.

* * *

The war news continues to sound good and—though I'm not as optimistic as some—I wouldn't be surprised if the European end were practically wound up this summer and the Asiatic in, say, another year and a
half or so. My guess is that, on the Eastern front in Europe, where the
final decision will probably be arrived at, Zhukov's First White Russian
Army—now crossing the Oder—will by-pass Berlin, leaving it to be
reduced in due course by Rokossovsky's Second White Russian Army—
now mopping up the Danzig-Gdynia area.[1] But they don't always do
what I think they're going to—or ought to—do.

I'm having a lot of fun with the novel-notions, but am, of course, not
yet ready to start actual production. That, I hope, won't come for a little
while yet. Me, I like to mull. When you start to put things down
on paper you, necessarily, start whittling them down and I like the pre-
writing period when all is grand and vast and majestic.

>Much love, darling…
>SDH

I've had a couple of letters from Nell, who thinks she may get a radio
spot for her Maisie stories.[2]

1. In April 1945 Marshal Georgy Zhukov commanded the final assault on Berlin
   and remained there as commander of the Soviet occupation force in Germany.
   Konstantin Rokossovsky was commanding operations in East Prussia and
   Pomerania in 1945.
2. Whitfield later added a marginal note: "'Maisie' by Nell Martin played by dear
   friend Ann Sothern."

TLS Stern

To Lillian Hellman

15 March 1945, The Aleutians

Lily darling,

Weather kept us home from the range this morning: there's not much
sense in trying to hit a 500-yard target with a rifle when—unless your
mother was an eagle your father happened to run into that time he went

up the mountain—you can't see 200 yards. We'll probably try again Sunday, or next month, depending on how other folks are scheduled.

* * *

I haven't seen any of the Hemingway war correspondence, but am told that he's dissatisfied with his contract or his treatment or something that he'd get sore at and in retaliation is burlesquing himself.

I know what you mean about Potter, who can be a very foolish woman, but me, as I said before, I got to kind of like very much…which may or may not be Alaska. (After a while up here everybody gets to believing most of their reactions are more or less colored by the place; that's what the Alaskan fear of going Outside largely comes from.)

I'm impatiently waiting for clippings on the *Chicago Tr[i]bune* House of Representatives shindig, visualizing great bales of them, but not to be surprised if the whole thing stirred up only the faintest of ripples. There's no way of telling from here at the moment.

It seems to me that I'm putting on some weight these days—not that I'm fat yet, but my face has filled out a little and my garments—or so I tell myself—are a bit tighter here and there. (I know, I know! I've thought this before and been made a chump of by the first pair of scales I climbed on.)

Now I ought to quit this and go down into Pneumonia Gulch to keep a 9:30 date with the barber before I start winnowing the night's news.

Much love, darling …
SDH

TLS LPT

To Lillian Hellman

18 March 1945, The Aleutians

Dearest Lily,

Today's white and cold after a blizzardish yesterday and life is white and nice and so are you and me as near as I can make out from this distance.

I don't know a damned thing I didn't know the last time I wrote you and haven't even got any new guesses worth passing on. I've got to start moving round more: chances are some of the finest rumors never reach this part of the island at all.

A couple of days ago I happened to run across a copy of Lenin's *Theoretical Principles of Marxism* (Vol. XI in the *Selected Works*) and am looking forward to a very fine time indeed with it. I had almost reached the point where there was nothing ahead of me but westerns and mysteries.

That's awful news about Maggie.

La Potter has sent me some manuscript chapters of the Alaska flyer book, so me and my editorial pencil will no doubt be having a high old time for the next few days. She's back in Fairbanks, and I suppose Miriam is too by now. Somebody told be they'd run into her at the Minneapolis airfield, headed that way.

The weather's starting to cut didoes again, out of doors, of course, but then that's where I've got to go presently. Last night we had to send out a couple of search parties to hunt for a chaplain who'd gone astray in the snow. Nobody's going to have to send any out for me. I'm against being lost like *PM*'s against people who push other people around.

* * *

>Much love, darling…
>SDH

TLS HRC

To Mary Hammett

20 March 1945, The Aleutians

Mary darling,

A very sweet letter from you yesterday did its best to make it a very sweet day, but I guess the weather—which was not what anybody could have called sweet—won the decision in the end, though, as a matter of fact, the days haven't been too bad lately. It's the nights that turn into howling monsters.

I'm pretty much in agreement with you on *A Tree Grows in Brooklyn.* It's readable enough, except maybe toward the end, but certainly not very profound, and when you get through it you have a kind of well-what-of-it? feeling. I didn't see the picture: I've seen only a couple of pic-tures—and those by accident—in a couple of years.

What happened to "My Brother Felix" is that it was pushed around into another book to be called "There Was a Young Man," which, about half finished, now rests in a trunk at Pleasantville, N.Y., from which it will one day be exhumed to be pushed around again and called some-thing else. The notion that occupies me just now is a new one.

Having gone through Saturday and Sunday with very little sleep, I got myself a good clean 9 hours of it last night and this morning and am now—for me—bursting with well-being and health and energy, so I'm going to try to apply some of them to work before they run out on me, which is likely as not to happen in, say, half an hour or so.

Much love, sweetheart, and how in hell are you spending your time these days?

Papa

TLS Marshall

To Lillian Hellman

Early in March, Hemingway visited New York for a week. The Hemingway anec-dote Hammett refers to is presumably Hemingway's boast that he was the first American to enter Paris after the Germans were driven out of the city in August 1944. Hemingway enjoyed telling the exaggerated story of meeting André Malraux at the Paris Ritz and asking him why he and the brigade he commanded did not help when Hemingway took Paris. Malraux, who had been active in the French resistance, led the Brigade Alsace-Lorraine late in 1944. From 20 December 1944 to 10 January 1945, his brigade defended Strasbourg against the German offensive led by Field Marshall Karl Rudolf Gerd von Rundstedt. Hemingway reported on the Rundstedt offensive as a war correspondent.

20 March 1945, The Aleutians

Dear Lilishka,

I'd heard the Hemingway story before and, surprisingly, with all the details pretty much the same. It's a pip, huh? About Malraux I'd only heard vague rumors and yours was good news. I guess we were right in always thinking him quite a guy.

This morning, starting at two o'clock, I loaded myself down with nine straight end-to-end hours of sleep and am practically a new man tonight, which may or may not be all to the good, depending on what you thought of the old one.

I liked the "lady who supplied the coffee and sandwiches" touch at your Medical Society affair. There must be something about the mere act of forming an organization that makes all of them act like all others at times, no matter how different their aims.

I'm still fumbling around with rosy nebulae, most of which I hope will presently merge to form a novel, and it's a lot of fun. I'll let you know the details as soon as I know them, but that's not yet.

(At this point I took time out to decide that, since tomorrow's the first day of spring, our front page might as well carry a picture of the traditional gauze-clad Spring with a chaplet of buds on her hair, shivering in a snowdrift. It's coming to weighty conclusions like that which really wins wars, though it's hard to explain it to civilians.)

Don't fret about not being able to squeeze the most out of your trip, not being able to do as much good as you hoped.[1] Miracles seldom happen in the best circles and steady does it. Unless I am politically a dope—which is always possible, but that wouldn't keep me from being mildly surprised by the proof—things ought to be tightening up along about now. Though God knows I'm no longer in close enough touch with what's going on Outside to set myself up as an expert.

To work, to work, now, my darling . . .

> Much love . . .
> SDH

Afterthought—enclosure—thanks.

1. In March 1945, Hellman returned from her five-and-a-half-month trip to Russia, the Middle East, and England. She had been invited to Russia by UOKS, the union of movie and theater workers.

TLS HRC

To Josephine Hammett

22 March 1945, The Aleutians

Princess darling,

Winter's still hanging around like somebody you owe money, though it gets in most of its dirty work at night and we usually manage to pick up a few rays of sunshine—that rarity—sometime almost every day. You understand, this here sunshine is not exactly hot enough to scalp you always, but still it's sunshine, and we are in no position to be finical about it. We take what we can get of it when we can get it and are glad in our groaning, snarling way.

Of news there isn't a whole lot. A couple of weeks ago the *Chicago Tribune* denounced me—along with some others—as a communist propagandist in the Army, inferring that I was up here scouting Alaska for the Soviet Union in case they wanted to take the Aleutians away from us, and there was a little to-do over it in Congress, but I'm not in the guard-house and nobody's taken away my dog-tags, so I dare say no great amount of harm's been done. There are a lot of people in the world, my brown-haired dear, who would have been helped by a year in the right kind of kindergarten.

All kinds of rumors of an early peace in Europe continue to float around and as soon as I can make a reasonable guess I'll probably start looking around for bets. From a military standpoint, I don't think we can smack Germany over before summer, but peace isn't always dictated by purely military considerations and—in spite of official denials—there's doubtless some kind of negotiation going on somewhere. If you can find a small but all-seeing crystal ball you might mail it to me.

> Meanwhile, much love, toots...
> Papa

TLS Marshall

To Lillian Hellman

29 March 1945, The Aleutians

Dear Lily,

A mean, mean day, my darling, with much filling of the military ear by the blowing slush and banshees wailing over the tundra now it's dark and hell to pay all along the line.

Next week I should know—as nearly as anybody can ever know anything in this Army—whether I'm going to be transferred to I & E or stay here. If the transfer goes through I should be able to pick off a furlough in a matter of a week or so. If it doesn't I'll settle cozily down here to do a novel, probably about a middle-aged painter in the Army. I've got a couple of other notions, but at the moment like that one best.

It seems like a long time—though it's probably only many many days—since I've had a letter from you. Do you think you're in London again? Or *are* you in London? Do I have to start communicating with you through Nancy again?

By the way, when you send the clippings, don't by any means omit the *New Masses* and *Daily Worker* if they should be available.

The war news continues to look swell, though I'm still one who doesn't look for the end in Europe much before summer—unless, of course, something unpredictable happens.

Last night I read Glenway Wescott's *Apartment in Athens,* which seemed to me an adequate enough description of how his grandmother in Minnesota felt when she had to take in boarders, and am halfway through Dick Wright's early autobiography, which seems to me the story of a blackface Cliff Odets who never had any roller skates either.[1]

It is that I now must work.

> Love, darling…
> SDH

1. Richard Wright's *Black Boy*; Clifford Odets was a proletarian playwright.

TLS LPT

To Lillian Hellman

1 April 1945, The Aleutians

Lili dear,

Yesterday was a nice enough day from the standpoint of weather and I spent most of it on the rifle range, having a pretty good time but hanging up no records that can be sent to Tokyo with the idea of frightening the people out of their wits.

So the other night I was in the mess hall and a comic who's down here with a USO troop came over to me and said he was Sam Levine's nephew and would write Sam he had seen me.[1] So I can't tell you what this meant to me, but, at least, I can tell you it happened.

By way of research—ah, there!—for my book I'm reading Henri's *The Art Spirit* and finding some very fine stuff indeed in it. Ever read it?

I'm looking forward to the *Collier's* with your story: we're never very far behind the States on the weeklies.[2] And I hereby authorize you to ignore anything sent to you by any one of my millions of "friends," unless accompanied by (a) money, or (b) advance warning from me.

Nancy sent me a copy of your letter to the southern columnist, my recent warning against writing letters to the editor having arrived, I'm afraid, too late. Meanwhile, or just the same, whichever I mean, I thank you for your nice words, though; looking back from '45, 48 seems plenty young for anybody to enlist.

I haven't made up my mind about the birthday gift yet. It'll no doubt depend on whether I'm staying here, going back to the mainland, or furloughing to the States.

The weather's mean but I'm not.

> Much love, darling…
> SDH

1. Sam Levine was a Broadway actor; Sam Levene was a Broadway and Hollywood actor who had appeared in *After The Thin Man* (1936).
2. Hellman did a series of travel articles for *Collier's* in 1945. Her article in the 31 March 1945 issue was about a long train ride to the Warsaw-Vistula front describing the hardships the Russian people endured and their warm treatment of her.

TLS LPT

To Mary Hammett

4 April 1945, The Aleutians

Mary darling,

* * *

I had a letter telling me that Maggie Kober—of whom I'm very fond—is down with multiple sclerosis (a disease of the spinal cord) and hasn't much chance of beating it. It's not painful, thank God, but she has to spend most of her time in bed and hasn't too much control over her right leg. A hell of a thing to happen to a girl in her twenties!

My mind's made up about this morning: I'll stick around, but not to write any more letters. I'll fuss around with the novel I'm going to do—if I stay on the island this summer—about an artist in Alaska. It's at that nice stage now when I've got nothing to do but fool around with notions and feelings and don't yet have to commit myself to anything by putting it down on paper.

Take care of yourself, blondie.

> Much love...
> Papa

TLS Marshall

To Mary Hammett

7 April 1945, The Aleutians

Mary dear,

A nice long letter from you was on my bunkside table when I came out of the ether late this afternoon and that's a very fair way to wake up.

* * *

Offhand, I can't give you much definite detail on Switzerland's position in the war, except, of course, that she's been tied up so closely with Germany economically that she can hardly be free otherwise. She's probably kept herself as "technically" neutral as possible, but that's not likely to help a great deal. The basis of the San Francisco Conference—where an attempt will be made to set up the post-war world—is that nobody who wasn't *against* the Axis should have much voice in world affairs.[1] It's quite rightly assumed nobody's been, or could have been, honestly neutral. When I say that Switzerland's not going to be sitting so pretty, however, I don't mean that anything so terrible will happen to her. The chances are nothing much will, except we should have to listen to less of that hogwash about her sturdy independence and rugged democracy and the like. Just as we can hope to hear less about the joys and delights of life in Sweden.

There's far from enough information lying around on which to base a decent guess as to the length of the war with Japan. The chances are the decisive factor will be our success against the Jap army in the industrial regions of north China and Manchuria. It might be that we'll go in there fairly soon...or we might wait till the Jap homeland has been pounded a bit. I can't see any advantage in waiting that long—to me it seems a matter of going in as soon as sufficient troops and materiel are ready, which may or may not depend on the end of the war with Germany—but they don't always bother about what I see or don't see. Whether Russia strikes at the same time we do has probably already been decided by us and them on the basis of what'll work best for everybody—the same agreed-on-by-both-sides basis that has kept them out of war with Japan till they'd finished polishing Germany off.

Anybody who claims he's "come to know that the mass of the people and their relation to the government can never change," is simply claiming that he's never bothered about history...or anthropology...or much of anything. In all periods of history there has been, among the ignorant, this same silly confidence that their mode of life was the final, fixed, everlasting ideal civilization towards which all earlier modes had been but steps. That *every* stage is only a step to another stage, and that this always will be true as long as man is capable of advancement is, I suppose, a little tough on people's vanity and maybe makes them feel less secure in themselves...but that doesn't keep it from being the most obvious and the most unmistakably true lesson that, not only history, but also most of the sciences, have to teach. We've only had three hundred years or so of this kind of social structure and that's far from being long enough, as time runs in history, to be considered even semi-permanent—nor was its forerunner, feudalism, any more permanent, nor the oriental slave state. You could make a better argument—though it would still be false—for the permanence of primitive communism, under which we once lived, under a similar form of which the American Indian was living only a couple of generations ago, and under which people still live here and there in the less progressive parts of the world. And in none of these stages did government in our sense exist and in all of them the relation of the bulk of the people to society as a whole was a good deal different. Recorded history goes back some 6,000 or 7,000 years—with some 180,000 years of Paleo- and Neolithic culture before that—so what kind of a sample of permanence is our two or three centuries of living this way? Unless, of course, you have the kind of egotism that makes you insist on your everlasting importance. It's as if you were to write a history of the world by starting with the date of your birth and the statement, "Before this day nothing of importance happened in the world."

The reasons so many people who considered themselves liberals or revolutionaries in youth become something else when they grow older are several. One of the most important is that too much of that kind of thinking among the young is actually no more than a form of personal resentment against authority—or sometimes against age as represented by authority—and the years of course remove its causes. Another is that most people have some sort of more or less vague flareup against injustice at one time or another—and unless they're blind they're likely to get around to it young—but are without either tough enough fibre or clear enough minds to stick it out when they find there are no easy solutions to what's wrong with the world, that it's a long, tough and unglamourous struggle. Then of course there's the chap who collects a little worldly goods and comes to think society has no other business except the protection of his property. And then others just get old and tired; but there is a surprising small proportion of earnestly sincere folk who've switched over. Their efforts may be a little weaker because of age and often their viewpoints may be dated, but those who were honest and straight when they were young stay honest and straight when old. (Honesty, as a matter of fact, is something that has to be learned and so it would seem natural for the old to be even more honest than the young. Increasing weakness, and the timidity that can come with it, however, too often work against that among the "reasonably honest.")

It's nearly ten o'clock and I should be getting to work on tomorrow's batch of misinformation for our readers; so I'll have to let your question about war criminals wait over till next time I write.

Much love, darling, and take care of yourself...
Papa

1. The San Francisco conference, officially the United Nations Conference on International Organizations, began on 25 April 1945 and ran until 25 June. It included delegates from fifty nations, who approved the United Nations Charter on the last day of the conference.

TLS MARSHALL

To Prudence Whitfield

9 April 1945, The Aleutians

Pru darling,

Well, no, sweetheart, I don't think you should marry a "conventional, strait-laced stuffed shirt—who thinks *PM*, the Administration and everything about Russia etc. stinkin', lousy and untouchable." The chief thing wrong with your marrying him, of course, is that you think of him—or at least describe him—in those terms; and he's no doubt an admirable catch for anybody who considers him a solid citizen with no nonsense about him.

Two letters from you were waiting for me when—bed-bound—I got to my hut after noon chow and that's a very nice way to go to bed. One of the letters was very lively and gay, the other—written early the morning of the 4th—just as down-in-the-mouth and woebegone. You do bounce around, honey.

It's nice news that the apartment will be waiting for you the first of May, and that actually isn't so god-damned far away, though maybe I'm saying that because there's no chance in the world that I'd be back to see it before that. They always told me men were selfish.

After loafing on the job for a few days, pretending there was no use trying to do anything on the book till I knew definitely whether I was going to stay here to finish it, I'm now back in harness, though still not ready to pin it down on paper. It's a little after four in the morning—another stinking morning—and I'll probably get in a couple of hours after I've finished this letter.

This afternoon I shall make more or less vague attempts to find out what cooks on my transfer, but it would be easier to put on an energetic campaign for information if I were not so almost certain I'll be lucky to get any answers that are less vague than the guesses I could make lying in bed.

So I'm off to the wars, sweetheart.

> Much love…and take care of yourself…and stop stewing …
> SDH

TLS STERN

To Prudence Whitfield

13 April 1945, Fort Richardson, Alaska

Pru dear,

This probably won't be any great shakes of a letter: I'm kind of disgruntled tonight. Nothing serious has gone wrong, but an accumulation of little nuisances has me in a small but compact pet. I've been too long away from the part of the Army that keeps its shoes shined and its hair cut and wears a necktie and makes neat beds—well swept and mopped underneath, with those god damned shoes lined up in a pretty row—and washes its windows and shows up punctually hither and thither in accordance with notices on the bulletin board. I'll get back into those tidy habits if the war and I last long enough, but meanwhile they irk my free and soggy Aleutian soul.

The I & E stand for Information-Education, darling, and what's supposed to occupy me nowadays—when I'm not barking my skinny shins on the items listed above—is nursing along a round-table program for enlisted men on the Post radio, editing a monthly magazine for I & E personnel and writing a pamphlet about Alaska and the Aleutians. At the moment it doesn't look as if I'm going to have any time to work on the novel, but I don't mind that so much: I more or less thought of the novel as something to keep me busy down on the island, where I didn't have a great deal to do, since the paper practically got itself out every night.

Maybe I should go over to the cafeteria and try to eat myself into a better humor. I could go into town and try it with both drinking and eating, but it's after nine and I'd like to hit the sack early tonight, since I rise at six. And when I go into Anchorage, no matter how pure my intentions, I practically always run into a late and damp evening. Maybe my moral fibre isn't all it should be.

> Good night, darling, with love…
> Dash

TLS PENZLER

To Lillian Hellman

23 April 1945, Fort Richardson

Lily dear,

There is a good deal to be said for and against life.

Spring is beautiful here, but here one views all the seasons through a haze of coal dust.

It is comfortable living in a barracks with a built-in latrine, but looking out for haircuts and shoeshines and neat bed-making and wearing neckties and sweeping and mopping floors and washing windows and showing up for classes are nuisances after a couple of years of nothing of the sort.

Nursing along a round-table weekly affair for enlisted men on the Post radio station, editing a magazine for Information-Education personnel, and writing another pamphlet about Alaska seem pleasant and respectable enough occupations, but keeping-office-hours-obeying-tiny-regulations sits uneasily on my free Aleutian soul.

Some things seem mighty silly for a man of my age to be doing. But I guess the same thing could be said about some of the things I do by my choice in my off-duty hours.

Ah, yes, my chick, there is a good deal to be said for and against life.

Whatever you think best on the Viking deal will be all right with me.[1] My advice on that sort of thing would be kind of unclear. Why don't you mull it over with Pindyck?

And don't forget that I probably have some sort of obligation to Cerf, though Fran would know about that. (And, carefully, you might break the news to her that my move up here means there'll be no time to work on the new novel in the immediate future.)

Poor baby, you do seem to have got yourself into a pretty pickle with the Colonel.

I had letters from Lois and Maggie today, and a postcard from Julie who'd just met her Bill in San Francisco and was taking off for Los Angeles with him. Maggie sent me that charming newspaper picture of Cathy swinging the doll in the park. I forgot what Lois wrote, though I'm sure it included the usual suggestion that you were slighting her.

Too many people write me about FDR's death as if their sorrow were based on the fact that without him in the driver's seat they might be driven by fear into having to *do* something themselves.[2]

> Much, much love ...
> SDH

1. Hellman was attempting to arrange publication for a volume of *Adakian* cartoons with the Viking Press.
2. Franklin Delano Roosevelt died on 12 April 1945.

TLS LPT

To Lillian Hellman

28 April 1945, Fort Richardson

Lily darling,

Under separate cover I'm sending you a dingus Fran Pindyck sent me, with her letter more or less explaining the set-up. I signed the contract, but don't take that as a hint that I want it especially, so if you've got any other notions in your pretty little head I hope you'll tear up the document and play your own string out.[1]

When they ask me, "But what did you do in the Second World War, Grandaddy?" I shall hem and haw and reply, "Well, now you take the last Saturday in April 1945 for instance. I got up in time for breakfast and then after making my bed and sweeping round it and tidying up with special care because Saturday is inspection day I went down to the latrine where it was my turn to be latrine orderly—or one of a couple of orderlies—and we washed bowls and scrubbed floors and such still with special care because it was inspection day, and so by the time I got to the office there wasn't time to do much but cut 1000 words out of an article somebody else had written before it was time for me to take off for my company again for chow, which is about a ten or twelve-minute walk. Well, then, bub, after I came back from eating there were a lot of British Information pamphlets on what the limeys had done in Burma and we figured it was only worth while to distribute 100 of them, so I spent all afternoon burning the rest of them because there were a hell of a lot of them and that thick coated paper burns slowly in bulk." That's what I'll answer...and let history sit in judgment if it's got nothing else to do.

The joint is jumping—as I suppose yours is—with rumors and counter-rumors of surrenders and non-surrenders in Germany. A new one has just come in, so I dare say its denial can't be far behind. I'd kind of like to see the European end wound up, so I'll know whether it really will tempt me to get out of the Army, something I haven't thought about hitherto but which I've been thinking about the last couple of days...probably only because I'm bored pissless just now with what I'm doing...or, perhaps, with the way I'm having to do it.

The life of a fighting man, my darling, is not all blood and skirmishes.

Much love, toots, and may the world be smiling on you ...
SDH

1. Presumably Hammett refers to contracts for collections of his stories published by Lawrence Spivak in 1945: *The Continental Op* and *The Return of the Continental Op*.

TLS LPT

To Mary Hammett

29 April 1945, Fort Richardson, Alaska

Mary dear,

I'm sorry you're having such a to-do about the house. I don't know what the 1938 government liens could be about as I'm sure all our income tax difficulties for that year were long ago straightened out. Or was it the State government? I'm not so sure how I stand with them...don't know whether I ever owed them anything or—if so—ever gave it to them. The ideal arrangement anyhow—it seems to me from this distance—would be to put the house in your and Josephine's names.

Today's a fine sunny Sunday and I should have gone out...only I was too lazy. However, after I finish this letter and another, I think I shall at least go over and watch a nearby baseball game. It's too lovely an afternoon to spend indoors and I feel I shouldn't waste sunshine after all those sunless days on the islands. It's a little before two in the afternoon and I've only been up about two hours. Last night I stayed in camp and was in bed by ten, though, between listening to a radio that was turned on too loud and a flock of tipsy barracks-mates who came rolling noisily in from town at all hours, I didn't get solidly to sleep till much, much later.

Tonight I shall probably stay in again. I haven't gone on the wagon, but I haven't had a drink for some three days and fe[e]l enough better for it to think I'll spread it out till along about Tuesday, when I've a date that will no doubt lead to at least a little drinking.

Now I reckon I'd better get at that other letter so I can get out to watch the athletes before the sun's too low.

Much love, toots ...
Papa

TLS MARSHALL

To Mary Hammett

3 May 1945, Fort Richardson, Alaska

Mary dear,

* * *

I can't give you a too satisfactory answer to your question about whether a man discharged from the Army for a serious mental condition is thoroughly cured. The army's supposed to keep him in till he's cured, *if* his condition is curable, but obviously they can't keep him in forever if he's incurable.

No, I didn't have anything to do with *The Searching Wind*. I was in the Aleutians when it was written. I haven't even had a chance to read it in its finished form, though I saw the first rough drafts.

There isn't going to be any good news about Maggie Kober's health, darling. It's pretty definitely incurable and about all they can do is try to slow up its progress a little.

No, the electric suit didn't make me nervous.[1] It was too cozy, and without it I'd've been too cold. Nothing that's comfortable is likely to scare me.

I don't expect any miracles of the San Francisco Conference, but I think it'll work out all right. Of course it'll be picked to pieces by those who don't want world organization. They'll call it a complete flop no matter what's accomplished—on the grounds that more should have been accomplished.

Of course I'm jealous of your going to the circus, just as I'm jealous of those who'll see you all glamored up in the blue dress and white coat...but I reckon my day for circuses and blondes in white coats will come again. They can't spread this war out forever, I hope, I hope.

* * *

Much love, cutie, and many kisses...
Papa

1. In a 20 April 1945 letter to his daughter Mary, Hammett wrote, "I had a nice trip up from the island in a B-25 bomber—cozy in an electric suit plugged into the wall like a toaster—and taking only about half the time it usually takes in a transport plane."

TLS Marshall

To Lillian Hellman

3 May 1945, Fort Richardson

Dearest Lily,

* * *

You don't have to worry too much about the titles: it's not very likely that I'll have time to do anything on the novel in the immediate future. I'm not too disappointed, since I had from the beginning thought of it in terms of *if* I stayed on the island.

* * *

My elderly statesman advice to you on the new President and international, as well as domestic, affairs is to wait and see before you start shivering.[1] He's not likely to become a great man, but, unless there is a lot I don't know about him (that's a hell of an *unless!* there are millions of things I don't know about him) he could turn out to be an able one. But all of this reminds me that I'm getting much less news of what's going on these days than I used to down on the island. So if Nancy isn't too busy, will you have her start sending me clippings just as she used to send them in the good old days? I should keep in touch—I mean for my work, outside of for myself—with what's cooking and neither the radio nor the *Anchorage Times* do much good.

I spent part of the morning trying to talk my way into a swift trips down the Chain, but am not optimistic about the results. These folks are polite, but what they want me to do is sit in the office and write, which is one of the things I'm not anxious to do. I'm afraid it's going to take a little time to convert them.

When should I phone you—what days of the week are best and what part of the day...morning, afternoon or night? And where...Pleasantville or New York? RSVP

Now I go to push my way through elements towards that food and that bed. Come to think of it, I should clean my carbine tonight. Tomorrow's weapon inspection day.

> Much love, baby...
> SDH

1. Upon the death of Franklin D. Roosevelt, Harry S Truman, less than three months into his term as vice president, was sworn in as president on 12 April 1945.

TLS HRC

To Lillian Hellman

4 May 1945, Fort Richardson

Lily darling,

We had one-degree-above-zero weather this morning, but the snow stopped and the sun came out to make everything fine and gay with distant mountains sharp against the sky and life kind of nice.

A letter from you did nothing to make life unnicer.

The *Little Foxes* folk back in reconstruction days should be a very satisfactory setup for a play.[1] It's a nice—theatrically nice—period and with a few exceptions only the worst things have been done with it.

The Ella Winter stories were very fine indeed, as most La Winter stories have a habit of being.[2]

I'm glad Wallis liked what you'd done of the script and I do not pay too much attention to your complaints about what you'd done.[3] I remember you.

Having managed my transfer up here on the truthful grounds that Bill Glackin, my right-hand man, could run the paper as well as I, I am now trying to get him up here on the less truthful plea that he is as easily replaced as I. I don't know whether I'm going to be able to swing it, but I've nothing to lose by trying and I could certainly use him. I don't know whether I've ever told you about him. I don't especially like him—by which I mean I've not much warmth toward him—but he's a good boy and I'd rather have him backing me up than anybody else I can think of in the Army. He'd come in mighty handy up here among these military will o' the wisps.

* * *

There isn't any news of the novel for reasons already conveyed to you. If I don't get some part of my way on how I think this job ought to be done and decide to sulk in my tent I may turn to the novel again. Other-

436

wise it's likely to rest in the egg for a while. (I've no immediate intention of sulking: it ain't that hopeless.)

While I've been writing this there has been going on, in the next office, a discussion of international affairs between a corporal who's a Harvard man and a captain who was evidently educated in the National Guard of one of the more backward states which I have never heard the like of and I am one, ma'am, who has heard a great deal of talking on very low levels. But this... It beats me and I shall go eat...

> Love and love...
> SDH

1. *Another Part of the Forest* is about the Hubbard family, the central characters of *The Little Foxes* set twenty years earlier.
2. Ella Winter, wife of Donald Ogden Stewart, was an active member of the Communist Party.
3. Hellman's movie adaptation of *The Searching Wind,* produced by Hal Wallis, was released in 1946.

TLS LPT

To Lillian Hellman

6 May 1945, Fort Richardson

Lily darling,

It's another sunny Sunday afternoon. I slept till noon, then breakfasted on a shot of bourbon—how do you pronounce that?—and roast chicken—pronounced chicken—and came over to the office to do this no doubt unworthy reply to the very nice as usual letter that came from you yesterday.

Last night I did Anchorage mildly, this evening I shall probably spend on the Post, unless, of course, some 1-volt temptation should ambush me.

Maybe I encouraged Maggie a little in the eccentric princess stuff, sweetheart, but I didn't invent it; after all she had got a fine start before I knew her aping her mother, the batty duchess. I must tell you about the m[ezuzah] some time. It is probably just as well if I don't write it.

There's plenty of reason for pessimism in international and domestic affairs, I dare say, but, perhaps through ignorance, I don't choose to be much influenced by it. What I say in my carefree soldier-boy way is come on, future, let's see what you've got for us in the way of rowdydows from which we can win a little something here, a little something there until we've got enough to put together a nice, neat and at least partially complete structure. Don't tell me I'm light-headed: I'm only light-hearted. (Ah, the gaiety of youth!)

I'm now in the midst of an attempt to render the Bretton Woods proposals into a language that Army personnel can be expected to understand: it's kind of fun.[1]

Yesterday, for an hour or two, I had a wrestling-match with the question of whether I should get out of the Army when they start whittling it down after the European War is over. It wound up by my deciding that even with 2,000,000 fewer men in it the Army will still represent the heart and guts of American manhood or something and I belong with it. I'm not sure to what extent my decision was influenced by personal desires, but, anyhow, there it is. And one thing I am sure of is that if I convinced myself I ought to get out and did so I could look forward to blackish periods of dissatisfaction with myself now and then.

The sun is poking a beckoning finger through the window (See, there's a bit of the poet in the boy!) and I think I'll go out and soak up some of it.

Much love, cookie...

SDH

1. The United Nations Monetary and Financial Conference, held at Bretton Woods, New Hampshire, from 1 to 22 July 1944, established an International Monetary Fund to stabilize national currencies and to promote trade and an International Bank for Reconstruction and Development to support developing countries.

TLS LPT

To Prudence Whitfield

2 June 1945, Fort Richardson

Pru dear,

* * *

I don't remember a hell of a lot about the 27th, except that it was in the main pleasant enough. Somehow this birthday seems to have meant less to me than any I can remember. I suppose after you've passed the half-century mark the odd numbers become dull and you're impressed only by the decades. If that's true my next significant one should be the sixtieth. When the time comes I'll let you know whether this theory is a true one.

* * *

Furloughs are frozen at the moment and in any event it's unlikely I could get away in the immediate future, so don't start looking for me too soon. In a couple of weeks I hope to get away for a run down the Chain to spend at least a few days each on Attu, Shemya, Adak, Amchitka and perhaps at Cold Bay. I've friends at all those spots and am looking forward to the trip. This is a nice time of the year down there. Not that it's bad here either. We've had almost continuous sunshine for some days and the temperature is just about right for me. The lack of darkness is an annoyance at times: this isn't exactly the land of the midnight sun and the sun does go below the horizon, but the darkest it gets just now is a sort of dullish twilight from a little after midnight till somewhere between two and three in the morning.

* * *

I don't think you should be depressed by the Pacific war news — or not too much. I take for granted it's the losses on Okinawa that bother you. The losses are pretty heavy and any of us who ever served under Buckner know him for a man who doesn't care a hell of a lot for those under him: there's every reason for supposing he'll chuck 'em in like confetti.[1] But it's quite likely he's playing it the right way on that island. Okinawa is the prize plum of the crop and is worth practically anything we have to pay for it. Every life lost there may be saving ten lives later elsewhere. It's tough on the boys (I know a lot of them in the 7th Division; they were in the force that took Attu) but sometimes war's like that.

Buckner is no Grant, but Grant too was a man who tossed 'em in there when the chips were down. (I know I'm talking from up here where nothing's happening, nothing seems likely to happen. We've had our hopes from time to time, but they are pretty thin these days.)

For the past few weeks I've been tottering along with a chest cold, a touch of grippe and a lame left shoulder, which may or may not be rheumatic. For a while I tried to cure them all with liquor, but that didn't work, so I gave it up and haven't had a drink for four or five days. None of them is really very bad, but just the same I think Monday morning—this is late Saturday night—I'll drag the accumulation around to the Infirmary and see what science thinks.

It's eleven-thirty, the latest I've been up since last Monday, so I think I'll call this off for the night and wander over to my barracks and bed.

> Good night, darling, and much love ...
> SDH

1. General Simon Bolivar Buckner was Commander of the U.S. Tenth Army.

TLS STERN

To Lillian Hellman

3 June 1945, Fort Richardson

Dearest Lily,

I know I'm a lowdown bastard not to have written you in all this time, and I've actually no excuse. A combination of life's, the Army's, and my own god damned foolishness had me on a sort of group of merry-go-rounds from which I've just managed to climb down.

For a while a couple of weeks ago it looked as if I were going to pull my age on the Army and walk out, but I think everything is going to be mildly all right now...I hope so anyhow.

I think I wrote you I was pretty dissatisfied with the layout here. And then I got myself a chest cold and some grippe and a lame shoulder that may or may not be rheumatic and foolishly tried to beat them with liquor, which of course didn't work out. Then one morning, between a hangover, my ailments and some additional annoyances in the office, I decided the hell with the whole thing—it wasn't worth it at my age—and announced I was going home. So the Major said sit down and have a cigarette and shut the door and just what's on your mind and we had it out as far as the Information-Education Section was concerned and wound up by deciding if I stayed in I could have a fling at doing things my own way and we'd see how that worked out. Of course I'm not having my own way completely, but then I didn't expect to, knowing the Army and being no dreamer, but it seems to be working out nearly enough to be satisfactory...and to make me glad I stayed in.

Well, that should have been enough for me, but some people, I always say, get more sense as they get older and others are named Hammett, so I went off on another wingding in town, which was all right as far as the Army was concerned, but it didn't do me any great amount of good. But anyhow that's water under the bridge now and I'm a good little boy who's staying on the Post o' nights and minding his p's and q's and hoping this time he'll continue to be, if not exactly sensible, at least not too silly.

My ailments are still a little with me and, while none of them is too bad by itself, I think maybe I'll drag the accumulation around to the Infirmary Monday morning and see what science thinks of them.

And tomorrow, which is Sunday, I'll try to write a fitting reply to your letters: I know this banshee wail isn't one.

Much love, cookie, and try to pretend you're not sorry you ever met-ten up with such an old fool.

> I kiss your hand ...
> SDH

TLS LPT

To Lillian Hellman

3 June 1945, Fort Richardson

Lily darling,

* * *

This afternoon I went out and sat in the sun watching a baseball game, but it seems to have done neither my grippe nor my team much good. Then I decided tonight might be a good time to get some work done and came over to the office only to run into one of my superiors who'd just come back from his first trip down the chain and had made a lot of brand new discoveries of things I'd been telling him about ever since I came into this office and I had to listen to him for hours before I could get to my work; and now I'm tired, I tell you, tired, tired, tired!

There ain't a hell of a lot of news on hand, except that if I can get through with my Aleutian jaunt in time I'll probably go to Edmonton for a week around the 9th of July.

* * *

Why didn't you tell me about the Pindyck contract, baby? I know now what the point was, but the notice from the Authors League on the reprint-book royalty fight didn't reach me till just a day or two ago and I had no idea of what was cooking.[1]

You're really having—and have had—trouble with those god-damned teeth, poor darling. I wish I could go through it for you.

Last night was Saturday—meaning I could sleep late this morning—so I worked and hung around the office pretty late...till about 1:30 this morning. But what I'm getting at is that walking to my barracks at that hour I had no trouble at all reading a typewritten memorandum I'd forgotten to look at.

Louis sent me a copy of his Viking anthology (for which I must remember to write him a letter of thanks) and I think it's a swell job.[2]

* * *

Much love, darling ...
SDH

1. Hammett's novels were published in paperback by Pocket Books. In summer 1945, the Author's Guild demanded a 25 percent increase in royalties on mass-market paperback reprints, most of which sold for 25 cents. The royalty had been 10% or 2.5 cents per copy. The Author's Guild asked for 12%, or 3 cents per copy.
2. Louis Kronenberger, *Reader's Companion: A Personal Anthology Selected for Re-Readability from the Writers of 2000 Years for the Readers of Today.*

TLS HRC

To Mary Hammett

17 June 1945, Fort Richardson

Mary dear,

Here I am, way behind in my letter-writing again, so I may as well make my usual apologies and my usual promises I'll do better. Excuse me, honey.

* * *

My lame shoulder—in spite of my having had it baked daily till every time it sees two pieces of bread it tries to crawl between them—still keeps me off the rifle range, makes typing difficult unless I balance a portable on my knees, and makes nuisances of morning chores like bed-making and sweeping and mopping; but it's no worse than that and I'd be lying if I claimed it had me in any agony.

The trouble with most writers on witchcraft and similar topics is that almost all of them are like Willie Seabrook and do sacrifice accuracy for sensationalism.[1] The only trustworthy stuff I know of in that field is done by anthropologists, who, of course, don't give it the old hubba-hubba. You ought to read Fraser's *The Golden Bough*, and, if you can find it in the library, Waite's *The Rosy Cross*, which is a history of Rosicrucianism back when it was linked with alchemy and is more or less in the field that interests you.

Today's been a pleasantly quiet Sunday. I got up in time for an eleven o'clock breakfast, then read proofs of a book a friend sent me till one, when it was time to go sit in the sun and watch my outfit's team play baseball. Then I came over to the office for a little work—the first in several days—and now as soon as I have written a couple of letters I'm going over to the cafeteria for something to eat, go back to the barracks, take a shower and flop on my bunk with a book on the Baltics till the lights go off at ten.

Much love, baby, and take care of yourself...
Papa

1. William B. Seabrook, who wrote several books on various forms of witchcraft and sorcery around the world, died in 1945.

TLS MARSHALL

To Reba Hammett

1 August 1945, The Macdonald Hotel, Edmonton, Alberta

Dear Sis—

I've been up in Jasper National Park for a couple of days, here a little more than a week—the first city large enough to have street cars in two years—and am now sitting around waiting for a plane ride back to Anchorage. It's not bad sitting—summer heat is a pleasant novelty and even suntan uniforms, which I never liked especially, seem nice. Living in a hotel again and having breakfast in bed is of course little if any short of heavenly. I'm supposed to be here on a job, but my orders let me avoid the local Army base and I'm practically a pig in clover.

I've been away from Fort Richardson for a brief while and things change fast with us, but the way they stacked up when I left should bring me a 45-day furlough in the fall. I shall probably spend a couple of weeks of it at Santa Monica with the youngsters, the rest of it in the East.

There isn't much other news of me. I stay surprisingly robust and reasonably content and shall in all likelihood stick it out up in Alaska till V-J Day—not knowing what else to do with myself.

How's Dad? And you? And what news is there of your part of the world?

Love,
Dashiell

ALS Judi Hammett

To Mary Hammett

V-J Day [15 August 1945], Fort Richardson

Dear Baby,

It's a hell of a while since I've written, but I had something cooking and didn't want to write about it until I was reasonably sure. It goes like this: last week I made a lucky guess and put in for my discharge. I haven't seen my orders but am told they were cut today, which should

mean—as nearly as anybody can predict anything up here these days—
that the rest of it is only a matter of sweating out transportation back to
the States, and that shouldn't take many days…though they'll probably
seem many. For the first time my three years—or that's what it would be
next month—in the Army seem kind of like a lifetime and even my two
years up here seem small eternities…which shows what can happen to
your point of view when you feel your job's over. Now I've got to dash
around winding up a lot of little odds and ends so I can spend the rest of
my time here lying on my bunk a-chewing of[f] my fingernails and waiting for word to take off. Much love to all of you and, while I'll probably
go to New York first, I hope to be out to see you before long.

   Papa

TLS Marshall

To Prudence Whitfield

25 August 1945, APO 462, Minneapolis, Minnesota

Pru dear—

 Half a step, half a step, half a step onward I advance towards Fort
Dix, N.J., and my discharge. I left Anchorage by air Wednesday, was
grounded overnight at Watson Lake in the Yukon and came on here—
this is Edmonton—the next day. I'm told I'll leave here either tomorrow
or Monday on the 36-hour train-trip to Minneapolis. How long I'll be
held there is anybody's guess, but it shouldn't take more than a day or
two to get me on a train for the East and—

 Meanwhile I'm letting the young do my share of the fretting over days
lost here and there. I concentrate on eating, sleeping and loafing and
should return to civilian life as fat and sleek as a suckling pig.

 See you soon (seems funny, writing those words!)

   Much love,
   Dash

ALS Penzler

To Mary Hammett

2 September 1945, Fort Dix, N.J.

Dear Mary—

Of course anything can happen in the Army, but as of seven-thirty this evening it looks as if tomorrow afternoon will find me on my way to Pleasantville with my discharge papers tightly pinned to the breast of my undershirt. I'll wire when it happens and you ought to have the wire long before you get this. The weather is hot as hell after two years in Alaska, but I'll get used to it, I suppose—or go back to my north country. The 4-day trip from Edmonton in a troop train was a bitch—this is no weather to be doubling up in Pullman berths. I'm in tip-top shape physically and without a plan in my head so far as the future is concerned. I'll let you know what's cooking as soon as anything is.

> All the love there is—
> Papa

ALS Marshall

PART FOUR

Activist
1945–1951

*Hammett testifying before the McCarthy
Committee, 26 March 1953*

"I can stand anything I've got to stand," he said
as he moved towards the door.

Ned Beaumont in *The Glass Key*, Chapter 1

WHEN HAMMETT returned home after World War II, he moved back into his room at Hardscrabble Farm in Pleasantville, New York (which remained his permanent residence until Hellman sold the farm in 1952), and he looked for an apartment in New York City where he could live during weekdays when he had business there. He found temporary living quarters on East 66th Street, but after six months, he moved to a studio apartment in Greenwich Village near the main office of the Civil Rights Congress and the Jefferson School, where he taught. He kept an office on the ground floor and had a living room–bedroom with a fireplace that overlooked a small garden. He kept the apartment cold in winter, because it reminded him of the Aleutians, he said.

His army experience provided Hammett a renewed sense of purpose. In the army he had served essentially as an educator, a role he liked, and he planned to enlarge upon it in civilian life. He wanted to be actively involved in politics, doing work he considered meaningful, making people aware of what he felt were abuses of power. The Civil Rights Congress, formed in April 1946 through the merger of three Communist organizations, offered Hammett the opportunity to engage in the kind of activism he relished most: defending the rights of working people by involving himself in specific cases. He was named president of the Civil Rights Congress of New York, a job that required him to respond directly to events of the day—protesting against the lynching of blacks in Georgia; providing for the defense of those accused of violating the Smith Act (which made it a crime to teach, advocate, or encourage the overthrow of the United States government); working to ensure voters' rights; and defending freedom of speech and political expression by actively opposing the House Committee on Un-American Activities. He organized, he spoke, he protested, and he educated. He built the CRC in New York into the most successful American Communist organization of its time, with a bail fund that had some $760,000 in cash by 1951. In the evenings, he taught mystery writing, among other courses, at the newly formed Marxist college, the Jefferson School of Social Science.

In addition to his political commitment, but clearly secondary to it, Hammett had vague plans to resume his career as a writer. He had ideas for several novels, one of which he may have come close to completing, though no evidence survives except for the mention of it in his letters. He was at least thinking about short stories, and he took an active interest in Broadway theater, where his opinion was respected. He invested in plays, edited Hellman's work, and acted as an advisor to Broadway producers. But he put off the writing when there was a chance to do anything else instead. There were many distractions. Politics made heavy demands on his time, and so did his daughter Mary.

In 1946 Mary's mental condition was so bad that Jose felt she could no longer cope. Jose had shielded Hammett from the worst of Mary's transgressions but now, in desperation, she wrote him asking for help. He flew out immediately and, after discussion with Jose and Jo, decided—reluctantly—to take Mary east with him. He would take care of her, find her the very best of psychiatric help. It was a decision that had severe consequences for him.

For a while Mary shared his apartment, and then he got her one of her own. They drank together, each feeding the other's weakness. He had seen brief episodes of her erratic behavior before, but now he realized how deeply disturbed she was and the hopelessness of her condition. His own drinking worsened; by 1947 Hammett was in a downward alcoholic spiral that took him near the point of death.

His last prolonged bout of uncontrollable drinking ended with his collapse and hospitalization in December 1948. His doctor was blunt: if Hammett did not quit drinking immediately, he would die. He chose to live. Beginning in January 1949, Hammett quit drinking for good. His recovery was slow and incomplete. Mary returned to California in 1952 after her doctors admitted there was nothing more they could do for her, and Hammett gave up any hope of a relationship with his older daughter.

As Hammett's health improved, Hellman encouraged him to continue working in the theater and in Hollywood. She cautiously arranged for Kermit Bloomgarden, her producer, to hire him as a script doctor in late fall 1949. When she saw that Hammett was up to the job, she asked William Wyler at Paramount Pictures to hire him as a scriptwriter for an adaptation of Sidney Kingsley's novel and play *Detective Story*. In January 1950 Hammett moved to Los Angeles and found the movie industry as shallow as ever and the city even more offensive. He was disdainful of the project and must have been dismayed by the spectacle of his leftist friends feverishly denouncing their pasts. After three months' work he returned the money that had been advanced him and went home to New York City, never looking back.

The political atmosphere of the time was tense, especially in Hollywood. In October 1947, the House Committee on Un-American Activities launched a sensationalistic investigation of Communist activities in Hollywood, and the next month cited ten writers and directors for contempt of Congress when they refused to answer questions about their membership in the Communist Party. In May 1949, the Hollywood Ten, as they were called, unsuccessfully sued the studios for violating their constitutional rights by firing them, and in August 1950, their appeals of their contempt charge exhausted, all of them were sentenced to prison. At the same time, the Justice Department was attempting to force the party underground, using the Smith Act to jail more than a hundred accused Communists. The blacklist, by which certain employers refused jobs to accused Communists, was even more pernicious than legal assaults. Hundreds of people, especially those in movies, radio, and television, had their livelihood stripped from them.

The blacklist affected Hammett first; the courts followed soon afterward. In the late 1940s he received $1,200 a week from the three radio shows based on his characters. By early 1950, two had been canceled due to his political affiliations, and in 1951, the last was taken off the air. He was undeterred, continuing to serve in a highly public way as president of the Civil Rights Congress, an organization formally designated Communist by the House Committee on Un-American Activities. When eleven Communist leaders were found guilty of violating the Smith Act in November 1949, the bail fund committee of the Civil Rights Congress posted their bail of $260,000, so they could be free during the appeals process. In July 1951, after all appeals were exhausted, four of the men failed to surrender themselves, and the Justice Department launched an inquiry. As chairman of the bail fund committee, Hammett was subpoenaed to testify in federal court to aid in efforts to find men still at large. When he took the stand, he refused to give even his name. He and three other trustees of the bail fund were sentenced to federal prison for contempt of court. Hammett served five and a half months.

His silence was predictable. A primary tenet of the Civil Rights Congress was that citizens had the right to their political beliefs without government interference, and that was a principle Hammett had embraced all his life. Now he did what he had to do without complaint. He went to jail and served his time as a model prisoner, without expecting or accepting sympathy. His letters from prison are unfailingly cheerful. Solitude never bothered him, and during his sober times he even sought it. Nonetheless, Hammett's confinement marked a turning point for him physically. His conviction was as resolute as ever, but after he was released from prison, he was a physically broken man with dwindling resources, and he acted the part.

To Josephine Dolan Hammett

25 October 1945, Hardscrabble Farm, Pleasantville, N.Y.

Dear Jose,

I'm a hell of a guy, I guess, but ever since I got out of the Army last month I've been trying to get myself to sit down and write letters, but this is the first day I have really managed to do it...and it'll probably take me some time to get my hand in again, so it's not likely this will be any great shakes of a communication.

Let's see what's happened. I went on a binge for three weeks or so to celebrate my return to civilian life and to try to get over its being kind of confusing to me. Then I came up here and decided to go on the wagon until I've finished a novel that I hope to start putting on paper either this week or the beginning of next. I'm still looking for an apartment or a hotel suite in the city, but they are hard to get as diamond mines. I could work here of course except that shooting ducks and squirrels and such small things seems to take up too much of my day and I think the book would go faster if I were locked in somewhere in the city...though god knows it's mighty fine here in the country this time of the year.

My health is swell, as usual, and I'm putting on a few pounds here and there, though I doubt if I'll have to make much change in my clothing sizes. (By the way, I've a lot of pre-war clothes and haven't bought much new stuff, though I find most of my old clothes are a little loose in the waist and a little tight in the shoulders.)

Will you give this check to Mary for her birthday and tell her I'm a mean old man to have let it come this late.

* * *

Love,
SDH

TLS Marshall

To Mary Hammett

31 October 1945, Hardscrabble Farm, Pleasantville, New York

Dear Mary,

It's a long, long time since I've written you a letter, undutiful father that I am, but I'm afraid you're going to have to be patient with me for a while. I'm working on a book and that kind of thing never leaves me with much inclination for doing anything like writing in my idle hours. But I'll do the best I can and I hope you'll not find any excuse for cutting down *your* letter-writing.

This book won't be a mystery. It's about a middle-aged painter who comes home from the wars and I'm not too sure what all's going to happen to him, though it isn't going to be one of those hard luck stories about how the returning soldier does or doesn't adjust himself to civilian life again. I haven't found a title yet. I'd use The Changed Lock if it weren't so hard and ugly to pronounce. The meaning fits, but that D-L sound is pretty bad.

Today's been like summer, though the radio promises below freezing weather for tomorrow. I won't be sorry to see it. Outside of my liking for cold weather there's also the matter of duck shooting to be improved: no birds are going to be foolish enough to pass overhead on their way south while the weather stays as nice as this. So far my murdering of the little creatures has been limited to a fair number of squirrels and a few wood ducks, which are wonderful eating but not as much fun shooting as mallards and blacks and such. Tomorrow I'll probably see if I can knock down some grouse.

I've been promised a suite at Delmonico's in New York later this month and will move in as soon as I can. Life won't be as pleasant in the city as here, but I'll probably get more work done: I have a hell of a time making myself stay inside the house here. Lillian and others usually come up here for weekends, but the rest of the time I'm alone and it's all very fine indeed...except it doesn't get any books written, and I'd like to get this one done this winter.

Remember Meg, Salud's daughter[1]...well, she has a very fine two-year-old daughter named Flora who is my constant companion these days—a very sweet, gentle and clowning type. We think Meg will have another litter in a few weeks.

> Much love, darling, and many kisses…
> Papa

1. Salud was a standard poodle owned by Hellman and Hammett.

TLS MARSHALL

To Josephine Dolan Hammett

5 December 1945, Pleasantville

Dear Jose,

Here's that infrequently heard voice out of the past wishing you all the happiness in the world in the new home, and hoping I'm sending this to the right address.

I've got a new home, too; I finally found a small apartment in the city and probably will move in the first of the week, so you might as well start sending my mail there. The address is 15 East 66th Street, New York City, and I think it's going to be comfortable enough—after I've bought a few odds and ends that are needed—to let me finish my book in peace and ease.

I'm speaking kind of boldly about "finishing" the new book, when the truth is I'm not a hell of long ways into it. The temptation to stay outdoors in the country has kept me away from the typewriter most of the time. But anyhow I've got a title now, or at least one I'm pretty sure I'll use. It's from a poem by Peacock and is, or will be, *The Valley Sheep Are Fatter*.[1]

Since the first day of October I've been on the wagon, but it was hard staying on the past couple of days. I'm getting new plates—the Army ones never fit me too well—and had to have some preliminary mouth surgery—all neatly sewed up just now with seven more or less neat stitches—with the result that I've been on a strictly liquid diet, and it's pretty easy to get tired of milk shakes and broths and such. I tried a little bread soaked in milk a few minutes ago, but couldn't manage it. Maybe I'll be able to do something with mashed potatoes and gravy tomorrow…or the next day …

Here's a check to divide three ways with those other people for your Christmas presents and I hope you all have the happiest of happy Christmases.

How did you make out on furniture and stuff for the house? If you're short I'm sure I can scrape up a few pennies, so please let me know. What I mean is, don't be stealing your Christmas money from yourselves to get things for the house, because it isn't necessary. I've got a hell of a lot of back income taxes to pay, but I don't expect to let that make me go short of anything and don't want you to.

My health, in spite of the gripe about my teeth—a point that had more to do with comfort than health—remains practically miraculous. I'm no fatter than ever, but otherwise I'm hale and blooming.

Kiss the youngsters for me and give them my usual promise that I'll try to write more often, and this time maybe I will manage it.

> Love to all ...
> SDH

1. "The mountain sheep are sweeter,/ But the valley sheep are fatter; / We therefore deemed it meeter/ To carry off the latter." From the novel *The Misfortunes of Elphin* (1829) by Thomas Love Peacock.

TLS MARSHALL

To Mary Hammett

11 December 1945, 15 East 66th St., New York City

Dearest Mary,

Tonight I'm taking time out from *The Valley Sheep Are Fatter*—it's more reassuring to me to write out the title instead of just saying "the book"—to try to do a short story—my first in god knows how long—for a new magazine called *Salute* which is to be started by some of the *Yank* lads in February. What I mean is I intend to get started on the short story as soon as I finish this ...

I haven't actually moved into the new apartment yet, so I've not much news about its comforts of lack of them. I had to buy bedding and kitchen ware and such and deliveries are slow as hell these days in this city, but most of my stuff should be in by tomorrow or the next day and I expect to be firmly installed before I go up to the country for the weekend. I've been promised a telephone next month.

If there's snow on the ground when I get up to Pleasantville Saturday I shall try to get a shot at deer with a bow and arrow—the only way it's legal to shoot them in Westchester County—but I'm afraid it's a little too late to start. The season ends that day and I will have to be awfully lucky to get anything the first day I try. I reckon it's my own fault for frittering time away. First I put off getting a bow and arrows, and then I let one thing and another put me off till now the thir[t]y days have about run out. Oh, well, there's always next year, and I'm no longer young enough to be impatient.

The cut in my mouth is healing well enough, though I'm still on a semi-liquid diet and am not likely to be eating much until next week at the earliest. It's a nuisance, but no worse than that.

My agent's trying to rig up another radio program for me: S[y]dney Greenstreet as *The Fat Man* or something of the sort and seems to think it could be hot stuff, though it seems kind of w[a]cky to your old man, who, however, readily admits he doesn't understand much about what's good and bad on the air waves.[1] The idea, of course, is for me to work out a detective character who'll be something on the order of Gutman— the fat crook Greenstreet played in *The Maltese Falcon*. I'm not supposed to do any work on it after I get the character set, and that part at least is OK by me.

Now it's time I turned from pleasure to business and got going on that god-damned short story, which, with customary delusions of grandeur, I hope to do tonight in one fell stroke. A couple of times many years ago I managed to do a complete story in one sitting and have never been able to get over it...I kind of go round with the notion that's par for the course.

> Much love, toots, and many kisses ...
> Papa

1. The *Fat Man* radio serial ran from 21 January 1946 until 1950 on ABC. Mary Hammett received a writer's credit, but she had no involvement with the show.

TLS Marshall

To Josephine Hammett

27 December 1945, Hardscrabble Farm, Pleasantville, New York

Dearest Princess,

Well, we got another Christmas past with nothing much worse than a leaking roof which kept me up emptying vessels till the small hours. Outside of that—and you'd have to be pretty flabby to call that bad—it was a pleasant day and I think I'll suggest to somebody that we have another Christmas this coming year. It might be nice, if enough popular support can be mustered, to make it an annual event...or am I just a dreamer?

I've been up here since the 21st, so I should have another Christmas waiting for me tomorrow morning. I'm going in to the dentist at eleven and shall of course pay a visit to 15 East 66th to see what goodies Santa Claus left there for me. There ought to be a lot of 'em because I've been a powerful good boy for a long time now...and it'll be a pretty ho d' y' do if I'm not well paid for my exemplary behavior.

The photo you sent me is a honey: you look very lovely, very warm and gay, and very Irish...all of which I dare say you are. Thank you, cookie!

The third or fourth of January should find me back in the city and more or less installed in my new apartment until the book's finished, which I hope won't be too many months away. I've got a couple of more in my head and may actually do at least one of them the same year. (All right, all right, I know that sounds alcoholic, but I haven't had a drink since October 1.)

Last week my mouth picked up a gum boil or something bulbous and tender under the lower edge of my lower plate and so, while others guzzled goose and venison, I Christmas-dinnered off 'n soups and such.

I saw that *Yank* story. They didn't misquote me about the new novel, but it is a lie just the same. When folks ask me what a book or story is about I usually tell 'em the first thing that pops into my head...what the hell else is there to say except maybe that it's about people? and nobody's ever satisfied with that kind of answer. The book *is* about a man who's just come out of the Army, but his family—such as he has—doesn't play a very large part in it... though I'm still not exactly sure what does. All I know about him so far is he's an artist named Helm and has been on a drunk since his discharge and has just been locked out of his hotel and he's got a son who's a Captain in the Eighth Air Force. I'm just finishing a short story about a couple of men just discharged from the Eighth Air Force, one of whom wants the other to marry his sister so they can hang around on the farm together and shoot ducks and stuff, and the other one likes the sister well enough only she reminds him of a girl he knows down South so he thinks he'll go down there and see *her*. I don't know what that proves, but I only write 'em … it's up to my readers to try to figure out what in the name of God they're all about, if anything.

Love and everything …
Papa

TLS MARSHALL

To Mary Hammett

26 January 1946 [no address]

Dearest Mary,

The opening night of our new radio program seems to have gone off well enough. Maybe it didn't exactly knock people off their chairs, but I never thought it was going to and the reports I've had on its reception thus far are favorable enough. So now we've got twenty-five more weeks in which to try to land a sponsor at, of course, more money. Your check should start reaching you every week now (I say "your check," but naturally you'll turn it over to your mother) and if you'll let me know what deductions are made for social security and withholding tax and the like I'll send along a monthly check to make up the difference. Tell Jose she'll get the usual check from the bank this month in addition to the radio dough and can probably use it for things you all need for the house. After that, though, there will only be the radio money, unless, of course, that should come to an end. (My agent, however, is pretty sure he'll have droves of sponsors fighting for it long before our sustaining period is over, and it's a cinch an agent has to be right sometime!)

The Valley Sheep Are Fatter goes along smoothly, but without any great speed, probably because I've been putting in a good deal of my time on other things. I came up to Pleasantville Friday and will stay till Tuesday, but after that I hope to settle down to a more or less day after day attack

459

on the book till it's done...which I still think will be before the winter ends.

My new teeth should be ready for me next week and I'll no doubt look pretty as hell in them. I haven't had any mouth trouble for a couple of weeks now—since the dentist patched up this Army set—and I'm eating well and often...even if mostly my own cooking. The new apartment is comfortable and I haven't been going out a great deal. I'm never too fond of society unless I've got a little liquor in me, and I'm still on the wagon. True, I went off for a couple of days two weeks ago, but that was just a temporary affair and I got right back on again.

I'm sorry to hear, at last, about your automobile accident and wish you would write me all the details including—or especially—whether you are *completely* OK now, and, if you aren't, just what's the matter. Don't brush this off: I really want to know in full.

(This god-damned typewriter doesn't seem to have been cleaned or oiled since it was born and it's driving me nuts with its sticking and jumping. I'm glad it's not the one I have to write a book on!)

Lillian has started a new play—about the same people who were in *The Little Foxes,* but back when they were younger and their parents still alive...kin[d] of how they got to be the way they were.

Just now I'm heels over head in figures, trying to get my income tax figures straightened out for the two years I was in the Aleutians, and I can't figure out whether I'm a rich old man or a pauper.

Whichever I am, I love you and miss you ...

> Kiss the Josephines for me ...
> Papa

TLS MARSHALL

To Mary Hammett

3 February 1946, New York

Mary darling,

It's early Sunday morning and I've just knocked off work on a short— lucky for me and the customers!—speech I'm to make at a Jefferson

School of Social Science dinner Monday night. It's all about the veteran's need of progressive education or something and will no doubt be very informative or stirring or pointless as the case may be. Tomorrow I hope to get that god-damned short story out of the mothballs and into the mail. It should have been done weeks ago. It'll only take me a couple of hours to finish it. That's what the trouble's been: I always hate like hell to work on things when I know ahead of time just what I'm going to say and have no little problems to worry my old white noggin. But this time I'm going to do it so I'll have nothing to keep me from getting back to *The Valley Sheep Are Fatter*.

Poor baby, you *did* have a jolly time of it with that smash-up! I know nothing ever permanently damages a Hammett, but just the same I don't like your "the only after effects are extreme nervousness, dizziness and high blood pressure," even if you do say you "feel fine." And, as you know, I have less than all the faith in the world in most Southern California doctors. So it would be just as well if you told me *exactly* how these things affect you nowadays and what you're doing about them and who your doctor is. Or do I have to threaten to come out there myself for a few days to find out? Or must I drag you East to have medical men I know and trust give you the once over? And let's cut out this nonsense of not saying anything you think will "worry" me. I should have known about all this months ago. You and Jose can both consider yourselves spanked and stood in corners: you're a couple of dopes!

The Employee's Withholding Exemption Certificate came and I filled it out—I didn't give you any dependents, which will make your income tax a little higher than if I'd put Jose and Jo down, but has other advantages—and am sending it on to your employers. Don't forget to let me know what deductions are made from your checks when they start coming. I'm still half-drowned in papers and things on my own tax problems and will have my man straighten out that lien thing. I know what it is: I paid the 1938 tax here and the New York income tax office evidently never got around to notifying the California boys. We wanderers over the face of the globe are always having troubles like that.

Here's something I've been meaning to send—a memento of the days when I was a soldier and wore you in duplicate around my neck. Later, of course, the Army stopped putting the names of next-of-kin on dog tags, but I was an old-fashioned warrior and never got one of the new models.

I'm now breaking in my new teeth. I like 'em a lot better than the old ones—which never quite filled my mouth—but the breaking-in period isn't exactly all one sweet dream, since they press in new and hitherto untoughened places. But, once this period is over, I hope I'm set for life. I'm also sun-lamping myself into a reasonable facsimile of a mild tan. I guess maybe I'm trying to turn myself into a thing of beauty...like an old Persian rug.

Now for a little reading in Shapley's *Galaxies*—I'm doing some astronomical research for my *next-after-this* novel—before I hit the sack.

> Love and love,
> Papa

TLS MARSHALL

To Mary Hammett

6 February 1946, New York

Dear Toots,

Here's your check for your first week's work on the *Fat Man* and I don't guess anybody's ever made an easier dollar. The form you filled out hadn't reached them in time for the tax deduction to be taken off, but they'll probably catch it in time for the next check, which should come to you direct.

The Jefferson School dinner went off well enough. We wanted to raise $14,000 and we raised $14,000 so I guess you've got to call that success. It's quite a school—a combination of the old Worker's School and the School for Democracy, with somewhere around 5,500 pupils who take everything from Marxism, foreign languages and dancing to shorthand, anthropology and history—and I'm probably going to give courses in something or other, starting with the April term.[1] It's not settled what I'll teach yet, but I'll no doubt wind up doing something about novel-writing or related subjects.

* * *

I guess that's all I know.

Much love . . .
    Papa

1. Hammett taught mystery writing at the Jefferson School for Social Science in lower Manhattan from 1946 to 1956 and served on the school's board of trustees from 1949 to 1956.

TLS MARSHALL

To Mary Hammett

8 February 1946, New York

Mary dear,

Jesus, am I becoming a faithful correspondent! I seem to be writing you every day, which is a lot better than you do for me . . .

* * *

No news has had time to happen since I last wrote you. Today's been sunny and crisp and I spent it conferring with folks at the Jefferson School, submitting my mouth to dental doings, lunching with Lillian, and trying on a couple of suits at the tailors. In between these exciting things I walked. I walk a good deal, but still don't get as much exercise as I've been used to. I'm going to have to do something about it, I reckon, even if only something dull in the way of setting-up gestures at home.

I've just finished—God knows why—*The King's General* and have decided Daphne du Maurier is probably the most inept novelist we've got. I suspected it after *Rebecca,* but this is the clincher. Even the Ruff girl who wrote *The Manatee* looks good in comparison.[1]

* * *

Much love, cutiepie . . .
    Papa

1. *The Manatee* by Nancy Bruff.

TLS MARSHALL

To Mary Hammett

11 February 1946, New York

Mary darling,

Money, money, money...keeps rolling in...and I guess that's good if most of what I hear is right. Anyhow, herewith another check, bringing us up to last week's program. Addlepate that I am, I forgot to listen to tonight's episode, which makes two in a row I've missed, since I was speaking at a dinner last week. However, I don't feel any the worse for not having heard 'em and imagine I can soon get myself in shape to pass 'em up as easily as I do *The Thin Man.*

* * *

Much love...many kisses ...
Papa

TLS MARSHALL

To Mary Hammett

3 March 1946, New York

Dear Toots,

Here are three more of those things that have been a-piling up while my back was turned. You'll notice that the tax has been figured out and deducted for those early instalments and I suppose the $163.10 figure is what your net will be each week from now on. That's some $1,700—I'm too idleminded to actually figure it out at the moment—a year less than I've been sending you all, so I'll let the bank send you the usual amount this month and next to make up for it. OK?

This has been a nice sunny spring Sunday which I've managed to pretty much fritter away thus far. Having read most of the night, I didn't get up till nearly two this afternoon. Then I got myself some breakfast, read a ton more or less of Sunday papers, opened and shelved a new set of the *Encyclopaedia Britannica* and now, at six-thirty, am doing this while I try to persuade myself that I ought to get out of pajamas, bathe and shave, and go at least as far as Ruben's for food. (I don't know how I'll make out with this argument: there's a lot of canned stuff in the pantry and fresh stuff in the icebox and shaving and dressing is almost as much work as cooking a meal. Chances are I won't be able to make up my mind either way for another couple of hours. I'm not the decisive type today...)

There ought to be a lot of not too important news around, if I could find it. Let's see ...

I've just lost an $1,150 investment in *Jeb,* a Shumlin production that ran for just seven days. I didn't see either it or the script till the opening night, but I wasn't surprised. Like most of Robert Ardrey's plays, it meant well, but didn't add up to a very dramatic evening in the theater. Oh, well, there's always the next time, and I've got a $1,200 piece of a Bloomgarden production which opens later this month, a fairly funny if trivial farce about Colonel McCormick of the *Chicago Tribune*...or at least that's the way it read and I'm told it's been tightened up a bit since I read it. It's called *Woman Bites Dog* and was written by Sam and Bella Spewack.[1]

Lillian's somewhere in Louisiana or Alabama digging up stuff for her next play. She's been gone about a week and I suppose the length of her stay will depend on what luck she has with her material. Frances Goodrich Hackett was in town a few weeks ago and I had dinner with her, though I didn't see Albert, who was abed with the flu. Frances wanted to be remembered to you and Jo. Lois Jacoby was in for lunch last week. She's now working for one of the committees raising money for the General Motors strikers. Dorothy Parker—in your part of the world—seems to have made up her mind to divorce Alan Campbell, who's still flitting merrily around London in an officer's uniform. Maggie Kober's in very bad shape—can't use her legs at all and has trouble doing anything with her hands—and the doctors seem to know as little about how to treat her as in the beginning. It's still a case of try this and that and the other hoping to God something will do some little good...and nothing has yet.

Well, well, well...I stopped to fiddle around with a chess problem on my desk (torn out of a newspaper: doing chess problems in bed at night is one of my new ways of killing time on the pretense that I'm putting myself to sleep) and here it is seven minutes past eight. Guess I'll scrape my face and dip myself in the tub and go down to Ruben's after all …

> Much love, sweetheart …
> Papa

I'm still not too satisfied with those vague reports you send me on your physical well-being—

> 1. *Woman Bites Dog* opened at the Belasco Theatre on 17 April 1946 and closed after five performances.

TLS MARSHALL

To Mary Hammett

27 April 1946, New York

Mary dear,

* * *

Of me there's not much news. I'm still healthy, of course, but am not sure I've yet got back into the groove, or whatever you want to call it, of civilian life. Or maybe it's just laziness…Anyhow, my list of accomplishments since getting out of the Army is still surprisingly small…or wouldn't that surprise anybody? Thursday I start giving my course in the Mystery Story at the Jefferson School and there's a faint chance that will wake me up. I'm ashamed of how little I've done on the novel …

Now I've got to dust myself off and go out to see some people about something or other.

> Much love, darling …
> Papa

TLS MARSHALL

To Mary Hammett

4 July 1946, Pleasantville, New York

Mary dear,

* * *

The chances are I'll spend most of the summer here, only going in when I positively have to, which will, I'm afraid, be oftener than I'll like, since I'm now president of something called the Civil Rights Congress of New York—roughly speaking, it's a sort of revival of the old International Labor Defense—and there's always something doing in that field.

Kober, Lillian and I went to see the Louis-Conn fight and had a pretty good time.[1] It wasn't much of a fight, of course, but none of us thought it was going to be. What you go to a Joe Louis fight for is to see a man who knows his business...to see him keep after the other guy till he finds an opening...and then pretty soon it's all over.

Maggie Kober seemed a little better when I saw her ten days ago, but she's actually in bad shape. She can no longer move at all except her head and arms a little. For a while it was a hell of a job trying to understand her when she talked, since she had trouble controlling her lip muscles, but she could speak fairly well the other day. The chances are, everybody knows, this improvement will be only temporary, but we all go around hoping and hoping for a miracle. Her daughter Cathy, now four, is a little honey.

* * *

Farm notes: the calf named Dashiell has been butchered and is now in course of being eating bit-bit by bit-bit, and very tasty he is too...the place is overrun with puppies just now: Meg had ten, of which eight lived, and her daughter Flora, whom you've never seen, had three giants...there are few if any large fish in the lake this year: stuff put in last year to kill weeds seems to have ignored the weeds and concentrated on the bass...I haven't caught any snapping turtles yet, but I haven't been working at it very hard...tomorrow I'm going to sandpaper and varnish a boat, and maybe the canoe...I'm back at work on the novel, which is now tentatively entitled *The Valley Sheep*...Lillian yesterday finished the second act of her play and is supposedly toiling on the third at this moment...I've just bought a crossbow, but haven't yet tried it out.

That'll have to do for now. The hour's late and I want to stir my stumps early in the morning.

Kiss the J's for me and take care of yourself.

Much love and many kisses …
Papa

1. Joe Louis knocked out Billy Conn in the eighth round. The audience was 45,266 and a ringside seat cost $100.

TLS MARSHALL

To Mary Hammett

1 August 1946, Pleasantville, N.Y.

Mary dearest,

There were a couple of letters from you in today's mail, the first mail I've seen in three or four days. I've been here practically by myself—even the Hermanns are off on their vacation—and have been too busy or lazy or something to go in to the post office. I've got to go into the city for a conference next Tuesday or Wednesday and shall probably hurry right back as soon as it's over. Actually I should have gone in for a mass meeting yesterday—to help raise hell about that Georgia lynching—but I wriggled out of it, letting one of the other officials of my organization do the dirty work.[1]

The weather's been pretty hot here too, though today's moderate enough and it started to sprinkle half an hour or so ago, which will interfere with some outdoor painting I had more or less vaguely in mind. Oh, well, maybe I can find something to daub inside. For the past week or so I've been counting that day lost in which I didn't besmear something with a little pigment, and I've just got in a new shipment of stuff that I'm anxious to try out. Next week I shall probably take up embroidery. Do you wish me to make you a bib?

* * *

There are a great many latent homos in the world and the arts attract more than a full share of homos, latent or active. God, it is to be pre-

468

sumed, knows why it should be so and it's done the arts a great deal of harm, since homos of either sex seem to have a tendency to substitute tenseness for vigor and sensitivity for feeling.

Now I'm off for a stroll in the rain.

Kiss the J's for me, baby.

Much love and stuff ...
Papa

1. On 25 July 1946, two black men, Roger Malcolm and George Dorsey, and their wives were lined up by a mob of twenty white men and shot to death near Monroe, Georgia. Malcolm had stabbed his white employer. Dorsey, the women, and a white farmer who was a friend had picked him up from jail after paying his bail. They were stopped on their way home.

TLS MARSHALL

To Mary Hammett

8 August 1946, Pleasantville

Dearest Mary,

Wednesday evening I went into the city for a few hours to attend a meeting and picked up the two checks I enclose. I see by the morning papers that *The Thin Man* goes back on the air this Friday night. If I remember rightly it's scheduled to move back to the Sunday night spot—but playing against Edgar Berg[e]n this time instead of Jack Benny, which is stiff enough competition, if not quite so tough as before—next month. The airwaves are sure-god getting themselves cluttered up with Hammett opera.

Lillian's spending this month up on Cape Cod. She gets nervous if she can't hit the seaside now and then. I may go up for a week before she returns, maybe I'll take off around the 19th. Meanwhile Jean Potter's been up here with galley proofs of her book on early bush-flying in Alaska—*The Flying North*—and I've been going over them with her. It still looks like a pretty good book, though I don't know how much real popular interest can be developed for that sort of thing. She's leaving for Paris next month to marry a chap who works for one of the American airlines in Berlin. They expect to be transferred to Moscow as soon as the American field there is ready. Nancy Bragdon, Lillian's former secretary, whom I don't think was around when you were East, left a couple of weeks ago for Wales, where she's to make her mind whether she's going to marry a Welsh lawyer. There seems to be a boom in the international marriage market.

My CRCNY organization has finally managed to get under the skins of the city administration on police brutality—especially towards Negroes—and we've hopes of maybe getting results.[1] Meanwhile I'm told the Police Commissioner denounced me as a meddler or something in the *N.Y. Times* yesterday morning and the *World-Telegram*'s red-baiting specialist had us on the front page as a Communist outfit yesterday afternoon. I haven't seen either story, but the clippings are on the way to me by mail and we're fixing up a press conference for Tuesday to try to give the papers our side of the story if any. Lynchings and such seem really on the upswing these days, the bastards ...

That's about all the news there is. The puppies are still thriving and there's a new calf to replace the Dashiell we've been eating. This one is light brown with a lot of white on its face and, of course, cute as they all are.

This typing looks pretty lousy for a man who hasn't had a drink for five or six weeks. Maybe it is the typewriter this time...it's one of the wrecks that Lily has around: the only good one on the place is up in Massachusetts with her. She finished the first draft of her play, by the way, and it reads swell, though the third act needs a little more working over.[2] I don't know whether I told you she's going to direct it herself.

Kiss those people for me and take care of your pretty little self.

Much love and the like ...

Papa

1. Hammett was president of the Civil Rights Congress of New York, which was formed in April 1946 by a merger of the International Labor Defense, the National Negro Congress, and the National Federation for Constitutional Liberties. Its purpose was the defense of individuals whose civil rights were violated. In practice, it was devoted primarily to support of Communists who came under attack for their political activities. The CRC was cited by U.S. Attorney General Tom Clark as a subversive and Communist organization. On 28 July Hammett asked New York City Mayor William O'Dwyer to take immediate

action to stop police brutality, which Hammett said was directed toward blacks. On 7 August, Police Commissioner Arthur Wallender responded that the charges were without foundation. In a 13 August press release, Hammett expressed dissatisfaction with Wallender's statement.

2. Hellman was working on *Another Part of the Forest*, which opened on Broadway on 20 November 1946, directed by her.

TLS MARSHALL

To Mary Hammett

13 August 1946, Hardscrabble Farm, Pleasantville, N.Y.

Dear Marykin,

Today I went into town for a couple of hours to be interviewed by some reporters about police brutality and such in the handling of Negroes—I'll no doubt be misquoted by everybody except *The Daily Worker* and maybe *PM*—and found the enclosed check waiting...so here it is ...

In the city the weather was cloudy, but not bad. Up here it's been an almost continuous thunderstorm since midmorning, with gallons and gallons of the rain we really needed. I hope tomorrow will be clear so I can get a little outdoor painting done. My projects are piling up on me. Of course I *have* got some indoor stuff I could get at ...

The OPA has cut my rent on 66th Street almost in half—within $7.50 of it—starting this month.[1] I don't know whether my landlord has committed suicide yet. And, what's more important, I don't know whether I'm going to stay on there for another year. My present lease expires the last of September. I'd like to move into the country for the fall and winter, or forever, but since I'm going on with my classes at the Jefferson School it'd probably be more convenient to have a base in the big city.

I've just finished a couple of novels—seems to me I haven't been reading much lately—*Independent People,* which is the kind of rural story I like, but pretty dull in spots, and *The Camelephamoose,* which was fairly amusing in spots, but a little too whimsical for my vinegarish taste, besides which it petered out in the end. After I finish this I'm going to bed with *Escape in Passion,* or whatever the thirteenth volume

471

of Jules Romains' long novel *Men of Good Will* is called. I don't think that either is going to be a really good novel, but I've found most of it pretty enjoyable reading...which is at least something.

Kiss the J's for me.

> Love plus ...
> Papa

1. The U.S. Office of Price Administration froze rents for 1.4 million domiciles in New York City on 1 March 1943, permitting landlords increases of 15 percent a year only in cases of hardship. A state-run system of rent controls replaced the OPA in 1947.
2. Halldor Laxness, *Independant People*; Donald Hough, *The Camelephamoose*.

TLS MARSHALL

To Mary Hammett

17 August 1946, Hardscrabble Farm, Pleasantville, N.Y.

Dear Mary,

Thunder is storming outside tonight, which scares the bejesus out of old man Salud but is cozy enough for a fellow like me who has a clear conscience, if any...I started to read Connolly's *The Condemned Playground*, but gave it up when I ran across my name spelled Ham*n*ett. The British, I told myself, are too inaccurate a people for me to fool with when I could be writing letters to California blondes...So maybe I'll carry Schlesinger's *The Age of Jackson* or Pearson's *Oscar Wilde, His Life and Wit,* off to bed when I've finished this. I'm already equally prejudiced against both of them, against the Schlesinger book because he does anti-Soviet chores for *Life,* against the Wilde book because fairies usually make dull reading...Maybe age is making me harder to get along with...I probably need the mellowing influence of a good woman or something...Do you know any good women or something?...I've been hunting for things to letter on a couple of trays I'm in process of refinishing and have finally settled on an English saying, "He who eats most porridge shall have most meat," for one and a Turkish adage, "Eat the fruit and don't inquire about the tree," for the other. For a while I hesitated over, "God provides and sends both appetite and the meat," but decided He had been getting publicity enough...In looking for something else today I ran across some old clippings and am tempted to start a scrapbook again. I haven't kept one since God knows when...Reading about yourself sometimes helps you to forget what you really were and I could use a few such props now and then...I never write anybody without mentioning the puppies: they're fine...Sometimes I hint that Cinq can spell a few simple words, but I wouldn't want to lie to my own daughter unless I had something to gain by it...I keep forgetting that I'm supposed to be looking for a secretary, which is no doubt why I haven't yet found one...Maybe next week...I actually prefer not having one, but then I let too many things pile up on me or go by default. I'd hate to guess how many deals I've passed up by simply not getting around to answering letters. I'm a slob...Lillian still writes that she's having a lousy time on Cape Cod and will probably be back late next week, though I wouldn't bet on it if the weather improves up there...I should buckle down next week to planning a money-raising campaign for my Civil Rights Congress in early fall. I hate that part of organization work, but it's as necessary as skin on a leg...It'd be nice if you could just go ahead and do things with the dough coming in of its own accord...But it's always going out a hell of a lot faster than it's coming in...It's past midnight and I've been up since six-something this morning. If I'm going to get any reading done, or even get up at a country-decent time tomorrow, I'd better put a stopper on this and, as they say in Alaska, git to gitting...I'm thinking about going up to Alaska and the Aleutians for a couple of months next year...Nobody can say I don't think about a lot of things...including you...Kiss those J's for me...

> Much love, baby ...
> Papa

TLS MARSHALL

To Nancy Bragdon

4 September 1946, Hardscrabble Farm, Pleasantville, N.Y.

Dear Nancy-pie,

I addressed your envelope first and already feel as if I had written you a long letter. If I'm going to have to put all that stuff on envelopes it's only fair that you should address me c/o Hellman, Hardscrabble Farm, Hardscrabble Road, Pleasantville, Westchester County, New York, U.S.A.... Lillian tells me, though you didn't tell me, you're going to take the fatal leap this month, so I reckon I'd better tell her and not you that I wish you all the happiness in the world and think you're a dear sweet girl who deserves it... The Zilboorg newlyweds came up Sunday with young Greg and the rest of the Stones and seem quite pleased with themselves.[1] I advised Peg to try to stick it out as long as she could. Dotburger and Artburger were here for the weekend, she recovering from a breakdown or something, he preparing to go to Hollywood or somewhere[2]... Liliburger went into town yesterday and will likely be back tomorrow night or Friday, I don't know with what grotesques lined up for this weekend... Mrs. Osborn took her puppy away yesterday, I'm sorry to report; two-thirds of the Hermann children returned to school today, I'm glad to report; I return to school on the 30th, I'm indifferent to report... The coffee prescription is simple: put it in cold water, put the cold water with coffee in it over a moderate fire, yank it off as soon as it comes to a boil. Some folks return it once or twice to the fire to come to a boil again, but nobody ever lets it sit there and boil—unless of course it's coffee that's been used several times before and he's trying to get the last bit of coloring matter out of it... On the fly rod I'm less helpful, but I don't think it's going to matter a great deal since they're still unobtainable. I'm on an A & F waiting list that reaches from here to there with no signs of any action till next spring. Britain's always had the cream of the bamboo-rod crop anyhow, so why don't you give it a try over there? You ought to try to find out, however, if it's a light, medium or heavy rod you want, and with stiff, medium or soft action; just saying "it's about 10 feet long" is like ordering "a piece of meat" in a restaurant. Don't make me have to speak to you about this again. By the way, the new spun glass rods—supposedly the last word in balance, flexibility, strength and stuff—should hit the market after the first of the year. Let me know if you want an early copy for anybody... One of the new bait-casting rods with a built-in reel arrived from A & F this morning. Now if I only had some fish to try it out on... Maybe I'll see if I can tease a pickerel tomorrow... "Our" dogs no longer do anything to the porch rug, though the Stones' Tony got to it for one spot Sunday. In spite of all their lying about him it turns out he's only vaguely housebroken. He's a nice puppy, though not of course to be compared to—see what I mean?...The grown dogs brought a dead and very ripe woodchuck up on the lawn this morning, where the puppies had a fine time with it till spoil-sport humans put in their two cents' worth... Lily's still on the second act rewrite; I still murmur insincerely that I'm going to get back to work on TVSAF (*The Valley Sheep Are Fatter*). Mrs. Carpenter was due to return today from *her* breakdown, but a state income tax inspector got to her first and now she's home relapsing like mad[3]...You can't say this isn't a hot-bed of activity...Take care of yourself, baby, and give my best to Craig...

> Love ...
> *Dash*

1. The Stones are presumably the family of I. F. Stone, who was then an editorial writer for *PM*.
2. Dotburger and Artburger are Dorothy Parker and Arthur Kober. Nancy Bragdon addressed Hammett as Dashburger.
3. Mrs. Carpenter is unidentified.

TLS HRC

To Marjorie May

Cuban-born Marjorie May was a girlfriend of and secretary to Hammett, working for him in the late 1940s. At the time of this letter, she was visiting Cuba. Rose is presumably Hammett's housekeeper, Rose Evans.

10 September 1946, Hardscrabble Farm, Pleasantville, N.Y.

Dear Marjie,

It was swell going into town yesterday afternoon, for the first time since Christ was a corporal or thereabout, to find a letter from you. But when are you coming home? When are you going to tear your dwindling buttocks away from the traffic jams, the dancing caballeros, the morticians' bars and the circling buzzards and come back to our nice civilized New York with its falling stock market, re-rationed cigarettes, closed chain stores and no-boats-no-trucks-no-much-of-anything? (If I sound as if I'm complaining don't pay any attention: I've been up here as utterly unaffected by all those things as if none of them existed, and, come to think of it, how do I know they exist? maybe it's just a lot of nonsense made up by the *Herald-Tribune*.) Anyhow what I'm trying to say is there's nothing to hurry home to but me and your black-faced virgin...I don't know what she's been up to—unless you choose to believe those unlikely stories about getting no nookie—but I've been up to practically nothing on a fairly large scale. Just now I've a sore ear from experimenting with a Zenith Radionic Hearing Aid—me, I'm so deaf I can't hear a fly walking more than fifteen feet away unless of course it's hurrying—to see if it's of any practicable value in picking up otherwise inaudible insect, bird and animal sounds in the woods. The results are not on the whole satisfactory thus far and there are folks who think I'm a leetle teched in the haid, but, well, that'll give you a rough idea of what I do while civilization totters...Once in a while, but not often enough to spoil the novelty, I add a line or two to *The Valley Sheep Are Fatter*, which by no means approaches *Men of Good Will* in bulk...Most of the summer has been spent tinkering with repair and refinish jobs on furniture—do you think television will offer a future to a cabinet maker?—and I'm about to give birth to a sort of bench for a bay window with three upholstered seats and/or three places for plants that can be changed around from time to time as he or she wishes. It still needs some thinking over, but I'd like to get it done so I can turn to watches and clocks, the idea of which makes my mouth water now...See what I mean?...Put that thermometer down; I tell you 104 degrees is perfectly normal for me!...I'm glad the show goes so beautifully and hope it keeps on thataway...My Jefferson School séances will be of a Tuesday this fall. All the courses have been set at ten weeks now—fall, winter and spring terms—and in January I'm to do a workshop in addition to whatever this one is I'm now doing. If inertia permits I'm going to take your advice and get myself ten sub-divisions for the ten fall classes...I reckon it's time I was letting some puppies out to wet the lawn ...

> Much love, cutiepie ...
> Dash

TLS Richard Dannay

1946

To Mary Hammett

10 September 1946, Hardscrabble Farm, Pleasantville, N.Y.

Dearest Mary,

* * *

A letter from Havana today told me—among other things—that there's an undertaking establishment in that city with a bar for the mourners.

Also in the day's mail was a letter from Wilkie F. Hammit of Denver who wishes me to help him find out something or other about his father, who later married a "neice of J. P. Morgans," became a motion picture actor in the silent days under the name of Ned Finley and was murdered on Long Island by "the Under World of New York City." Wilkie F. says he first learned all this from a "spiritulist," but it was all later confirmed by his stepmother. It would seem, sweetheart, that a man doesn't have to spell his last name with an e and two t's to be utsnay.

Yesterday I ordered a new shotgun and a small-caliber rifle. I hope I don't have to wait too many months for delivery. A fishing rod I ordered in May arrived two days ago, in plenty of time for next year. Things to amuse the idle are scarce.

Variety reports that Goodrich Rubber may sponsor The *Fat Man* program, but I haven't heard anything from my producer, so...We've got till February to find a customer.

I'm off to bed meanwhile.

> Love and kisses ...
> Papa

TLS MARSHALL

To Mary Hammett

16 September 1946, Pleasantville, N.Y.

Mary darling,
As anybody ought to be able to tell from the enclosed check, I went

into the big, big city for a couple of hours this afternoon and then hurried back here to do myself a nice quick-warm-up dinner of leek soup, baked beans, salad and some kind of pudding—originally made, I suspect, for four-year-old Cathy Kober this past weekend—I found in the ice box, all of which I've just finished eating with Salud snoring at my feet.

New York's a strange town these days. The truck drivers have been on strike for long enough to at least partially empty most grocery stores—some of the big chains have shut up entirely—and the newspapers can't get enough paper for more than very skimpy issues, with no space for advertising. The businesses that haven't been hit by the truck drivers have been smacked by sailors' and longshoremen's strikes, and today all the barbers from 34th Street to 59th—the heart of the town—were supposed to walk out. My Civil Rights Congress has a fund to supply bail money for strikers who are arrested—one of the new gadgets in breaking a strike is to arrest as many picketers as possible in an attempt to make the unions use all their money for bail—and the chances are we'll have plenty of business in the weeks to come, unless, of course, the Maritime Union should settle its difficulties. I'm now also on the National Board of Directors of the Independent Citizens' Committee of the Arts, Sciences and Professions—it was at one of our meetings that Henry Wallace made the speech there was, and still is, so much fuss about—which ought to mean that I'll be busy as a skinny white-haired bee putting in my two cents' worth here and there through the coming elections.[1] Also I've promised to work a little at trying to get one Hulan Jack re-elected to something or other.[2] (Maybe that's why it's nice being up here all alone—no servants, no nothing this week—where nobody'll know if I just pay no attention to the telephone when it rings.)

* * *

My recent reading hasn't been too hot: a piece of junk called *Sea Change*, by a woman called Hunt, and Cross's *The Other Passenger*, which has a couple of good ideas in it but is pretty wretchedly written, and *The Innocents of Paris*, by Cesbron, which has some kind of cute child stuff in it but doesn't hold up any too well and a dullish novel called *The Magnate* by a man named Harriman who should go back to stock brokering or whatever it was he did before he started writing. I may never finish this one, though I'm not expecting a whole lot from the next one on my list, Charles Jackson's *The Fall of Valor*. He wrote *The Lost*

Weekend, you perhaps remember, and this one, which is about a dope who doesn't find out he's a homo till he's in his forties, is generally supposed to be more or less autobiographical too. Sherwood Anderson's short story "Hands" is the only piece of fiction about homos that I remember *ever* thinking any good.[3]

That, I reckon, brings us pretty well up to date, and now I've got to do some telephoning and such before I settle down with either a book or a woodworking tool for the rest of the evening, so ...

> Much love, baby ...
> Papa

1. U.S. Secretary of Commerce Henry Wallace criticized President Truman for "promoting a dangerous arms race" in his conduct of Soviet relations. Wallace advocated instead "friendly, peaceful competition" with the Soviets. He was forced to resign on 20 September 1946.
2. Hulan Jack was borough president of Manhattan from 1953 to 1960, the first black to hold that position, and the highest elected black official in the nation.
3. "Hands" is one of the stories in Anderson's *Winesburg, Ohio* (1919).

TLS MARSHALL

To Mary Hammett

24 September 1946, Pleasantville, N.Y.

Mary darling,

Yesterday afternoon I busted into the big city—hence the enclosure—to attend an ICCASP National Board meeting and hung around till late this afternoon, coming back in a small cloudburst.[1] Tomorrow night I'm due in the city again—for a CRCNY Executive Board meeting and to listen to the music for a new rev[ue] some people I know are doing—and Friday I'm supposed to take off for Chicago, where there's to be a weekend conference of various labor groups, including the CIO, and various progressive political organizations. If we're lucky we'll come out of the conference with a unified political program on which we can all work during the coming elections, but as likely as not there'll be quite a bit of scrapping to be done before it's managed—and there's always the possibility that it won't be managed at all. I should be through in Chicago by Sunday afternoon—though you never can tell—in time to get myself all set to start my classes at the Jefferson School Tuesday. I keep scolding myself for not making more preparations for each class, but somehow …

The Wallace resignation and the Harriman appointment are still creating a great to-do.[2] Many people are of the opinion that Harriman, the dope, who liked being Ambassador to Britain, wouldn't have accepted the Commerce secretaryship unless he'd been promised that when Byrnes resigns because of "bad health" Harriman will be moved up to the Secretary of State post. He's had his eye on that job for quite a while. Meanwhile a lot of people are getting quite a laugh out of the fact that yesterday, following the news that the "radical dreamer" Wallace had been replaced as Secretary of Commerce by the "solid business man" Harriman, 126 stocks on the NY Exchange—including such biggies as A T & T, General Motors, Pennsylvania RR and Harriman's own Union Pacific—went down to new low prices for 1946, and some railroad bonds went down to their lowest in two years. One New York paper (*PM*) has picked up the news that Harriman is under indictment by the Department of Justice, along with half a dozen other railroad magnates, for conspiracy in restraint of trade or something. She's a very, very cute world, honeychild …

Newspapers are still largely playing down the fact that the atomic bomb is no longer the No. 1 world threat. Various devices of biological warfare are now the big stuff. Our Army and Navy now consider the atomic bomb primarily as an aid in that warfare rather than as a big destructive blast. This new stuff is a hell of a lot cheaper, can be made on the sly in breweries and other small establishments, which is of course just dandy for little nations. Most of the formulas are common knowledge in scientific circles, known even by all laymen who are interested enough to read the sort of scientific publications anybody can get hold of. The hush-hush about all this seems to come from two reasons: (a) we've been working like hell on them, especially the Navy, and I'm told that at one of the Geneva Conventions we definitely signed an international treaty outlawing the manufacture of biological weapons, and (b) if the people continue to think that in the atomic bomb we've got a complete stranglehold on the rest of the world they won't worry so much about our bungling foreign policy.

Well, that's all the great intellectualizing you'll get from this source right now. I'm going out and broil myself a steak for dinner.

Kiss the Js for me. Much love, toots...
Papa

1. ICCASP: Independent Citizens Committee for the Arts and the Sciences and Professions.
2. In 1946 W. Averell Harriman was recalled as ambassador to Great Britain after six months to fill the vacant position of secretary of commerce previously held by Henry Wallace. James F. Byrnes was secretary of state from 1945 to 1947.

TLS MARSHALL

To Mary Hammett

2 October 1946, Hardscrabble Farm, Pleasantville, N.Y.

Dear Mary-pie,

The Chicago weekend was fairly satisfactory, taking one thing with another, and if the conference didn't go as far to the left as some of us would have liked to see it, it didn't, on the other hand, go as far to the right as some of us were afraid it might. I think we came out of it with a pretty good set-up for trying to goose the Democratic Party back into the footsteps of the late FDR...the rest is a matter of a lot of work between now and this fall's elections and still more work between then and the '48 elections. There's no possibility of getting anywhere in the near future except by working in the ranks of the Democratic Party and the reactionaries in that Party are pretty much in the saddle at the moment, and they aren't giving any help to progressive candidates like DeLacy in Seattle and the boys in the Dakotas.[1] They'd rather see them defeated this time so the '48 Democratic convention candidates will be "safe" men, and they'll probably succeed in a few states. DeLacy may squeeze through, though he's got a tough battle ahead of him. I met him at lunch today in New York, for the first time, and rather liked him...but then I'm likely to be prejudiced in favor of any congressman with a good record, there not being a hell of a lot of 'em left.

This time I liked Chicago more than I usually do, perhaps because I had a room at the Stevens Hotel with a view out over the Lake .... and a very lovely view it was. I made the trip both ways by train and was dope enough to sit up both nights (Friday and Sunday) playing poker till breakfast time. The seventy-five dollars or so I won didn't, I think, make up for the loss of sleep, though I seemed to feel spry enough at the time. However, I went around all day yesterday feeling kind of grippy—I'm all right today—and blamed it on the all-night stuff.

My new class at the Jefferson School started last night and was, as usual, very pleasant. That School has become one of my favorite institutions. After the elections I'm going up to Boston to give a lecture at a similar school up there.

Lillian finished her play yesterday and goes into rehearsal the first of the week.[2] It's scheduled to open in New York about the 20th of November, with out-of-town try-outs in Wilmington, Detroit and Baltimore before then. I'll not be able to make the Detroit trip, but will catch it for at least a night in the other two spots. I haven't seen the finished third act, but the first and second are swell.

Now I'm for bed. Kiss the J's for me. Here's a clipping and a check.

> Much love, blondie,
> Papa

1. Hugh De Lacy led the left-wing Washington Commonwealth Federation, which supported reforms advocated by Upton Sinclair. De Lacy was elected U.S. Representative from Washington State during World War II. He was defeated in his 1946 reelection bid.
2. *Another Part of the Forest.*

TLS MARSHALL

To Mary Hammett

6 October 1946, Hardscrabble Farm, Pleasantville, N.Y.

Mary dearest,

I enclose one of the results of a quick run into the city Friday...the only result I can remember...Lillian's play goes into rehearsal tomorrow, so I shall go in to see the first run-through, which gets me out of a trip to Albany to sit in on some election doings. The city's got me trapped this week. I've got my class and a board meeting Tuesday night, some kind of social affair to help launch a new left wing quarterly—*Mainstream*—Wednesday and another board meeting Thursday.[1] Things are closing in these days, though sometimes they cancel themselves out...for instance, my having to speak at an anti-Bilbo dinner on the 17th keeps me from having to go to New Haven to speak at some kind of rally there[2]...You can usually count on October being the loveliest month of the year in this part of the world and the one we're having now is no exception...the days are hot and sunny, the nights cool and crisp...At the moment I'm afraid there's not much chance of my getting to California, cutie, but we'll see how things work out...Or maybe we could fix it so some western Hammetts could come east for a visit...I'm still taking an occasional shot at red squirrels and crows—both nuisances that are outside the game laws—to get my eye and hand in for the coming shooting season, now only about three weeks away, though I'm by no means sure I'll be on hand much of the time after it opens...I can try, though...Now I've got a little work to do before sleepiness crawls all the way up my back—it's at about the third vertebra now and moving fast—so...Kiss those people for me ...

                Much love, cookie ...
                Papa

1. *Mainstream* was a magazine founded by members of the cultural section of the Communist Party U.S.A. to publish literature, art criticism, and aesthetic theory. It merged with the *New Masses* in 1948 to form *Masses and Mainstream*.
2. Senator Theodore Gilmore Bilbo, U.S. senator from Mississippi, was known for his strident white supremacism.

TLS MARSHALL

To Frederick Dannay

Frederick Dannay and Manfred B. Lee wrote and edited jointly under the pseudonym Ellery Queen. Presumably "The Living Library Anthology" was a working title for their Twentieth-Century Detective Stories *(1948), which includes Hammett's "Mike or Alec or Rufus" under the title "Tom, Dick, or Harry."*

18 March 1947
    In connection with my story to be used in *The Living Library Anthology*,

I agree to accept a fee equal to the highest fee paid to any other contributor to this anthology.

> Dashiell Hammett

ALS COLUMBIA

To Mary Hammett

26 March 1947, Pleasantville

Dear Mary,

It's a long, long time since I've found myself doing this, which only goes to show, I dare say, what a lousy old man I am.

Between one thing and another this has been a hell of a winter—though I suppose, taking it all in all, I've had a better time than I admit—and I'm not at all sorry to see it over...if it is over...for the past couple of days the wind, snow and temperature—hanging around 18 degrees—have been trying to make a liar out of the calendar.

The one thing and another I'm complaining about—but take my bellyaching with a grain of salt—are chiefly one of my recurring periods of low blood pressure (with low blood pressure you live forever but you're mostly too tired to do anything); a couple of weeks of semi-invalidism with a sprained back or something from foolishly trying to hoist a jammed window while leaning over a piece of furniture; a full schedule of meetings and other doings for the Civil Rights Congress (I'm New York State president) on behalf of the Jews, Negroes, trade unionists, Communists, pseudo-Communists, suspected Communists, imaginary Communists and god knows who all the Trumans, Tom Clarks, Tom Deweys, Vandenburgs, Bilbos, Rankins, Hoovers big and little, and other so-and-so's of the sort choose to jump on;[1] another fairly full schedule on the executive committee of Progressive Citizens of American, where we're still in the throes or something of successfully merging the Independent Citizens Committee of the Arts, Sciences and Professions with the National Citizens' Political Action Committee (Jesus, the petty jealousies that spring up here and there among former rivals!);[2] the two classes a week I was giving at the Jefferson School, now over till fall since I decided I'd have to skip the spring term this year; my play; and various odds and ends of speeches and other chores for what sometimes seems to me like every Tom, Dick and Harriet and his or her organization.

Well, that's out of my system now, toots, and the rest of this letter shall be cheerful as all git-out.

I've been up here in the country alone for a few days trying to get in some honest licks on the play. I'd hoped to have it finished long before this, but I kept putting it aside for too many other things; but I'm going to get it finished this spring or else. I still think it's going to be pretty good...maybe. Next week I have to go into the city for a Madison Square Garden rally Monday, a farewell dinner to Henry Wallace Wednesday and a board meeting Thursday—that's the way I've been going most of the winter—but hope to get back here for another week or maybe two immediately afterwards.

My health is fine again. The blood pressure is up to pretty near normal again—which is normal for me—and my back is as good as new. I still sleep on a bed board—not directly on it, of course: it goes between the springs and the mattress, as you probably know—but only because I've come to like it and not because my ailing frame needs propping.

This afternoon I tried my first fishing of the year, but gave it up before the fish had much of a chance to show me anything. It was too cold on the fingers—you can't cast with gloves on—and too windy for any kind of accuracy. Perhaps tomorrow will be milder. It's too early for bass, I imagine, but there's no reason why the pickerel shouldn't be biting. Most of the afternoon I spent sitting on the cottage porch watching things through field glasses. There are Mallard and Black ducks nesting near the lake as usual this spring and also—for the first time—a pair of wild geese...one of the smaller variety of Canada goose. Yesterday I thought I saw some baby ducks near the end of an island, but it was snowing too hard for me to be sure. I'll probably put the boats—hauled up for the winter—in the water tomorrow and take a closer look at things.

This is a hell of a late date to be thanking you all for the lovely Christmas presents, and for the candy more recently, but anyhow I do thank you. And I also thank Jo for the glamor-puss photograph. I guess I haven't any children left, just a couple of grown-up cuties.

My lonely bed is calling me.

Kiss the J's for me.

> Much love, sweetheart ...
> Papa

1. Tom C. Clark was attorney general in the Truman administration, appointed to the U.S. Supreme Court in 1949. Thomas E. Dewey was governor of New York and ran for president in 1944 and 1948. Arthur H. Vandenburg was a Republican senator from Michigan with presidential aspirations who vigorously opposed the New Deal. Theodore G. Bilbo was a Mississippi senator who bragged, "We tell our Negro-loving Yankee friends to go straight to hell." Representative John Rankin, a Democrat from Mississippi, was an avid anti-Communist who proposed the legislation in 1945 to make the House Committee on Un-American Activities the only permanent investigating committee in the House of Representatives. Former president Herbert Hoover and anti-Communist crusader and FBI director J. Edgar Hoover were "big and little" Hoover.

2. The pro-communist Progressive Citizens of America, associated with Henry Wallace, replaced the popular-front-era Independent Citizens Committee for the Arts, Sciences, and Professions. The PCA served as a rival to the anti-Communist liberal Americans for Democratic Action, associated with President Truman. On 31 March 1947, the PCA held a rally in Madison Square Garden to protest the anti-Communist foreign policy initiatives of the Truman Doctrine, announced three weeks earlier. The event was sold out.

TLS MARSHALL

To Mary Hammett

30 April 1947, Pleasantville

Dear Cutiepie,

I've been up here—all nice and alone—for four or five days and am hoping things will allow me to hang around for another undisturbed week...or maybe two. But the chances are of course that this, that or the other will conspire to drag me into the city along about the first of the week for at least a day or two. I can always hope, however, and even if I do get dragged in I can still hope to escape the first time anybody turns his, her or its back.

* * *

Dorothy Parker was up Saturday and asked about you and Jo—very surprised to know you were both in your 20's: people always have a notion that other people stand still until they see them again—and wished to be remembered.

The terry robes have gone forward—so my secretary tells me—and I hope you both find them what you want. I'm sorry I didn't have time to pick them out myself, so I don't know too much about what they're like. My Marjorie sometimes goes a little overboard on the elaborate side— Latin American raising, I guess—but I'm hoping for the best. Tell Jo her book on dialectical materialism has also—at least that's my belief—been forwarded. The loom is still on my list of things to look after; and I have not yet been able to get hold of the name of the man for you to see...but I hope to in a day or so and will shoot the news to you right away. Meanwhile, cut out your goddamned foolishness and behave yourself. (That's the second correction I've had to make thus far: I'm typing like some of the Hammetts I know!)

The AYD meetings at the University of Buffalo and Cornell went very well, I think, though both groups are under a lot of pressure.[1] We picked up half a dozen new members at the Buffalo clambake, which wasn't bad in view of the fact that the AYD president had resigned the day before, giving Hoover's outburst as his reason. It was still winter up there, had snowed the day before I arrived and the evidence was still on the ground.

My trip back from the Coast was nice enough to make up for the one West. We ran ahead of a tailwind at about 19,000 feet of altitude all the way and got into New York half an hour ahead of time, though we'd been at least half an hour late in leaving your part of the world. Once again I was lucky enough to pick up a nontalkative seat-neighbor. This one was a deaf man on his way to Maine to buy—among other things—lobsters for one of your local eateries.

I'm sorry to hear about Jo's tooth-outedness, but hope and trust it all came out okeydokey. Wisdom teeth hardly ever do anything but give work to dentists, which may be, for all I know, what God designed them for. Tell Jo I'll write her in a day or two...or maybe before that...maybe I could write her tonight to keep from having to work on my play.

Lillian's play closed Saturday night...till early fall, when it will go on the road. We would like to have kept it open for another month, but this has been a hell of a tough year on serious shows and it didn't seem worth while risking the money.[2]

My recent reading has been mostly miscellaneous crap: *He Dared Not Look Behind,* a dopey item about a man who killed his wife because she had a wooden leg and then was driven to suicide by the ghost of the artificial gam; *Write Sorrow on the Earth,* a so-so French resistance novel by a correspondent I used to know; *Dario,* a trivial and politically evil job about an Italian Fascist by another correspondent I know; *A Murderer in the House,* another flimsy study of a maniacal killer; *Miss Agatha Doubles for Death,* a foolish whodunit; and *Comrade Forest,* a more or less standard-formula novel of Soviet guerrillas. Last night, luckily, I remembered I had never read Scott Fitzgerald's *Tender Is the Night,* so things aren't so bad at the moment[3] . . .

The weather's been not untypical of this time of the year in this part of the world; fairly sunny most of the time, a bit breezy, hazy, and not so warm as it was last month. Wild flowers as well as tame are popping up and things smell good. I have been loafing on my chores, but expect to stir myself in a day or two. There's a boat to be repaired, another to be calked, and both of them and a canoe to be painted and varnished. Also there's fishing equipment and such to be overhauled, and I reckon I ought to paint at least the porch of the cottage at the lake. A man's life is not always an easy one . . .

* * *

At the end of that last page I was stopped again by the possibly brilliant idea that perhaps the telephone strike—which isn't going so well: weak unions—could be helped out by a movement to convince telephone subscribers that, since their service has been either cut off entirely or severely limited by the strike, they shouldn't pay the telephone company's bills for this period . . . or should only pay part of them. At the moment it seems good to me, but I'll have to mull it a little more before deciding whether it's worth while shaving and going into the big city about tomorrow. Maybe there's something to it . . . maybe it's at least worth discussing with somebody on the inside . . .

Speaking of strikes, you may have to give up your Camels for a while, which would only mean shifting to another brand of cigarettes. Some five thousand employees of the company—R. J. Reynolds—voted yesterday to go out if their demand for a 15¢-an-hour raise isn't met. The company, which only had a $9,000,000 *increase* in profits last year, is offering them a 5 1/2¢ raise, the bastards. I'll let you know how it turns out: I doubt that your local papers are going to tell you much.

Campbell's Soup is another item you may have to go without, too; but that also is still in the works, and on that too I'll let you know. (What the hell are you turning out to be? My Western Representative for consumer support of the labor movement?)

I forgot to tell M.M. about sending along those withholding slips — if they still come with the checks — but will try to remember the next time I talk to her.[4] She's now in process of dickering for that studio apartment I told you about — or did I? — and I'm never too sure what will happen if I put two things on her mind at one time. (As a matter of fact, she's not nearly as rattlebrained as I pretend . . . it's only that she's an enthusiast at times and thinks with her glands instead of her head.)

Much love, toots, and many kisses . . . of which you might spare a few for those people whose names begin with J . . .

Papa

1. American Youth for Democracy (AYD) was the successor to the Youth Communist League disbanded in 1943 with the dissolution of the Popular Front.
2. *Another Part of the Forest*, which opened on 20 November, ran for 182 performances. There is no evidence of a play by Hammett.
3. *He Dared Not Look Behind* by Cledwyn Hughes; *Write Sorrow on the Earth* by Charles Christian Wertenbaker; *Dario* by Percy Winner; *A Murderer in the House* by Kate Clugston; *Miss Agatha Doubles for Death* by H. L. V. Fletcher; *Comrade Forest* by Michael Leigh
4. M. M. is Majorie May, Hammett's secretary.

TLS MARSHALL

To Josephine Hammett

30 April 1947, 15 East 66th St, New York City

Dear Princess,

I'm in Pleasantville of course, but I just got some new station[e]ry from Tiffany and have to show it off, don't I? And who — or whom, if you want to act like a junior at UCLA — better to show it off to? I've got to start impressing you now, haven't I, if I'm going to count on your supporting me in my old age?...And don't be too sure that's what I'm not counting on...And don't be too sure my old age is more than a week or two away...Most of what I call news I've already written to Mary—a couple of hours ago—and I'm sure you can get it out of her by simply twisting her arm or putting burning splinters under her fingernails—ah, those sweet old childish pranks!—or perhaps working a little with pliers on her fingers and toes. (I've got to stop reading those books about underground movements in Nazi-occupied countries!)...Our thunderstorm has quit for the time and I've been thinking of a short story—anything, it seems, to keep from working on the play I've promised Kermit Bloomgarden—I may do to while away the time, which is a true artist's way of saying he's badly in need of money[1]...Meanwhile, Cinq—the 11-month-old black poodle you've never seen—has come in to shake himself like a shower-bath over everything; but, just to show you I never lose my head completely, I used his wet back to moisten—or moisturize, as the Raleigh cigarette people say—the postage stamps for this letter ...pretty shrewd, eh?...But none of that is what this letter is really about...It's about you...I don't suppose it's been a secret that I've loved you since I first saw you half-an-hour-fresh from the womb and looking very much like my father whom I don't love; but now you've grown into the kind of woman I'd always hoped you'd grow up into—only better, of course. Once, while I was in California, I said fumblingly that I was proud of you, which sounded a little like the parent taking some sort of credit. I didn't mean that, honey: I meant I was proud of being your father, which, if you understand me, is a bit different...The other things I said—that you're not only lovely to look at, but also lovely—I stand by; and when your face lights up with laughter you are to me the loveliest thing I've ever seen; but if, on that account, you go round lighting up your face all the time like a Cheshire cat all the time I can see how people are going to think you're a gibbering idiot...

> I love you, darling, deeply and completely ...
> Papa

1. Hammett acted as a script consultant on plays produced by Kermit Bloomgarden, but he did not write a play for him.

TLS MARSHALL

To Mary Hammett

10 July 1947, Hardscrabble Farm, Pleasantville

Dear Marynik,

The Chicago trip went OK, except that the temperature had a tendency to hang around 96, and now I'm back up here, I hope, till I get the play finished. I've got to go over to Katonah Saturday night for some kind of doings for and with Henry Wallace, down to Baltimore on the 25th to make a speech about something to some kind of youth, and probably won't escape having to show up in the city now and then for a day, but otherwise I hope to consecrate myself and the rest of the summer to what you might call my art if you wished to be funny. Lillian leaves on the 19th for an international theatre conference in Paris and most likely will be gone at least a month, which may give me a chance to clean the filthy type on this here machine ... or maybe I could use my own and stop looking gift horses in the letters.

This afternoon I went fishing for the first time in ages—chiefly to try out some new and fancy equipment: you always think of new sports tackle as fancy—and managed to catch only one lousy medium-sized bass. Tomorrow is another day—or has somebody said that before?— and it may happen I'll be ambitious enough also to set out some entrapments for turtles, though it wouldn't be wise to bet on it unless you found somebody who'd give you fancy odds.

* * *

The two new puppies are marvelous little rolly-pollys. The female has been named Saramurf—after Sara Murphy, who's married to the chap who owns Mark Cross—and we're hunting for a name for the male. They're seven weeks old now, very brash, and follow me around—by which I mean they get under me feet—as much as I'll let 'em. They've got the usual poodle liking for being around people.

The hospital let Max Hellman out for one day last week and he came up here and we all had a very good time. He was in better physical shape than I've seen him since I got out of the Army and very happy. There seems to be a pretty good chance of his leaving the hospital—though he'll always have to have a nurse with him—this fall.

That's the news, toots. Kiss the J's for me.

Much love and stuff …
Papa

TLS Marshall

To Josephine Hammett

29 July 1947, 15 East 66th St, New York City

Dear Princess,

This paper's a liar. I'm in Pleasantville. It's getting so you can't trust anything nowadays…I've just finished what I call a hard day's wok on the play—which means I fooled around with it for a while this evening after I got through listening to baseball games on the radio—and am doing this in bed preparatory to turning out the light so I can get a good night's sleep and be all fresh to do no more tomorrow than I've done today…Last week I went down to Baltimore with Canada Lee for some PCA doings and had a good time and, for all I know, may have done a little good[1]…The old home town is moving a little: we had a dinner at one of the fairly prominent hotels, at which something like a third of the sixty-some who attended were Negroes. That could never have happened in my day!…The weather's been hot and nice the past few days. I spent most of this afternoon on the lake, with no great results as far as catching fish is concerned, but with a lot of fun trying out some new tackle…Also tomorrow I must take some ticks out of some puppies' ears…LH is in Paris now, having stopped over in London for five days.[2] After she gets through with the UNESCO conference she's going to take a motor trip through the south of France with Willie Wyler and his frau…for some people I guess life is just a round of pleasure…I'm in course of reading Upton Sinclair's Lanny Budd novels.[3] There are eight or nine of them and I've finished only a couple, so I wouldn't want to make any official reports yet… A moth just flew out of Cinq, the black poodle who shares my bedroom when I'm up here…This r belongs somewhere up in the third line: I don't know how it got down here…What I do know, though, is that it's getting along toward four in the morning and I'm heading for the bedding…I've been dreaming about half-tamed black bears lately. Do you want to tell me what that means? ... Kiss those people for me and take care of yourself because you're the only one of you we've got ...

> Much love, cutey-pie ...
> Papa

1. Canada Lee was a highly respected black stage actor involved in radical theater. PCA was Progressive Citizens of America, which called on the left to resist anti-Communist hysteria. The group broke into three divisions: Youth; Women; and Art, Science, and Professions. Lillian Hellman, a member of the last, was vice president of PCA in 1946.
2. Hellman accepted the invitation of UNESCO head Julian Huxley to the International Theatre Institute in Paris.
3. There are eleven Lanny Budd novels, tracing the political history of the Western world from 1913 to 1950.

TLS MARSHALL

Public Letter

Soviet Russia Today was a political magazine founded in 1932. The 1948 California House Committee on Un-American Activities described it as among the "more important" Communist front organizations, publishing its magazine "for the sole purpose of carrying on propaganda on behalf of the Soviet Union." Hammett was on the editorial board.

October 1947 New York City

Dear SRT Reader:

The circulation figures are in the rate directories. But you don't have to look them up. All you have to do is stop, for a minute, at the nearest newsstand.

Look over the headlines. Not even double murders and socialite divorces are allowed to crowd anti-Soviet smears off the front page.

Look at the magazines—at least one feature, per issue, designed to panic America into fear of the Soviets—the sort of fear that fattens munitions profits—until war zooms in.

And against all that *Soviet Russia Today*, one small American magazine, courageous, determined, carrying on the fight for sanity and truth in American–Soviet relations.

Small, perhaps, but don't underestimate it. History is a continued story of the recurrent triumphs of little David Truth over Goliath Big Lie.

The important thing is to keep David in the fight.

Not a penny of the big advertising on which the anti-Soviet press grows so huge, goes to *Soviet Russia Today*.

Yet this amazing magazine keeps going—and growing!

All because whenever it is in danger, *you* lend a hand, you do without something else for a while, you send what you can to keep David in the fight.

Your helping hand is needed right now. Rising costs in printing and all along the line have brought a new emergency. Send in whatever you can, *at once*.

Keep David in there, fighting!

> Yours,
> Dashiell Hammett

TLS Published in *Soviet Russia Today*, October 1947

Public Letter

28 October 1947, Civil Rights Congress of New York

Dear Friend:

Hollywood writers and artists are fighting back against the "thought-control" attacks of the Thomas-Rankin Committee.[1] Their bold action is turning the movie inquisition into a boomerang for the inquisitors.

Labor and organizations of the people are in the front ranks of the fight. More than three hundred such organizations were represented at the CRCNY Conference for Abolition of the Committee held on October 11. All pledged their support to the campaign.

A central point is support of the resolution introduced by Representative Adolph Sabath of Illinois, under which Congress itself would abolish the body. CRC is pledged nationally to secure half a million signatures to a supporting petition. In New York, a minimum of 100,000 signatures must be obtained.

Won't you do your share in this campaign?

A petition is enclosed. Get it signed. Send it in as fast as possible with the contributions of the signers—to provide the sinews for widening the campaign and defending the victims of the Thomas-Rankin Committee.

You undoubtedly have friends you can enlist in this signature drive. Please use the order form enclosed to get petitions for them.

To spread this campaign, we need funds, quickly. Your own direct contributions will help to speed it.

> Sincerely,
> Dashiell Hammett

DH:el

Uopwa 16-83

1. The House Committee on Un-American Activities, whose leading Democrat was John Rankin, was chaired in 1947 by J. Parnell Thomas (R-New Jersey).

TLS Schomberg

To Reba Hammett

1 February 1948, 28 West 10th St., New York City

Dear Sis,

Here I am, the demon correspondent with all the latest in news. I don't know what's so terrible about letter writing nowadays, but if I can get myself to knuckle down to it for half an hour every month or so I'm doing nobly. This is the first letter I've written anybody in a least two months...I'm glad you saw the old man, and that he's in good shape, all things considered...About that matter of turning his wealth over to me when he dies: I wouldn't argue with him if I were you; you know I think you're entitled to all of whatever it amounts to...As you can see by this paper, I've a new address. Somebody gave me a bloodhound puppy for Christmas and I had to move into a larger place to accommodate her. At six months she's the size of a small calf, only with more energy... I'd heard that Dick is living in these parts, but I haven't got around to looking him up yet... Mary is East with me now, about to undergo as much as she can stand of a psychoanalysis; Jo has reached the dizzy eminence of senior at UCLA. I don't know what she wishes to do after she graduates in the spring: I'd like her to go on with postgraduate work till she makes up her mind, but she seems to think she'd like to work at something for a year or so before deciding whether to return to the academic world, which seems sensible enough too... Poverty and debts having descended on me in equal proportions, I now have to settle down to doing some short stories or something, not a nice prospect after all these years of evading that kind of stuff... Naturally us Yankees, remembering our 28 inches of snow one day last December and our below-zero temperature night before last, are inclined to be a little snooty about winter-weather complaints from the Carolinas: once while I was in the Aleutians I got a letter that went pretty thoroughly into a descri[p]tion of the chill and dampness of Georgia... It's nearly one in the morning, so maybe I'd better stop this and pretend I'm going to think about those short stories or something I've got to manufacture.

> Much love,
> Dashiell

TLS JUDI HAMMETT

To Richard Hammett

17 March 1948, 28 West 10th St., New York City

Dear Dick,

Dad died Friday night — apparently without much pain — at the Morgan County Memorial Hospital in Berkeley Springs, West Virginia, and was buried this morning.

Since the Navy has taken over the Saint Nicholas churchyard where Mama and his mother are buried, and no more burials are permitted, it seemed useless to send him up to St. Mary's to another burying ground, so he was buried in West Virginia. I couldn't get down for the funeral: Reba went up from Charlotte and arranged everything, and told me over the phone tonight that all went well.

She'll probably write to you in more and better detail when she gets home Friday.

Sometime when you feel up to whatever kind of small family reunion you and I could manage you might give me a ring. The number is GR 3-5747.

> All the best,
> Dashiell

TLS JUDI HAMMETT

To the Veterans Administration, New York

A holograph note in Hellman's hand at the top: "Left this letter with DH at Apt— do not know if sent." The letter is unsigned.

2 June 1948 [no address]

Gentlemen:

Please note change of beneficiary on my policy No. N-4 099 278. At present, beneficiary is Miss Josephine Hammett, 2624 Purdue Street, West Los Angeles 34, California. I now wish to divide the policy, that is, to add another beneficiary who is to share with the first, equally. This means that the policy will have two beneficiaries, each to receive one-half. They are:

Miss Josephine Hammett, as before
Miss Mary Jane Hammett of 28 West 10 St, NYC.
Please advise me that the change has been made.

> Thank you.
> Dashiell Hammett

TLU MARSHALL

To Josephine Hammett Marshall

Following their marriage on 6 July 1948, Jo and Loyd Marshall lived for about a year in Honolulu, where he worked as a mechanical engineer, a civilian employee of the U.S. Navy. Hammett stayed with Mary and Jose in Los Angeles for a while before returning to Pleasantville.

29 August 1948, West Los Angeles

Dear Princess,

It's nice hearing from you and if your old man weren't such a lazy slob he'd've written you long before this, but if he were not such a lazy slob how do you know he'd be your old man and in any case what right have you or anybody else got going around interfering with the dubious ways of nature?...We all miss you a great deal and speak of you often—whenever we happen to think of it. Some of us remember you quite clearly—a plump redhaired girl with two ears, as I recall.

Mary and I expect to head back to the United States next Sunday, that is if we can get around to making reservations in time. Our plan—if that's what you want to call it—is to take a morning plane so we'll have daylight with us most of the way.

Things have been kind of quiet around here since you left: no marriage or giving in marriage or amusements of the ilk. It may be you young matrons should speak to the spinsters of your generation. Do they think it equitable to live off the old folks forever?

* * *

Feeling restless today, I thought up a plot for a novel, which I hope one day to get around to doing. Meanwhile it's swell having a new novel not to do: I was getting pretty bored with just not working on that half a dozen or so old ones...I've been reading a lot of things called *City Boy* and *Silent Children* and *No Bugle Tonight* and *The Heart of the Matter* and such like and can truthfully say they are for the most part competently printed on good enough paper and well bound to boot. Tonight I shall probably try *The White Goddess*, or maybe the Beards' history.[1]

Everybody sends love, I guess, or would if I asked them. Anyhow, I send mine, honey, and my best to Loyd ...

Pop

1. *City Boy* by Herman Wouk; *Silent Children* by Mai-Mai Sze; *No Bugles Tonight* by Bruce Lancaster; *The Heart of the Matter* by Graham Greene; *The White Goddess* by Robert Graves.

TLS MARSHALL

To Josephine Dolan Hammett

9 January 1949, 28 West 10th Street, New York

Dear Jose,

Thanks for the Christmas gifts. They came in mighty handy. I was in residence at the Lenox Hill Hospital when they arrived, with nothing much to do but eat and smoke my head off, and you helped me a lot on both.

I didn't tell you—and told Mary not to tell you—about the hospital till it was all over because there was no sense in worrying you when there really wasn't much to worry about. I went in four or five days before Christmas and didn't come out till three or four days after New Year's, so there's a rumor around that I was only dodging the holidays. That's a lie, but it is not a bad idea. I'll remember it.

As of now I'm supposed to have something called a "potential" cardiac condition—whatever in hell that is—and something else is happening in or to my lungs that's too complicated for me to understand but has nothing to do with t.b. and in any event is said to be painless and relatively harmless. Then there's some faulty co-ordination—nervous-muscular—in hands and legs, but that seems to be untangling itself all right. What this stuff seems to add up to is I'm a wreck who'll live as well, as actively and as long as anybody else if I stop drinking and—and this promises to be more trouble—settle down to a life of regular meal-times and bedtimes. So that is what I'm doing now. I came up to Pleasantville Friday and will probably stick to the farm for at least a few weeks, going into the city only Thursdays—I've a class to teach at the Jefferson School that night—and scooting back to the country Fridays. I'm still a little woozy, but otherwise feel fat, fit and fine, and am actually gaining a little weight for the first time in years. I've had to start buying shirts with size 16 collars and it's going to take a little exercise—sawing wood will most likely be what I choose—to get my waist back where 32-inch waistbands don't bind.

That's the story of my young life. Mary has a cold, but seems in pretty good shape outside of that.

> Love,
> DH

TLS Marshall

To Mary Hammett

10 January 1949 [Pleasantville]

Dear Mary,

Here's that letter you complained about not getting. If there's not much in it I can only say there's not much in me and that no doubt goes for some other people I know too.

* * *

I've got a very pretty Freudian slip for you and Doctor T.[1] Writing to somebody about my difficulties in sticking to a regular schedule of meals and so on, I said the not-drinking was not a problem at the moment—only I inadvertently spelled problem "probablem". Want to make something of it?

Strange things have been happening to me; I've been writing letters, for the first time since God knows when. Do you suppose that's going to be my new vice? I remember writing bales of them when I was in the Aleutians with nothing to drink.

All the day wasn't spent letter-writing—it hasn't got completely out of hand yet—and I got in a little reading. I'm now in the middle of *The Dukays,* a novel by a Hungarian named Zilahy, which I don't think is to be published till the 17th. So far it's a very amusing job.

* * *

This, I guess, is about as far as I can go at the moment and it's after eleven, a time when all good men should be in bed with a warm book.

Love and stuff ...
SDH

1. Dr. Joseph D. Teicher was Mary Hammett's psychiatrist in New York.

TLS MARSHALL

To Josephine Dolan Hammett

21 January 1949, 28 West 10th Street

Dear Jose,

Yesterday afternoon I went into the big city, had lunch with Mary, stopped in to let my doctor poke at me, did my nightly—I mean weekly—chore at the Jefferson School, put in a while at a left-wing conference on the National Maritime Union's trouble[s]—which are plenty—and went home to bed.[1] After the quiet rural life I've been leading since I escaped from the hospital it seemed a regular merry-go-round of doings.

Today I got up at nine, breakfasted, talked to our daughter on the phone, listened to the troubles of a budding novelist, and came back here to Pleasantville, where the snow that started earlier today has got everything looking like something out of a book of fairy tales.

Mary seemed in very good shape yesterday and (over the wire) today; my doctor's report on me was nothing spectacular, but things seem to be coming along OK. My only present complaints are a slight shortness of breath and a tendency to tire too quickly...and neither are too bad. That's my news.

SDH

1. In a backlash against the Communist leadership of the National Maritime Union (NMU), more than three fourths of the board, those associated with the Communist Party, were voted out of office.

TPS Marshall

To Josephine Hammett Marshall

25 January 1949, Pleasantville

Dear Reader;

This, from Heda Hop's column in today's *Daily News,* should answer the question in your letter.[1] But it would be just as well to bear a few things in mind:

> ...Lillian Hellman almost finished adapting "The Naked and the Dead" for the stage. She's working on another script, "Montserrat," dealing with the life of Simon Bolivar, for Richard Conte.

for instance, the stage version of *The Naked and the Dead* is not almost finished. It was put aside for the nonce because it couldn't have been done in time for this spring's production and also because Litvak—who directed *The Snake Pit* and so on—is trying to persuade LH and Mailer to skip the play form and do it straightaway into a movie, and they haven't been able to make up their minds yet;[2] for instance again, *Montserrat* doesn't deal with the life of Simon Bolivar, though he—at that time, 1812, only a budding revolutionary—is mentioned importantly enough; and, for a last instance, the play's not being done for Richard Conte, though I suppose he's somewhere in the list of possibilities: everybody else is, so I don't know why he should be left out. Monty Clift is, I think, at the head of the list, but he, as usual, can't make up his mind...or whatever it is actors use for minds.[3]

Going further into the *Daily News,* one of my few sources of accurate information about the great outer world, I then reached the horoscope column—without it I wouldn't think of trying to get through one of these troublous days—and am doing my muddled best to be piloted by it, though I have not noticed any great degree of sensitiveness in Salud, the only being who could possibly be classified as my co-worker.

Another item shakes my confidence in the press a little too: about the slips showing here. I took a good gander at Betty, the farmer's wife, this morning, but nothing was showing. However, Lillian's coming up for dinner—I had told her to feel free to drop in at any time while I was here as a guest—and maybe her petticoats will be dragging. But I'm not easily

> WHAT TO EXPECT TODA.
> Sun in Aquarius
> General Tendencies—Temper may be too sensitive today—watch this in your co-workers and make sure that you are not acting in the same manner. Romances would be affected by careless words, and would need time for recovery. Best interests for today seem to be mechanical or scientific doings—and this includes housekeeping, which is truly a science these days—also the planning of research or any detailed writing or study. Be sure that your performance equals your standards today, as there are slips showing here.

daunted. After a stiff slug of White Rock spiked with lemon juice I went at it again.[4] "Affecting" a "romance" seemed like nice work, but I couldn't think up a "careless" word: they all seemed so sort of premeditated. "Housekeeping" I just sneered at in passing. "Planning" was attractive enough except what else have I been doing exclusively for years and years? So I settled for "mechanical or scientific doings," which, by a process of reasoning with which I need not bother you, led to my going out to saw some firewood. The sawing went well enough, especially since luckily I still am somewhat short of breath, tire easily and speedily. (That kind of good fortune keeps you from getting blisters on your hands.) But when I came back to the house I opened a newly arrived copy of a magazine called *American Forestry* and my already weakened faith in the public press got another bop in the nose.

There, purporting to illustrate an advertisement, was this picture. Now I use this particular bow saw, and I've never seen anybody else use one, so I can only go by what I know. And the plain truth is that by the time I've got the saw-blade that far into the tree trunk my tongue is hanging out too far to be omitted from any drawing pretending to a modicum of honesty and my legs—always thinner than the ones shown—have taken on a pronounced sag, often suggesting that I'm holding on to the saw to keep from falling. (I won't say anything about my not wearing plaid shirts, or whatever the guy in the picture's got on: it is well known that a certain type of artist is likely to use shading of one sort of another to cover up faulty draftsmanship...)

You lucky, lucky girl! L. Hellman has just arrived so I'll put this up a while.

Next day

It's been snowing merrily—I put merrily in because I'm a writer and can't leave the plain facts alone: the truth is I can't see any expression at all: it's just blank white—since mid-morning and things are whitening up all around. L. H. took off for Manhattan around ten; I'm still in pajamas and robe—it's after two—and may not choose to get out of them— much less into anything else—all day; and I ate too much lunch.

Tomorrow's my big day in the big town—probably lunch with M. Hammett, perhaps a haircut, maybe some shopping, certainly the Jefferson School and just as surely an NMU conference thereafter. I can hardly wait till Friday, when I'll be coming back here for another week of nothing much to do except deciding whether to let Salud in the house.

Love to you and Loyd ...

> Respectfully yours,
> Samuel Dashiell Hammett

1. Hedda Hopper was a Hollywood gossip columnist and actress.
2. Russian-born Anatole Litvak directed *The Snake Pit* in 1948. *The Naked and the Dead*, Norman Mailer's best-selling World War II novel, was not adapted for the stage, though Hellman worked on the project. It was made into a movie in 1958, directed by Raoul Walsh, with a screenplay by Mailer and Denis Sanders.
3. Hellman adapted and directed Emmanuel Roblès's play *Montserrat*. It opened at the Fulton Theatre in New York City on 29 October 1949 and ran 65 performances. Neither Richard Conte nor Montgomery Clift appeared in the production, whose cast included Emlyn Williams and Julie Harris.
4. White Rock is a brand of nonalcoholic mixers.

TLS MARSHALL

To Josephine Hammett Marshall

13 February 1949, Pleasantville, N.Y.

Dear Jo,

Today's been Sunday, a warmish thawy day with sun-sun in the air most of the time. Mary came up at noon and went back to the big city around ten o'clock—a dentist or something to see in the morning. I'm in process of trying to bind a battered cookbook in sole leather, a job for highly skilled titans.

Lillian's in Washington over the weekend, being fêted by the Yugoslav and Russian embassies, I think, and possibly by other subversive elements, as well. I was going along, but got myself involved in some left-wing NMU doings and had to stay home to concoct attacks on what we call the reactionary and war-minded leadership of Phil Murry, Tom Curran and the ilk.[1]

Lee Cobb got his voice back in plenty of time and *Death of a Salesman* opened Thursday night to a burst of enthusiastic—even somewhat hysterical—huzzas from most of the critics.[2] I wasn't on hand and as an investor I'm mighty glad the show's in solid, but just the same I doubt if it's quite the world-beater most of the lads seem to think. Arthur Miller can't have improved *that* much.

I've just finished some lousy detective stories (I mean finished reading them, I write nothing but wonderful ones) and Barnett's *The Universe and Dr. Einstein,* which I liked a lot except for god's being dragged in too much along towards the end. A little while back, when Einstein was sick and didn't know how seriously—it turned out to be nothing likely to shorten his life—he seems to have completed the "Unified Field Theory" he's been struggling with some twenty-five or thirty years. This at the moment is supposed to be a close secret, so . . . .

This kind of thing ain't either getting that cookbook bound or making trouble for CIO heads . . . . . .

My best to Loyd.

> Love,
> Erle Stanley Gardner

1. Philip Murray was president of the CIO. Joseph Curran was president of the National Maritime Union.
2. Lee J. Cobb played Willie Loman in *Death of a Salesman*, which opened on 10 February 1949 at the Morosco Theatre and ran for 749 performances.

TL (FACSIMILE SIGNATURE OF ERLE STANLEY GARDNER PASTED AT BOTTOM)
MARSHALL

To Josephine Dolan Hammett

28 February 1949, Hardscrabble Farm, Pleasantville, New York

Dear Jose,

Winter came back to us today with about a foot of snow up here and the temperature in the low twenties. I did my first real snowshoeing of the winter and my legs feel like it tonight. But it was fun.

Mary phoned this morning to say she'd had a letter from you and you might go to Honolulu before summer. I hope you won't let your foolishness keep you from letting me know about whatever money you need for the trip.

I had a dinner date in the big town tonight, but used the weather as an excuse to postpone it. I have to go in for my class at the Jefferson School Thursday nights—usually I go in a day ahead and come back after the class.

It seems to have started snowing again—it stopped a couple of hours ago—so maybe I'll be snowed in and won't have to go anywhere anytime. The deep freeze is full of food and the cellar's full of firewood; I've got plenty of books to read and at least a week's supply of cigars, cigarettes and pipe tobacco.

Last week I went in to see my doctor for my monthly check-up and everything seemed OK. I'm still gaining weight—though now only a couple of pounds a month—and, except for a tendency to tire easy, seem as good as new. The not drinking—I'm now in my third month with not even so much as a glass of beer with meals—hasn't bothered me yet and the tougher job of eating three meals a day…Well, sometimes it's pretty tough, but most of the time I manage it.

I guess that's all.

> Love …
> SDH

TLS Marshall

Public Letter

1 March 1949, New York State Civil Rights Congress
To All Labor, Fraternal, Civic and Religious Organizations

Dear Friends:

In the death block of the state prison in Trenton, N.J., six innocent Negro men await death—for a crime they did not commit.

On January 27, 1948, a man by the name of William Horner was attacked and killed in his store in Trenton. Following the murder, the police established an illegal curfew in the Negro community, and intimidated the entire neighborhood by a special police bandit squad armed with tommy-guns. Subsequently, the six young Negroes were arrested and charged with the crime.

Enclosed for your information is a complete chronology of the case. As you will see for yourself, the case of the Trenton Six has all the earmarks of another Scottsboro frameup.

* No witness reported more than three men at the murder scene. Yet six were convicted.
* The six Negro men were tried by an all-white jury.
* The only evidence against the prisoners consisted of five "confessions" which the police admit were forced. These "confessions" were repudiated by the men in open court. Police Captain Delate testified: "I knew the truth and I insisted on Collis English (one of the Trenton Six) making a confession in line with the truth as I conceived it to be."
* None of the Trenton Six fit the witnesses' descriptions of the actual criminals. All of the men have proof that they were not anywhere near the scene of the crime.

The case of the Trenton Six is now pending appeal before the Supreme Court of the State of New Jersey. To make sure that this shocking travesty of justice is not allowed, and that six innocent men do not die, we earnestly urge you and your organization to do the following:

* Call upon Governor Driscoll of New Jersey through letters, telegrams, resolutions and petitions and urge him to use his executive power to free the innocent "Trenton Six" immediately.

* At your next regular membership meeting, place on your agenda the case of the "Trenton Six". We will be happy to supply a speaker to present the facts in the case. If you prefer, we will supply all the necessary background to the speaker of your own choice. If your order of business at your regular meeting is too crowded, may we respectfully urge, if possible, that you arrange special meetings around the case. Mrs. Bessie Mitchell, sister of one of the defendants is ready to appear before your membership in behalf of the "Trenton Six".

* Join officially with the Committee to Save the Trenton Six in the planning and the carrying on of the fight to see that justice is done, and that the six innocent Negro men do not die.

* Rush defense funds to the COMMITTEE TO SAVE THE TRENTON SIX—CIVIL RIGHTS CONGRESS. All monies collected for the "Trenton Six" will be earmarked and used exclusively for their defense.

Time is short. Six lives are at stake. It is for these reasons that I appeal to you and your organization to act at once.

May we hear from you soon on these matters.[1]

        Fraternally,
        Dashiell Hammett,

Chairman
Uopwa#16 - 83

1. In June 1949 the New Jersey State Supreme Court ordered a new trial, and four of the Trenton Six were found not guilty in 1951. A second successful appeal on behalf of the two found guilty in 1951 led to a third trial at which one of the remaining accused was found not guilty. The other defendant died of a heart attack before the third trial.

TLS SCHOMBERG

To Josephine Hammett Marshall

6 March 1949, Hardscrabble Farm, Pleasantville, New York

Dear Princess,

Mary told me your Mother was going to visit you this month and I think it's a nice time of the year for the trip. I wrote J last week: there'll probably be a reply waiting for me when I get to town along about Wednesday. She usually writes me there...I haven't seen Mary for a week or so—I had a million (less some hundred thousands) of things to do when I was in NY last week—but she seemed all right when I talked to her over Alexander Graham Bell's Folly. I think she's still fooling around with the dentist but I don't know whether he's got back to serious stuff like drilling and such...The dramatization of *The Maltese Falcon* seems all set for the fall *if* we can get a good script and *if* we can get a good cast: I guess what I mean by its being all set is that—though papers haven't been signed yet—my greedy end has been agreed on.[1] I'm no longer so hot on Howard Duff to play Spade. Have you got a favorite for the part? (Now forget about Fred MacMurr[a]y for the moment!) If we can get Peter Lorre for Gutman I think we'll ignore the written-in fatness: He should do a pretty good job on it, used to be a fine actor...Spring is back again and it's been mighty nice outside these last few days. A calf was born while I was away. He's a little frail but will, I'm sure, grow into first-rate veal. Anyhow when I let him suck my finger for a while yesterday it was with the thought that before long the situation would be very much turned around...That's about all the news I've got. Lillian and a portrait painter friend of ours—George Bergen—came up Friday and stayed till late this afternoon and none of us did anything much except sit around and talk. It came up somewhere in the course of conversation that in one of the prominent bars in St. Louis there's a picture by the Spanish painter Miró. I think he was the chap who invented Dadaism and was later a surrealist. Anyway we concocted a rumor for George to spread in art circles that what the proprietor of the bar really wanted was a mirror, but he was misunderstood over the phone when he ordered it and then—probably sensitive about his accent, a Greek maybe—let it go at that when, after a great deal of searching, the Spanish painter was found somewhere in Europe and brought to St. Louis.

That'll give you a rough idea of the week-end's intellectual level...It's time I was tucking myself into bed...Give my best to Loyd ...

> Much love, cutey ...
> Pop

> 1. No stage dramatization of *The Maltese Falcon* was produced. Howard Duff was a movie and radio actor who was the voice of the title character on the radio serial *The Adventures of Sam Spade*. Peter Lorre played Joel Cairo in the 1941 movie version of *The Maltese Falcon*.

TLS MARSHALL

To Josephine Hammett Marshall

14 March 1949, Hardscrabble Farm, Pleasantville, New York

Dear Jo,

I had a letter from Jose the last of the week, full of anticipation and things. Don't let her hit the bean-games too heavy in those Chinese gambling houses. And don't trust her with too many secrets of a military nature: the Irish were neutral in the last war, but there's no telling what they'll do in the next.

Mary phoned this morning, so I can report that as of that time she was breathing. I haven't seen her for a couple of weeks and don't know whether I'll be able to manage it this week. I'm going into the city Wednesday as usual, but my engagement book's got a lot of things listed...a lot of nice dull things.

Lady Chatterl[e]y's Lover was a pretty foolish book, and I suppose it's even sillier now that Lawrence is dead and you know he's never going to manage to do what he was trying to do.

My weight still goes up, though slowly. A few more overfeedings on stewed goose—like tonight's—ought to step it up. Did I tell you Henry Wallace and I made a date to meet at 165 pounds? I saw him at dinner Saturday night and (he claims) he's already got himself down (from 199) to 182. I've still got something in the neighborhood of 10 pounds to pick up. But last year's election shows he's not too hard to beat.

I've just finished a dullish book called *Thieves' Market* and shall now get going on F. L. Green's *Mist on the Waters.*[1] He's the man who wrote *Odd Man Out.*

My best to Loyd.

>   Love in chunks …
>   Pop

1. *The Thieves' Market* by A. I. Bezzerides.

TLS Marshall

To Josephine Dolan Hammett

7 April 1949, Pleasantville

Dear Jose,

You sound as if you're having a wonderful time on that island—what's the name of it? I keep forgetting. Alcatraz, isn't it?—and I hope you stay with it till you've worn the young Marshalls to a frazzle. Show 'em what our older generation is made of, if anything.

* * *

At the moment my weight-gaining seems at a halt—I hang around the low (and I mean low) 150's—but I'm eating well and feeling well, so I have nothing except the usual few hundred things to complain about. It's well along towards five months since I had my last sip of Virginia Dare, and it's been anything but bad, thanks chiefly to a god-given ability to be practically as silly out of my cups as in 'em.[1]

Now for the outdoors.

>   Love to all …
>   SDH

1. Virginia Dare was a brand of scuppernong wine introduced in 1835 and named for the first English child born on American soil. It was a slang term for alcoholic beverages.

TLS Marshall

To Josephine Hammett Marshall

18 April 1949, Pleasantville, New York

Dear Jo,

* * *

Your Mother wrote me she was hunting for plane reservations. I dare say it's just as well she's heading back towards the States, unless you want a native step-father. In the same letter she wrote, "The Hawaiian men have wonderful healthy bodies and are nice."

Last week I picked up where I'd left off misinforming the Jefferson School students. I've a small class this time. Either I'm not so great a draw as Olivier, for instance, or the school's registration is falling off. I didn't stay in town for the faculty meeting Friday and haven't got the real lowdown, though I imagine poor old Jeff continues to take a beating. Red-baiting's kind of rife these days in these parts and it keeps the space between floors and beds fairly well filled with otherwise intrepid characters.

Mary came down for a while Friday afternoon and seemed much as usual only possibly a little fatter. She was in some sort of quandary having to do with going or not going to California for a couple of months this summer. I haven't made up my mind what I'm going to do when the school term ends this June. Maybe I'll skip the next term and go up to Martha's Vineyard for a pair of months; maybe I'll skip the term and just loaf here; maybe I won't skip the term and just loaf here. It's a tough problem that's sure to take fifteen minutes of my time when I get around to facing it.

The last couple of days have been cool and rainy, but flowers are out to hell and gone all over the place. I've been planting, transplanting and probably deplanting like crazy.

Thursday I visited my sawbones for the bi-monthly checkup and all seems well. The weight-gaining has stopped, but I attribute that to my getting more exercise these days. If he attributed it to anything I wasn't listening: I go to him—as all sensible patients go to their doctors—for miracles; let him keep his science for medical conventions and such. (Does a guy have to go through all those years of college and internship and so on just to tell me what I always knew—I'd be in a lot better shape if I stopped drinking and ate more?) But he did talk intelligently about television sets, of which he has some practical knowledge, and I promised to look at a Fisher set before buying an RCA-Victor.

Now I've got to go downstairs and see about something to eat: this pounding a typewriter and chewing on gumdrops is hungry work.

Give my love to everybody.

Love ......
Pop

TLS MARSHALL

To Josephine Hammett Marshall

25 April 1949, Hardscrabble Farm, Pleasantville, New York

Dear Madam,

It doesn't seem there's much news around here except your Mother's due to leave for the States tomorrow, but that ought to be more news around there than here and what have you got to do but sleep for a couple of weeks afterwards?...A lot of Yugoslavs—most if not all of the UN delegation—were here for the weekend, cluttering the place up with the international situation—which for the Y's is quite a situation—but otherwise doing no harm...Nearly all of them speak pretty good English and have a nice kind of ga[ie]ty...Henry Wallace came over, among other people, for dinner Saturday night, seeming a little tireder and older than usual, but he has been dieting, and that may be to blame...Willy and Tally Wyler were here Sunday—they're east for a couple of weeks while he looks around for a play or something to manhandle into a picture before tackling Dreiser's *Sister Carrie*—and they asked (I've forgotten what, but I didn't tell 'em anything) about you[1]... I saw your friend Mike Romanoff at the St. Regis a couple of weeks ago, but he didn't ask about you.[2] Should I phone him and tell him anyhow?...Tally told me her little boy—remember him? he's not quite three I guess—had asked their butler, "Which do you like best, bosoms, or sit-ons?"...Lillian's been in bed all day with grippe or Virus X or something, though it may be that she's sulking a little because the newly published Congressional Committee on UnAmerican Activities pamphlet on the recent Peace Conference lists her in the group of sponsors who have been affiliated with 31 to 40 red-front organizations while I'm in the smaller and more elite 41 to 50 group, including something—where I seem to be alone—called the Crown Heights Committee For A Democratic Spain...From now on whenever I get involved in one of those Committee arguments I'm going to mow down the opposition by pointing out that, "Now, up in Crown Heights (I wish I could remember where it is or was) we always did it thisaway"...Wednesday I go into town as usual and shall try to escape after school Thursday night, but, unless my duties in Crown Heights interfere, shall certainly be back here by Friday... The weather's coolish but nice and so do I try to be... I'll probably phone your Mother Wednesday night...give my best to Loyd ...

Love,
Pop

1. William Wyler directed *Carrie*, the 1952 movie based on Theodore Dreiser's novel *Sister Carrie*.
2. Michael Romanoff was a restaurateur who claimed Russian nobility.

TLS Marshall

To Josephine Hammett Marshall

24 June 1949, 28 West 10th St, New York City

Dear Toots,

Here I'm again in this great big city which I'll be glad to make you a present of any time you (and those who own the property) are willing. It's a hot day, but not as hot as it has been...probably saving its real strength for tomorrow when I have to spend the morning chairmaning a Conference for Civil and Human Rights at the City Center Casino, which is supposed to be air-conditioned if you wish to be optimistic. I'd intended opening the Conference and then turning it over to Mary Van Kleek to manipulate while I loafed till my afternoon chores on the resolutions committee reared their red heads, but she developed a dead or dying brother somewhere out of town and so ...[1]

I don't know much about the ins and outs of your waterfront strike. In ordinary times most unions shy away from arbitration—remembering how many times they've been screwed that way—but when times start to get hard and the heat's really turned on labor, then business tends to take the don't-let's-discuss-it: it's-this-or-else stand. The shipping interests have always leaned in that direction: they're cuties.

* * *

Now I've got to write a few thousand well-chosen words to open up tomorrow's doings by knocking the audience, if any, so cold they'll never hear whatever else is said, if anything, the rest of the day.

My best to Loyd.

> Love ...
> Pop

1. Mary Van Kleek was a dedicated fellow traveler involved with the Civil Rights Congress after her 1948 retirement as director of the Russell Sage Foundation.

TLS MARSHALL

To Josephine Dolan Hammett

30 June 1949, Hardscrabble Farm, Pleasantville, N.Y.

Dear Jose,

It seems—and I guess it is—a hell of a long time since I've written you, but I've been working pretty hard and...you know all those usual excuses of people who are just lousy correspondents.

* * *

My Civil Rights Congress had some Conferences, Mass Meetings and the like over the weekend, so I spent five or six days in town for a change, and didn't like it too much. Cities are for the young, I guess, or maybe for the very old.

Mary phoned me this afternoon to ask me if it would be all right for her to go to California early in July instead of waiting till August. It doesn't make much difference to me, of course, but it sounded a bit like one of those sudden childish brainstorms she gets, so I told her to wait till Doctor Teicher gets back Tuesday—he's been away for a week transporting his family to California—and I'd talk it over with both of them. I saw her two or three times while I was in town, just for an hour or two each time.

* * *

I still haven't got back the weight I lost when I had a week's flu in the spring and I've got all kinds of complaints like my legs not feeling springy enough and my tiring too easily and shortness of breath and occa[s]ional slight vertigo; but my doctor doesn't pay too much attention to my squawks. He seems to think I'm coming along fine and all that's wrong with me is I think I ought to feel too well too soon. Actually I seem to be in better shape than I've been in the past ten years, certainly in better shape than when I went into the army, so I reckon I'm still a few steps from death's door.

I'm trying to get a book—tentatively entitled *Man and Boy*—started and am fumbling around with a couple of television shows for the fall, so I guess I can call myself fairly busy.

* * *

Love ...SDH

TLS MARSHALL

To Josephine Hammett Marshall

15 July 1949, Hardscrabble Farm, Pleasantville, New York

Dear Jo,

Of course you can ask what the new novel's about. It's about people. People are interesting and I've always thought somebody should write about them some day...or have I said that before? One of the troubles with being an elderly writer is you're likely to go round stealing from yourself, plagiarism at its lowest.

Lillian didn't go to England after all—they found an actor here to play opposite Williams—so instead she went out to the Coast to talk about possibly doing the screen treatment of Tennessee Williams' *A Streetcar*

Named Desire.[1] She's been gone just about a week, will probably come back next week. I've talked to her on the phone a couple of times, but since she's staying at the house of the prospective producer she couldn't speak freely enough to let me know how things really stack up. Willy Wyler will direct if she does the script. (I think she's just hunting up things to do so her conscience will let her keep putting off the dramatization of *The Naked and The Dead.*)

* * *

My best to Loyd.

Much love, honey …
Pop

1. Emlyn Williams played the villain Izquierdo in Hellman's adaptation of *Montserrat*. Oscar Saul wrote the screenplay for the 1951 movie adaptation of *A Streetcar Named Desire*, directed by Elia Kazan.

TLS MARSHALL

To Mary Hammett

10 August 1949, Hardscrabble Farm, Pleasantville, N.Y.

Dear Mary,

It was nice getting your letters and I'm glad your trip was the usual pleasant one. It's been hot as hell here the past couple of days. But I haven't minded it too much and—anyhow—am moving north the day after tomorrow. The new address, so far as I know, will be *c/o Webster, Gay Head. Martha's Vineyard, Mass.* If that isn't all of it I'll send you the rest later. We'll probably stay up there until Labor Day, September 5, and then come back here.

Max Hellman died last week; Abe Abeloff has been sick for a week or two and is off to Europe Friday for a short rest; Sam Rosen has been in the hospital a couple of weeks with a broken kneecap, a broken rib and some smashed teeth he got in an auto accident and will probably stay there a few weeks longer; George Bergen is growing a beard which makes him look very much like a European art student of the '90s;[1] Cary

Grant was up for dinner the other night; Lillian's play goes into rehearsal just about a month from now; our *Fat Man* movie deal is still hanging fire, as it has been for nearly a year; I just turned down a Mutual offer to put the *Thin Man* radio show on five fifteen-minute periods a week; the Continental Op Radio Show (I mean television show) is still in process of doing whatever it's in process of doing; I've a couple of other radio or television ideas—based on characters invented in the dim past—in more or less formative stages; there's a possibility—not too big—that I may have to fly out to the Coast sometime around the 9th of September to testify in Warner Bros.' suit against us on the *Sam Spade* show; I've just finished a good lunch; and that's about all the news I have.[2]

I left that yellow terry jacket rather than hunt for last moment space to pack it; if you have room for it bring it, if not do what I did and leave it for next time. It doesn't eat much.

Give my best to your Mother.

> Love …
> Pop

1. Abe Abeloff was Hammett's doctor. Sam Rosen, also a physician, and his wife, Helen, supported political causes Hammett endorsed. George Bergen was a portrait painter.
2. On 28 May 1948, Warner Bros. sued the broadcaster, sponsor, director, and producer of *The Adventures of Sam Spade* for copyright infringement. The studio argued that its contract with Hammett for movie rights to *The Maltese Falcon* included exclusive rights to the characters. Hammett was later added to the suit. It was settled on 28 December 1951 in Hammett's favor.

TLS MARSHALL

To Marjorie May

10 August 1949, Hardscrabble Farm, Pleasantville, New York

Dear Marje,

I'm afraid I wouldn't be much help to you with the play: it's simply not my kind of theater. My kind—if I can be said to have any—is the playwright's theater: the playwright says as much as he can of what he wants to say and then hunts for a director and actors who can make it come alive on the stage. He hopes they'll add to it, but, unless he's casting in Paris perhaps, he usually plays safe by not demanding too much of them. It's not much fun to write a part for the wittiest, handsomest, most urbane, most charming, most intelligent man in the world and then wind up with Dennis King playing it.

Your kind of theater in this play is the actor-director theater in which the ms is only a vehicle for them. I've got nothing against this kind of theater—and God knows directors and actors like it—but I've never been interested in it and know practically nothing about it. If I remember I liked Robert Morley—is that right?—very much in the act of *Oscar Wilde* I saw but couldn't see any reason for going back after the intermission:[1] I read *A Streetcar Named Desire*—quite like your play in structure—with the feeling that I was going through a too-long draft of a first act, vehicles just ain't my meat.

I'm off to Martha's Vineyard Friday.

Yours,
Dash

(who advised Courtney Burr not to produce *Sailor, Beware!*)[2]

1. Dennis King was a British actor who was in the Broadway production of *The Searching Wind* in 1944; he was part of the repertory company of *The Philco Television Playhouse* in 1948. Robert Morley starred in *Oscar Wilde*, which had runs on Broadway in 1936 and 1938.
2. *Sailor, Beware!* ran for 500 performances at the Lyceum Theatre in New York, beginning 28 September 1933.

TLS Richard Dannay

To Mary Hammett

29 August 1949, c/o Webster, Gay Head, Martha's Vineyard, Mass.

Dear Mary,

* * *

We'll probably stay here till Wednesday, September 7, make the

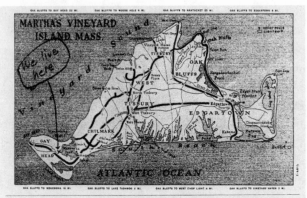

Enclosure in 29 August 1949 letter to Mary

Pleasantville place by the 8th, and come into New York along about Friday the 9th. I may stay in the city over the weekend. Willie Wyler phoned the other day to ask if I'd be interested in doing the movie script of the Kingsley play, *Detective Story,* and I promised him I'd at least go take a look at it when I get back to the city.[1] His studio, Paramount, bought it a month or so ago. I also talked to Hunt Stromberg about maybe doing some work on *The Fat Man* if the deal with Columbia goes through...at the moment that deal looks like a sleeping duck. Meanwhile I'm putting in a little—and I do mean little—work on Sean O'Casey's *Purple Dust* for Kermit, who wants to stage it this winter.

Kermit and Ginny were up for the weekend. He went back to town last night—he's busy getting the Chicago company of *Death of a Salesman* ready—and she'll probably leave us tomorrow night.

This island is some eighteen miles long by nine wide, full of bays, inlets, ponds, with almost as many good sandy beaches as it has people, so that you feel crowded if there are any other people within a hundred yards of you on the shore. I'm fat, sunburned and contented.

* * *

Give my love to your Mother.

　　　Much love ...
　　　Papa

1. *Detective Story* opened on 23 March 1949 at the Hudson Theatre and ran for 581 performances.

TLS Marshall

To Josephine Hammett Marshall

10 September 1949, 28 West 10th St, New York City

Dear Jo,

Well, here I am back in what I guess you got to call the old home-stead though it looks more like an ivory basement to some of us and unless I can think fast I'll most likely be stuck here for a few weeks…God forbid.

I got in yesterday, go to the theatre tonight to see *Detective Story*, will have to spend tomorrow grinding away at the O'Casey play, have confer-ences on the movie sale or non-sale of *The Fat Man* Monday, forget what it is I have to do Tuesday, and so on and so on and t'ell with it.

* * *

I'm not sure I accepted, but I think I'm on Marcantonio's finance com-mittee: he's running for Mayor with no chance of winning that anybody can see right now but American Labor Party inner politics make it neces-sary to run him.[1] Anyway out of Bugs Baer's column yesterday I got a swell piece of advice for campaign finance committees: "A campaign contribu-tion is a voluntary donation from a twisted arm. The pressure should be applied gently and smoothly. You are after money and not cuff-links."[2]

* * *

My usual best to Loyd.

My usual love to you …
Pop

1. Vito Marcantonio, a member of the American Labor Party in 1949 and U.S. Congressman from New York. A supporter of the American Communist Party, he ran for mayor of New York in 1949, winning 13.8 percent of the vote.
2. Arthur "Bugs" Baer was a syndicated humor columnist for the Hearst newspapers.

TLS MARSHALL

To Kermit Bloomgarden

After seeking Hammett's advice about a New York production of Sean O'Casey's 1940 play Purple Dust, *Bloomgarden abandoned the project. The play was later produced without Hammett's or Bloomgarden's involvement at the Cherry Lane Theatre off-Broadway, opening on 27 December 1956 and running for 430 performances.*

2 October 1949, 28 West 10th St., New York City

Dear Kermit,

Here's what I think ought to be done to *Purple Dust,* boiled down as far as I can, because I don't imagine you feel like reading a book about it at the moment, but you can have as much act-by-act detail as you want whenever you want it, and as far as I know I'll be available for talking about it almost any time that suits you within the next few weeks either here or in Philadelphia.

Still seeing the play as a slapstick allegory with music, I've tried to resist my natural tendency toward tight plotting: I think a lot of the play's charm hangs on its seeming haphazard quality.

About the music: the three pieces in Act I are jammed together (pages 1-5, 1-11 and 1-17) in the first third of the act, and then there's no more music until O'Killigain's brief song to Souhaun far along in Act II (page 2-31). In Act III there's a work chant (far too short) on page 3-16 and the "Faraway o!" song on page 3-35. If O'Casey can't be persuaded to write—or permit—more songs, then the songs in Act I should be put further apart—which shouldn't be very difficult—because they—especially "Deep In the Bosky Country"—prepare the audience for a good deal of music. If, as I hope, O'Casey agrees to more songs, here's a rough schedule of possibilities, though there are other spots that would do just as good. (1) A work-song or ballad by workmen, off-stage at first and then brought on by the 1st and 3rd Workmen as they entered, top of page 1-32. Instead of peering around the corner hunting for Poges, as now, they would of course, be surprised to find him there, but I don't think that need make any difference to the following scene. (2) Avril and Basil do a riding-song (parallelling the "Bosky Countrie" song) as they set out for the horses on page 1-38. (3) In the beginning of—or early in—Act II, "Deep in the Bosky Countrie" might be done again, bitterly, perhaps by Cloyne and Barney. O'Killigain's song to Souhaun (page 31) should be lengthened. (4) Poges's and the 1st Workman's conversation about past glories could wind up (page 2-20) in a song. (5) In Act III, I think the scene between Poges and the Canon would be helped by bringing Avril,

Souhaun and Basil on (page 3-6) singing a bawdy song. (This scene both-ers me a little in its present form: Avril seems to step out of character—anything for a laugh,—but I don't think that would be true if she and the others were tight—and the Canon has already included drinking among the things he disapproves of.) (6) The workmen's shanty on page 3-16 should be longer of course.

The rains, the rising of the river, the expected flood are mentioned too casually—and too infrequently—to make enough impression on the audience, so that the inundation at the end of the play now seems—or will seem to an audience—more fortuitous than inevitable. This doesn't need much fixing. The 1st Workman in his opening speech (page 1-2) could include marks of water among the things hidden by the black and white paint; and again in his first speech on page 2-18 he could put the water in with the wind; and so on wherever there's an opening. (I think the thing to get across is that the house is generally uninhabitable when the water rises during the rainy seasons—some years worse than others—and it's only a matter of time before a fullgrown flood will knock it over.) The rain should begin in Act II.

Of the Irish mistresses, Souhaun is the larger character—as she should be—but I think Avril's running-off with O'Killigain at the end of Act I is passed over too lightly, and, in any event, I think there should be one, or possibly two, hair-down scenes between the pair. The first one could easily be spotted by keeping them on-stage instead of withdr[a]wing (bottom of page 2-4) after Stoke and Poges have gone off. They should discuss Avril's adventure, with Avril possibly attaching no importance to it or seeming not to. The relationship between them remains the same, of course, mentor and pupil, mother and daughter. Souhaun, as I see her, would realise that they had about played their string out with the two Englishmen and—a point of pride with trollops—shouldn't want to wait for Stoke and Poges to come to the same conclusion. Since Avril won't admit that she cares too much about O'Killigain—a point of pride with young trollops—Souhaun makes a play for him (just as it's now written) but when that's no go she turns to the 2nd WORKMAN as her next best bet. (To keep this from seeming too abrupt—as her turning to him is in the present version—she could very easily stay on stage instead of exiting (page 2-23)—Poges going off at that point—and play pretty much the same part Poges now plays with the 2nd Workman until Poges comes in at top of page 2-28 with, "My own great-grandfather was Irish, etc.")

The second scene between Souhaun and Avril could come right at the end of Souhaun's scene with O'Killigain (page 2-31), Avril coming on right after the kiss, Poges's entrance with the roller being held off to interrupt the scene between the two women when we've had enough of that. Souhaun now knows that, warm as he is to her, O'Killigain has no more interest in her than he'd have in any goodlooking woman who was handy, and that the real thing—if there is any real thing involved—is between him and Avril. She urges Avril to run off with him, but Avril—perhaps because she does think her feeling for O'Killigain is real and has had no experience of that sort of relationship—can't make up her mind until—in Act III—the whole situation, including the flood, push[es] her into it. Souhaun, I think, should wait till after Avril's gone to clear out with the 2nd Workman—a sort of guardian according to her lights till the end. (The 2nd Workman, if he needs any explaining, patiently waited until Souhaun had made her play for O'Killigian, knowing the younger man would make off with the younger girl in the end and Souhaun would fall in his lap.) None of this stuff, of course, should be on any higher emotional level than is necessary to carry it off.

Now I've got some production difficulties for you that you're going to love—live stock. In the beginning of Act II, where there are now off-stage animal and bird noises, I'd like to see chickens, ducks, pigs, perhaps a sheep, roam into the room where the two Englishmen are abed. Where the "Bull puts a stylized head with long curving horns over the barricade and lets out a loud bellow" (page 2-13) I'd like to see the head and shoulders of as pretty and gentle cow as you can get hold of. And at the finale of ACT III I'd like to have the 2nd Workman ride in on a very big white plowhorse—with water from the rising river sloshing around its legs—haul Souhaun up behind him and ride off.

The Act I and Act II curtains are weak, but I'm not sure that isn't as it should be. (I like the buildup of the "naked" stuff at the end of Act I—it's very Irish and is why other folk always think the Irish are liars—and wish there had been more of that sort of thing throughout the play. This is an anti-British play but the Irish will find it more insulting to them than to anybody else: all good Irish writers manage to do that.)

The "precious vase" sequence didn't hold me very well, and I think it could very well be either cut out completely or whittled down to a mere additional catastrophe. A good deal of cutting could be done throughout—many of the funny scenes are too long—but perhaps you can get a kind of blanket permit out of O'Casey to cut that stuff to fit.

The telephone troubles should be increased throughout to build to the Postmaster's entrance, but that's simply a matter of spotting them wherever there's a hole and I can easily do that when I get down to details.

I don't know just what you think the best way to deal with O'Casey— I mean I don't know what shape you want to put your suggestions in or how much detail you want to go into—so if you'll let me know...as I said in the first paragraph of this letter ....

Yours,

TLU HRC

To Josephine Hammett Marshall

Beginning on 13 January 1950, Hammett worked on the movie adaptation of Sidney Kingsley's play Detective Story *for Paramount, with William Wyler directing. After working for nearly two months, and unwilling to complete a script, Hammett returned the money paid him by Wyler. He had given $1,000 of his advance to his daughter Josephine. The movie was released in November 1951. Screen credit went to Kingsley for the original story, and Robert Wyler and Philip Yordan for the script. Hammett did not receive screen credit.*

29 December 1949, 28 West 10th St., New York City

Dear Jo,

Many thanks to you and Loyd for the lovely grey pajamas, which I am now wearing and which reminded me that I'd better sit to hell down here and write you this whatever-it-turns-out-to-be.

After going through more ifs and whereases than the original negotiations for the Louisiana Purchase, my contract to do *Detective Story* for Paramount seems finally settled. My present plan is to fly out of here on the evening of Tuesday, January 10th. That'll put me in Los Angeles on the 11th. I'm due back here on the 19th—my class at the Jefferson School starts then—so the Chamber of Commerce will be just wasting its time if it tries to persuade me to stay longer. (I don't remember their going to any trouble the last time I was out there but you can't tell.)

I'll probably stay at either the Beverly Hills Hotel or the Beverly Wilshire—wherever Paramount puts me up—but I'll let you know about that when I know about it.

My boyish diffidence about furniture for your new house will disappear like a miracle as soon as Paramount's first check—I should get it next week—comes along. It's not only actresses who lose their modesty when they get movie money.

Tomorrow night I shall probably go up to Pleasantville for the longish weekend. Tonight I've got to sweat over a put-off-and-put-off-doctoring job on a play called *The Man*. I saw the first run-through at rehearsal the other night. It's pretty much of a stinker, even if not quite as much of a stinker as *Detective Story*. (I made the mistake of reading the script last week and it's a pip! If Sidney Kingsley is a writer I'm the president of the NAM. Lookie, that's man spelled backwards...very backwards!)

Love to your Mother and Loyd and to you, and no matter what happens to the rest of you, take care of our grandchild ...

Pop

TLS Marshall

To Reba Hammett

29 December 1949, 28 West 10th St., New York City

Dear Reba,

I'm sorry you couldn't get up for Christmas, but many thanks for the gifts, one of which is decorating my bathrobe pocket right now. The holidays were pleasant but uneventful, by which I suppose I mean pleasantly uneventful.

A couple of days ago I had a wire from Dick asking me to phone him, so I did, thinking maybe something was the matter, but I reckon it was just a combination of approaching age and the holiday spirit because all he had was a suggestion that we get together, resulting in a dinner date for next week. Come to think of it, I don't think I've seen him since 1931.

Along about the tenth of January I'm going out to the West Coast for a week to talk to Willie Wyler about *Detective Story*. Later in the spring I'll probably go back there for a month or two to do the movie script. Paramount and I finally seem to be ending negotiations that went on longer than the Louisiana Purchase preliminaries. Willie is going to direct the picture. He's in Sun Valley now and I'd've gone there to talk to him—I've never been there and I like winter—but my younger daughter Jo is now back from Hawaii and living in Los Angeles and I'd like to see her. I suppose I haven't told you I've been nagging her since her marriage to make me a grandfather, and if all goes well she's going to do that along about the twelfth of May. I'm very happy about it.

This is typed on my newest toy, an IBM electric—some stuff, eh? Look how I can even s p r e a d w o r d s o u t i f I w a n t t o f i l l s p a c e o r s o m e t h i n g !

Now I've got to put in a night's work on a put-off-and-put-off play-doctoring job on *The Man*, a none-too-good melodrama Kermit Bloomgarden's got in rehearsal now. I've a feeling it's not going to be much better when I get through with it, but I promised him I'd have a try, and if I don't get it done tonight I'm likely to be trapped in town over the weekend.

> Mary sends her love and so do I …
> Dashiell

TLS Judi Hammett

To Kermit Bloomgarden

Bloomgarden hired Hammett as an advisor on the production of Sidney Kingsley's play The Man, *which opened at the Fulton Theatre on 19 January 1950 and ran for 92 performances.*

29 December 1949, 28 West 10th St., New York City

Dear Kermit,

Here are my notes—such as they are—on *The Man*. Page numbers here refer to the revised copy I have. You probably have later scripts by now, so I am sending along mine to make it easier for you to find out what the hell I'm talking about—in case that makes any difference.

In her scene with Ruth (1-1-13 to 1-1-19) Mrs Gillis shouldn't, as I think you agreed, be quite so bustling, nor do I think she should be so superior; but practically all the present dialogue could stay in if it were made clear—by a couple of false starts here, and more explicitly later in her conversation with Armstrong—that she at least partly saw things from the girl's viewpoint but felt she had to back up the girl's mother, presumably her own sister. And it should be more obvious when (1-1-9) she sends Ruth off to church that she's not only escaping a monitor's role she doesn't like, but also playing a trick on both Ruth and the old ladies.

In her scene with Armstrong, Mrs Gillis, when she speaks of Ruth (1-1-11 and 1-1-12) should show definitely that she's on the girl's side, thinks the girl's semi-delinquency a harmless, if sometimes annoying, part of her adolescence, and looks on the girl's mother as a dope for not being able to handle it better. (What I'm trying to get at is that she can't be so callous with Ruth, so friendly to Howard. The key to her attitude toward Howard in the first act at least must lie in her attitude toward the girl— whom he actually somewhat resembles—and not in her memory of Donald—whom he doesn't resemble at all. When she talks to Howard later about her son it should be as a model rather than as a lad who was like him.)

Mrs Gillis shouldn't talk to Armstrong about her son (1-1-13 to 1-1-15) except perhaps to mention him in passing. These speeches should be saved and addressed to Howard later. They are clumsy here and give the whole play a false slant, making the audience expect a boy-and-girl story. (If you hadn't told me the plot ahead of time I would've expected the son of a bitch to come back from the grave disguised as Howard!)

I'd like to know more about Armstrong: she talks too much about her own affairs and not enough about his. This trip is obviously an event— the argument over the room-rent shows he's never been away for any length of time before. Where is he going and why? What does he do for a living? There's too much unneeded exposition in the scene, not enough needed characterization. In spite of a reference to her "fussing over him" they seem no closer together than the ordinary hotel resident and the ordinary hotel proprietor.

I don't think he should laugh at the window: Howard's belief that he was laughed at should be pure fantasy. (That dog stuff is a lot of crap to me too, but I guess we won't go into that: there are probably a lot of theater-going old ladies who believe in Fido's instincts.)

I agree with you that after the dog talk following Howard's entrance, Mrs Gillis should take a well-let's-get-to-work line and I think his speech, "And it's not only dogs that dislike me ...people are the same..."(1-1-20) comes to[o] soon. Perhaps it should come in instead of his "Would you like me to go look for her?" (1-1-25). I think she should have mentioned Sarah's having been her son's dog (1-1-19) perhaps with something else about her son, consciously or unconsciously holding him up as the normal boy. Through the early part of this scene Howard should be asking questions, looking around, while Mrs. Gillis's mind is on the work they have to do. He should see the son's photo on the piano, and perhaps that's the spot to use her earlier speech to Armstrong about Donald.

In Scene 2 Mrs. Gillis should start to worry a little, but she's also genuinely interested in him. His similarity to Ruth is fairly pronounced throughout this scene, same chip on shoulder, same feeling the adult world is an enemy, same juvenile stubbornness. She tries to talk to him—she does this as it's now written—as she thinks the girl's mother should have talked to her. (I don't want to push you too far on this, but I'd have a photo of the girl on the piano and have her (Mrs. Gillis) mention her niece.)

Howard's army-rejection speeches (1-3-48 and later) read strong enough to me, but they didn't hit hard enough when I heard them the other night. They have got to hit hard, because the rejection has become his symbol for everything that's wrong with him and the world. I think somewhere along in here Mrs Gillis's desire to help him should become a little mechanical; even she can see she's getting nowhere and—whether she knows it or not—she'd be satisfied to quiet him down. When he gets to "and sometimes you're looking down at someone, etc..." he frightens her, but she makes herself believe he's talking the sort of nonsense-fantasy that the young often engage in (Ruth again) and goes back into her mechanical soothing act until he flies up again (1-3-53) when he starts talking about Armstrong. Genuine fear starts with her with the discovery the doors are locked.

Throughout Act II she should be a really frightened woman and, though she doesn't want to harm him or anyone else because she's never thought in terms of harming others for her own advantage, her desire to escape from this trap fills her mind to the exclusion of everything else. Her hysterical flare-up when she learns the dog has been killed is OK, though I think it was overdone the other night.

Getting Ruth on-stage and keeping Mrs Gillis quiet in the closet (2-2-13 and 2-2-14) seem to me too contrived in the present form. But suppose Mrs Gillis had told Howard a little about Ruth, that she was coming back among other things, and suppose he was curious about the girl, perhaps about the similarity Mrs Gillis had seen between him and her. (All right, so Howard's a budding homo! Don't even budding homos have moments of co-educational groping? Or haven't you ever been one?) So he wants her in. Mrs Gillis, pretty well beaten down by now, is ready to clutch at straws, but, in this set-up, Ruth seems like a pretty sturdy straw: Mrs Gillis likes the girl, thinks she's good stuff under the bobby-sox surface, easily convinces herself Ruth's the ideal person to handle Howard—essentially the same world, talks the same language, thinks along the same lines and so on. So she promises to be quiet and the girl comes in.

The first part of the scene between Ruth and Howard (2-2-14 to 2-2-17) could be lengthened, but needn't be essentially different in dialogue. The chief difference would be in its playing. She would be the wise-cracking drug store coquette, his manner would have less finality, more of that there groping, than his words. Her speech about doing a woman's work (bottom of 2-2-17) would be flattering in intent—you great big strong man—but would have the same result as in the present version and the rest of the scene between them would be pretty much as is. (I'm prejudiced, but I think this whole scene could be a honey.)

On 2-2-25 and 26, Howard should be trying to remember things, but Mrs Gillis should be trying to stop him from thinking back. Even she must have learned by now that that sort of thing only leads to more trouble for her: her only hope is to keep him placid until he wanders off...if he ever does. Her "Don't think about it now" (2-2-26) is the line she should stay with.

You said the knife was coming out, which is good.

Stevens's "That's strange...we've had several reports...maybe I'd better run back and check my books in the car." (2-3-48) is untelephone-manny and should read something like, "Those people are always getting their reports mixed up. I'll phone in and tell 'em plenty this time," and he should start towards the phone. Mrs. Gillis, who sees in anybody and especially in a man this big, her savior, should start to throw herself on his mercy—she can hardly be worrying too much about Howard's comfort at this stage—but Howard, who has seen it's either raining or snowing and is fussy about getting his clothes wet, says it's ten blocks, or whatever it is, to the car line and asks Stevens to drive him there. Stevens says, OK, jump in the car while I phone in, and Mrs Gillis takes him back to the phone. Howard, who is turning up his coat collar or something of the sort before dashing out to the curb, sees her whispering to Stevens as in present version and goes upstairs. Mrs Gillis tells Stevens Howard is nuts and Stevens quite reasonably disturbed wants to know what he's going to do with a homicidal maniac in his car. Mrs Gillis, hustling the telephone man to the door, says take him to the police station. By the time they reach the door Stevens can see, with due relief, that Howard's not in his car, not in sight on the street. Mrs Gillis hurriedly—she wants to get that door locked—tells Stevens to go tell the police: Howard can't be allowed to roam around. Stevens halfheartedly points out that the phone still needs fixing. She says he can come back after he's told the police, come back with the police, and hustles him out, slamming and locking the door after him.

Then she does her stuff and goes upstairs.

I think you're going to need that final scream.

> Yours,

TLU HRC

To Mary Hammett

12 January 1950, Beverly Wilshire, Beverly Hills, California

Dear Mary—

The way things look now—if we can adjust our contract—I'll stay out here for six or eight weeks and finish the picture in one more or less fell swoop—instead of coming back in a few months to do it.

I had dinner with your Mother, Jo and Loyd at Chasen's tonight. They all seem in blooming health and send you their love. Your Mother says most of her trouble with her teeth is over.

The weather's been lousy—cold and rainy—since I've been here but looks as if it might clear up now.

Tomorrow I start functioning—if that's what it is—at the studio. I've decided to try working there this time, but will most likely wind up working at home as usual.

Love—
Papa

ALS MARSHALL

To Jean Potter Chelnov

Hammett lent Potter money in Alaska, which she paid back over the next decade.

23 January 1950, Beverly Wilshire

Dear Jean,

Thanks for the checks, but I still wish you wouldn't get yourself so lathered up over that lousy debt. So you haven't written anything for three years. So what? So a lot of people skip a lot of years. There's always plenty of time: No one dies young anymore.

I've been out here a couple of weeks—and most likely will stay a couple of months longer—doing the movie script of Sidney Kingsley's play, *Detective Story*. It's pretty much a piece of cheese but I think maybe it'll work out all right. Anyhow I let myself be talked into putting aside my book—now entitled "December First"—and having a try at it.

If things work out good I'll be a grandfather in May. My younger daughter—back here now after a year in Hawaii—is pregnant. I've been looking forward to this a long time...kind of pantingly since she got married a year and a half ago.

Love,
Hammett

TLS MARSHALL

To Lillian Hellman

27 January 1950, Beverly Wilshire, Beverly Hills, California

Dear Lily,

It was nicenicenice hearing your voice on the phone this afternoon: it seemed weeks since we had talked. There's something unbecoming about our not being garrulous.

There isn't much news I didn't give you earlier today. The weather's been brisk and coolish, but kind of nice. Wednesday I took Jo to Santa Anita and didn't cash a bet, though it took a photo finish to beat me out in the sixth race, an eight-to-one shot that would have put me ahead. The *Compass* had a not-too-bad piece about anti-Semitism on the Sam Spade show: they had phoned me about it earlier in the week.[1] Hearst's INS wanted me to do a special feature story on the Boston million-and-a-half holdup.[2] The local *Mirror* wants to syndicate a Sam Spade comic strip. My clothes came, so I've got a little more of something to wear and you need no longer fear I won't be so well dressed as Billy Wilder. Jo is coming in to have lunch with me tomorrow: I don't go to the studio Saturdays. I'm going to the Gershwins for dinner Sunday. I've talked to Lee twice—once when I ran into her by chance and again when she phoned today—and she hasn't yet mentioned your name: I'm waiting her out. Other things are possibly happening, but nobody tells me about them.

Willie's still scraping around on the bottom of the barrel for a Hurstwood.[3] Gary Cooper says he wants to do it. Charles Boyer would, but his accent's a toughie, would turn it into the fall of a su[p]erior sort of head waiter. The gimmick seems to be that Willie's got to have a big name in there or the studio will insist on cutting his budget in half...a fate worse than death.

I'm staying in and eating dinner here tonight and it's about time I started doing it.

> I love you very much, Lilipie ...
> Dash

---

1. *The Daily Compass* was a short-lived leftist newspaper that succeeded *PM*.
2. On 17 January 1950 a group of armed masked men robbed Brinks, stealing $1.218

million in cash and $1.557 million in securities. The crime became known as the "Fabulous Brinks Robbery."

3. Hurstwood is a main character in Theodore Dreiser's *Sister Carrie*. Laurence Olivier played the part in the movie *Carrie* (1952), with Jennifer Jones in the title role.

TLS HRC

To Lillian Hellman

31 January 1950, Paramount Pictures, Hollywood, California

Dear Lilishka,

Here's the television layout, which you'll find quite simple if you don't rattle yourself by starting out with the notion you're not going to understand it. The chief things to remember are that you start off A, B, C, D in simple order, and that a little turning of a knob or ring usually goes a long way.

Sister Carrie looks like a very dead pigeon at the moment and Willie's starting to worry about getting going on *Detective Story;* so I staid home today to see if I can start knocking it out in big chunks. So far, no, but presently, of course.

I had a pleasant if unexciting evening at the Gershwins. Irwing was there, still saying fortuitous when he means fortunate: he sent his regards or love or something to you. The How'd Benedicts and her mother were there; Howard was tight and amusing.[1] He looks old. The Dick Brooks—he is directing his first picture, with Cary Grant—and I guess that's all.[2] Ira looks no older than ever and seems positively lively. Lee spoiled our game by asking right off if you'd got back from New Orleans yet.

Last night I took Pat Neal to dinner and had a nice enough time.[3] We made a tentative date for dinner with Jean Hagen and her husband later in the week.[4] Jean's working in a Lana Turner picture. Pat's an awfully pretty girl if you don't look at her hands and feet and can ignore that incredible carriage. She's very much the earnest future star at the moment and thus not too entirely fascinating if you don't think her career the most important thing in the world. She's studying under somebody and says she's now a hundred per cent better as an actress than before; claims she's learned nothing from the movies and is a bit proud of the fact that she's difficult to direct and won't do as told unless she agrees with the director; asked if I thought she ought to go back to the stage for one play if she found the right one (I said yes); all of which was less dull than I'm probably making it sound, but wasn't too all-fired exciting either. She sent her love to you and seemed genuinely glad you weren't mad with her.

I'm phoning you later tonight and so shall most likely tell you everything I've written here. That's the way things go. Now I'm going to have dinner sent up.

> Much love, honey, and I miss you …
> Dash

1. Howard Benedict was a producer of the Sherlock Holmes movies for Universal, among other projects.
2. Richard Brooks directed and wrote the screenplay for *Crisis* (1950), starring Cary Grant.
3. The actress Patricia Neal was a special friend of Hammett's. On Broadway she played in Hellman's *Another Part of the Forest* and the 1952 revival of *The Children's Hour*.
4. Jean Hagen, who had played on Broadway in *Another Part of the Forest*, was married to the actor Tom Seidel.

TLS HRC

To Lillian Hellman

2 February 1950, Paramount Pictures, Hollywood, California

Dear Lilishka,

It's much warmer out today—so a hand put out the window tells me—and I miss you. I'm still sticking indoors trying to toil with indifferent results. There must be some way of writing less dully than I'm doing: I guess there is, but the result would probably be poetry and not a movie script. Anyhow I miss you. I've been kind of jittery about the script for the past couple of days, but I wouldn't be surprised if that was a good sign. It's no doubt all wrongheadedness and delusion to think what you're doing is pretty good; the only trouble is I'm not doing enough, good or bad. I think Willy—whom I haven't seen this week—is more worried about it than I am, and he hasn't even seen any of this dullness I'm putting down on Paramount's paper. And I miss you.

Tonight I pursue my butterfly career by going over to Pat's for dinner. Jean and Tom and another couple whom Pat says I know but whom I don't of course remember are to be there and Pat's to broil steaks, she says. It may turn out good or it may turn out bad but in either case I shall miss you.

Last night I had dinner with my family, which was pleasant enough and I got away early. Jo's still in fine shape and is very busy just now picking out furniture and refrigerators and the like for the new house, which they hope to move into this month. I haven't heard from Mary for a couple of weeks—I imagine she's sulking again, God, as usual, presumably knowing why—but Muriel had lunch with her last week and didn't report anything bad, so I take for granted everything's what we carelessly call all right.[1] Of course I miss you.

Now I reckon I ought to try to get in a few licks on this here script before I start duding up for the evening. Maybe if I had some coffee sent up ...

> I love you and miss you, cutie ...
> Dash

1. Muriel Alexander was Hammett's secretary in New York.

TLS HRC

To Lillian Hellman

12 February 1950, Beverly Wilshire, Beverly Hills, California

Dear Lilishka,

If I didn't say anything I should've this morning it's probably because I'd read till eight o'clock and was kind of foggy about what was going on at ten-thirty when you phoned. All I remember is it was nice as usual talking to you.

* * *

I had a long and customarily unreal letter from Mary telling me she had just got over an attack of jaundice, had been firmly put on the wagon by Doctor Teicher, had lost ten pounds (she's always losing ten pounds, just as my Father always had just succeeded in getting his weight down to 130 again) and so on...Maggie Phillips is coming out for a part in the picture Jean's doing, a Lana Turner dingus called *A Life Of Her Own* or some such, which J says is a stinkeroo...I've just finished reading an elegant novel, which you wouldn't like, called *The Horse's Mouth,* and another not bad one called *The Vintage*[1]... Now let's see what comes of a projected movie script of a play called *Cops and Robbers* or something by a writer named Sydenham Kinsey or something...I love and miss you, cutie ...

Much love,
SDH

1. *The Horse's Mouth* by Joyce Cary; *The Vintage* by Anthony West.

TLS HRC

To Lillian Hellman

14 February 1950, Beverly Wilshire, Beverly Hills, California

Dearest Lillest,

I just got in to find a very nice telegram and a very nice letter from very nice you. It's very nice out too, warm and balmy, but not as nice as you, nor as warm and balmy. And stop getting headaches and sick stomachs; if FDR could deal with Henry without getting things like those so can you and if you don't choose to then you'll simply have to stop playing around with that Iowa yogi and his fringe of impracticals.

I went to lunch with a couple of agency-folk—talk of a future Hitchcock picture with a piece of the take—saw Charlie Bracket[t] and Louis Shur[1]—though not together—started over to Maggie's and was yelled at by Cathy in a car with Arthur's sister on her way to a doctor and ice skating, stopped to talk to her for a few minutes and found her as delightful as ever, went on over to Maggie's and had as lovely a time as I had yesterday, which was very lovely indeed. So I'm going back tomorrow. Maggie was young and gay and full of talk about practically everything.

For some reason I got very hungry and stopped this to eat what now seems to me a great many pork chops and salads and custard pies. Full of food, I'm now trying to think up reasons for going light on my labors tonight and getting myself early into bed with a book or two. I'm now reading something by a Frenchman called *Special Friendships,* which isn't too bad in its way and have just finished Munro's *The Gift of Glory,* which I kind of liked: it's about Eugene O'Neil[l] as a playwright but not, I hope, as a man. Not too deep, but readable...or maybe I'm getting mellower...it seems to me I've liked several books lately.

Now I'll play tricks on my conscience by working just a little before I pretend I'm too sleepy to do anything but read till six in the morning or so.

Much love, cutie: I miss you but am not going to miss you any longer than I have to.

Dash

1. Charles Brackett was a screenwriter for Paramount in 1950, the year he collaborated with Billy Wilder on the screenplay for *Sunset Boulevard.* Louis Shur is unidentified.
2. *Special Friendships* by Roger Peyrefitte.

TLS HRC

To Mary Hammett

22 February 1950, Beverly Wilshire, Beverly Hills, California

Dear Mary,

Thanks for the Valentine candy; it arrived late but was good enough to make up for that and I'm still nibbling on it.

* * *

There's some talk of my doing a picture for Hitchcock to direct, either later this year or next, but as of right now I don't think I'm going to be interested in tying myself up to it. Movies, I think, ought to be written by people who like seeing movies; I try not to feel as if I were slumming but that's about what it amounts to. There are a great many people who like to write nonsense and I think it's wrong for other people to butt into their field, especially since these other people aren't likely to do as good a job at it as the others.

I'm still having a very pleasant time here; somehow it seems as if I were on vacation, though God knows what from. Maybe from the world.

Much love, toots …
Papa

TLS Marshall

To Josephine Hammett Marshall

This is Hammett's first letter to Josephine after the birth of her daughter Ann on 24 May 1950.

22 June 1950, 28 West 10th St., New York City

Dear Jo,

The first two pictures of the baby (there ought to be a lot more waiting for me up in the country: I've been in town since Tuesday) were very fine, especially the scowling one. She looks exactly like Loyd, though I can't remember having seen [him] scowl like that, but she must have got that expression somewhere …

Tonight I wound up my summer stint at the school and am now a free man till fall, which means nothing much except that I won't have to come into town that one day a week unless I want to.

Mary was in for a couple of hours a couple of days ago and seemed in pretty good shape. I think she's due to arrive in your part of the world around the third of the month. I saw Teicher this afternoon and he seemed a little more optimistic—if not too cheerful—about her than the last time I saw him. Mostly, however, we talked about a book he's writing. What else do people ever talk about? It's on child psychology—or something of the sort—of course.[1]

I fixed up that account at the Beverly Hills Saks Fifth Avenue, so you can feel free any time to walk in and buy out the store. They'll gladly charge it to me.

* * *

That item you saw in the paper about Olivier in Willy Wyler's *Sister Carrie* seems to have been right, though I don't think he's definitely decided on the girl yet. He seems to be full of idiotic ideas about bringing the background up to date, making Carrie more important, and so on. I had dinner with the writers the other night: they're in a dither with visions of being asked to change the book to a Betty Grable musical. I advised them to be firm with Willy: what have I got to lose?

This electric typewriter is making what sound like hissing noises. It must be hissing just on principle: I can't believe it's able to read what I'm writing.

My love to ANN and Loyd and you of course, honey. I had a wonderful time with you all.

> Love ...
> Pop

1. *Your Child and His Problems: A Basic Guide for Parents*, by Joseph D. Teicher, M.D. (Boston: Little, Brown, 1953)

TLS Marshall

To Josephine Hammett Marshall

27 June 1950, Hardscrabble Farm, Pleasantville, New York

Dear Jo,

* * *

Korea's the big news just now, which makes conversation pretty tough, since nobody seems to know what happened or is happening. I'm old enough to be pretty placid about the whole thing: it's not difficult for me to be placid about unpleasant things happening to Dr. Rhee's government: he's a stinker even among Koreans and generally speaking I've never been able to consider them God's masterpieces. The truth is, I suppose, I'm not too appalled by the thoughts of a possible World War III. We've had two of those World War things and both were silly and wicked, but not much more silly and wicked than most large-scale things we tackle in our present childish state. The way we live, I dare say war can be considered as normal as peace.

There's nothing like that kind of deep thinking to rest up your back and legs: now I feel able to face that walk to the pond.

My love to everybody, and keep those photos coming, honey.

> Love ...
> Pop

TLS Marshall

To Josephine Hammett Marshall

20 July 1950, Hardscrabble Farm, Pleasantville, New York

Dear Jo,

It's kind of late at night and I'm kind of tired from not doing much of anything all day except a couple of hours of fishing that didn't inconvenience anybody except a couple of medium-sized pickerel that got themselves attached to a hook, pulled to a boat, freed from the hook and tossed back into a pond.

Yesterday I went into the big city and spent most of the afternoon wrangling over terms in contracts for the outright sale of a couple of radio programs. The current "red scare" has the radio industry all upset or something and for months both the *Spade* and the *Fat Man* programs have been teetering on a very slack wire. At the moment we're going through another crisis and it may be I can save something out of possible ruin by selling them lock, stock and barrel. The chief thing standing in the way seems to be my greediness, or—as I look at it—my reluctance to let myself be scared into taking any price I can get.

Also while in town I went around to show my left foot to my doctor. It started cutting up on me a couple of weeks ago. We vaguely decided an arch or something was to blame and I ought to stop running around in flat-soled moc[c]asins, no-heeled sneakers, bare feet and the like. We were much more definite about his troubles, which come from overwork. A week's vacation in California did not do him much good: I think he wants me to p[re]scribe a month in Europe for him, but I may give him up and start treating only healthy doctors, if there are any.

Today I took my nose out of theoretical physics and started Stendhal's *The Green Huntsman,* which I'm enjoying. I like Stendhal's way of being a novelist, whatever that means.

Want to prop Ann's eyes open for at least one picture?

> Much love to all ....
> Pop

TLS MARSHALL

To Mary Hammett

30 July 1950, Hardscrabble Farm, Pleasantville, N.Y.

Dear Mary,

The weather's been fine, hot and sunny and I've been—as usual—going into the city as seldom as possible, which always turns out to be too often anyway. I'll have to go in once this week and then hope not to see it again till I get back from Martha's Vineyard around the middle of September. The present plan is to leave here Friday morning, stop over night in Stonington, and get to the island on the afternoon of the 5th. The address will be the same as last year: "c/o Webster, Chilmark, Martha's Vineyard, Mass."

My radio programs are still all in a hubbabubba and I don't know any more about how they stand—or how they'll come out—than anybody else. At the moment it looks as if I'll be off the air completely by September, but it could work out differently. Outside of the money involved, which is nice to have, I don't care too much. Maybe I'll know something more definite later in the week, or later in the month, or later in the year.

Muriel is off on her vacation, but will be back on the 14th, I think.

I've had a nice weekend all by myself without servants or anybody except dogs, and a fish or two, though I still don't go fishing as much as I used to. I guess I'm beginning to look on it as an old man's sport.

Now I've got to go cook myself some dinner, mostly lamb chops and coffee, I reckon, and I think there's a piece of watermelon in the icebox.

Give my best to Doctor T. when you see him. And my love to your Mother.

> Love ...
> Papa

TLS Marshall

To Josephine Hammett Marshall

9 September 1950, Martha's Vineyard

Dear Princess,

The weather's changed from good to better lately and that's about all the prodding we needed to start making ferry reservations for later dates. We've still got the one for Tuesday the 12th, but now also one for Wednesday the 13th and if tomorrow dawns pretty there's no telling what'll happen in re the 14th, 15th, 16th, et al. There's no reason why this shouldn't be a nice place to spend Christmas, though I guess we've got to go back sometime ...

In the great outer world, I understand from occasional peeps into the New York newspapers and some e[a]vesdropping on the radio, there's some to-do over what we're doing to the Soviet Union and what they're doing to us and I gather there's some sort of wrangling going on some-where on the Asiatic Coast, and I reckon I will be somehow affected by these things when I get back to the mainland, but meanwhile it's easier to concern ourselves with such more intimate matters as the complete shortage of local lobsters and the promised coming to this—the Gay Head—end of the island of electricity this fall and the new road west from Lobsterville. Also the Vineyard Haven Laundry's driver quit and the dirty linen wasn't picked up Friday. I tell you, it wasn't like this when I was young: the world's going to hell: some people claim radio and movies are responsible, but I think it started with the invention of the wheel. If man had been meant to revolve he wouldn't have been born with flat feet.

Lillian's finished the second act of her new play and it reads awfully good.[1] I haven't finished the first chapter of my new book and so it doesn't read at all. I sometimes feel it's hardly worth while having books if you have to write them. (Actually, in my torpid way, I'm kind of high on the book: it's a monstrously good conception, if only I don't bitch it up more than eighty per cent.)

I'm very sunburned so I must be very well. The fact that most of the dead and dying on Okinawa were quite sunburned did nothing to unlink sunburn and health in the popular mind and I am far too cowardly to go against the popular mind. I am very well. I don't wish to listen to any suggestions that I am not.

* * *

That, I think, takes care of what news there is.

Love to all, honey …
Pop

1. Hellman was working on *The Autumn Garden*.

TLS Marshall

To Josephine Dolan Hammett

28 September 1950, Pleasantville

Dear Jose,

Earlier in the week I was in town and saw Mary, who seemed to be in pretty good shape, though she said she hadn't been sleeping very well. I'll probably see her doctor when I go in next week: we're about due for our more or less semi-annual conference.

Don't go to too much trouble to look it up, but if you have the address of Carrol[l] John Daly will you send it to me?[1]

* * *

The new novel I'm working on goes along slowly, but fairly satisfactorily, I think. I'm having a good time with it; it's not at all like anything I've done before.

* * *

Now I'm off to bed with every intention of getting up and out at 5:30 in the morning…but I had the same intentions this morning and went back to sleep till nearly 9:00. Well, we'll see …

Love,
SDH

1. Carroll John Daly was a detective fiction writer who, like Hammett, began writing for *Black Mask* magazine in 1922. His *The Snarl of the Beast* (1927) is credited as the first hard-boiled detective novel.

TLS MARSHALL

To Josephine Hammett Marshall

19 November 1950, Pleasantville, New York

Dear Princess,

* * *

The fortunes of war in my hassle with the anti-red radio forces seem to have swung a little in my direction at the moment—NBC has put *Spade* back on as a sustaining show—but it's too soon to know what the final outcome—if there ever is one—will be. It'll be nice if I don't have to go to work for a living, but meanwhile I'm taking no chances and am working—if more intermittently than I should—on that there new and outstanding novel.

There's nothing definite to say about Mary yet, so perhaps it would be just as well if you didn't say anything at all to your Mother. Mary had some sort of convulsions—seemingly non-alcoholic in origin—and spent a week in the hospital being checked up on. The medical men don't altogether agree on what happened or on what's the best thing to do about what happened, and the chances are she'll have to take some more tests. (I don't think she knows about this.) None of this seems too immediately serious. The chief thing to decide at the moment will be whether she's most in need of physical or psychical treatment, or both; and I don't want to make any unnecessarily silly decisions. So I'm listening to the experts, hoping I won't do what practically everybody always does in such cases—take the opinion of whichever expert comes closest to my own. I hope to know more about this—I can hardly know less—later in the week and will let you know. Meanwhile, this information—such as it is—is only for the occupants of 6521 West 87th Place, and I don't altogether trust that kitten either.

The virtually final version of Lillian's first act is kind of wonderful; she's now having at Act II. She and a few others think I ought to direct it and, while I construe that sort of thing as "popular demand," I don't feel too sure that I should start a new career till I'm in my sixties and I'm three years away from that.

> Love to all, honey …
> Pop

TLS MARSHALL

To Josephine Hammett Marshall

4 December 1950, Hardscrabble Farm, Pleasantville, New York

Dear Princess,

This morning it rains much rain and blows much wind, but not on the grand scale of a week ago so—except for such cheap advantage as it can take of things crippled by the earlier gale—it isn't likely to do much damage. The tree expert who looked the place over last week turned in an estimate of somewhere between $30,000 and $40,000 to restore things to prestorm shape. I imagine that includes replacing the original platinum on birches and the aquamarines that no doubt give blue spruces their blueness. The birds seem to like trees being down: it gives them more thickets to fool around in or whatever it is they do in thickets.

My final—for the moment—medical consultation on Mary should take place later this week (I don't actually believe it will, but that's what I've been promised) and then maybe I'll have some idea of where we stand, or at least what we do next. I had dinner with her Wednesday night and she seemed well enough, whatever that means. I'll probably see her again this Wednesday. There isn't anything for anybody to worry about: it's just because she *isn't* so badly off that all this fuss is necessary. If she were sicker things would be clearer.

At this time my best guess on when I'll make that trip to California is between the fifteenth of December and Christmas, though I won't be able to stay for Christmas Day. And I don't too much know what's what.

Last month I had a sort of omnibus published in England—five novels and four short stories — and the London *Times Literary Supplement* gave it a very nice full-page review.[1] (Oh, all right, there *were* some ads on the page, but don't let's quibble: I choose to think of it as a full page.) *The Times* is awfully stuffy and pompous, of course, but I guess it's still the most influent[ia]l publication in the world, so...It makes me out quite a fellow in a writing way...and this is a time in history when I can stand being made out quite a fellow. If I can get hold of an extra copy I'll send it to you because I do not wish you to go through life not thinking I'm quite a fellow, and there is Ann, too, who must be taught to think the same thing without any foolish juvenile notions of her own.

Ann in her pictures gets lovelier and lovelier. Lillian, who keeps some of the snapshots on her bedside table and has a tendency to bore me now and then with talk about them, is afraid the baby can't be as pretty as her pictures though I've explained that the photos are absolutely unretouched except for painting out the hare lip and other little things that a mother would naturally do. Lillian thinks it's practically criminal of you not to bring the child East at some early date for a long visit here on Hardscrabble Farm.

The Times said, "Mr. Hammett has not published a novel for more than 16 years, and it is to be hoped that he will soon complete the major work on which he is rumored to be engaged," so I reckon I'd better [page torn] engaged. Love to everybody, Honey ...

Pop

1. *The Dashiell Hammett Omnibus* (London: Cassell, 1950) was reviewed in "A Man Called Hammett," *Times Literary Supplement*, 17 November 1950, p. 728.

TLS MARSHALL

To Josephine Hammett Marshall

11 December 1950, Pleasantville, New York

Dear Jo,

The check's for Christmas. I decided in my elderly wrong-headedness that I ought to give you and Loyd a television set this year. (Now wait a minute; the descent from radio to television is certainly not as great as from bridge to canasta!) Anyhow, that's what I decided. The kind of set you all are to pick out is up to you, though I'd suggest you get one with a large screen—the little ones are nuisances—and my more or less irrelevant advice is to get a RCA Victor set, not that it's better than some of the others but RCA repair service seems better than any other and repair service is by far the most important item in television owning, as you'll find out. You can buy some kind of yearly service guarantee with the RCA and they seem to back it up pretty well. I don't know what the price—including installation and the all-essential service guarantee—will be, of course, so I haven't filled in the amount. My guess would be that the set you should have would run over $500 but probably, I hope, not over $1000, so you have a free hand in that range. (If this whole idea is too repulsive to you and you'd rather use the money for something else I'll no doubt be willing to listen.)

* * *

I sent you—for Ann—a few toys from Schwarz's, including the only one I had any real interest in, a large doll; and I guess I was chiefly interested in that because I've always though[t] every little girl should at some time have a doll larger than she is and, naturally, it's a lot easier to do that to her before she's grown too much. I'm going to get her some more toys, but also, from me to her and your only part is to go pick them out, I'd like you to raid that baby department at Saks 5th Avenue for me: let's really deck her out! (If you don't do well by her I shall tell her you gypped her as soon as she's old enough to understand and she'll always hold that—along with the other things children pick up along the way—against you: children like to hold things against their parents.)

Ann in her photographs is getting kind of monotonously lovely: I've just been gloating over the two teeth with a magnifying glass, through which, of course, they look larger.

* * *

Now I've got to slide down to the pond to see if perhaps a duck or two may have come in under the mistaken impression that somebody was showing a movie there this afternoon.

Much love to everybody, toots ....
Pops

TLS Marshall

1951

To Josephine Hammett Marshall

11 January 1951, Pleasantville, New York

Dear Princess,

* * *

We finished the last—and I think practically final—revision of Lily's play yesterday afternoon and I came on up here, where I hope I'll be allowed to stay till I have to go in for the new school term next week. The play reads pretty doggone swell, though you never really know till you see actors act it out. It hasn't a title yet. At the moment *Some of Us*—my suggestion—looks most likely. And it isn't cast yet, though I think it's been decided to use Freddy March and Florence Eldridge if their present show—*An Enemy of the People*—closes within the next two or three weeks.[1] *An Enemy of the People* has been losing money right along, but it's always anybody's guess how long the management of any flop will try to drag along hoping for miracles. Anyhow the present plan is to take LH's show to Philadelphia for a ten-day or two-week tryout in time to open in New York on March 7th. God be with us.

* * *

I love you, toots, and send my love to those people you're closely related to by marriage …

Pop

1. Fredric March and his wife Florence Eldridge starred in Hellman's *The Autumn Garden*, directed by Harold Clurman. The play opened at the Coronet Theatre on Broadway on 7 March 1951 and ran for 101 performances.

TLS Marshall

To Josephine Hammett Marshall

2 February 1951, Pleasantville, New York

Dear Jo,

This afternoon I escaped a mild conspiracy to have me stay in town to see Williams' *The Rose Tattoo* open tomorrow night and got back here

549

where I belong. Nine full twenty-four-hour-long days I spent in that damned city! Why, I even went places to dinner, I went to a night club, I went—of all things—to the theater, to see Odets' *The Country Girl,* an empty and dull collection of clichés.[1]

Lillian's play is now in its second week of rehearsal and, I'm told, coming along all right. I listened to actors read their parts the first day but haven't been back since. I'll probably start haunting the place late next week when they get further along; the early days of puttering gestures and tentative movements can be pretty dull. Freddie March—who loves every line of the play, especially those lines dealing with Florence Eldridge, who plays the part of a foolish woman whose husband (Colin Keith-Johnson) is tired of her—should be mildly terrific in it.

* * *

I've been gotten hold of by a young composer named Kubik—Prix de Rome and all that kind of stuff—who wants me to do a melodramatic opera with him.[2] I may do it if I find out that he's any good as a composer. I've got my spies working on him now.

There's a prize fight that I ought to be looking at on the television set—Durando vs Green—so …

Love to all, honey, and much, much love to you …
Pop

1. Odets's *The Country Girl* was at the Lyceum in Manhattan, where it ran for 235 performances.
2. Gail Kubik (1914–1984), a prolific, Pulitzer Prize–winning composer of concert music and movie scores, was music director of the film division of the OWI during World War II.

TLS Marshall

To Josephine Hammett Marshall

Hammett was under intense FBI scrutiny at this time. His 278-page FBI file, which began in 1934, indicates that agents shadowed Hammett with some difficulty and on at least one occasion broke into his and Hellman's house at Hardscrabble Farm in search of incriminating evidence.

9 February 1951, 28 West 10th St., New York City

Dear Toots,

* * *

Last weekend burglars broke into this apartment—I was in Pleasantville, as all sensible people are whenever possible—and carried off
three watches and a forty-pound strong-box, which they broke open in
somebody's backyard three or four houses down the street from mine.
There was nothing in the strong-box—naturally: who puts stuff in
strong-boxes?—except some papers that hadn't seemed important
enough to put in the files. I'm not even sure the box was locked. Clowns!

* * *

I'm going back to P'ville tonight and come in the first of the week to
take up rehearsal-going in earnest. I saw half of the first act last night
and it looked all right for this stage, but it's pretty hard to form any opinion of how things are going till they start running all the way through the
play; they should be doing that by the first part of the week.

> Love to all and much to you …
> Pop

TLS MARSHALL

To Maggie Kober

Sunday, 18 February 1951, 28 West 10th St., New York City

Dear Maggie dear,

I've just come from putting Madame aboard a train for Philadelphia,
where her opera—God and several other people willing—will open
Wednesday night. I'm going down tomorrow afternoon.

The play looks wonderful, but all of the acting still needs a lot of work
and some of it needs a great deal. It's not so much a matter of things
being done badly as of being done mechanically, as if nobody knew very
well what sort of character he was supposed to be. Barker is good as Carrie Ellis and Florence Eldridge—while not always everything anybody
could ask in the Rose Griggs part—really works at it and is going to be
theatrically successful. The rest of the cast, thus far, tapers down from

there to Carol Goodner, who says her lines as if she were reading them for the first time from the script. There's no reason to suppose everything won't be find and dandy for the New York opening on March 7, but things don't look too hot for the Philadelphia opening. I suspect that Clurman likes to do the bulk of his direction in front of audiences and rather likes the role of the director who opens out of town with a shambles that he whips into shape for the big city. I'm more of Madame's opinion, that when you take people's money—even if on the road—you ought to try to give them something for it. Well, we'll see. It's always possible to postpone the Philadelphia opening...and Madame thinks—as she's thought right along—that it's in worse shape than I do. But it's a good play, honey.

What you should do about Cathy's wanting a collie seems simple enough: let her pick out one and buy it for her. She ought to be kind of nice with a dog: she's got the kind of bossiness that most dogs like: by nature most of them are leaners.

There doesn't seem to be much local news. Madame's Pleasantville farmer is in the hospital with pneumonia. I found that three watches vanished with that stolen strong-box. Last week I hope I finished giving my deposition in that idiotic Warner Brothers suit. Washington's Birthday gives me an off-night from my teaching chores this week, so I won't have to hurry back from Philadelphia unless—as I probably will—I want to hurry back. I guess that's the crop.

> Much love, darling ...
> Dash

TLS HRC

To Josephine Hammett Marshall

24 February 1951, Pleasantville, New York

Dear Jo,

There were a couple of letters from you—and that Valentine—with nice snapshots of the baby waiting for me when I got back here from

Philadelphia last night for what I like to think of as a well-earned rest. I'm going back there tomorrow afternoon, probably to stay till Thursday.

Lillian's play looks pretty good, though there's a lot of work still to be done on it, chiefly in the way of getting actors in shape. You nearly always have to change characters a little to fit the abilities or hamminesses of those sterling folk (lice, all of 'em, male and female) but you hate like hell to make any changes that will affect the play as a whole, so ...

All the Philadelphia reviews were good and attendance has been a lot better than expected, though nobody's expectations were too modest. I saw the show when it opened Wednesday night and again Thursday. The performances as a whole were fairly good, though Kent Smith—who's turning out to be the sex-appeal boy, at least for Philadelphia—is making a loveable character out of what was meant only to be a kind of pleasant inoffensive drunk; Joan Stanley, as a young European who wants to get to hell back home, is hopelessly cute; and Colin Keith-Johnson, who's sup-posed to be a gruff, quiet, strong—at least strong in comparison with the others—man is rabbitty. Freddy March was pretty good; Florence Eldridge was quite good, if a little hammy; Ethel Griffies is at least better than she was in rehearsals; Margaret Barker has been all right through-out; and so it goes. If something can be done with Keith-Johnson—and I think it can—we'll be all right, though I wouldn't mind having Joan Stan-ley replaced, though the only young actress—she has to look seventeen or eighteen at the most—I can think of for the part is well-cast in a hit...Julie Harris in *The Member Of the Wedding*. Oh, well ...

I think the play's due to be a hit—when we get to New York, I mean: nobody in the theater ever actually pays any attention to other cities—but not a smash hit. Audience reactions will most likely be the same as in Philadelphia: they'll like it while it's going on but be left wondering what it was all about when the final curtain comes down. It's a good play, though—easily Lillian's best and—what's more important—points at better ones to come...if she'll keep her nose to the grindstone.

I'll send you a copy of the play when Little, Brown publishes it, which should be shortly. They got the corrected proofs Friday and seem in a hurry to bring it out.

There doesn't seem to be anything in this letter but the play, but I guess that's about all there is in me at the moment. Don't think that means I've given up liking to talk about myself; it just means other things are pushing my affairs aside for what I hope is a very brief interlude. Then I can get back to my favorite topic.

> Meanwhile, love to all, and much love to you ...
> Pop

TLS Marshall

To Josephine Hammett Marshall

11 March 1951, Pleasantville, New York

Dear Jo,

Well, we got *The Autumn Garden* launched Wednesday night— though for a couple of days it didn't look as if we'd make it—to fairly good mixed reviews—as good, I guess, as any Hellman's ever had with the exception of *Watch On the Rhine*—and now it's almost entirely up to God or whoever it is that is responsible for the theater. Business is pretty good, but it's too early to say how it's going to be in the weeks to come. Ordinarily there'd be nothing to worry about, but summer—when business usually drops off—isn't very far away and—more important—the play's loaded with high-priced actors: a box-office take that'd be fine and dandy for most shows won't be enough to meet the payroll on this one. We can't drop much below $20,000 a week without running into trouble and I guess that's a lot of money. (I have, I'm glad to say, no investment in this piece and my share—small though it is—comes out of the take and isn't dependent on profits.)

The company—who'd turned in such lousy performances just before the opening that we were seriously thinking of dropping them and the director and starting all over in the fall—perked up on the big night and turned in a pretty good job, though still far from what it should have been. Audiences thus far seem to enjoy the show, but go away—as was expected—wondering what the hell it was all about. (If they were told most of them wouldn't like it, so I suppose it's just as well to leave them dangling, but just the same it's kind of an unsatisfactory state of affairs.)

Ann's latest snapshot was wonderful, as usual, and—wolf! wolf!

wolf!—I hope to be out to take a gander at her in person very soon. Tentatively, again, I hope to leave here on the night of the 29th—or sometime the 30th at the latest—for a couple of weeks in your California.

Mary came in for a couple of hours last week—the first I'd seen of her in some time—and seemed in pretty good shape. I didn't ask—and don't exactly know—what her homecoming plans are at the moment.

Spring's been peeping around the corner for the past week, but the last couple of days have been coldish, though bright and sunny, so I don't know what's going to happen. Snow birds—juncos—are still with us. They usually head for the north again as soon as snow gets off the ground for good, but I'm not silly enough to base any expectations on birds: the dopes are always heading north or south, as the case may be, on false alarms. People make mistakes, but they don't make nearly so many as birdies and beasties.

Now I've got to take a quick run through a book—*The Eyes of Reason*—that in a moment of weakness I promised to review.[1]

> Love to all, and much to you, honey …
> Pop

1. No review by Hammett of Stefan Heym's *The Eyes of Reason* has been located.

TLS Marshall

To Maggie Kober

11 March 1951, Pleasantville, New York

Dear Maggie dear,

* * *

Madame and I came up here yesterday. She goes back to town in the morning; I hope to stay till I have to go in for my regular Thursday chores. She's upstairs now with a heating-pad against her back: she fell on the cellar steps this afternoon but I don't think did herself much damage.

I saw Arthur opening night, but only to say hello to so I can't report much except that he seemed to be alive and seemed to be breathing and there was—as well as I can remember—no noticeable chill on his flesh when I shook hands with him.

* * *

I've got a stack of work I'm supposed to do tonight, like writing a review of Heym's *Eyes of Reason* for the Liberty Book Club and an opinion of a Warner Brothers' affidavit for my lawyer and a letter of criticism to a former pupil and such like, but I'm not a fellow who feels like tackling a stack of work tonight and I'm sure if I put my mind to it I can easily think up half a dozen good and sound reasons why I shouldn't, so ...

* * *

As I thought, I've already thought up some at least good enough reasons for not tackling work tonight, so I'd better sneak off to bed with a book while they still seem good enough to me.

> Much love, honey, and see you soon ...
> Dash

TLS HRC

To Josephine Hammett Marshall

19 March 1951, Pleasantville, New York

Dear Jo,

For some reason—chiefly, I suppose, because I can't ever actually learn from experience—I really believe I'll be in Los Angeles on the morning of the thirtieth. It seems almost like tomorrow...I'd hoped to be able to stay in California a little longer this time, but I'm afraid that's no soap: I've got to be back before the twelfth of April.

The Autumn Garden wobbled a little last week, but looks as if it were going to pick up now. Most of the weekly reviews—*Time, New Yorker, Cue,* etc.—gave it a fair break and some of the daily reviewers who didn't like it too much have mended their ways in later stories—I don't think it was as much a matter of their changing their minds as it was of thinking that maybe as time went on the play was going to be considered a good one and they might be thought dopes for panning it—and so we seem to have a pretty good chance of lasting awhile. The real test, however, won't come till summer opens.

* * *

Kefauver's Senate Crime Investigating Committee has given television a much-needed reason for existing back here.[1] The hearings seem to be the hottest things the medium has had since the early days of Howdy Doody. Actually they are not too bad to watch, but what this sort of audience response is doing to any sort of justice that might be involved is another story. Former Mayor O'Dwyer was on the screen most of today and, since I've always been prejudiced against him, his spitting image and very-own words only deepened my prejudice.[2] I dare say those lookers and listeners who started out with a bias in his favor had *that* confirmed.

Now I've got to go look at some prize fights on television, where I'm not prejudiced in favor of anybody—only against whoever is the announcer.

* * *

There's a book I ought to read before going to bed tonight, so if I can find it under a bed or wherever it is I guess I'd better get at it.

Love to all, toots …
Pop

1. Tennessee Senator Estes Kefauver headed a Senate committee to investigate organized crime, specifically to determine whether organized criminals used interstate-commerce facilities to circumvent federal law; the manner and extent of organized crime; and whether organized crime was spreading. Hearings were held in fourteen cities. Those in New York City were televised.
2. William O'Dwyer was mayor of New York from 1945 to 1950. He was forced to resign because of accusations of involvement in organized crime.

TLS Marshall

To Josephine Dolan Hammett

20 March 1951, Pleasantville

Dear Jose,
    Spring kind of looks like it's here these past few weeks, with buds and birds popping out hither and thither and one thing and another.
    Mary—as you probably know, because I suppose she has written you—

is due to leave New York Saturday night, which should put her home Sunday morning. I talked to her on the phone this morning and she said she was in the middle of packing or closing up her apartment or whatever it is people have to do when they move. I'm going into the city either Wednesday night or Thursday and will most likely spend a few hours with her then.

She is, I think, in better shape than when she came east three years ago, but you shouldn't expect any miracles.

After all the maybe-this-months-and-maybe-nexts I've been doing I think I'm finally going to get away from here for California on the night of Thursday the twenty-ninth, which should put me in your part of the world on Friday morning, March thirty. I'd hoped to be able to stay for a month this time, but the way things look now I'll have to be back in New York before the twelfth of April. Oh, well, better luck next time.

* * *

Financially, this year's going to be a holy terror and so—from the looks of things right now—are the next few years to come, but there's nothing desperately uncomfortable about the situation. It just means not much money. You and Mary are going to have to get along on that hundred a week I send you, which shouldn't be too difficult. I hope to know within the next week or two how I really stand.

That's about all the news there seems to be in these parts.

See you late next week.

> Love …
> SDH

TLS Marshall

To Maggie Kober

16 April 1951, Pleasantville, New York

Dear Maggie,

So we got on the plane twenty minutes before take-off time and Ann screamed her head off till we started moving, sobbed while we taxied up and down runways and was sound asleep before we were twenty feet in the air. A few minutes later I stuck her into the berth and she slept without moving till refuelling and reloading noises awakened her at five o'clock in the morning at the Chicago airfield; then she lay there amusing herself till I changed her clothes and gave her a bottle at seven and went back to sleep till I picked her up to take her off the plane in New York at eight-thirty—we were just about an hour late. So it was all mighty fine. She went to sleep again in the taxi going over to Lillian's, but woke up cheerfully as usual to make a kind of regal entrance.

Lillian's quite nuts about her, of course, and sometimes bores the bejesus out of even me, who doesn't bore too easily where my granddaughter is concerned. We didn't bring her up here till Saturday morning, but she's just like a permanent installation by now, and a nice baby to be around, since she seldom fusses very much and wears very well indeed.

* * *

I had an invitation from the Comite National des Ecrivains to go to Paris on May 20, spend three or four days there, then go down to Renaud de Jonvenel's château in the Correze district for a week before returning to Paris for some kind of doings about "Intellectual Comfort vs Conscience," on the 5th or 6th of June.[1] Since it's one of those all-expenses-paid trips, Madame is a little bitter about my not thinking I'll go. Madame has a firm belief that one should go almost anywhere for almost any purpose if it's free, and of course she's been trying to get me to France for years. I am tempted, since I'd like to see some of the people who'll be there—especially, I guess, Pablo Neruda—but on the other hand I'm far from sure I could get a passport or care to go to all the trouble involved. I've got to make up my mind this week…which isn't going to be too hard, since I already doubt that I've any intention of saying yes.

It was awfully nice seeing you, honey, and I miss those afternoon visits: the days seem to have a big hole in them around three or four in the afternoon now. Oh, well, maybe before too long …

And I miss Cathy too.

> Much love, sweetheart …
> Dash

1. The reference is presumably to Renaud de Jouvenal, a Communist journalist from a prominent French family. His father, Henry de Jouvenal, was Colette's second husband.
2. Pablo Neruda was a Chilean poet and prominant member of the Chilean Communist Party, who later won the Nobel Prize for Literature in 1971.

TLS HRC

To Maggie Kober

23 April 1951, Pleasantville, New York

Dear Maggie,

Today's been kind of all right, with sun and springness in pretty adequate quantities. Madame had to go into the big city this morning, but she should be back here early tomorrow afternoon, so the baby and I press on more or less bravely without her. This morning we took a longish walk—of course I had to do the walking, toting her—to the pond and around through the woods, and after we came back to the house she picked up her first bee between thumb and forefinger. It scared the bejesus out of her getting away, but doesn't seem to have stung her and— quite naturally and arrogantly—I felt very good about that. A true descendent, I told myself, who can handle bugs and such without harm coming to either!

Later this afternoon the child's nurse fell off the terrace steps and is now lying upstairs with what the doctor hopes isn't a sprained ankle, which now leaves us with only a couple of maids to take care of us. We'll no doubt use them up tomorrow and then start in on the farmer's wife, who has high blood pressure anyway and shouldn't cause us much trouble. We hope to have the ground pretty well cleared by Thursday noon, when the child's mother arrives.

If there seems to be a great deal of Ann and little of anything else in this letter it's because that's the way my life seems to be arranged just now: I wonder what I did with my time when I didn't have her to waste it on. I seem to spend most of the day either fooling around with her or waiting for her to wake up so I can fool around with her, and Madame is a very willing assistant, though I must say I think she's sometimes a little too maudlin. She actually asks people—it's more like a demand as a rule—if they don't think the child is beautiful and when, as they feel they have to if they want to stay off her son-of-a-bitch list, they say, yes, it's one of the most beautiful children they've ever seen, she looks at me as if to say, see, what did I tell you? I'm afraid Madame is boring a great many people.

I go into town Thursday, as usual, but earlier this week, to deposit the baby at 63 East 82nd Street, to pick up Jo at the airport and deposit her at 82nd Street and then to do my usual chores at the Jefferson School in the evening. We shall probably come back here in a group Friday afternoon for the weekend. I'm hoping things will work out so I can spend most of the next two weeks up here with the youngster, but I may have to take days off to beau her mother around the big city. We'll see; maybe I can work up some minor ailment...I can't use my age as an excuse: Jo knows I ran around quite chipper in California earlier this month...It seems longer ago than that.

This is the time of the year when—except for a few robins and a small flock of chickadees the other day—there are few birds around the house and it always makes the immediate outdoors seem sort of vacant, the way the absence of insects always seemed to leave holes in the atmosphere in the Aleutians. Most of the summer birds haven't arrived yet and the year-rounders are busy with new spring-stuff in the woods: business will pick up in a couple of weeks, I know, but just the same I'm always afraid they'll take their trade somewhere else. I must put out a couple of new wren houses tomorrow, and a couple of shelters for either robins or wood thrushes to nest in.

> Much love, honey ...
> Dash

TLS HRC

To Josephine Hammett Marshall

On 9 July 1951 Hammett was subpoenaed by U.S. District Court Judge Sylvester Ryan to testify about his knowledge of the whereabouts of four men convicted of violating the Smith Act whose bail had been posted by the bail fund committee of the Civil Rights Congress of New York. Hammett was president of the CRC and chairman of the bail fund committee. The court had in evidence the minutes of the committee, initialed by him. After being sworn in Hammett refused to answer any questions asked of him, pleading protection under the Fifth Amendment even when asked his name. Judge Ryan found him in contempt of court and sentenced him to six months in jail or until he purged himself of contempt. At 7:30 that evening he was taken into custody by a federal marshal, who escorted him to the West Street Federal House of Detention in Manhattan to begin serving his term. Three days later, Judge Learned Hand of the U.S. Court of Appeals granted the petition of Hammett's attorneys for bail in the amount of $10,000 pending an *appeal. Hammett's secretary, Muriel Alexander, attempted to post bail for him, in cash. Federal marshals refused to accept it unless she would disclose the source of the money, which she still refuses to do nearly fifty years later.*

On 28 September, the order to set bail having been revoked, Hammett was transferred to the Federal Correctional Institute at Ashland, Kentucky to serve the balance of his sentence. He was allowed to write letters only to a designated relative—he chose his daughter Josephine—and his incoming mail was censored. He received a four-week reduction in his sentence for good behavior, and on 9 December 1951 he was released. Ten days later the second appeal of his conviction to U.S. District Court was denied.

12 October 1951, PMB8416, Ashland, Kentucky

Dear Jo,

This is the first letter I've written since I've been in the clink, so if it's no better than usual let's pretend I'm out of practice... It's getting kind of fallish down here, with frosty nights, mostly foggy mornings and sunny afternoons—the kind of weather that makes me think I ought to be out in the woods with a gun. With thirty days off for good conduct, I'm due to get out of here on Dec. 9—I'll phone you when I get back to New York either that night or the 10th—so I'll at least get a couple of weeks of duck shooting... Your letters and the enclosed pictures have been mighty welcome. You're a nice girl. From now on it'll be better if you write me direct—to the address above. Regulations seem to say your name and address should be at the top of your letters... The cold that's been with me for a couple of months now still hangs on, but it's never been too much of a nuisance, though I seem to have been sort of run-down or something when I arrived here. Right now I'm in my usual pretty good shape... I had to shave off my mustach[e] when I got here. I think I'd been wearing it for some twenty-five years and I miss it esthetically, but actually feel more comfortable without it... Not knowing what the world's like outside, I haven't made any plans for the future, but the chances are I'll be in California either before or after Christmas. I'd like to bring Ann back with me as originally planned, of course... Lily, from whom I hear now and then, told me she had written you. She's still in either France or England and should be returning any week now. She seems to be having a pretty good time in spite of her worrying about things. She wrote me that André Gide had said among other things that I was as good a writer as Balzac, which of course pleased me immensely... On the 14th of last month three judges of the Circuit Court heard our appeal against our present sentences and have not yet handed down their decision. Actually, we have never expected much help from them—at very most some chink through which we could sneak out on bail while waiting the results of another appeal to the Supreme Court—but it's nice once in awhile to imagine they might see things the way we see 'em and turn us loose pronto. There are a great many legal technicalities involved and the whole thing is at least as dull as that civil suit you sat through an afternoon of in California—and I haven't heard the verdict on that case either. I guess judges just aren't in any hurry when I'm involved. Maybe I overdo it in giving an impression of patience...Now I've got to go off someplace or other to see about something or other...Give my love to everybody ...

> Much love, honey, and kiss that Ann thing for me.
> Pop

Dashiell Hammett
#8416

ALS Marshall

To Josephine Hammett Marshall

18 October 1951, PMB8416, Ashland, Kentucky

Dear Jo—

I don't have to tell you it was mighty nice having a letter directly from you, and the photo of Ann was nice too—the first I've ever seen of her in feminine clothes where she didn't look like one of those displaced persons getting off a boat...The same mail also brought a letter from your Ma, who has written fairly often...One of those dopey columnists seems to have reported me in the hospital here, but there isn't, of course, any truth to or in it: I'm feeling fine...The government, in its infinite unwisdom, hasn't yet decided to let me correspond with Lily or Muriel the only two who know anything at all about my affairs. Muriel used to come to see me once a week while I was in the West Street clink in N.Y. and tell me what was doing, but I haven't heard from her in more than a month now and have no idea of what goes on in my business. Will you tell her to let you know everything as soon as it happens? And then pass it on to me? You can't send enclosures, of course, which means you'll have to boil it—whatever it is—down for me. (I am all in favor of that. Muriel—as you'll find out—dulls things up a good deal in an attempt to make them interesting. She's a nice girl, but her ideas of "interesting" are god-awful. It's not always easy to pry out of her what's important to me rather than interesting to her, but I'm sure you'll manage wonderfully.)...While you are resting from this delightful chore you might also do some go-betweening between Lily and me. First-off I'd like to know if she's back from Europe yet and, if not, when she's due...Also you could phone Pat for me (if you haven't her number you can get it from Muriel) and give her my love and tell her sometimes I've found it awfully easy to be in love with her in jail...That's all I can think of right now... The time still seems to pass quite swiftly, I don't even seem to get much time to read, though I've reread *Les Misérables* and liked it better than I remembered, which is also true of some Thomas Hardy I've been rereading—*Jude the Obscure, Return of the Native,* and *Tess of the D'Urbervilles*...One of the nicest features of this place is that chewing tobacco is available, which wasn't true of West Street...I'm glad you got over your cold—let's cut out doing things that might make things tough for junior!...Give my love to everybody and kiss the monster for me ...

     Much, much love to you, honey—
     Pop

Dashiell Hammett
#8416

ALS Marshall

To Josephine Hammett Marshall

27 October 1951, PMB8416, Ashland, Kentucky

Dear Jo—

    I don't want to sound too much like the doddering grandfather I am, but it seems to me that Ann becomes lovelier in almost every snapshot you send. She's kind of something—For God's sake, don't you start worrying about my health and well-being!—My lawyer finally got down to see me yesterday and as usual, I learned nothing from him and he nothing from me. I think he's a pretty good lawyer but he's a foolish fellow to talk to, a sort of five-and-ten cent store man-of-the-world who's always sure he knows what I mean as soon as I give up trying to make him understand me. About Christmas, it's too early for me to say whether I'll be in California by then. I'll have to let you know later—I'm quite sold on my mustach[e]less state by now and only popular pressure could make me regrow liphair. In any event, I'll wait till you've seen me nude-faced and have had a chance to cast your vote before I do anything—(I just stopped this to be counted and to draw socks and a handkerchief: we get fresh ones every night except Saturday and Sunday)—Looking back, I see I forgot to finish what I had to say about my health and well-being, which is that I'm probably no less healthy than any Marshall you're likely to see and certainly no more unhappy. Being in jail is a damned dull nuisance, but that's about all, and sometimes I'm not even sure the "damned" belongs in there. I don't know how a longer sentence would be, but, as the boys say, you can do five months without taking your shoes off —Muriel will write you once more that everything is under control and you, I hope, will tell her that isn't what I want to know; that I want to know *what* is or isn't under control and that I'm not in need of "interpretive" information but of information

[illegible]. It's not always easy to get news out of her!—That last letter of mine was kind of brief because I was called away—and probably didn't have anything to say anyhow—I'm now about to read *Crime and Punishment*,[1] tackle Cooper's *The Last of the Mohicans*, which I've never tried, and read Derleth's *Wind Over Wisconsin*. I've read his short stories but have never had at one of his novels—you might show this letter to Lily—

Love to all and much, much love to you, honey, and that Ann-thing—

Pop

1. *Crime and Punishment* by Fyodor Dostoevsky.

ALS HRC

To Josephine Hammett Marshall

31 October 1951, PMB8416, Ashland, Kentucky

Dear Princess—

Today has been one of those days when I feel 57 years old instead of only 55 or 56, but I do not feel any older when I finish the day than when I started it so I guess I'll be all right.... Somebody reported that somebody else had heard on the radio that the circuit court had upheld our conviction, but we haven't been able to verify it yet. There won't be anything surprising about if it's true, since we've never been hopeful of an up-set—only we'd like those three old judges to come to life long enough to say one thing or another, they heard our appeal on September 14...It rained this morning, was gloomy most of the day, and cleared along towards sunset. Sweeping, wall-washing, dusting, window-washing and brass polishing kept me indoors most of the day, so it didn't matter greatly, and I was too lazy to go out for my usual half-hour walk, but I may try to go after supper. We had bacon and corn fritters for supper—there were other things too, like cream pie and coffee and the odds and ends of overcooked vegetables that I customarily ignore—and they were pretty good. The bacon—from prison-farm pigs—is always pretty good, but the fritters and hotcakes and rolls and such here usually come out awfully doughy...It's almost seven in the evening, so in a few minutes I'll stand up to be counted, then I'll swap my socks and handkerchief for clean ones, then maybe I'll take a bath—though I've got till nine o'clock to make up my mind about that—then I'll spread myself on the bed with today's Charleston W. Va., paper and yesterday's *NY Times* and a couple of books with nothing much else to do till lights go out at ten o'clock. Ah, this is living!...Give my love to all and kiss that child for me...

> Much love, honey—
> Pop

SDHammett
8416

ALS HRC

To Josephine Hammett Marshall

3 November 1951, PMB8416, Ashland, Kentucky

Dear Jo—

   Snow tonight, the first of the winter. It was mostly mixed with rain earlier, but managed to get itself straightened out by the time we were coming back to our dormitory from supper at around half-past five...The mop-handle felt kind of good in my hands this morning— Monday, Wednesday and Friday are mopdays—and I realized I'd been looking forward to it: I guess either I was feeling good or I'm going crazy—or both...The radio-rumor about our appeal turned out to be true: the Circuit Court upheld our conviction last Tuesday with one small dissenting voice occupying itself with some sort of technicality which may (or may not) do us an eensy-weensy bit of good in a strictly academic way. We've got a couple of days to decide whether we'll go on up to the Supreme Court with it. I dare say there'll be lawyers down to see us next week, but I won't be too broken hearted if mine can't make it...We drew our winter underwear this afternoon, but I'm not likely to feel ambitious enough to bathe and get into them tonight...The pictures of Ann walking around in the pale coveralls were wonderful as most of her pictures are...I don't have to tell you, I hope, how glad I am your doctor can't find much wrong with you beyond the usual ravages of age, and how I am looking forward to your second off-spring. You're a nice girl, that's what you are, and I love you...The local talent has just left for the auditorium where they'll rehearse for an amateur show to be given presently. Most of the inmates here are from the hills of this state, West Virginia and Tennessee—guitars and hillbilly music are likely in for one hell of a beating ...

   Give my love to everybody and especially to you and Lily and Ann.
          Pop

SDHammett
8416

ALS HRC

To Josephine Hammett Marshall

5 November 1951, PMB 8416, Ashland, Kentucky

Dear Princess—

    Today's been a lazy sort of Sunday, bright and sunny and only reasonably cold, with some snow still hanging on the grass and on the nearby hills. I seem to have slept most of the day away—an hour-and-a-half's nap between breakfast and dinner and maybe a little longer on in the afternoon—though I did go out for what I guess you could call a brisk 30-minute walk around the yard...I'm due to leave here five weeks from today. The time goes very rapidly, though I had expected it to drag a little along here towards the last...There is of course no news unless you would like to know that I had fresh pork steak for dinner and grilled cheese sandwiches for supper and haven't yet changed into my winter underwear and things like that...When you write to Muriel again ask her how Willy the turtle is. I don't think I've told you about Willy. She's a she (so I suppose her real name is Wilhelmina) wood-turtle spotted alongside the road to the lake at Pleasantville by Willy Wyler on his birthday (which is why she's named Willy) and picked up by me. I brought her into the city a week later to turn her loose in my yard. Wood turtles are quite tame and make nice pets if you like stupid pets. Turtles are also traditionally considered bad luck. The day after I brought Willy into the city I was thrown into the clink and so you can see she has a special place in my heart. (On the same day we found Willy I caught a snapping turtle that made a very nice soup, which is by no means bad luck. Well, wood turtles, though small are edible too. Maybe...)...It's getting a little chilly in here—some cluck turned off the heat a while ago—so maybe I'll stop this and try a hot shower and some blankets...

        My love to everybody and in an especially noisy way to you, Lilly and the Ann-thing—
        Pop

    SD Hammett
    8416

ALS Marshall

To Josephine Hammett Marshall

8 November 1951, PMB8416, Ashland, Kentucky

Dear Jo—

That lawyer fellow came down again to see me Tuesday, with news of our failure to win an out-on-bail plea to the Circuit Court earlier in the week—as expected, of course. He and the others' lawyers take our troubles up to Jackson of the Supreme Court Friday afternoon (this letter won't get to you in time or I might ask you and Ann to be praying your heads off at about two-thirty Eastern Time that afternoon) at which time another plea will most likely be made to let us out on bail while the Supreme Court decides whether it wishes to hear our troubles.[1] The lawyers seem to think there's some chance of us getting out for a while, but don't bet any money on it. However I've already ordered dinner in New York City for next Tuesday night—oysters on the half shell, quail and sweetbreads...Letters from your Mother and Mary came yesterday, one from you with the usual—but only one—darling snapshot of that child...Lily finally managed to blackjack some sort of information out of Muriel [] about my affairs and sent a resume down by Haydon, so I'm not so completely in the dark as I was[2]... God, or who ever is in charge, worked most of the day trying to whip up some more snowier and colder weather, but with only moderate success—unless persuading me finally to put on winter underwear can be called success...I'm now in slow process of reading Charlotte Brontë's *Jane Eyre* for the first time, after which I have on my bedside table for re-reading Gogol's *Dead Souls* and Meyer Levin's *Citizens*, which I'm not sure I've read before, though it seems likely...I have a remark for you: in the course of a brief discussion of the Negro question this afternoon, one of my fellow inmates whom I rather like—originally form South Carolina, I think, though he's lived in Kentucky for some years—said, "It's not that I'm prejudiced, because I've got no reason to dislike niggers, but I just hate 'em!"...Now to book, bed and, eventually, sleep. I no longer drop off as soon as the lights go out. Now it usually takes me a couple of hours to get to sleep, but they're seldom unpleasant hours; as a matter of fact, I sometimes look forward to them: I lie there and think pleasantly about things to which I don't have to come to any conclusion...

Much, much love to you, darling, and give my love to everybody—
and especially to Lily and Ann—
>Pop

SDHammett
8416

1. Robert Houghwout Jackson was associate justice of the U.S. Supreme Court.
2. Charles Haydon was hired by Hellman to file the appeal of Hammett's convic-
    tion. She dismissed Mary Kaufman and Victor Rabinowitz, who had represented
    Hammett initially.

ALS MARSHALL

To Josephine Hammett Marshall

12 November 1951, PMB8416, Ashland, Kentucky

Dear Jo,

Thanks, honey, for the information about what we call business and
stuff: with what dope I got from Haydon I think it fills me in pretty well
and—unless, of course, something unexpected turns up (if anything
turns up it will be unexpected)—I'll be OK until I get out of here in what
seems like a very few short weeks—The line in your letter about my
"friend with the pearls" has me stumped though. Want to give me some
additional clue? I'm probably a dope—it's probably not true that jail sentences sharpen the wits—but no amount of mulling has helped me
guess whom you mean— The weather this long weekend has been quite
wonderful and I've spent a bunch of both mornings and afternoons out
in the yard, even though it's sometimes better to pretend I don't hear the
sounds of somebody in the nearby woods with a shotgun— Our lawyers
had their chat with Supreme Court Justice Jackson Friday, and Jackson,
in turn, promised to repeat the chat to other members of the Supreme
Court the next day to find out whether they wanted to hear us out—and
that's how it stands now. We should hear how it comes out on Tuesday or
Wednesday. I've half a notion—with not much to base it on—that Fred
may get out on bail while they listen to his tale of woe, and I may not.[1]
But we'll see—It doesn't make a great deal of difference to me whether I

finish out my time now or go out on bail for a while and most likely have to come back and give 'em the three or four weeks I'll owe—Bed now and Gogol's *Dead Souls*, a very funny book—

Much of the nicest kind of love to you, sweetheart, and give me love to everybody, especially, of course, L and A—
Pop

SDHammett
8416

1. Frederick Vanderbilt Field was one of three other trustees of the CRC bailfund jailed along with Hammett for contempt of court.

ALS Marshall

To Josephine Hammett Marshall

27 November 1951, PMB 8416, Ashland, Kentucky

Dear Princess—

I let last week slide by without writing you. I don't know whether laziness was to blame, or short-time slackness, or a combination. I'll be out of here a dozen days from now and it's easier and easier to tell myself there's no use writing when I'll soon be talking to you on the phone—only you're not to start thinking the same thing. Your letters have been wonderful and you're a darling and you're by all means to keep them coming to the last minute...As nearly as I understood my lawyer—by no means as easy a task as it may seem to those who don't know him—the last time he was down, L. is not coming to meet me and my airplane transportation from Charleston, W. Va. (which is only a couple of hours from here by bus), is either to be mailed me here ahead of time or be waiting for me at the airport in Charleston. Will you check on this with L. for me? Anyway, I should be in NYC in plenty of time for Sunday night's dinner, and I'll phone you at such time as I imagine you come home from your roaming but are not yet in the hay...The Supreme Court was to have had our tale of woe last week and we may get some sort of peep out of them this week or next. They aren't going to do me personally a hell of a lot of good at this late date, but I'm a fellow who's mighty grateful—so I say—for any small crumb that falls my way...The news from L. was very good in that it all sounded very Lillianesque and she doesn't always sound Lillianesque unless she's in good spirits... I still haven't—and won't have until I've had a chance to look the situation over in NYC—any idea of what I'm going to do when I get out or when I'm coming to California. Being in jail is really being out of the world, since even your friends seem to think they're helping you by not telling you anything that might "worry" you, and even when they do try to tell you something they are either so cryptic, or so take for granted your knowledge of things you don't know, that you can't make heads or tails of what they're saying...

      Much love to you, honey, and give my love to all, especially not forgetting L and A—
      Pop

SDHammett
8416

ALS HRC

To Josephine Hammett Marshall

4 December 1951, PMB8416, Ashland, Kentucky

Dear Jo—

If there's any god, this should be the last letter I send you from this address: you should next hear from me via telephone Sunday evening or Monday morning—My lawyer sent me a wire this afternoon saying the Supreme Court (with Justices Black and Douglas, long may they live, dissenting) had denied our plea for bail, and we heard the same thing on the radio half an hour later.[1] Now all we've got to do is read about it in the newspapers and we'll begin to believe it. The news wasn't, of course, any great surprise to us as we had figured it at most a four-to-one chance—My lawyer came down to see me last week, with no great amount of news, but with a topcoat to go home in, which is no doubt better—I had a letter from your Mother this afternoon. She was on her way over to Ann while you and Loyd took off for your northern flight. I hope you had a good time—

Much love, honey, and give my love to everybody, not forgetting of course, to shout it most loudly at L and A—

Pop

S. D. Hammett

8416

1. Justices Hugo Black and William O. Douglas.

ALS Marshall

PART FIVE

Survivor
1952–1960

Hammett in Vineyard Haven,
Massachusetts, 1960

She talked for five minutes straight...while she tried to hit upon the safest attitude to assume. And before we could head her off, she had hit upon it—silence! We got not another word out of her; and that is the only way in the world to beat the grilling game.

The Continental Op in "Zigzags of Treachery"

HAMMETT WAS RELEASED from jail in December 1951, but his troubles had only begun. The blacklist was in full force, and it operated both in government and in the private sector. Hammett's radio programs had been canceled, his books went out of print, and his name lost the cachet it had held for twenty years. Now, in the public eye, he was a convicted Communist, with no means or earning potential.

Hammett had considered taxes an annoyance since the 1930s, though his letters provide evidence that he did not ignore them entirely. Nonetheless the cost of his disdain for money finally came due. The IRS presented him with a bill for $111,008.60 in back taxes, an amount that grew to $140,795.96 by 13 December 1956, when the matter was settled in federal court by default judgment. New York State presented additional bills. Hammett never saved, except by buying war bonds, and these he had liquidated and exhausted after the war. The interruption of his income had immediate effects.

Hellman, also beset with tax problems, sold Hardscrabble Farm, a terrible blow to Hammett. Although the farm was legally hers, Hammett had shared its expenses, and it had been his refuge. When he could no longer afford to keep an apartment in the city, his friends came to his aid. Samuel Rosen, a socially active leftist physician, and his wife, Helen, offered Hammett free use of a four-room cottage on their estate in Katonah, New York. Hammett insisted on paying $50 per month rent. He moved there in fall 1952 and stayed until his last illness, six years later.

Senator Joseph McCarthy was at the peak of his demagoguery in the early years of the 1950s. Rather like the gossip columnists who had milked Hammett's name since *The Maltese Falcon* was published, McCarthy seized the opportunity to make a headline by questioning yet another celebrity. He subpoenaed Hammett to testify before his Senate Committee on Government Operations on 26 March 1953 as part of an inquiry into the use of federal funds to purchase books by known Communists for State Department libraries abroad. Hammett surprised the senator and spectators alike by acknowledging that McCarthy's position was tenable given his goal. When asked whether he would favor the adoption of Communism in the United States, Hammett answered no; it would be impractical if most people did not want it. When McCarthy asked Hammett whether he would buy books by Communist authors to be distributed throughout the world if he were in charge of fighting Communism, Hammett answered: "If I were fighting communism I don't think I would do it by giving people any books at all."

Hammett still felt the urge to write, and he struggled to shape his novelistic ideas. His theory of writing included the basic concept that each word had to matter. He struggled with every paragraph he wrote, and when he revised what he had written, he edited most of it away. His last attempt at a novel is a 21,500-word fragment called "Tulip," the only one of his attempts at a sixth novel that has been located. The title character is an ex-soldier who had been stationed in the Aleutians during World War II with Pop, who is transparently Hammett himself. After the war, Tulip visits Pop, who is trying to write a novel, and they talk, often about literature. Pop says "if you're careful enough in not committing yourself you can persuade different readers to see all sorts of different meanings in what you have written, since in the end almost anything can be symbolic of anything else, and I've read a lot of stuff of that sort and liked it, but it's not my way of writing and there's no use pretending it is." A writer writes, Pop says, for "fame, fortune, and personal satisfaction.... that is and should be your goal. Anything less is kind of piddling."

Hammett's working draft for "Tulip" has not been located. Lillian Hellman had a fair copy typed, which served as a setting copy for her collection of Hammett's stories published after his death, *The Big Knockover* (1966). The fragment ends, she says, with the words "If you are tired you ought to rest, I think, and not try to fool yourself and your customers with colored bubbles." By all evidence, with that thought Hammett ended his writing career in the summer of 1953.

The spirit of the McCarthy era lasted for the rest of the decade, though its figurehead self-destructed a year later. In 1955 Hammett was subpoenaed to testify before the New York State Joint Legislative Committee investigating philanthropic organizations. But by that time the threat of the Communist hunters was blunted, and testifying was simply an annoyance to Hammett.

He was now very ill. Although he was only sixty-one in 1955, he had the appearance of a man much older. In August 1955 he suffered a heart attack, and as he recovered, he mentioned with increasing frequency a pain he attributed to rheumatism in his shoulder. Hellman was less of a presence in his life after he got out of jail; she had other interests. He relied increasingly on Josephine and her growing family for gratification, but also withdrew more and more, preferring a quiet, solitary evening at home to anyone's company.

In the summer of 1958 it was apparent that Hammett was unable to live alone, though he resisted pressure to move back in with Hellman. With collaboration from the Rosens, who said they needed the guest cottage Hammett was staying in for their daughter, Hellman arranged to have him move into her New York apartment. They spent summers in Martha's Vineyard, where she had a home. He grew steadily weaker, and after lung cancer was diagnosed late in 1960, the end came swiftly.

To I. F. Stone

V. J. Jerome was the cultural director of the American Communist Party. The Alien Registration Act, known as the Smith Act, was passed on 28 June 1940. An amplification of existing immigration laws, the act also made it a crime to advocate or teach the overthrow of the government by force or to belong to any group that advocated the violent overthrow of the government. The Smith Act was used to limit the activities of American Communists.

18 March 1952, Committee to Defend V. J. Jerome, 799 Broadway, New York City

Dear Mr. Stone:[1]

Our committee is planning a "Culture Fights Back" rally in tribute to V. J. Jerome, one of the sixteen New York Smith Act defendants. The rally will be held at Hotel Diplomat, Thurs, April 17th at 8:30 pm. It will be sponsored jointly with Masses & Mainstream, publishers of Mr. Jerome's new novel, *A Lantern for Jeremy*.

The evening will be devoted largely to a cultural program together with a number of brief addresses. We should be honored to have you participate in this meeting as a speaker. The basis of the gathering is a common front against the Smith Act threat to intellectual and cultural freedom.

We look forward to your acceptance of this invitation. An early reply will be appreciated.

> Sincerely yours,
> Dashiell Hammett

Chairman
dh:sg

1. I. F. Stone was a non-Communist libertarian political journalist who wrote for *The Nation*.

TLS SCHOMBERG

Form Letter

4 April 1952, Committee to Defend V. J. Jerome, 799 Broadway, New York City

Dear Sir or Madam:

The enclosed article "Grasp the Weapon of Culture" threatens to send its author V. J. Jerome to prison for five years. This article was cited by the government as the single "overt act" in its indictment charging Mr. Jerome with violation of the Smith Act.

V. J. Jerome is a well-known Marxist scholar, whose works on culture, such as *The Negro in Hollywood Films, Culture in a Changing World,* and *Intellectuals and the War,* have been widely discussed here and abroad. Unquestionably, Mr. Jerome's ideas differ from those of many other Americans. Nevertheless, Americans of varying beliefs are joining in defending his right to express his ideas.

To dramatize the threat of the Smith Act, to artists, scientists, educators and other professionals, the Committee to Defend V. J. Jerome plans to reprint this article along with the attached statement on freedom of expression to be signed by cultural figures of varying political persuasions.

We invite you to join the signers of the statement. Among those who have already signed are: Charlotta Bass, Peter Blume, Morris Carnovsky, Russell Cowles, Howard da Silva, Philip Evergood, Lloyd Gough, Carroll Hollister, Leo Hurwitz, John Howard Lawson, Robert Morss Lovett, Dorothy Parker, George Price, Anton Refregier, Jacob Lawrence, Paul Robeson, Rev. Ernest Trantner, Dr. Gene Weltfish, Charles White and Rev. Eliot White.

We look forward to your supporting this democratic action.

> Sincerely yours,
> Dashiell Hammett
> Chairman

W. E. B. Du Bois   Alfred Kreymborg
Honorary Chairmen

TLS Schomberg

To Josephine Hammett Marshall

In the fall of 1951 the IRS ruled that Hardscrabble Farm could not receive favorable tax treatment as a working farm, because it had lost money for eleven years running. That and other adverse rulings left Hellman owing $110,000 in back taxes. She sold the farm and moved out in April 1952.

10 April 1952, 28 West 10th St., New York City

Dear Jo,

This is cheating in a way, because I promised my doctors—I haven't as many as Camel cigarettes, but I've more than one—I'd stay in bed till my temperature went down to normal, and it's still in the 99s. It's never been very high, which is a nuisance: if you're going to have any at all you ought to have enough to brag about. Something called "that virus that's going around" has had me down for the past couple of weeks, though I'm not sure anybody knows what they're talking about because I haven't had a cough or headaches or diarr[h]ea, which seem to be the principal symptoms: all that's happened to me is I ached everywhere and felt lousy and had a day of not being able to keep food down and a temperature that fluctuated feebly between the 90s and the 100s. The worst of it was not being able to read the first few days, but now that I can read...

Lillian's been moving P'ville this week, will probably wind up the job this weekend. I haven't thought about it much except to know it's going to leave quite a hole in life. I think she suspects me of having taken to bed to avoid the unpleasantness of helping her move. She's coming down for dinner tomorrow night: I haven't seen her since last Sunday, haven't seen anybody: I'm not a man who likes his friends when he's sickish.

I miss hearing from you and miss photographs of the youngsters and hope this sounds pathetic enough to touch you into doing something about it such as forgiving me for seeming to be such a non-caring non-corresponding father for so long...

Now I'm going to make a pot of tea and crawl back into bed with a very dull novel called *Down All Your Streets* that I'm reading.[1] God knows why I'm wasting my time on it—maybe because it's a thick book and I like thick books when I'm invaliding—when I've got Hauser's *The Social History of Art* to work on.

Love to all, honey, and much, much to you ...
Pop

1. *Down All Your Streets* by Leonard Bishop.

TLS Marshall

To Josephine Hammett Marshall

16 April 1952, 28 West 10th St., New York City

Dear Princess,

The enclosed clippings from, you might say, friend and foe alike give, I guess, some sort of picture of how I stand legally just now. I send 'em along chiefly because, having written you I'd been sickish and not knowing what—if anything—the papers printed out there, I wanted to be sure you didn't think I was having trouble: I'm certainly in no particular trouble now and have no reason to foresee any. One of my doctors took a gander at me Sunday and pronounced me in good enough shape to do what I had to do—I'd been up since Friday—and I felt OK. Monday morning I had—as the papers say—a little session with the Grand Jury, but it was by no means a difficult session and—though I was told to hold myself ready for a possible recall—I have no special reason for supposing anything will happen in the immediate future.[1]

I've got to run now, honey, so...

Give my love to everybody...and a great deal to you...
Pops

1. Hammett testified before a federal grand jury about the bail fund committee of the New York Civil Rights Congress.

TLS Marshall

To Lillian Hellman

28 April 1952, 28 West 10th St., New York City

Dear Lilishka,

That letter I wrote Saturday was dated Sunday because I took the date from the *Post,* which now in a fairly successful attempt to achieve one hundred per cent inaccuracy dates its Saturday edition that way.

Muriel finally had her baby Saturday, a ten-pound boy, and both seem to be doing all right, though they had to take it out with a Caesarean, which I suppose she knew about ahead of time, though she said nothing about it.

You'll probably be glad to know the weather's still lousy in these parts. It continues to rain, and while it's not cold it's very rawish.

Oscar's Becky phoned me this morning and I am going there for dinner tomorrow night.[1] Charlie also phoned me that the will and power of attorney were ready for my signature any time I'm ready.

Hypochondria notes, to get 'em over with: my temperature bounced a little yesterday but was back at normal today; and if the scales are to be trusted I've gained some weight. Tomorrow—depending on whether I feel like going out in the afternoon—I may go up to see Abe.[2] Taking one thing with another I'm a fairly spry old man today.

There was something I was to remind myself to say about missing you, but I don't remember what it was except that I do miss you, so maybe that was it.

Now I'm going to look at some fights on television and then see if I feel like having a go at the book.

> Much love honey, and I hope you're having fun.
> Dash

Later: I was hoping I'd do enough on the book to brag about in this space. I did some, but not enough to brag about. So ...

1. Oscar Bernstein was Hellman's attorney. Becky was his wife. Charles Haydon was Hammett's attorney.
2. Abe Abeloff was Hammett's physician.

TLS LPT

To Lillian Hellman

18 August 1952 [no address]

Dear Lilishka,

These decorations are partly decorations,[1] of course, but mostly they are to let you know that things of some sort do go on in our part of the world regardless of who is or who isn't in town at the moment even though you can't believe everything you read in the newspapers, like that thing in Hy Gardner's column about me this morning in the *Herald-Tribune* and it's looking a good deal like rain this afternoon although rain wouldn't make a great deal of difference since there are no local baseball games scheduled for today, which leaves me very little to do except maybe work at my writing, which is in good favor with me nowadays. I looking on the book as something that might turn out to be very worth while having done, though I'd be one of the first to admit that my optimism may be based more on what I intend and hope to inject into it than what I've managed to get into it thus far, but that, I dare say, is more or less true of any writer's any book at any given time, and I hope that is true because I naturally—or it seems natural to me—wouldn't want to be—or to consider myself that, though after looking at this—as drunken-looking a page as was ever typed by a probably sober man I think I shall have to stop and brood over the whole tactical situation. But I love you anyhow.

　　　　Dash

1.   Hammett pasted a "Peanuts" comic strip on the top of this letter.

TLS HRC

To Lillian Hellman

20 August 1952, 28 West 10th St., New York City

Dearest Lilipie,

Let's see now what's news today that wasn't news some other day if any, outside of the fact that I've done very little work, which, while not setting the day off from all others as much as might be supposed still is generally speaking unsatisfactory and if you, as I can understand, don't like this way of writing you might just as well let the rest of this letter go unread because this seems to be my way of writing just now, so there!

I had a postcard from Nancy, sending her love to you, of course, and asking me to try to persuade you to come up and visit them. She says the need of buying a new refrigerator will keep them from any New York holidays.

I still haven't got up to your neighborhood, haven't been out of the house since along about this time last week, but I'll make it one of these days for sure. I stay in because I think I've got a lot of work to do—and I have, time's a-wasting—and then I don't get it done anyway. Explain that to me, Miss Hellman, though not just by saying it's too much like me to need explaining; make up some fancier stuff even if it isn't perhaps as truthful. After all, what is truth? (I don't put quotation marks around things like that—me and Adlai take what we want where we find it, counting on our hearers being too uneducated to see that our stuff lacks freshness.)[1]

It's not too late to still do some of that work I'm bragging about not having done, but the chances are I'll find some more or less Proustian reason for not doing it. For instance, my watch just stopped—because I'd forgotten to wind it since God knows when—and it[s] stopping upset me. Do you think I can do my best work when I'm upset? (Do you think I can ever do my best work?)

I enclose some things, perhaps so the postage on this letter won't be altogether wasted.

> Love,
> Dash

1. Adlai Stevenson was the Democratic candidate for president in 1952.

TLS HRC

To Lillian Hellman

On 16 July 1952, Mary was briefly committed to a hospital in California for mental illness.

21 August 1952, 28 West 10th St., New York City

Dear Lily,

I couldn't find a single damned thing in the *Herald-Tribune* about me today (Sunday, Sandoe; Tuesday, Hy Gardner; Wednesday, John Crosby) and begin to feel like a defeated candidate for the Prohibition Party's nomination. Tell me, do you think obscurity is nice after one gets used to it?

Mary's home from the hospital, I hear, and perhaps in better shape than before, though, as I suppose was to be expected, she doesn't love her mother too much for having sent her away. I don't know what the hell good I could do out there, but I really feel uncomfortable—as if I were dogging it—about not going. Oh, well, I've got better places to go next week anyhow!

* * *

The rain it is sounding outside quite in a brisk way presently as it is I write. (I like that style and may adopt it.)

I haven't been able to tear myself away from this work I keep thinking and talking about but not doing long enough to get outdoors to the 80's or the barber shop or anywhere, but it is possible that if it does not rain tomorrow—what could rain possibly have to do with it, I wonder? Will you ask Gregory (the physician, not the poodle) why I put that in?—I may get around to both. Since you are the gambling type I must warn you, however, not to make any very large wagers on it, unless, naturally, you are given very big odds.

Now my conscience tells me that I ought to clear this typewriter for possible work on the novel that I'm supposed to be writing.

I love you with the utmost extravagance even if I do set the "Expand" key so that not too many words will take up a great deal of room when I write, but it does not always seem to me that such words as run through my head are at their best when embalmed in black on white, and what are your problems as a writer, Miss Hellman?

SDH

TLS LPT

To Lillian Hellman

24 August 1952, 28 West 10th St., New York City

Dear Lilishka,

This is the day I start looking forward to Wednesday with real excitement, though you say I ought to have started that a long time ago and I say I ought never to have had to do it at all this time because being back here in New York seems to have been more of a waste of time than anything else as near as I can figure out, but that's the way things go or something sometimes I suppose, and if Proust doesn't get through with Albertine pretty soon now—I'm almost up to "The Flight of Albertine" chapter and very hopeful—I'm afraid he's going to lose a customer. Writers, not only Proust, nearly all writers, make too much of things as a rule: it's as if they took for granted that their readers lived in vacuums, which may be true some of the time, but is at least an impolite assumption and very often leads to boredom. At the moment I take a dim view of writing and writers in general, but may feel better about it after I've scrubbed the little hand-shaker's teeth, shaved and bathed and had my little dinner—steak tonight, I guess, and maybe I'll go crazy and whip up a mess of potatoes, onions and lima beans to go with it. There's nobody around to dog-eye me if I don't eat much of 'em after I've cooked 'em—if I do—so why not? Isn't this Liberty Hall or something? On the other band I barely may—after I've done those things that end with bathing—dress and go[] out for dinner, in which unlikely case I could mail this and you'd probably get it Tuesday whereas if I don't mail it till I go out tomorrow then you won't get it till…of course, the chances are I won't go out tonight, telling myself I should stay home and get some work done and— who knows?—maybe even telling myself that with some truth in it. I'm having a mess of trouble with my book, but it's the kind of trouble I suppose I ought to be having—what I hope and think I mean by that is that I'm having a hard time making it as nearly as good as I want it in the way I want it—so I guess there's nothing to do except go along sulking and cursing and writing and tearing up and writing and not tearing up and thinking I ought to be working harder on it and finding sulky reasons for not working on it at all and thinking it's going to be better than it's going to be and worse than it's going to be and different from what it's going to be and one minute sure that tomorrow or the next day I'll be better and the next minute just as sure that I'd've been better off writing it a few years ago when I had more stuff...all nice cute silly stuff that, I dare say, helps pass the time while the novel will get done—little better or worse than it ought to be—somehow somewhen. And with that bit of solemn bellyaching I leave you, my child, for what I hope is just a little while.

> Love,
> [end of paper]

TL LPT

To Josephine Hammett Marshall

9 October 1952, 28 West 10th St., New York City

Dear Jo,

The photo of Evan was magnificent![1] Outside of being nice people yourselves, you and Loyd certainly produce wonderful children!

I'm moving next Tuesday up to Katonah. Remember we went over there to the Rosens' one afternoon? They've a four-room guest cottage, with ten acres, near the entrance to their place, which is what I'm moving into. It's only an hour and twenty minutes from the city. So my new address is: Arcady, Orchard Hill Road, Katonah, N. Y. Telephone: Katonah 0324.

Lillian's about to go in rehearsal with a revival of *The Children's Hour* as soon as she finishes casting it, which should be fairly soon.[2] Pat Neal, Kim Hunter and Iris Mann are already signed up for the principal parts, so what's left shouldn't take long.

Pat has taken an apartment on Park Avenue, is thinner than ever, but otherwise seems to be in pretty good shape. She sends her love to you and tells me Jean Hagen—not to be outdone by you—has a boy baby too. A lot of breeding seems to go on in this world.

I expected to have my book finished before this—I guess all writers always think they're going to dash off whatever they're starting to work on in no time—but it's still less than half done. However, I think what I've got down is pretty good—when you're writing you have to think it's pretty good or commit suicide—and I'm in no real rush. I'll get it finished this winter, anyway, and that's soon enough. I've lost weight again—the scales hardly know the difference when I step on them—but I feel, sleep and eat fine, so I reckon any complaining I want to do has to be pretty academic.

My fall term at school starts tonight, so ...

Give my love to everybody, kiss the children for me, and try to forget that I've been such a lousy correspondent.

> Much love, darling...
> Pop

1. Loyd and Josephine Marshall's son, Evan, was born on 4 January 1952.
2. The revival of *The Children's Hour* opened on 18 December 1952 at the Coronet Theatre in Manhattan. It ran for 189 performances.

TLS Marshall

To Josephine Hammett Marshall

20 October 1952, Arcady, Orchard Hill Road, Katonah, New York

Dear Princess,

Well here I am all more or less installed in what looks like it's going to turn out to be one of the nicest homes I've had, though I suspect the nearby shooting—most of the open season gets under weigh this week—isn't going to be so hot, and I'm not a man who's likely to go far afield for his sport, but they tell me you can't have everything...

Officially I moved up here Tuesday afternoon, but since I had to go back to the city over Wednesday and Thursday, I didn't truly get going till Friday—there was a nice letter from you with nice photos of the youngsters waiting here for me when I arrived—and am just about now in the final stages of shaking down. My twice-a-week cleaning woman comes for the first time tomorrow, so that should make it official. I brought up some of my own junk—beds, chairs, tables, rugs, lamps and so on—and since the place was already furnished I've been busy as hell storing stuff in the toolshed and garage.

* * *

Tomorrow I hope to get back to work on the book. My aim in life is now to be out of the trenches for Christmas, though the truth is I'll be more than satisfied if I've the first draft done by then. It[s] title—permanent I think—is "Tulip," which is the principal character's last name, or, anyhow, what he says his name is.

That's just about all the news there is, unless you want all the fascinating details about how my desk fit into this corner of my new quarters and a chest of drawers wouldn't fit into that one and so on and on at whatever length you can stand.

My love to everybody and lots and lots and lots to you…
Pop

TLS MARSHALL

To Josephine Hammett Marshall

14 June 1953, Arcady, Orchard Hill Road, Katonah, New York

Dear Princess,

Oh, it's news about little old me that you want? Well, well, that's right up my alley. Since there's practically none of any importance I shouldn't have any trouble going on at great length, embroidering little things till they look big, using my imagination when I haven't even got the little things to blow up, and creating a great todo in general. Take my right shoulder, for instance: I've had rheumatism or arthritis or something in it since along about 1940 or 41, but the funny thing about it was that it never bothered me—or not enough to make me notice it—unless I was doing something I didn't especially like to do. I don't like shooting at targets particularly, so I used to have to go over to the infirmary and have it baked before I went on the rifle range in the Army. On the other hand, it never bothered me when I went out with a shotgun for fun in the woods or on the water, though the recoil from a shotgun puts just as much strain on the shoulder as an army rifle and much more than the carbines. Carrying firewood bothers my shoulder too, and putting on coats, and sometimes when I can't get to sleep at night my shoulder hurts. Understand, it's not the other way around: it's not my shoulder that ever keeps me awake, it only seems to hurt when I can't sleep. Come to think of it, I don't remember its bothering me any while I was in jail. I've got a great many doubtless fascinating things like that I'd be glad to go into very deeply and lengthily if I could be sure of having an audience stupid enough to be interested in them …

The novel—"Tulip"—has been untouched for a long time now, though I think I have only a couple of months' work at most on it to finish it up. Not working on it is partly a sort of stage fright, I think—putting the finishing touches on a book can be kind of frightening, because that's that then—partly that I feel—most of the time—that it can be a very good job and I don't want to botch it—and partly that from a financial standpoint there's not much use in my publishing anything till my income tax troubles get straightened out. That last reason is only half valid, though: I could finish the book without publishing it. And I really ought to because I've got another book in my mind that I should get at…

I haven't heard from Lillian since she got back to Rome—if she's back yet: she said she was spending a few days travelling en route—but maybe I'll get a letter tomorrow.

The snapshot of the youngsters together was wonderful. Ann looks as if she's doing an imitation of Louise Glaum or Ma[e] Murray, blonde vamps of the silent picture days who were much given to looking under lowered lids.

> Much love, honey, and give my love to everybody …
> Pop

TLS MARSHALL

To Josephine Hammett Marshall

25 June 1953, Katonah, New York

Dearest Jo,

The enclosed enclosure—taken just last week—purports to show that if I no longer look exactly like a plump and well-tended teenager still

I don't look as if the years had battered and beaten me too much, at least that's the way it looks to me but I could be biased.

I had a letter from Lillian this morning saying she'd had lunch with the Goldwyns in Rome the day before. There seem to be a great many of those people who go to make up that group that are called—at least by the members of that group—"everybody" in Rome this year. Lillian, busy on her screen version of a Nancy Mi[t]ford novel for Korda, will be back here in August to rehearse the road company of *The Children's Hour,* going back to Europe to finish up her stint there if necessary.[1] Pat, who is going on the road with *The Children's Hour* in the fall, is now doing a couple of plays for the Theatre de Lys, just a week in each. Last week she did *The Scarecrow* and this week *School for Scandal.* I meant to see her in them, but haven't got around to it thus far and probably won't. It may be that I'm sulking about her marriage, which takes place, I suppose, early next month.[2]

* * *

My love to everybody including perhaps especially you…
Pop

1. Hellman was working on an adaptation of Mitford's novel *The Blessing* for Alexander Korda. He rejected it, and the project was suspended until 1959, when another screenwriter finished the script. The movie was released as *Count Your Blessings.*
2. Patricia Neal married the British writer Roald Dahl on 2 July 1953. Hammett did not like Dahl.

TLS MARSHALL

To Josephine Hammett Marshall

7 July 1953, Orchard Hill Road, Katonah, New York

Dear Jo,

Thanks for that "gaunt but indestructable"—it's the kind of thing I like—but I guess I also like pictures of your children more than I do pictures of my parents' children, maybe because they've got a longer future ahead of them with more looks to start with.

How's the house-hunting coming along? Is it still as tough a job as it was not so long ago in Los Angeles, or has it eased up a little? The chief trouble with house-hunting as I remember it was that it didn't seem to make much difference w[h]ether there were lots or few vacancies, finding something you wanted was always difficult.

I haven't seen Pat for some time but I saw her picture in the paper last week with her new husband and the announcement of their marriage so I guess they're either in Europe on their honeymoon now or on the way there. It was a pretty good picture of both of them.

I had a letter from Lillian this morning, who is now in Paris, by way of London, and seems headed for the south of France with a probable return to Rome from there, though it was all pretty vague. She said she thought the script was coming along all right.

It's too early of course to see whether Eisenhour's—among other things I have given up spelling this year: let the letters fall where they may, the word or the name's the same as far as I'm concerned—mentioning my books has helped sales, but his position seems to me very vulnerable from his standpoint and I imagine he'll be slapped down, politely perhaps but slapped down just the same.[1] The gent at times seems to talk a little like Adlai Stevenson and it's not known that that kind of thing helps anybody's political career.

The weather's been very good for some days now, especially for those of us who enjoy not doing very much of anything in the country, and if anybody comes along taking a poll you can tell them you have a father who definitely belongs to that group. I have to go into the city next week for my annual meeting with income tax folk in which we usually agree pretty well on how much blood you can get from a turnip but except for that trip I hope to go a few weeks more without having to move.

Now I've got to stop and do some chores like heating a cup of coffee and seeing how a small spider that has trapped a large wasp in its web in a window-corner is making out and maybe watching part of a baseball game on television—you know, the kind of thing that keeps one on the go all day long.

Much love, sweetheart, to you and everybody ...
Pop

1. After Hammett testified on 26 March 1953 before the Permanent Subcommittee Investigation of the Senate Committee on Government Operations, chaired by

Joseph McCarthy, as part of the inquiry into books by Communists in State Department libraries overseas, his books were removed from State Department library shelves briefly. When asked his opinion, newly elected President Dwight D. Eisenhower said he saw no threat from Hammett's novels, and they were restored to the libraries.

TLS MARSHALL

To Josephine Hammett Marshall

11 July 1953, Orchard Hill Road, Katonah, New York

My Dear Mrs Marshall,

It's been a nice week here as far as the weather was concerned, and as far as everything else was concerned, I guess, though of course things may have gone wrong that I don't know about and never, I hope, will find out about.

Lillian when last heard from was about to start circulating in the south of France and I've no reason to suppose that isn't what she's up to. Pat, so far as I know, is now Mrs R[oa]ld (pronounced Rule) Dahl and honeymooning somewhere in Europe. I, so far as I know, am here though I remember once in 1936 when I thought I was in Princeton, N.J., but the *Hollywood Reporter* said I was in Spain. Anyhow, next Tuesday I will go to New York, which seems quite an adventure to me, not that it is so long since I've been there but that I so easily fall into ruts and a week or two of not doing something constitutes a rut for me.

My clipping service sent me a great deal of stuff from various newspapers on the "book-burning" question and I spent a couple of hours reading it and trying to make some sense out of it, but without too much luck: it seems just another fuss in a vacuum—the kind of thing that "liberals" on both sides get all excited about—so I stick to my original hope that the publicity will help my sales. I don't see what else there could be in it for anybody.

I got the "Tulip" manuscript out today, after a lengthy holiday from it, and am staying home tonight—I usually go up the hill for dinner with the Rosens on Saturdays—with the intention of putting in some more work on it—but there will be the Yankee-Washington ballgame on TV, and some boxing—from Los Angeles this time—and...well, we'll see how things work out. There is—fortunately—always tomorrow!

Speaking of TV, I watched Tom Fool win another easy race this afternoon. He's quite a horse so I hope you won't bet against him if he gets to your part of the world as he probably will in time; Royal Vale—now in your part of the world—is the only horse I've seen make him work to win. Royal Vale looked pretty good both times, but wasn't good enough, as what horse is? though maybe Native Dancer by next year...well, we'll see how things work out.

Now I'm off kitchenward to broil some lamb chops and sauté some mushrooms and fry some potatoes and onions and slice some tomatoes and pour some milk for my dinner, only that reads like too much and I'm already thinking of eliminating maybe the tomatoes.

> Much love to you and to everybody ...
> Pop

TLS MARSHALL

To Josephine Hammett Marshall

18 July 1953, Orchard Hill Road, Katonah, New York

Dear Jo,

It's been sunny and very hot for a few days—kind of nice actually—so we're beginning to scream about dry spells and water shortages, though it was only a few weeks ago that we claimed we were getting far too much rain. Water seems to lack permanency under capitalism. I hope that explains things because I can't think of anything else.

I just took time off from this to peep at Native Dancer on TV beating horses in a Chicago race. He's quite a colt, though I suspect Tom Fool will beat him when they run against one another this fall—probably because it's hard to think of anybody beating Tom Fool just now—but maybe next year...

I'm in self-exile from the Rosens' again today. Barrows Dunham, author of *Man Against Myth* and *Giant in Chains* and in course of losing his lease on a professor's job at Temple, and Jack McManus, editor of

The Guardian, are there for dinner and there will be much intellectual conversation about progressive political matters and I can get a belly-ache just thinking about it. Outside of the necessary talk that goes with most of the things you work at, while you're working at them, I'm not sure talk oughtn't to be limited to women and sports...and I hope that's a sign of age because that way I can count on the notion staying with me and not being just a passing fancy. (I always get testy like this when I'm working, and I've been working a little—I never seem to work very hard, and do you want to make something of that?—on the book.)

Here's a clipping for you and don't tell anybody that I'm more or less inclined to agree with Lawrence.[1] The argument goes on gaily and I'm of course glad to see my name in print—even though it's beginning to cost me a pretty penny for clipping service—but I still can't see where it's likely to do anybody much good or much harm however it turns out: it has all the down-to-earth reality of the old theological disputes over how many angels could dance on the head of a pin. Meanwhile things seem to be going along all right.

> Much love to you and to everybody ...
> Pop

1. In the *New York Herald Tribune* of 7 July 1953, syndicated columnist David Lawrence wrote: "The question is not whether Mr. Hammett's books should be put on the shelves of libraries generally in the United States—they should of course be available to those readers who wish to select any detective stories they like. The real question is whether the government of the United States itself should give recognition or prestige to Mr. Hammett in Communistic circles abroad by putting his books in overseas libraries paid for by the American tax-payer."

TLS Marshall

To Josephine Hammett Marshall

30 July 1953, Orchard Hill Road, Katonah, New York

Dear Princess,
  So here it is already getting along towards the first of August and I

guess I'd better stir my neglectful bones a little and get that "Tulip" manuscript finished because I said I was going to get done with it this summer so I could get to work on another.

Of course I can get hold of a projecting machine to look at movies of
the youngsters and would be glad to. So could you folks too, I dare say, if
you'd just phone a local Eastman dealer or other retailer of movie films,
who usually has or can tell you who has a projection room for just that
purpose.

How is the househunting coming along? You've sounded as if you
were getting warmer in the last couple of letters.

Earlier this week I suddenly, for the first time in I guess more than
15 years, woke up with a touch of pleurisy. It was a slight enough touch,
God knows, and Doc Rosen couldn't find anything else wrong with me
except the slight temperature that duos with it, and the whole thing
was well on its way somewhere else by the next day, so the most I got
out of it was a sort of halfwitted nostalgia: I used to have it two or three
times a year from the late 20s to fairly late in the 30s. Maybe my youth's
coming back, and I'm not sure I want to go through all that mishmash
again.

Lily's still in Rome, though she's looking for a place by the water to
dodge the worst of the Italian heat. The chances are she'll stay over in
Europe till the middle of fall. I think she'd be foolish to come back for a
few weeks just to direct the road company of *The Children's Hour.*

Flora, the brown poodle, was chloroformed this week. She had had a
couple of operations on her jaw—for osteomyelitis—and could probably
have stood another but she was nearly ten years old and it didn't seem to
make much sense just keeping her alive to show it could be done.

That's about all the cheerful news I have and I'm sure you don't want
me to write gloomy stuff.

> Much love, honey, and my love to all…
> Pop

TLS MARSHALL

1953

To Josephine Hammett Marshall

12 August 1953, Orchard Hill Road, Katonah, New York

Dear Princess,

There was a nice letter from you with a couple of cute snapshots of the kids waiting here for me when I got back this afternoon from yonder great big city where I had had to go on Miss H's and not my business, but hurried back on mine.

Lillian's now summering in some improbably named village—part of St Jean de Luz, I think—on the French part of the Basque, which I guess is on the Mediterranean because it's my notion that all European beaches are, and will most likely stay there till she has finished at least the first draft of the script she's doing for Sir Alex, and the road company of *The Children's Hour* will have to be cast without her—there's still new Marys (though I think that's taken care of now) and Karens and Mrs. Tilfords (though Fay Bainter may do for that) to be found—and it's likely that she may not get back in time to direct it either, so I guess I'll be running into town and out again like mad for a little while. (You can figure out how I exaggerate, if you want to, by just asking when I have to go in again, and then I'll say not till the middle of next week, and then you'll know.) Pat's going on the road with the show, but the plan's now to have her switch back and forth from the Karen to the Martha part—I don't know at what intervals—so that means or ought to mean that the new girl will have to be able to switch too. The most likely candidates at the moment seem to be a girl named Barbara (?) Baxter, who played in *Camino Real* and Priscilla Gil[l]ette, who played in *Regina,* Marc Blit[z]stein's operatic version of *The Little Foxes.*[1] Anyhow I'm going to listen to them read when I go in next week.

Take care of yourself, toots, and give my love to everybody and keep a lot for yourself…

Pop

1. Neither Barbara Baxley nor Priscilla Gillette got the part. Blitzstein's opera *Regina* premiered in 1949.

TLS Marshall

To Josephine Hammett Marshall

21 August 1953, Orchard Hill Road, Katonah, New York

Dear Jo,

This stationery might mean I'm staying here more or less permanently—I don't see any reason for moving in the for[e]seeable future—
but the chances are it only means that I finally got around to getting
some new stationery.

Yesterday was another day of giddy whirling in the big city, listening to
a lot of part-readings. I don't know where actresses get their names: they
all sound like actresses' names. Patricia Wright, Lynn Thatcher, Mary
Lee Dearing, Doreen Lane, Patty Foster, Toni Halloran, Sandy James,
Carol Lee! Priscilla Gillette turned out to be a little too fat of face and a
little too inexperienced, but I think maybe both things can be fixed up
and she might make an all right Karen-Martha for the show. There was
another very pretty girl who gave a better reading—Diana Douglas—but
was, I'm afraid, a little too pretty-pretty for the part.[1]

I saw Dorothy Parker for a moment in Frankie & Johnnie's, where I
went for lunch, but didn't have much chance to talk to her.[2] She's casting, too, as were, I dare say, Rodgers and Hammerstein, who were also
having lunch there.

This morning I had a postcard from Lillian, mailed at Arles when she
was en route to that place where she's supposed to be now. Now that—
or so I hear on the radio—the French government's postal employees
have gone back to work I'll probably hear from her. Today's card is the
first news I've had from her in a couple of weeks. She picked the right
time to move over into France!

The youngsters look wonderful, as usual, in their snapshots.

> Give my love to everybody, and chunks to you …
> Pop

1. None of the actresses named were hired.
2. Dorothy Parker's *Ladies of the Corridor* opened on 21 October 1953 at the Longacre Theatre in New York City.

TLS MARSHALL

To Josephine Hammett Marshall

16 September 1953, Orchard Hill Road, Katonah, New York

Dear Princess,

Fall feels kind of with us these days and I like it of course but I suppose in my decadent world it means chiefly that baseball is over except for the World Series—the Dodgers look best on paper, but then so did Cleveland in the American League, so I guess I'll have to string along with the Yankees as usual—and now football begins. (I hear UCLA looks kind of good this year.)

Lily's still in Paris—I had a letter from her this morning—and will probably take her finished first draft over to London to show it to Korda this Sunday or Monday. She talks about maybe coming home before long, but doesn't really know, of course. A first draft can be anything—or any combinations—from a simple and me[re] outline to something that you only have to go over to fix up the punctuation; and a producer's attitude toward it can be as varied. So we'll know when we know …

Monday I went into town to look at the first reading and first semi-rehearsal of the *Children's Hour* road company. It looked all right, but you can't tell much from those firsts, so I came back here to wait till next week when things should sort of begin to jell. I'll probably spend most of next week in the city and perhaps go down to Wilmington for a couple of days when the play opens there the following week.

I had lunch with Pat Neal who looks and acts as if she was having a good time with her new marriage. She said that in London she was talking to a painter named Wood who was telling her something or other about Jacob Epstein, the sculptor, and mentioned that Epstein was currently interested in a mad way in Smuts and Pat said it was probably stupid of her not to know, but what was a smut?[1] My guess would be that Pat deep in her mind thought maybe Epstein was going in for pornographic statuary.

And here now more than a week has passed—it's the 24th—and I haven't finished that letter to you. Oh well, much MUST have happened since then. Let's see…

I went into the big city Monday and came back last night, having seen two run-throughs of the *Children's Hour* road company and several partial rehearsals and it begins to look all right, though it still needs a lot of work but that, presumably, is what rehearsals are for and there's still another week before it opens in Wilmington next Thursday. I'll probably go back into the city tonight and look at a couple of more days, then come back here for the weekend and perhaps go down to Wilmington for the final touches and the opening. You never can tell at this stage of the game—things going good may turn out to be lousy and things going lousy may turn out well—but the play looks in better shape than it did at this stage last winter...I mean the new people: there's no reason why the others shouldn't. Janet Parker isn't going to be any Iris Mann, I'm afraid—not that Iris was ever up to expectations in the part—but I shouldn't be too surprised if Fay Bainter and Priscilla Gillette turn out to be better—taking it all in all—than Katherine Emmet and Kim Hunter. I think perhaps Pat will play better opposite this girl than she did opposite Kim. Well, this time next week we'll be about ready to maybe soon know[2]...

Fall started out here nice and bright and fallish and people are looking at caterpillars and grandma's arthritis and things and predicting a hard winter the way they always do and then we get whatever kind of winter we get as we always do, leaving one with the thought that caterpillars and grandma's arthritis and squirrels and things always prepare for a hard winter so why shouldn't prophets? How are you going to get anywhere by predicting that things are going to be just slightly bad and just slightly good, the way they ordinarily are?

Lillian's in London now—or was the first of the week—seeing Korda about the picture, half-hoping to be able to talk him into letting Ophuls—who's going to direct it—come back to New York with her while she finishes it up. I tried to phone her the other night, but there was a six- or eight-hour delay on the lines so I gave it up. I may try again tomorrow.

Much love to all, toots...
Pop

1. Artist Wood Gaylor was the former director of the Salons of America, which sponsored non-juried, no-awards art shows in Manhattan from 1922 to 1936.
2. Janet Parker, Katherine Emmet, and Kim Hunter played in the revival of *The Children's Hour*.

TLS MARSHALL

To Josephine Hammett Marshall

3 October 1953, Orchard Hill Road, Katonah, New York

Dear Jo,

I went down to Wilmington earlier in the week for final rehearsals and the opening—Thursday night—of the *Children's Hour* road company and it looked very good to me, better, I think, than the New York company, which, if true, would make it the best of all the tries at it, since I think the revival was done better—with one exception—than the original showing. The Wilmington morning paper's critic gave it what seemed a fairly intelligent rave notice, but of course you've got to bear in mind that the Wilmington theater is owned by the Duponts and it's not likely that the local newspapers are going to come out and say much against anything that plays there if they want to stay in business because those nylon people haven't got much doubt about who owns and operates the state of Delaware and don't fool around much with those who think different. But it did look pretty good. Pat is better in it, I think, more relaxed and sure of herself and has put on a little weight and looks very, very lovely, and does a better job playing against this Karen—Priscilla Gillette—than she did opposite the other one, Kim Hunter.[1] And I think Priscilla makes a better Karen than Kim did, though of course she's not as good an actress. Up to now she had chiefly played musical comedy cuties and it was hard work getting that out of her, but I think she made it. Del Hughes, who directed the road company, did a nice job and everybody loves everybody else within reason, though I'm not sure how Pat's going to take it when she finds out that Priscilla Gillette has a remarkably fine stage voice. Pat likes her own voice a good deal, which I had counted on to keep her from paying any attention to Priscilla's, but that dope of a drama critic in the Wilmington paper had to go and comment on how nice Miss Gillette's voice was, so...I am very glad you are not an actor: they are capable of sillinesses unknown to the rest of the world and if I ever find out that I am wrong and that the rest of the world is capable of the same sort of silliness I am going to give up all political activity designed to benefit mankind and take up knitting.

Lillian is still in London as far as I know though I heard a rumor in Wilmington the other night that she was really mad with Kermit and only pretended to be in Europe while she hid out up in Pleasantville. I'm going to be very sore it if turns out to be true.

My class resumes fall operations this Thursday, so I guess I'll be going into town as least once a week for a while now.

The weather's been kind of perfect for a long time now, bright and sunny and reasonably warm in the daytime and just chilly enough to be nice at night. It probably won't stay like this for more than a year or two, though.

After the opening in Wilmington the other night I sat up and talked till after five in the morning, then decided I wasn't sleepy, wrote a letter, and caught the seven o'clock train north, arriving here in time to look at Friday's World Series ballgame on TV, was still up to look at the fights that night, then went to bed with the usual book and read till the usual time, all of which was very much like years ago and gave me quite a feeling of youthfulness...probably second childhood.

And now it's two-thirty of a Sunday morning so I guess I'd better take my second childhood to bed and tuck it in with a good toy or book or something.

> Much love, honey, and give my love to everybody...
> Pop

1. Priscilla Gillette did not appear in the Broadway revival. The role of Karen was played by Kim Hunter.

TLS MARSHALL

To Josephine Hammett Marshall

20 October 1953, Orchard Hill Road, Katonah, New York

Dear Princess,

It seems like a long time since I've heard from you but I don't worry too much about it since they tell me God can be trusted to punish those who neglect aged parents so I guess I can leave it up to him if he isn't too busy with some other of the jobs that those who claim to know give him...and I don't understand that sentence too clearly and I don't exactly know which side it leaves me on, but...

Lillian got back home last week, slimmer and more rested-looking than when she left, but just as full of troubles naturally. She liked London this time, which may have been because she was on her way home and could only stay there a week or two. Outside of that, she seems to have liked Rome a great deal and none of the other places too much. She's currently in Cleveland looking at the play, and probably will be back either tomorrow or Thursday unless of course there seems to be some reason for spending a few more days with *The Children's Hour*. Reviews on the road have been swell, box-office receipts not so swell.

Last week they ran the Humphrey Bogart version of *The Maltese Falcon* at the school and I sat through it again since I had promised to talk a little while afterwards. I liked it this time and wondered why I found it a little boring last time till I remembered that I'd seen it then at the Warner Bros.' studio in Burbank after looking at the two previous versions—both horrible jobs—during a lawsuit and while Maggie was dying over at the Cedars of Lebanon hospital, so I guess I would have found practically anything tiresome to sit through.[1]

The weather's been wonderful and I feel good and the world is not at all as bad a place as some of its weak-stomached critics make out...

> Much love, honey, and give my love to everybody ...
> Pop

1. Maggie Kober died in summer 1951.

TLS MARSHALL

To Josephine Hammett Marshall

13 November 1953, Orchard Hill Road, Katonah, New York

Dear Princess,

I'll of course by all means send Ann her yellow birthday card right away as soon as I can get to a store and find one and I hope I'm far too well trained in the ways of this world to ask why a birthday card? And why now? And why yellow? I just do what I'm told.

Lillian's just back from Chicago where she's been putting some new people into *The Children's Hour* company for what may turn out to be a fairly successful run there—that's one of the cities you stay in as long as there's any hope of making money. Janet Parker, who was playing Mary Tilford on the road, had to be replaced by Iris Mann—she was in the New York company—because Chicago has laws or something against girls under 14 working in the theater and Janet's only 13 and children of that age can probably only work in Illinois at jobs like farmwork and bootblacks and selling newspapers...maybe as bartenders, too, or messengers for racketeers. The law is often confusing.

I saw Jean Hagen in her new TV stint and thought her cute but too smug, which has always been one of her faults. That Danny Thomas has always been one of the unfunnier comics to me.[1] TV has a great many unfunny comics, or so it seems to me, but then I might be getting bilious from age and think it's from comics, which is the kind of thing that happens sometimes.

That reminds me that I've got to stop this now for a little while and go watch the Gavilan–Bratten fight on TV, they being two of my favorite fighters for watching purposes. Well, it was a fairly interesting fight—though a little one-sided—because Gavilan, who usually dances around a lot, fought mostly flat-footed, and Bratton, who boxes well enough but hits better if he's fighting a guy who lets him hit from around the waistline or lower, which Gavilan wasn't likely to let him do much, decided to box, and there went his fight, if I make myself clear[2]...

But the chief thing that was good on TV tonight was that there was a Campbell's Soup program on just before the fights and I dialed in in time to catch the credits and there was one for production or set designing or something for *Fidelis Blunk*.

I hope you're all over your flu epidemic. It couldn't have been much fun even if you more or less took turns. I haven't had anything since spring, not that I feel neglected. The weather's been pretty nice here thus far—except for a lot of wind and wet snow last Friday—and prospects seem good for at least the next few days, and looking ahead much further than that always seems like crystal-ball stuff to me.

I went into the big city yesterday to welcome LH back from Chicago and to do my usual weekly session at school and came back here this afternoon. I'm going in again Sunday and will probably hurry back home that same night.

The pictures of the youngsters were wonderful, as usual.

I've got to run now to do something or other.

Give my love to everybody and keep a lot for you …
Pop

1. Jean Hagen played Danny Thomas's wife in *Make Room for Daddy*, a situation comedy that ran on ABC from 1953 to 1964.
2. Gavilan won, retaining his welterweight championship.

TLS MARSHALL

To Josephine Hammett Marshall

23 November 1953, Orchard Hill Road, Katonah, New York

Dear Princess,

Danton Walker said in his column in *The Daily News* Saturday, "Dashiell Hammett has bought a home in Mexico, where he plans to live permanently," but it's thirty years since I've been to Mexico and I have no deed to any house, though I watch my mail hopefully, and today Walter Winchell says in his column in *The Mirror* that the State Department is very sore at somebody for giving Lillian a passport last spring when the truth seems to be that they were so unsore about it that they gave her an extension on her passport without any todo when time ran out on it in early fall, so I guess you just can't believe much of anything you read in the papers except maybe the paid advertisements and please don't tell me that people who are trying to sell you something might be tempted to lie…

I had a nice letter from you this morning with nice photographs of the youngsters, which is probably much nicer than the deed to Mexican real estate that I was looking for, and I'm glad the youngsters are over their flu attacks: they certainly don't look unwell in the pictures.

This week—Thanksgiving Day falling on Thursday (am I pretending this is something new?)—I take a vacation from school. I think Lillian's coming up Wednesday so she'll be here to set off the firecrackers or whatever you do on this particular holiday. I went into town yesterday to have dinner with her. She seems well, except for some trouble with her back, but is of course full of complaints about this, that and the other. I like her, so her complaints often seem cute to me, but the truth is as I grow older I have less and less understanding—of which I never had much, though I suppose I thought I did because the young hate to think they're mudheads—of either the reason behind complaints or the reason for them. They seem to me just talk, or quotations from the scripture or something. You improve an automobile or a civilization or a way of making soup because you think it will be better that way, not because you didn't like it the way it was: if you're disgusted with it it's a lot easier to walk or become a hermit or commit suicide or change your diet or something. I don't know what got me started on all this, but anyhow that's my sermon for the day.

The Children's Hour seems to be doing fairly well in Chicago, but is not what theatrical circles call a smash.

I saw your UCLA play those people Saturday on TV and, after what seemed to me a shaky start, they looked pretty good, though I wouldn't at the moment bet too much on them when they meet those other people at the Rose Bowl. In spite of Saturday's tie, which I didn't see, Notre Dame this year looks to me like the best single-platoon college team I've ever seen, though I have not seen Maryland, which, discounting those early soft touches, figures better on paper and may well be.

I do not seem to have anything else to say to you at the moment except that I love you...and give my love to everybody...

Pop

TLS MARSHALL

To Lillian Hellman

Hellman's The Lark, *adapted from Jean Anouilh's* L'Alouette, *opened at the Longacre Theatre on 17 November 1955, starring Julie Harris, Boris Karloff, and Christopher Plummer. Leonard Bernstein composed the music. It ran for 229 performances. This note is transcribed as Hammett wrote it, errors included.*

[about August 1955, no address]

About music of *The Lark,* being what Hammett remembers of telephonic conversation with L. Bernstein;

7 unaccompanied voices, featuring solo by counter-tenor

608

Before curtain rises voices are heard in kind of solemn, perhaps alternately aggressive and reverand, rendition of "exaudi oriatem meam Domine" or something.

1st after curtain rise is a motet (or should it be motel?) from the Mass—or based on the Mass—"quietollis, etc"

2nd, Joan does a dance or something to off-stage shepherds singing a motet or something based on 13th Century stuff

This is intereuppted by counter-tenor singing "Laudette something-or-other"—

later on they sing in unison

Later points in first act:

Court song is based on Early Rennaiscance secular text of "fide etc"

Last of first act: Benidictus is a free ecclesiatical setting of benedictions in the style of the 14th Century

2nd act:

Before curtain rise solders' voices singing "Viva la Joan" or something to another borrowed tune...and then whistling same tune after curtain rises.

Repeat "Quietollis" for confession.

Burning: sanctus from Mass in 14th Century manner

Chanting of requiem

Coronation (and he seems pretty sore about having his music reduced to just a "gloria")—setting of Gloria of Mass to music of prelude to Act I.

He wants to know why, if you want to say anything about music at all, you don't print it in your book, since, he says. it's all vocal and easily done.

TLU HRC

To Josephine Hammett Marshall

13 October 1955, Orchard Hill Road, Katonah, New York

Dear Princess,

This is a fine late date to be welcoming you into your new home and stuff, but anyhow I do and it sounds pretty good and I hope you will be happy there and so on...

* * *

Last month I had some sort of heart attack—an *unseri[ou]s* coronary embolism—and spent part of last week and part of this in dear old Lenox Hill Hospital and came back here yesterday on the promise to my doctors that I'd play invalid for at least three weeks, which is what I'm doing. So I can't go to Lily's rehearsals and I can't go in to my Jefferson School classes, and the truth is that I don't want to much anyhow, feeling kind of weak and thus far very willing to spend most of my time in bed. Weakness is about all I do feel, however, and nobody seems to have any doubts that I will be as good as new once this take-it-easy period is over and I can go back to smoking and taking it easy again in my own way.

Now I've got to go lie down. Give my best to Loyd and kiss the youngsters for me.

> Much love, honey…
> Pop

TLS Marshall

To Josephine Hammett Marshall

14 October 1955, Katonah, New York

Dearest Jo,

That letter yesterday was just so you'd know I wasn't too badly off in case you heard that I'd had a heart attack because that can be made to sound sort of ominous—it has nice bullying possibilities that I must explore for possible future use—and there wasn't much news in it—the letter—so here I am trying to bring you up to date about what's been going on in my world since long long ago when I last wrote you…only nothing much of anything seems to have happened…but we can't all live full lives, I guess …

Pat had a baby last spring, a kind of cute little girl that I saw when she was maybe a week old, christened Olivia Twenty Dahl for God knows what reason. Pat, whose new show, *A Roomful of Roses,* opens here next week, phoned me while I was in the hospital and promised to send me the youngster's picture—she says she looks like Ann, but then that's probably the only baby Pat ever saw—but it hasn't come yet. (It seemed to me that when Pat spoke of the baby it was a little remotely, as if she were speaking of last month's baby, but I'm probably doing her an injustice.)

Judy Rosen, now Judy Rubin, also had a baby in London last week, a boy named David as a great many boys seem to be named. A lot of other people I know seem to be breeding too, but I don't guess there's much use of telling you about those you don't know like Felicia Monte[ale]gre, who's an actress married to Leonard Bernstein, who's a composer-conductor married to her, so I'll just stick to my statement that a lot of people I know seem to be breeding. I was up before some kind of state joint-legislative committee in the spring to keep up my franchise and the income tax people both federal and state bother me just enough to keep my blood more or less circulating and that heart attack—I'm beginning to roll that phrase around in my mouth quite unct[u]ously—made me skip this term at the school and I haven't done much work on the book for more or less obvious reasons, none of which has to do with publishers, because, regardless of what's often said, they're folks who have nothing against making an honest dollar and are always willing to print anything that'll sell, and have been taking life easy.

Lily is up to her ears in rehearsals of *The Lark*, which opens in Boston in a couple of weeks and comes into the big city some time next month, and in conferences with Tyrone Guthrie, who is going to direct the opera that she and Lennie Bernstein made out of *Candide,* probably next year. I miss all this fun, if that's what you want to call it, by being on the sick list, though I've hopes of getting up to Boston in time to see *The Lark* before they bring it to town.

Franc[e]s Goodrich and Albert Hackett got smash-hit notices for the opening of their *Diary of Ann[e] Frank* and everybody is very happy about it—those that aren't jealous—and that's every last bit of news I can remember unless you want me to make some up for you.

My best to Loyd and kiss the children for me—isn't it about time you sent me a snapshot of them?—and take care of yourself for me…

> Love—
> Pop

TLS MARSHALL

To Josephine Hammett Marshall

25 January 1956 [no address]

Dear Jo,

Well, I'm all right as far as the heart is concerned according to the doctor who doesn't want to see me again—bored, I guess—until the middle of March unless I can think up some kind of complications meanwhile, which I have no intentions of doing just to interest him. I like him, but not that much.

The Xmas ties were nice and the only reason I've only worn one of them so far is that I haven't been going to the big city very often and us rural characters don't tie down our Adam's apples much unless we're showing off for strangers. Thanks.

Lily will probably be along in an hour or so and we'll drive up to Martha's Vineyard for three or four days—stopping maybe tonight at Providence—for a look at her new house there—in Vineyard Haven, just down the road a little from the place she rented last summer—to decide on improvements and things. You know how people are when they've just bought a new house; they get fidgety to move the attic into the basement and so on. The new place looked good last summer and I think it's going to be all right.

I'm still skipping the school and will most likely take the rest of the year off. There doesn't seem to be much sense in going back just for the late spring and early summer terms.

The youngsters look grand in the snapshots.

> Love to everybody including you too...
> Pop

TLS Marshall

1956

To Josephine Hammett Marshall

5 February 1956, Katonah, New York

Dear Princess,

The Martha's Vineyard trip was nice, though Lily's furniture hadn't arrived so we'll have to go back again next month to see how it looks in the new house and what else she needs and stuff, which is what we went up for in the first place, but we stayed three or four days and filled in the time with going over things with the architect who['s] supposed to make alterations and picking out wallpaper and such and had a good time. New England is nice in winter if you like winter in places like New England, which I do. That's a nice island.

You were right about that being me in the *Time* photograph, though with *Time*'s usual inaccuracy they managed to place it in Sardi's when it was actually taken in the Oak Room at the Plaza, and that wasn't as easy a mistake to make as you might think, since they took the pictures themselves, but they manage all right. I think it was in the same story that they had Julie Harris's eyes grey, though they're as startling a blue as you're likely to find, if I remember them rightly.

I went into the big city yesterday and came back this afternoon, and will probably go in again later in the week—maybe Thursday—to see Lily off to the southland—some place in Florida or one of the West Indies, where she's going for ten days or so to try to get her voice back to par, on the theory that she may have a trace of virus or something to interfere with her complete recovery from having the polyps taken off her vocal c[o]rds. The oven of her gas range blew up on her at breakfast this morning and banged up one of her ankles—which seems to be all right now—and the big toe on her other foot, which seems to be giving her trouble—or was when I talked to her on the phone a few minutes ago—right now. She's going to have it x-rayed tomorrow to make sure it's nothing more than a bruise, which God knows can be painful [e]nough when you get them there.

Nothing untoward happens to me however: I just go along in my usual on-this-hand-not-too-good-on-that-hand-not-too-bad shape, looking forward to some sort of gradual decline till I die in my eighties, though I'll spread it out as long as I can because having been born in the last century I'd naturally like to see this one through and die in the next, but since I was six years old when this one came in I'd be pretty old and people around me would probably get pretty impatient and you cou[ldn]'t blame them too much...though I guess I would.

> Love to everybody...and take care of yourself for me...
> Pop

TLS Marshall

To Josephine Hammett Marshall

24 April 1956, Orchard Hill Road, Katonah, New York

Dear Toots,

It's kind of nice today, though still not quite spring, and I feel pretty good and will probably go down to the big city this afternoon and have dinner with LH and come back here tomorrow.

The heart thing's all cleared up and all I've got to worry about now is that my lungs or something don't manufacture enough oxygen for my great big muscles—that's the way I try to make myself remember them now—and so I'm pretty weak sometimes and have shortness of breath and stuff to keep me from leading that fantastically active life to which I try to make myself remember I was accustomed. The doctors don't seem to take this thing with as much seriousness as I'd like—I suspect they more or less write it off as just one of those incurable things that go or come with advancing age—but I have no intentions of playing *that* game. As soon as I've got time from other things—I'll probably go up to Martha's Vineyard for another week in a few days—I'll see what I can do about pestering the be-jesus out of them.

> Much love, honey...and my love to [e]verybody ...
> Pop

TLS Marshall

To Josephine Hammett Marshall

5 June 1956, Orchard Hill Road, Katonah, New York

Dear Princess,

It was nice up in Martha's Vineyard and I spent nearly a month up there, coming home the day before Decoration Day last week and tomorrow I'm to phone my Doctor Abeloff to find out what couple of days he's got me a room in the hospital for so I can go over there and let them examine me to try to find out if they can do anything about that shortness of breath and accompanying general weakness that bothers me into thinking that I'd like to climb mountains or something—which isn't too bad, but the trouble is I get to thinking that I used to climb mountains or do many equivalent things (and you don't have to tell me I never did: I know it) and that's a kind of softening of the brain that probably does a lot of harm in the long run. The world's too full now of old fuffs who go around believing—or at least saying in the absence of witnesses—that they were once hell-a-mile. My guess, of course, remains the same, that old age is catching up with me a little prematurely and I'd better find out about it so I can nurse myself along and try to do at least a little better than my father, whom I'd like to beat at the longevity racket and who was about 83 when he popped off.

Lily's coming down from the Vineyard tomorrow and I'll probably go in to the big city and have dinner with her. She's up to her neck in work on *Candide,* which i[s] due to open in November. I think *The Lark* closed for the summer—Julie Harris' contract read that she was to get a month off—and will go on the road this fall.

That's about all I've got time for now.

> Much love, toots, and to everybody—
> Pop

TLS Marshall

To Josephine Hammett Marshall

30 July 1956, Orchard Hill Road, Katonah, New York

Dearest Jo,

Your letter telling me you are going to have another youngster in February got to me just a minute ago and of course to me, who doesn't have any of the bother, it seems like the most wonderful news imaginable, and, speaking as one who grew up in that size family, three children seems to me the ideal number, and, speaking as one who had an older sister and a younger brother, I can assure you of course that the newcomer will be a boy. Anyhow, what you and Loyd are doing is nice and the child will be nice and I feel nice about it—only why do I keep making these typos?

A couple of weeks ago my medico put me on a saltier diet and I imagine I feel pretty good from it.

This clipping from a local newspaper I send along because though the story makes me sound a little too pathetic I think I look good in the picture.

That'll have to be all for now, except love to everybody...and it's nice what you're doing and I love you...

    Pop

TLS Marshall

To Josephine Hammett Marshall

7 August 1956, Orchard Hill Road, Katonah, New York

Dear Princess,

You're a dear sweet girl and I'd love to see you and the youngsters but the plan your letter suggests doesn't, I'm afraid, seem practicable just now, for various reasons, none of which has much to do with the things "covered" by that dopey newspaper story I sent you, and which I foolishly took for granted you'd take with a grain of salt. I guess I forgot the power of the press. Anyhow, I'm not yet the pathetic figure the story makes me seem with its "ill and penniless" angle. So I'm ill! Well, I have had a cou-

Now Ill, Penniless Recluse

Hemingway Talks Too Much, Says Creator Of 'Thin Man'

BY HERBERT GELLER

SOMERS—The man who earned a million dollars as creator of Sam Spade and the Thin Man is penniless and ill today, living quietly at the home of a friend in a secluded section of this town.

Dashiell Hammett, once the darling of mystery readers the world over, lives a solitary life at the home of Dr. Samuel Rosen of Orchard Hill Road, with whom he has made his home for four years.

The money he earned as creator of Sam Spade and the Thin Man is gone, and Hammett is faced with a federal income tax claims for thousands of dollars, as well as a $316 judgement he was recently ordered to pay a newspaper clipping service in Westchester County Court.

Hammett has shunned the spotlight since he was convicted and served a six-month sentence for contempt of court in 1951. The writer was jailed on the contempt count after he refused to disclose information about the Civil Rights Congress, listed by the United States Attorney General as a communist front organization, of which he was an officer.

Hammett has been so removed from public life since then that he learned about the county court judgement from a reporter who called to ask about it. The judgement was handed down by County Court Judge Hugh S. Coyle of Lewisboro, who ordered Hammett to pay $316 and $10 costs to Burrelle Press Clipping Service of New York.

Second Contempt Count

When Hammett failed to appear in court for examination on payment of the judgement, Judge Coyle fined him another $250 for contempt of court. The judge then ordered Hammett to pay the judgement, costs, and contempt fine at the rate of $10 a week.

But this is only a drop in the bucket to the claim for thousands of dollars in back taxes which the federal government has lodged against Hammett.

Hammett is plagued by health troubles as well as financial woes. He was hospitalized several times in 1955 for heart trouble and has a lung ailment acquired during military service in World War I. But he does not attribute his poor health to his Army services in the Aleutian Islands in World War II.

The health problem stands in the way of completion of a current novel, says Hammett. He has two books in the works, "just about people."

But he hasn't written detective stories for some 20 years. His detective best sellers like "Red Harvest," "The Maltese Falcon," and "The Glass Key" were written years ago, and the author says he didn't particularly enjoy writing them. He based his detective stories in part on his experience as a Pinkerton detective, and, though he felt they were something of a dead end, they made money; so he continued writing them.

The hardboiled "Mickey Spillane" school of detective stories does not arouse Mr. Hammett's

DASHIELL HAMMETT

admiration. He dislikes violence for the sake of violence and prefers the subtleties of George Simenon's "Inspector Maigrete" to the bloodthirsty tales of Mike Hammer.

In fact he feels a good writer is heading down a cul de sac if he concentrates on detective stories.

Anderson The Best

On the subject of American literature Mr. Hammett is more at home, but he feels the golden day in this country's writing is past. The 1920's were the boom period of American writers, when such giants as Sherwood Anderson (whom none of today's authors approaches, in Hammett's eyes), and Ernest Hemingway were crashing into new literary fields.

About Hemingway Mr. Hammett has mixed feelings.

"Everything he writes is an embodiment of himself," says the former mystery author. "He can write very good stories and very bad stories."

Novels like the recent "Over the River and through the Trees" are "a picturization of Heming-

way's habit of talking too much," he declares.

"The Old Man and the Sea" on the other hand is a good story which shows Hemingway's best writing qualities, Hammett feels. But the story is not new. Hemingway has been telling it to friends for years.

Best of today's writers, Hammett feels, is William Faulkner. His books like "Absalom, Absalom" are the finest examples of literary technique, although "they have nothing to say to the reader."

A man whose views on politics and world affairs have been bitterly assailed, Hammett still keeps an eye on international news. The cold war does not distress him, for he feels the issue at stake between the free world and the Soviet Union are "only a family quarrel."

Hammett is glad the neutralist bloc of nations favoring neither the United States nor Russia is growing larger. "It will help maintain peace," he says.

For the mistakes which put him in prison and destroyed his career he has no apology.

ple of years of more or less progressive breathlessness and weakness—
and a heart attack or something that certainly wasn't very bad and seemed
to have nothing to do with the other things—and it was a nuisance, but
not as much of a nuisance as it would have been if I'd had to do things
when I didn't feel like doing them—like working for a living—and I had
been sick before—for longer periods—and no doubt will be again—and
could wait it out even if I got a little impatient now and then, and I did,
and I seem to be on the mend now and have felt stronger for the past
month or so and how strong do you expect to get anyhow? So I'm broke!
Well, I am, but I still move around New York City when I go there by taxi-
cab and usually have a steak and some caviar and whatever I happen to
think of in the ice-box and don't have to worry about the price of anything
unless it's fifty dollars or something—phooey on that kind of being broke!

Lillian's still on Martha's Vineyard, working on *Candide* with her
col[l]aborat[o]r and the director, and will pr[o]bably be down to New York
later this month when they start rehearsals or wind up the casting or something.[1] She sounded all right when I talked to her on the phone last week.

Now I've got to go down to Katonah to get my hair cut. Give my love
to everybody, and I'm sorry about this summer, but maybe I'll see you
before too long anyhow.

> Much love, honey...
> Pop

1. *Candide*, a comic operetta based on Voltaire's satire, opened on December 1, 1956,
   and ran for 73 performances. Leonard Bernstein wrote the music; Richard Wilbur,
   John LaTouche, and Dorothy Parker wrote the lyrics; Tyrone Guthrie directed.

TLS MARSHALL

To Lillian Hellman

Katonah, N.Y., along about the seventh of January in the year of 1957 A.D.

Dear Lishka,

It's cold and sunny with an inch or two of snow that fell last night and
more promised in flurries this afternoon and tonight and I guess I'll go
into the village presently and mail this and get my shopping done.

Sam Rosen phoned Saturday night to say they weren't coming up that week-end because Friesy had had to have his appendix out and was all right now and how was I? and he'd had a lovely trip and things like that and that they'd be up next week.

Yesterday that rheumatic shoulder wasn't so good so I spent most of the day lying on the bed looking at television, which wasn't so good either, but better I dare say than on most Sundays, or maybe I was more docile. Anyhow I started off with a girl singing "The Saint Louis Blues" straight on a church show and the Revernd Albert Kershaw explaining afterwards that God was implicit in the song, which is just about what they did to the Song of Solomon years ago so I guess it's all right; and then I saw *Camera Three* doing—they only had half an hour to do it in—high spots of the Chaucer and Shakespeare versions of *Troilus and Cressida* and, for all of it[s] deadpan gooeyness, I liked the Chaucer version better; and then I looked at somebody called Sonny Fox escorting somebody called Pud and somebody called Ginger through a sort of trip to the Indonesian E[m]bassy in Washington and was mildly amazed as usual by the slick bad manners of television folk and the way people put up with it; and then I listened to a woman named Elizabeth Boyd talk about *Madame Bovary* in neither an interesting way nor an uninteresting way on a program called "Re[p]ort From Rutgers"; and then looked at something called "Odyssey"—I guess it's Channel Two's answer to "The Wide Wide World" on Channel Four, which would seem dull enough not to need an answer—which dealt at great length and that sort of time-wasting that television almost always has with the Comstock Lode and Virginia City, which couldn't have been *that* dull; and then I watched Christopher Plummer do a Walter Kerr version of *Oedipus Rex* on Omnibus, which was not bad except maybe for a kind of repulsive over-doing of makeup after he'd blinded himself. Carol Goodner played J[oca]sta and was just a kind of puppet, as was a guy named Goodier who was Creon, but I guess that didn't matter much.

Love,
Dash

TLS HRC

To Lillian Hellman

17 January 1958, Orchard Hill Road, Katonah, New York

Dear Lilishk,

It looks like all right today, sunny and stuff, so maybe I'll give Katonah my business.

It was hot spit talking to you last night, though maybe I didn't sound so bright, but then I ask myself, when do I? and I don't know about that answer I keep getting.

I had a letter from Jo today saying she liked the pocketbook and Julie was nuts about the panda and Ann and Evan wore their pajamas all day Christmas and Ann wore hers out that night and Evan's lost his first tooth and things like that and they look mighty good in the snapshots.[1]

There's a popular song called "You're My Destiny" that has a second line I kind of like... "you are what you are to me," because it's got that kind of nice ambiguity that I like.

> Now for Katonah...
> Dash

1. Julie Marshall, Hammett's third grandchild, was born on 19 February 1957.

TLS LPT

To Josephine Hammett Marshall

21 January 1958, Orchard Hill Road, Katonah, New York

Dear Princess,

Thanks a lot for the book of photographs: that guy's quite a photographer!

You and Loyd really turn out good-looking youngsters. They're all of them really dreams in the snapshots. I'm glad they liked the stuff I sent them.

Lillian's in England seeing about the local *Candide* show and will probably be there for another couple of weeks.

I've been laid up for a couple of weeks with a cold, which, while little enough in itself, made breathing tough for me. I had no pain—which I guess was goood. but—oh, boy!—was I uncomfortable? It's better now or I am or something.

> Love to everybody ...
> Pop

TLS MARSHALL

To Josephine Hammett Marshall

17 May 1958, 63 East 82nd St., New York City

Dear Toots,

After five years and a half I finally tore myself, or got torn, I'm not sure which, from Katonah and came back to the big city where my address will be this until next month when I'll try Martha's Vineyard for awhile and my address will he in care of Lillian Hellman, Vineyard Haven, Mass. After the summer I don't know ...

Julie sounds like quite a kid and the others looked good too in the slides you sent me. It's a nice family!

> Love to all of them ...
> Pop

TLS MARSHALL

To Lillian Hellman

The note at the bottom, signed "Lillian," is to Diane Johnson. Hellman wrote it when Johnson was working on her biography of Hammett, which Hellman authorized. Hammett and Hellman had met thirty years before, at a party in Hollywood, on November 22, 1930.

25 November 1960 [no address]

Nov 25, 1960
    7:10 AM.
    On this thirtieth anniversary of the beginning of everything,
    I wish to state:
    The love that started on that day was greater than
    all love anywhere, anytime, and all poetry cannot include it.

    I did not then know what treasure I had, could not,
    and thus occasionally violated the grandeur of this bond.

    For which I regret.

    But I give deep thanks for the glorious day, and thus
    the name "Thanks-giving".

    What but an unknown force could have given me, a
    sinner, this woman?

    Praise God.

        Signed.
          Dashiell Hammett

If this seems incomplete it is probably because I couldn't think of anything else at the time.
        DH

Oct 1978

Dear Diane
    I wrote this and presented it to Dash for his signature.
        Lillian

TLS WITH AUTOGRAPH NOTES LPT

Nov 25, 1960 (64) ✓
7:10 A.M.

On this thirtieth anniversary of the beginning of everything,
I wish to state:
      The love that started on that day was greater than
all love anywhere, anytime, and all poetry cannot include it.

      I did not then know what treasure I had, could not,
and thus occasionally violated the grandeur of this bond.

      For which I gegret.

      But I give deep thanks for the glorious day, and thus
the name "Thanks - giving".

      Who but an unknown force could d have given me, a
sinner, this woman?

      Praise God.

                  Signed.
                  ~~Dashiell Hammett~~

If this seems incomplete it
is probably because I
couldn't think of anything
else at the time

                              DH

Dear Diane   Oct 1978
    I wrote this and presented it to Dash for
his signature

                  Lillian

CODA

HAMMETT DIED ON 10 January 1961 in Lenox Hill Hospital. He was sixty-six. The cause of death was lung cancer complicated by emphysema and pneumonia, in addition to disease of the heart, liver, kidneys, spleen, and prostate gland. There was a memorial service at Frank E. Campbell's Funeral Home on Madison Avenue. Lillian Hellman delivered the eulogy.

Hammett's only income in the last years had been his veteran's pension of $131.10 per month. He died broke, with liens against his estate of more than $220,000, mostly for back taxes. His primary assets were his short stories and five novels, all written between 1922 and 1934—and a portion of at least one of the novels he had been promising since 1934.

As executor of the will, Lillian Hellman settled his income tax debt and gained control of his literary estate. The blacklist was over by then, and she revived his literary reputation, arranging republication of his novels and editing *The Big Knockover,* a collection of his short stories which included "Tulip," a 21,500-word fragment of the last novel he attempted.

It is tempting for sympathetic observers to draw a melodramatic picture of Hammett's final decade, but to do so does him an immense disservice. He was not a man who tolerated pity, especially pity directed toward him. Following Benjamin Disraeli's dictum, he never complained and never explained. In that dark political age of the 1950s, Hammett avoided the acrimony and hatred and self-righteous indignation that consumed many of his colleagues and close friends. He was too proud, too self-sufficient to seek either approval or vindication from others. He believed in self-affirmation, and he held on to that basic principle to the moment of his death.

APPENDIX: HAMMETT'S READING

Hammett refers to the books listed below in his letters, usually in the context of commenting on his current reading. Most of the books were new publications when he referred to them. When he was in the army, Hammett had access to Armed Services Editions; thus those publications are cited, in addition to the first edition.

Allen, Hervey, *Bedford Village* (New York: Farrar & Rinehart, 1944).

Arnold, Thurman Wesley, *The Folklore of Capitalism* (New Haven: Yale University Press, 1937).

Auden, W. H., *The Double Man* (New York: Random House, 1941).

Bardeche, Maurice, *The History of Motion Pictures* (New York: Norton/Museum of Modern Art, 1938).

Barnett, Lincoln, *The Universe and Mr. Einstein* (New York: Sloane, 1948).

Beard, Charles and Mary, *A Basic History of the United States* (New York: Doubleday, Doran, 1944).

Bezzerides, A. I., *Long Haul* (New York: Carrick & Evans, 1938).

Bezzerides, A. I., *Thieves' Market* (New York: Scribners, 1949).

Bishop, Leonard, *Down All Your Streets* (New York: Dial, 1952).

Bojer, Rowan, *The Everlasting Struggle,* trans. Arna Heni and Louise Rourke (New York: Century, 1931).

Bowen, Catherine Drinker, *Yankee from Olympus: Justice Holmes and His Family* (Boston: Little, Brown, 1944).

Boyle, Kay, *Plagued by the Nightingale* (New York: Cape & Smith, 1931).

Brontë, Emily, *Wuthering Heights* (1847).

Browder, Earl, *The People's Front* (New York: International Publishers, 1938).

Brown, Harry, *A Walk in the Sun* (New York: Knopf, 1944).

Bruff, Nancy, *The Manatee* (New York: Dutton, 1945).

Carlisle, Harry, *Darkness at Noon* (New York: Liveright, 1931).

Carlson, John Roy, *Under Cover: My Four Years in the Nazi Underworld of America; The Amazing Revelation of How Axis Agents and Our Enemies Within Are Now Plotting to Overthrow the United States* (New York: Dutton, 1943).

Carpenter, Margaret, *Murder Perilous* (Boston: Little, Brown, 1943).

Carse, Robert, *There Go the Ships* (New York: Morrow, 1942; published in an Armed Services Edition in 1943).

Cary, Joyce, *The Horse's Mouth* (New York: Harper, 1944).

Cesbron, Gilbert, *The Innocents of Paris*, trans. M. Waldman (Boston: Houghton Mifflin, 1946).

Clugston, Kate, *A Murderer in the House* (New York: A. A. Wyn, 1947).

Comfort, Will Levington, *Apache* (New York: Dutton, 1931).

Connolly, Cyril, *The Condemned Playground: Essays 1927–1944* (New York: Macmillan, 1946).

Cooper, James Fenimore, *The Last of the Mohicans* (1826).

Cummings, E. E., *1 x 1* (New York: Holt, 1944).

Dalí, Salvador, *Hidden Faces* (New York: Dial, 1944).

Derleth, August, *Wind Over Wisconsin* (New York: Scribners, 1938).

Dooley, Roger B., *Less Than Angels* (Milwaukee: Bruce, 1946).

Dostoyevsky, Fyodor, *Crime and Punishment* (1866).

Du Maurier, Daphne, *The King's General* (Garden City: Doubleday, 1946).

Du Maurier, Daphne, *Rebecca* (Garden City: Doubleday, Doran, 1938).

Farrell, James T., *No Star Is Lost* (New York: Vanguard, 1938).

Fast, Howard, *Freedom Road* (New York: Duell, Sloan & Pearce, 1944).

Fast, Howard, *The Last Frontier* (New York: Duell Sloan & Pearce, 1942).

Faulkner, William, *Sanctuary* (New York: Cape & Smith, 1931).

Fitzgerald, F. Scott, *Tender Is the Night* (New York: Scribners, 1934).

Fletcher, H. L. V., *Miss Agatha Doubles for Death* (New York: Messner, 1947).

Ford, Ford Madox, *The Good Soldier: A Tale of Passion* (London & New York: John Lane, 1915).

Frank, Waldo, *The Death and Birth of David Markand: An American Story* (New York & London: Scribners, 1934).

Franklin, Francis, *The Rise of the American Nation, 1789–1824* (New York: International Publishers, 1943).

Fraser, Sir James George, *The Golden Bough* (12 vols, 1890–1915; one-volume abridgement by Fraser, New York: Macmillan, 1922).

Gaither, Frances, *The Red Cock Crows* (New York: Macmillan, 1943; republished in 1944 in an Armed Services Edition).

Garston, Crosby, *China Seas: A Novel of the East* (London: Chatto & Windus, 1930; New York: Stokes, 1931).

Gogol, Nikolai, *Dead Souls* (1842).

Gorky, Maksim, *The Magnet*, trans. Alexander Baksy (New York: Cape & Smith, 1931).

Graves, Robert, *But It Still Goes On: An Accumulation* (London: Cape, 1930).

Graves, Robert, *The White Goddess: A Historical Grammar of Poetic Myth* (New York: Creative Age, 1948).

Green, F. L., *Mist on the Waters* (New York: Harcourt Brace, 1949).

Green, F. L., *Odd Man Out* (New York: Reynal & Hitchcock, 1947).

Greene, Graham, *The Heart of the Matter* (New York: Viking, 1948).

Harriman, John, *The Magnate* (New York: Random House, 1946).

Hauser, Arnold, *The Social History of Art*, 2 vols., (New York: Knopf, 1951).

Hauser, Heinrich, *Thunder above the Sea* (New York: Liveright, 1931).

Hecht, Ben, *The Florentine Dagger: A Novel for Amateur Detectives* (New York: Boni & Liveright, 1923).

Henri, Robert, *The Art Spirit* (Philadelphia: Lippincott, 1923).

Heym, Stefan, *The Eyes of Reason* (Boston: Little Brown, 1951).

Hobson, Laura, *The Trespassers* (New York: Simon & Schuster, 1943).

Hoke, Henry Reed, *Black Mail* (New York: Reader's Book Service, 1944).

Hough, Donald, *The Camelephamoose* (New York: Duell, Sloan & Pearce, 1946).

Hough, Donald, *Snow above Town: A Story of Wyoming* (New York: Norton, 1943).

Hughes, Cledwyn, *He Dared Not Look Behind* (New York: A.A. Wyn, 1947).

Hunt, Barbara, *Sea Change: A Witches Brew* (New York: Rinehart, 1946).

Jackson, Charles, *The Fall of Valor* (New York: Rinehart, 1946).

Jackson, Charles, *The Lost Weekend* (New York: Farrar & Rinehart, 1944).

Jeans, Sir James, *The Mysterious Universe* (London: Macmillan, 1930).

Jerome, V. J., *Culture in a Changing World* (New York: New Century, 1947).

Jerome, V. J., *Intellectuals and the War* (New York: Workers Library, 1940).

Jerome, V. J., *The Negro in Hollywood Films* (New York: Mainstream and Masses, 1950).

Karski, Jan, *Story of a Secret State* (Boston: Houghton Mifflin, 1944).

Kronenberger, Louis, editor, *Reader's Companion: A Personal Anthology Selected for Re-Readability from Writers of 2000 Years for the Reader of Today* (New York: Viking, 1945).

Lamb, Harold, *Genghis Khan: The Emperor of All Men* (New York: McBride, 1927).

Lancaster, Bruce, *No Bugles Tonight* (Boston: Atlantic Monthly Press/Little, Brown, 1948).

Lawrence, D. H., *Lady Chatterley's Lover* (1928).

Laxness, Halldor, *Independent People*, trans. J. A. Thompson (New York: Knopf, 1946).

Leigh, Michael, *Comrade Forest* (New York: Random House, 1947).

Le Sage, Alain-René, *Gil Blas* (1715–1735).

Levin, Meyer, *Citizens* (New York: Viking, 1940).

Manhood, H. A., *Gay Agony* (New York: Viking, 1931).

Markham, S. F., *Climate and the Energy of Nations* (New York: Oxford University Press, 1942).

Marx, Karl, *Das Kapital* (1867).

Mazaline, Guy, *The Wolves*, trans. Eric Sutton (New York: Macmillan, 1934).

McCormick, Renée de Fontarce, *Little Coquette: The Story of a French Girlhood* (Boston: Houghton Mifflin, 1944).

McCoy, Horace, *I Should Have Stayed Home* (New York: Knopf, 1938).

Meredith, William, *Love Letter from an Impossible Land* (New Haven: Yale University Press, 1944).

Millay, Edna St. Vincent, *Wine from These Grapes* (New York & London: Harper, 1934).

Moley, Raymond, *Our Criminal Courts* (New York: Minton, Balch, 1930).

Munro, W. Carroll, *The Gift of Glory* (New York: Scribners, 1950).

Nathan, George Jean, *Monks Are Monks: A Diagnostic Scherzo* (New York: Knopf, 1929).

Neumann, Alfred, *The Hero: The Tale of a Political Murder*, trans. Huntley Paterson (New York: Knopf, 1931).

O'Hara, John, *Hope of Heaven* (New York: Harcourt, Brace, 1938).

Pearson, Hesketh, *Oscar Wilde: His Life and Wit* (New York: Harper, 1946).

Pennell, Joseph Stanley, *The History of Rome Hanks and Kindred Matters* (New York: Scribners, 1944).

Peyrefitte, Roger, *Special Friendships*, trans. Felix Giovanelli (New York: Vanguard, 1950).

Powys, C. F., *The White Paternoster* (London: Chatto & Windus, 1930).

Price, Willard, *Japan's Islands of Mystery* (New York: Day, 1944).

Proust, Marcel, *Remembrance of Things Past,* trans. C. K. Scott Moncrieff (originally published in 16 volumes, 1920–1937).

Rinehart, Mary Roberts, *The Circular Staircase* (Indianapolis: Bobbs-Merrill, 1908).

Romains, Jules, *Death of a World*, trans. Gerard Hopkins (New York: Knopf, 1938), vol. 7 of the *Men of Good Will* series, which comprised 27 volumes, the last published in 1946.

Romains, Jules, *Escape in Passion*, trans. Gerard Hopkins (New York: Knopf, 1946), vol. 13 of *Men of Good Will*.

Romains, Jules, *Work and Play*, trans. Gerard Hopkins (New York: Knopf, 1944), vol. 11 of *Men of Good Will*.

Rowan, Richard Wilmer, *The Pinkertons: A Detective Dynasty* (Boston: Little Brown, 1931).

Rukeyser, Muriel, *Beast in View* (Garden City: Doubleday, Doran, 1944).

Sandoz, Mari, *Old Jules* (Boston: Little, Brown, 1935).

Schlesinger, Arthur M., Jr., *The Age of Jackson* (Boston: Little, Brown, 1945).

Seabrook, William B., wrote a series of books about witchcraft, including *Magic Island* (1929), *Voodoo Island* (1929), and *Jungle Ways* (1931).

Selsam, Howard, *Socialism and Ethics* (New York: International Publishers, 1943).

Sforza, Carlo, *Contemporary Italy: Its Intellectual and Moral Origins* (New York: Dutton, 1944).

Shapley, Harlow, *Galaxies* (Philadelphia: Blakiston, 1943).

Sigerist, Henry, *Civilization and Disease* (Ithaca, N.Y.: Cornell University Press, 1943).

Simenon, Georges, *On the Danger Line*, trans. Stuart Gilbert (New York: Harcourt, Brace, 1944; republished in 1944 in an Armed Services Edition).

Sinclair, Upton, *Mammonart: An Essay in Economic Interpretation* (Pasadena: Upton Sinclair, 1925).

Siodmak, Curt, *Donovan's Brain* (New York: Knopf, 1943; republished in 1944 in an Armed Services Edition).

Smith, Betty, *A Tree Grows in Brooklyn* (New York: Harper, 1943).

Spain, John (pseudonym of Cleve F. Adams), *Dig Me a Grave* (New York: Dutton, 1942).

Spring, Howard, *My Son, My Son* (New York: Viking, 1938; republished in 1943 in an Armed Services Edition).

Stegner, Wallace, *The Big Rock Candy Mountain* (New York: Duell, Sloan & Pearce, 1943).

Steig, William, *All Embarrassed* (New York: Duell, Sloan & Pearce, 1944).

Stendhal, *Lucien Leuwen* (1855).

Stoker, Bram, *Dracula* (1897).

Sze, Mai-Mai, *Silent Children* (New York: Harcourt, Brace, 1948).

Thayer, Tiffany, *The Illustrious Corpse* (New York: The Fiction League, 1930).

Tolstoy, Leo, *War and Peace* (1865–1869).

Untermeyer, Jean Starr, *Love and Need: Collected Poems 1918–1940* (New York: Viking, 1940).

Van Paassen, Pierre, *Days of Our Years* (New York: Hillman-Curl, 1939).

Waite, Arthur E., *The Brotherhood of the Rosy Cross* (London: Rider, 1924).

Walpole, Hugh, *Fortitude* (1913).

Warner, Sylvia Townsend, *A Garland of Straw: Twenty-eight Stories* (New York: Viking, 1943).

Wertenbaker, Charles Christian, *Write Sorrow on the Earth* (New York: Holt: 1947).

Wescott, Glenway, *Apartment in Athens* (New York: Harper, 1945; republished that year in an Armed Services Edition).

West, Anthony, *The Vintage* (Boston: Houghton Mifflin, 1950).

White, Victor, *Peter Domanig: Vienna in Morning* (Indianapolis: Bobbs-Merrill, 1944).

Williams, Ben Ames, *Leave Her to Heaven* (Boston: Houghton Mifflin, 1944; republished that year in an Armed Services Edition).

Winner, Percy, *Dario, 1925–1945: A Fictitious Reminiscence* (New York: Harcourt, Brace, 1947).

Wise, Herbert A., and Phyllis Fraser, eds., *Great Tales of Terror and the Supernatural* (New York: Random House, 1944).

Wouk, Herman, *City Boy* (New York: Simon & Schuster, 1948).

Wright, Richard, *Black Boy* (New York: Harper, 1945).

Zilahy, Lajos, *The Dukays*, trans. John Pauker (New York: Prentice-Hall, 1949).

INDEX

NOTE: Italicized page locators denote photographs and figures.

Index

Index

Index

Index

Index

Index

Index